# IF YOU'RE CRACKED YOU'RE HAPPY

PART WON

## ALSO BY MARK ARNOLD:

*The Best of The Harveyville Fun Times!*

*Created and Produced by Total TeleVision productions:*
*The Story of Underdog, Tennessee Tuxedo and the Rest*

BearManor Media

2011

Published in the USA by BearManor Media
P O Box 71426 • Albany, Georgia 31708
*www.bearmanormedia.com*

Cover artwork by John Severin from the collection of Jerry Boyd. Color and additional layout by Mort Todd. Interior graphics courtesy of Mike Arnold, Greg Beda, Jerry Boyd, Dan Fiorella, Marten Jallad, John Severin, B.K. Taylor, Mort Todd, and from various issues of *Cracked* magazine and other sources. Typesetting and layout by John Teehan.

ISBN 978-1-59393-644-0

Printed in the United States of America.

# TABLE OF CONTENTS

IF YOU'RE CRACKED

YOU'RE HAPPY!

Iron-On detail from *Cracked* #123, March 1975.
Artwork by John Severin.

# DEDICATION

This book is dedicated to the various people who believed in me during the past year and who put up with my devotion to completing this book in a reasonable amount of time, considering all of my other obligations. Your respect and loyalty is appreciated, and you are all acknowledged by name below…

Sylvester Phooey Smythe (1925-    )

# ACKNOWLEDGEMENTS

**SPECIAL THANKS** to Ellen Abramowitz, Jim Amash, Rick Altergott, Noel Anderson, Sergio Aragonés, Mike Arnold, Peter Bagge, Ron Barrett, Jerry Beck, Greg Beda, Bobbie Bender, Dave Berns, Ray Billingsley, Michael Ian Black, Luciano Blotta, Oskar Blotta, Bruce Bolinger, Jerry Boyd, Christie Brehm, Walter Brogan, Gary Brodsky, Roger Brown, Dan Budnick, Brian Buniak, Daryl Cagle, Joe Catalano, Dan Clowes, Ernie Colon, Terry Colon, Frank Cummings, Barbara Dale, Susan D'Antilio, Jack Davis, Michael Delle-Femine, Carson Demmans, Stephen De Stefano, Steve Ditko, Heather Durham, Barry Dutter, Don Edwing, Douglas Everett, Andrew Farago, Al Feldstein, Gary Fields, Bob Fingerman, Dan Fiorella, Pete Fitzgerald, Charles Foster, Kent Gamble, Grant Geissman, George Gladir, Stan Goldberg, Scott Gosar, Greg Grabianski, Murad Gumen, Charles E. Hall, Larry Hama, Russ Heath, Rich Hedden, Sam Henderson, Lee Hester, Troy Hickman, Todd Jackson, Al Jaffee, Marten Jallad, Eric Johnson, Oren Katzeff, Mike Kazaleh, Milton Knight, Dick Kulpa, Alan Kupperberg, Aron Laikin, Paul Laikin, Andy Lamberti, Kit Lively, Jay Lynch, Norma Martin, Nick Meglin, Grant Meihm, Cliff Mott, Rick Nielsen, Dan O'Brien, Ben Ohmart, Don Orehek, Rick Parker, Tom Richmond, Mike Ricigliano, Kevin Sacco, Jim Salicrup, Frank Santopadre, Warren Sattler, John Scrovack, J.J. Sedelmeier, John Severin, Dan Shahin, Scott Shaw!, Lou Silverstone, Andy Simmons, Joe Simon, Lenore Skenazy, Ricky Sprague, Bill Sproul, Howard Stern, Steve Strangio, Tony Tallarico, B.K. Taylor, Roy Thomas, Mort Todd, Angelo Torres, Rurik Tyler, Jim Vadeboncoeur, Sam Viviano, Jim Warren, Rob Weske, Samuel B. Whitehead, Marv Wolfman, Jeff Wong, Bill Wray. I apologize to anyone I didn't get into contact with for this book. Your work on *Cracked* does not go unappreciated or unnoticed.

Dedicated to the memories of Bernard Baily, Henry Boltinoff, Frank Borth, E. Nelson Bridwell, Bernie Brill, Sol Brodsky, Carl Burgos, Pete Costanza, Jerry De Fuccio, Bill Elder, Bill Everett, Sururi Gumen, Lennie Herman, Bill Hoest,

Joe Kiernan, Jack Kirby, Larry Levine, Lugoze, Joe Maneely, Don Martin, Vic Martin, Marian McMahon, Howard Nostrand, Jack O'Brien, Paul Reinman, Charles Rodrigues, Syd Shores, Jerry Siegel, Robert C. Sproul, Bob Stevens, Chic Stone, Bill Ward, Ed Winiarski, Basil Wolverton, Pete Wyma, Bob Zahn. There may be more, and I honor them, too.

Interviews conducted specifically by the author for this book were completed on the following dates:

Rick Altergott, February 28, 2010
Noel Anderson, April 27, 2009 and November 24, 2009
Mike Arnold, March 15, 2009
Ron Barrett, February 1, 2010
Ray Billingsley, April 17, 2009
Bruce Bolinger, November 24, 2009
Walter Brogan, March 10, 2009
Roger Brown, February 3, 2010
Dan Budnik, June 4, 2009
Brian Buniak, April 4, 2009
Daryl Cagle, March 9, 2009
Frank Cummings, November 24, 2009
Jack Davis, May 22, 2009
Carson Demmans, March 3, 2009
Barry Dutter, August 29, 2009
Michael Eury, November 14, 2009
Gary Fields, April 28, 2009
Bob Fingerman, March 11, 2009
Dan Fiorella, February 2, 2010
Pete Fitzgerald, February 28, 2009
Kent Gamble, March 10, 2009
George Gladir, March 21, 2009
Scott Gosar, March 23, 2009
Greg Grabianski, August 12-14, 2009
Murad Gumen, March 31, 2009
Charles E. Hall, March 2, 2010
Larry Hama, February 22, 2009
Russ Heath, March 8, 2009
Frank Jacobs, January 24, 2010
Al Jaffee, May 8-10, 2009
Milton Knight, April 26, 2009
Todd Jackson, February 3, 2010
Marten Jallad, March 8, 2009

Mike Kazaleh, July 28, 2009
Dick Kulpa, November 23, 2009
Alan Kupperberg, February 1, 2010
Aron Laikin, May 9, 2009
Paul Laikin, May 4, 2009
Andy Lamberti, March 10, 2009
Kit Lively, March 25, 2009
Jay Lynch, February 25, 2009 and November 22, 2009
Grant Meihm, March 5, 2009
Cliff Mott, April 2, 2009
Rick Nielsen, August 28, 2009
Don Orehek, March 10, 2009
Rick Parker, January 28, 2010
Steph Ramsay, February 3, 2010
Tom Richmond, May 7, 2009
Mike Ricigliano, February 19, 2009
Kevin Sacco, March 14, 2009
Warren Sattler, March 12, 2009
John Scrovak, February 23, 2009
Michelena Severin for John Severin, March 11, 2009
Lou Silverstone, March 14, 2009
Andy Simmons, March 3, 2009
Joe Simon, March 16, 2009
Ricky Sprague, February 2, 2010
Bill Sproul, January 20, 2010 and February 1, 2010
Steve Strangio, February 1, 2010
Terry Colon, February 3, 2010
Tony Tallarico, March 8, 2009
B.K. Taylor, December 9, 2009
Mort Todd, April 4, 2009
Angelo Torres, May 8, 2009
Marv Wolfman, February 27, 2008

# FOREWORD

## BY STEVE DITKO

M.A.

I can't supply your wanted information.

S.D.

# INTRODUCTION

**2008** would have been *Cracked* magazine's (or should I say "mazagine's") 50th anniversary. Even though the print version had ceased publication over a year before, I thought the current owners of Cracked.com would be interested in making one more visit to the past and issue a brand-new coffee table book featuring the best of almost 50 years of *Cracked*. I sent them an inquiry/request through the website, but it was ignored. Flash forward another year, and my publisher Ben Ohmart and I discussed what I could do as a follow-up to my book, *Created and Produced by Total TeleVision Productions: The Story of Underdog, Tennessee Tuxedo and the Rest*, and Ben came up with the idea for a book about *Cracked*.

Now, I've been a black-and-white humor magazine fan and collector since I was seven years old in 1974. Back then, I collected *Mad*, soon *Cracked* and eventually *Crazy*. I bought *Mad* and *Crazy* regularly, but I didn't buy *Cracked* all that often. (Although it was still being published, I never saw *Sick* on the stands except in one instance, but it was so pathetically bad by the late '70s, that I probably wouldn't have purchased it even if it were easily attainable.)

I felt *Mad* had great artwork and writing; *Cracked* had great artwork and lousy writing; *Crazy* had great writing and lousy artwork; and *Sick* had lousy artwork and writing. There were exceptions, but this was my general assessment.

I started reading *Cracked* with #125, the July 1975 issue with Sylvester's *Earthquake* cover. While I instantly fell in love with John Severin's artwork, the writing was just not in the same league as *Mad* and was at best amusing, but never laugh-out-loud funny.

I didn't even pick up #126 because of this. The next issue I purchased was #127 due to its *Star Trek* cover. I tried to like *Cracked*, but the humor was so lame and obvious that I grew tired of collecting it after a few issues. I would quit buying it for months at a time. This went off and on until 1983 by which time *Crazy* and *Sick* were canceled and there were few other options. Sure, the occasional *Wacko* or *Laugh Factory* came out, and I did start buying and collecting *National Lampoon* as well, but by the mid-'80s, humor magazines were on the way out, culminating in a downward spiral that unfortunately has not stopped to this day.

Fortunately, from 1986-2000, the writing in *Cracked* improved and was just as enjoyable, if not more so at times than *Mad*. During this period, I really enjoyed picking up both magazines and looked forward to see how each publication would treat a particular movie or TV show it was parodying.

*Cracked* was also the most consistently published American humor magazine other than *Mad* from 1958 through 2000, when yet another ownership change upset the regularity and the content. I knew something was up when a year passed between issues in 2001-2002. The regular series limped along coming out with alarming infrequency until the magazine breathed its last in 2004. The entire enterprise changed hands once again, and a short-lived attempt came out in 2006 with (what turned out to be) a three-issue series that more closely resembled *Maxim* than *Mad*. By 2007, it too was gone. As a result of this and the advent of eBay, I purchased the missing issues for my collection because of my hunger for any humor magazines during a time when barely anything was being published was insatiable.

As I said, Ben suggested I write the history of *Cracked* for my next book and I, like a lot of those whom I have interviewed for this book, said, "Why? Did anyone even like *Cracked*?" Sure, it was published for 49 years, but it never got the press, the readership and moreover the respect of *Mad*. It was always the butt of jokes and the publication you bought when you couldn't wait for the next issue of *Mad* during its eight-times-a-year publishing schedule from the late-'50s through the mid-'90s. More importantly, did anyone else besides me remember it or care?

*Mad* has had the luxury of still being published after 57 years despite the fact that it has reduced its frequency from monthly to quarterly in recent times. To most people when the subject of *Mad* is mentioned, they ask, "Is *Mad* still being published? I used to read that as a kid." Even the decade-long run of *MadTV* on FOX didn't seem to give the connection that *Mad* was still a viable publication.

So, before I agreed to write this book, I put out a few feelers and the response was overwhelmingly positive. Not only did people remember *Cracked*, they actually wanted to talk about it! There were memories of *Shut-Ups* and *Great Moments* and John Severin and *Spies and Saboteurs* and the endless parodies of *M*A*S*H* and Fonzie and Bill Ward's sexy women and Don Martin's bailing out of *Mad* to work for *Cracked*. After the response I got, I thought, "This is going to be fun."

*Cracked* was an also-ran to be sure, but it is an important also-ran because without it, *Mad* wouldn't have had any serious competition and competition breeds the need to excel. I seriously doubt that *Mad* would have continued to achieved the high standards it continually set for so long without the competition of *Cracked, Crazy, Sick, National Lampoon, Help!* and so many other short-lived attempts. It would have eventually rested on its laurels and its ongoing reputation, which unfortunately in recent years, is happening now.

So now, without any more fanfare, like it or not, here indeed is the history of *Cracked*...

# 1957 B.C. (BEFORE *CRACKED*)

**FOR** those younger readers born after 1990, the thought of obtaining your humor fix through the pages of a black-and-white pulp magazine featuring drawn and painted parodies and satire may seem very quaint, but for roughly 50 years that was one of the prime ways for people to get a subversive point of view on life in America, and to get a humor "fix." Television was still in its infancy and the comedy shows that existed at the time were mainly Vaudevillian-type variety shows or domestic situation comedies; definitely not anything featuring biting social satire or parody. The closest would be something like Sid Caesar's *Your Show of Shows*, which did the occasional parody, such as their infamous *This is Your Life* parody, but those were the exception and not the rule, and appeared roughly about the same time as *Mad*'s debut.

The origins of this type of satirical humor is commonly attributed to *Mad*, which debuted in October 1952 and featured the genius of Harvey Kurtzman who had already made a name for himself at EC (Entertaining Comics) for his war material in *Two-Fisted Tales* and *Frontline Combat*. Legend says that Kurtzman was envious of Al Feldstein who wrote and edited three horror titles (*Tales from the Crypt*, *The Vault of Horror* and *The Haunt of Fear*), two science-fiction titles (*Weird Science*, *Weird Fantasy*) and two suspense titles (*Crime SuspenStories*, *Shock SuspenStories*), among other things, and that Kurtzman wanted more money. EC publisher William M. Gaines suggested adding a humor magazine to his two war titles in order to give him a larger paycheck and figured that Kurtzman could dash off the new title in his sleep, as he had a keen sense of humor, a side that he couldn't show very well in his war titles.

Of course, Kurtzman didn't just "dash" anything off and soon put as much effort into his work for *Mad* as he did for his other titles and eventually *Frontline Combat* fell by the wayside and *Two-Fisted Tales* was turned over to future *Cracked* artist John Severin. Kurtzman's dedication eventually caused *Mad* to be one of EC's strongest selling titles and also their only monthly, lasting for 23 issues as a comic book before transitioning into a "slick."

Future *Cracked* editor Mort Todd claims, "You know that Severin, Elder and Kurtzman had a studio together? To hear it from Sev, he was pretty key to the creation of *Mad*. I don't know if Michelena [Severin] told you about it, because Severin hasn't said much about it in the past."

Though humor magazines existed long before *Mad* became one in 1955, *Mad* is often cited as the first humor magazine focusing on the satire / parody element. Previous humor magazines that paved the way for *Mad* were Britain's *Punch* and *The Harvard Lampoon*, which featured comedic stories that occasionally had a satirical bent, but more so after *Mad* became a mainstream success. Another type of *Mad* antecedent was a magazine called *Bunk* featuring various gag cartoons and pages of jokes and humorous short stories, and there were many more of this type. Other *Mad* ancestors include *Foo*, *Puck*, *Judge* and *Ballyhoo*.

*Mad* transitioned from a 10-cent color comic book into a 25-cent black-and-white magazine with its 24th issue (July 1955). Though rumored to have changed to avoid the newly established Comics Code, the real reason is that Kurtzman demanded the change or he was going to walk. Kurtzman commonly made similar threats. The final straw came later when Kurtzman demanded 51% of *Mad* in order to stay on as editor after it was changed to a magazine. This time, Gaines turned him down and Kurtzman walked. He went to Hugh Hefner to start *Trump*, a deal that was already planned when Kurtzman made this final demand of Gaines.

Gaines had recently retired all of his other 10-cent comic books since the Comics Code Authority was watering down his material and sales were equally dismal. A recent foray into black-and-white magazine versions of his other canceled comics (*Terror Illustrated*, *Shock Illustrated*, *Confessions Illustrated*, *Crime Illustrated*) was a resounding flop. The editor of these titles was Al Feldstein. Recently let go from EC, Feldstein was now searching for work, when a call came from Gaines to get Feldstein back to head the now staffless *Mad* as Kurtzman took all of his artists save one (Wally Wood) with him.

Determined to make *Mad* a profitable venture, Feldstein initially filled its pages with the work of famous comedians like Wally Cox, Ernie Kovacs and Bob & Ray. Eventually, the call went out for not-so-well-known artists and writers who did have a keen sense of humor, not necessarily Kurtzman's sense of humor, but definitely inspired by Kurtzman's style of humor. Feldstein did have some experience with this sort of thing briefly before at EC with its own homegrown *Mad* rip-off entitled *Panic*. This experience was enough as

Feldstein proved to be an excellent choice for *Mad*'s editor; a role he retained for almost 30 years.

John Severin's wife, Michelena, sums up the two original editors of *Mad*: "Al Feldstein was *Mad*'s head, but Kurtzman was its heart."

Of course, success always begets imitations and shortly after *Mad*'s 1955 debut, the imitations began, the first being Stan Lee's *Snafu* magazine for Atlas Comics in 1956. *Snafu* lasted only three issues before being canceled. Soon, Kurtzman's *Trump* also became a short-lived *Mad* rip-off casualty, lasting only two issues in 1957. These early failures did not dissuade other imitators and between 1956 and 1958, where over a dozen different black-and-white humor magazines debuted, including *Lunatickle, Crazy, Man, Crazy* (aka *This Magazine is Crazy*), *Humbug, Nuts, Frenzy, Thimk, Panic* (not the EC comic), *Loco, Frantic, Shook Up, Zany* and, of course, *Cracked.*

Comments Mort Todd about *Snafu* and Marvel / Atlas: "They probably did at least a half-a-dozen color humor comics. Those were fun, too. There was a lot of Joe Maneely and Severin, and then Stan Lee did a series of 'Photo Funnies.' Stan always tried to get something going. It's strange that they didn't do another standard *Mad* format magazine after *Snafu* until *Crazy*."

Marten Jallad contributed a list of all the black-and-white humor magazines that came out in 1958 alone:

| | |
|---|---|
| **NUTS** | Feb. 1958 – #2 April 1958<br>Health Knowledge |
| **CRACKED** | Feb. 1958 – #365 November 2004<br>Major/Larken/Globe/American Media/Mega Media |
| **FRENZY** | April 1958 – #6 March 1959<br>Bimfort Magazines Inc. |
| **THIMK** | May 1958 – #6 May 1959<br>Counterpoint Inc. |
| **PANIC** | July 1958 – #6 July 1959<br>Vol. 2 #10 Dec. 1965 – Vol. 2 #12 1966<br>Panic Publications |
| **LOCO** | Aug. 1958 – #3 Jan. 1959<br>Satire Publications |

| | |
|---|---|
| **ZANY** | Sept. 1958 – #4 May 1959<br>Candar Publishing Co. |
| **FRANTIC** | Oct. 1958 – Vol. 2 #2 April 1959<br>Pierce Publishing Co. |
| **SHOOK UP** | Nov. 1958 #1<br>Dodsworth Publishing Co. |

More about them in the next chapter…

# MAN'S ACTION

## THE ACE/CANDAR/ MAJOR MAGAZINE STORY

THE magazine empire that eventually formed *Cracked* had its origins with the Ace paperback publishing line. Founded in 1952 by Aaron A. Wyn, Ace had published a line of science-fiction paperbacks that are now regarded as some of best in the business. Eventually, the publisher expanded to include a line of magazines in 1957. They were science fiction and a number of "sweat" magazines that were popular in the late '50s through the 1970s. Ace's magazine publishing line was christened Candar and although Ace editor Donald A. Wollheim was the original publisher and editor, soon the publishing and editorial chores for all the Candar magazines were handed over to a new hire, Robert C. Sproul.

Sproul's son, Bill, takes up the story: "My grandfather, Joseph Sproul, was Circulation Manager of Ace Books. My father had extensive circulation experience working for Hearst and Pocket Books and went to work with my grandfather. My father hated the corporate life and wanted to be his own boss and so he looked into publishing. There was a small publisher my father knew who died and had a few titles that my father took over. He taught himself the publishing business by becoming a "Field Publisher." Field publishing is putting out many different types of magazines and keeping ones that make a profit and nurturing the ones that catch on, while 'stirring with your left hand' the others. The biggest challenge was finding the talent to run / edit these titles while much time was spent working on the printing, and circulation end.

"The early offices of his publishing days were space he rented in Manhattan. He struggled along trying to make a buck by publishing small circulation magazines. *Cracked* was just one of twenty or more. He had a family with two kids, my older sister and I, and struggled with alcoholism. My mother gave him 'the ultimatum' and he quit drinking in 1959. In 1962 my younger sister was born. He was successful at getting people to work for him because he was a good guy and treated people fairly. Bill Ward, John Severin, Don Orehek, Charlie Rodrigues, all had a mutual respect for each other."

Paul Laikin remembers Sproul: "He was a nice man. His father was in the magazine business, also. He knew the ins and outs of marketing. That was his thinking. He wasn't an editorialist. He never stood in the way and say, 'This isn't funny.' He never said that to me. If I came into the office, he trusted me that I wrote the best material that I could, but he handled Severin. The only thing that Severin did in those days was the big movie spoof. I used to write the entire issue. There were no writers. *Mad* had Frank Jacobs, but I couldn't ask Frank to write for *Cracked*."

Tony Tallarico also remembers Sproul: "He was a very loose publisher. If he gave you something and you thought of something better, he let you go ahead and do it. That's what made Sproul the kind of person he was. People liked to work for him. He was not a pain in the ass where he went over every page and said, 'Hey, you gotta do this and that.' It was never like that.

"Because of his distributor, he had to put out a number of magazines, and some of them could be around a very bad sell period like around Christmas, which is a very bad magazine sell period because people are spending their money on other things, so then he would try to cut corners by doing that. The summer months were the best months for sales, but Bob Sproul was not cheap. I wouldn't characterize him in a bad light. Now, if it were others…no Bob, he was straight."

Warren Sattler adds, "Sproul was fine. I loved him. They were wonderful, except when he came to pay. I had to wait three months, but that's typical of almost every magazine I have ever worked for."

Taschen's excellent overview of the genre, *Men's Adventure Magazines*, discusses a basic history of the publications, replete with dozens of magazine cover images of both Sproul-edited and non-Sproul-edited titles. It turns out by reading the book's biographical overview that most if not all comic book publishers dabbled in this sort of publication at some point in their histories, mainly because of the staggering popularity and income they generated. This allowed many publishers to thrive and to keep publishing low-end, loss-leader publications such as comic books and magazines like *Cracked*.

Bill Sproul explains, "Aha, the skeletons in the closet. I often wonder what happened to these titles. Of course, many of the women in their pages were my buddies' moms and my teachers, so moving to Florida did wonders for the quality of the photos ... ONLY KIDDING!!! My father left the editorial offices for these titles in New York. I was not kept abreast (pun intended) of the inner workings because I was only 14 years old. All I remember is my father working on his distribution ledgers for them. We had *For Monsters Only*, *True Frontier*, *Real Frontier*, *Crosswords*, *Cracked* and all the associate publications here in Madeira Beach. You have to keep in mind that my father was a hands-on publisher coming out of the circulation end of the business. One of his greatest talents was controlling the distribution of all his titles. The ledgers I mentioned were pure genius and gave him unbelievable control issue to issue. To look at them today you would think it could only be done by computer.

"We didn't talk to others about the men's magazines. I am still uncomfortable talking about it with my mother still alive. It has nothing to do with the *Cracked* story. I truly hope you agree. There was nothing wrong with them, in my eyes, but we moved to the south in the '70s and it still had a Bible belt mentality. My father was very private, very protective, and really never spoke about his business, any of it. We had our fan-kids that came to the office on their way home from school. They were fanatical *Cracked* readers and we would bounce ideas off them. But, all in all, we didn't want people to know what we did at Coastal Magazines. We lived in a smaller beach community and there was nothing to gain by notoriety.

"My sister edited *True Frontier* for some years and both of us worked on *Cracked* on and off. I did some paste-up and layout for most of *Cracked* associated publications (annuals, *Collectors' Editions...*) and wrote a lot of photo captions, posters and cover ideas when I was in high school (It was a good source of income as a kid, I also worked gas stations, bussed tables, etc.). I was associate editor of *Cracked* when I got out of high school, and then went back after two years at Eckerd College, when my dad lost his editor. We had many different editors over the years; most of them didn't last very long. It is funny just the other day I heard of an art teacher at the prestigious Ringling School of Art, in the late '80s; main claim to fame was that he had been an artist and editor of *Cracked* magazine. I think he lasted a month with us. It was a fun job; Elaine Ozimok was hired out of college as an office associate and was with us for a decade or so. I lost touch with her, but believe she is still living around here."

There was, however, a different side to Sproul, as evidenced by Murad Gumen's comments: "There was a seedy side to *Cracked* under the domain of Robert Sproul, and in my case, they didn't even offer a rotten kill fee; I was forced to part ways. Sproul had promised my father a guaranteed number of pages each issue, but didn't follow through. That is what broke my father's relationship with the magazine."

According to *Men's Adventure Magazines*: "Bob Sproul – the successful publisher of *Cracked*, the only enduring competitor to *Mad* magazine – debuted *Man's Action* in 1958. Sproul took well to the market, expanding to five magazines, most of which were published into the 1970s."

While sales figures are not available, the book states: "In the early '60s, the sweats continued to flourish, with most of the lower-tier magazines selling in the range of 100,000 to 250,000 copies every month."

The magazines that Sproul published in this genre include *Man's Wildcat Adventures*, *Man's True Danger*, *Man's Exploits*, *Man's Daring*, *Lion Adventures*, *Man's Peril*, *Rage for Men* and the aforementioned *Man's Action*.

There were also science-fiction magazines: *Saturn, Web Detective Stories* and *Web Terror Stories.* This title was really three separate magazines in one. It started life in 1957 as a science-fiction/fantasy magazine under the title *Saturn, the Magazine of Science Fiction*, but only lasted for five issues. It then switched to a detective magazine, first as *Saturn Web Detective Stories* for five issues and then as *Web Detective Stories* for a further nine issues. Finally, it became a weird-menace terror title under the name *Web Terror Stories* for a final eight issues.

Tony Tallarico remembers working on the men's magazines: "Yes. The men's magazines. I did some illustrations for them. These were really men's magazines. They would have pin-ups in there; they'd have some nudes. They would have where the Germans took over and beat up the women. You know, that type of stuff. I did inside illustrations. It was like a half-a-page illustration, double-page illustration, realistic, black-and-white half-tones. It was not a kid's magazine. It was an adult feature."

Though Sproul was listed as the publisher of *Cracked* and the other Candar / Major magazines, the "real" publisher was a man named Bernie Brill. Bill Sproul: "Bernard Brill was in the garment business with a retail store in Manhattan and was the guy who put up the money to start my dad in the business. He was not a magazine guy and did little to influence anything my dad did. His office paid the bills and paid my dad a salary plus bonus on percent of profit. My dad published in many different genres: crossword, horror, men's adventure, cartoon, sci-fi, monster and western. Some lasted for years, others for just a few issues."

Says Don Orehek, "He was the money man, and was the 'silent partner' behind the Candar / Major empire. Yes. Brill. Right. He was the money guy. I don't know too much about him, though, but I know the name. I don't think I ever met him."

Tony Tallarico adds, "He had a partner who was the money man. He was very sharp. I'm sure they had different type of corporations for different types of publications."

Paul Laikin offers his recollections: "Before they did *Cracked*, they did the men's magazines. I don't remember if they came to me, or I went to them. I have them all. I would write humor pieces and fillers. You know, 'I Climbed Mt. Everest in my Shorts' or whatever, so that would be their humor piece to break up the monotony. 'Ten Ways to Seduce Your Mistress in an Open Convertible.' They had one office of the four offices in the *Cracked* compound, and he did the men's magazines. He put them together and Harry Chester was the layout man.

"Bernie Brill was a very successful agent. I'm a little vague about who he was, but I remember him being around. He worked with Bob Sproul on the men's magazines under Candar Publishing Company and *Cracked* was a part of it at that time.

"Brill was just a front really for Sproul. He was just a name – a financier. Sproul had his desk and was there 9-5 at 45 West 45th Street. It was a nicer office. There were more girls there. It was a better place to visit. It was over a newsstand on the corner. They had a nice spread of offices.

"They were slow in paying, and every once in a while when I was hard up for a buck, I would get in touch with them and they would ship out some money to me. He would always pay, but sometimes he was slow. It was just one of those things. I think he was trying to get some interest on his buck. So anyway I would call him up and have him get me a check right away, but he was slow in paying."

Sproul was not good at innovation of magazine titles. What he was good at was creating popular imitations of successful magazines. Martin Goodman's Marvel Comics (then publishing as Atlas Comics) had fallen on hard times and the majority of the staff had been laid off. This has been often called "The Atlas Implosion."

Goodman discovered a closetful of completed-yet-unused stories, and forced Stan Lee to end offering freelance work. He essentially fired the entire steady bullpen staff one by one until finally, by the end of April, the implosion was in full effect.

*Comic Book Comics* #4 (November 2009) describes the implosion in succinct terms: "In the wake of the Wertham purge, Goodman transferred distribution of his comics to the industry leader, American News Corporation…right before the Feds trustbuster it for also owning America's largest chain of newsvendors, Union News.

"When ANC ceased operations, it left nearly half of America's comic book publishers without any way to get to market…including Atlas.

"Lee wrote, 'It was like we had been the last ones to book passage on the Titanic!'

"In 1957, Goodman ordered Lee to fire the entire Atlas staff except himself."

Mort Todd adds, "Martin Goodman was his uncle-in-law or something, so Stan always had a job. I guess they had a big inventory of stuff, so they spent over a year working through that inventory, and didn't hire except for occasional covers here and there.

"Atlas had big sales trouble and basically fired pretty much everybody except [Jack] Kirby and [Steve] Ditko as freelancers, and Don Heck. The production crew was out, [which had been] run by Sol Brodsky, and all the artists were out of work. I'm not exactly sure about who approached who, but as you are well aware, there were dozens and dozens of *Mad* rip-offs in the '50s; first, when it was a comic book and then when it became a magazine, and you know Sproul himself put out a couple other *Mad* rip-offs (*Zany*, *College Laughs*, *French Cartoons and Cuties*, *Monster Howls* and *Pow!*).

"Brodsky hooked up with Sproul and they put together *Cracked* and if you look at the first couple of issues of *Cracked*, it was mostly all Atlas artists. Incredible stuff. There was Russ Heath, Al Williamson, and even Al Jaffee, who were working at Marvel back then. Brodsky designed the original *Cracked* logo."

At the end of 1957, the core group of Atlas artists scrambled to find steady work. One of many new ventures they find is a new publication seeking to imitate the success of *Mad* magazine. Atlas production manager Sol Brodsky approached men's magazine publisher Robert C. Sproul with an idea for a *Mad*-like magazine and Sproul hired Brodsky as his new editor. Many of Atlas' artists and writers ended up at *Cracked*, mainly due to the fact that Brodsky put the word out to all of his former staff. Soon, artists like Carl Burgos, Paul Reinman, Russ Heath, Bill Everett, Jack Kirby, Joe Maneely, Al Williamson, Ed Winiarski, Syd Shores, Pete Costanza and Bernard Baily came on board, and of course, John Severin.

# ACE MAGAZINE COVER GALLERY

BIGGER THAN EVER
French
CARTOONS and CUTIES

Man's
Action
I WAS MEAT FOR BLOODTHIRSTY SHARKS
THEY BUTCHERED FOR POWER
19¢
MONSTER SPIDERS COVERED MY FLESH

TO HELL WITH FREELOADING VETERANS
MAN'S ACTION
19¢

AMERICAN MEN ARE SEX SAPS
MAN'S ACTION
25¢

SEX PROBES THAT SHOOK THE WORLD
MAN'S ACTION
25¢
TRAPPED IN A DERVISH HAREM
SGT. FRANK'S HELLSHIP
ESCAPE TO EDEN

NINE SEX PITFALLS YOU FACE!
MAN'S ACTION
BLUE MURDER WEARS HORNS
25¢
The PARADISE MAIDENS of SNOWBOUND JONES

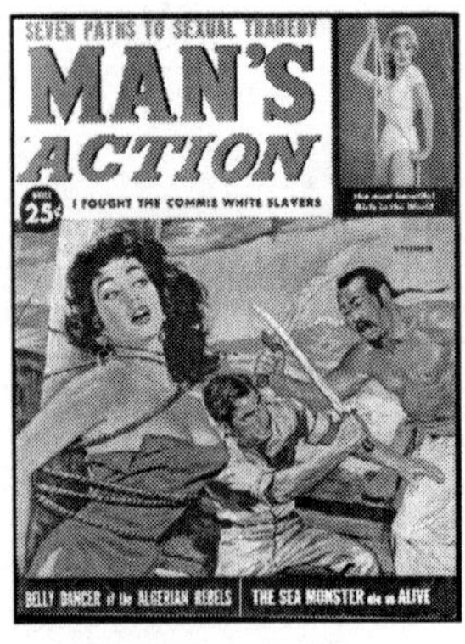
SEVEN PATHS TO SEXUAL TRAGEDY
MAN'S ACTION
25¢
I FOUGHT THE COMMIE WHITE SLAVERS
BELLY DANCER of the ALGERIAN REBELS
THE SEA MONSTER ate us ALIVE

VIRILITY DRUG: GREAT NEW DISCOVERY!
MAN'S ACTION
25¢
TRUE REPORT: STONE AGE SAVAGES KILL SCIENTISTS!
Combat History of the 1st Infantry

AT LAST! THE TRUTH ABOUT APHRODISIACS
MAN'S ACTION
25¢
MY MELANESIAN BRIDE OF TERROR
Combat History of the 2nd Division

BLOODIEST FIGHTS IN BOXING HISTORY!
MAN'S
ACTION
25¢
COSSACK DOUBLE-CROSS OF THE NYMPHO BARONESS

SMOKING CAN MAKE YOU IMPOTENT!
MAN'S
ACTION
SEPT.
25¢
EXCITING COMBAT HISTORY
FIRST IN A NEW SERIES

THE SECRET LOVE LIFE OF WOMEN
MAN'S
ACTION
PIRATE ORGY OF THE RENEGADE SUB
25¢
THRILLING COMBAT HISTORY

MAN'S
ACTION
$1,000,000 IN GOLD FREE!

LOVE PRACTICES OF IMMORAL COEDS
MAN'S
ACTION

MAN'S
ACTION
CASTRO'S EXECUTIONER

CONFESSIONS OF A TEEN-AGE WHITE SLAVER
MAN'S
ACTION
THE NUDE CAT-WOMEN OF FRANCE

A NIGHT OF LUSTFUL HORROR
MAN'S
ACTION

MAN'S
ACTION
THE TATTOOED NUDES OF OKLAHOMA JOE
AFTERMATH TO CORREGIDOR

THE UNHOLY, NAKED GERMAN WITCH CULTS
MAN'S ACTION
FIGHTING 5th ARMORED DIV.
HE WAS FINGERED FOR MEMBERSHIP IN THE DEPRAVED
FRAT HOUSE OF DEATH

SCANDANAVIA: THE WORLD'S FREE LOVE PARADISE
MAN'S ACTION
$1,000,000 TREASURE
NAKED DANCER
79TH INFANTRY DIVISION

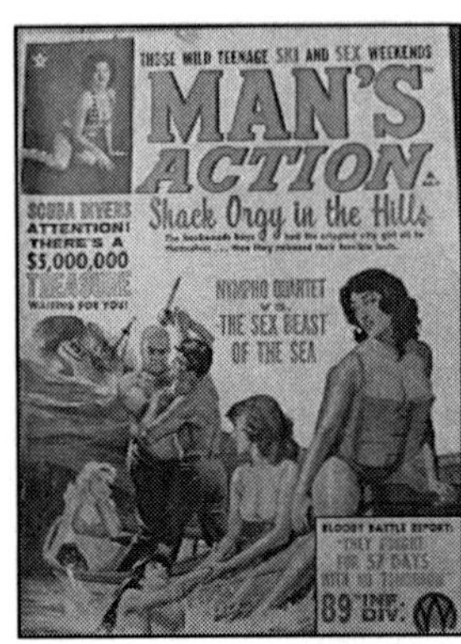
THOSE WILD TEENAGE SKI AND SEX WEEKENDS
MAN'S ACTION
Shack Orgy in the Hills
ATTENTION! THERE'S A $5,000,000
NYMPHO QUARTET VS. THE SEX BEAST OF THE SEA
89TH INF. DIV.

WARNING! YOUR LOVE LIFE CAN KILL YOU!
MAN'S ACTION
ISLAND OF SHAME
"TIGER" TARNOWSKY THE MADMAN WHO MASSACRES REDS
WAR KILL
NEW YORK'S LOST MILLION DOLLAR TREASURE

CAN HEAT AND SUNBURN RUIN YOUR VIRILITY?
MAN'S ACTION
PAUL DEAN REPORTS ON: BEATNIK JOYGIRLS OF RED SQUARE
JAKE MACON'S SUICIDE DIVE OFF OMAHA BEACH
32nd
JUST FOUND! $10 MILLION PIRATE TREASURE
THE LUSTY BUCCANEER

WILL YOUR JOB WRECK YOUR SEX LIFE?
MAN'S ACTION
PAUL DEAN REPORTS ON "CHOPPER" BUSANO— THE MAD MAJOR WHO BUTCHERS REDS
GOLD IN TEXAS
The "LOVE-YOU-JOE" GIRL WHO DOUBLECROSSED A WOUNDED AMERICA

SEX DRUG THAT DRIVES LOVERS CRAZY
MAN'S ACTION
EXOTIC NUDES in a GOVERNMENT SIN PALACE
THE WORLD'S WILDEST NYMPHOMANIAC
Death Crush of the SAVAGE SEA MONSTER
CHARGE of the LUSTY BRIGADE
I HAD TO SATISFY 3 WOMEN—OR FACE A FIRING SQUAD

DO VIRGINS MAKE LOUSY LOVERS?
MAN'S ACTION
STREETWALKERS VS. RAPISTS
TRAMP STEAMER DECOY GIRLS
SAVAGE LUST OF THE JUNGLE BRIDE
CAPTIVE NUDES
SLAVEGIRL ISLAND

DOCTOR'S MACHINE MAKES LOVE BETTER THAN MEN!
MAN'S ACTION
WIN A TICKET TO WEEKEND BLISS!
HOW AND WHERE TO FIND MILLIONS IN GOLD AND JEWELS!
SQUEEZE PLAY WITH THE BLONDE VICE COP
THE BLOODY DIAMONDS OF THE GREEN HELL MAIDENS!

HOW TO BOOST YOUR LOVE PERFORMANCE!
MAN'S ACTION
NAKED SHAME OF THE WANTON STARLET
$5,000,000 LIES WAITING ALONG THE OLD OREGON TRAIL!
PLEASURE GIRL BUSTOUT
THE JET SET DOLL VICTIMS OF THE SEX BEAST SWAMI!

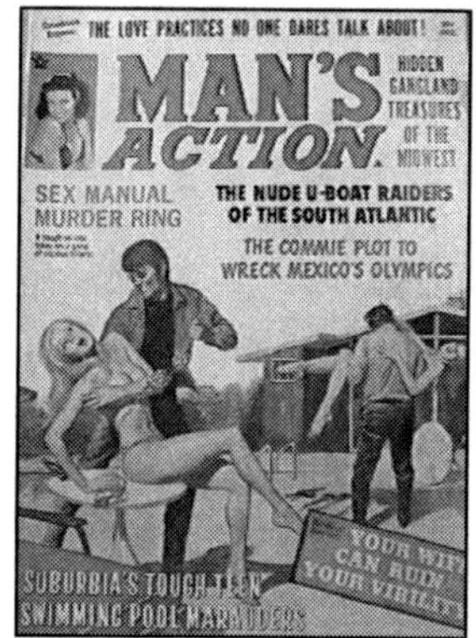
THE LOVE PRACTICES NO ONE DARES TALK ABOUT!
MAN'S ACTION
HIDDEN GANGLAND TREASURES OF THE MIDWEST
SEX MANUAL MURDER RING
THE NUDE U-BOAT RAIDERS OF THE SOUTH ATLANTIC
THE COMMIE PLOT TO WRECK MEXICO'S OLYMPICS
SUBURBIA'S TOUGH TEEN SWIMMING POOL MARAUDERS

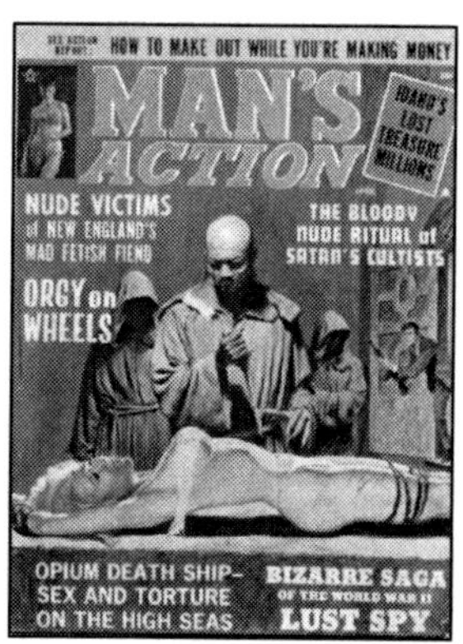
HOW TO MAKE OUT WHILE YOU'RE MAKING MONEY
MAN'S ACTION
IDAHO'S LOST TREASURE MILLIONS
NUDE VICTIMS of NEW ENGLAND'S MAD FETISH FIEND
THE BLOODY nude RITUAL of SATAN'S CULTISTS
ORGY on WHEELS
OPIUM DEATH SHIP– SEX AND TORTURE ON THE HIGH SEAS
BIZARRE SAGA OF THE WORLD WAR II LUST SPY

WOMEN WHO BUY SEX!
MAN'S ACTION
ORGY TRAP OF THE COMMIE BRAINWASH GIRLS
SCANDINAVIA: THE WORLD'S FREE LOVE PARADISE
GIRL SKIN-DIVERS RAID CASTRO'S FORTRESS
RHODE ISLAND'S SUNKEN SUB TREASURE
THE DOLPHIN: MAN'S LINK WITH OTHER WORLDS
NUDE JUDGE, NUDE JURY!

PART-TIME JOY GIRLS OF SUBURBIA
MAN'S ACTION
TOUGH TEEN SWIMMING POOL MARAUDERS
BLOODIEST TREASURE IN THE SEA!
NUDE COMMANDO THUNDERBOMB RAIDERS
THE STRANGE ORGY OF GUN RUNNER SLADE

SCANDINAVIA: THE WORLD'S FREE LOVE PARADISE!
MAN'S ACTION
THE NAKED WITCHES OF STUD ISLAND
THE GRINNING HORROR OF HAITI'S TONTON MACOUTE!
THOSE GOLDEN-LEGGED JOY GIRLS OF LAS VEGAS
THE BLOODIEST TREASURE IN THE SEA!

ARE YOU A LOVE WEAKLING?
MAN'S DARING ACTION
25¢
THE SACRED ORGY OF THE WHITE RHINO

DARING

MAN'S
WILDCAT
ADVENTURES
WE RAIDED THE BORED WIVES BORDELLO

SIN INSIDE A DIME-A-DANCE HALL
Wildcat
ADVENTURES
WOMEN ARE BETTER LOVERS THAN MEN
THE ORGY OF THE KAMIKAZE

BOOK BONUS
FRISCO V-J DAY ORGIES
WILDCAT
ADVENTURES
COUNT PERIORINI
STREET QUEENS
TEENAGE GANGS

EXPOSED SCHOOLS OF LOVE FOR RICH MEN'S SONS
WILDCAT
WOLF TORTURES OF THE NAZI KILLER QUEEN
THE BARON OF NEVADA AND HIS BRANDED BROADS

LOVE GADGETS CAN KILL YOU!
WILDCAT
ADVENTURES
DEATH CRUISE OF THE
2 NUDE CUBAN CUTIES
AMERICANS AM STILL YOUR ENEMY

BOOK BONUS
"THEY TOOK MY MANHOOD!"
WILDCAT
SLUGGER HELLENHART'S STRIP TEASE COMMANDO RAID
THE NIGHT THE GIRLS RAN WILD

TEN WAYS TO KEEP IT
WILDCAT
ADVENTURES
THE PHONY TEENAGE DIRTY PHOTO SWINDLE
RODEO IN THE RAW
NAZI TORTURE THEATRE

WARNING: SMOKING CAN DESTROY YOUR LOVE LIFE!
WILDCAT
ADVENTURES
HOLLYWOOD'S DANGEROUS TEEN TEMPTRESSES
PT BOAT ESCAPE
NAKED DAUGHTERS
REVENGE OF THE PASSIONATE TORSO

A FULL SEX LIFE CAN HELP YOU STOP SMOKING
WILDCAT
ADVENTURES
BLACK LEATHER LIBRARY LUST RAID
NUDE MOVIE
The MAN-HANGING WOMEN
THE SAMPAN PLEASURE GIRLS OF KOULOON

SEX KEYS THAT UNLOCK HER HIDDEN DESIRES
WILDCAT
SEDUCE HER WITH AN ORGY
HIPPIE SEX KITTEN TELLS IT LIKE IT IS
TAKE OUR REVEALING SEX TEST WITH YOUR MATE
HIGH AND DRY....

WILDCAT
SQUEEZE THOSE FEMALE SEX TRIGGERS!
THE NAKED DELIGHTS OF THE SEX CARNIVAL
FIND HER FAVORITE POSITION
THE WORLD'S MOST SENSUAL NUDES!

LONGER LOVE MAKING: WOMEN BEG FOR IT!
WILDCAT
DOES SHE HAVE SEXUAL HEAT?
LEARN HER SECRET SEX SIGNALS
GIRLS NEED IT THE OLD-FASHIONED WAY
THE WILDEST NUDES WE'VE EVER SHOWN!

SENSUAL EXERCISES TO POWER YOUR SEX MUSCLES!
WILDCAT
SPECIAL
YOUR SEX SCORE— GET IT UP!
THE NAKED EXPERIMENTS OF BEDMATES
A NEW WAY OF DOING IT
NOW
BIG GATEFOLD

SATURN
THE MAGAZINE OF SCIENCE FICTION
MAR
Eternal Adam
by
JULES VERNE
A NEW FIND
NOEL LOOMIS. ROBERT SILVERBERG. ALAN BARCLAY

SATURN MAGAZINE OF
WEB
DETECTIVE STORIES
DAUGHTERS OF HELL
SCREAM BLOODY MURDER
Jim Allen. Tony Phillips.

SATURN
SCIENCE FICTION AND FANTASY
JULY
ACE 35¢
By
JULES VERNE
GORDON DICKSON . AUGUST DERLETH . IRVING COX

SATURN
SCIENCE FICTION
AND FANTASY
OCT.
CALIFORNIA IS DOOMED!
ROBERT A. HEINLEIN - FRANK BELKNAP LONG - ALAN BARCLAY

SATURN
SCIENCE FICTION
AND FANTASY
MAR
RED FLAG OVER THE MOON
ROBERT SILVERBERG. CHARLES STEARNS. CHARLES FONTENAY

SATURN
WEB
DETECTIVE STORIES
A LONG VIOLENT NIGHT
SHORT CUT TO HELL

SATURN
WEB
DETECTIVE STORIES
HELL'S DEADLY LOVER
CROSS ME AND DIE
Don Unatin-Al James-Buc

JUST KILL HIM, DARLING!
SATURN
WEB
DETECTIVE STORIES
LADY FROM HELL

HOT SLUG – COOL DAME!
WEB
The Hunger of Death
35¢ JULY
DETECTIVE STORIES
NEVER LOVE A HELLCAT
Buck Grimes-Bill Ryder-Don Unatin

FEAR FINDS A MATE
WEB
NO GUTS TO DIE!
DETECTIVE STORI
SEPT. 35¢
LOVE NEST IN HELL
Luke Hogan
Al James
Pete McCann

MY LOVE IS DEATH!
WEB
DETECTIVE
DUMB BLONDES ARE MURDER
TERROR TOWN
AL JAMES
JIM BARNETT
R. HARDWICK

TEASE ME AND DIE!
WEB
A GANG JOB!
SHOW HER HIS BLOOD
35¢
MAR
Al James-Bill Ryder-Don Unatin

SISTERS OF SLAUGHTER!
WEB
JUNE
LUST STEALS THE SCENE
YOU'LL DIE LAUGHING
MURDERER WANTED
Frank Cannon · Hal Crosby · Art Crockett

THE TRIPLE CROSS A Manville Moon Thriller
WEB
DETECTIVE
LUST ISN'T FUNNY
MODEL OF MURDER

HANG BY THE NECK! A Chester Drum Story
WEB
35¢ JAN.
THE SOFT ARMS OF MURDER
DETECTIVE STORIES
EVIL IS A READHEAD
Stephen Marlowe - Hal Elson

WEB
DETECTIVE STORIES
ART CROCKETT

THE MISTRESS OF HORROR CASTLE
WEB
THE AZTEC PAIN-PRINCESS
LING-TSU'S EXPERIMENTS IN FEAR
OH, BUT TO DIE

TORTURE CHAINS OF VENGEANCE
WEB
DESTROY ME!
TERROR STORIES
THE FANATIC JUSTICE OF SATAN'S CULT

WEB
TERROR STORIES
DANCE WITH THE DEVIL
MISTRESS OF THE 6 GATES OF HORROR
NIGHTMARE ISLAND
THE PURIFYING LASH
HELL'S HAREM
DRUMS OF TORMENT

WEB
CALL ME VICTIM
THE WHIPPING STONE
TERROR STORIES
EVIL is the NIGHT
JAWS OF DOOM
HAVE TUX: WILL SUFFER
ISLE OF THE DAMNED
MISTRESS OF THE STEEL MASQUE

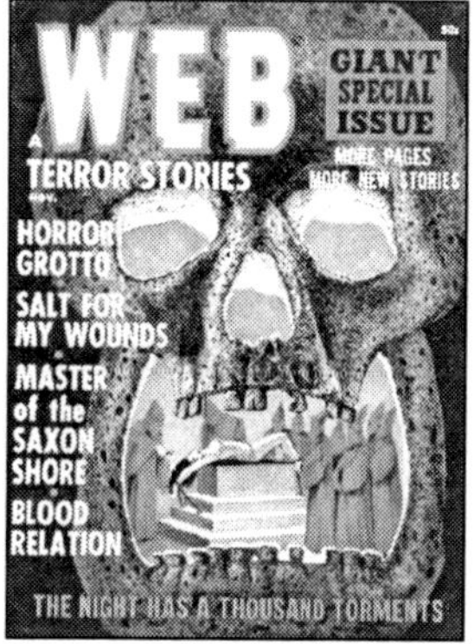
WEB
GIANT SPECIAL ISSUE
MORE PAGES MORE NEW STORIES
TERROR STORIES
HORROR GROTTO
SALT FOR MY WOUNDS
MASTER of the SAXON SHORE
BLOOD RELATION
THE NIGHT HAS A THOUSAND TORMENTS

WEB
MORE PAGES MORE STORIES
ANGEL OF HELL
SATAN'S SPAWN
PREY ON ME
REPENT AT LEISURE
COME, KISS THE LASH
MY LOVE, MY PRISONER
TERROR STORIES

WEB
GIANT 50¢
SPECIAL ISSUE
TERROR STORIES
THE LEATHER MASK
VENUS OF THE CLAWS
THE WHIPPING CURE
LASH OF THE AVENGER
SEE YOU IN MY NIGHTMARE
THE NIGHT OF THE HUNTRESS
MORE PAGES
MORE NEW STORIES

# JOHN SEVERIN

**JOHN** Powers Severin was born on December 26, 1921, in Jersey City, New Jersey. Much has been written about Severin regarding his various careers at EC, Marvel and other publishers. Strangely, Severin has contributed more work to *Cracked* than any other single project in his lifetime, yet precious little is mentioned about this fact, such is the stigma attached to *Cracked* and humor magazines in general, in regards to artistic integrity and accomplishment. Severin, at times, has achieved major successes with *Cracked* - namely with his caricaturing ability, which is incredibly lifelike rather than the exaggerated Mort Drucker-style.

Mort Todd explains that Severin had previous experience with humor before settling in on *Cracked*. "Severin did *The Hobo News* as a kid and art when Atlas did some *Mad*-a-likes, after he had a falling out with *Mad*. I guess he left while Kurtzman was still running the magazine, so he started looking for other work." He did work for *Riot* and the short-lived *Loco*, among other humor assignments.

Severin was offered the assignment of drawing the first cover of *Cracked*. He drew his cover layout idea and brought it in for approval. The problem was, Sproul was not about to pay as much as *Mad* (which by this time had converted to a magazine), so Severin passed on completing the assignment, and close friend Bill Everett came on board to paint the first cover, using much of Severin's layout. Michelina Severin remembers, "Yeah. He did the layout sketch for it, and he was so caught up in things, he gave the sketch to Bill." Thus, Severin's cover debut for *Cracked* began with issue #2.

Ultimately, *Cracked* probably wouldn't have survived if it weren't for the talents of John Severin. There were many issues almost entirely drawn by him. For instance, Severin singlehandedly drew the entire issue of *Cracked* #26, minus a one-page Bill Elder reprint and a subscription ad by Bill Ward, totaling 50 new pages!

Michelina Severin remembers how John was able to do it: "He was fast; much faster than he is now. He used to sometimes change styles because he would do so much at *Cracked*; he thought it might get boring seeing so much from him, 'cause John can change styles. He used to do things under other names."

Michelina explains the origin of John's many pen names: "Powers is John's middle name. LePoer is French for Powers. There's 'Nireves,' which is 'Severin' backwards. 'Sigbjorn'? That's Swedish for Severin. I know he did a cover during the time of James Bond and he signed it 'O.O. Severin.' It was because James Bond was so popular and it was a pun on 'Double-O Seven.' Sometimes he'd put 'Noel' because he's born the day after Christmas. He had great fun with it, doing those things."

Artist and friend Russ Heath agrees. "I think *Cracked* survived mostly due to Severin. He could do serious and crazy. No matter what it called for, he had a number of different styles. It was basically a one-man magazine for 40 years or something like that. He seems very unemotional when you talk to him about that. He won't answer the phone half the time now because he doesn't want to be bothered."

Michelina Severin continues, "John was a separate entity. They would pay John regularly whether he did work or not. Sproul set it up that way. I know other people would have problems getting paid. They were slow, but they did get paid. No, we never had a contract. When Michael Delle-Femine became editor, it was the same thing with Michael and then same with everyone else, later. One fee for the original and a separate one for reprints.

"We had an agreement. It's funny now; there was no contract. He did the work and then he got paid. And, all through the years when he worked at Marvel Comics, he would go in and give it to Stan Lee and then Stan got the check from Mr. Goodman. Also, we own *Sagebrush* and *Hang Ups*. The way it works, I think we own the rights to them, but not the ones that were published."

John sometimes did the coloring on his art. What isn't well known is that John Severin is colorblind. The most blatant example of this is on the cover of *Cracked* #192 in which Sylvester visits the planet inhabited by the characters from *E.T.* In *E.T.*, the characters are brown; on John's *Cracked* cover, they are green!

The obvious question is if John Severin was such a vital part of *Cracked*, why didn't Al Feldstein lure Severin back to *Mad*, thus effectively putting *Cracked* out of business? Feldstein certainly lured Angelo Torres and Jack Davis from *Sick*, thereby crippling one of *Mad*'s most enduring competitors into ultimate cancellation. Michelina Severin confirmed that John and Al weren't exactly buddy-buddy and proved this by stating that John never worked on any of Feldstein's books while at EC. Severin only worked on *Mad* when Harvey Kurtzman was in charge, and then only on the first 10 issues. Paul Laikin adds, "Severin left them, and he was one of *Mad*'s great artists."

Apparently, the feeling was mutual. In an interview in the *Crime Illustrated* volume of the Picto-Fiction box set published by Gemstone;, Feldstein was asked, "Why didn't you get John Severin to illustrate anything for the Picto-Fiction magazines?" Feldstein replied with a dry, "No comment."

Writer and future *Cracked* editor Lou Silverstone commented about whether *Mad* ever try to lure Severin away from *Cracked*: "I don't think so. They could have put *Cracked* out of business had they done that. That's why Jack Davis and Al Jaffee had to leave these books—I think it was called *Trump*—they withdrew it and they couldn't work for *Mad* for a long time after that. I had a bunch of scripts that they had accepted after the second issue. They never put that out."

Mort Todd adds, "Severin told me that if he went back to *Mad*, he would be lucky to get four pages a month. He'd be paid better than he was at *Cracked*, but he really enjoyed the fact that he could do the cover paintings and, like, 10, 15, 20 pages a month. What I thought was cool of him was that he would use all these pseudonyms to do all these different styles as 'LePoer' and such to lend some variety to the pages. He even did some Don Martin-type pages that Jay Lynch wrote. A minority of the contributors came into the office to bring their stuff in. The whole time Severin lived in Colorado. I didn't meet a lot of the out-of-town artists face-to-face until we had a party for the *Cracked* 30th anniversary in 1988. We brought Severin out and tons of other cartoonists."

Russ Heath has only kind words for Severin: "John Severin was a friend of mine since the beginning—I don't know—'46 or '47 or somewhere in there. He would come over to my house. One time with his wife and with my wife, we went to dinner in New York. I had actually broken up with my wife; I couldn't think of anybody else to go, so I asked her. We had to wait for a table so they put us in a bar. The four of us were in there and then some guy starts hitting on my ex. Severin comes over to interfere, and I said, 'I'm a free agent and she's a free agent, you can't mess with that,' but it never went anywhere from there, anyway—just an interesting sidelight.

"We usually talk about twice a year. I went over to his house one time for dinner. I guess that's why he's still married. I remember Michelina was cooking chicken in a paper bag or something or it was lasagna in a paper bag and the paper bag blew up because we were late."

Mike Ricigliano offers his appreciation for Severin: "He could do everything. You could go through some issues of *Cracked* and John Severin would have ¾'s of the art in the magazine using different styles or whatever. He was phenomenal.

"My favorite thing that I ever got to do for *Cracked* was a cover for one of the *Collectors' Editions*. I had the idea of doing like a *Gulliver's Travels* type of cover with the Saboteurs and Sylvester and so John and I worked together on it over the phone. He did the artwork and then I did overlays on it. I did all sorts of little things with ladders and ropes and it really was a fun cover. It's one of the *Crackeds* I actually have in my portfolio. I was so fond to work for John on it. I was very proud of it.

"I think it's great that John's still around and doing stuff. I just wasn't aware of it. I am such a big fan of his—he and his sister, Marie. She's such an amazing artist and she worked all those years for Marvel, also.

"At the time I was there, John did at least half the book. Joe Catalano was the main writer there when I was there. He did a lot of the work. Whatever the main features would be. He wrote funny stuff as well."

B.K. Taylor responds about Severin, "I was a big fan of John Severin, and of course some of the other big names that passed through—but Severin was always there and always turned out great art."

Tony Tallarico adds, "Severin's artwork was a lot, but he was the star. He was getting more than $40 a page."

Paul Laikin concurs: "John Severin, he was the only one that I didn't handle at the time. Bob Sproul, I guess, was afraid that John would take offense if I directed him. When I had written things for him, I sent things to Bob and he sent it to John. He handled John Severin himself. I don't even know how he handled all of that. He was handled by the boss himself, Bob Sproul.

"John was in Colorado and we were in New York, although he came to my engagement when I got married in the 1960s. John Severin came to my bachelor party, and Bill Everett and other people...a few people from *Cracked* and Bob Sproul.

"Unbelievable, that guy. He was great. I loved his stuff because it wasn't far out like Jack Davis and Will Elder; they were also very good."

In the John Severin interview with Gary Groth from *The Comics Journal* #215, August 1999, Severin said, "Even in *Cracked* today, if you picked up a *Cracked*, the people draw funny funny-pictures that to me, defeats the purpose of the humor. What I was saying was, you look at the stuff and then you look at mine, you see my stuff was almost serious.

"And the reason is, I think the thing is funnier if you have a serious person getting pie in the face than if you have a silly looking jackass acting like a goon. He gets hit with a pie, you figure, 'To hell with it? Who cares?' So in my vague attempts to do it that way, I probably don't hit the mark with as many people as I could if I were to change, alter it. Still I enjoy doing it my way.

"Well, I like it. But I'm willing to take any kind of criticism along those lines because sometimes it helps. And other times I realize that I just couldn't change. If I end up by being wrong I just would have an awful time changing it."

Though Severin can and has drawn humorous drawings, his style was almost too realistic when it came to drawing horror, which is why he seldom drew for the EC or Warren horror books. Comments Mort Todd, "John told me that he did sample drawing for the EC horror books, and it was just way too gruesome. Way too anatomically correct. He did a severed limb with every single vein and bone, and torn flesh and everything. It was like 'Yaaah!' His drawings were too photorealistic.

"Before I was at *Cracked*, I think a lot of Severin's stuff there had gotten stiff and he might have been just kinda cranking it out. I believe to a degree it was due to my fan-boy attitude that I got more inspired work out of him and other artists. Once I got the artwork I was like, 'Aww, man! I love that panel!' I feel his stuff was much more animated during my stay, and then after I left I felt 'Why waste Severin doing a *Simpsons* parody?' Gary Fields can do a better job with that, and have more feeling for it. You've got to use Severin for his strengths, the money shot!"

## JOHN SEVERIN ART GALLERY

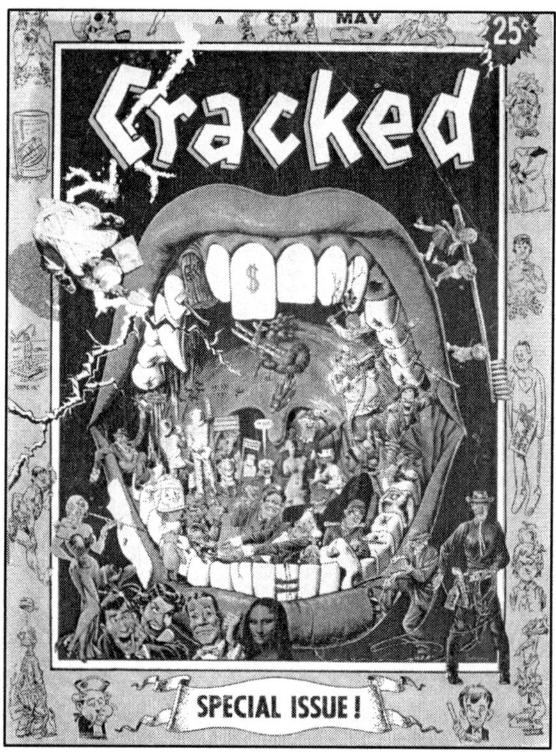


*Cracked* #2, May 1958, Severin's first cover for *Cracked* (although he did design the cover for #1).

This is from an article called "Rejected *Cracked* Covers" from *Cracked* #21, September 1961. Strangely, one of the images was eventually used for issue #31.

. . . And here is the revised version used as *Cracked* #31, September 1963.

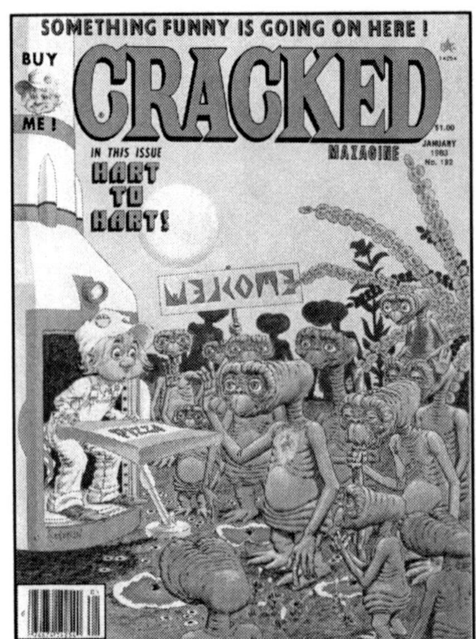


*Cracked* #192, January 1983. Although it is in black and white, this is the cover that shows that Severin is colorblind as all the E.T.s are green.

Detail of cover from *Cracked Collectors' Edition* #86, April 1991, one of Mike Ricigliano's favorites, which he still keeps in his portfolio.

The original art for "Lowering the Mental Level of TV Programs"... Image courtesy of Jerry Boyd.

And final form as published in *Cracked* #70, August 1968.

The original art for the cover of *Cracked Collectors' Edition* #112, September 1997... Image courtesy of Jerry Boyd.

And final form as published.

John Severin's final cover for *Cracked* #342, March 2000, that Mort Todd feels artwork like this should have been done by Gary Fields.

Severin at work on yet another *Cracked* cover from *The Comics Journal* #215, August 1999.

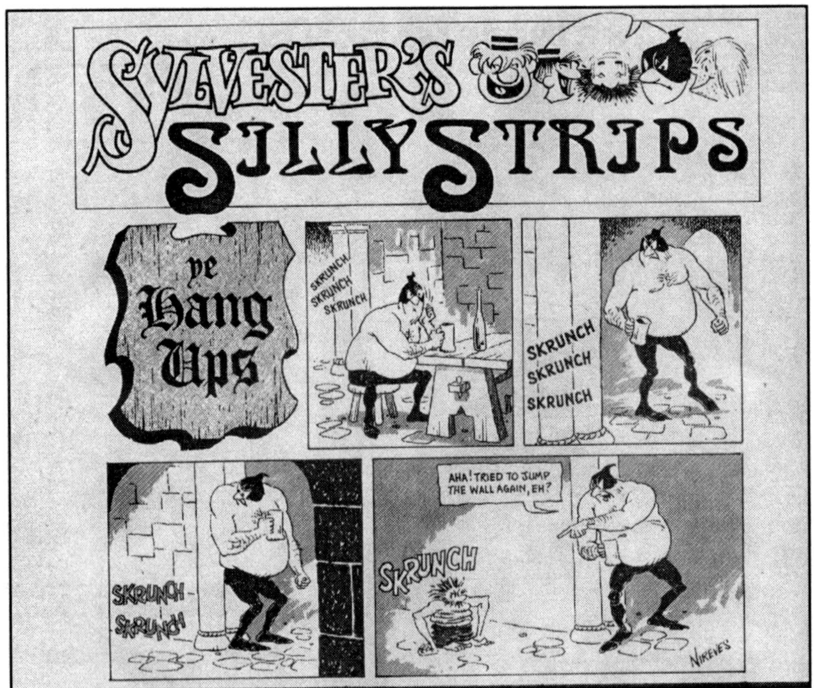


The 1st *Ye Hang Ups* strip from *Cracked* #114, January 1974.

Severin draws himself and other *Cracked* regulars in "*Cracked* 30th Anniversary Party!" from *Cracked* #238, September 1988.

Severin draws Severin for the article "Artist John Severin: The Granddaddy of *Cracked*!" from *Cracked* #347, September 2000.

The 1st *Sagebrush* strip from *Cracked* #78, August 1969.

# THE SOL BRODSKY YEARS

ON January 3, 1958, the new magazine hit the newsstands. *Cracked* would become the most successful *Mad* competitor ever published, bearing a cover date of March 1958.

Michelina Severin recalls, "Sol Brodsky set it up, but Bernie Brill was the main money man. He was the owner of it. Bob Sproul had a part ownership of it. Bob had about a quarter of it. I think the way it was, Sol went back to Marvel and Bob took over as publisher and editor."

Don Orehek adds, "Sol Brodsky was a good guy and I worked with him."

As *Cracked*'s original editor, Brodsky helped originate some *Cracked* staples, including the magazine's original three mascots: the sexy lady with cigarette holder named Veronica, the disheveled magazine editor referred to as "Der Editor" and janitor Sylvester P. Smythe. Veronica and Der Editor were dropped after Brodsky departed.

Russ Heath was one of the first artists Brodsky recruited to draw for the fledgling publication. Heath explains his brief tenure at *Cracked*: "I wasn't in the office, so I had no personal contact other than with Brodsky, who was up in New York. I do recall seeing Sproul physically when he was up here. I remember he was a tall, lighter figure. I assume that I'm remembering him. I'm not sure of anything anymore.

"I had a bunch of dumb, fun jokes that I was glad to get rid of doing those 'comic' ones. I got to throw all that crap in the backgrounds once that was out of my system. I didn't pay any attention about when I worked on *Cracked*. You'd learn as much by just reading the dates on the publication.

"I was supposed to go to work for them again, [but] I guess it was a misunderstanding. He called back on a second call to give me some stuff on a short deadline. Most people understand that you're working for more than one editor at a time. I said that I could start on it next week. They said, 'You can't start on it immediately? Well, then I don't want to talk to you.' That was the end of that. I don't know who that was I was talking to."

Another *Cracked* legend that was there at the beginning was Don Orehek. "Don's a little more zany," recalls Artist Aron Laikin.

Mike Ricigliano agrees. "I don't remember talking to him that much, but I did some whenever we needed to get some gags, too. Of course, Don Orehek's stuff was in *Playboy*, so his stuff was in a lot of different places, too, but he, like a lot of the rest of us, had a regular gig in *Cracked* that he counted on; a certain amount of pages per month, too."

Orehek describes how he got started with the magazine: "I started working for Sam Beerman for Crestwood Publications when I first got that job after school. They did *Broadway Laughs* and all that stuff, then *Mad* magazine came out and around this time there was Bob Sproul and he thought of *Cracked* and that's how I started with *Cracked* from the very beginning.

"The *College Laughs* and then *French Cartoons* came later, and the stuff that I did for *Cracked* was stuff that they bought from writers and then farmed it out to the different cartoonists, myself and Severin, Vic Martin, and all those guys."

Returning to comics for the first time since the Comics Code, Bill Ward did not sign his work as "Ward" for a number of years, preferring to use the name "McCartney," and debuting in issue #2. It is not known whether this change was made because of Ward's previous "blacklisting" from comic books as one of the casualties of the Comic Code Authority. Whatever the reason, Don Orehek explains where the name "McCartney" came from: "His wife. He was married to a British gal. He used to use her maiden name. I don't know if it was McCartney. I never met him. I knew that one of the names he used was his wife's maiden name."

Mike Ricigliano offers his memories of Ward: "I remember this conversation with him that his audience was just a little younger than *Mad* and because of it, his writing and the way he conducted business was targeted just that way, where there would be writing that was a little too sophisticated, he would actually purposefully—I don't want to say he dumbed it down—he'd pick things out of it that he thought would be too adult or whatever. All this was being done while this guy Ward was drawing girls that were half-undressed all the time in the magazine, so that was a contradiction of whatever he wanted, I would think."

Mort Todd comments about Ward when he brought him back to *Cracked* during his later years: "Ward wasn't working for the magazine for a couple years and I loved his stuff from way back. Ward must have introduced millions of kids to sexuality. You know, if your dad didn't have *Playboy* or something, here was some pretty exotic stuff. I can remember being seven years old and looking at a *Cracked* and then some 15 years later, I'm going through these back issues and I was like, 'Oh my God!' I saw a panel by Ward that I hadn't seen since then and I remembered every square inch of it, 'cause

I had been absorbing it then. Forget simple breast cleavage, with Ward you would get toe cleavage, too! It was fetished out to the max. I sincerely think for a lot of young boys and young girls that was definitely their first sexual awakening, going, like, 'Why do I really, really like this drawing?'

"He hadn't worked at *Cracked* for awhile because Sproul dicked him over. Ward had just bought a house and Sproul owed him checks. Sproul always took care of Severin, and from what I hear from a lot of other artists, checks were often late, but he couldn't afford to lose Severin. Bill didn't work for *Cracked* after that until I tracked him down to pay him for reprints and started commissioning new work from him. A few people I called were like Ward, who asked, 'Er, is Sproul still there?'"

Unfortunately, Ward's final pieces were quite shaky and were printed during the Lou Silverstone era, "Yeah, they were in inventory. I commissioned them, but they were printed after I left. They wouldn't give Ward work." Ward passed away in 1998.

Special mention should be made of a few early *Cracked* regulars, who were best known for other projects. Joe Maneely was an Atlas refugee who was contributing regularly to *Cracked* until a commuter train hit and killed him in an unfortunate accident on June 7, 1958. His last work appeared in *Cracked* #5, October 1958.

Paul Reinman was an inker for Jack Kirby who also worked on many books for Marvel, DC and Archie. He passed away in 1988.

Bill Everett was the creator of the Sub-Mariner for Marvel Comics and drew the front cover for *Cracked* #1. He died in 1973.

Carl Burgos was the creator of the Human Torch for Marvel Comics. He worked on a few other Sproul publications and died in 1984.

Ed Winiarski was an animator and a funny-animal cartoonist, mainly for DC. It is believed he passed away in 1975.

Al Williamson drew for EC, Warren and many comic strips. He lived in New York City until his death in 2010.

Bernard Baily created the Spectre and Hourman for DC Comics. He did some art direction with Harry Chester on *Cracked*. He retired in 1980 and died in 1996.

Syd Shores was best known for his work on *Captain America* and died in 1973.

Pete Costanza worked on Fawcett's *Captain Marvel* and a number of other comic book companies before passing away in 1984.

Gray Morrow worked for Warren and had two brief tenures at *Cracked*; the Sol Brodsky period and again when Mort Todd was in charge. He took his own life in 2001. Says Mort Todd of Morrow: "Gray Morrow was an incredible guy. I don't know if he was credited in the early issues. He did some beautiful gouache stuff that looked like gorgeous paintings, and I think

*Overstreet* miscredits him as Wally Wood. The *Price Guide* says Wally Wood was in, like, #9. Wood was never in *Cracked*, but Davis and Elder were, and how that came about was they were all blackballed from *Mad* after they left with Kurtzman, and then Humbug went out of business."

Basil Wolverton is best known for his crazy drawings that filled the pages of various comic books. His most famous creations are the cover to *Mad* #11, the covers to many issues of *Plop!*, and his winning entry to the Lena the Hyena contest for the *Li'l Abner* comic strip. He died in 1978.

Chic Stone was another Jack Kirby inker who did a lot of work on *Fantastic Four*. He passed away in 2000.

Jerry Siegel is best known for being the co-creator of *Superman*. He wrote for *Cracked* with his name spelled "Siegal." He died in 1996.

One of the happy accidents of the Brodsky era was the folding of Harvey Kurtzman's *Humbug*, which was self-financed by Kurtzman and his team of artists: Al Jaffee, Bill Elder, Jack Davis and Arnold Roth. As the final issue of *Humbug* rolled off the presses, Jaffee, Elder and Davis all bailed out for the greener pastures of *Cracked*, albeit briefly.

Today, Al Jaffee is so strongly associated with *Mad* that he no longer remembers that he did work briefly for *Cracked* for three issues in late 1958: "I wish I could help but the fact is I never did anything for *Cracked* that I know of. All I do know that relates to *Cracked* is that John Severin (an old schoolmate) was there and Don Martin joined in later years. Jerry De Fuccio also had some connection there after leaving *Mad*. He had a close relationship with Severin."

Mort Todd adds, "Jerry De Fuccio was Michelena Severin's cousin."

After receiving scans of his *Cracked* work, Jaffee was genuinely beside himself: "My memory, which is nothing to brag about, is very vague about these titles. Of course, after *Humbug*'s demise, I would have been happy with the work if it was offered.

"I really don't know what to say. My name is there and the stuff looks somewhat like my style, yet I don't remember it. I do recall Paul Laikin talking to me about doing something or other. It's a mystery to me. One thing sure, I have no problem admitting I did work for *Cracked*, if indeed I did. They had excellent artists and writers and were good competitors to *Mad*." Jaffee soon returned to *Mad*, contributing regularly to this day.

Fellow *Mad* artist Angelo Torres also had difficulty remembering his short stint at *Cracked*. Said Torres, "Sorry to say, I never did any work for *Cracked*, either. Prior to *Mad*, I worked with Joe Simon on *Sick* magazine. Good luck with your history of *Cracked*. It should be great fun going back over all that wonderful work by John Severin and others."

He, too, was sent scans of his work: "I guess I was wrong after seeing my name on the *Cracked* masthead. I couldn't figure out where Al Jaffee came in, though. I drew those pages, but I can't recall doing much else for *Cracked*. The masthead says 1959 and it was about that time that *Sick* was launched by Joe Simon and I worked for *Sick* from issue #1 until August 1967. I don't remember anything about working for *Cracked*, how I got the work or whom I dealt with at the publication. During that period I was doing a lot of different things and work came from many directions and I have lost track of most of it.

"Regarding *Sick*, it was Joe Simon's idea to put together another humor magazine to compete with *Mad* and *Cracked*. They came up with the idea, loosely inspired by Jules Feiffer's *Sick Sick Sick* cartoon feature which was hot at the time, settled on one *Sick*, and went on from there. Joe, being one of the nicest people in the business, I had no problem working for him all those years. In 1969, I went to work for *Mad*. I hope this helps a bit. This all took place so many years ago it's hard keeping track."

Bill Elder worked slightly longer at *Cracked* than Jaffee or Torres, even contributing a cover painting for Brodsky's last issue, #10, but apparently working for *Cracked* wasn't the most ideal situation for Elder as he soon rejoined Kurtzman with his next project, *Help!*, as did Jack Davis.

Jack Davis was not a fan of *Cracked*. In a brief interview with Davis, he revealed, "I hated it! It was low pay and low prestige, but I was afraid to go back to *Mad*. It was not a happy environment at *Cracked*. I did not have a good time. The pay rates were not good, but I was afraid to go back to *Mad* after leaving for *Trump*, so I worked for both *Cracked* and *Sick* before Stan Hart suggested I go back to *Mad* in 1965 and everyone approved. The positive aspect of being away from *Mad* is that it allowed me to work on projects that I probably wouldn't have gotten otherwise had I stayed like movie posters for United Artists and magazine covers like *Time* and *TV Guide* and many albums covers for RCA records."

Brodsky edited the first ten issues of *Cracked* before Martin Goodman made a lucrative offer for Brodsky to return to the Marvel Bullpen. Brodsky jumped at the chance and the rest is history where Marvel was concerned. Soon, people like Carl Burgos, Paul Reinman, Russ Heath, Bill Everett, Syd Shores, Bernard Baily, Gray Morrow, Jack Kirby, Chic Stone, Basil Wolverton, Jerry Siegel departed as well, by either joining Brodsky, or moving on to other projects. Comments Mort Todd on Brodsky's return, "I would imagine it was because Marvel got back on its feet. They were in need a full-time art department and once Marvel Comics officially started, he was already back there."

As for *Cracked*, Sproul searched around for a suitable replacement for Brodsky, but discovered that his replacement was already *Cracked*'s top writer, Paul Laikin, who had written for *Cracked* since issue #2. Laikin tended to edit his own material anyway, so coupled with the fact that Laikin became the sole writer for *Cracked* after Brodsky's departure, the promotion to editor seemed natural.

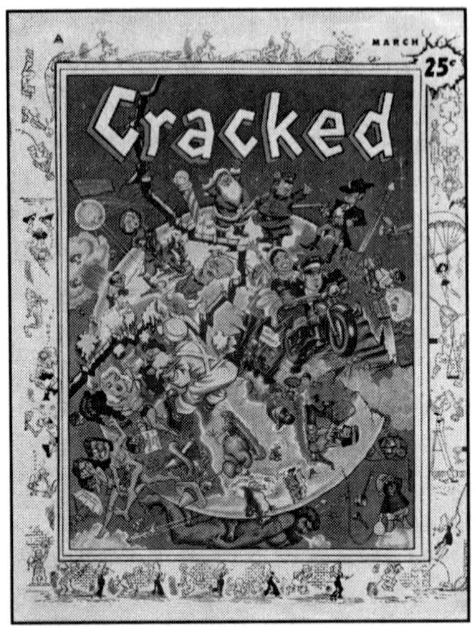


This is it, the very first issue of *Cracked*, March 1958.

The very first article drawn by John Severin in *Cracked* #1.

Der Editor, one of the three original mascots.

Veronica, one of the three original mascots.

Sylvester, one of the three original mascots.

Don Orehek, one of the best free-lance cartoonists around, has been a CRACKED artist for many years. He also contributes to some of America's other best-known magazines, ranging in audience, from GOOD HOUSEKEEPING to PLAYBOY. We at CRACKED are proud to introduce you to Don Orehek, in our series of . . .

GUEST APPEARANCES BY THE WORLD'S TOP HUMOR

ARTISTS

Being a very serious-type person, I shall tell it like it is. I have been drawing cartoons since 1956 and, to get away from my work, I have a hobby . . . drawing cartoons.

Aha, but these are different: They are in watercolor, and framed, and are shown in art shows; and they sell too . . . sometimes.

My beautiful wife and two beautiful children and I live on Long Island and, in the summer, I cook out on the barbeque grill almost every day. My steak is raved about from one end of the redwood deck to the other.

We have two cats, Biki (the baby named him when he tried to say "kitty") and Pinkie (who is brown but has a very pink nose). I like pigs too (the four-footed kind) but, for some reason, the city won't let me keep them.

Back in 1966, two other cartoonists and I went to Vietnam to entertain wounded G.I.'s. We were the first artists to go into an actual war zone. When we returned, we were invited to the White House and met President Johnson who thanked us for boosting the morale of the wounded servicemen.

Other than drawing to relax, I enjoy watching old movies, the older the better. But, on a Sunday afternoon, when they run five hours of Laurel & Hardy on TV, don't call me . . . I'll call you!

"HERE COMES A CUSTOMER."

42

Don Orehek as featured in the first of two "Guest Appearances by the World's Top Humor Artists" articles from *Cracked* #106, January 1973.

Don Orehek photo from *Cracked* #239, October 1988.

The very first *Shut-Ups* from *Cracked* #2, May 1958, art by Bill Ward.

Al Jaffee does *Shut-Ups* from *Cracked* #5, October 1958.

"Easy, Exciting Way to Earn Money in Beautiful Mexico" from *Cracked* #6, December 1958, art by Al Jaffee.

"Learn While You Snore!" from *Cracked* #6, December 1958, art by Al Jaffee.

"How a Rumor Gets Started" from *Cracked* #7, February 1959, art by Al Jaffee.

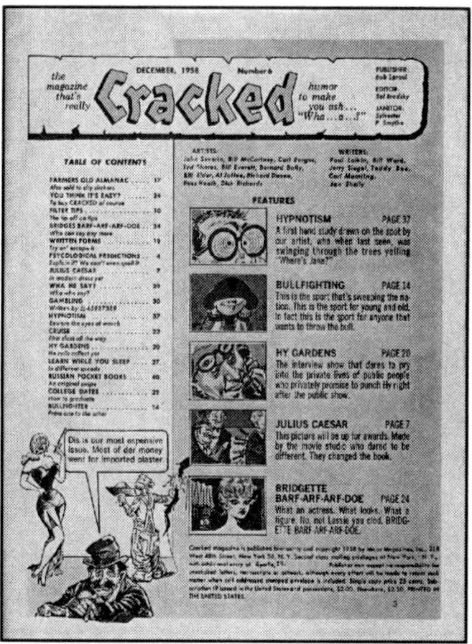

DECEMBER, 1958 Number 6

the magazine that's really **Cracked** humor to make you ask... "Wha...a...?"

PUBLISHER: Bob Sproul
EDITOR: Sol Brodsky
JANITOR: Sylvester P. Smythe

ARTISTS: John Severin, Bill McCartney, Carl Burgos, Syd Shores, Bill Everett, Bernard Baily, Bill Elder, Al Jaffee, Richard Doxsee, Russ Heath, Dick Richards

WRITERS: Paul Laikin, Bill Ward, Jerry Siegel, Teddy Bee, Carl Memling, Joe Shelly

TABLE OF CONTENTS

| | |
|---|---|
| FARMERS OLD ALMANAC | 17 |
| YOU THINK IT'S EASY? | 24 |
| FILTER TIPS | 10 |
| BRIDGES BARF-ARF-ARF-DOE | 24 |
| WRITTEN FORMS | 19 |
| PSYCOLOGICAL PREDICTIONS | 4 |
| JULIUS CAESAR | 7 |
| WHA HE SAY? | 29 |
| GAMBLING | 30 |
| HYPNOTISM | 37 |
| CRUISE | 22 |
| HY GARDENS | 20 |
| LEARN WHILE YOU SLEEP | 27 |
| RUSSIAN POCKET BOOKS | 40 |
| COLLEGE DATES | 23 |
| BULLFIGHTER | 14 |

FEATURES

HYPNOTISM PAGE 37
A first hand study drawn on the spot by our artist, who when last seen, was swinging through the trees yelling "Where's Jane?"

BULLFIGHTING PAGE 14
This is the sport that's sweeping the nation. This is the sport for young and old. In fact this is the sport for anyone that wants to throw the bull.

HY GARDENS PAGE 20
The interview show that dares to pry into the private lives of public people who privately promise to punch Hy right after the public show.

JULIUS CAESAR PAGE 7
This picture will be up for awards. Made by the movie studio who dared to be different. They changed the book.

BRIDGETTE BARF-ARF-ARF-DOE PAGE 24
What an actress. What looks. What a figure. No, not Lassie you clod. BRIDGETTE BARF-ARF-ARF-DOE.



3

Al Jaffee mentioned in *Cracked* #6, December 1958.

FEBRUARY, 1959 Number 7

the magazine that's really **Cracked** humor to make you ask... "Huh?...?"

PUBLISHER: Bob Sproul
EDITOR: Sol Brodsky
SCRIPT EDITOR: Paul Laikin
JANITOR: Sylvester P. Smythe

TABLE OF CONTENTS

| | |
|---|---|
| GREAT BATTLES | 28 |
| RUMORS | 32 |
| POSTURE STRAIGHTENING | 16 |
| THE MILLIONEARS | 9 |
| THINGS ARE TOUGH ALL OVER | 21 |
| IMAGINARY FEARS | 12 |
| COMPANY NAMES | 36 |
| OUR TWO FACES | 34 |
| RUSSIAN SCIENTISTS | 39 |
| ANNIVERSARY | 22 |
| CHRISTMAS CARDS | 4 |
| SOMETHING TO BE THANKFUL FOR | 24 |
| SUPERMARKETS | 36 |
| KNOW YOUR AMERICA | 18 |
| CIGARETTE PACKS | 30 |
| DON SWANSON | 8 |
| LITTLE KNOWN FAMOUS PEOPLE | 7 |
| PHOTO CONTEST WINNERS | 38 |
| SHUT-UPS | 42 |

FEATURES

IMAGINARY FEARS PAGE 12
An article which plainly tells you how to get rid of your imaginary fears—and get some good, real, earthy ones.

THE MILLIONEARS PAGE 9
The only television program where they give away a million dollars—and you don't have to answer any questions.

RUSSIAN SCIENTISTS PAGE 39
A startling report on Russia's revolutionary new machine—a machine that starts new revolutions.

SUPERMARKETS PAGE 35
The latest news on a growing American phenomenon that is sweeping the country, drawn by an artist who should himself be out sweeping the country.

RUMORS PAGE 32
A rumor can be vicious and ugly. It is never very funny. Neither is our two page article on it.



3

Al Jaffee and Angelo Torres mentioned in *Cracked* #7, February 1959.

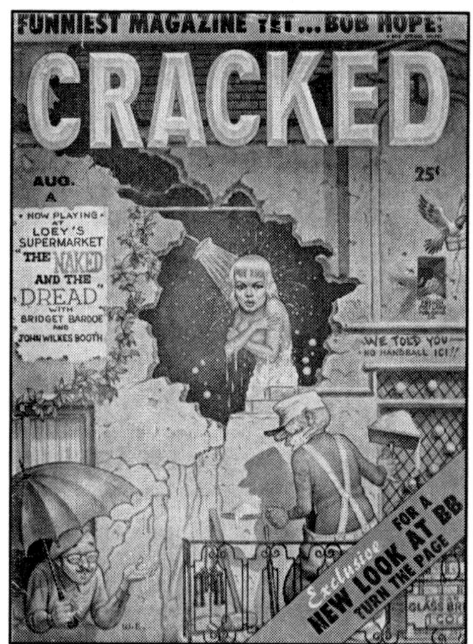


*Cracked* #10, August 1959, art by Bill Elder. This was also the final issue edited by Sol Brodsky and Elder's only cover for *Cracked*.

B.K. Taylor with Bill Elder. Image courtesy of B.K. Taylor.

*Casual Format* from *Cracked* #10, August 1959, art by Angelo Torres.

*Casual Format* from *Cracked* #12, January 1960, art by Angelo Torres.

Cracked Artists' Portfolio from *Cracked Collectors' Edition* #79, July 1989.

John Severin did the first Nanny Dickering interview in *Cracked* #99, March 1972. Bill Ward's rendition did not begin until *Cracked* #117, July 1974.

Bill Ward does Dave Berg in "*Cracked* Looks at Dating," from *Cracked* #76, May 1969.

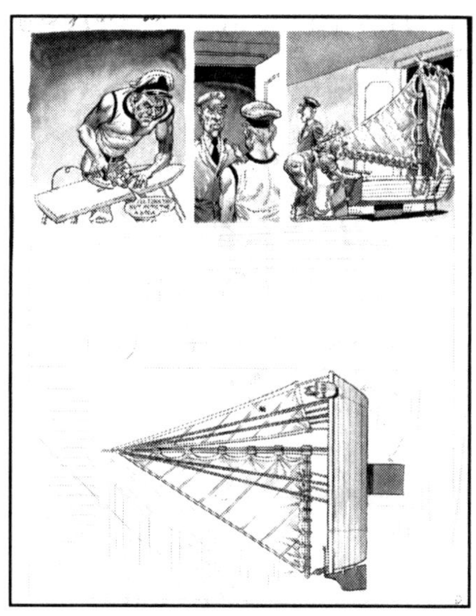

Three pages of Ward original art. Images courtesy of Greg Beda.

# PAUL LAIKIN

**WHILE** it was Severin that was the artistic and visual "glue" that held everything together at *Cracked*, it didn't start out that way. Initially, the pages of *Cracked* were populated by a virtual who's who of top talents rivaling those of *Mad*. In fact, some of the same artists and writers worked for both *Mad* and *Cracked* until *Mad* editor Al Feldstein put his foot down on the practice. He decided quickly after a rash of imitators popped up that having the same artists and writers appear at *Mad* and elsewhere would "cheapen" the *Mad* brand, and people would soon not know the difference. Most *Mad* people claimed an allegiance to *Mad*; some continued on appearing in both, using a pen name for other publications; still others, like Paul Laikin, defected to *Cracked* and other publications.

Laikin explains how he got into *Mad* and eventually *Cracked*: "When Harvey Kurtzman left *Mad* magazine, Al Feldstein took over. Kurtzman was writing *Mad* magazine, but when he left, there was nobody to write it. It was just artists that were doing it. Al Feldstein didn't know anybody, so he put an ad in the paper looking for writers. I went up and no one else was there and they sent me to do a movie spoof on *The Bad Seed*. Remember that, with Patty McCormack? I called it, *The Bad Seat*. The picture was so bad, so that's why it was *The Bad Seat*. [Note: This piece originally appeared in *Mad* #32, April 1957, but Paul Laikin's name was not mentioned until *Mad* #33, June 1957.]

"That was my first as a writer. I started writing for *Mad*. I did a piece. I was the first writer at *Mad* because it says, 'Bob and Ray,' but they took one of their radio spoofs and they illustrated it; and Paul Laikin, you'll see it in one of them. There was one guy that came in the same time as me, Frank Jacobs. Frank and me were the only in-house writers. Anyhow, I worked there for two years. It was going to end soon, but when *Mad* came out, it made such a big splash with Al Feldstein. When Harvey Kurtzman had it, it was still a comic book and 10 cents, but when it went to a slick—25 cents—that's when they called for writers. Frank Jacobs and I were the only two people who answered that ad, 'cause there were no writers.

"Previously, I saw it as a comic book. Harvey was writing it. Harvey's humor wasn't my kind of humor anyhow, but I saw the potential when this fellow showed me—I think it was issue #24—when it turned into a slick. When I went up there, there wasn't much time elapsing between when the guest showed me the book and when the ad in the *Times* appeared.

"When I wrote for *Mad*, Al Feldstein would look at a page and say, 'This is a little weak,' and give me comedy pointers and I was already in my 30s. He was just a horror comics' writer. What does he know about comedy? He's editing my pieces. That was a big part of it. He had about 12 scripts in his drawer of mine that weren't in. I asked, 'You're passing on my material?' I admit it wasn't great stuff, but that was a key feature of why I chose *Cracked*. I could put whatever I wanted, they didn't edit me, and I didn't have to work so hard. At *Mad*, you had to work for your pay. They went through every line. They did a good job and Al Feldstein was a good editor, but I just didn't want to work that hard.

"I started writing other stuff like a cannibal's menu with roast shoulder and some other things. When *Mad* came out at that time, they started to become a hit and sold immensely and then *Cracked* came out, because *Mad* made such a splash. Soon as I saw issue #1 of *Cracked*, I said, 'Wow! This is a phenomenon!' So, I went to *Cracked* and I started writing for *Cracked*. I was in issue #2 and 3. Sol Brodsky was the editor and Bob Sproul was the publisher. So when *Mad* found out I had put my name in it, they said, 'You can't be writing for *Mad* and *Cracked*. Sorry, but you have to choose one.' So me—which shows you the choices I've made in life—that I'm here in West Babylon and not on the Riviera—chose *Cracked*. *Cracked* was easier to do. There were a lot of reasons. I don't remember. Illogical reasons. *Cracked* took everything I wrote, because there was no one really to edit you.

"About issue #7 or so, Sol Brodsky got a call from Stan Lee to take him over to Marvel Comics. So he left for Marvel, and Bob Sproul called me into his office and said, 'Sol is leaving. Would you like to be editor of *Cracked*?' I said, 'Great!' 'Crazy' is what I should have said. 'How much do you want?' 'Well, how much do you want to pay?' I came up with a figure like $200, I didn't care, and it wasn't about the money for my day job. 'I'll give you $400,' which shows you how far off I was. I could probably live on $400 a month. I couldn't live on the other, but I didn't take it to live on. So, I became the editor I think with issue #11, and Sol Brodsky went on to do Marvel Comics. I left *Mad* because they didn't want me writing for *Cracked*, even if I used a different name. I used my own name and I must have quit my day job."

Basically, Laikin was given a choice. Although a quick writer and one that was frequently published, Laikin enjoyed the freedom writing for *Cracked* and the other publications that *Mad* did not offer him. Ultimately,

Laikin is the unsung hero of the black-and-white humor magazine genre. Although he did not originate the form or create any of the spin-off titles (save for *Wacko* in 1981), Laikin did write for virtually every black-and-white humor magazine that was created from 1956-1986 and edited three of the four magazines with the lengthiest runs (*Cracked, Crazy, Sick*) at one point or another.

Laikin explains, "When *Mad* made the big splash and then *Cracked* came out, there was *Thimk*, then I got calls and then I saw *Frantic*. As soon as I saw that, I went there, too. There was no one to stop me. I could write for all of them. I was writing for *Thimk* and every one. All I had to do is see the first issue and I went over there. I couldn't write it with *Mad*'s kind of criteria with every word checking this. My own level of humor was sustainable in these magazines and there really was no one else to question it. They had to take me. Only *Mad* objected and with Bill Gaines, they paid good money and were #1. The rest didn't care. The readers didn't care. Just change your name, which I did. I would change my own name. I was writing for *Thimk*, *Frenzy*, *Loco*, all while writing for *Cracked*. I was writing for *Zany*, too, yeah. Right, Bob Sproul had another one. It was a written type of thing. I think it was beneath me at that time. I still have all the issues. I don't remember the reason. I guess he felt there was enough market for two humor magazines.

"As a matter of fact, I did a book with *Mad* magazine, one of their writers. You know Arnie Kogen? He came to my house to do something with me. That was the worst writing experience I had ever had. We did an article for *Mad* and we were up until two in the morning in my living room. It had to be this way. I would have finished it at seven o'clock and it was work. To do it the right way was work, especially when you had to write with another guy. He was bigger and did TV work with *The Johnny Carson Show*. I went back to my day job, eventually. So, who was right? Anyhow, that was the *Mad* type format vs. the *Cracked* type, which I enjoyed. It was perfect for my temperament and writing and how I do things. I wanted to be a comedy writer and buckled down and went into television. I eventually did anyhow, but this was right up my alley, because it wasn't hard work at all."

Jim Warren of Warren Publications fame (*Creepy, Eerie, Famous Monsters*) had this to say in David A. Roach and Jon B. Cooke's *The Warren Companion*: "Paul Laikin wrote for *Cracked*. Then later on he replaced Harvey Kurtzman as my satirical editor for *Wildest Westerns*. He is now seen, or used to be seen, in *New York* magazine. He has one of the funniest minds in the world. He hung around our office a lot. He was a joy to be around. Paul and I palled around together. I loved his sense of humor."

Some dismiss Laikin as a hack, but understanding his unique brand of humor and consistency despite excessive corniness and predictability, his was the backbone of this particular genre that succeeded quite well until younger upstart magazines, like *National Lampoon*, paved the way for a more mature or adult-type of print publication comedy. Fans of the genre owe him a great deal for perpetuating a comedic style that could have died in the late '50s or early '60s.

Laikin explains how he worked: "I came in about once a week. I told them I couldn't be in the office everyday. When I went to the office, I didn't come in; there was no office to come into. I did everything from home. I had an office at home. My desk was the kitchen table. I wrote my stuff in longhand, not even a typewriter. Although later on I used a typewriter because it's clearer. The people sent me the art and then I took the art and my typewritten copy or my penciled copy and gave it to Harry Chester or Charles Foster, whoever was the paste-up man at that time. It was the only time I ever came into the office. Otherwise, I wouldn't have to be there. There was no reason for me to be there. I wrote all my stuff at home. Artists sent me the stuff to my home.

"It was a little more formal. I wrote a script. I blocked it out. I would let loose as I was, I could spot three words that were out of place in a paragraph. We blocked it out—everything. 'Man with discouraging look talks to other fellow who reacts in horror.' I wrote the balloon dialogue and had the whole thing blocked out. I sent it to the artists and they sent the script and took my copy and the other scripts and I gave it to the paste-up man. The guy who went to Marvel, Sol Brodsky was the first paste-up man. I gave it to him and that was the only time I went in, except for covers. 'What are we going to do about the next cover?' 'Oh, there's *Butch Cassidy and the Sundance Kid*. Let's have Butch Cassidy swinging the Sundance Kid around on a bayonet or whatever,' and then they'd approve it. Bob Sproul would. Covers were their thing. Stan Lee, too, would let me do whatever I wanted, but the cover; you had to come in for the cover.

"All the artists. There were artists around. A few lingered from the older *Cracked*. Then I hired my own people. If I had any trouble or if they didn't return my phone call, I'd never call them again."

When asked whether he felt overworked by working on too many projects for *Cracked* and other publications at the same time, Laikin responded, "Never. Never! If I felt overworked, I couldn't have done it."

Laikin's first change was to "clean up" *Cracked*. Early issues of *Cracked* seemed very cluttered with lots going on on the cover and little marginal drawings of Sylvester cleaning up cracked patches throughout the magazine, and two additional mascots, which Laikin summarily dropped.

Though ultimately Severin's redesign, Sylvester P. Smythe also received a facelift that made him—well, more friendly. Early images of Sylvester showed him busy at work with nary a smile on his face and showing much disinterest in what he was doing, and with his back to the camera. With the redesign of Sylvester, strongly in evidence with Severin's cover for issue #11 in 1960, Sylvester emerged as a more "happy-go-lucky" everyman, with a personality that seemed more outgoing and friendly.

His redesign has caused this author to suggest that Severin had Harpo Marx in mind when it came to Sylvester's redesign, but this suggestion has not been substantiated by Severin: "I would say no, but I will ask John." It was probably more a happy accident, but the similarities are there. Severin remembers, "He tried to make him more friendly. It was the same thing he did with the Hulk. The Hulk was still mean until he did it."

John Severin said of his inspiration for Sylvester in *Cracked* #347: "Jackie Gleason used to have a skit on his TV show where he played a guy who ran a moving company, and there was a little guy who worked with him. Bob Sproul, the publisher, said, "Let's do a take-off on the little guy from Gleason's show. So we put him in *Cracked*. The only problem was, the guy was ugly as sin. So I changed the look of Sylvester to make him look more like an elf. He's not a little old man. I made him happier looking, more pleasant looking."

Mike Ricigliano adds his two cents about Sylvester: "I have my loyalties to Alfed E. Neuman, but I always thought that Sylvester was a great character in his own right. He was a janitor and he worked in well with the *Cracked* stuff."

With such restructuring also came an overhaul of talent. Many of *Cracked*'s early artists migrated back to comic books and Marvel specifically, or to the comforts of the more lucrative in both style and pay, *Mad*.

After this 1960-streamlined version of *Cracked*, the years 1960-65 brought fresh new faces into *Cracked* and some old favorites that endured lengthy "tours of duty." These included Vic Martin, George Gladir, Jay Lynch, Charles Rodrigues, Joe Kiernan, Lennie Herman and Pete Wyma.

Paul Laikin began his long association with the late Vic Martin at this time. Martin originally did spot gag illustrations and the occasional *Shut-Ups*, but eventually came into his own with the popular *Hudd & Dini* pantomime strip starring two prisoners (closely resembling Laurel & Hardy in their 1927 silent film *The Second Hundred Years*) always intent on escape, but with one exception, not succeeding, always foiled by a unnamed mustached cop. Comments Laikin, "Vic Martin tried to imitate a little *Mad*. Like Don Martin, we had our Vic. That wasn't my style. I wasn't a pictorial person, really. I would prefer the verbal layouts and things. Vic Martin, I gave him a page or a page or two. I didn't give him anything more, because his style was out of the *Hispano el Diario*. You know what I mean." Martin went on to appear off and on in *Cracked* for the duration of its run.

Jack "King" Kirby made his sole contribution to *Cracked* in issue #14. Comments Mort Todd about the entry: "Yeah! And he rarely inks his stuff, too, and this one is." In an article Todd wrote for *The Jack Kirby Collector*, he states: "One can imagine Brodsky offering Kirby regular work at *Cracked*, but by the time he contributed his one piece to the magazine, Kirby was busy drawing western, romance and monster comics for a newly reinvigorated Atlas, and just a little over a year away from creating the Fantastic Four, thereby ushering in the Marvel Age of Comics.

"Like his *From Here to Insanity* work, Kirby inked his own art on duo-shade paper that provides camera-ready cross-hatching tones when a chemical is applied to it.

"As Editor-in-Chief of *Cracked* from 1985 to 1990, it was my main regret that I couldn't get Jack Kirby back into the fold."

Charlie Foster began production on *Cracked* in 1961 and remained in that capacity until the end of the decade. Tony Tallarico remembers Foster, "The only one left who was really on the inside is Charlie Foster, but he's kind of an oddball so you got to be nice. You know what I mean; you have to be polite, like it's a big deal that he should be in this book." Unfortunately, Foster declined to be interviewed for this book.

George Gladir made his lengthy *Cracked* writing career debut in 1962. His work appears in more issues than any other writer. Laikin comments on why the need to hire more writers came about, and that he hired Gladir, "Yeah, I believe I did hire George, but Bob Sproul did, too. At first the issues would say, "All material written by Paul Laikin, Pula Kinlai, etc." (This legend appeared in issue #11-23.) "I spelt my name different ways subtly to try to disguise the fact, but they were very observant. Bob, rightly said, 'You can't write and edit the entire magazine. It's a book! You have to have contributing writers.' So, I had to go out and search for a few writers."

Gladir takes up the story: "When I first started writing for *Cracked* in 1962, Bob Sproul was both the editor and publisher. It was his astute eye and judge of talent that enabled *Cracked* to initially survive against all the magazines that wanted to follow in *Mad*'s footsteps.

"I tried out at *Cracked* first, but I did sell an article to *Mad* sometime in the '60s about yacht flags. At the time they told me *Mad* was trying to reach the college crowd. I certainly would have liked writing for *Mad*, but it seems I was more in tune with *Cracked*'s slightly younger audience. Also, at *Cracked*, I was given free reign to write about anything I wanted to."

Mort Todd says of Gladir, "Oh, George is the best! With George, you knew you were going to get a great story with great gags, and what he did that was really important was send every article with tons of reference pictures. In those pre-digital days, it was really gold. I had to scour magazines to clip out reference for artists, but George would do that for his own articles. Have you ever seen George's layouts? He wouldn't only write a script, he would give you superb layouts. You can tell which ones George wrote if you look closely at Severin's stories. It's the same when you check out his Archie Comics, or closer to the *Cracked* would be if you look at *Archie's Madhouse*. You'll see the same precise layout if it was Orlando Busino doing George's stories in *Madhouse* or if it's Severin doing it at *Cracked*. He started out as a gag cartoonist and I guess it didn't work out even though he's a master at gags and design. Layouts are great for artists because they can follow them if they want or they can ignore them. For the most part, Severin would have to produce so many pages per issue that I think George's layouts were a good thing. It would be a launch pad for him. George did a rough layout that would serve as a springboard, which Severin would elaborate on."

Gladir continues, "I have no horror stories, but there is one unusual article I wrote for *Cracked* in 1965 (*Cracked* #46). The article was 'What Are the Celebrities of 1965 Doing Today in 1990?' ... sort of a backward glance at the present from the standpoint of the future. In it, I predicted John Lennon would die at the hands of his souvenir-hungry fans in NYC ... only a few miles away from where Lennon actually met his unfortunate demise a number of years later. I took no satisfaction in being so prophetic."

Not so prophetic was *Cracked*'s unfortunate situation in regards to articles appearing in late 1963 and early 1964. John F. Kennedy was a much loved and highly revered President of the United States and on November 22, 1963, was assassinated in Dallas. As issues were prepared well in advance many articles passed through too late to salvage them from the printers. As a result of the tragedy, none of these articles (except the last one mentioned) were ever reprinted.

The first was "Getting the Gate in '68" from #32 with art by John Severin. The article discusses what will happen to JFK in 1968 after the end of his second term. Ironically, the cover date of this issue is November 1963, the month JFK was assassinated, though the issue was on sale before that time.

In #33, December 1963-January 1964, had "At Home with the First Family" with art by Severin. #34, February 1964, had "JFK Now and Then" with art by Severin and finally #35, April 1964, had "It All Depends on the Point of View" with art by Bill Ward. It is obvious that glasses and a goatee were added to the JFK profile drawing in order to salvage this post-assassination article. Unfortunately, although the article was salvaged (and eventually reprinted), the joke was ruined because now it was an unidentified beatnik thinking of Castro as a nut instead of JFK.

Another latter day example appeared in #183, "What Christopher Reeve Will Be Like When He Gets Old," drawn by Samuel B. Whitehead. It is a sad story now since Reeve died young after being paralyzed after being thrown from a horse. In fact, later reprints of this article were changed to read "What SUPERMAN Will Be Like When He Gets Old," after Reeve's unfortunate accident.

"Sylvester Meets the Mets," from #64, had a reversal of fortune. Considered the lousiest team in baseball for a number of years, of which this article was based when it first appeared in 1967, the Mets became the "Miracle" Mets two years later by clinching the World Series title in 1969. As such, the jokes don't seem as funny today.

Jay Lynch also began writing for *Cracked* around 1962: "I sent some roughs for articles to Dee Caruso at *Sick* around 1962. So I was writing for *Sick* then. Paul Laikin had given Joe Pilati's *Smudge* mag a plug in *Cracked.* So I sent some roughs to *Cracked* and they printed them. I wrote lots of stuff for *Cracked* in 1963. My name was on the masthead. I don't think the individual pieces are credited, though. I did a lot of one-page gags that were drawn by Ward and Severin. One of them was called 'The Chicken Killer.' They reprinted that one so much in later years that Ward's original art must have worn out. They eventually reprinted the gag again in the '80s and had Nostrand redraw it. I got $15 for the gag in 1963. But in 1963 $15 could buy you a week's worth of groceries and a few cartons of cigarettes.

"I wrote a lot of the mag in '63. I went to NYC and met with Bob Sproul and Bette Martin, who were editing it. Sproul told me what kind of stuff they wanted. It was all very casual. And it was quite a kick to see Severin and Ward's final versions of my stuff, since I worshiped those guys' work since I was in grade school.

"Before that, it was a letter in the letter column of the Paul Laikin-edited *Cracked* that originally got me together with Art Spiegelman and Skip Williamson, in a roundabout way.

"Around '65 or '66, Spiegelman, with whom I did the fanzines when we were kids, got a job at Topps. Severin did some stuff for Topps. Wally Wood, Jack Davis and all the Kurtzman *Mad* guys were doing stuff for Topps. Artie hired me to devise gags for Topps then, and I have been doing it ever since. My *Cracked* stuff I did mostly while Sproul was the editor. Later, Joe Kiernan was the editor. I met him once ... but I didn't do stuff for Kiernan, only for Sproul.

"So when we did Wacky Packages at Topps, Len Brown, Woody Gelman and Art Spiegelman hired Paul Laikin to write some of the early Wacky Packages gags.

"His son Aron, who also worked on *Cracked* at one point, did some paintings for the Topps Garbage Pail Kids a few years back. So I'm still in touch with the Laikins, and also I'm still in touch with Charles Schneider, who used to write the *Shut-Ups* back in the era when Dan Clowes was doing *Cracked* stuff.

"At one time or another EVERYBODY either wrote or drew stuff for *Cracked* in its various incarnations.

"I remember when I was doing stuff for *Cracked*; there was this article somewhere that said Elvis Presley preferred *Cracked* to *Mad*. It was some mainstream article on Elvis. I have never been able to find it since it first came out, though. Somehow, *Cracked* was hipper in making gags about what was then the current music scene. *Cracked* had gags on Gene Chandler or Gene Pitney at a time when *Mad* only acknowledged what were then the household-word rock stars like Ricky Nelson or Elvis."

Don Orehek recollects the late Pete Wyma, who started at *Cracked* in 1963: "Pete Wyma, yeah, I knew him. He was the one who asked me to join up to the Cartoonist Workshop in Lincoln Center when Orlando was there with a bunch of other guys and that was when I quit my job at Crestwood in 1956. I used to drive in to Manhattan with him to look for parking spots and luckily I would always find those spots, and then of course when Ike or Eisenhower, they were going to build the Lincoln Center, which is a beautiful place, they kicked us out of there and that's when I started to work at home. He was in the Pacific and got malaria in the islands during the war down there and he used to be treated for malaria and I don't think he's alive anymore."

It was also at this same time that Paul Laikin left *Cracked*: "I left *Cracked* for *Sick* because I thought it was a better opportunity. It was a bigger outfit. It was a natural segue. There was no difference at all. I reported to 48th Street for *Cracked* and then I reported to Pyramid Publications, and there were more girls. I wasn't married. There were no women at *Cracked*. I thought I'd meet my future wife.

"Joe Simon never bothered me. I submitted everything. There was no one around to say no, because nobody did any of this stuff. They couldn't do it themselves. They could only say that they liked it. I don't know what criteria they used, but they sort of trusted me, and I looked like I knew what I was doing. Actually, I was. I knew exactly what I was doing. Well, not exactly. I was doing something that wasn't a hassle and was fun and I did things that way later, not in the Arnie Kogen way. I imagine if I partnered with a writer, it would happen that way. I have to do it this way. It wasn't that important. It was a fun thing. If it might have been important, I might have considered it, but since I didn't have them, it wasn't important." Laikin returned to *Cracked* on various occasions and became editor again in 1985.

People from The Marvel Bullpen that also worked for *Cracked* as shown in *Fantastic Four Special* #7 from 1969. Here's Dick Ayers, Sol Brodsky, Gene Colan…

…Bill Everett, Stan Goldberg, Jack Kirby…

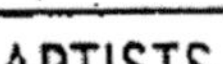

ARTISTS

MAD MAGAZINE is looking for top-notch free-lance humor artists to illustrate satire articles. If you know MAD, and you think you can match our art work, bring samples to:
Room 706, 225 Lafayette St. NYC

The classified ad that Paul Laikin answered in 1956 from *The New York Times* to work for *Mad*.

…Paul Reinman, Stu Schwartzberg, John Severin, and Syd Shores.

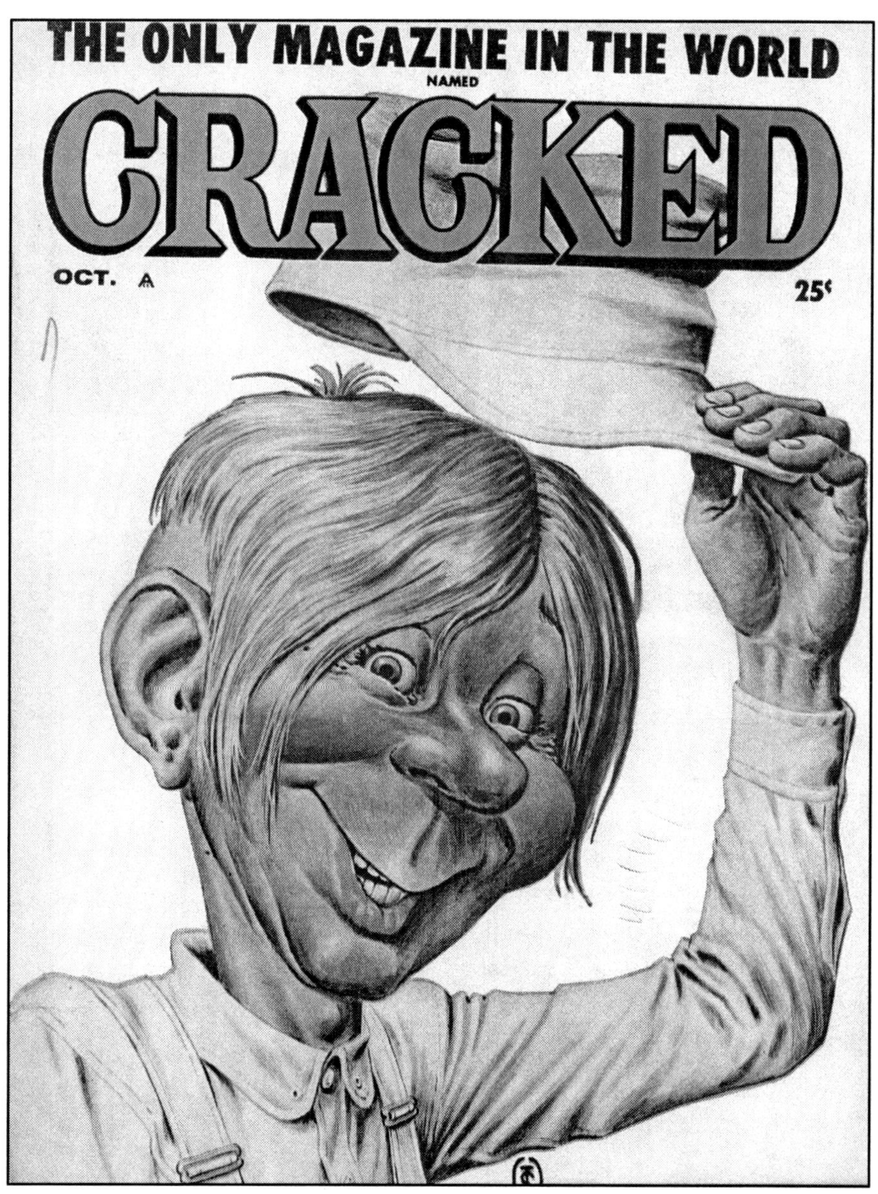


Sylvester P. Smythe gets a major facelift for *Cracked* #11, October 1959.

Though not proven, the revised version of Sylvester seems to be inspired by Harpo Marx as seen in The Marx Brothers' *A Day at the Races.*

The first appearance of *Hudd & Dini* from *Cracked* #76, May 1969, art by Vic Martin.

Though also not proven, Hudd, Dini and the cop's design seemed to be inspired by the Laurel & Hardy short *The Second Hundred Years* from 1927.

Jack "King" Kirby's only artwork for *Cracked* appeared in #14, June 1960.

George Gladir began his lengthy run writing for *Cracked* with #24, April 1962.

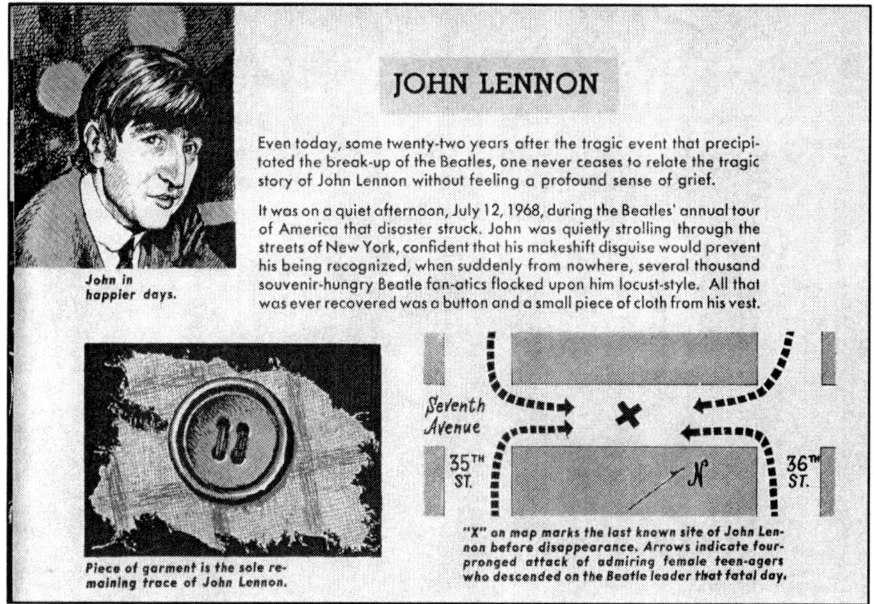


George Gladir is not proud of the fact that he was so prophetic about John Lennon in "What Are the Celebrities of 1965 Doing Today in 1990?" from *Cracked* #46, September 1965, art by John Severin.

Many articles appeared in the aftermath of the Kennedy assassination that were produced before and were never reprinted. "Getting the Gate in '68" from *Cracked* #32, November 1963, art by John Severin is one such example that tells what will happen after John F. Kennedy retires after his second term as President.

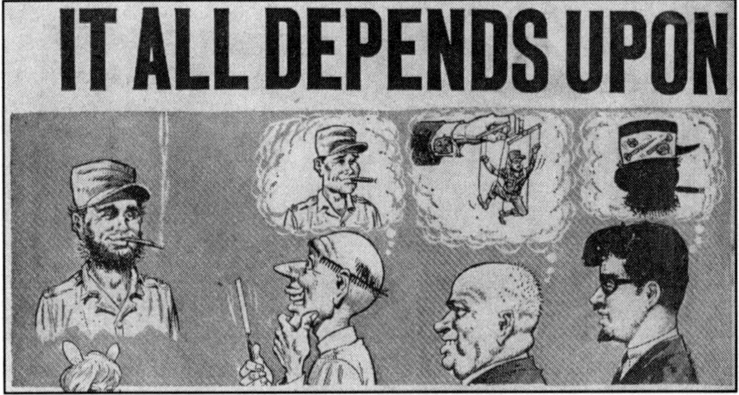


A good post-Kennedy example appears in "It All Depends on the Point of View" from *Cracked* #35, April 1964, art by Bill Ward. JFK is transformed into a beatnik in order to salvage the post-assassination article.

Jay Lynch claims that "The Chicken Killer" from *Cracked* #30, July 1963, art by Bill Ward, was reprinted so many times, they had to redraw it later.

And it was in *Cracked* #168, May 1980, with new artwork by Howard Nostrand.

# FINANCIAL DIFFICULTIES

**THE** late Joe Kiernan became editor of *Cracked* from 1964-1968, and was also a sometime artist and writer. Orehek remembers his colleague: "Joe Kiernan was a very funny cartoonist. He had beautiful ideas. He used to sell ideas to a guy on the radio and would get $10 a piece for an idea. One of his ideas which was really great had a Martian that comes ashore and he comes onto land and he says, 'Take me to your leidercranz.' You know the cheese? I thought that the funniest thing in the world, and Joe Kiernan was one of those funny guys. He was a good friend of mine. I introduced him to his wife, which he later married. I was a godfather to his daughter. He died and his wife and his grandkids are still alive. I still keep in touch with them."

Lennie Herman was a writer better known for his extensive work on *Richie Rich* and *Casper* for Harvey Comics. He contributed many articles and occasional gag cartoons for *Cracked*, beginning in 1964. Orehek recalls, "Lennie I knew very well and I was going with a girl who worked for a publication that IAL put out. It was something to do with Israeli Airlines and she worked for this guy and one day she told me that the editor was a cartoonist. I said, 'No kidding, really.' So I figured he probably did these corny drawings that young kids do and so one day I went up to the magazine. So I opened it up and there was a drawing from Lennie Herman and I knew his style. It wasn't signed. So I says, 'Wilma, see this cartoon?' She says, 'Yeah, my boss did that.' I said, 'Bullshit! Lennie Herman drew that damn thing. I know his style. Tell this guy that he owes Lennie Herman money.' She said, 'If you say anything to him, I'll never see you again.' It was getting late and I didn't want to make any problem. Finally, I see Lennie and I say, 'Hey. Lennie, don't get in touch with him. I never did.' Then finally I met another girl. I figured I'd break off with this offer. I called her up and I said, 'I told Lennie Herman.' Of course, it was ended. That is an easy way to get rid of women." Herman passed away in 1984.

Charles Rodrigues worked for many years at *Cracked*, also debuting in 1964. His sketchy art style complemented his work on *Shut-Ups* and the later *Great Moments*. He passed away in 2004. Mike Ricigliano remembers his late pal: "In *National Lampoon*, Charles did *The Aesop Brothers*, the twin brothers, and he had a comic strip for a while called *Charlie*. He was a great talent, I always thought, a very funny cartoonist and a funny person. He told me when I first got there that I would be working out of McDonald's in about two months and that most *Cracked* editors that had this job didn't last very long, and couldn't take it in Florida. The thing in Florida was very strange because *Cracked* was originally based in New York and it was much easier to get at the time without scans to get the artwork to the art director and everything else. This way was even crazier. The artwork would come into Florida. Then it would have to go from Florida to New York to get typeset and then back again. It was very insane."

Said Mort Todd of Rodrigues: "I called him once about doing work and he was CROTCH-E-TY!! As a kid, I had been reading *Lampoon* and loved his weird stuff in that. I remember one *Lampoon* cover where this grocery cashier had been shot by a mugger and he was reaching for a box of tampons to plug the wounds. I came across some Rodrigues originals once and they were outrageous! They were drawn on thin, crinkly onionskin paper and there was literally two inches of Whiteout on each drawing. He had such a spastic line style that appeared very loose and freehand, but he was such a nut that he would pile on all this Whiteout and do a wild amount of corrections to get that look. It was crazy! So, I called him and he was, well, I don't know what his story was, but he was just really angry about something and didn't want to be involved."

Joe Kiernan remained editor through 1968, when Bob Sproul himself took over. He remained in that capacity as both editor and publisher (with occasional breaks) through 1979. The years 1965-1970 were lean ones for *Cracked*, and as a result they are some of most difficult issues to find. In fact, with *Cracked* #38 (August 1964), the page count was reduced back to 44 pages, something that hadn't happened since issue #9 in 1959. The page count wasn't increased to 52 pages again until issue #70 in 1968. Also, reprints began to appear more frequently.

Despite the financial problems, there was some new talent during this period, including Oskar Blotta, John Langton, Tony Tallarico, Arnoldo Franchioni, Bob (B.K.) Taylor, Warren Sattler, and even an attempt to bring *Cracked* to the TV screen.

Also, 1965-1970 began the expansion of the *Cracked* line with a series of annual publications beginning with *The Giant Cracked*, later simply known as *Giant Cracked* and *Giant Cracked Fun-Kit*. *Biggest Greatest Cracked* and *Cracked's for Monsters Only* (a *Famous Monsters* rip-off) followed soon after and in succeeding years *King-Sized Cracked* and *Super Cracked*. Initial offerings had semi-decent inserts, including the *APE Comic Book* and a *Playboy* parody entitled *Boysplay*. Later inserts were highly repetitious and the main distinguishing feature was that they were printed on yellow paper. Even the postcard and sticker inserts in some regular issues of *Cracked* were of better quality than this.

Oskar Blotta is the second of three generations of humor writers and illustrators. His father, Oscar, was the creator of *Satyricon*, Argentina's leading magazine, which revolutionized humor in that country. Son Oskar contributed pieces to that magazine and also to other publications that eventually caught the eye of Sproul. Oskar soon began appearing semi-regularly from 1966 through the duration of *Cracked*'s run. Later, Oskar's son, Luciano, also began contributing with his father.

John Langton also started with *Cracked* in 1966 and appeared regularly through 1985. Langton was a commercial artist whose work also regularly appeared in *Crazy* and he was also considered one of Paul Laikin's regulars. In early appearances in *Cracked*, he went under the name of Johnny Langton.

Meanwhile, an article called "The Krantz Connection," Curt Ladnier mentioned *Cracked* magazine's brief attempt to get into the animated television field: "Steve Krantz established Krantz Films in 1960. He did not begin to devote his full professional attention to its development until 1963. The defining moment in Krantz Films' history came in 1965, when Krantz signed a deal with Marvel Comics' Stan Lee to produce and distribute animated versions of a number of their comic book properties, collectively titled *The Marvel Superheroes*. The actual animation duties for the show were subcontracted to Grantray-Lawrence Animation in California, with the exception of the *Mighty Thor* segments, which were animated by Paramount Studios. Krantz Films distributed the finished product to broadcasters, and the series premiered on television in 1966.

"In June 1966, *Cracked* featured a segment copyrighted to Krantz Films titled *The Flipsides*. The magazine promoted *The Flipsides* as an upcoming television series, but the show never materialized. Despite this early misfire, the coming year proved to be a busy time for Krantz Films."

"I do not recall ever seeing an animated *Flipsides* cartoon," recalls Bill Sproul. Krantz later went on to the *Spider-Man* animated TV series and the animated theatrical film *Fritz the Cat*, among other projects.

Tony Tallarico started in *Cracked* in 1967, mainly doing the "bonuses" for the various *Cracked* annuals: "I did a little activity insert, which I always thought was kind of nice. It was printed on a yellow sheet and inserted into one of the *Cracked* issues. I was doing a lot of activity books for publishers and this was really a take off on them. One of them, for example, was a dot-to-dot and you follow the dots and it kept crossing each other and what it was was a piece of Brillo. What you saw was a lot of lines and then it was Brillo. I don't remember any of the others.

"Years ago when they were in the city, I did some paperback cover paintings for them, and then we started drifting. He went his way and I went my way. And then I heard that there was a publisher in Valley Stream, which was where I lived, so I looked into it and for crying out loud, it was right across the street from the public school where my kids were going. So one day I just dropped by and it was walking distance from the house. There was Joe Cannon there. He was the editor. He was a writer. We even did some books together. I did a concept called *Sportsmania*. It was about the size of a paperback only it had about 150 pages. It was a humor book and he wrote it and I illustrated it. We did some other things together, but nothing really well. It wasn't anybody's fault. Things don't happen sometimes."

One memorable Tallarico piece was "Build a Gorkel House." It was reprinted many times. Tallarico recalls: "Oh yes. Oh my goodness. That was Sproul's idea. I forgot all about that and he loved it. When I thought of it, I thought it was kind of stupid and he loved it, so I went ahead and built him a Gorkel House."

Arnoldo Franchioni was born in Argentina and currently lives in New York. He has the distinction of few *Cracked* artists/writers to have his work appear simultaneously in *Cracked*, *Crazy*, *Sick* and even *Mad*. Why this overlapping was accepted for "Francho" (as he usually signs his name) and not for others is not known. What is known is that everyone asked about Francho appreciates his work and that alone was probably enough for editors to publish his work. Most recently, Francho contributed to *Nickelodeon* magazine.

Bob "B.K." Taylor started at *Cracked* in 1969 after a lengthy tenure at *Sick*. Taylor reflects upon his tenure at *Cracked*: "I sent my work everywhere, and eventually I received an acceptance from *Cracked*. I was excited to be working for national humor magazines, but I was really quite green and had so much to learn about the publishing world. I didn't know much about printing either, and I'm sure I drove the art directors crazy.

"I worked for *Cracked* when they moved from New York to Florida. There were a couple editors that more or less came and went. The real pillar of the magazine was Robert Sproul.

"I remember going down to Florida on vacation and dropping by the *Cracked* office in Madeira Beach. The office was closed at the time, and I remember thinking, 'This can't be the office!' It was on a canal off the ocean, with windows that looked out on the water. I peeked in and saw the different issues of *Cracked* on the wall and on desks and thought, 'This has to be the greatest editorial office anywhere—I want a job here!'

"The biggest horror story is when I look back at some of the artwork I did for *Cracked*. I was still pretty inexperienced, and one of my biggest problems was with page layout. The way they did it then—the artist drew the art and estimated where speech balloons would be placed. I think someone reprimanded me for having the artwork run into the balloon dialogue area or something. Consequently, sometimes I overcompensated. So there are a few examples where you can see the characters are scrunched down too far, or the art feels confined. (What I wouldn't have given for a computer back then!) I don't really think I found my style until the latter years of the *National Lampoon*.

"In New York laying out the magazine was Harry Chester Productions. I didn't realize it at the time, but Harry was the former right-hand man of Harvey Kurtzman—ironically, the creator of *Mad*, *Trump* and *Humbug*. Harvey Kurtzman's influence had a huge impact on my work, as did the other artists in his stable (Davis, Elder, Jaffee). With the exception of Harvey, they all worked for *Cracked* at one time or another."

Comments Mort Todd of Taylor, "BK! Yeah, I don't know why I didn't contact him about work, but I do love his stuff. He did the *Appletons* stuff for *Lampoon*. That was hilarious."

In 1969, John Severin created a strip about a small prospector and his mule called *Sagebrush*. The strip ran for many years in *Cracked* and even spawned its own *Cracked Collectors Edition*. Severin didn't comment much about this strip except it proved his love for the Old West, but Warren Sattler remembered a similar project he worked on at the time that was eerily familiar: "I really enjoyed comic strip work and that's what I really wanted to do. I did two strips, one called *Grubby* and one called *Swamp Rat*. *Grubby* was an interesting one. I've got to tell you that it concerns John Severin. I created it and I had a similar kind of sense of humor. I created this little grubby character that was a prospector and had a mule. I didn't sell it. I had a book printed up and I sent it off to a syndicate. I didn't sell it at the time; it was the end of the '50s and I would leave it around when I would go looking for work to see if anyone would pick it up. Then in '64 I sold it to the Al Smith's Syndicate and it was syndicated until the mid-'90s. Now, I start working for *Cracked* magazine and I noticed that John Severin has *Sagebrush*, which is a little prospector with a mule. I had no idea when John created it, or if he ever saw mine, but it was a total coincidence. The mule looked similar, but my character was totally different than his. I'm not accusing John or anything else; it was just a coincidence that we thought of the same thing."

It was around this same time that Warren Sattler did his first piece for *Cracked*, which ended up being a mainstay for about 15 years. Coming from Charlton Comics, Sattler explains why he didn't end up as a regular for *Sick*, which was published by Charlton from 1976-1980: "A cartoonist's job is pretty lonely. You sit alone and then you draw alone. I don't work in a bullpen or anything. I work from home. I'd get the jobs mainly through the mail and I'd talk to editors that way. Charlton was here in Connecticut so after I'd finish a job, I'd deliver it in person. I got to know Joe Gill, who was one of the writers, and George Wildman, who was my editor. Other than that, I'd just go in.

"I did a couple of pages for *Sick* and it was so badly printed it wasn't worth it. The comic book I liked, because I loved to do Westerns, and I had a chance to do Western comic books and I loved that. How it happened that I got the *Cracked* job: I had delivered a piece of artwork to DC, and I was with my son and I said, 'Down on Park Avenue is somewhere where *Cracked* is. Let's take a walk down there and see if I can get some work.' So, I walked all this way to Park Avenue South. It was quite a long way and when I get there, it's a warehouse. They had nothing to do with *Cracked* except that they printed the book or stored them there. Somehow, one of the people there told me the actual address in Florida. Well, I made up a package and at that time *Have Gun, Will Travel* was popular on television. So, I made up a lead cartoon that had 'Have Pen, Will Draw,' and I put that in the package and I got work after that. Bob Sproul called me up and said, 'Yeah.'

"I never did try to work for *Mad*. I spent my energy always trying to get into the comic strip field. I guess I should have gone there, but I was not that crazy about doing that kind of work. When I had it with *Cracked*, it was fun. I suppose it would have been the same over at *Mad*, I imagine.

"I wrote absolutely nothing for *Cracked* except for the little doo-dads, like a sign in the background. One of the things I used to notice: I'd get my work from Florida. I'd do my work and then I'd send it to New York, where they'd put it together and glue in the words. I don't know what his name was, but whoever that was used to put a little tiny character saying, 'Where's spot?' in the backgrounds. So I caught on to that and I started drawing a fish in a frame in various scenes and write underneath 'spot.' It was just one of my running gags. We did all that. We used each other's names on books and on signs."

Aron Laikin comments on the environment in the late 1960s, when he was a child: "I noticed something when I used to go to the early Christmas parties, and things like that when I was a kid, a guy like Harry Chester who did all the typesetting for most of the magazine. He used to host parties for *Mad* and some of his other clients like *Reader's Digest*. He would have these guys from *Reader's Digest* who you would imagine would be very low-key and boring at a party, but it was actually the opposite. The *Mad* guys were very low-key and the *Reader's Digest* guys were cracking jokes left and right, and I think part of that was because the *Mad* and the *Cracked* guys, we all got our humor out in our art and we weren't used to socializing. We're in our own world. We got to a party environment. It wasn't our comfort zone."

Lou Silverstone comments on the humor magazine environment at the time: "The best was in the '60s and '70s. It sort of went downhill after a while. *Cracked* was considered an imitation, but eventually it was recognized like

*Newsweek* was an imitation of *Time*. The truth about *Cracked* is that *Mad* didn't approve of *Cracked*, but they didn't worry about it, either. We weren't allowed to write for other magazines that used our bylines so for years I did under pseudonyms. I guess the other guys did, too."

Tony Tallarico mentions page rates for the various black-and-white humor magazines at the time: "The page rate was all about the same. It was really quite poor—$35 a page, maybe $40. It was all poor, but you could do it easily. It was an easy job and other than that, they were all basically the same. A guy I went to high school with, Angelo Torres, he was working for *Mad*, and he got real page rates. He got $300-400 a page. And every time the pages were used again, he got a royalty on it. Gaines, he was very good about that, when he made a paperback out of it. He always shared the money. He knew that without these guys, he would be nothing. He'd be doing *Bible* stories, which is what he started out with."

Mike Ricigliano adds: "They didn't pay badly, but I didn't know what *Mad* paid, but I always assumed it was lower than *Mad*. I think mine fluctuated over the years. I think I got paid more when I was with Sproul, then less, then it rose again. Mine was more of a roller coaster. I don't think I ever got $400 a page, but I probably got $250 a page at some points and something similar for writing, or something where the writing and artwork was a package deal or something. I've honestly forgotten."

Mort Todd confirms that by the time he took over in the 1980s, *Cracked,* too, was paying reprint royalties, even posthumously: "If the artists weren't alive, I did my best to track down the wife or the kids and stuff. I think it was like $25 a page, which doesn't sound like a lot, but if you got like a 4-8-page story, that's a couple hundred bucks you didn't expect."

Charles Rodrigues as featured in the second of two "Guest Appearances by the World's Top Humor Artists" articles from *Cracked* #107, March 1973.

One of the better inserts was in *Biggest Greatest Cracked* #1, 1965, art by John Severin, Bill Ward, Don Orehek and Vic Martin. It was a full-color comic book size insert called *A.P.E.*

The first of many, many, many *Cracked* annuals was called *The Giant Cracked* from 1965.

Another good insert was a revamped parody of *Playboy* called *Boysplay*. The original version appeared in *Cracked* #24, April 1962, while this expanded full-color comic book size insert appeared in *Biggest Greatest Cracked* #4, 1968, art by John Severin, John Langton and Vic Martin and written by George Gladir.

Comedian Steve Allen proudly shows off the cover of *Cracked* #34, February 1964, on his 1962-64 syndicated TV series. It was assuredly the biggest plug for *Cracked* up until that point.

*The Flipsides* article from *Cracked* #52, July 1966, art by John Severin. I could have sworn that I've seen this pilot at one point, but did not connect it to *Cracked* as the Sylvester character was referred to as Clyde Flipside.

Portion of the front cover of *Cracked* #52, July 1966, art by John Severin, promoting the unsold pilot for *The Flipsides.*

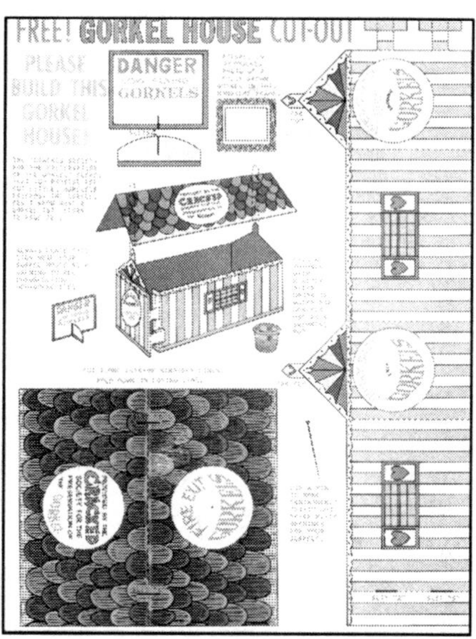


Bob Sproul apparently loved the "Gorkel House" feature by Tony Tallarico. It originally appeared in *Cracked* #64, October 1967.

Recent photo of B.K. (aka Bob) Taylor.

Some original art by Warren Sattler from *Cracked* featuring Sylvester as seen for sale on eBay.

# FLORIDA: MORE SUCCESS AND MORE COMPETITION

AS the new decade of the 1970s began, Bill Sproul describes the major operational changes for *Cracked*: "I started working for my dad when I was a kid. My father hated the commute from Rockville Center, Long Island, to Manhattan, so sometime in the mid-'60s; he moved his office to Valley Stream. After that move, he realized that if he could do it there, he could just as easily do it in Florida. We moved to Florida in February 1971. He opened an office on the water, bought an architectural award-winning house on the water and now he commuted to work by boat. We lived a dream life in Florida with membership at a private beach club across the street. (The Bath Club. Marilyn Monroe and Joe DiMaggio hung out there in the '50s.) We had a cabana on the beach and eventually moved the office to cottage on the property. Then my dad's commute was on his bicycle." Sproul's first issue published after moving to Florida was #93. The New York offices moved to Park Avenue and were just a warehouse and mail stop, not a true editorial office. Distribution had also been recently changed from Ace to Dell, and then changed to Select Magazines in 1975. Meanwhile, the adult magazines now renamed *Wildcat* and *Daring*, changed their distribution to PDC.

Comments Sproul about the distribution change: "Changing *Cracked*'s national distributors was vital to the success of *Cracked*. Dell was doing a good job for us but when it was time to really step up circulation Select Magazines had the power and the people to make it happen. They had most of the top magazines at the time. They pledged to my father an army of people out in the field and they delivered on all of their promises.

"It takes a bunch of dedicated people to increase newsstand circulation nationwide with good proprietary location. They helped us surpass 1.25 million in circulation and we sent our own guys out in the field to help and oversee it. It didn't hurt that my father knew so many wholesalers out there also. This is when the cases of Mumm's Champagne became legendary."

Shortly after Dell began distribution in 1971, Sproul introduced another long-running title to the *Cracked* fold. Originally, it was a one-shot reprinting all the previously published *Shut-Ups*, which had become *Cracked*'s most popular recurring feature. A second edition appeared the following year; then, in 1973, a reprinting of some of *Cracked*'s best movie parodies. By 1974, the series was finally christened *Cracked Collectors' Edition* and ran for 125 issues through 2000, becoming *Cracked*'s second most-successful publication.

Many issues from the *Collectors' Edition* series also featured completely brand-new material. Standouts include #9 (*Sagebrush*), #16 (*Fonz for President*), #26 (*Sharks!*), #29 and #35 (*Mork*), #48 (*Great Moments 'n' Shut-Ups*), #50 and #56 (*Video Games*), #60 (*Michael Jackson*), #69 (*Nanny Dickering*), #74 (*30 Years of Cracked*), #79 (*Artists' Portfolio*), #82 (*Jack Davis*). The latter three consisted of reprints but sported unique themes instead of the usual random reprint packages.

Issue #69 bears particular notice as it featured singer, actress and model Bebe Buell in a fumetti-style photo comic of Nanny Dickering called "Cracked Interviews the Rock Video King!" Ms. Buell was a *Playboy* centerfold in 1974 and also had a brief affair with Aerosmith's Steven Tyler that resulted in the birth of actress Liv Tyler (who also appears in this story). At the time, Liv was named Liv Rundgren as Bebe claimed that singer Todd Rundgren was Liv's father to protect her from Steve who was battling a severe drug problem. Mort Todd and Charles E. Hall also appear in the story.

Mort Todd comments on his "discovery": "You remember that 'live-action' Nanny Dickering photo comic with Bebe Buell? That was the 'acting debut' of Liv Tyler. That little nine-year-old was Liv Tyler. Bebe was a *Playmate* model and Liv's mom. I've known Liv since she was two, and we put her in there way before she became a big star."

Mike Ricigliano describes Bob Sproul after *Cracked* moved to Florida: "He was a New York guy and he used to bring me into his office at the time to tell to me about the old days in New York. I was always interested in part to listen to these old stories about New York and I always suspected that he missed New York, or missed some aspects of New York. His whole thing was that he was going to go down to Florida where he liked it and figured that his operation would work just fine if he lived in Florida and all the other stuff was up there. You know, the magazine always got out. It was just a little more difficult at the time to get it out, I thought, from Florida."

There was a time in the 1970s when *Cracked* was seriously being considered by Jim Warren of Warren Publications fame (*Creepy, Eerie, Famous Monsters*). In David A. Roach and Jon B. Cooke's *The Warren Companion*, Warren relays the details: "I didn't know Robert Sproul, but I do remember *Web of Horror*. Unfortunately, I also remember an incident involving *Cracked* magazine that is plenty painful. It's been about 25 years and I just stopped thinking about it last Tuesday. Here goes: During the middle or late '70s, *Cracked* was for sale. I believe it was due to the death of the owner, or one of the owners. As I recall, there was a widow involved who wanted to sell the property. The president of our printing company, World Color Press, telephoned me to ask if I was interested in buying *Cracked*. I didn't have to think about it—I told him, 'Absolutely.' The asking price was in the millions. I thought the magazine would be a perfect fit for the company. I could easily assemble the talent to take the quality up a notch or two. I would edit it myself. It would be a fun job! At the time, *Cracked* was 48 pages plus covers. We'd add another 16 pages and fill them with our Captain Company ads. We wouldn't compete head-on with *Mad* because *Mad* was in a class by itself. With talent like Sergio Aragonés, Mort Drucker, Dave Berg, etc., I couldn't top *Mad*'s line-up. But I figured we could mount a respectable product—and it would be a hoot! The downside would be, having to compete with Bill Gaines—whom I liked and was friendly with.

"I went to our bank, our printer and our distributor, and told them I'd buy the magazine if they loaned me half the purchase price, knowing that all three would benefit from the deal. I was also counting on getting the price down by about 25%. But two things happened: they wouldn't drop the price, and my distributor wouldn't give me terms that were acceptable to us. Time ran out. The deal collapsed.

"Later I realized I should have been more aggressive about it, even if it meant paying full price. It would have been a good addition to our family of titles. Instead, someone else eventually acquired it. That was the downside. The upside? Bill Gaines and I remained friendly. And I didn't have to go through the trauma of having a magazine that could never be better than second-best."

Though Warren would have definitely added advertising, such a thought was not unfavorable to Sproul. Mike Ricigliano explains, "I always remember Sproul talking about using advertising in the magazine and he was not adverse to doing that at all and of course *Mad* always seemed to be, but now they've done as of lately. I haven't checked lately, but I know that they were doing it for a while there. They were using color and these were all things that Sproul had no problem doing any of those things."

Sometime earlier, in the late '60s, Bob Sproul *did* start a competition to Warren's horror magazines, the aforementioned *Web of Horror*. *Web of Horror* was able to get some of the hottest young artists, including Jeff Jones, Mike Kaluta, Bernie Wrightson, and Ralph Reese. "The reason they didn't go to Warren was because Warren wasn't buying any new art. We couldn't afford it. We were using reprints at the time. If you look at our 1968-1969 issues, you're going to see a lot of reprints. We couldn't afford the $35 page rate," said Warren of the publication. Unfortunately, it came out later that Sproul wasn't paying properly either and many of the artists apparently were shortchanged.

Mort Todd comments, "Those guys have a bad taste in their mouth about Sproul. Wrightson and Kaluta and Jeff Jones really got screwed. I talked to a few of them about monster magazines, and they had horrific reminisces. Writer Bruce Jones called me when I was doing *Monsters Attack!* for some advice about reusing his Warren stuff. Before I started *MA!* I looked into buying *Creepy*, *Vampirella* and *Eerie* from Harris Publications. It turned out that Harris didn't buy the copyrights, they only bought the physical assets, so we passed on it. I would assume that if the publisher doesn't have the work-for-hire receipts, the stuff is owned by the creators. I told Jones they can sue you for reusing it, but that's OK, let them try and sue you for it. You've got your name on the story. Let's see what they've got as proof of ownership. Copyrights are a funny thing."

Warren considered retaliating with a humor publication, but it was not economically feasible at the time: "Not in the '60s. In the '70s, after we had recovered from the downturn—after *Creepy*, *Eerie*, *Vampirella* and *FM* were healthy—I thought about a humor mag. Still, I didn't want to get into it unless we had a chance to be the best. I considered buying *Cracked* magazine. My idea of doing a humor magazine was to have Harvey Kurtzman as the editor and then come out with something that was not *Mad*, but was something on a higher plane. 'Higher' meaning not intellectually higher, [but] age level higher. *Mad*'s average reader, let's say, was 12-14. What Harvey and I were striving for was 22-24 and my crack at humor was with *Help!*" By 1970 came the *National Lampoon*, which did target a college-age reader, but says Warren, "That's not exactly the type of humor that Harvey and I had in mind."

The ongoing success of *Mad* and *Cracked* and the new upstart, *National Lampoon*, caused a stir at Marvel Comics, who recruited Marv Wolfman to head up a new black-and-white humor magazine in 1973. Wolfman relates, "Stan Lee and Roy Thomas called me in to create *Crazy* and edit it. They wanted to get into the *Mad* field. Marvel had done a humor magazine back in the '50s (*Snafu*) as everyone copied *Mad* when it was a hit. I think between the success of *Mad* and *National Lampoon* they just decided to do it again. Stan wanted it to be more *Mad / Cracked* where I wanted it more *Lampoon*.

"I had far too much work and because of the situation there I had to pretty much do *Crazy* by myself, which made it impossible. I was also editing most of the other black-and-white books at Marvel and writing. Something had to go so the mag that took the most time and made me the least money had to go. Those things aren't our decisions to make. Those decisions come from the publisher. I think they were very happy with what came after us since the magazine lasted for 94 issues."

Meanwhile, *Cracked* continued on during the 1970s and recruited a number of new artists and writers as others departed, including Joe Catalano, Sururi Gumen, Mike Ricigliano, Howard Nostrand, Randy Epley,

Andy Lamberti and Samuel B. Whitehead. Others, like Howard Cruse and *Famous Monsters* cover artist Basil Gogos, contributed very little to *Cracked* despite their bountiful resumes. In fact, Gogos' major contribution was cover paintings for the newer *Cracked* paperbacks as published by Dell.

B.K. Taylor remembers, "*Cracked* was fun because it was there that I did some of my first writing. As I remember, 'The *Cracked* Guide for First Aid' was my first written article. I also recall a cover idea where all these weird monsters are leaving a theater, and the marquee on the theatre reads 'Monster Movie' (*Cracked* #105, November 1972). Now this was comedy gold! It was illustrated by the great John Severin, and, ironically I saw that actual cover for sale at a Comic Con, and I now own it! There was a subscription ad also for the magazine that read, 'Have *Cracked* delivered right to your face.' The illustration was of a man with a *Cracked* magazine stuffed in his mouth and you could see the mailman in the background who had just delivered it. *Cracked* was a great training ground."

Joe Catalano started a lengthy run at *Cracked* just a few months prior to this in 1972. He eventually was promoted to consulting editor. Comments Mort Todd about Catalano's return to *Cracked* in 1986: "He called me up after I had been there a while. He had written about a couple hundred issues before, but I felt the need to heavily edit most of his new work. Sometimes in the credits I added a continuity credit for myself, because it often went beyond the call of editing duty and I had to do a bit of unpaid rewriting. No slight on his talent, but I was uncomfortable leaving his scripts as received."

Murad Gumen comments about his own career at *Cracked* as well as his father's, the late Sururi Gumen, who began at *Cracked* around 1974; Murad a little later: "My father prepared some wonderful samples for *Mad* in the late 1960s, and despite what the *Mad*-men claimed, the usual gang members were not all idiots, as far as I was concerned; they were impressed enough to call him in and make a fuss. But they stopped short of trying him out, partly because the failure of the great caricaturist Bruce Stark was fresh in their minds, as they indicated, and perhaps partly because my father was humble and quiet, and maybe failed to impress them on a personal level. This disappointed my father greatly, and persistence was not in his nature. I was on his back for years to get him to prepare new samples for *Mad*'s chief competition, and it took my father a long time to do so. Once he did, the call came immediately from Robert Sproul to bring my father on. Sproul was so bowled over with the quality of my father's work, he said, 'Now we can race with *Mad*.' I remember after a two-page start, my father was quickly assigned to do the movie satire for *American Graffiti*. The movie and TV satires primarily served as the crown jewels of these magazines, and I was very happy that my father quickly made it to the 'top.'

"Not long after, I began to write as well as draw. *Crazy* constituted the bottom of the humor magazine barrel. I submitted scripts to the higher-paying *Cracked*, and they took me on right away. Once in a while, father would be assigned my scripts, which was weird but wonderful. One great thing with *Cracked*, as opposed to *Crazy*, was that my scripts would survive intact, with no editing. The bad thing was that at the time, no credit would be offered the creative people (save for in the masthead), although sometimes the artists would get around this by signing their names. One time, one of the artists—Howard Nostrand—gave me credit as the writer, in a back cover where an astronaut sticks a flag pole on the planet's surface, making the planet fly off balloon-style. I thought that was so nice of him!

"Two of my favorite pieces for *Cracked* were the satires for the television shows *Three's Company* and especially *Fantasy Island*. I was of the 'jam-pack' mindset, inspired by the Harvey Kurtzman style of the older *Mad* comics, and I would be happiest when I could stuff not one gag in every panel, but however many I could get away with, at least two, if not three or more. At this stage, I would supplement whatever I came up on my own with joke books, but I soon came to realize the scripts were richer when I relied solely on my own head; sometimes it was easy to tell that a borrowed joke was tired and old, and I soon dispensed with outside sources almost entirely. (Especially when I wrote the TV satires for *Crazy*, under editor Larry Hama.)

"What made these two scripts very special for me was that they were illustrated by John Severin, who will occupy a special spot in the heart of any kid who grew up with *Cracked*. Not only did Mr. Severin give life to these scripts in his inimitable way, but also he followed my storyboarded panels almost to a tee, which flattered and delighted me no end.

"It was also interesting to see how other artists handled my scripts, for example, Bill Ward and his Nanny Dickering (a character each artist would give his own interpretation of) interviews; but of course, John Severin was in a league of his own. One of the interview scripts that was close to my heart was to the tune of '*Cracked* Interviews the Animation King.' As an animation buff, this one allowed me to throw in a few homages, while making fun of Hanna-Barbera at the same time.

"During my *Cracked* days I was attending college, and whenever I'd come across some school-related stupidity, I'd make a note of it. Soon I had a collection, and I was very proud of my original observations. I decided to make an article of it, one of those 'You Know You're in School When' types of things, and once the article appeared anonymously, soon to be lost into *Cracked* oblivion, I could not help feeling a sadness. This was a very special effort on my part, built up over a long while, and its fate was just another forgettable article.

"My break with *Cracked* came with an assigned article, a satire for the movie *The Swarm*. They decided not to spotlight this film, as its box-office turned out to be a bust. As a result, they killed my article after it was completed. The publishing world can be exploitative, and some publishers justify as an industry practice 'kill fees' in this kind of situation, a policy I don't agree with; as the artist or writer, you're going to spend the same amount of time doing the assigned work, whether it winds up being used or not. (Since rates are usually low, if your work isn't used, that's enough of a blow in itself, for those of us who do the work for more than the money. Kill fees are akin to calling in a plumber to do a job, and after the job is finished, you tell him that you changed your mind, and will thus only give him a small part of what was agreed on. What professional would put up with that?)"

During this time, *Cracked* also kept introducing more and more regular features, one of which was originally drawn by Charles Rodrigues and then continued by a host of others: *Great Moments*. Mike Ricigliano discusses his contributions to the feature: "It was a combination. I couldn't tell you which ones I wrote—a good amount of them, some of them Joe wrote—Joe Catalano. I probably wrote a lot of the *Great Moments* ones.

"The one with the caveman giving nose jobs might have been Sproul's idea. He came up with a couple of ideas on the *Great Moments*, too. I don't know who did it, but he came up with some of them and that might have been one of them. He wrote some too and he was a fun person to work with sometimes and he would be like a kid also. He'd come up with concepts and share it with me and I'd sit there and enjoy it. Part of that time when I was down there and doing the art, he enjoyed having an artist in house to kind of collaborate on some of those things. He would never put his name to the credits. He'd share his concepts and put it down on paper for me, so yeah, some of those he wrote."

Howard Nostrand and later Warren Sattler took over the *Great Moments* feature. Sattler comments on his time doing the feature: "I'll tell you that was my favorite thing because I liked to paint and got to do color work then. Really, all of *Cracked* was fun to draw. They never told me how or what. Well, what yes, but not how."

Mike Ricigliano had quite a lengthy tenure at *Cracked* with occasional breaks. He describes his unique way of how he got hired: "The way I got started in *Cracked*. I knew of *Cracked*. I had tried to get in *Mad* and couldn't and I had a nice conversation with the people down there and I just started sending them belongings of mine every day.

"This was around '76 and they were based in Madeira Beach, Florida, and so I started mailing them an object of mine a day, thinking this would be off the wall enough to get me a job. It culminated at the last day of that month of sending them stuff; I sent them this life-size papier-mâché mannequin of Sylvester and got him a plane ticket and they picked it up at the airport and they hired me the next day. It was an offbeat kind of way to get a job.

"It was actually his son and daughter that I did most of my appeals to. I sent stuff to them basically. Their dad picked up on the energy level and saw the humor in it, and thought I would be a good fit for an associate editor type of thing. So that's what I did. I went down there and that seemed to help and got a title, which was associate editor.

"I think they did see my work in *Crazy*, and along with all this dirty laundry and everything else I was sending them over the course of time. I would also send them tear sheets of the work I had done. I didn't get a job as an artist. I got a job as someone who would be a liaison between the artists and the editorial staff at the time.

"The first time I went down there, they had all the—I was very much of a novice in the field—I knew *Mad* as a reader, but not as someone who knew original art or what it looked like or anything like that, so the first time I was down there, it was like being a kid in a candy store because I'm back there and they had all the envelopes full of John Severin art, Jack Davis art, and a number of *Mad* guys had done stuff for *Cracked* early on and so I was just loving all of that and over the course of time, my job was to basically talk to these artists and writers and make sure that the art was there and throw out concepts for them and work with them that way. One of the artists was Charlie Rodrigues, who did *Shut-Ups* and the *Great Moments* back covers, which I'm sure were his original concepts to begin with. Charlie Rodrigues was this very sarcastic, fun guy. I was always a huge fan of his and I think the publishers didn't really get along with him that well, so at one point I think they just basically said that they weren't going to use his stuff anymore and they walked over to me and asked me if I wanted to do these features. I said I would do it and that's how I got my first artwork into *Cracked*, after he notified Charlie that he wasn't going to use his stuff anymore."

Warren Sattler comments about Howard Nostrand, who had a lengthy comic book career at Harvey Comics before landing a position at *Cracked* for the last decade of his life beginning in 1976: "The only one I had contact with and that was a half-hour conversation and that was with Howard Nostrand. He was funny. I learned stuff about him after the fact because I only knew him from *Cracked*, but he did a comic strip—I think he did *Roy Rogers* or something like that."

Adds Mort Todd, "Ohhhh! I would have loved to have worked with him. His art was great. I don't know why some people didn't like Nostrand's style."

While at Harvey, Nostrand drew stories for their various horror comics in his inimitable Jack Davis style. Nostrand even acknowledged his similar drawing styles in a *Cracked* article from issue #151 called "If Frankenstein's Monster Did Guest Appearances on T.V." In it, Nostrand gives apologies to Jack Davis and draws an image of the Frankenstein monster similar in style to Davis' life-size poster as sold in the back pages of Warren magazines. Nostrand passed away in 1984.

Randy Epley was a longtime comedy writer with tenure similar in length to that of George Gladir and Joe Catalano, among others. He began writing for *Cracked* in 1978, writing off and on until nearly the end of the run. He also wrote for other publications before turning his attentions to delivering comedy on stage.

Andy Lamberti also started at *Cracked* in 1978: "In the mid-1970s, I saw an ad in *The New York Times* requesting a need for writers. I signed on with my first appearance in *Cracked Collectors' Edition* (*Shut-Ups*), December 1978. I wrote for them from then until the magazine was put out by American Media in Florida.

"When I first signed on, my editor was Joe Catalano, who was extremely helpful. Sadly, throughout *Cracked*'s history, writers and artists were never given 'script credit' for pieces. Why, I don't know. (At least through 1985 there was no 'script credit.')

"My prime time at *Cracked* was in the late 1970s and early 1980s. I was also selling much material to *Crazy* and *Wacko* and had to use pen names, since it was the way to go then. These magazines were very competitive. (For example, when Paul Laikin was doing *Crazy*, he'd use the names of his family members on articles.)"

Samuel B. Whitehead worked at *Cracked* from 1978-83. He also worked concurrently in other humor magazines, including Scholastic's *Bananas*. He currently resides in Pennsylvania and is friends with B.K. Taylor.

In the late '70s, a longtime *Cracked* artist was asked to assume the role as artist of one of *Cracked*'s most durable features, *Shut-Ups*. Orehek tells the story of how he got the lucrative assignment originally drawn by Bill Ward, John Severin, Vic Martin, Charles Rodrigues and Mike Ricigliano: "I was asked to do it. Of course, somebody else was doing it before me. And then after that I started doing them all. I enjoyed doing them. It was easy to think up the ideas, and then when I was teaching cartooning for kids here in Port Washington, this kid came up to me and he had this idea for *Cracked*, and there were three on a page, and one of his was on there. I don't remember if I was getting $300 for it or what, so I sold the kid's thing and I sent him a check for 25% of a $100 and he never cashed that check! I finally got in touch with him and he said, 'Oh, I don't want to cash it.' I told him, 'Cash it and when I get it back, I will give it back to you with the original drawing.' And I did that and he was happy as hell, you know. Then his parents used to eat at the Palm—the old Palm—and I did a lot of drawings in there for those people. If you go in there now, you will probably see my name in there. They were in there and they saw my name and they were happy as hell in there."

As far as ideas for *Shut-Ups* were concerned, Orehek explained how they were written: "I would show rough drawings and then from that I would do good drawings from that. I would have to trace it because the original thing was done in pencil. [In regards to writing], it was half-and-half. My wife would write a lot of stuff, too. She's a good writer. Her name is Suzanne Orehek or Suzanne Whitney. Usually, Suzy or Suzanne Orehek or Suzanne W. When she wrote a story for *Woman's World*, which was a mini-mystery, she would use her full name 'Suzanne Whitney Orehek.'"

Don Orehek's wife wasn't the only case of nepotism in *Cracked*. Michelina Severin explains, "Three of our daughters at different times worked on *Cracked*, like on the *Hang Ups*. They didn't do a whole lot because they were so young, but they were able to do it because of John. I'll tell you a story about one of the covers. There was one about 1978 that was signed 'C.E. Severin.' That was our teenage daughter, Catherine. What happened was that John had an unexpected surgery and he was supposed to be working on the cover, but of course he wasn't able to do it. I said to Bob that we would be happy to let one of our daughters draw it. He said, 'Well, do you think she could?' and I said, 'Well, let her try it.' So, Cathy did do the cover while John was in the hospital. Howard Nostrand was an artist over at *Cracked*. What happened, unbeknownst to her, was that Bob said to Howard, 'I don't know how well this young girl can do the cover. Could you draw something in case we can't use it?' So Howard did and he called up later and said that it was the first time he had ever been knocked out by a girl. And Catherine did the cover. Three of our daughters (Catherine, Margaret and Ruth Severin) also were in *Cracked*, like *Hang Ups*.

"One thing that *Cracked* did that no one else did … where at *Mad* if they did a parody of *Happy Days*, they did it once and never did it again, but at *Cracked*, if they did one, they'd say, 'Eh, let's do one again! There are some new characters. Let's do another parody.'"

Mike Ricigliano explains: "I know the one year I was there; I believe every cover that I did—10 covers—had Fonzie on the cover. That was the thing that just blew me away was that it was kind of a real revelation to pull at the time. Here we were doing this magazine and had been successful, but then the Fonz thing—the *Happy Days* thing came along. I remember the cover and everything where he puts Fonzie on the cover and when he did, the sales must have gone up because he tied in to all those ABC shows at the time that were hits: *The Six Million Dollar Man*, *Laverne and Shirley*. All of the kind of pop culture shows that were on at that time, but every cover—and you can talk to John Severin because he'll remember this—every cover we had to figure out a way to get Fonzie on the cover. It was amusing to me, but we did it. We always had Fonz in there. We had Fonz posters. We had Fonz special issues. It just happened to be during that one year. I believe that they were still doing Fonz covers when I left, but that one year they did, maybe one or two they didn't.

"The thinking was, 'Let's ride a good thing while we got it!' and so if they had a really hot issue or if they had a really hot show, it would be 'Let's figure out another way.' I remember doing a Fonz Cinderella one that I had the concept for that I gave to Joe Catalano, and Joe wrote a really funny piece on it and John did a great job illustrating it. Whatever way we could come up with to put Fonzie in there and put a different take of it. If there was a hot show, *M*A*S*H* or whatever, we had no qualms about putting it in there again, whatever way we could put it in there again. I think what he did when I was there, was find his audience. It was just a coincidence that I was there when this was going on, but I think he realized then."

Writer Barry Dutter adds, "Early *Cracked* was so shameless because they did their period where they put *The Six Million Dollar Man* on every cover. Then they had *M*A*S*H* every issue because *M*A*S*H* sells. Then it was Fonz. Then it was Mork. It was whatever was the hot thing at the moment; they'd put on the cover. In the late 1970s, they put *Star Wars* on the cover so many times; they actually got a cease-and-desist letter from Lucasfilm. True story. Then during the Silverstone/Andy Simmons era, then they started putting *The Simpsons* on the cover, every single issue. So then, as a goof, when we took over *Cracked*, I made a joke to Kulpa at the time, if Andy and Lou ever were to do a spoof of *The Sopranos*, they'd probably call it *The Simpranos*, and Kulpa goes, 'Yeah, yeah. Do it, do it!' That was kind our spoofing the old Andy Simmons *Cracked*, a blatant attempt of mooching off the success of *The Simpsons*. That was our proud way of continuing our *Cracked* history, which was shamelessly exploiting whatever was popular at the moment."

Tony Tallarico comments on *Cracked* and other black-and-white humor magazine sales figures during the 1970s: "They were all marginal. There was nobody like *Mad*. *Mad* was selling a million. DC was selling 250,000 and down. Like *Cracked* was probably in the 250,000 range. All the others were also-rans."

Tony's figures relate closer to the early '70s. By the late '70s, with the inclusion of the Fonz, *Star Wars* and *M*A*S*H*, *Cracked* hit a peak average sale of 473,801 as mentioned in the March 1978 issue. *Cracked* also drove up sales with the inclusion of various inserts into the regular issues, including stickers, postcards and iron-ons. These inserts were of higher quality than the ones that actually appeared in *Cracked's* various annuals and specials. They were full-color on heavy card stock for the postcards and had actual adhesive on the backs of the stickers. And of course, the iron-ons really worked. The most famous of these was used for the title of this book: "If You're *Cracked*, You're Happy," originally from issue #123, March 1975.

Sproul delighted in these sort-of catchphrases. Others commonly used were "The World's Humorest Funny Magazine," "Something Funny's Going On Here," "Order Now—Chaos Later," "We Prove Humor Can Be Funny," "What's Up Front Our Cover," "Buy Me!" and of course the intentional misspelling of "magazine" as "mazagine," which had been going on since issue #30. Another catchphrase used in the '70s and early '80s was the name of the letters' page, now called "Lettuce from Our Readers."

One of Mike Riciglianoʼs duties was to "write" the letters' page. He explains: "We were getting feedback from kids in actual letter form. We got lots of letters. We never used the letters the kids wrote because they weren't old enough. The kids that read *Cracked* were a younger demographic than the *Mad* reader. That's my guess, anyway. A lot of the letters wouldn't have made for good letters on the letters page. Not interesting letters, so that was one of my jobs, making up letters and coming up with an interesting enough letter and then a funny answer to the letter, and maybe something that we could use artwork with. I actually think a few of them were real, but while I was there, there was very few of them. Where we worked, that was an actual deadlined thing for me and the secretary that was there and maybe Bob would have one that he'd come in with, but a lot of it was done in-house, at the time. I cannot vouch for all the time. I can just vouch for my time down there, which was one year of being very strong.

"I actually had an assumed name at *Cracked*. When I left *Cracked* after the one year I was the editor there, Bob Sproul was not happy. He was upset that I was leaving. He wanted me to stay as the editor. So I left, and he told me that I couldn't do stuff anymore. I kept submitting stuff and I made a papier-mâché dummy and I made a few years back here in town for the owner of the Colts and it got a lot of play, nationally. My 15 minutes of fame as an artist. I also had a dummy of myself called Joe the Dummy spelled Thadummi like an Italian name, so I was submitting stuff under the name Joe Thadummi!! After a while, Sproul caught on. I wasn't very good at hiding and banished me for a few more issues until he finally let me do stuff again."

Although *Cracked* was generally regarded as skewing to a younger audience than *Mad*, it did have its share of somewhat adult or at the very least "offensive" humor. Though such items were the exception and not the norm, it is worth pointing out the article "The Hitler Nostalgia Craze" from #117 with art by Bill Ward, the photo captioned "Watermelon Jokes to End Them All!" from #97 and the covers of #171 and 184, both featuring Gary Coleman from *Diff'rent Strokes*, all could be up for debate in regards to taste. One wonders how suitable they were for younger eyes. As usual, hindsight displays their flaws, and if an anthology of the *Best of Cracked* were to be created, it is doubtful that these items would make it in, due to today's politically incorrect environment.

The three issue *Creepy* rip-off series by Bob Sproul appeared in 1969 called *Web of Horror* and featured artwork by some of today's top horror comic talents.

Joe Catalano began his career at *Cracked* in 1972. Here is a brief appearance drawn by John Severin from "*Cracked* 30th Anniversary Party!" from *Cracked* #238, September 1988.

B.K. Taylor wrote and John Severin drew this classic cover from *Cracked* #105, November 1972. The original artwork is now proudly owned by Taylor.

Howard Nostrand tips his hat to Jack Davis in this swipe from the classic *Frankenstein* poster that used to be sold in the back of Warren magazines that originally appeared in *Cracked* #151, July 1978.

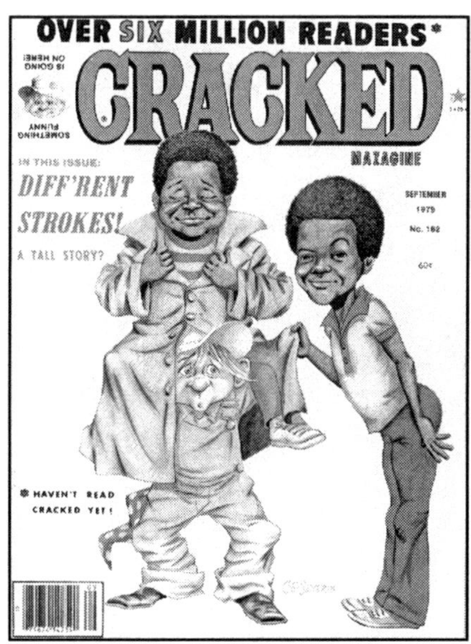


John Severin was out of commission, so he recruited his daughter Catherine to fill in for him on the cover of *Cracked* #162, September 1979.

The long-running *Great Moments* feature first appeared in *Cracked* #118, August 1974, art by Charles Rodrigues.

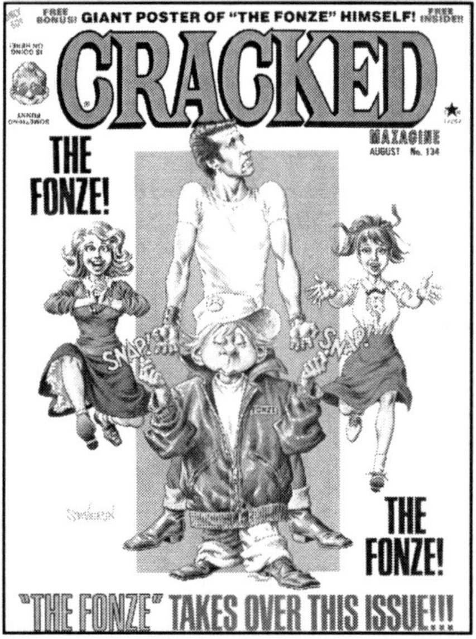


One of the best-selling issues of *Cracked* was the first to featured the Fonz from *Happy Days* very prominently. This is *Cracked* #134, August 1976, art by John Severin.

The first Fonz appearance in *Cracked* was in the first of many *Happy Days* parodies. This is from *Cracked* #118, August 1974, art by John Severin.

The Fonz first appeared on the cover in the background of *Cracked* #133, July 1976, art by John Severin.

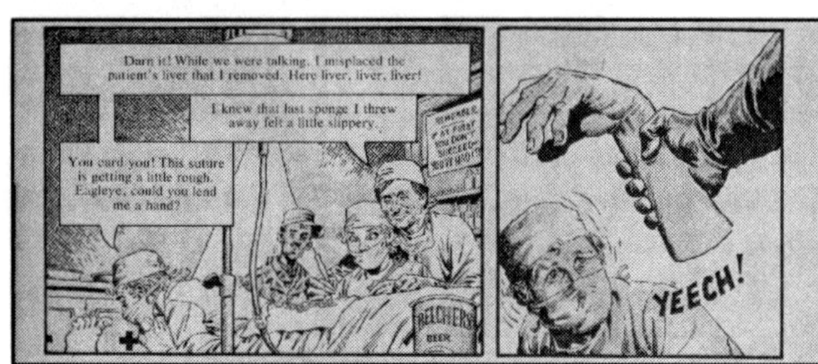


*M*A*S*H* was another Bob Sproul favorite with at least eight parodies leading to its own *Cracked Collectors' Edition*. This is a classic scene from the first *M*A*S*H* parody from *Cracked* #115, March 1974, art by John Severin.

The original artwork by Samuel B. Whitehead for the *Three's Company* parody called "Three'sa Company" from *Cracked* #186, May 1982. Images courtesy of Greg Beda.

TV
FLOUR

AAAHHH!

Shortly after appearing in *Cracked* #123, March 1975, Iron-Ons were offered for sale in *Cracked* #126, August 1975. Artwork by John Severin.

The catch phrase "Something Funny is Going on Here" first appeared on *Cracked* #61, July 1967. This one is from *Cracked* #62, August 1967, featuring Sylvester.

Full color inserts started appearing in *Cracked* # 144, September 1977. These stickers came complete with pre-glued backs or in the case of the postcards, printed on card stock.

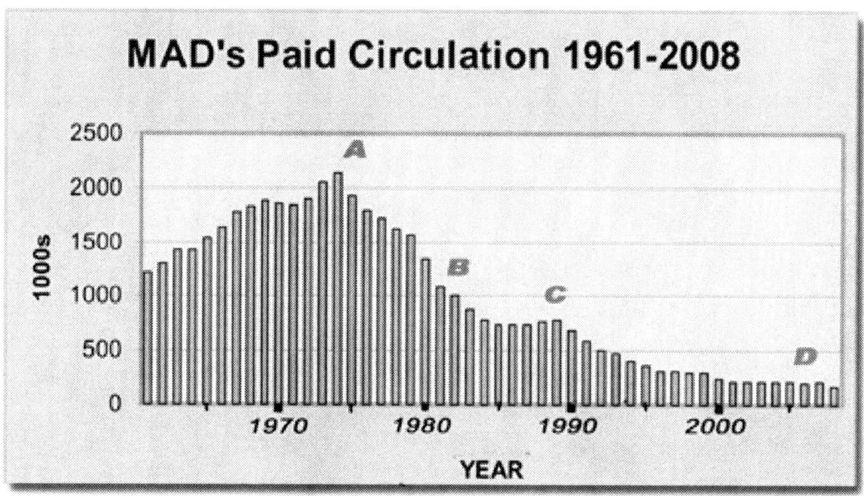


A chart found on the Internet showing *Mad's* declining sales over the years. *Cracked* sold at best half that and was totally gone by 2004.

The Tragedy-Tragedy shield appeared briefly on *Cracked* starting with issue #39, September 1964.

Bob Sproul added the word "Magazine" to cover of *Cracked* #22, November 1961.

Then with issue #30, July 1963, it became "Mazagine" virtually forever more.

The long-running *Cracked* Bookstore ad featuring the catchphrase "Order Now – Chaos Later" first appeared in *Cracked* #123, March 1975.

Some questionable material ended up in *Cracked*. This is from "The Hitler Nostalgia Craze" from *Cracked* #116, art by Bill Ward.

Here's "Watermelon Jokes to End Them All" from *Cracked* #97, November 1971.

Sylvester painted in blackface from the cover of *Cracked* #171, September 1980, art by John Severin.

# THE 1980s

## THE END OF *SICK*, *CRAZY*, AND THE ORIGINAL *CRACKED*

THE remaining black-and-white humor magazines started falling on hard times as the 1980s began. There were a number of reasons for this: one, other forms of entertainment began making an impact, even before the days of the Internet, including video games and home video. Two, the advent of the direct distribution system created a situation where magazine dealers were not allowed to return unsold magazines, thus causing them to be more selective in their ordering. Three, many of the artists and writers for these publications had been in place for over 20 years and were not getting any younger. Four, *National Lampoon* and more "mature" and "adult" forms of humor had made major inroads. *Lampoon* had one of the most successful feature film comedies of all time with *Animal House*. *Mad* tried to follow suit with the abysmal *Up the Academy*, seemingly cementing the fate of the two publications. Any attempts at a *Cracked* TV show or movie were stillborn, but an ongoing series of *Cracked* Movies appeared in the magazine that featured a caricature of Bob Sproul.

*Sick* was the first casualty, ending in 1980. After being more successful than *Cracked* in the 1960s, by 1980 it was a pathetic shadow of its former self, primarily due to Charlton Publications assuming publication of the title in 1976 and ultimately running it into the ground, both quality and distribution-wise. Creator and owner Joe Simon was not part of this dismal version, which really consisted of Charlton licensing the name *Sick* from Simon and the results bore no resemblance to the *Sick* Simon originated.

Next, Marvel threw in the towel on *Crazy* in early 1983. After a valiant attempt to revitalize the magazine to its earliest glories in 1980, the magazine struggled to find an audience and the title was summarily canceled. Strangely, except for the continuing *Savage Sword of Conan* title, it was the only title still being published from Marvel's early '70s black-and-white magazine line.

Larry Hama was the final editor of *Crazy* during this time, and he offers his perspective of *Cracked* and *Crazy*: "I was always envious that they had John Severin! I must admit, though, that I never really read *Cracked* or *Mad* during that era. I read *Cracked* and *Sick* as a kid, though, along with *Mad* and *Help! Help!* was my favorite and still is to this day. How can you miss with a combination of Harvey Kurtzman, Terry Gilliam and Gloria Steinem, with contributions by Gil Shelton, Robert Crumb, and Woody Allen?

"I probably read *Cracked* pretty regularly in Jr. High. Then I discovered Mark Twain, Sid Perelman, Barthelme and *Punch* magazine.

"We had Jack Sparling doing fairly regular stuff for us. I don't really know who was working for *Cracked* at the time, so I can't say for sure who overlapped. Maybe Arnoldo Franchioni. I know he did stuff for *Mad*. I didn't see *Mad* or *Cracked* as being the competition in that way. We were trying to do something kind of different.

"I thought we came up with some good, new stuff. We had a foul, cigar-smoking clown way before *The Simpsons* did, we did a different take on movie parodies by having two jerky teenaged boys sneak into all the theaters in a multiplex and make snide remarks about the movies instead of doing straight parody. These concepts may have been free-floating in the zeitgeist, but we were there before the others. I was least happy about having to do the same old movie and TV parodies. That seemed so yesterday, even way back then!

"I miss *Crazy* because I think we were on the verge of being able to take it in some very original directions when video games came along and all those kid quarters went into slots instead of across the newsstand counter."

Ray Billingsley never worked for *Cracked*, but talks about his time at *Crazy*: "I remember hearing *Cracked* was a rip-off of *Crazy*, which was a rip-off of *Mad*. We were glad that we were at least Number Two. We were good, just not good enough for *Mad*.

"There was no rivalry or competition among us artists as I remember it. It's not like we met all the time at the office. We all worked from home or our studios and mailed in the finished product, or like myself, just walked it in. I was extremely lucky because they never rejected my work. I did not have to redraw anything. I do believe that we [the artists] all liked and respected each other's work. I was and am a fan of everyone, and truly like everyone's work. We saw *Mad* as a height to reach for.

"I think I was the least proud of my very first work there. It was only one page - almost like 'filler,' and I think I could have done better, As the issues went on, I got better and better artistically."

Many of the artists and writers retired after *Crazy* and *Sick* folded, but a few fled to *Cracked*. There were a few new ones during the last part of the Sproul era from 1981-85, including Brian Buniak, Roger Brown and Rurik Tyler.

Mike Ricigliano began his second tenure at *Cracked* in 1981 and during the second one was instrumental into the creation of the *Spies and Saboteurs* features and sketches. Ricigliano describes their origins: "That was mine and it was really when I was down there when I was the editor [that] Bob Sproul was kind of asking me or telling me to do something like the marginals. Some of the things I used to do while I was the editor: I used to write the letters page, the letters and the answers to the letters, that's how *Cracked* used to do their letters. At the time, he let me put these little things in the margins and then he let me expand it and so it's pretty much right out of Aragonés, but kind of a combination of Aragonés and *Spy vs. Spy*. I think it was more Sproul's idea than mine. Once he let me have my head with it, I kind of made it mine. It was more about the saboteurs than it was about the other characters. It was about the saboteurs doing things to the art on the pages. He would let me use them right on the art. I don't know if Aragonés did that or not, but he used to let me like 'tug on' someone's clothing in the panel."

Says Mort Todd of the feature and Ricigliano, "I did not want to overtly copy *Mad*. You can't get away from some elements like the format and stuff, but as far as going to the extent of doing headlines like 'The *Star Wars* Dept.,' or have a Mort Drucker swipe artist, I mean, some humor magazines just slavishly followed *Mad*'s features. I was inspired by the manic Kurtzman era, which *Mad* wasn't even doing anymore. That's more what I was aiming for. I was kind of against using Sergio Aragonés-type cartoons in the margins, but Ricig was such a nice guy and came up with such clever stuff for the *Spies and Saboteurs*, I kept it and tried to mix it up a little bit. He would send us a couple sheets of all these little gags and Cliff would paste them up throughout the magazine. We tended to put them more in stories themselves, rather than in the gutter or on the sides. Ricig was great. He's another guy who's pretty damn funny. A real talent."

Brian Buniak also had two tenures at *Cracked*, the first in the waning days of the Bob Sproul era, starting in 1983. Buniak explains the environment at the time: "Probably that first decade where there was *Mad* and *Cracked*. Marvel later had *Spoof* and *Crazy* or *Not Brand Ecch*. There was humor all over the place. By the end of the '70s, humor was being replaced by all the gritty superheroes. Most of the comics by then had very, very little to do with humor. By that time, stuff like *Cracked* were really hard to get into at all, but once you got in there, you stuck. I have a real thick memory of my first tour of duty at *Cracked*. They were in Florida, because I sent things in. I had no idea of who the editor was, but I recalled a very pleasant woman who always answered the phone. I would always ask for this guy and she would always put me on hold and asked me to call back. No matter when I called, it was down in Florida. I could see it on my phone bill, how many times I called. I would do this and she would always come back and say,

'He's in a meeting.' The second time around I would try to leave something that would make them call back about *Mad* about *Cracked* collections. I said, 'Why not come up with *Cracked* comics?' similar to what they did at *National Lampoon* where they would let artists do anything they wanted. Give them the freedom rather than doing an advertising parody. And they said, 'No.'; it's not spectacular at all to them."

Roger Brown also started at *Cracked* in 1983 and usually wrote pieces illustrated by Mike Ricigliano. He comments, "Mike Ricigliano was great to work with, we seemed to just blend well together. I could just give him a bare-bones idea for a skit and he 'got' the idea and knew what I envisioned as the final gag. You don't get that kind of connection very often. The *One-Shots* features and one-pagers were my favorites. I was a regular with the magazine from 1983 through 1993 until the magazine changed hands. I still get e-mails today from people that read the magazine and enjoyed our features. Working with *Cracked* really got my mind used to thinking on multiple concepts at the same time. I use that same method today in my inventing/product development work. You can see the products I have licensed on my website as well as some of the other comics I wrote.

"One of the cartoonists, Orlando Busino, I was gag-writing for loved my work and told me I should submit material to *Cracked* magazine. I was already a fan of the magazine, but had not tried submitting to them. I put together some material and sent it in and was thrilled when they picked up over half of my material. That prompted me to get rolling submitting to them regularly. Which led to me being a regular contributor for 10 years.

"I wrote for *Cracked* from 1983 through 1993. Mike Delle-Femine was editor at the time. He was great to work with and had a fantastic sense of humor.

"Early in my career with *Cracked* magazine they did a parody of *Mad* magazine which resulted in *Mad* trying to sue *Cracked*. Their lawyer notified me that I was named in the lawsuit and I could end up owing some huge amount of money if the suit went through. I believe the final outcome was that *Cracked* pulled that issue off the store shelves.

"I loved both magazines, but tried out for *Cracked* first because I had a working relationship with some of the artists writing gags for them. Then once I was working for *Cracked*, *Mad* had a policy that I would have to quit writing for *Cracked* before they would even look at my material. That wasn't something I wanted to do so I stuck with *Cracked*.

"I did an ongoing feature called *One-Shots* with artist Mike Ricigliano that seemed to be one of the fan favorites. Anytime I was at a comic book convention that was the pages they wanted me to sign.

"I looked forward to getting the newest issue each month and would read it cover to cover as soon as I got it. I would tear out the ones I thought were funniest and put them on my wall in my room."

Mike Ricigliano comments about his former partner: "There was a guy that I was doing some drawing with that they kind of teamed me up with named Roger Brown and he did kind of other panel gags called *One-Shots*. I had met him a couple of times and he would do the writing and send me the gags. He had little *One-Shots*. This is really jarring my memory. I was probably doing in the 20 years I worked for *Cracked* about seven or eight pages an issue. I was still doing a number of other freelance stuff at the time, but *Cracked* was my main client. They gave me plenty of work."

Rurik Tyler (whom at times also wrote for *Cracked* under the name of Bo Badman), was the last new major writer that got his start in 1985 at the end of the Sproul era. He also worked for *Mad* for a few years before returning to *Cracked*. Later, he went on to write various comic books.

In 1985, artist Warren Sattler ended his long association with *Cracked* around this time. He explains: "It went to New York after that and I did one job and I was working on a second job when I got my check from them, and I noticed it was light, so I called them up and said, 'You're not paying me well enough.' Well, the editor says, 'I'm taking a cutback from the artists. You give me $100 or whatever works.' I don't know who the guy was; I don't know if he was an assistant editor or anything, I just know that's that what happened to me. I finished the job, sent that one in, and again I got shorted when my check came, so I just quit then and there."

Comments Mort Todd, "Laikin worked with Sattler but I never got the chance. I enjoyed his *Lampoon* stuff! He did one there that was a violent 'Tom and Jerry,' with the bloody results of their antics, like 'Itchy and Scratchy'. I made a point of trying to get as many of the excellent people from *Cracked*'s past, though Warren was one I missed."

Sattler continues, "Jerry De Fuccio after that called me up when he took over and he was going to do *Cracked* and he tried to get me back and I told him the incident then and he said, 'Well, that's too bad. It won't happen with us.' I said, 'No, I had bad luck with it and I'm not going to come back.' Later on, in the '90s, at the end of his life, he called me up again. I was too tired and my eyesight had gone bad and I did do work with him then, but that was just private stuff."

Around 1985, there was a major shake-up at *Cracked* which led to the departure of Bob Sproul, whose association ended with issue #212, July 1985, after 27 years of faithful service, the longest tenure of any publisher on *Cracked*, and, ironically, the same year Al Feldstein stepped down from *Mad*. Bill Sproul completes the story: "In the early '70s, *Mad* and *Cracked* were spoofing TV and movies more on their covers and lead parodies. We found that for reasons still not clear to me we could beat *Mad* to the punch every issue by months. They would spoof a movie eight months after release and TV shows after the season was over. We started to increase circulation as sales improved. By now *Cracked* had developed its own personality. It was the cleaned-up version of *Mad*. We sought a younger audience, and the editorial theme was there would be nothing in it that a parent of a 10-year-old child would object to his child reading. This was the harder way to be funny. No sex, drugs or scatology. Dad continued to increase circulation and sales were really picking up. He had started spending more money on paper quality and cover stock, making *Cracked* look better. He made the big gamble when he decided he could sell at every newsstand *Mad* sold in and began to double and triple the circulation; this doesn't just happen on its own. He had to call in all the people he knew in the wholesale and national distribution part of the business. He also had to increase his credit with the national distributors and the printers and basically mortgaged the whole damn thing. He then became known as the 'champagne publisher' because he rewarded the reps and guys who helped him accomplish this with cases of Mumms Cordon Rouge Champagne. (He began drinking wine and beer after moving to Florida.)

"*Cracked* upped its circulation to 1,250,000. We published nine issues a year and 14 *Collectors' Editions* and annuals. Then, Bernie Brill died. His wife took over his duties and my dad and her sold the magazine to *The Globe*. My dad was not optimistic about the longevity of *Cracked*. Paper and printing cost were skyrocketing; *Mad*'s sales were dropping. The drug 'Crack' was in the news, and he figured even unconsciously parents don't want 'Crack-ed.' He also was ready to retire, which he did. He spent summers in Switzerland (my mother's homeland), traveled the world, fished and became a beach bum. He was a fabulous writer, an intellect, with an unequaled wit. He had larger-than-life persona. He died September 30, 2007, at 86 years old."

Instead of filming an actual movie, *The Cracked Movie* started appearing semi-regularly beginning with this appearance in *Cracked* #178, July 1981, art by John Severin. Bob Sproul appears as himself.

It started off as a simple take-off of *The Blob* called *The Talking Blob* from *Cracked* #149, March 1978, art by John Severin. The Talking Blob then started making cameos in the various *Cracked* Movies and in other features and even got his own issue of *Cracked Blockbuster* #2, Summer 1988, featuring all of his previous appearances.

Lo Linkert's *Your "Ugh" Ancestors* first appeared in *Cracked* #107, March 1973.

Mike Ricigliano's *Spies and Saboteurs* made an unannounced first appearance in *Cracked* #179, August 1981.

Murray Ball's *Stanley* first appeared in *Cracked* #112, October 1973.

A strange piece of merchandise was the *Cracked* Blow-Up Poster that featured your head photo atop a drawn body. It first appeared in *Cracked* #77, July 1969, in the ongoing house ad featuring various novelties.

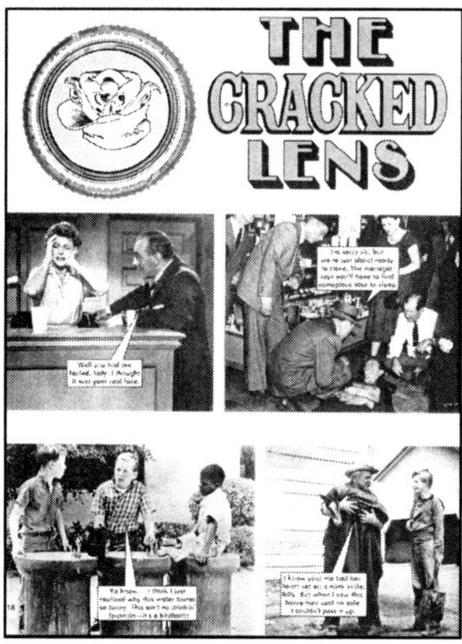


*The Cracked Lens*, an age-old photo caption feature with a new title debuted in *Cracked* #154, October 1978.

The final issue of *Cracked* produced by Robert C. Sproul. This is issue #212, July 1985.

The very first piece of *Cracked* merchandise was the "Who's *Cracked*?" T-Shirt, which first appeared in *Cracked* #7, February 1959. Does *ANYONE* have one of these?

A sample edition of the German version of *Cracked*, called *Kaputt*.

By the 1970s, the merchandise got a little better. Here's the first of two *Cracked* Binder and Notebook ads. This one first appeared in *Cracked* #119, September 1974, featuring the covers of *Cracked* #98, 80 and 105.

And here is the second *Cracked* Binder and Notebook ad, which first appeared in *Cracked* #127, September 1975, featuring the covers of *Cracked* #97, 86 and 93.

The *Cracked* Reporter ad ran for quite a while in *Cracked* and featured Bill Sproul. It debuted in *Cracked* #163, October 1979, but Bill's debut didn't appear until #167, March 1980.

One of the final bits of merchandise from the original Sproul run was The Official *Cracked* Fan Club Kit, first advertised in *Cracked* #195, July 1983.

Strangely, these *Cracked* cards and stickers produced by Fleer were never advertised in *Cracked*, but appeared in stores in 1978.

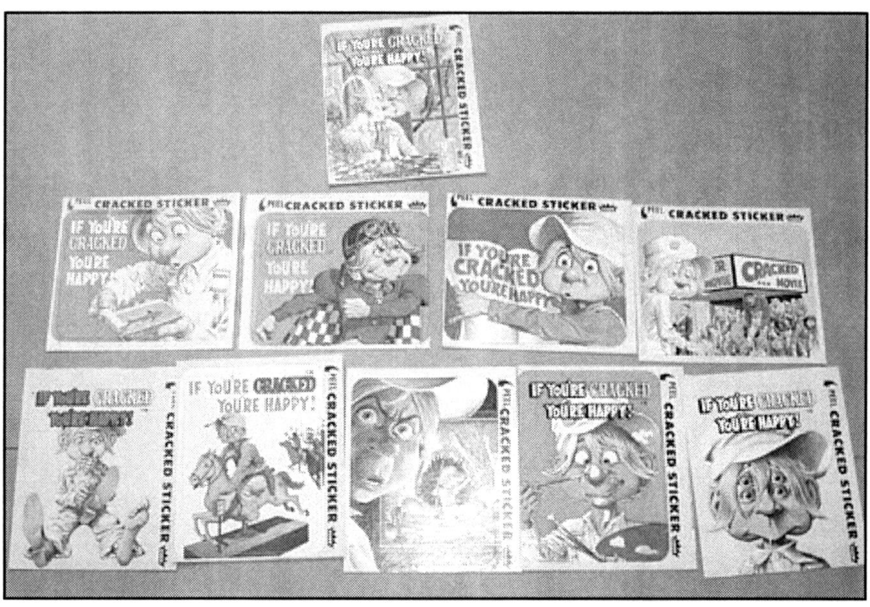


These are the stickers for the series.

# LARKEN, LAIKIN AND GLOBE

MICHELINA Severin reflects, "*Cracked* was sold after Mr. Brill died. His wife eventually took it over and sold it off." Brill died in October 1977, and the sale to Larry Levine and Kenneth Baratto led to the formation of Larken Communications. Larry and Ken's first job was to recruit Paul Laikin to head up the revitalized venture in 1985.

Severin continues, "This guy named Ken bought it and Michael Delle-Femine took over as editor at that time and he really brought *Cracked* back. Later, they began to get vulgar.

"Bernie Brill owned it and then it was sold to Globe. In between Michael Delle-Femine, a man with an Italian name owned it, Kenneth Baratto. Mrs. Brill sold it to those two guys and Michael came in and revitalized it and brought John back. Paul Laikin had edited some of them. There was a year before Michael. At that time, John had opted out of it, actually. Bob was still involved and Paul Laikin was the editor. What happened was they decided that they didn't need to use John and Bob Sproul almost threw a gut when he found out. He was very anxious to get John back, and when Paul was back, he was getting pushed out."

Mort Todd offers his version of the story, as he understands it: "I understand that Sproul's son was editor for a while. I felt the magazine was running on fumes after Brill passed and they had no real direction, so by the mid '80s, they got rid of it. I don't know what the shopping process for it was, but there were two business partners in Manhattan named Larry Levine and Ken Baratto. Their main business was doing ad placements for a bunch of tabloid magazines, specifically the Globe, and all of Globe's other newspapers, along with some teen, astrology, hair, black and porn magazines. Back in the day Globe had four or five papers, like the *Star*, *Examiner*, *Weekly World News* and junk like that. So this company would do corny ad placement for them that were close to scams and hoaxes and get them into the pages. Levine also had a background in publishing. He used to have a paperback line imprint called Zebra. It was really the poverty row of books, but they did do some Robert E. Howard books. Anyway, they had this opportunity to get *Cracked* and they figured that they could parlay it into something. I think if you look at the first half-dozen issues or so, it'll say, 'Published by Larken Communications' and that was Larry and Ken. Then after a while they got Globe to invest or buy half of it, so though most of the time I was there, it did say 'Globe Communications,' in the indicia, I personally had nothing to do with Globe. Globe handled printing, making it cheaper by tacking it on to their other publications, and most importantly did the distribution and newsstand display. Soon after I left, Globe took it over completely and then it ran it out of Globe's offices. We had our own separate offices, which was really a blast.

"Until we took it over, Cracked was packaged in Florida. There was some sort of editorial address in Manhattan. It was weird because it was right across the street from my friend, Dan Clowes' apartment. I think it was a New York mail drop for the magazine. I ended up having two different offices up on 5th Avenue; the first one was on 35th and 5th, which was right in the shadow of the Empire State Building. We shared a floor with some porn magazines, which was pretty amusing. They put out all these rip-off digest books similar to *Penthouse Forum* called *Intimate Letters* and stuff like that. They had filing cabinets filled with tons of really gross porn magazine photos from the '70s with all of this bushy hair and bad hygiene, and they just regurgitated these books, reprinting them constantly. They had dozens of these titles. Anyway, that was the first office. It was a kick having a 5th Avenue address across from the Empire State Building. It wasn't where the publishers were; it was down the street from them, so I was pretty much left alone.

"As publisher, Ken Baratto tried to put his finger into the soup and burned it plenty of times. You'd think the publisher would have the final word, but I pulled some shenanigans that always turned out profitable for them despite their initial protestations. What happened was, they get the magazine and they don't know nothin' 'bout humor, so they're looking around trying to find an editor. They called up Marvel and talked to Larry Hama because he did a pretty damn good run on *Crazy*. Larry! I can't say enough about how cool Larry is. *Crazy* wasn't as good after he left it. Towards the end when they just did slim parodies of *X-Men* comics. Anyway, they were desperate and Hama was pretty busy at Marvel and happy there, so he wasn't gonna quit to work at *Cracked*. I'm pretty sure he suggested Laikin. He probably didn't have 1000% confidence in Laikin, since he was the guy who replaced Laikin on *Crazy*. So, they hired Laikin to package the book and gave him pretty free rein. He worked out of his home, which was up in Long Island instead of being at the office.

"You know Laikin's background. He used to edit Sick, as well. His one Marvel Comics credit, outside *Crazy*, was where he did the dialogue for

*Avengers* #9 over Stan's plot; he seemed pretty proud of that. He brought it in once, a worn-out, battered copy. He was trying to impress me as hip to comics, I guess.

"The thing I remember him doing in Mad was a parody of *If* by Rudyard Kipling, and he subsequently used it again in every magazine he edited."

Murad Gumen adds, "After Sproul lost control of his magazine, which sounded incredible (it was his baby!), Paul Laikin came into the fold. By this time, I got the feeling Mr. Laikin had lost some of his passion, and in addition to the low rates (as was the case with *Crazy*), the legacy of *Cracked* suffered. He wanted very much for me to do a cover for his big premiere issue (I had done covers for the short-lived *Wacko*, under Mr. Laikin). I felt uncomfortable, as *Cracked* covers were John Severin territory. Mr. Laikin was phasing Mr. Severin out in any event, I believe because Mr. Severin was too expensive, but I got the feeling whether I did the cover or not, it would have been a moot point as far as Mr. Severin was concerned; and I felt a loyalty to Paul Laikin, who had given me my start. Yet, I still felt bothered, and I didn't do any more covers. I felt compelled to dig up Mr. Severin's address and to write him, giving my apologetic reasons, as well as taking the opportunity to tell him what his work meant to me, but I never heard back."

After leaving *Crazy*, Paul Laikin formed his own black-and-white humor magazine, with the advent of *Wacko*. Again, he called on the services of his "cabinet" and they produced another in a long line of black-and-white humor magazine "product" that lasted for three issues. *Wacko* might have continued after its three issue run if it wasn't for a call to return to the pages of *Cracked* as editor for a second term.

Comments Mort Todd on Laikin's reliance of regulars: "It works out that way: I likewise have a cadre of people that I can rely on to do the work. Maybe it's like a movie director using a troupe of actors and knowing they can be counted on. I know what to expect from these artists and use them whenever possible, whenever I have a good budget."

Aron Laikin picks up the story: "They needed someone to take the helm and he seemed like the ideal person. They brought him in and he's really like a one-man show. He was able to take over in many different areas with both the writing and the editing and the layout; just the whole coordination of it. There wasn't much of a big environment. Most of the work was actually done at home. He enjoyed that freedom and it added to his creativity. He would lie down in his bed and take a pen and pencil and that was his office. I worked at home. Most of us did. It wasn't like Marvel where they had the Bullpen. Even *Mad* magazine, most of the artists worked at home."

The reason for Laikin as a choice was because of his previous experience with black-and-white humor magazines. The new publishers were very aware of Laikin's prior tenure at *Cracked*.

Aron Laikin continues, "Yeah, they knew. They wanted to make it more corporate and more organized. They were more business-minded in that second run. They were very familiar with that. It was one of the big reasons for bringing him on as the editor. They really needed to revive the magazine and they had certain ideas about the direction they wanted to go and they felt my father would be the one to lead him down that path. I started assisting him as an art director and doing some of those spot illustrations inside and then John Severin and myself alternated on the covers, in 1985.

"Art has always been my strength. I've been around the writers as well, so I'm familiar with that side of it, so yeah, I am a writer. I do everything from writing ad copy to business plans to animated cartoons. I do it sometimes in conjunction with my father. Both of us would sit around in a room and spat ideas and it started with ideas. I used to come up with the ideas, but I didn't know how to structure it, so I would just put out bullet points and he would put it into a paragraph or dialogue. While I started learning, and got more comfortable with it and then I would start doing the full writing part of it, and then he would edit, and then we would go back and forth and brainstorm, so we're a good writing team."

Another Laikin relative also was along for the ride during Paul Laikin's years at the black-and-white humor magazines, Eden Norah. Says Aron Laikin, "That's my sister. That's her first and middle name. Since my father wore so many hats, he would basically take the helm and cover so many different areas, so he didn't want to put his name as doing everything, but he did get input from so many different people but on a less official level. That's how that happened, but my sister is a Pulitzer Prize-winning author. She's an investigative reporter for *Newsday* and she's been a well-known writer for about 25 years and she's also written some books and other things, but her full-time thing is working for *Newsday*. She also won another big award there just a couple of weeks ago and she had to go to your neck of the woods. She went to UCLA and had to make a speech and get the award.

"It was just the three of us and we did have a lot of input on all projects so if you wanted to stay home and do that. My mom passed away at an early age. I was probably three. That was another reason my father worked at home was to take care of the magazines and us. So, he would go into the offices a couple times per week, to make sure everything was being put together properly."

Paul Laikin had this to say about using his son Aron at both *Crazy* and *Cracked*, who sometimes used the name Aron Mayer: "He was about 16 or 17. He went to do the Art Students League. In fact, that's what he does now. He's an artist and caricaturist and goes to parties. He did covers for *Cracked*. He's a fine artist, too. He can do oils. He's another New Yorker. When he was 18 or 19, he did those things for me. With *Cracked*, some Wall Street guys and a Madison Avenue guy bought it. They called me in again and I did it again with another associate editor dropped on me. That was *Cracked*."

Laikin's second go at *Cracked* was not as prosperous as his first. Although he did recruit his usual gang of cronies, it was more than obvious that his heart wasn't quite with the product as the quality was not up to the level of previous times. This, coupled with the fact that John Severin was no longer appearing in new pages and the fact that Laikin had a propensity to utilize material originally appearing in *Sick* hastily rewritten or retitled to reflect that it was now a piece from *Cracked*.

Aron Laikin reveals his side of the story, "He basically wanted to do other things and had written several books. He did a Reagan coloring book with Mort Drucker and they were bestsellers and he also got involved with writing for feature films, so he just wanted to get out and do different things. He had 30 years of doing *Cracked* and *Sick* and *Wacko* already. The new people that came in were young and like myself wanted to get a new fresh approach to the magazine at that point, so it was sort of mutual. My father was doing some writing as well after he was editor. We were both working on a freelance level."

Murad Gumen continues, "Paul Laikin was replaced not long after, and I worked a little with his youthful successor. At the time, I was in a different state of mind (employed by Walt Disney), and I wasn't feeling the same zest for humor magazine work. The last *Cracked* job I did was a half-hearted satire script for *Married With Children*, which was not one of my finer hours; especially since this television show was satirical to begin with.

"*Cracked* changed hands a few times afterwards and I wouldn't have minded working for Lou Silverstone, a *Mad* writer I was a fan of. (But I never pursued it; once I spoke with him on the phone, and he sounded like a great guy.) I did, however, approach one of the magazine's later owners, evidently richly financed through angels in Kuwait. When I met with them, I couldn't get a handle on what they were going for (more or less a sexually de-emphasized *Maxim* type of magazine); I didn't feel like preparing written work on spec, especially since the odds for rejection seemed high; and their need for artwork appeared low. It is a sign of the times in American publishing where illustration and cartooning now take a big backseat to photographs, since many cookie-cutter art directors feel artwork is less sophisticated and perhaps in line with 'kid stuff.' Even a magazine designed to follow in *Cracked*'s footsteps appeared to choose such a philosophy, which was pretty ironic."

Artist Kent Gamble adds, "When Paul left *Crazy* and at some point not too long after that, Paul surfaced at *Cracked*, I still worked for Larry Hama. I worked at *Crazy* until it folded. And of course he called me and he asked if I wanted to do something, and I said, 'Sure! Why not?' But it seems like Paul didn't last at *Cracked* very long as the editor. When he was dismissed, that was the end of my run, too, because I was one of his guys.

"When I was drawing for *Crazy* I just assumed since I was drawing for *Crazy*, that none of the others would want me and they would be like, 'Well, you're with that magazine, why would we want you over here?' So I just sort of assumed that they didn't want me and was happy to be at *Crazy*, and I just dreamed in the back of my mind, that I would be in *Mad*. I always followed *Mad*. That was my dream, to be in *Mad*."

Gamble did pay attention to parodies that were done in *Cracked* and *Mad*, while at *Crazy*: "Oh yeah, I paid attention to it. I would look at it to see what parodies they were doing. I would say, 'Oh gosh, they're doing the same parody I'm working on right now.' I was constantly looking to see what the others were doing. I prayed that Mort [Drucker] wouldn't do one for *Mad* that I was doing, because it would make mine look like garbage. That was always my fear, too; that his would come out first and make mine look really bad.

"It seems like after Paul surfaced at *Cracked*, I did *Rambo II* for Paul at *Cracked*, but soon after I had sent it off, then Mort had done it for *Mad*. Afterwards, I said, 'Oh my God. Mine looked horrible!' Richard Crenna was in it, and Mort's anatomy is perfect. That was one I remember that I did and he did. I did *Grease* one time and mine came out first and I said, 'Hey, that looks pretty good,' and then his came out and I felt, 'Mine isn't very good.' His stuff makes everyone's look bad."

John Reiner worked for Laikin at *Crazy* and at *Cracked* and also was inspired by Mort Drucker's style. Says Aron Laikin of Reiner: "I just remembered some of the artists like John Reiner, he would work late hours and he would drop off his art at three in the morning. It was a lot of different experiences in how we coordinated with all the other people involved in the magazine. Tony Tallarico was another kind of one-man show. My father never had to worry about him. He'd turn in the art and he let him be. Murad was a great draftsman and brought a nice line to his work. That's why he worked with Disney for so many years. I also worked for Disney and did some of their murals at their stores. I come from more of a painter background. That's why I did more of the covers. The cartooning was actually much easier for me and was a nice departure. I do much more realistic portraiture stuff. At the same time Murad was doing licensing, I was doing the murals for the stores. At the same time I was doing licensing for Warner Bros. John Reiner's doing *The Lockhorns* and *Howard Huge*."

Don Orehek recalls another story about Reiner long before he worked professionally: "In 1967, when I was living in Manhattan with my wife and son Errol (who was born in '67), a good friend of mine whom I knew from the navy, a guy by the name of Bill McKuen, was selling stuff at Greenwich Village art shows. I was living in the area so why not show some of my stuff, so I started doing drawings of New York military people and from that I started to do package drawings of military guys, marines and different things like that and they were selling for like $20 a piece. Then from that I started doing more cartoons in the Village and I did a cartoon of General Custer with all the Indians were flying around and everyone was getting shot up and Custer was blowing the Indians away, and other guys were getting shot with arrows, and there's this one guy with the nose in the air and a pencil, he says to Custer, 'Make mine pastrami with a kosher pickle to go.' There was a lawyer who bought that thing for $20 with the frame and everything, and after that I started doing things with lawyers and things. Before that I was doing seascapes with acrylics and was selling some really nice pictures, and this one kid comes up to me and asks, 'How much do you want for that lighthouse?' I looked at him and he was a kid like 16 years old and I wanted $75 for it. He doesn't have $75, he's a kid, and so I looked at him and asked, 'Where do you live?' and he said, 'Here in Greenwich Village.' So I figured he could go home and get $75. So, I said, '$75,' and he whipped out $75 for it! Many, many years later, was the first cartoonists meeting we had, on Thursdays. We still do it, you know, all the guys like Sy Barry and all these name guys, we'd meet once a month at a restaurant. So this is the first meeting we had. This guy comes up and says, 'You know, I bought a lighthouse from you in Greenwich Village and you only used four colors.' I looked at him and guess who that guy was? It was John Reiner. I almost dropped dead. He was a kid when he bought that thing from me. I never asked him how he had $75, but I see him every once in a while. He loves that painting. He still has it. It's amazing. Anyway, so after this I started doing lawyer and dental gags. People thought I was a lawyer and they also thought I was a dentist, so I did that for a long time. I stopped doing it about 1980. They gave me a crappy street to work on so I figured, the hell with it, so I stopped doing it after that."

Kevin Sacco followed Paul Laikin from *Crazy* to *Cracked*. He describes the events that led to his tenure at *Cracked*: "I was doing advertising storyboards in New York City. I had worked a little bit for *Crazy* magazine, and that was under the auspices of Marvel. What the deal was then was you kind of graduated from *Crazy* if you were lucky to go work at *Cracked*. So, what happened was—if memory serves, Paul Laikin went from editing *Crazy* to editing *Cracked*."

Tony Tallarico also came along for the ride. He comments, "Whenever Paul went into another magazine, the same format, but with another publisher, we would do some things together. That was his contacts that he would call and then one time Martin Goodman, the Marvel owner. He sold Marvel and went around with a Xerox copy of the check he had, which was for—I don't know $15 million—and a cheap son of a bitch, cheap! I mean, if you had lunch with him, you'd get stuck with the bill! And not just with me, everybody! He wanted a magazine like that, like a *Mad* for his own ego and he contacted Paul Laikin and Paul couldn't do it. He was busy with the Marvel stuff and he didn't want to have anything interfere with that. He recommended me and I think we did about 4 issues. It was called *Trash*, but it was not Marvel. It was by Goodman after he had sold the business and he did this on his own.

He had a little office and he was playing publisher. I mean, he had so much money he did not know what to do. It's true.

"Ironically for me, Paul was called the poor man's Harvey Kurtzman. Later in life I did run into Harvey Kurtzman and wound up doing work for him, so that's how I remember Paul. Paul was always a sweetheart to me, because he took a try on me without any knowledge of what I was going to do and he sort of brought me along. The first few jobs I did certainly weren't as good as what I did later. He really did go to bat for me. I really appreciated that.

"He wasn't that critical. He was more like he would say things like, 'Oh, by the way, Stan Lee was asking about you and saying, 'Who is this guy?" and that would be like jumper cables and you'd feel just great. He'd always find something nice to say about what you were doing. He wasn't particularly critical.

"To me, *Cracked* was the magazine you read just before you got to *Mad*, and there was *Cracked*. It was #2 like the Avis, 'We Try Harder.' When I was working for *Cracked*, I was really quite happy.

"I remember when Paul got to *Cracked*, he was really—from what I remember at that time—he was less relaxed, working hard, more stressed, in order to get it together, than when he was at *Crazy*.

"After Paul left, I tried to pursue them to keep going after that, because I loved the gig, but they never returned the phone calls. They just basically disappeared. I think they were running the business through some other business. You used to call up and get this other business. It was folded into another business. I think it might have been Globe, and you could never get these guys to call you back. As a sensitive artist, I thought they hate my stuff and they're not going to call me anyway, so I gave up on it.

"The interesting thing about that they were the generation after me and all Harvey Kurtzman students, or at least I knew [Drew] Friedman was. I think he also worked on comic book art at the SVA as students. Harvey had pointed these guys out to me, and so when I saw them appearing in *Cracked*, I wasn't surprised because they were up and coming. These guys were probably friends with the editor as this kind of new, younger crowd."

Paul Laikin adds, "When I left *Cracked*, I thought that was the end of them. I found out that *Cracked* was flourishing without me, which I couldn't believe. Somehow, I got a little time on my hands between jobs doing some articles, sending some in to another editor of *Cracked*. I'm not sure when I didn't contributed, not as vividly as the early years. My thoughts are crystal-clear about day one. I remember the first day, but not further down the road. I may have had a free period that I was doing that and my son was becoming an artist."

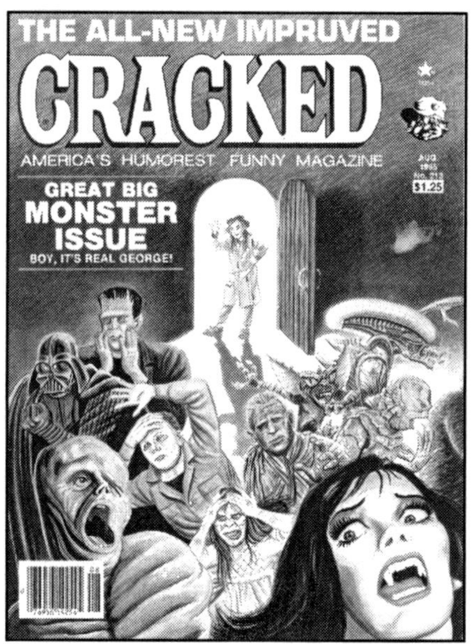


The first issue of the Larken Communications *Cracked* #213, August 1985, art by Murad Gumen.

IF

(WITH APOLOGIES TO RUDYARD KIPLING)

The notorious *If* parody by Paul Laikin, which Mort Todd claims was printed in all the black and white humor magazines Laikin worked on. This appeared in *Cracked* #214, September 1985.

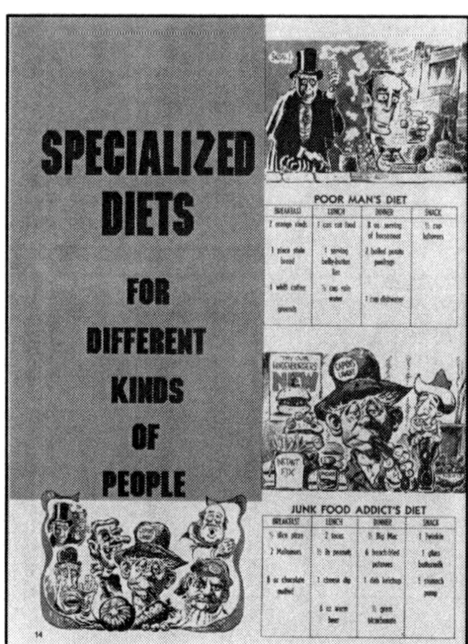
SPECIALIZED DIETS FOR DIFFERENT KINDS OF PEOPLE

POOR MAN'S DIET

JUNK FOOD ADDICT'S DIET

A possible example of a *Sick* article revised and updated to becoming a *Cracked* article due to its amateurish paste-up job from *Cracked* #214, September 1985.

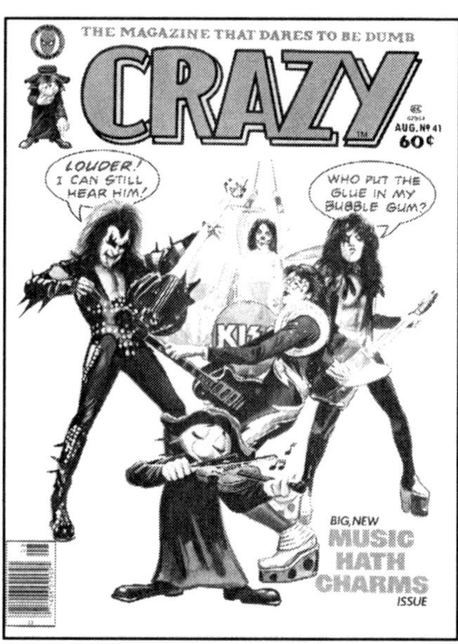


*Crazy* #41, August 1978, art by Bob Larkin, transformed itself into…

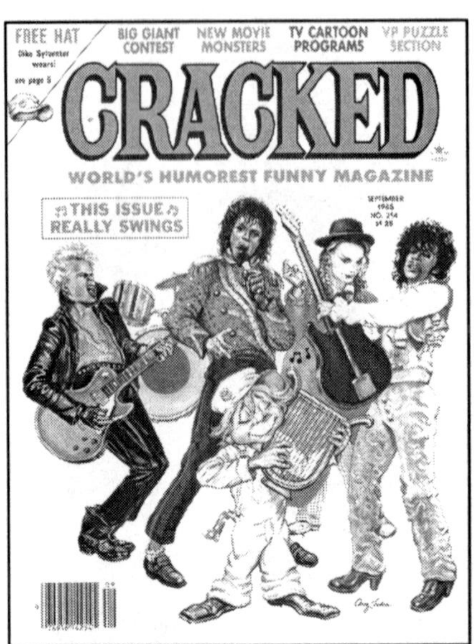


*Cracked* #214, art by Aron Laikin.

The *Cracked* hat as worn by Sylvester first appeared in #214, September 1985.

Aron Laikin from *Crazy* #19, August 1976.

Eden Laikin from *Crazy* #27, July 1977.

# MORT TODD AKA MICHAEL DELLE-FEMINE AT THE HELM

MICHAEL Delle-Femine a.k.a. Mort Todd was disgusted by Laikin's reliance on reprinting old material. After becoming editor with #219, one of his first tasks was to hire new talent. Initially, Todd kept on much of Laikin's staff, but soon discarded most of his art staff save for Walter Brogan, Al Scaduto and Vic Martin. Todd brought back people like Mike Ricigliano and George Gladir, and hired a new staff of up-and-coming and legendary artists and writers, including Dan Clowes, Rick Altergott, Steve Ditko, Milton Knight, Bob Fingerman, Bill Wray, Peter Bagge, Rick Parker, John Arcudi, E. Nelson Bridwell, Cliff Mott, Gary Fields, Rob Orzechowski, Charles E. Hall, Gray Morrow, Jerry De Fuccio, Don Martin, Dick Ayers, Henry Boltinoff, Lou Silverstone and Pete Fitzgerald, for lengthy runs. Other legends made token appearances, but include Kurt Shaffenberger, Stephen De Stefano and Gene Colan.

Mort Todd explains how the transition occurred between Laikin and himself: "I have to say that his stuff was horrible! Laikin's stuff was like really bad Sick material, and as it turns out, some of it actually was *Sick* material. The publishers had Laikin do an issue or two, and even those guys could see that it wasn't really what they wanted. It wasn't too appealing to kids; it was actually Ken's kid, who was probably about 10 or 11 then, who voiced his opinions a lot and probably said something like, 'This sucks!' So they wanted to get an assistant editor, one younger and in touch with what the kids would want. So again through Larry Hama, they were looking for someone that would handle stuff in the office and be accountable, instead of Laikin bringing his yellowed pages every now and then. Larry's assistant editor at the time was Pat Redding, who I had known from school and we were good friends. I don't think we had worked on many comics at the time, but we sure hung out a lot. When I met her in school, I was going to Parson's School of Design. She wasn't really into comics, but she got into comics and ultimately she was Larry's assistant. We would have all been about 21 or 22. I guess Larry asked her if she knew anybody funny.

"By then, we had already put out *Psycho Comics*. That was, like, 1981, I guess. Me and Dan Clowes and Rick Altergott put out our own comics with Pete Friedrich. We put out two issues and some other goofy titles. This was just as direct sales was starting, so we slipped in there and got it into comic shops. We were doing riffs on Atlas/EC-type crummy crime and horror and romance comics. We were all these little punks doing these short little horror stories, thinking that we were pretty dang clever. I had then done a few other comics and written *Superman* for *Action Comics* and sold cover sketch ideas to Julius Schwartz.

"I got interviewed at *Cracked* by Larry Levine and Ken Barratto. They asked me, 'Well, if you were working on the magazine, what would you do?' I wrote and drew a three-page 'pilot story' for them which was 'Hu-Man vs. G.I. Joke' ('He-Man vs. G.I. Joe') to show that I could be 'cutting-edge topical.' Naturally, I was more influenced by Kurtzman than anything *Mad* or *Cracked* was doing currently. I was trying to emulate Kurtzman and Wood gone wild, and I guess they liked it. I got hired and they put me in that office next to the porn guys.

"My first job was to go through letters and write the letters page and crap like that. All the mail was forwarded from Florida and it was all hate mail about how *Cracked* is a rip-off of *Mad*. One letter even had a rancid anchovy in it. I guess the guy couldn't afford a bigger fish! It had corroded through the letter and envelope. It was like the Mafia sign of death. It was all hate mail at first, but it didn't take long to change to where we were getting letters about *Mad* ripping us off. It was very funny. At first, I was just writing the letters pages and doing the low-end editorial work and inventory. Then I started looking at Laikin's stuff, and I guess I was a real snotty kid, I started telling the publishers that it stank in no uncertain terms. Almost every story had a Nixon gag in it. It was 1984 and kids don't even know who Nixon was anymore. Get over it! Then, I found some 'original' art with *Cracked* logos peeling off and it said *Sick* under it. It turns out he was double-billing the publisher for old stuff. There was one where he tried to pass off this non-descript whitebread Johnny Langton chick as Nanny Dickering!

"Rebilling for this stuff, was not only ethically challenging, but *Cracked* could have gotten sued for reusing it. The publishers wanted me to find some new artists and I said, 'Most importantly, the first thing you gotta do is get Severin back!' Severin wasn't in those Laikin issues. *Cracked* is Severin. It wouldn't have lasted as long as it did without John's unequaled contributions. There're no two ways about it. I called Severin (probably got the number from Pat at Marvel) and tell him what's happening and ask if he would please return to the fold. I think Laikin mentioned that Sev wasn't interested in returning. As it turns out, Laikin offered him a poor page rate and demanded kickbacks from all the artists. If you want to draw for *Cracked*, you've got to pay him part of your page rate. Of course, Severin's, like, 'There's no way I'm doing that!' The page rate offered was probably nothing, perhaps under $100. I was able to get Severin $500 a page and no kick-backs, along with the promise that he wouldn't have to deal with Laikin at all. Once the publishers found out about the kickbacks and the reused material, they wanted to get rid of him, but they wanted to find another editor to run the magazine first. I was like 22, so they weren't about to give it to me.

"They interviewed a bunch of people and none of them fit the bill. One had the last name 'Zahn,' and I'm pretty sure he did some *Crazy* stuff. He was a red-haired guy and all of these people, prospective editors, would come in and talk to Ken and Larry and say, 'The first thing you got to do is change the title of the magazine and get rid of Sylvester.

"Here they just spent, I don't know how much they bought it for—I couldn't imagine that they spent more than a couple hundred grand, if that—so, here they just blew this money and people are saying, 'You've got to change the name and the mascot.' That didn't fly too well with them, and in fact, these wanna-be editors totally anticipated the feeling they had during the 21st Century *Cracked* attempt.

"Zahn had brought in some samples by Steve Bissette. I dig Steve's stuff, and even met Steve before, at conventions and stuff. Bissette did some super-bloody caveman gags. Tons of blood and I can see the equal amount of blood drain from the publishers' faces in horror. That wasn't the type of stuff they were looking for. They thought it was too much for a kid-friendly magazine.

"This is where I pulled some sneakiness; while they're looking for an editor, some prospective hires were asking me—and the publisher asked as well, because I handled the publishing schedule—'Well, when is the next issue due to print?' I gave them a date for TWO issues away, not the one that was due immediately. I put the book together myself and then when the book was due, I went to Ken and Larry and go, 'Here's the next issue.' I showed them, 'Yeah, I can do this,' and they ended up hiring me as Editor in Chief.

"There were a couple issues of the Laikin run where I packaged half the book. Once I got Severin back, I was in charge of Severin. So I got Severin and a few other people in there. I think there might be two, maybe three issues where it's half-and-half, and then finally I took over. I might have put two books together secretly just to show them 'Look, you don't have to hire nobody else!' They surely got me for a lot less than they would have had to pay a real editor. That was the first of my many sneaky maneuvers at *Cracked*. But the thing is, I saved them money, I saved them grief and sales picked up. I obviously knew the magazine and the audience.

"My favorite *Mads* were the early ones, the Kurtzman books, in color or black and white. I devoured all the *Mad* paperbacks as a kid. I learned a lot about history and politics from the old *Mads* and I realized, as a fan, I'm wasn't going to gear *Cracked* for kids only. It's gonna be fine for kids to read, but I'm not going to write down to them. That's been the main fault of so many humor magazines. I just did what I liked and it worked and sales were picking up super quick. I was only 10 years older than the average reader and I'm still fairly juvenile.

"We had bound volumes of every issue, and I read them all to be more familiar with its history. There were certain articles that had stickers on them saying, 'Do not reprint this article.' *Mad* sued *Cracked* more than anybody. I think it was the 202nd issue of *Cracked* that has Sylvester hulking out as Alfred E. Neuman and there were spoofs of *Mad* features. There was a big lawsuit and a lot of legal intimidation. When I was working there, my publishers would have loved the publicity garnered from controversy and lawsuits. How can you take a public domain character like Neuman that's a couple hundred years old, and also purport to be a humor magazine, and sue anybody that makes fun of your mascot?

"I released a *Cracked Collectors' Edition* (#77) that I titled *Rad*, with big letters from the *Cracked* logo. I reprinted and listed every name on the cover of artists that had worked for *Mad* and *Cracked*. I went out of my way to piss them off, and wanted them to sue, because I wanted to expose the hypocrisy. They can make fun of anybody, but when somebody makes fun of you, it's time to get the lawyers. I reprinted all the stuff that said, 'Do not reprint.'

"One lawsuit was over a *Planet of the Apes* article that featured stills from the movie. Fox said, 'You can reprint the article, but not the photos.' There were also a couple of lawsuits of cease and desist in relation to *Star Wars*. They went beyond parody to unlicensed exploitation.

"Starting with Severin's first cover, which may have had Schwarzenegger's 'Commandope' or something like that, I did the layouts for every single friggin' cover I edited. I'm of two minds with cover layouts, I either like hyper-simple, sort of like *Famous Monsters*, where you've just got a big-ass head, or what I did with *Cracked*. I wanted to do it scattershot with as many pop culture references as possible, so that if you didn't like Schwarzenegger, maybe you would like Max Headroom or something. Most of the covers I did would have 20 characters in some sort of fight and then have tons of copy, too. Cover as many bets as possible, so if they don't like one thing, they might like another. I started putting artists' names on the cover and hyping features like *The Uggly Family* or *Shut-Ups*, so if you didn't like the movie we're making fun of, then it would be, 'Oh, there's Don Martin or *Hang Ups*.'"

Walter Brogan was a *Cracked* artist who came in during the second Paul Laikin tenure, but remained on staff long after Laikin's departure: "I did storyboards for the *Galaxy Rangers*, and that's when I got a call to work for *Cracked* magazine again from Michael Delle-Femine. That's when he had taken it over from Paul. I think Paul was still working there, though. I think Paul had called me. He was working there and Michael was working for him. I don't know what his real name; it was Mort Todd or something.

"At the time, Michael Delle-Femine had taken over. I couldn't give you the timeline on that at all, but he was my editor for a good amount of time and he was a lot of fun, and after him came Lou Silverstone and Jerry De Fuccio and some of those guys who were also great guys to work with, so there's been a few editors who worked there. Like I said they were all really nice people to work with. I'm sure Mort Todd has some stories. When he was working there, there were two owners and I was roaming around the office and I didn't know he was the owner of the magazine. He had a really dirty, stained shirt and he came up to me and asked, 'Who are you? What are you doing here?' And I said, 'Who are you? What are you asking me these questions for?' He had this stained shirt and he said, 'I own the magazine.' And I said, 'Oh, I work here.' You've got to ask Mort Todd about that."

Brogan discusses the incredible pressures he faced in meeting the deadlines at *Cracked*: "The only problem I had was because I was also working in advertising at that time was that I was doing storyboards all day and I couldn't do the *Cracked* work until I got home at night, and I only got 7-10 days to do about 10 pages, and I felt that the work suffered. I was always pressuring these guys to give me the story quicker. That way I could have maybe five more days to work on it, an extra five days. That was a lot of work. I had to get by on about five hours sleep.

"I would finish a cover in a day. I would get the idea. I'd finish the pencil in a couple of hours, bring it in the next day, get the ok, and then finish the color in a couple of hours and finish it in about a half a day. The advertising paid so much more that I really didn't want to jeopardize that. It paid like 10x more than working on *Cracked*.

"I had a certain love for that type of work. It was enjoyable. I always wished I had at least five extra days to work on the *Cracked* stuff. I was always pressured. Mort and Lou would try to get me the stories sooner and for some reason they didn't. I guess they knew I was fast and I could get it done. It would look ok, but out of all of them, there were probably three or four stories that I was really happy with. All the rest, I wasn't really all that happy. That was a lot of work. I would average between 8 and 10 pages per issue. Thank God I was young. I don't know if I could do it now. Well, that's that love for it. I would finish like 2 in the morning, go to sleep and get up at 7. It took me like an hour and a half to get to work and then I would storyboard all day. Sometimes I had to stay late doing the advertising. Then I'd get home and sleep maybe an hour, an hour and a half. The *Cracked* stuff, I had always wished that they gave me five more extra days."

Al Scaduto was a Laikin loyalist who also stayed on and contributed occasionally through the end, usually with single-page cartoon strips. He also is noted for his work on the newspaper strips *Little Iodine* and *They'll Do it Everytime*. He passed away in 2007.

Vic Martin, of course, was in the early days of *Cracked*, but had left and become a Laikin loyalist, working on *Crazy* and *Wacko*. When Laikin returned to *Cracked*, so did Martin, and when Laikin left, Mort Todd kept him on and helped him revive his *Hudd & Dini* strip for *Cracked*, which had been drawn on occasion by Don Orehek during Martin's absence.

Mike Ricigliano returned to *Cracked* during the Delle-Femine era. Here, he explains the circumstances of his return: "What had happened was after a year of being an editor at that point I knew I could write and draw. I did some writing for them. I did drawing for them. There was a shortage of artists and writers and Mr. Sproul was charging me with finding more artists and writers and my thought was, 'Well, I can do some art and writing. Let me do it,' and he kind of took those duties away from me. I felt that the only way to write and draw for this magazine was to leave the magazine. I did it. I wasn't that happy doing the editorial stuff anyway. I kinda left. I ended up working for American Greetings and the highbrow greeting cards for a year, and then I ended up in newspapers for the bulk of that time, but then somehow got back with *Cracked* a few years later, and then started doing things very regularly."

George Gladir also returned to *Cracked* at this time: "Things went smoothly until 1985 when *Cracked* was sold to another publisher and a new editor took over. After a brief but serious problem period still another editor was installed—Mort Todd (a.k.a. Michael Delle-Femine). Mort came along at the right time. He was both knowledgeable and innovative, and helped save the magazine. Some time later when Mort left the magazine a new editor took over, Lou Silverstone, a former *Mad* writer. I got along with all the editors, but Mort was something special. He always had the interests of the writers and artists uppermost in his mind. We became steadfast friends, and our friendship continues to this day."

One of Mort's first new hires was a young Dan Clowes, who achieved greater fame with the movies *Ghost World* and *Art School Confidential*. For *Cracked*, he is best known for his *Uggly Family* feature. Clowes discusses his days at *Cracked* in an interview by Mike Sacks: "I contributed to *Cracked* from around 1984 to 1989, though I think I only published one piece under my own name. After that, I was 'Stosh Gillespie'—Stosh was the name my father originally wanted for me. He worked in a steel mill when I was born, and several of his Polish co-workers had that name. Also, I think he was trying to bum out my mom. As for Gillespie, it's my middle name.

"No one was ever a fan of *Cracked*. Growing up, my friends—okay, 'friend'—and I used to think of *Cracked* as a stopgap. We would buy *Mad* every month, but about two weeks later we would get anxious for new material. We would tell ourselves, Okay, we are *not* going to buy *Cracked*. Never again! And we'd hold out for a while, but then as the month dragged on it just became, okay, fuck it. I guess I'll buy *Cracked*. Then you'd bring it home, and immediately you'd remember, Oh yeah, I hate *Cracked*. I don't understand any of the jokes, and Sylvester P. Smythe is the most unappealing character of all time.

"I don't know if you've ever seen *Sick* magazine, but they actually had an even uglier mascot: Huckleberry Fink. He was just so ineptly drawn that you didn't know what the hell he was. I think he was a freckled hillbilly. And instead of 'What, me worry?,' his was something like: 'Why try harder?'

"My friend Mort Todd was the editor-in-chief for several years, and we created some truly ridiculous material. We did parodies of TV shows that nobody our age, much less the nine-year-olds reading the magazine had ever seen – stuff like *Ben Casey* and *The Millionaire*. I don't think we ever bothered with a show from our own era (the '80s), or even the '70s. Oddly enough, nobody ever wrote in to say, 'What in the hell are you doing parodying *Dragnet* and *My Little Margie*?'

"*Cracked* was a strange place. They had a consistent, revolving audience of nine- and ten-year-old kids who would innocently pick it up at the grocery store for a year or two before moving on. In the front section of each issue there would be photos of children holding up their issues of *Cracked*, or posing in front of giant Sylvester P. Smythe birthday cakes. The kids always had these confused, lukewarm smiles."

Mort Todd comments on his friend, Dan Clowes: "The publisher really liked Fingerman's work, which was odd because he didn't really like a lot of other new artists, like Dan Clowes. He haaaated his work. He just hated it and we did this one strip called, *The Uggly Family* and 'Ouch!' He despised it so much, I had to slip it into the magazine without him knowing it, and he was livid. We immediately started getting positive fan mail, and then he loved it, so he had to backtrack on that. He still didn't like Dan's art that much. We used a fantastic cartoonist named J.D. King, who was doing a lot of innovative, alternative stuff. He hated J.D.'s work, too."

One of Dan Clowes' friends was Rick Altergott, who also worked for *Cracked* starting in 1985. Altergott went on to produce *Doofus* for Fantagraphics. Due to the similarities in Altergott and Clowes' drawing styles, some have suggested that Altergott is a pseudonym for Clowes. This is untrue.

Altergott comments on his time at *Cracked*: "I was friends with cartoonists Dan Clowes, Michael Delle-Femine and Cliff Mott before the time I began freelancing for *Cracked*. We had a common interest in comics, and I went to Pratt Institute with Dan and Cliff.

"Dan and I began the short-lived imprint *Look Mom Comics* with Pete Freidrich and his pal, Mort, when we were freshmen in college. Years later, Mort became the assistant editor at *Cracked*, and slowly his writing and art showed up in the pages of the 'New' *Cracked*. He brought along some great talents, such as Peter Bagge, Dan Clowes, Bob Fingerman and Bill Wray. There were a few transitional issues before he got involved that had no Severin art and a masthead of either unknowns of ghostwriters; they were terrible! (Pula Kinlai = Paul Laikin.) The whole thing might have folded right then if the issues hadn't become stronger.

"Mort soon became the full editor of *Cracked*, and brought along Cliff Mott. Soon he also was able to have Steve Ditko and Don Martin as contributors! That was quite a coup. Ditko was never a very good fit, but who cares; it was Steve Ditko!

"The early stuff I did for *Cracked* was pretty terrible. I remember drawing a caricature of Lionel Richie in a lame two-page article. I also was tried out as an artist to draw *Hurry-Ups*; the companion page to the long-running *Shut-Ups*. As a kid, I always liked that feature, as drawn by Charles Rodrigues, and later Don Orehek. I was a regular reader of *Cracked*, but I was a much bigger fan of *Mad*.

"And if *Cracked* wasn't as good as *Mad*, it was better than *Sick*. Some later issues of that mag gave me the creeps, when Jack Sparling took it over and gave it a soft-porn vibe that was completely inappropriate with his *Cher D'Fleur* material. I knew something was seriously wrong over there!

"Later at *Cracked*, I would get a chance to draw some of the movie and TV spoofs that had always been my favorite from *Mad*. I put everything I had into those jobs, but my cartooning chops at the time were still developing. They still are to this day, but even so, I am proud of a few of the jobs I turned in. I scripted and drew *Cracked*'s spoof of *Young Guns*, which came out ok. Some others were: *Leonard Part 6*, *Star Trek V*, *Bill and Ted's Excellent Adventure* and a few others."

One of Todd's biggest coups was hiring the legendary Steve Ditko to do some new material for *Cracked*. Ditko, co-creator of *Amazing Spider-Man* and notorious for not being interviewed since 1969, has always stated that his art should speak for itself. Todd takes up the story of how he acquired the services of Ditko: "Initially I was thinking, 'How the hell am I going to fill 48 pages a month?' But there are a lot of freelancers out there that want to work! I called a wish list of my favorite artists and writers, and hired them, just out of the blue, like Ditko.

"With Steve, I found his number in the phone book. I called his studio and told him that I wanted to talk to him about work. Ditko was about two blocks away, dropped by and we talked for hours. He'd come in like once a week and Cliff and I shut down whatever we were doing and we would rap for hours.

"Steve would prefer his work to speak for itself, and we could all take a page from him, but obviously, we had a lot of questions and he's got opinions on everything. I knew there were some issues he didn't really want to talk about, like the *Spider-Man* era, but we would sort of segue into it. Did you ever read any of his self-published stuff in the late '60s and '70s like *Avenging Worlds* and *Mr. A*? I read that in junior high. There was a story that was quite anti-U.N., and I remember reading this as a kid and going, 'Gosh, what's so wrong with the U.N.?' and it made me question things and think. Reading and talking to Ditko developed me philosophically and politically. It was mid-'80s, Ronnie was in office and here I was, making money for the first time in my life. I got more interested in government and political opinion. I spent many hours a week being exposed to and agreeing with Ditko and Severin's views, confirming my conservative punk attitude.

"Ditko's just really private, unlike most comic book people. I continued to work with Steve after *Cracked*, including my stint at Marvel Comics. I called a few years ago about doing some work and he'd officially retired, commercially, but he's putting out some excellent books of his more personal work with Robin Snyder. He's a comics pioneer, a living legend and still creating intense work.

"He has a strong love of the medium and we would talk about cartoons and comics and other cartoonists' work. He had actually done some humor before *Cracked* like Charlton's *From Here to Insanity*. So, despite people thinking he didn't fit in to the genre, he's done humor and it's always a large aspect of his writing.

"One thing that interested him in working for *Cracked* magazine was the black and white art aspect. He had done some Warren pages in incredible washes and then did some really nice work, at *Cracked*, with the duo-shade paper. Severin's the master of that. We would get art in from Severin, and Ditko would be in the office and he would just pore over it. Literally, put his finger on it and go over the lines, processing Severin's artwork. For the longest time I was always trying to get a piece where we could have Severin ink Ditko, because Steve would've enjoyed it. In fact, years later at Marvel I got permission from the Ayn Rand Estate for an *Atlas Shrugged* graphic novel mini-series, but Ditko wouldn't do it. I was going to get Severin to ink it and I was hoping that would interest him. Steve said he didn't want to be responsible for designing how these characters looked, because every reader had their own impression of how they should appear. The estate was so keen to have Steve do it they said they would approve whatever he came up with but he still had no interest in the project. It could have been a classic! The book ends up much like a *Doc Savage* novel. It's about the producers of the world, the masters of every trade and industry being overtaxed, overregulated and overburdened, so they all decide to just drop out. They create a super secret society in the mountains and the government raids them. At the end of the book, there's a big shoot-out. It's a total *Doc Savage* novel. People think since it's in six-point type and a couple thousand pages, and weighs a lot, that it's too much to contemplate, but once you get into it, every chapter is like a pulp or a serial. Ditko was a student of Ayn Rand in the '60s when she used to give classes in the Empire State Building. Later he came up with the character Mr. A, based on Aristotlean philosophy. After *Cracked*, I optioned *Mr. A* for film and comics. We shot a video short and shopped a script but unfortunately, nothing came of it.

"It was fun to cultivate new talent at *Cracked* but the thrill for me was working with the professionals whose work I grew up on. I dug up a lot of people, some I'd worked with, like Kurt Schaffenberger (who drew my *Superman* comic at DC and drew *Supedupman* for *Cracked* in the '50s) and some I hadn't at all like Gene Colan, whom I respect immensely as an artist and a man. The attraction to the artists was that, compared to doing 17 pages or 20 pages a month for comic books, this was a three or four page gig! I see it sort of like actors who do TV ads. It's short work and it pays a lot better. The black and white factor wasn't limiting; it was just the opposite. It allowed them to be a little more creative. You could really go to town with a wash, zipatone, duoshade, rubylith or whatever technique. And with the added incentive of a better page rate, allowing them to keep their copyright and returning the originals to them (along with a fanboy editor who would fawn over the art), I felt we got a more inspired result. Another thing I started were no work-for-hire contracts. As an artist I could relate to not 'selling your soul to the man.' The creators would get and own all their work. Why not? We could get just about anyone we wanted that way. "

"I wrote and drew the first couple *Robot Wars* strips and it was admittedly on a *Spy vs. Spy* bent. I was totally trying to think of a one-pager we could do in that vein and I moshed it up with the *Transformers*. Steve picked up on it and I think it was his idea to take it over. That was, I believe, his initial work for *Cracked*. I was going to draw it out for a couple more issues but was more than happy to pass it on to Steve.

"I'm pretty sure I gave him layouts for the first few. When you gave him scripts or layouts—I don't know if you've heard that famous 'Bernie Krigstein' story—basically, you would give him a script with six or eight panels per page and it would come in with, like, 12 panels, which was fine by me. He would break the story down and tell it in his own way. Some of it was wildly esoteric, but that is Ditko at his best. I deeply admire his work and enjoyed interacting with him very much.

"He didn't do any covers for us, but I should have gotten him to do a monster cover or something. He did a parody of 'Blundercats,' done in wash and that was beautiful. And, he also did 'Transdeformers vs. Boltron,' that was something spectacular done in duo-shade. Around that time, he was doing a few coloring books. He did *Go-Bots, Transformers*; things like that. He certainly could draw on model if he had to, and I think if it's a challenge, he loves to go for it.

"I reprinted a strip Steve did at Charlton in the '70s he owned called *Killjoy* in a *Super Cracked.* He was a guy in the comedy mask of comedy-tragedy. It was a pretty straight superhero story, but I reprinted that in two-color and then apart from *Cracked*, he was in every issue of *Monsters Attack!* I let him run with that and he wrote and drew. It was a gas. When Severin's and Steve's pages came in or the monster mag, I was tripping. Checking out the layouts, looking at the brush lines. I took advantage of my position on one of Steve's stories for *Monsters Attack!* I actually inked it under a pseudonym, and he hated it. I was inking with rapidograph pen then, not brushes, and I was trying to emulate the look of brush with a pen. It looked really, really crusty and crummy."

Milton Knight offers his insights when he worked at *Cracked*: "It was, I believe, 1985 or '86 when Michael Delle-Femine (a.k.a. Mort Todd) became editor and invited me to contribute. We had become acquainted through involvement in New York's independent comics publishing 'scene,' and would regularly meet at conventions and parties. I dug Michael's work for the 'Look, Mom' group. Creatively, we were quite simpatico; all young'uns inspired by Golden Age art and sensibilities. My contributions stopped when he left the editorship, I think '87 or '88. Mike/Mort was a fun editor. I just did my work and handed it in.

"I had submitted to *Mad* first, and got their standard list of writers' requirements. Like *Playboy*, *Mad* has a very specific editorial philosophy, and to get into the magazine, you must subscribe to it. Beyond the paperback reprints of the '50s comics, I was never a fan of the magazine, and was not strongly inspired to resubmit. *Cracked*, on the other hand, had seemingly no editorial philosophy except to be funny and broadly topical.

"Prior to working at *Cracked*, I barely paid attention to it; once I started contributing, I started enjoying the work of other artists in it. For that brief period, the magazine was so loose that there was conceivably 'something for everyone.'"

Another one of those first hired was Bob Fingerman. Fingerman describes, "I started at *Cracked* when I was 21 years old. I was like really fresh. *Cracked* was pretty much my first regular gig. It was certainly the gig that got me enough money to leave home. I was still living at home and working for *Cracked*. It helped me afford to move out. I worked for them from 1985 to 1987. It was almost three years. I think I was in every single issue and often more than one story per issue. They were my bread and butter during those years, for better or worse.

"It was Mort who hired me. I knew Mort socially. It was not like we were pals or anything, but we traveled in similar circles. We had a lot of friends in common, including some people that were from his years at SVA. I think he went to SVA. He knew a guy named Pete Friedrich who published a comic anthology called *Pure Entertainment*. I had met Pete when I was still in [Will] Eisner's class, because he would come in there looking for new talent for *Pure Entertainment*. And actually I think that was the first published comic I did, I think it was for him. Then I met Mort.

"It was certainly an interesting bunch when I was working there. It was the beginning of Dan Clowes' career and Peter Bagge. They were doing stuff for them. They were using some interesting people. They were definitely a younger generation of underground cartoonists.

"The first thing I did for them was a take off on *Mad Max*, with the very clever title of 'Cracked Max.' Ha ha. Get it? I think the only cover I did for the regular magazine was that *Hollywood Squares* one with like the Beastie Boys and Pee-Wee Herman was on it, too. The rest were for the specials. I was proud of some of the covers I did. They felt like a triumph because I was getting some work in color and also they paid better.

"It was almost three years, so it didn't feel that short. I did a lot of work for them, but honestly. I know one I was proud of—and I have looked at this stuff in 20 years, and I probably wouldn't like looking at any of them anymore—but the one I felt was a triumph which was one of the one I wrote, was *Pee-Wee's Playhouse*, and the main reason I felt that that was a triumph was because Mort fought me on that one. He didn't want to do it. He thought it was lame and he thought it was a fad that was going to go away, and all he did was make a lot of fag jokes about Paul Reubens and I said, 'No, no, no, no. This is good stuff.'"

Mort Todd comments about Fingerman, "He was such a young, green lad at the time! Did you ever read Fingerman's thing in *Minimum Wage* about his *Cracked* days? It's such a barbed satire of Cliff and me but it was a bit out of context. It was about his character having to work for 'Whacked' magazine and the porn magazines. For years, I'd see him at conventions and for the last five years, he's been pretty friendly. He was pretty young but so was I. Can't remember who came in first, but he and Bill Wray basically came in together. I think it might have been Wray that suggested Fingerman but it might have been the other way around. Being a comic geek, I was familiar with Bill Wray's work. I was happy to get the chance to use him. What soon happened with both of them was that even though they were new to the field, they kept wanting page rates on par with Sev."

Fingerman corrects the account about his graphic novel: "I did a graphic novel called *Beg the Question* which is a fictionalized account of my youth and working for a magazine called 'Stacked'...very subtle. Anyway, if you take a look at that book, there are parodic mentions and drawings of Mort Todd. If you take a look at that book, there are parodic mentions of Mort in the third chapter. I bear him no ill will, whatsoever. I feel that he gave that magazine more than it deserved. He worked very hard for them. It was the classic water under the bridge. Any bad feelings I may have had at the time are long since dissipated. He did a great job."

Fingerman was one of the few people at *Cracked* over the years that did not have an enjoyable experience. Fingerman explains, "Oh, I'm not the only one. I'm sure if you talked to Bill Wray, he would also tell you it was pretty lousy. He and I are good friends and I would imagine that he would have a very similar take on it, although he lasted a lot longer than I did. I at least remember it unless someone would tell me different; I left on my own accord, because I couldn't stand it anymore. It was a very seedy enterprise that itself wasn't a bad thing. I've worked for a hell of a lot of seedy publications. Fortunately, I don't anymore, but certainly for the first 10 years of my career. It was all *Cracked* and working for men's magazines. It was not always exactly high-caliber environments. I remember literally when I first worked for *Cracked*; they were in an office that was also doing porno digests. I just thought, 'What grubby little office.' They were doing these little digest-sized newsprint porno mags called; *Intimate Letters* and *Human Digest* was one." (Stuff much more hard-core than what Sproul used to do.)

"I think this was pre-Globe. I think they sold to Globe and I think that's when my troubles began. I couldn't swear to this, but I think they were with a different publisher [Larken]. They also were publishing a porn magazine devoted to gargantuanly obese ladies. I think that one was called *Hub*. It was kind of a grimy little office, very cramped with piles of stuff everywhere and then at some point about six months after I started working there, they moved to nicer offices and I think that would be when Globe took over. Either that or they just decided to move to a nicer spread. It was not like it became suddenly really classy, but it wasn't grimy anymore. It was a more professional-looking setup."

Bob Fingerman recollects the events that ultimately led to his exit from the publication: "In terms of the actual work, it was fine. It was generally pretty easy going and by and large they appreciated my work, and when I say 'they,' I mean Mort and the art director, Barry Shapiro. He was kind of an anxious, slightly older guy. He was one of these guys that seemed to be slightly defeated by life. It was actually one of the Globe people, because there was a publisher at that point who took a hands-on interest. He was a real greasy guido-ish Italian guy with really bad hair plugs, Kenneth Baratto. It was when this new publisher came in and took an interest and that's always a problem. When the higher-ups want to get their own hands dirty and they don't have any understanding or flair for what they've purchased. They think they're a writer and all that's going to do is fuck everything up. This is kind of my best story of what I can give you as an example. I was fired because this publisher guy thought that I was trying to crowbar subliminal satanic messages in the work, which is about as ludicrous as anything I can imagine. I mean, you couldn't make that up. The reason he thought that—do you remember the band Mötley Crüe? Back then, they wore makeup and they were sort of a poor man's KISS and they had lots of skulls and crossbones and pentagrams and all that kind of stuff as their costume. They wanted to look dangerous. If the references here don't date this story, nothing will. It was a thing called 'ZZ Slop vs. The Space Pirates' and it was this little space opera where ZZ Top were the heroes and Mötley Crüe, they were the Space Pirates. I think Pat Benatar was in it and other rockers of that era. Anyway, I drew this thing and because Mötley Crüe was in it, I just drew it the way they looked. They had pentagrams and I drew pentagrams. If anything it wasn't subliminal, it was right there, because there were skulls and crossbones because they were pirates, and there were some pentagrams. In any case, Mort called me one day and said, 'We don't need your services anymore,' or words to that effect, and I said, 'Why?' And he said, 'The publisher thinks you are putting satanic messages into your work,' and he knew that was ridiculous. Honestly, my first instinct was, 'Well, fine, fuck him,' but I needed the work. They were paying my rent. So I said to him, 'Did you go to bat for me?' cause at that point, I had been with them for over two years, and he hadn't. So I said that I had to go talk to this guy. I've got to convince him he's wrong, and I ended up having to go to their main offices to go plead my case. It was in a different building in New York. I think it was more midtown. I don't remember the exact address. I really think that this was pre-Florida. I think Globe was mainly headquartered in Florida. I don't know. It's where the old New Yorkers go to retire because it's a better climate. But anyway, I had to go down there to plead my case and did it successfully. I could have been totally honest and said, 'Hey, I'm an atheist. I don't care about Satan, nor do I care about God, so…' It was not a good thing. Atheism has not been a good selling point for anything. Look, I am not pushing forward an agenda. I was just drawing them as I saw them. This is what they look like and the pictures of Mötley Crüe. Hey, look, I didn't make it up. Look. It's what I used for reference. And he saw the costumes and pretty much gave me the no bless oblige and said, 'Ok, but don't let it happen again,' and left off with a warning. And I said fine, but after that I was ticked off and I did start putting subliminal things in. In another issue, I wrote the word 'cunt' in the background, but I did it as a rebus but they never caught that. I don't remember what the article was, but I know I did it as a rebus around a blackboard. The kind of things that they would have above the chalkboard in a classroom. I don't remember the exact rebus, but I did remember that that was my little revenge, and I didn't stick around much after that, because it left such a bad taste in my mouth that I decided to redouble my efforts to find better work.

"I do remember once Bill Wray, Walter Brogan and I, went to the executive offices because we weren't getting paid on time, and I think Bill, being the one with the strongest personality, we would go to the offices and demand our money, and that also caused grief, and this predated the 'pentagram' incident. That also probably helped management not lean in my favor, and of course freelancers are supposed to be grateful for the crumbs that we get, so the fact that we would actually have a little *Norma Rae* moment and go marching off to say, 'We want our money!' made them hate us. They hated all three of us.

"I was definitely hurting for a little while after I left, but it was absolutely the best thing that I ever did. It's not really a great resume builder. It's definitely prejudiced some people against me to have *Cracked* be the most tear sheets in my portfolio back when people went around with a portfolio. Nobody does that anymore now with the Internet. Back then when you went traipsing around with your book, it really did not impress art directors, cause they didn't even look past where you were even published, it was whether the artwork was any good or not. *Cracked* is the only place this guy has worked. What a loser.

"I honestly didn't try to work for *Mad* because here's my own modesty. I didn't think I was good enough. I definitely thought I was good enough for *Cracked* and indeed I was. But *Mad*, I was intimidated by *Mad*, especially back then, they still had all the really good guys working for them. Those were the days of Mort Drucker and Jack Davis. All the old-school guys were still there and I felt, 'There's no way could I get my foot in the door.' So, the thing is, Bill Wray definitely would be the guy to talk to because Bill did work for *Mad* for many years after *Cracked*. If you worked for *Cracked* you were persona non grata at *Mad*. They did not to know from you, and that was partly because Mort Todd took it upon himself to be fairly antagonistic with *Mad*, so beyond being competition, he was also being the little thorn in their side, and they took that personally."

Mort Todd adds his comments about Fingerman's exit: "The story with the satanic symbols, I'm pretty sure that Fingerman inked over some panels. What happened with Fingerman was his own undoing. I tried to get these guys raises regularly and but I don't recall too many late checks. Fingerman at 21 or 22 was easily making $250 a page, which in the '80s, John Romita wasn't making that. Bob started billing and increasing his rate on the invoices, and I think he might have even double-billed once or twice. So, I would just basically turn the bills in to get checks cut and I wasn't noticing it, but the accountants noticed it. I could pretty much set the page rates, but for raises, I'd have to get the publisher's OK. He got something like two raises within one year, but then he jacked up his own rate again, and so that's what killed him. I think the publisher called him in on it, and he had to come in once to see that 'greasy Italian.' I was in a bad spot because I should've paying attention and he got himself fired and there was some bad blood. I heard that it irked him that I used to say 'adaption' instead of 'adaptation.' I heard a movie director say adaption in a commercial the other day, which reminded me of it. I've seen him in recent years at cons and we have friendly chats. You gotta admit he's made his mark in the medium."

Bill Wray started working at *Cracked* in 1985. Wray declined to be interviewed for this book, so Mort Todd takes up the story: "Wray and Fingerman were buddy-buddy and would often commiserate together. They'd smolder about all the injustices the world handed to them. All the roadblocks in their life.

"Out of respect, I would never redo artists' work. Except in the case of Bill Wray, I had to because he delivered it unfinished. He was always late with his work, and sometimes work would come in days late, and the pencils weren't erased. That's just sloppy and unprofessional and we'd have to erase them. For the *Star Trek IV* parody (#228), he drew that and it was so late that he brought it in without backgrounds. So, I had to stay up all night and fill in the backgrounds in duo-shade. I couldn't even try to match his style.

"That's when I would have to start lying about deadlines to him. I'd say, 'We definitely need this by the first of the month,' when it was actually going out at the end of the month. One fine day, I got a call from Bill Wray. He said, 'Oh man. I know I have been slacking off. I really want to prove to you how good I can be. I want to do the best job I've ever done for you!' and that set off my Spidey sense. I was all, 'What? Why all of a sudden do you want to be on time and do a good job?' Over the course of his working for the magazine, each time he turned in a job his signature got bigger and bigger with a 'Walt Disney' riff and a big copyright symbol next to it. He was saying, 'I'm going to do the best job I'm ever going to do for you or anybody.' I was all, 'Well, that's very nice, Bill. Thank you.'

"I then got a call from one of my sleeper agents at *Mad* saying, 'You know, Bill Wray was up here looking for work.' I said, 'Oh, really?' It turned out he brought over his portfolio and the editor agreed with me and said, 'Well, this looks kind of sloppy. How about this? You go back to *Cracked* and do some more work and show us what your real potential is. How good you can be and then come back to us.' After I got that underground dispatch from *Mad*, I was thinking, 'Ok, so what kind of script can I give Bill to show off to *Mad*?' At the time, you might perhaps remember that there was a little HBO series called, *Tales from the Crypt*. So I was thinking, you know what, why don't we do a *Tales from the Crypt* parody, and prominently feature our buddy Bill Gaines? So, I got writer John Arcudi, one of my favorite writers with a wicked sardonic bent who later wrote *Hellboy* stuff. He wrote and created *The Mask*, the character that made Jim Carrey and got screwed over for royalties. I told him to come up with a parody and to write a script called 'Tales from the Creep' (#250).

"As an editor, I was kind of like an old-school editor where I would give a rough plot and a lot of gags and titles to the writers, because I already knew what direction I wanted and what the writers were capable of bringing to the material. So, I get the script from John and Bill came in and I told Bill, 'Here's your story where you're gonna show me how much you can shine!' The cover for 'Tales from the Creep,' had Bill Gaines, of course, as the Creep instead of the host, the Crypt Keeper. 'I want you to make him as fat and as ugly and disgusting as possible.' Bill was sweating and, like, 'Oooohh kaaayy.' He drew the script, brought the art back and it was passable. It was his regular, pedestrian stuff. I looked at the first page and I go, 'Bill, where's your signature?' Like I said, with each job he turned in it was just getting larger, and all of a sudden, it wasn't there anymore. 'What's that about?' He wanted to come up with something like 'Hack Davis' or something corny. So, I ended up having one of his other signatures put on an overlay. It was very petty of me. I don't blame him for wanting to go to *Mad*, but his way of doing it was cheesy. He wouldn't have gotten more pages than we gave him. He might have gotten a little better page rate. As it turned out, he only got one page, that Monroe thing, or whatever. It wasn't fun to look at.

"He tripped out that we put his name on it and I called him on it and was like, 'Bill, I know that's why you wanted to do such a good job for us. Maybe it was time that we should part company and you can go on to *Mad*.' I guess it took him a couple of years to do that. A few years later at a convention, he tries to pick a fight with me! He started trying to push me around. He's a tall guy with quite the gut and a shiny dome and he got into a shoving match at a comic convention. All I could do was laugh at him. Luckily, Arcudi was there to back me up if things got rough! Basically, that's why those Fingerman and Wray didn't like me. It used to really bother me, as I usually got along well with all cartoonists I worked with. It wasn't until John Kricfalusi of Spumco told me that it was natural for people in 'positions of power' to have to make some enemies. John later had his own problems with Bill Wray.

"For a while, I would always get such scowls at conventions when I saw them. Since then, Fingerman, and me, we've have had various casual conversations and it's no prob. Also, it was like a quarter of a century ago now, but Wray may still harbor a grudge."

Peter Bagge discusses how he started working for *Cracked*: "I was acquainted with Mort Todd at the time he took over as editor back in 1985 or so. He asked me to contribute—though he doubted the publishers would be okay with my art, so I just submitted scripts. I only dealt with Mort, off and on for as long as he was there. 3 years? 4? I forget. I also only wrote stuff for him at his request, and never sent unsolicited ideas to him. He'd say 'Write a spoof of *The Phil Donahue Show* for me,' and I would. It was all very no fuss, no muss."

Rick Parker, who later on had a lengthy run on the *Beavis and Butt-Head* comic book for Marvel, did a few pieces for *Cracked* at this time, but it was short-lived. He contributed again later during the Dick Kulpa era.

John Arcudi was another Todd discovery from 1985, who went on to greater fame after leaving *Cracked*. He is best known for creating *The Mask*, which went on to become a major hit feature film for Jim Carrey. He also wrote under the pseudonym "Archie Falbo."

E. Nelson Bridwell was a longtime writer for DC. His contributions to *Cracked* are few, but his previous notoriety warrants his mention here. He died in 1987.

Gary Fields also started in 1985, during Todd's era: "I probably found *Cracked* on the newsstand, bought it and found out where they were to drop off some samples. I also think that Frank Caruso (who's a bigwig at King Features) was being published in *Cracked*. I went to high school with his brother and that was most likely the driving force of me going to see them.

"I only went to *Cracked*. I think I heard back then (in the mid-'80s) that *Mad* was a closed door. They had their usual gang of idiots.

"I roughed out and wrote a four-page story and spoofed a Barry Smith *Conan* cover and Michael bought it as *Canine, the Barkbarian*. That was my first piece for *Cracked* and it appeared in an issue of *Super Cracked*.

"I worked for *Cracked* from 1985 to 2000. When I started there, Michael Delle-Femine was the guy to see. He's a great guy. Lots of ideas and really was passionate about *Cracked*. He and I were young guys at the time and I think he brought some new blood to the magazine. Whenever I told people that I was working for *Cracked*, the usual response was, 'Oh, they're still around?' Michael really pushed to get everyone aware of *Cracked*. Michael was the guy who got under *Mad*'s skin and there was a little battle of the humor mags going on. Michael was instrumental in bringing Don Martin and Lou Silverstone over.

"Barry Shapiro was the art director. He was an older guy who I think worked at Marvel years earlier. He seemed to know everyone at Marvel. He was replaced by a talented cartoonist/designer, Cliff Mott.

"Years later, I believe the magazine was sold to a publishing company that did bridal magazines (*Bridal Guide*). Lou Silverstone came over and he and Andy Simmons were the new editors/writers. Todd Jackson was the assistant editor. Cliff stayed on as the art director. In the late '90s, *Cracked* was sold to the *Weekly World News* company. That didn't last too long because I was told it didn't make enough of a profit. It was sold again to Dick Kulpa, a staff artist who worked there. I think he had good intentions of continuing *Cracked*'s legacy but it didn't work. Whether it was too much for him or whatever, it became a pale imitation of what it once was."

Says Todd of Fields, "Gary Fields and I think Darren Auck, who later ran the Marvel Bullpen and became a great friend of mine, along with Michael Kraiger, they all just got out of Joe Kubert School and they showed up at the office—the one sharing porn space—and they showed me their work and I'd went, 'Yeah!'"

As mentioned above, Cliff Mott replaced Barry Shapiro in 1986. Mott describes how he attained the art director position at *Cracked*: "After moving to New York to attend Pratt Institute I became friends with fellow comic obsessives, Mort Todd, Dan Clowes and Rick Altergott. We shared our appreciation for the ridiculous and sublime in all forms of media. Several years later Mort became editor at *Cracked*, and after a few freelance jobs, he hired me as art director, and since there were only two of us, associate editor.

"I was woefully unprepared to work there when I started. I was aware that it existed but I was a *Mad* man all the way. Once I saw the acres of gorgeous work that Sev and others had done since the '50s, I grew to have a much greater appreciation for the title.

"I had a tremendous run at *Cracked*. Everything I learned professionally grew out of my time there. I was able to assist great talents that I never dreamed I'd meet, let alone work with: legends like John Severin, Don Martin and Steve Ditko. Later on, through the magazine I was able to meet personal heroes like Ed Roth and John Holmstrom. As an added value, having a cushy art job allowed me the opportunity to develop my own personal style in a leisurely fashion.

"I never dreamed I could work at either one, but fate stepped in and dealt me the *Cracked* card. I would love to do some work for *Mad* someday, if no hard feelings remain. I know they hated our guts over there for a while. We just tried to be competitive ... plus pull a couple pranks.

"The very top-tier talent we had come from *Mad* in the first place. Sev, Don Martin, and in terms of writing, Lou Silverstone, whom Mort hired after Don defected, who went on to edit with *National Lampoon* alum, Andy Simmons, and write for the mag for years. As one might guess, the more experienced artists and writers were a pleasure to work with and never, ever missed deadline. As for the younger guys, what they lacked in timely response, they made up for with enthusiasm and creativity. Not a small number eventually made their way into the pages of *Mad* itself!

"I'm most proud of becoming competitive with *Mad* against massive odds. I derived the most pleasure from working with the artists and encouraging them to try different visual approaches, even under tight deadlines and budgets. There was nothing to be unproud of, but I was disappointed that we were unable to spin off the magazine into other media, although we were close on several occasions.

"I don't miss the job. I do miss the camaraderie we enjoyed as a group of underdogs, fighting to bring humor to a satire-starved world!"

Rob Orzechowski began at *Cracked* as a replacement for Bill Wray in 1986, who was doing his various *Sylvester Celebrity Posters* on the back covers of the magazines, then abdicated to *Mad*. Orzechowski's skills in drawing Sylvester as various movie monsters got him the job in drawing much for *Cracked*, and especially *Cracked Monster Party*. He also has done work for *Hustler* and was brought to *Cracked* by Gray Morrow.

Charles E. Hall was a writer for *Cracked* during the Mort Todd era starting in 1986, and has worked with Todd on various post-*Cracked* projects. Says Todd about Hall: "He's a very talented individual who did writing and layouts. Was also a steady partier that remembers a lot of funny stuff about those days that I sure don't. He was responsible for the debauched theft of a Styrofoam *Mad* logo from a comic con, which I then prominently displayed in my office. He also did some writing for me at Marvel. Primarily he is a musician and played the *Cracked* 30th anniversary party and recently recorded the theme song for *The Diabolikal-Super Kriminal* film I produced, and recorded songs for the *Playboy* animation Cliff Mott and I did (along with doing some sick voices). A colorful character!"

Hall continues the story: "Bebe Buell, best known as a *Playboy* centerfold and high-profile girlfriend to a select group of rock stars, and possessed with her own musical aspirations, would come around to see my band. Bebe had been a lot of places, known a lot of famous people, and her interest in me confirmed suspicions I had been harboring about my own talents. It wasn't too long before I moved in with her, we started a band, and I left The Moguls. Or maybe they threw me out. Now, the thing is, Doug and Mort didn't see much of each other at that time, but Mort and Bebe were very good friends. So I really got to know Mort through Bebe.

"Bebe had met Mort shortly after she moved to Yarmouth, Maine, just outside of Portland, to get her cousin's help in raising her daughter, Liv, then known as Liv Rundgren, now known as Liv Tyler. Bebe was at the Maine Mall outside Portland with her niece and there she spotted Mort, clad in black leather, wearing, even then, in the late '70s, his trademark Ray-Ban Wayfarer prescription sunglasses. Bebe thought that Mort looked like somebody who would know where to get pot. Bebe's niece knew Mort from school, and Bebe looked him up in the phone book, and called him out of the blue, asking if she could drop by sometime. Of course, Mort was still living at home with his mother!

"Mort moved to New York City but he and Bebe stayed in touch, and I believe that she introduced Mort to her then-boyfriend, Stiv Bators, of seminal punk band The Dead Boys. Some of Mort's first professional work was doing the logo for Stiv's solo album *Disconnected*.

"After Mort scored his gig at *Cracked*, he would often fly up to Maine to visit Bebe and Liv, spend the weekend, take them out to dinner, and generally show them a good time. After I moved in he kept coming up. We got along well together from the start. Mort liked my collection of comics, largely weird Charlton science-fiction and off-brand horror. I knew him then as Michael. Bebe still calls him that.

"It was Bebe's idea that I do something for *Cracked*. She was interested in me making money with my talents, whatever they might be. She talked to Mort first, and talked to me second, so it was rank crony-ism from the get-go. I usually drew in pencil, had never drawn much for print, and there was no shortage of experienced cartoonists eager to work for *Cracked*, so Mort offered me work writing to start, with the prospect of getting my cartoons published later on.

"Mort made it easy for me to write for *Cracked*. I would do a pencil version of my piece, and Mort would send it along to the artist. I never went near a typewriter. Sometimes I would send in bits of script on the first snippet of paper that I had scribbled on. Once I asked Mort if he had any suggestions for me. He replied that it might be helpful if I sent in my work on whole pieces of paper. I worked from a desk on the glassed-in back porch of my apartment in Portland, and sent my stuff in by the regular mail, so there was no direct communication between the artists and me; I got to know them through the work. Of course, you can learn a lot about someone this way. This would have been in the mid-'80s, probably around '86.

"I was reasonably convinced at this time that I was going to be a big rock star, or at least big enough not to have to worry about the rent. Indeed, all the evidence pointed in that direction, so I wasn't too worked up about writing for *Cracked*. Mort appreciated that attitude. He would say that most people in my position would be bragging about writing for *Cracked*, but I wanted to keep it quiet.

"My first piece for *Cracked* was a real corny how-to kind of guide for guitar, drawn by John Severin. One of Mort's great strengths as an editor, and something that really showed during his subsequent tenure at Marvel Comics, is his ability to match creators with projects. He knew that it would be easiest for me to make fun of something I knew. I was familiar with John Severin's work, and would have to say that I really started out on top in the comic writing business, in terms of whom I got to work with. I was fortunate enough to work with Mr. Severin often during my stint at *Cracked*. It was always a pleasure to see his work come back. I wrote quite a few *Hang Ups*.

"Mort would let satirize pretty much anything I liked, but as often as not I would work from some suggestion or concept of his, Mort was always coming up with concepts, or something would arise from some conversation we were having, or something we were already making fun of anyway. Mort always appreciated the subversive potential in humor comics, as well as their potential for instilling healthy skepticism in young minds. I got to work with a lot of great artists.

"I did a bleak think piece entitled 'How The Future Turned Out' with Gray Morrow, the incisive 'Nanny Dickering Interviews The Fast Food King' with Bill Ward, that anticipated *Fast Food Nation*, albeit with more puns, and *Shut-Ups* with Vic Martin, which inspired me to do some 'Shut-The-Fuck-Ups' for in-house use only. I did a *Honey, I Shrunk The Kids* parody with Wally Brogan, two *Batman* parodies with Rick Altergott, who researched real rare jelly jars for the opening panel where Bruce and Dick are sorting their collection, and a 'Skateboards Of The World' overview with Pete Fitzgerald that referenced Glasnost and Apartheid. It was all a lot of fun.

"I've never heard of Mort getting credit for it, but he is responsible for Liv's first acting appearance in the national media. Mort came up one weekend with photographer Kevin McMahon and shot a photo-funny in which Bebe played Nanny Dickering. Liv, Mort, and myself all had roles. Kevin had a lens that could take reasonably undistorted full-length pictures at close range, and we shot the whole thing in our apartment. The photos were cropped and dropped in over drawings.

"It was around this time that Mort came up with the idea for *Monsters Attack!*, black-and-white horror that would be a sister magazine to *Cracked*. He used many of the same artists that worked for *Cracked*, and I got to do a couple short stories. One, illustrated by Gray Morrow, more of a *Twilight Zone*-type piece than horror, was inspired by Mort. It featured a successful magazine publisher named 'Mick Dellasandro,' who runs afoul of his own passions.

"In June 1989, Bebe and I moved to New York with our band, The Gargoyles. We got a sublet. Liv was to follow a few months later, after we'd gotten our own place.

"Now I was in a position to drop in to the *Cracked* offices regularly. When I had first visited the *Cracked* offices on a trip from Maine, they were located not too high up, with extensive windows overlooking a busy midtown street. Now, Mort and art director Cliff Mott shared a cramped, windowless room located in an airless maze of cheap carpets and pre-hung doors that was the offices of the publisher. As I remember, he publisher also produced some fairly questionable pornography, so there were generally boxes and piles of it in the hallways.

"Mort showed me around the city: Japanese steak houses in midtown, peep shows on $42^{nd}$ Street, Forbidden Planet, Billy's Topless—all the high points. He also came to our shows at places like CBGB's. Mort threw parties for his magazines. There was a *Monsters Attack!* party at Mars, and an anniversary party at 'The Tunnel,' where The Gargoyles performed as

'Nanny Dickering and the Martians.' I don't think Bebe stayed in character for a moment, and we did our regular set, with no *Cracked*-related, or even comics-related, songs. I'm pretty sure no one noticed. A lot of creators had come from out of town, and this was the one time I met John Severin, who was very kind, and gave me words of encouragement.

"Later, at a release party for *Monsters Attack!* attended by a large number of artists, Vic Martin and Sergio Aragonés pretended to hurl insults at Cliff and Mort. 'Poo! I spit! Enemies!' said Mr. Aragonés. Mort told me he would have to meet with certain creators that worked for both magazines in clandestine, out-of-the-way places, and hand off folders and envelopes like spies, and this was all before Mort 'stole' Don Martin!

"Well, strangely, in terms of all the attention Mort had generated for the magazine, the new talent he'd brought in, people like Dan Clowes and Pete Bagge, the ties he'd strengthened with the older artists, and the huge increase in sales, Mort's relationship with *Cracked*'s publisher was deteriorating seriously by this point. One should really ask Mort about this, but indicative of the situation, and this is what Mort told me, as sales increased the publisher upped the print runs, then blamed Mort when the *percentage* of books sold dropped!

"To make matters worse, Mort had moved in with Bebe and myself. Living with us wasn't working out for Mort, and living with each other wasn't working out for Bebe and me. Mort left *Cracked*, The Gargoyles broke up, Mort moved out, Liv moved in, and Bebe threw me out, which I have to say was a good move on her part. I went to live with Mort in the East Village on a block that functioned as an open-air heroin market. That stuff was never our style, but the block was known as one of the safest in Alphabet City. Not that we were worried.

"I heard through Cliff that the new editors—they hired two to replace Mort!— decided that I wasn't funny, and that was it for me and *Cracked*. To Bebe's credit, she always pushed me to sell my art, and she encouraged me, when things started falling apart at *Cracked*, to send a package to *Mad*. So I did. I waited, gave a call, and the women I spoke to said something to effect that they hadn't received any such package or she didn't know about it. I stepped out of the apartment for a few minutes, and Bebe got right on the horn to *Mad* and asked them what they meant: she knew damn well they got the package. According to Bebe, and she is my only source on this, the woman on the other end of the line admitted that they had received my package, but said that all the examples of my work were from *Cracked*, and that they wouldn't even consider me! I don't think that they could have possibly connected me to the disappearance of their sign—I was just a package and a voice on the phone—so I have to put it down as another example of their professional pettiness.

"My favorite *Cracked* piece was actually one I did for *Monsters Attack!* It may have been the last thing I did with that company. Mort knew I had an interest in aviation and military history, so he suggested I come up with a World War One flying piece and throw in a couple monsters. He had John Severin in mind for it from the start, knowing his encyclopedic knowledge of uniforms, war machines, and period detail. I was especially excited to work on this story, looking forward to seeing the art.

"I came up with a German vampire in a Fokker tri-plane and French werewolf in a SPAD having a dogfight using silver bullets. Severin did a fantastic job: the planes were right, the period detail perfect, and the characterizations broad but not absurd.

"Unfortunately, before the piece was completed Mort left the magazine. The replacement editors looked at my story and figured they could improve it. I had the vampire get a case of blood lust / target fixation, and become so obsessed with pouring hot silver into the werewolf that he doesn't pull out of his dive in time, and gets skewered on a stake in no-man's land. I guess this wasn't clever enough, because the re-write had the vampire shooting off the werewolf's propeller, which then flies back into his cockpit and spears him. Really! I never heard of that happening! Vampires and werewolves are one thing, but let's not mess with physics or the laws of probability. That ending really takes me out of the moment, but 'Transformation Flying' remains my favorite piece.

"My least favorite piece was also for *Monsters Attack!* It was an adaptation of Edgar Allen Poe's "The Cask Of Amontillado." Much to my surprise in reading the original story I found that it wasn't set in Poe's own time, but during the Italian renaissance, so I did my layouts and costumes accordingly. Wally Brogan, who is a very nice guy, and an artist that actually would come around the *Cracked* offices frequently, as he lived on Staten Island, got the gig. When the art came back, it bore no relation at all to my layouts. It was back to early 19$^{th}$-century America, all top hats and high collars, and my script needed to be re-written to fit the new panel arrangement. I was puzzled. It was as though my old buddy Wally hadn't even glanced at my script. It was quite some time later that Cliff Mott, I believe, ran across a version of the tale that had been done in *Creepy* or *Eerie* in the '70s. Wally had copied it frame by frame! Nothing against Wally, perhaps he preferred working from that version, but I was quite disappointed, as I had felt that I'd done a scholarly job on my adaptation.

"Once Mort and I took Wally out for sake. I don't think he'd ever heard of it. Anyway, he didn't think too much of hot wine in a tiny cup, and made faces one would imagine a cat would make licking soap.

"I guess I feel that my second *Batman* parody was a little weak, but I've only myself to blame for that, although the artist did miss the gag when I put

The Artist Formerly Known As Prince, then known as Prince, in a 'Hefti' bag in the final panel. The artist corrected the spelling to 'Hefty'!"

Gray Morrow made a brief, but lengthier return to *Cracked* starting in 1987. As mentioned before, he is remembered for his horror artwork for Warren before taking his own life in 2001.

Jerry De Fuccio, Don Martin and Lou Silverstone all defected from *Mad* during this period after Editor Al Feldstein retired in 1985, but more on them later.

Dick Ayers has been drawing comic books since 1948. He's best known for his work on *Sgt. Fury and his Howling Commandos.* He made occasional appearances in *Cracked* from 1987 to the end.

Henry Boltinoff did literally dozens of short comedy features in various DC Comics. He did single-page gags for *Cracked* beginning in 1988. He died in 2001.

Pete Fitzgerald was the last major new hire during the Mort Todd era and he relates the story of how he got started at *Cracked*: "Shortly after graduating from the Kubert, I attended one of Fred Greenberg's comic conventions in NYC, at the Roosevelt Hotel—this was sometime in June 1989, I think—with my portfolio and Xeroxed samples of my black-and-white work in tow. Michael Delle-Femine (a.k.a. Mort Todd) and Cliff Mott had a *Cracked* table there, promoting both *Cracked* and their then-upcoming spin-off mag, *Monsters Attack!* I remember the debut issue of *Monsters Attack!* wasn't completed yet, but they were giving out copies of John Severin's color cover as a flyer to promote it.

"They liked my samples, especially a pun-filled joke map of a mythical continent done as a school assignment. They put copies of my samples on file, and a few months later, I got a call from them, asking if I'd like to do a try-out assignment, which was 'Skateboards of the World.' I added lots of peripheral gags to the main gags in the script, emulating two of my cartooning heroes, Bill Elder and Wally Wood. The results pleased them (and got a fan letter that saw print a issue or two later), so I was in!

"I worked through three regimes. The first was headed by Mike Delle-Femine (a.k.a. Mort Todd) and Cliff Mott, plus former *Mad*-man Jerry De Fuccio. I arrived during the tail-end of Delle-Femine's editorial reign, which I believe lasted about four or five years, in fall 1989. Great times. I was fresh out of school, and full of energy and enthusiasm. Mike seemed to both revere *Cracked*'s history—like putting out a special issue of Jack Davis' work at the mag, and reprinting great stuff from Wolverton in the regular pages—and cultivating newer talent, such as Dan Clowes, Bill Wray, Peter Bagge, Gary Fields, Wally Brogan, Rurik Tyler. I'm sure a young whelp like me would've had a much tougher time getting my foot in the door without Mike and Cliff running things. Plus, they hired the great Don Martin away from *Mad*! They also made sure *Cracked* had a table at comic conventions, at least the ones held in NYC. They turned me onto some cool movies, too, like John Woo's pre-Hollywood action films (*The Killer*, *Hard-Boiled*, *A Better Tomorrow*, etc.) and movies directed by Jack Webb (*Dragnet* [1954], *The D.I.*).

"*Cracked* was my first choice. Shortly before graduating from Kubert School, Joe Kubert arranged a portfolio review at the *Mad* offices for myself and another third-year student. It was cool, taking place at the old *Mad* offices (before they moved to DC), but they let it be known that there were no openings at that time, and they were doing the critique as a favor to Joe.

"At the time, some of my friends, who knew about the business, said *Cracked* was a better deal anyway, despite its somewhat-lower profile and cheaper rates. This was mainly because you'd get your original artwork back, and would receive a small licensing fee in addition to the page rate; whereas you signed everything away if you worked for *Mad*. Also, I think you had to 'pay your dues' elsewhere before *Mad* would consider hiring you, unless you were some kind of cartooning genius right out of the gate, which I certainly wasn't.

"I've always freelanced, so it's just me at my drawing table at home, transmitting the layouts by fax or e-mail, and either shipping or e-mailing the finished artwork. I've never had to work in an office environment, so I can't compare different companies in that way. *Cracked* was perhaps a little freer, in letting me add content beyond the writer's script—in fact, they often encouraged that—although I've been fortunate to have worked for people who have mainly let me be free to do my own thing.

"I don't have a single favorite piece, but some I think are a cut above include: * 'Skateboards of the World,' Issue #253, May 1990—a sentimental favorite; my first job, brimming with enthusiasm, even if some of the ink wash is too heavy and dark. * 'Nuked Kids on the Block / New Kids on the Chopping Block' (color cover and inside poster for *Cracked Blockbuster* #4, Summer 1990)—Delle-Femine gave me my first *Cracked* cover assignment (and my first color job) to mock the then-popular teenybopper group. I did two rough concepts, he liked them both so much he had me do both, making one of them the cover, and both as pull-out posters! A major ego-boost, and a nice payday as well! * 'Who's the Most Important Person of the 20th Century?'—Silliness I originally did for a fun cartoon APA. I still belong to, *Cartoon Loonacy*, that Cliff Mott liked and convinced *Cracked* to buy when they needed a filler page. * 'Rush Hour on Venus' * 'Married Couples in Space' * 'The X-Files Paranoia Quiz' * 'The Cracked Student Profile' * 'TV Game Shows Through History' * 'New Muppets' * 'Modern-Day Creatures We Could Do Without' Among the Worst: * 'The Last Issues of Popular Comic Books'—too much of it was rushed. * 'Drink Coasters from Quark's Bar'—some of the actual drawing is okay, but the finishes were way too rushed, and the slap-dash wash tone I put over the whole background looks terrible."

Besides totally revitalizing and revamping the magazine, Mort Todd canceled a number of long-running annuals that had outlived their usefulness or became misnumbered and replaced them with new ones that ran through the end of Lou Silverstone's run. Gone were *Giant Cracked*, *Biggest Greatest Cracked*, *King-Sized Cracked*, *Super Cracked* and *Extra Special Cracked*. New were *Cracked Blockbuster*, *Cracked Digest*, *Cracked Party Pack*, *Cracked Spaced Out*, *Cracked Summer Special* and *Cracked Super*. Many of the inserts included into these newer specials were also of higher quality, many in full-color on glossy paper stock. Even a special issue of *Cracked* was done entirely in 3-D!

Todd comments on the revamp of *Super Cracked* to *Cracked Super*: "I relaunched it after I did an issue with the old numbering. I started doing themes for the reprint books (inspired by E. Nelson Bridwell's stewardship of the DC *100 Page Spectaculars*) and said to no one in particular, 'This is going to be all superhero humor now!' I'm pretty sure there wasn't a #27 in our file copies. I looked at that website with all the covers and #26 was a Sproul issue and #28 would have been a Laikin issue. I must've worked on that one. I think the cover said 'Stickers' inside and they weren't sticky and the 'iron-ons' were printed on regular paper. I'm blamin' Laikin for the misnumbering on that one."

The ongoing *Cracked Collectors' Edition* remained untouched except that it became a giant-sized publication instead of the standard 52 pages it had been since its inception. It also begat the *Cracked Monster Party*, as the various monster-themed *Collectors' Editions* had done quite well over the years.

"I came up with the title *Cracked Monster Party*. You know the movie *Mad Monster Party* by Kurtzman and Davis? That's why I called it *Cracked Monster Party*… 'for those who know how to look' as Dr. Wertham said. After seeing the earlier reprint books I was determined to give the issues a singular theme, instead of just conglomerating any junk together, and before long I noticed Mad doing it more. I've always been a monster fan and did some *Collectors' Editions* called *Monster Party* and they really sold like a mutha. The publisher was numbers savvy and said, 'Why don't we start a *Monster Party* magazine?' I was totally in to it and we began some other neat ideas like the digests. Them reprints really brought in a lot of easy money for the publishers. I tried to make extra value for the readers by sticking cool shit in them.

"We had 30 years of film of some incredible art to reprint, a veritable *Who's Who* of comic creators. Back then, artwork was photographed for printing so you can imagine there was a bit of it. Larry Levine created a job for his deadbeat son by making him in charge of the film. Because we were printing through the Globe, we changed printers from Canada to an American company. We actually had censorship problems when it was printed in Canada because we called them a third-world nation and *Monster Attacks!* almost ran afoul of their anti-crime & horror comics laws still on the books. We find out the film got delivered to this plant in Nebraska and it was in no order whatsoever. If we needed to reprint books, which we did a wicked lot, it would be impossible to figure out. So, Cliff, associate editor Roger D. Crosby and I flew out to Nebraska and had to hand-sort 30 years of film. It was only through my knowledge of every issue of the magazine and previous reprints—and I don't have that knowledge now—that we could basically tell where every page was from originally. Levine's son just screwed up our inventory and there was water damage and stuff. I also found some film from '60s issues of *CAR-Toons* mixed in with it. Later they relocated it all down to Globe in Florida where it was part of a diabolical, post 9/11 attack and it got anthraxed and then destroyed.

"Sproul had an interesting way for cataloging reprints. They had this card catalogue that was done, sorted by genre in semi-chronological order. It listed the contents of every issue and where reprinted. When we didn't have the original film (especially of the early issues), it was helpful, because then I could find it was in, say, *Collectors' Editions* #13, and we could use the film from that issue. In some instances, like when we were reprinting Cracked #1, we didn't have all the film, so we actually made large Xeroxed pages and Cliff mostly hand cleaned them."

*Cracked Monster Party* begat *Monsters Attack!*, a *Creepy*-inspired title that Todd had quietly slipped into the mix. He explains: "Since the *Monster Party* magazine did so well, I decided that I really wanted to do a 'serious' monster magazine. Here I am working with Severin and Colan and Ditko and I'm like, 'We can get all the best horror artists, these EC, Atlas and Warren artists. Let's do a kick ass magazine.' The publisher considered it but kept putting it off and putting it off, so behind his back, I ordered a UPC, reserved printing time, put a book together, and actually released it without him knowing about it until it came out! I look back and I have no idea how I got away with it. So, we had this magazine on the newsstands and he just had a shit fit. Then he saw the numbers and we sold a quarter of a million of them."

The title ran a further four issues, the last not produced by Todd.

Adds Todd, "I had commissioned most of the stories for #5 and Silverstone and De Fuccio edited the stories to no good advantage by my thought. Their heart wasn't in it and they didn't have an unhealthy attraction to monsters as I did. They let it die but since it was all creator-owned, I still have the rights to my work. I started my own publishing company, but at that time, no way could I have gotten a newsstand deal.

"The newsstand back then was run like the mob. You've got to put up a million to get the distribution and clearance and the same for printing costs. My company, AAA, didn't last too long and it was direct sales only so sales were bleah (except for a Bill Ward book plugged in *Playboy*). I still have the *Monsters Attack!* stuff and have been pushing to do like a *Tales From the Crypt* or *Creepshow* anthology movie or something like that.

"I have agents still pursuing some production companies. That's one of the reasons I put out my Weird Menace comic. In that, I reprinted a Gray Morrow story that I wrote and a Severin story I penciled, and other stories that I wrote and drew."

As far as sales figures during the Mort Todd era are concerned, Todd confirms, "There was the *Batman* issue for the first *Batman* movie with a cool Rurik Tyler cover that had the 'smiley face' spotlight on the 'Dark Knught.' (#248). There's an amusing story behind that issue, too. When *Batman* was in production, I was on the closed set in England. My girlfriend at the time, Charlotte Skene-Catling, was the granddaughter of DC Comics founder Major Malcolm Wheeler-Nicholson (the family had no connection with DC since the '30s), and had a friend who was the associate art director to A.D. Anton Furst on the film. Through her, I got to sneak onto the film lot at Pinewood. I took all kinds of pre-production shots and saw all kinds of top secret bat-shit. Here was DC owning *Mad*, and we beat them to the newsstands by six months! Our issue came out when the movie came out. We didn't do the actual parody that month, but we did do an all-*Batman* issue. (The parody actually appeared in the next issue, #249.) I had taken pictures of the Batmobile model and other designs. I also continued my one-sided rivalry with *Mad* on that issue, too. Back in the '60s, their classic Silverstone/Drucker parody of *Batman* was called 'Batsman' and so in the '80s, Hall and Altergott did an Adam West *Batman* parody that we called 'Battyman.' Then *Mad* came out and called their '80s movie parody 'Battyman,' so I called our official movie parody 'Batsman.' I would name-check every parody in *Mad* and in *Cracked* to make sure that we didn't use the same goofy title. When I saw that they stole the *Cracked* name from '67, I said, 'Screw it!'"

"We had other traitorous *Mad* creators who worked with us under cover, and now THEY were regularly getting the hate mail saying, '*Cracked* came out with this movie two months ago. You're ripping them off!' I heard the gang of usual editorialits got all upset. An advantage with us, was that *Mad* had seven editors, and during editorial meeting they would stomp the life out of any script, where everyone would want to put their own two cents. Plus, they would wait for numbers. 'Let's see how the box office or the TV ratings are before we do a parody,' and they had a longer lead-time than we did. They probably had a four-month lead-time on theirs and I cut ours down to a little more than a month .

"I worked it out with the printers. Realistically, when you have a year or a couple years of printing booked on a schedule, and the presses are reserved for you, you know your deadlines and I cut it as close as possible, in order to be semi-topical, so that a month after we closed the book, it's on the stands."

Todd comments as to why he finally left *Cracked*: "Towards the end they were just really unreceptive to doing licensing deals for merchandise that

I had arranged. That was the next step for the magazine, and I was always interested in expanding the brand. For years I was the only editor, and also did tons of free publicity and promotion for them. I had the able Clifford P. Mott as my art director, and that was it. We were putting out, like, 40 books a year, and hundreds, maybe thousands of pages per year. A couple times I had short-term assistant editors but always part-time. Around 1988 or '89, I asked for a raise and a full-time assistant. And I really wanted the merchandise stuff to happen and get maybe a percentage of the books I created or something. *Monsters Attack!* was selling a quarter of a million, (and we were about to launch a second sci-fi/fantasy magazine that had gone as far as a Gray Morrow cover painting) and some of the best issues of *Cracked* were doing like 600,000, and that *Batman* issue, sold some 660,000 copies.

"I used to go into my publisher's office at night (worked a lot of nights. It wasn't always parties on the *Playboy* yacht, right, Cliff?) and look at the 'real' figures. For the most part, he would only show me percentages of sales, not how many sold issues the percentage represented. He would have all the covers of past issues on the wall the percentage tagged on them. Based on that he would say, 'Hmmm, we need more covers with red on them.' He also worked on the 'thumb rule.' If he could place his thumb on the page and it didn't cover some part of the art he thought he was being shortchanged. Quantity over quality!

"I hired Lou Silverstone and Jerry De Fuccio and also anointed them as my successors. Lou is the perfect gentleman of comics and beyond his seminal *Mad* work, he also did wild TV stuff and *T.H.U.N.D.E.R. Agents* for Tower. It was a great experience collaborating with him. And Jerry was from the first generation of comic fans, knew every cartoonist living and dead and probably had a piece of artwork by each of them. He was a wealth of information and a more influential figure in comics than people are aware.

"Why I basically left is that I had done that horror magazine and it sold like hell. After a false start, it came back from the grave, and was doing great. And, before *MadTV*, I also talked to a production company about doing a *Cracked* TV show. We had a script and I had all kinds of merchandising lined up, like toys, video games, T-Shirts. And for some reason they were dragging their heels on it.

"There was some merch. Did you get the Sylvester plush doll advertised in the mag? Did you get one of the *Cracked* painters cap? Or the square egg maker? That last one resulted through Larry and Ken's mail-order thing. 'We just bought 10,000 square egg makers. Let's give them away through *Cracked*.' We still had *Cracked* flying discs from Sproul era and were called such because they couldn't use the word 'Frisbee®'. We manufactured some of our own product later, We did a *Cracked* 30th Anniversary T-Shirt that had all the characters on it by Severin."

Mort Todd recollects one final tale which led to an encounter with the infamous William M. Gaines in the *Mad* offices: "I had little respect for my contemporary *Mad* editors. I heard that *60 Minutes* was going to do a puff piece on *Mad*, so I found out who the producer was, and told him, 'Ok, you're going to do this *Mad* thing. Do you want the real story?' This is *60 Minutes.* They could have done an startling exposé about how everyone's favorite humor magazine was a slave pit for the artists. *60 Minutes* didn't want to hear it. When I finally saw the show, Morley Safer was glowing over Ficarra at his drum set, 'Oh, we made a joke! Here's the proof: badump-dump.' You know, I just went, 'Yeccchhh!'

John Ficarra is the editor of *Mad*, who did write for *Cracked*, briefly in the late '70s, Todd reveals, "Yeah, but, no, Ficarra will probably deny it to his death. Many people who were at *Mad*, worked for *Cracked*. At the time it reminded me of Soviet Russia, having a Politboro of editors, who step on every freakin' gag and I was in pain. I took it very seriously back then! The two guys I did like were Charlie Kadau and Joe Riaola. They're kind of funny, but Nick Meglin, Ficarra, ohhhhh. I met them once when I was still editor and got the cold shoulder. It was at some art opening at the School of Visual Arts and someone introduced us.

"For a few years, before I ever imagined being at *Cracked*, I kept bumping into Gaines in place like the South Street Seaport Mall or the circus! Gaines may have used bad voodoo against his competitors but *Cracked* must have had bigger juju! Yeah, he hated us. Bill Gaines figured that every issue we sold was a buck-forty-nine out of his very pocket. Unike at Marvel and DC, artists and writers would lunch and hang out with people from both publishers, but not with *Mad* and *Cracked*.

"There was one time at a con when writer Charles E. Hall, who had been in a lot of bands, had some *Cracked* t-shirts and merchandise and said, 'You know, I want to go over to the *Mad* table and see if they'll trade t-shirts or something, because bands do that all of the time.' So, Cliff and me are going, 'Dude, it ain't gonna happen,' and sure enough, they just sneered at him. Back then at every convention Cliff and I usually hung out with a pile of cartoonists and drank for hours (as opposed to our usual work day). So, we were at this bar, with Gray Morrow most likely, and the Con closed and Charles had the subversive idea of sneaking into the Con and swipe their six-foot *Mad* logo made out of Styrofoam. I can have a clear mental picture of his skinny ass booking up the escalator with it. We ended up putting it in our office and people coming into our office would see this big *Mad* logo. I think I heard from Lou that they didn't necessarily suspect that we swiped it, but they were really upset because Bill Gaines' son Chris spent so many hours carving and coloring it."

Charles E. Hall takes up the story: "Sometime around then I got my first taste of how little humor there could be in the humor comics business.

I attended my first comic convention at the Hotel Pennsylvania across from Madison Square Garden. *Cracked* had a table, and *Mad* had a table. I thought that maybe the *Mad* folks would like to swap a little merchandise with their compatriots at *Cracked*. I think I had my eye on an Alfred E. Neuman coffee mug. Mort and Cliff both warned me that *Mad* wouldn't be interested, but I didn't believe them. How could *Mad* take themselves, and the whole humor comic racket, so seriously? How could they harbor a grudge for decades, directed now at people who weren't even born when *Cracked* started ripping off *Mad*? It's not like anyone ever bought a copy of *Cracked instead* of *Mad*. So, I disregarded my pals and chugged over to the *Mad* table with my offer. Plus, I was curious, and wanted to find out for myself what the deal was. Also, I didn't really care in the slightest what anyone thought of me, and certainly wasn't thinking ahead to perhaps ever wanting to work for *Mad*. Not if they were going to be jerks, anyways.

"Chris Gaines was at the table, and he would scarcely even look at me. His verbal response was monosyllabic, and his whole demeanor was that of a bound man being tormented by a buzzing insect. I was amused and insulted in equal proportions.

"Now, behind the *Mad* table was a *Mad* sign that carried the *Mad* logo in red. It was on white poster board, around four feet-by-two feet. Mort had learned that Chris Gaines had colored in the letters by hand with magic marker. As the convention was winding down for the night, I made my way to the deserted *Mad* table, took the sign under my arm, rode down the escalator and walked out the front door with it. No one paid the slightest attention to me. I later presented it to Mort as a trophy, and it sat behind his desk at the *Cracked* office for the rest of his time there. Next day at the convention we heard that Chris Gaines was really bummed out, especially as it had evidently taken him a long time to color the sign in. Supposedly, he was overhead saying, 'I *know* it's those guys at *Cracked*!' Well, I was only freelance, so I'm not sure that's completely fair. I was never compensated directly for my efforts. Still, we were all sort of offended by his attitude: after all, no witnesses had come forward!"

Mort Todd continues, "At another convention we went to, Chris Gaines was running the *Mad* table. So me and Cliff saunter up, look around their wares and we say, 'Gosh, you've got a lot of cool stuff.' I was a big skateboarder then, and they had a really lame Alfred E. Neuman skateboard for $35 so I bought it as a company expense. I said, 'You know when I was a kid I'd heard that *Mad* had tours of the office,' and he was like, 'Yeah, yeah, we sure do.' I said, 'Awesome,' so he gave me his business card saying, 'Give me a call sometime, we'll set up a tour.'

"We were always getting accused of ripping off *Mad* and my publisher wanted us to make *Cracked* business cards, so I handed Chris Gaines' business card to Cliff, 'Here, copy this for our business card.' It was black and red ink with the *Mad* logo and Alfred's head, so I was like, 'Put Sylvester's head there. Put the logo there. Put our names there.' We're ripping them off, so why not rip off their business card?

"A week or two later—this is like right after Don Martin came over—a couple weeks later we call up Chris Gaines and set up a tour of *Mad*. We go over there, I bring my *Mad* skateboard and we're all pretty young looking. It was Cliff and I and Ian Wheeler-Nicholson, another one of the Major's grandkids. In the 1930s Major Wheeler-Nicholson had worked with Bill Gaines' dad in comics publishing. They graciously give us the tour and show us all kinds of original art they're hanging on to. We're asking questions about EC and *Mad*, so they knew we were very knowledgeable about their legacy. They show us a whole bunch of Don Martin's pages and I asked, 'Gee! Why did Don Martin leave the magazine?' And they said, 'Well, 'cause his wife's a bitch!' And we said, 'Gosh, it wasn't because of copyright? It's not because of his original art?' We get the whole $5 tour and then Chris takes us to Bill Gaines' office.

"So we're in his tiny office and he's not there, but then we hear these thundering footsteps. It was almost like Godzilla coming down the hall. 'Cause we were going on about EC, Chris Gaines is all, 'Bill, we've got some old EC fans here.' Gaines the Elder stops and looks at us. Bill and I have had encounters before, like at a the memorial service for E. Nelson Bridwell, but I was in the guise of mild mannered Michael Delle Femine, with normal glasses, suit and tie. Not the post-punk skateboarder Mort Todd. He walks in, blocking the one exit and goes, 'Those aren't old EC fans!' Me and Cliff look at each other, we're almost breaking into a sweat and there's no way to get out of here and we're all, 'Fuck! He's gonna kill us!' and then he continues, 'Those are young EC fans!' Phew! I get him to autograph my *Mad* skateboard and we took photos and I thought it was a little too skeezy to print the photo in *Cracked*, so I sent it to *Thrasher* magazine—a skateboard magazine—and they printed it in full color. 'Why is the *Mad* man signing the *Cracked* man's deck?' So, of course, I heard from Lou that Gaines just went ape shit. He hit the roof! He was so pissed and said, 'That guy's got brass balls!!' It was all fun and games until *Thrasher* hit the fan. I also got another photo of me standing in front of the *Up the Academy* statue. That was *Mad*'s attempt to rip *National Lampoon's Animal House* and turned out so crummy that Gaines had to buy it back from the movie studio. I thought it was pretty funny that they had the statue in the waiting room.

"In the end I split *Cracked* because they weren't going to hire an assistant and weren't going in the direction that I interested in outside the magazine. All right, time to pack it up."

**To be continued in Part II**

The first thing Mort Todd did after becoming editor was to scour bound volumes of *Cracked* just like these and educate himself on all the previously published material. It is here where he found out about certain articles that were never to be reprinted for legal reasons, but he reprinted them anyway.

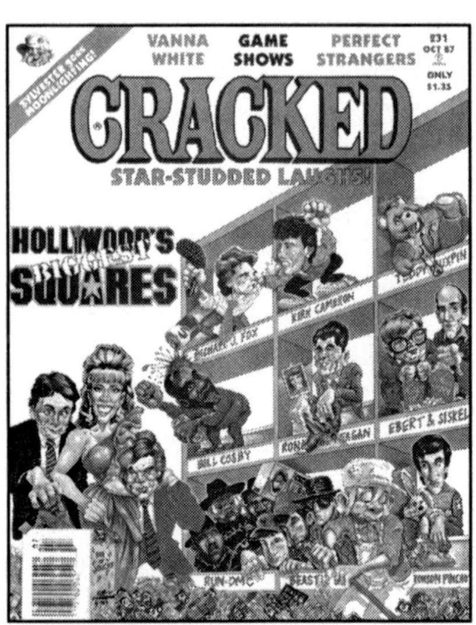


Although he had many covers on the various *Cracked* specials and annuals, this was the only cover of regular *Cracked* drawn by Bob Fingerman, #231, October 1987.

This was the notorious "ZZ Slop vs. the Space Pirates" article from *Cracked* #223, October 1986, which got Bob Fingerman fired for supposedly having satanic messages.

The first *Robot Wars* from *Cracked* #216, November 1985, art and script by Mort Todd, loosely based on *Mad's Spy vs. Spy*.

The first Steve Ditko artwork for *Cracked* was in #218, March 1986, where he took over the art chores from Mort Todd for *Robot Wars.*

The first Dan Clowes artwork for *Cracked* from #216, November 1985.

The first *Uggly Family* story was snuck in the back pages of *Extra Special Cracked* #9, Winter 1985.

Like *The Uggly Family*, *Canine the Barkbarian* first appeared in an annual. This is from *Super Cracked* #32, Fall 1986, art by Gary Fields.

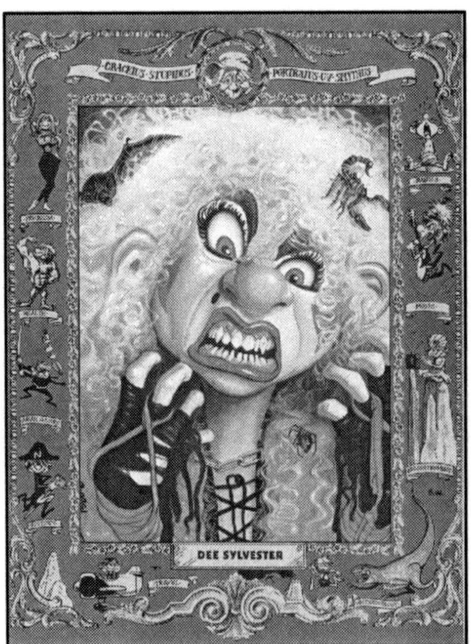


Before bailing out to *Mad*, Bill Wray contributed the Sylvester Celebrity Poster on the back cover of every issue. Here is the first one from #221, August 1986.

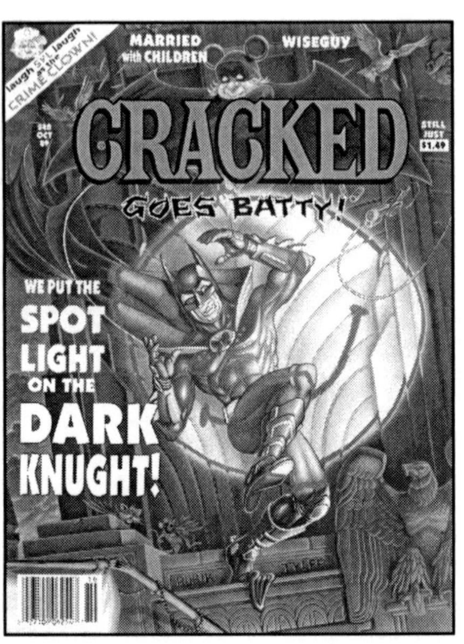


The best-selling *Cracked* issue from the post-Sproul issue was #248, October 1989.

*Cracked 3-D Classics* was published by Ray Zone and is actually *The 3-D Zone* #19, 1989, in that series. The issue features older *Cracked* articles now presented in 3-D, and features this new cover by Bill Wray.

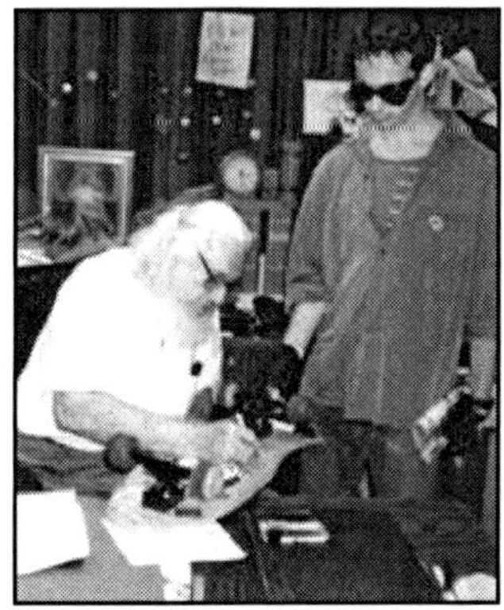

When titans clash? Anyway, here is the photo of Mort Todd getting his Alfred E. Neuman skateboard signed by William M. Gaines at the *Mad* offices. Gaines was not pleased when this photo appeared in *Thrasher* magazine soon after. Image courtesy of Mort Todd.

John Severin draws Mort Todd in "*Cracked* 30th Anniversary Party!" from *Cracked* #238, September 1988.

Mike Ricigliano started the *One-Shots* feature that eventually was assisted by Roger Brown. Here is the first one from *Cracked* #227, April 1987.

Many *Cracked Collectors' Editions* featured all-new material as #69, December 1986, pictured here did.

John Severin did the first Nanny Dickering interview in *Cracked* #99, March 1972, a role more suited for Bill Ward.

Former *Playboy* centerfold Bebe Buell starred in the Nanny Dickering fumetti, which also featured her daughter, a nine-year-old Liv Tyler, in her first public appearance from *Cracked Collectors' Edition* #69, December 1986.

The advertised but never filmed *Cracked* TV Show from the back of *Cracked Digest* #3, April 1987.

*Cracked Collectors' Edition* #82 (The Comedy of Jack Davis), April 1990, reprinted every article drawn by Jack Davis including Jack Davis' first cover for *Cracked* #12, January 1960, pictured here. Mort Todd really wanted to get Davis to return to *Cracked*, but Davis politely declined.

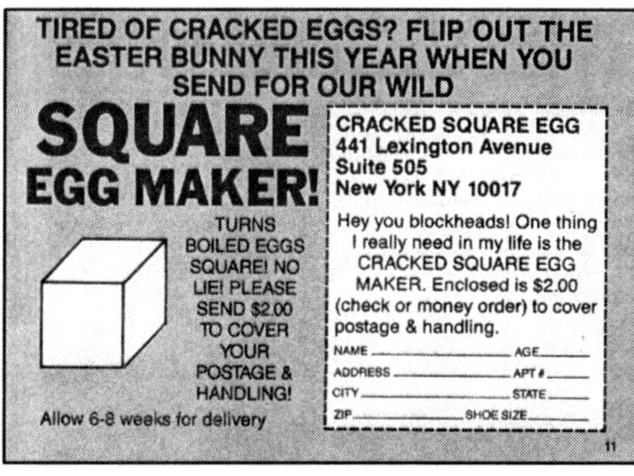


One of the strangest pieces of *Cracked* merchandise was Larry and Ken's Square Egg Maker as featured in *Cracked* #220, July 1986.

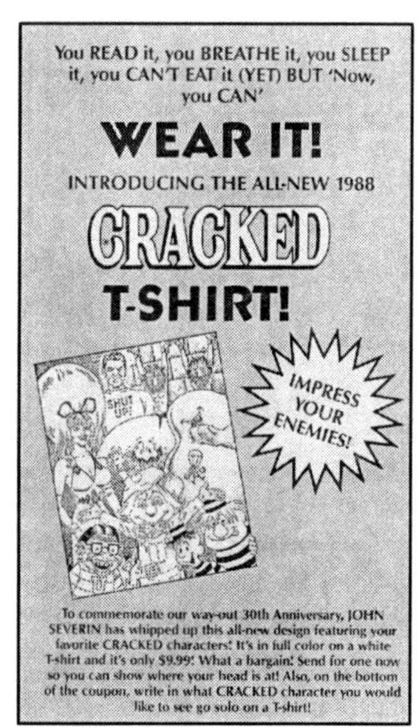


Finally, after 20 years a new *Cracked* T-Shirt was offered for sale in *Cracked* #233, January 1988, art by John Severin.

The Sylvester P. Smythe Plush Doll, now hard to find as he first appeared in *Cracked* #232, November 1987.

A black T-Shirt and a Don Martin T-Shirt soon appeared.

A little cheesecake to promote the new Cracked merchandise never hurt anyone.

More cheesecake.

Still more cheesecake.

Ok, knock it off with the cheesecake! What is this, *Wildcat*?

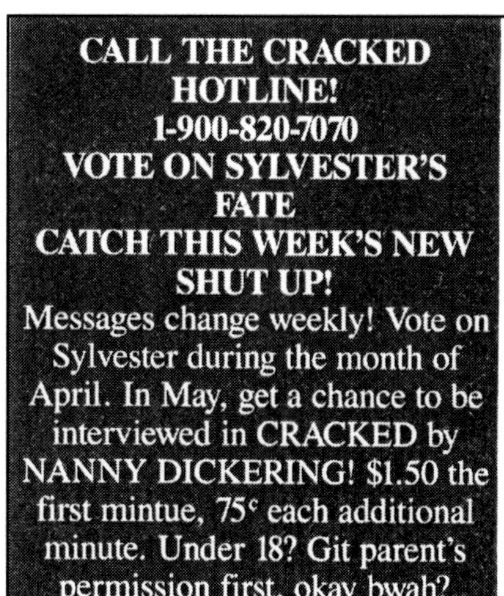


Yes, there was a short-lived *Cracked* hotline with various jokes told, as mentioned in *Cracked* #254, July 1990. Ask your parents permission if you can call…

*Cracked* as it appeared on *The David Letterman Show* in *Cracked* #234, March 1988.

**JASON HERVEY, star of ABC-TV's WONDER YEARS and many movies, dropped us this pic of himself enjoying our BLUNDER YEARS parody in CRACKED 239! Thanks, Jason and continued success with your hit TV show and career!**

*The Wonder Years'* Jason Hervey reads his favorite magazine in *Cracked* #243, March 1989.

Pee-Wee Herman discusses the important issues of the day with Joan Rivers on *The Late Show* and in *Cracked* #232, November 1987.

**From THE Wiseguy to a bunch of wiseguys: Ken Wahl got a big kick over the parody we did of his show, WISEGUY. His manager said he was reading it on the street and rolling on the ground (in laughter, we hope)!**

*Wiseguy's* Ken Wahl shows off his Walter Brogan artwork in *Cracked* #255, August 1990.

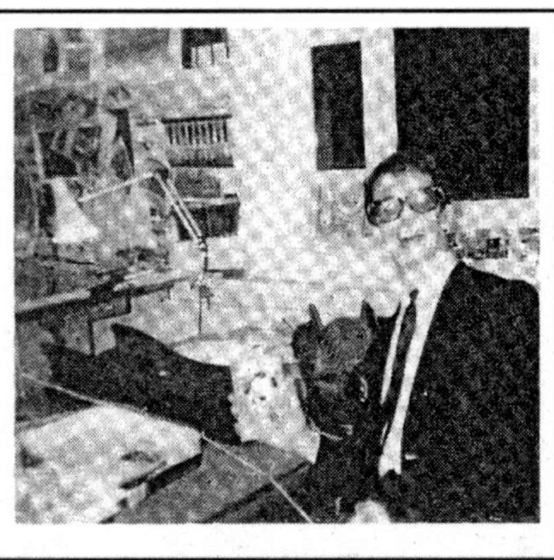

Mort Todd flew to the *Batman* set in England and scooped *Mad* in the process in *Cracked* #247, September 1989.

And #248, October 1989.

Mort Todd with Archie and Betty in *Cracked* #247, September 1989.

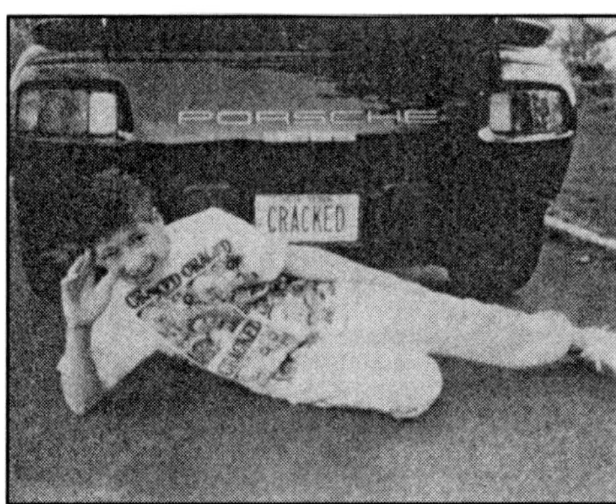


Publisher Ken Baratto got his son, Mark to pose in *Cracked* #239, October 1988.

**Here's a photo of CRACKED writter/artist JEREMY BANX modeling the CRACKED T-Shirt in front of the CRACKED Building! Actually, Jeremy is pictured here in Knossos, Greece at the palace of King Minos (owner of that way-out minotaur). Who says we ain't a educational magazine?**

Artist Jeremy Banx appeared in *Cracked* #244, May 1989.

As did Bebe Buell.

# CRACKED PARTY PIX!

## A CRACKED LENS EXCLUSIVE!

All captions made up by Mort Todd

Guess what? After 30 years of continual publication, CRACKED is more popular than ever!... And 1989'll be even bigger! We'll produce over 1500 pages to amuse you...more than any humor magazine anywhere! 30 years is a long time for anything, let alone a crummy humor magazine. The event was covered by TV, newspapers and magazines...Don Martin's coming to CRACKED even made MTV! To celebrate CRACKED's third decade, contributors came from all over the world to convene in New York City for the CRACKED PARTY at the trendy TUNNEL night club! Guests included people from TV, radio, publishing and rock with music provided by NANNY [illegible]

John Severin, you rascal! I haven't seen you in over 20 years!

Don Orehek, you bum! You still owe me $1.45 I lent you in 1963!

A HISTORIC MEETING: Two CRACKED veterans (both habitual since issue #1, 1958) meet after some 20-odd (very odd) years! Orehek, the SHUT UP KING, lives in New York and Severin in Colorado.

Bebe Buell in action as the rocking and rolling NANNY DICKERING

ANOTHER HISTORIC MEETING: John Severin meets his idol, Don Martin (who is fairly new contributor from Florida).

Don Martin...Now I've heard that name!...Did you used to work with Jerry Lewis?

...An' then Ron Reagan himself goes over the edge and comandeers the fantastic Ron Rover, initiating a destructive rampage that...

INTERESTING! (yawn)

Hurry up and get to the finish, Altergott!

THE YOUNG TURKS: RON ROVER (and HURRY UP) artist Rick Altergott amazes CRACKED artistes Peter Bagge (left) and Dan Clowes (middle) with a potential plot.

23

The *Cracked* 30th Anniversary Party was documented in *Cracked* #241, December 1988.

MORE MISH-MASH:
Sober and clean-cut CRACKED art director Cliff Mott discusses a cover sketch with artist Walter Brogan and writer Dan Knotts.
Now Wally (hic), thish is the first sketch I've seen by you that makes sense!
What's he talking about? That's my subway map!
ON THE RUN:
Peter Bagge (also writer & artist for the NEAT STUFF magazines and book), Dan Clowes ("Stosh Gillespie" of the UGGLY FAMILY and LLOYD LLEWELLYN magazine creator) and CRACKED editor-in-chief Michael Delle-Femine share a laugh as they limo to that Manhattan night club The TUNNEL!
Did ya see the look on Wally Brogan's face when we stuck him with the bill?
Hyuck! Hyuck!
Haw! Haw! That was rich!
Randy! You say you've written the CRACKED LENS for over 10 years and never been in it?
...Well, surprise! You're on the CANDID CRACKED LENS, now!
The much-respected CRACKED humorist and chief ARCHIE Comics writer George Gladir (center), flanked by writer Randy Epley and editor Delle-Femine.
HUDD & DINI co-conspirator and creator Vic Martin plots!
Heh heh! The TUNNEL! What a nice place for Hudd & Dini to... tunnel to!
John, in a hip place like this, ya gotta take your tie off and let your hair down!
Artists Bill Wray and John Severin discuss techniques. Have you seen Bill's work on DC's THE CULT or John's work on Marvel's SEMPER FI? Well, do it!
Mike, as talented as you and your son are, I don't think he's ready to ink my art, yet!
REAL-LIFE SABOTEUR: The Son of Ricigliano strikes as Severin confers with writer Joe Catalano (left) and SPY & SABOTEUR creator Mike Ricigliano!
Wicked wild party, eh, Cliff?
Yeah, but Sylvester couldn't make it... That means I'll have to clean up this place tonight!
THE END?:
Bemused art director Mott talks with GARGOYLE guitarist and CRACKED contributor Charles E. Hall. Charles wrote the ROCK 'n' ROLL SHUT UPS in this issue!

# THE CRACKED MAGAZiNE INDEX PART I

(Please note that reprints commonly were featured in regular issues of the magazine. Every attempt has been made to identify when an article has been reprinted and what issue was the original source. Also, art and writing credits are identified when known with the art credit first, followed by the writing credit. Finally, it has been confirmed through a number of sources that *Pow!* #3 and *Super Cracked* #27 do not exist. *Pow!*, *Zany*, *For Monsters Only* and *Don Martin's Droll Book* are included in this index due to the majority of the material either being reprinted in or reprinted from *Cracked*. The reprint information will only list the magazine title if it is anything other than *Cracked*.)

**1, March 1958 (44 pages) (25c) (©1957 Major Magazines. on sale date: January 3, 1958)**

Cover – Cracked World – Bill Everett (1st appearance of Sylvester P. Smythe and the Sexy Lady with cigarette named Veronica.)
Page 2 – Wincin Cigarette ad – Paul Reinman
Page 3 – Contents
Page 4 – Editor's Press Interview – Russ Heath (1st appearance of Der Editor)
Page 6 – Letters From the Editor
Page 7 – Gunsmokes – Russ Heath (1st TV parody)
Page 10 – How to Build a Hot Hot Rod
Page 12 – Brave Guy – Paul Reinman
Page 13 – Ad Slogans
Page 14 – The $64,000,000 Cracked-Pot Question – John Severin (1st Severin art)
Page 16 – Little Mercurochrome
Page 17 – Max Wallis Interviews Jayne Womansfield – Russ Heath (1st *Cracked* Interview)
Page 20 – Chef of the Month – John Severin

Page 22 – News Flash From Behind the Iron Curtain
Page 24 – Science Fiction – Don Orehek, Bob Campbell, J. Kiernan
Page 25 – How I'll Beat the Champ – John Severin
Page 28 – Cracked Brings You Greetings – Bill Everett
Page 30 – Your Christmas Shopping Guide – John Severin
Page 31 – Marjorie Morninglory
Page 33 – Shakespeare
Page 36 – Sixteen and a Half Tons of Friendship – Paul Reinman
Page 38 – Famous Proverbs
Page 40 – So You're Going to College?
Page 42 – Why Doesn't This Ever Happen? – Bill Ward
Page 43 – Subscription Ad – John Severin
Back Cover – Voto ad – Paul Reinman

**2, May 1958 (44 pages) (25c)**
Cover – Big Mouth – John Severin (1st cover by Severin)
Page 2 – Grand Old Daddy ad – Paul Reinman
Page 3 – Contents
Page 4 – The Breaking Point – Bill McCartney (Bill Ward)
Page 5 – Behind the Hand!
Page 6 – Advice to the Lovesick / Westinghut ad
Page 7 – Fling a Wing-Ding – Russ Heath
Page 10 – Build This Beautiful Yacht – Bill Everett
Page 12 – Soupedupman
Page 13 – Honestly True Confessions – Paul Reinman
Page 15 – Bridge on the River Kweer – John Severin
Page 19 – Cracked Shut-Ups (Europe) (1st *Shut-Ups*) – Bill McCartney (Bill Ward) (Bill Ward's 1st post-Comics Code Authority work.)
Page 20 – Travel – Bill Everett
Page 22 – American Grandstand – John Severin
Page 24 – Stop – Bill McCartney (Bill Ward)
Page 25 – Highway Parole – Bill McCartney (Bill Ward)
Page 28 – Hollywood's Fairy Tales
Page 30 – The Story Behind the Satellite Science Non-Fiction – Paul Reinman
Page 32 – Foreign TV Commercials – Bill McCartney (Bill Ward)
Page 35 – Keeping Up With the Joneses – Paul Reinman
Page 36 – How Times Have Changed
Page 38 – Frankenstein and Rock 'n Roll! – Joe Maneely
Page 41 – Rock 'n Roll Buttons
Page 42 – Letters – John Severin
Page 43 – Subscription ad – Paul Reinman
Back Cover – Bar-Lament Cigarette ad – Bill McCartney (Bill Ward)

**3, July 1958 (44 pages) (25c)**

Cover – Cracked Building – John Severin
Page 2 – Miss Clearoil
Page 3 – Contents
Page 4 – New Look Magazine Covers
Page 6 – Letters
Page 7 – Baseball 1958 – John Severin and LePoer
Page 10 – Cracked Shut-Ups (send me in) – Bill McCartney (Bill Ward)
Page 11 – The Jack Faar Show – Russ Heath
Page 15 – Medical Specialists – Joe Maneely
Page 18 – The Origin of Nicknames
Page 20 – Inside Small Businesses – Pete Costanza
Page 22 – The Sky of Tomorrow – John Severin
Page 24 – Early Good Morning Husband and Wife Radio Show – Bernard Baily
Page 26 – Rexell ad
Page 28 – Unknown Inventions of Known Inventors
Page 30 – Cracked's Observation Test
Page 32 – New TV Formats – Joe Maneely
Page 35 – Cultural Exchange – Bill McCartney (Bill Ward)
Page 37 – How to Meet Your Next Door Neighbor
Page 39 – Billionaire – Bill McCartney (Bill Ward)
Page 42 – A Case of Mistaken Identity – Bill McCartney (Bill Ward)
Page 43 – Subscription ad – Joe Maneely
Back Cover – Polka Dot Toothpaste ad – Paul Reinman

**4, September 1958 (44 pages) (25c)**

Cover – Cracked Beach – John Severin
Page 2 – Miss Cracked 1959
Page 3 – Contents
Page 4 – Cracked Calendar – Bill Everett
Page 6 – Letters Page
Page 7 – Real Ad (Ad page that appeared for years featuring various novelty items.)
Page 8 – The Hollywoodization of Sopheeya Luring – Bill McCartney (Bill Ward)
Page 10 – It Shouldn't Happen to a Dog – LePoer (John Severin)
Page 11 – French Forlorn Legion – John Severin
Page 14 – Who'd She Expect…Elvis? – Bill McCartney (Bill Ward)
Page 15 – Best Selling Records
Page 18 – Stickers
Page 19 – Meet the Author – Carl Burgos
Page 21 – OKKO Corral – John Severin

Page 24 – Where Do We Go From Here?
Page 26 – Saturday Night Dance – Joe Maneely
Page 29 – Try This Cracked 5-Day Diet
Page 31 – Lifer Magazine – Bill McCartney (Bill Ward)
Page 34 – Are you a Shnook?
Page 36 – Summer Jobs – Carl Burgos
Page 38 – How I Rebuilt My Punk Lawn
Page 40 – Ancient Egypt
Page 42 – Cracked Shut-Ups (diamond ring) – Bill McCartney (Bill Ward)
Page 43 – Subscription ad – Joe Maneely
Back Cover – Maulbury Cigarette ad

**5, October 1958 (44 pages) (25c)** (This issue came out after the downfall of Harvey Kurtzman's *Humbug* magazine. As a result, you see the addition of Jack Davis, Bill Elder and Al Jaffee in this issue's credits. This issue is also the last to feature artwork by Joe Maneely, longtime Atlas artist who was killed in a commuter train accident on June 7, 1958, so the addition of new art staff was welcome.)

Cover – Cereal Box – John Severin
Page 2 – Angle Touche ad
Page 3 – Contents
Page 4 – Foreign Car Concious (sic)
Page 6 – Letters
Page 7 – Have Gun Won't Travel – Bill McCartney (Bill Ward)
Page 10 – The Joker's Wild – Bill McCartney (Bill Ward)
Page 11 – Madame La-Zanya / Mureyene ad
Page 12 – Modern Day Monsters – Joe Maneely
Page 14 – 'Enry 'Iggins of Scotland Yard – John Severin
Page 17 – The Barbecue – Bill Elder
Page 19 – Cracked Shut-Ups (daddy run) – Al Jaffee
Page 20 – Cracked Rogue's Gallery
Page 22 – All Weather Drive-In Movie – Jack Davis
Page 24 – Exclusive Pictures from Darkest Africa
Page 26 – TV Programs of the Future – Joe Maneely
Page 28 – Illustrated Proverbs
Page 30 – Top Model Agency – Bill McCartney (Bill Ward)
Page 32 – Modern Kiddie Books
Page 34 – New Uses for Comics
Page 37 – Secrets of Crashing Highbrow Society
Page 39 – Cracked Photo Contest
Page 40 – Impressing the Opposite Sex – Carl Burgos
Page 42 – Character Bumps – Joe Maneely

Page 43 – Subscription ad – Bill Elder
Back Cover – Elvis Enlistment ad – John Severin

**6, December 1958 (44 pages) (25c)**

Cover – Eggs – Russ Heath
Page 2 – Travlrs Checques ad
Page 3 – Contents
Page 4 – Psychological Predictions – Bill Elder
Page 6 – The Old Cracked Barrel (Letters page)
Page 7 – Julius Caesar in Modern Dress – John Severin
Page 10 – Filter Tips
Page 12 – Written Forms for All Occasions
Page 14 – Easy, Exciting Ways to Earn Money in Beautiful Mexico – Al Jaffee
Page 17 – Farmer's Old Almanac
Page 20 – Hy Gardens Calling Collect
Page 22 – Luxury Cruise – Bill Everett
Page 24 – Bridgette Barf-arf-arf-doe – Bill McCartney (Bill Ward)
Page 27 – Learn While You Snore! – Al Jaffee
Page 29 – Wha? Wha-d He Say? – Bill McCartney (Bill Ward)
Page 30 – Gambling Pastime
Page 32 – Male College Types to Be Wary Of – Bill McCartney (Bill Ward)
Page 34 – So You Think It's Easy to Buy Cracked? – John Severin
Page 37 – Hypnotism – Richard Doxsee
Page 40 – Original Best Selling Russian Pocket Books
Page 42 – Cracked Shut-Ups (Bwanna Jim) – Bill McCartney (Bill Ward)
Page 43 – Subscription ad – Bill McCartney (Bill Ward)
Back Cover – Bubble-Nut Sparemint Gum ad

**7, February 1959 (44 pages) (25c)**

Cover – 1st Anniversary (Pictures all six previous covers) – John Severin, Russ Heath, Bill Everett
Page 2 – Who's Cracked T-Shirt ad (Does anyone have one of these?)
Page 3 – Contents
Page 4 – Christmas Cards of Celebrities
Page 6 – The Old Cracked Barrel
Page 7 – Little Known Famous People
Page 8 – Introducing Don Swanson – Don Swanson
Page 9 – The Millionears – John Severin
Page 12 – Imaginary Fears and Complexes
Page 16 – 10-Day Posture Straightening Exercises – Bill McCartney (Bill Ward)

Page 18 – Know Your America
Page 21 – Things Are Tough All Over! – Bill McCartney (Bill Ward)
Page 22 – Happy Anniversary Cracked – John Severin
Page 24 – Everybody's Got Something to Be Thankful For – Angelo Torres
Page 26 – Company Names – Al Jaffee
Page 28 – Great Battles of Yesterday and Today
Page 30 – New Look Cigarette Packs
Page 32 – How a Rumor Gets Started – Al Jaffee
Page 34 – Our Two Faces
Page 36 – Traffic in the Supermarket
Page 38 – Announcing the Winners of the Cracked Photo Contest
Page 39 – Russian Scientists Invent Amazing New X-Ray – Richard Doxsee
Page 42 – Cracked Shut-Ups (beastly hot) – Bill McCartney (Bill Ward)
Page 43 – Subscription ad – Bill McCartney (Bill Ward)
Back Cover – Schleppes ad

**8, March 1959 (44 pages) (25c)**

Cover – Frankenstein Snowman – John Severin
Page 2 – Who's Cracked T-Shirt ad
Page 3 – Contents
Page 4 – Interplanetary Magazines – Bill Everett
Page 6 – The Old Cracked Barrel
Page 7 – Ya Pays Yer Money and Ya Takes Yer Cherce – Bill McCartney (Bill Ward)
Page 8 – Modern Movie Monsters
Page 10 – Situations Wanted
Page 12 – You Call This a Shape? – Bill McCartney (Bill Ward)
Page 13 – Romeo and Juliet – John Severin
Page 16 – Personalized Cigarette Lighters
Page 18 – Tips to the World Tourist
Page 20 – Do's and Don'ts
Page 22 – The Last of the Hollywood "B" Pictures – Gray Morrow
Page 25 – Horror House ad (real ad) – John Severin
Page 26 – It Never Happened…But Someday It Might! – Bill McCartney (Bill Ward)
Page 27 – Alaska – John Severin
Page 30 – A House for Every Pool – Don Orehek
Page 32 – Everyday People to Advertise the Product
Page 33 – It Could Be Verse – Richard Doxsee
Page 36 – Restaurants to Make You Feel at Home!
Page 38 – Home Town Confidential

Page 40 – Superstitions
Page 42 – Cracked Space Shut-Ups! (most beautiful girl) – Bill McCartney (Bill Ward)
Page 43 – Subscription ad – Bill McCartney (Bill Ward)
Back Cover – Gloom Toothpaste ad

**9, May 1959 (44 pages) (25c)**
Cover – On the Moon – John Severin (Last cover with original logo.)
Page 2 – Viceboy Cigarette ad – John Severin
Page 3 – Contents
Page 4 – Diplomas for the Man in the Street
Page 6 – Who's Cracked T-Shirt ad / Old Cracked Barrel (Statement of Ownership)
Page 7 – Carmen – John Severin
Page 10 – Yoga – John Severin
Page 13 – When it all Started (No kidding, ranger) (1st *When it all Started/Ended*)
Page 14 – Directions – John Severin
Page 16 – Make up Your Own Story
Page 18 – First Impressions – Bill McCartney (Bill Ward)
Page 20 – Horoscope
Page 22 – Modern Art – John Severin
Page 24 – There's One in Every Crowd – Bill McCartney (Bill Ward)
Page 26 – Develop a Sense of Humor – Carl Burgos
Page 28 – To Tell the Truth
Page 30 – Push Button War – Bill Everett
Page 32 – Horror House ad – John Severin
Page 33 – Huff n' Puff – Bill McCartney (Bill Ward)
Page 34 – Un-Togetherness
Page 37 – Cinema Movie Life TV Photo Screen Magazine
Page 41 – Cracked Shut-Ups (driving in the country) – Bill McCartney (Bill Ward)
Page 42 – When it all Started (consented to pose)
Page 43 – Subscription ad – John Severin
Back Cover – Hilo Shampoo ad – Bill Everett

**10, August 1959 (52 pages) (25c)** (1st 52-page issue although reprints from #1 and #3 helped create these eight new pages. Last issue edited by Sol Brodsky.)
Cover – Bridget Bardoe in Shower – Bill Elder (new logo. Elder's only cover for *Cracked*.)
Page 2 – Bar Doe Soap ad – Bill Elder
Page 3 – Contents

Page 4 – Fraternity Keys
Page 6 – Who's Cracked T-Shirt ad / Old Cracked Barrel
Page 8 – When it all Started (The Laretta Young Show)
Page 9 – The Home Life of a TV Moderator
Page 10 – Whatever Happened to These Movie Scenes?
Page 13 – Charge It
Page 16 – Ancient Psychiatry – Bill Elder
Page 18 – It All Depends on the Point of View (snake) – Bill McCartney (Bill Ward)
Page 20 – New Highway Signs for the Speed Age
Page 22 – Be a Movie Director
Page 23 – Cracked Sportslants
Page 24 – Tipping
Page 26 – Enlistment Posters – Gray Morrow
Page 28 – Casual Format – Angelo Torres (1st *Casual Format*)
Page 33 – Cracked Brings You Greetings – Bill Everett (reprint from #1)
Page 35 – Celebrity Song Sheet for Celebrities
Page 37 – Horror House ad – John Severin
Page 38 – How to Meet Your Next Door Neighbor (reprint from #3)
Page 40 – Heart on Sleeve Section – Bill McCartney (Bill Ward)
Page 41 – Baseball Statisticiatic – John Severin
Page 44 – Flashes from Outer Space – Basil Wolverton
Page 46 – Observation Test (reprint from #3)
Page 48 – Perry Masonry – John Severin
Page 50 – When it all Started (The Telephone) – Angelo Torres
Page 51 – Subscription ad
Back Cover – Clorex ad – John Severin

**11, October 1959 (52 pages) (25c)** (1st issue with modern logo and major overhaul of staff. No Editor credit. Paul Laikin writes entire issue for this and every issue through #23.)

Cover – Sylvester Tipping his Cap – John Severin (1st redesign of Sylvester)
Page 2 – Bull Telephone System ad – Bill Elder
Page 3 – Contents
Page 4 – Old Cracked Barrel
Page 5 – Who's Cracked T-Shirt ad
Page 6 – If Racketeers Took Over the Children's World – Jack Davis
Page 10 – State Posters to Lure the Beat Generation – Bill Elder
Page 11 – Giant Book Sale ad
Page 13 – Story of the Month (I'm afraid) – Jack Davis (1st *Story of the Month*)
Page 14 – Creative Housekeeping – John Severin
Page 16 – Endings for Old TV Shows – Jack Davis

Page 19 – Believe it or No! – Jack Davis (1st *Believe it or Not!* parody)
Page 20 – Handshakes – John Severin
Page 22 – Way Out West! – Jack Davis
Page 24 – Cracked Annual Awards – John Severin
Page 26 – Trade School for Misfits
Page 28 – How to Tell You're in Love – John Severin
Page 30 – Restaurants – Jack Davis
Page 32 – The Way That Movie Should've Ended – Jack Davis
Page 33 – Judo – Jack Davis
Page 36 – The Charge of the Light Brigade – John Severin (1st *How it Really Was*)
Page 38 – National Advertising – John Severin
Page 41 – Bop Shut-Ups (I'm floatin') – John Severin
Page 42 – Popoff
Page 43 – Horror House ad – John Severin
Page 44 – When it all Started (take the nice gun) – Jack Davis
Page 45 – French Forlorn Legion – John Severin (reprint from #4)
Page 48 – Are Comics Ruining Our Children? – Bill Elder
Page 50 – Stickers (reprint from #4)
Page 51 – Subscription ad – Jack Davis
Back Cover – Thousands Now Play ad – probably Bill Elder

**12, January 1960 (52 pages) (25c)** (No Editor credit) (Paul Laikin writes entire issue.)

Cover – Sylvester Jig-Saw Puzzle – Jack Davis (Jack Davis' 1st cover for *Cracked.*)
Page 2 – Oases Cigarette ad – John Severin
Page 3 – Contents
Page 4 – Old Cracked Barrel
Page 5 – Who's Cracked T-Shirt ad
Page 6 – Mixed Up Pocketbooks – Bill Elder
Page 8 – Casual Format – Jack Davis
Page 9 – Awards from the Syndicate – Bill Elder
Page 12 – How Different Nationalities Make Marriage Proposals – Bill McCartney (Bill Ward)
Page 14 – Rate Your Personality – LePoer (John Severin)
Page 16 – Realistic Children's Games – Jack Davis
Page 18 – Architecture – Bill Elder
Page 20 – When it all Started (I'll buy you a drink) – Bill McCartney (Bill Ward)
Page 21 – Sunshine Healthy – John Severin
Page 24 – Illustrated Little Willies – LePoer (John Severin)
Page 26 – Do-it-Yourself Cartoons (1st *Do-it-Yourself Cartoons / Captions*)

Page 28 – Story of the Month (You look terrible!) – Jack Davis
Page 29 – Civil War Facts – Jack Davis
Page 32 – Casual Format – Angelo Torres
Page 33 – Peter Goon – Jack Davis
Page 36 – A Beatnik Goes to a Party – Jack Davis
Page 38 – Russian Shut-Ups (eat) – Bill McCartney (Bill Ward)
Page 39 – Perry Coma is a Fraud! – Bill Elder
Page 42 – Marriages Are Made in Heaven – Jack Davis
Page 44 – Brigitte Bardot as Seen by Different Artists – John Severin
Page 47 – Medical Specialists – Joe Maneely (reprint from #3)
Page 50 – Horror House ad – John Severin
Page 51 – Subscription ad – Jack Davis
Back Cover – Brand X Cigarette Box Cut-Out

**13, March 1960 (52 pages) (25c)** (No Editor credit. Page numbering changes with this issue to not include covers; reverts back with #17.) (Paul Laikin writes entire issue.)

Cover – The Smythe Family – John Severin
Inside Front Cover – The National Geagraphic Magazine – John Severin
Page 1 – Contents
Page 2 – Letters (Statement of ownership)
Page 3 – Who's Cracked T-Shirt ad
Page 4 – Ignited Air Lines ad – John Severin
Page 6 – HIP Alphabet Book – Vic Martin
Page 9 – Believe it or Nuts!! – Jack Davis
Page 10 – Modern Appliances Have Overshot Their Function! – John Severin
Page 12 – Cartoons of the Year – Jack Davis
Page 14 – Send Out Your Own Greeting Cards
Page 16 – 10-Day Posture Straightening Exercises – Bill McCartney (Bill Ward)
Page 18 – Are We Civilized? – Russ Heath
Page 21 – Story of the Month (finish your oatmeal) – Don Orehek
Page 22 – Sick Unions for Sick People – John Severin
Page 24 – Memorial Tribute
Page 26 – Wild Record Albums – Bill McCartney (Bill Ward)
Page 28 – Russian Magazines – Bill Elder
Page 30 – Be Different Buttons
Page 31 – If Different Poets Had Read Cracked – John Severin (Alfred E. Neuman appearance. 1st in *Cracked*.)
Page 36 – Remember! Forest Fires Can Prevent Bears! – Russ Heath
Page 37 – Bat Masteyson – Jack Davis

Page 41 – When it all Started (First World War) – John Severin
Page 42 – Horror House ad – John Severin
Page 43 – Freezing People – Jack Davis
Page 48 – Shut-Ups (I'll find you) – John Severin
Inside Back Cover – Subscription ad – Jack Davis
Back Cover – Cracked Book Jackets

**14, June 1960 (52 pages) (25c)** (Paul Laikin writes entire issue.)
Cover – The Descent of Man – Jack Davis
Inside Front Cover – Who's Cracked T-Shirt ad
Page 1 – Contents
Page 2 – Letters
Page 3 – Commercials in Real Life – John Severin
Page 7 – The Searcher – Jack Davis
Page 8 – How to Break Bad Habits – John Severin
Page 10 – Kookie Songs for Other Stores
Page 12 – Why People Move to the Suburbs – Jack Davis
Page 16 – Do-it-Yourself Cartoons
Page 17 – When It All Ended (go to the police) – John Severin
Page 18 – Sea Haunt – Jack Davis
Page 22 – Jig-Saw Puzzle – John Severin (1st *Jig-Saw Puzzle*)
Page 23 – Band-Aides for Weird Color Skin – Jack Davis
Page 24 – How They Got the Stars to Jump – John Severin
Page 26 – TV and Real Life Western Heroes – John Severin
Page 30 – Celebrity Shut-Ups (shampoo) – John Severin
Page 32 – Old Ideas for New Panel Shows – Jack Kirby (This is the only artwork done for *Cracked* by Jack Kirby. Strangely, he did not sign the work, nor is he credited on the contents page.)
Page 37 – Thumbprints of Famous People
Page 38 – Sylvester P. Smythe As Seen by Different Artists
Page 40 – Travel – Bill Everett (reprint from #2)
Page 42 – (Picasso painting) – Russ Heath
Page 43 – Story of the Month (Court of Domestic Relations) – Vic Martin
Page 44 – Family Albums of Celebrities – John Severin
Page 48 – Horror House ad – John Severin
Inside Back Cover – Subscription ad – John Severin
Back Cover – Coco-Colo ad – Bill McCartney (Bill Ward)

**15, August 1960 (52 pages) (25c)** (Paul Laikin writes entire issue.)
Cover – Sylvester Joker Card Hand – John Severin (This cover gag predates *Mad* #69's by almost two years!)
Inside Front Cover – Who's Cracked T-Shirt ad – John Severin / *The Cracked Reader* ad (1st *Cracked* paperback book)

Page 1 – Contents
Page 2 – Letters
Page 3 – Hollywood Life Stories from the Pages of History – John Severin
Page 8 – Thousands Now Play ad – probably Bill Elder (reprint from #11)
Page 9 – How Family Life Would be if the Sexes Changed Places – John Severin
Page 11 – If Literature Were Written in the Gossip Columns
Page 16 – The Banana Man – Jerry Kirschen
Page 17 – Sports Oddities (Hank Luckeezi) – Jack Davis (1st *Sports Oddities*)
Page 18 – Viceboy cigarette ad – John Severin (reprint from #9)
Page 19 – 3 Stories – Jerry Kirschen
Page 20 – Famous Proverb Shut-Ups (small packages) – John Severin
Page 22 – Do-it-Yourself Captions – John Severin
Page 24 – Great War Heroes – Jack Davis
Page 26 – Cracked's Intelligence Test
Page 29 – When it all Started (blood pressure) – Jack Davis
Page 30 – Cracked Headlines
Page 32 – How Some of Our Customs Began – John Severin
Page 34 – They Shoulda Listened – Jack Davis
Page 37 – Cut! Cut! CUT! – John Severin
Page 38 – Illustrated Limericks – Jack Davis
Page 41 – Sports Oddities (Fullback Arnold) – Jack Davis
Page 42 – Nursery Rhymes
Page 44 – I Got My Job Through The Daily Times ad – John Severin
Page 45 – Smell-O-Rama – John Severin
Page 47 – When it all Started (Ponce DeLeon) – Jack Davis
Page 48 – Horror House ad – John Severin
Inside Back Cover – Subscription ad – Jack Davis
Back Cover – Ocean ad – John Severin

**16, October 1960 (52 pages) (25c)** (This issue contains the most new material drawn by John Severin for a single issue so far – at least 30 pages!) (Paul Laikin writes entire issue.)

Cover – Trick Mirror – Jack Davis
Inside Front Cover – The Unsociables ad – John Severin
Page 1 – Contents
Page 2 – Letters
Page 3 – Untouchybulls – John Severin
Page 10 – Cracked's Handy Guide to Self-Analysis – John Severin
Page 12 – Magazine Covers – Jack Davis
Page 16 – People Who Get on Our Nerves – John Severin
Page 19 – When it all Started (speaking to you as a sister) – John Severin

Page 20 – How Infantile Are You? – John Severin
Page 24 – What They're Really Saying? – John Severin
Page 26 – Television and Real Life – John Severin
Page 28 – Digest Magazines – John Severin
Page 32 – There's One in Every Crowd – John Severin
Page 35 – Cracked Dartboard
Page 36 – *The Cracked Reader* ad – Jack Davis
Page 37 – The Jungle Book ad
Page 38 – Stories of the Month (I don't mean to be nosey) – Jerry Kirschen
Page 39 – Who's Cracked T-Shirt ad – John Severin
Page 40 – Cracked Marquees
Page 42 – Horror House ad – John Severin
Page 43 – Ye Olde Shut-Upf – Jack Davis
Page 44 – Hip Talk Taken Literally – Chic Stone
Page 48 – Occupational Calendars – John Severin
Inside Back Cover – Subscription ad – Chic Stone
Back Cover – Cracked Playing Cards – Jack Davis

**17, December 1960 (52 pages) (25c)** (Page numbering reverts back.) (Paul Laikin writes entire issue.)

Cover – Cracked Bookends – John Severin
Page 2 – Bam ad
Page 3 – Contents
Page 4 – Who's Cracked T-Shirt ad / Letters / *The Cracked Reader* ad
Page 6 – Western Onion ad – John Severin
Page 7 – The Tightropers – Angel Martinez
Page 11 – When in all Ended – Russ Heath
Page 12 – Cracked's Applied Psychology – Angel Martinez
Page 16 – Historical Telegrams That Never Got There
Page 19 – If – John Severin
Page 21 – Stories of the Month – Angel Martinez
Page 22 – Cracked Looks at Old-Time Songs – Angel Martinez
Page 26 – Sequels to Best-Sellers – Chic Stone
Page 28 – If TV Shows Weren't Rigged – John Severin
Page 31 – Fine Art Captions – Jack Davis
Page 34 – Shakespearean Shut-Ups (Romeo) – John Severin
Page 36 – Things We Shoulda Done – Jack Davis (1st *Things We Shoulda Done*)
Page 39 – Subscription ad – John Severin
Page 40 – Union Cards for Organized Crime – John Severin
Page 42 – Illustrated Slang – Chic Stone
Page 45 – If Some Famous Married Couples had Divorce Hearings – John Severin

Page 48 – Horror House ad – John Severin
Page 49 – Ivery Soap ad – John Severin
Back Cover – Brand X Beer Labels

**18, February 1961 (52 pages) (25c)** (Logo slimmed down to the most familiar version.) (Paul Laikin writes entire issue.)
Cover – Wanted Poster – John Severin
Page 2 – Beautyrester ad – John Severin
Page 3 – Contents
Page 4 – Who's Cracked T-Shirt ad / Letters / Subscription ad / *The Cracked Reader* ad
Page 6 – Cracked Cut-Out Calendar for 1961 – John Severin
Page 10 – Future on the Spot Reporting – John Severin
Page 14 – Redesigning Ads to Appeal to Children – John Severin
Page 17 – The Discovery of America – John Severin
Page 21 – When it all Ended – George Peltz
Page 22 – Historical Headlines
Page 26 – Famous People Do-it-Yourself Captions – John Severin
Page 29 – A Cracked Hip Primer – John Severin
Page 32 – If Women Did Men's Jobs
Page 35 – The Shooting of Dan McGrew – John Severin
Page 38 – Interior Decorating to Fit Your Job – Jerry Kirschen
Page 40 – If Shakespeare Had Read Cracked
Page 41 – The Sailing of the Vikings – John Severin
Page 43 – Stories of the Month (The Panhandler) – Jerry Kirschen
Page 44 – Real Cracked Books – Vic Martin
Page 47 – Jack Paar Makes Up With the Press – John Severin
Page 50 – Horror House ad – John Severin
Page 51 – Cold ad – John Severin
Back Cover – Reward Poster

**19, April 1961 (52 pages) (25c)** (Paul Laikin writes entire issue.)
Cover – The Millionaire – John Severin
Page 2 – A Diamond is Forever ad – John Severin
Page 3 – Contents
Page 4 – Letters (Statement of Ownership: Average number of copies sold: 140,676) / Subscription ad / *The Cracked Reader* ad
Page 5 – Ads You Never Get to See – John Severin
Page 11 – How to Prepare a Job Resume
Page 14 – Russian TV Shows – John Severin
Page 18 – Political Record Albums – John Severin
Page 21 – When it all Started (Oscar! Don't do that!) – John Severin
Page 22 – Specialized Eye Charts (1st *Specialized Eye Charts*)

Page 24 – Fine Art Shut-Ups (lopsided hat) – John Severin
Page 25 – Informal TV Shows – John Severin
Page 26 – Draw Your Own Conclusion – John Severin (1st *Draw Your Own Conclusion*)
Page 29 – Cracked Paste-On Tattoos – John Severin
Page 30 – Horror House ad – John Severin
Page 31 – When it all Ended (don't go near the cage) – Vic Martin
Page 32 – How to Cure Superstitions
Page 34 – The Little World of Don Swanson (rocket) – Don Swanson
Page 36 – Summer Festivals – Vic Martin
Page 39 – The Cremation of Sam McGee – John Severin
Page 43 – The Revels of Ancient Rome – John Severin
Page 45 – Stories of the Month (My problem, Doctor) – Vic Martin
Page 46 – Educational Motion Pictures – John Severin
Page 50 – Cracked Fun Shoppe (real ad) – John Severin
Page 51- Levenworth Mutual ad – John Severin
Back Cover – Cracked Million Bills – John Severin

**20, July 1961 (52 pages) (25c)** (Paul Laikin writes entire issue.)
Cover – Frank Sinatra, Dean Martin, Peter Lawford, Sophia Loren – John Severin
Page 2 – Great Moments in Medicine – John Severin
Page 3 – Contents
Page 4 – Letters / *The Cracked Reader* ad
Page 5 – How Madison Avenue Can Make Unpopular Subjects Popular – John Severin
Page 6 – If Different Comedians Played Shakespeare – John Severin
Page 11 – Real Wildlife Nature's Oddities (1st *Real Wildlife Nature's Oddities*)
Page 12 – Handwriting Analysis – John Severin
Page 14 – Lose Weight by Exercising Right on the Job – John Severin
Page 16 – Undeliverable U.S. Mail
Page 18 – Stories of the Month
Page 19 – King Arthur's Round Table – John Severin
Page 21 – Autobiographies of Animal Stars
Page 22 – New Designs for Business Cards
Page 24 – Subscription ad – John Severin
Page 25 – What Has Happened to Merchandising? – LePoer (John Severin)
Page 28 – The Little World of Don Swanson (chinning hanger) – Don Swanson
Page 29 – The Face Upon the Floor – John Severin
Page 33 – Celebrity Cut-Out Stamps

Page 34 – Is the Ink Blot Test Reliable?
Page 36 – Madison Avenue Shut-Ups (no cavities) – Vic Martin
Page 38 – Great Women of History – Oswaldo Laino
Page 40 – Cracked Sympathy Cards
Page 42 – Horror House ad – John Severin
Page 43 – The Ride of Paul Revere – John Severin
Page 45 – Real Wildlife Nature's Oddities
Page 46 – If Political Figures Did TV Guest Shots – John Severin
Page 50 – Cracked Fun Shoppe ad – John Severin
Page 51 – Grand Old Daddy ad – John Severin
Back Cover – Cracked Popularity Kit – John Severin

**21, September 1961 (52 pages) (25c)** (Paul Laikin writes entire issue.)
Cover – Abominable Snowman Sylvester with Sir Edmund Hillary – John Severin
Page 2 – *More Cracked* ad
Page 3 – Contents
Page 4 – Letters / *The Cracked Reader* ad
Page 5 – Blech Shampoo ad – LePoer (John Severin)
Page 6 – On-the-Spot Test Commercials – John Severin
Page 11 – That Wonderful Year 1930 – Oswaldo Laino (1st *That Wonderful Year*)
Page 12 – When it all Started (Look at that)
Page 13 – Neurotic Magazine – John Severin
Page 20 – The Little World of Don Swanson (poster) – Don Swanson
Page 21 – Television Shut-Ups (cashier's check) – John Severin
Page 22 – Rejected Cracked Covers – John Severin (The interesting thing about this article is that one of the covers deemed "rejected" was actually used later on as the cover of *Cracked* #31. There is also another Alfred E. Neuman appearance.)
Page 24 – Great Lovers of Fiction – Oswaldo Laino
Page 26 – Cracked Wrappers – John Severin
Page 28 – Stories of the Month (The Psychiatrist) – Vic Martin
Page 29 – Jig-Saw Puzzle – John Severin (reprint from #14)
Page 30 – Men That Don't Fit in – Sam Hayle
Page 32 – Signs of the Times
Page 33 – The Charge Up San Juan Hill – John Severin
Page 35 – When it all Ended (We're safe now) – Vic Martin
Page 36 – A Cracked Gallery of New Artists – Oswaldo Laino, John Severin
Page 40 – Subscription ad
Page 41 – Pages That Didn't Get Into Cracked – John Severin (1st *Pages That Didn't Get Into Cracked*)

Page 42 – If Different Comedians Played Shakespeare – John Severin
Page 43 – If Political Figures Did TV Guest Shots – John Severin
Page 44 – Sequels to Best-Sellers – Vic Martin
Page 45 – Cracked Look at Old-Time Songs – Oswaldo Laino
Page 46 – Specialized Eye Charts
Page 47 – Horror House ad – John Severin
Page 48 – Cracked Fun Shoppe ad – John Severin
Page 49 – Real Abominable Merchandise ad (real ad) – John Severin
Page 50 – Letters
Page 51 – Callidac ad – Severin
Back Cover – Abominable University Diploma

**22, November 1961 (52 pages) (25c)** (1st issue to state "Magazine" boldly on cover.) (Paul Laikin writes entire issue.)
Cover – We Need New Quarters – John Severin
Page 2 – Cutt'r Sank ad – John Severin
Page 3 – Contents
Page 4 – Letters / *More Cracked* ad / *The Cracked Reader* ad
Page 6 – Russian Ads Along the Kremlin – John Severin
Page 10 – That Wonderful Year 1917 – Oswaldo Laino
Page 11 – Neighborhood Confidential Magazine – John Severin
Page 18 – How to Make and Art of Your Job – Oswaldo Laino
Page 21 – When it all Ended – Vic Martin
Page 22 – If Different Poets Had Read Cracked – Oswaldo Laino
Page 24 – Popular Songs Shut-Ups (smile umbrella) – Bill McCartney (Bill Ward)
Page 26 – Madison Avenue's View of America – Oswaldo Laino
Page 28 – The Little World of Don Swanson (pterodactyl) – Don Swanson
Page 29 – Instant Living – Oswaldo Laino
Page 32 – You Too Can be an Optimist
Page 35 – Grin! – Bill McCartney (Bill Ward)
Page 37 – The Little World of Don Swanson (Pisa) – Don Swanson
Page 38 – Great Enemies of Fiction – Oswaldo Laino
Page 40 – The Rationalizer – Stuart Sloves
Page 41 – Gunfight at OK Corral – John Severin
Page 43 – Pages That Didn't Get Into Cracked – John Severin
Page 44 – Handshakes of Different People – John Severin (partial reprint from #11)
Page 45 – Hollywood Life Stories – John Severin
Page 46 – Mixed-Up Pocket Books – Vic Martin
Page 47 – Commercials in Real Life
Page 48 – Cracked Fun Shoppe ad – John Severin

Page 49 – Special Instant Merchandise ad – John Severin
Page 50 – Horror House ad – John Severin
Page 51 – Subscription ad – John Severin
Back Cover – Cracked Cut-Out Paste-On Matchbook Covers – John Severin

**23, February 1962 (52 pages) (25c)** (Paul Laikin writes entire issue.)
Cover – Unfinished Sylvester a la Washington – John Severin
Page 2 – Which One is a Banker? Ad – John Severin
Page 3 – Contents
Page 4 – Letters / *The Cracked Reader*, *More Cracked* ad / Subscription ad
Page 6 – Madison Avenue Conformity Products – John Severin
Page 9 – Great Moments in History – Oswaldo Laino
Page 10 – The Little World of Don Swanson (chopping tree) – Don Swanson
Page 11 – If Big League Business Takes Over Little League Baseball – John Severin
Page 16 – Columbus – Bill McCartney (Bill Ward)
Page 18 – Stories of the Month – Vic Martin
Page 19 – Famous Quotations Shut-Ups (Don't give up the ship) – Vic Martin
Page 20 – The Tipsy Mother Goose – John Severin
Page 25 – When it all Ended (What can happen) – John Severin
Page 26 – A Cracked's-Eye View of Paris! – Bill Everett
Page 28 – Draw Your Own Conclusion – Bill McCartney (Bill Ward)
Page 30 – Theme Songs for Celebrities – Bayon
Page 32 – Progressive Child Psychology – John Severin
Page 34 – Accessories for Your Car – John Severin
Page 37 – There's One in Every Crowd – John Severin
Page 38 – Horror House ad – John Severin
Page 39 – People Who Get on Our Nerves – John Severin (reprint from #16)
Page 40 – Cracked's Illustrated Limericks – Brutus
Page 42 – Interior Decorating to Fit Your Job! – Bill McCartney (Bill Ward)
Page 43 – Redesigning Ads to Appeal to Children – John Severin
Page 44 – The Little World of Don Swanson (clock) – Don Swanson
Page 45 – Magazine Covers Just a Little Bit Different – Oswaldo Laino
Page 46 – More Things We Shoulda Done – John Severin
Page 47 – Cracked Fun Shoppe ad – John Severin
Page 50 – Illustrated Slang – Bill McCartney (Bill Ward)
Page 51 – White Horses ad – John Severin
Back Cover – Cracked Paint Sign

**24, April 1962 (52 pages) (25c)** (1st issue to feature new writers besides Paul Laikin. In this case, George Gladir, who had a lengthy association with *Cracked*)

Cover – Four-Eyed Sylvester – John Severin
Page 2 – Ramington Shavers ad – John Severin
Page 3 – Contents
Page 4 – Letters (Statement of Ownership: Average number of copies sold: 159,113) / *Completely Cracked* ad / Subscription ad / Back Issues ad (#20-23)
Page 6 – If Madison Avenue Advertised Crime – John Severin
Page 11 – Hollywood Miscasting – John Severin
Page 13 – Shotgun Slayed – Bill McCartney (Bill Ward)
Page 17 – Great Inventions in History – Oswaldo Laino
Page 18 – Advance of Civilization – John Severin
Page 20 – Home Sweet Home – John Severin
Page 22 – Celebrities Libraries – John Severin
Page 24 – Celebrities Checkbooks – John Severin
Page 26 – Free-For-All-Land – Bill Everett
Page 28 – Past, Present and Future Changes in Sports – John Severin
Page 31 – Boysplay – John Severin (Revised for *Biggest Greatest Cracked* #4 as a full-color insert.)
Page 40 – Whither Specialists? – John Severin
Page 43 – Stories of the Month – John Severin
Page 44 – The Balanced Diet – Bill McCartney (Bill Ward)
Page 45 – When Doctors Advertise! – Jack Davis, John Severin (Although this piece is signed Jack Davis, it is obvious that John Severin finished it up. Davis by this point had moved on from *Cracked* to Harvey Kurtzman's *Help!* magazine.)
Page 49 – When it all Ended (The Science Fiction Movie) – John Severin
Page 50 – Horror House ad – John Severin
Page 51 – Robert Booms ad – John Severin
Back Cover – Push Button for Service

**25, July 1962 (52 pages) (25c)** (Another record Severin issue with 37 pages of Severin art.)

Cover – Patching up the Logo – John Severin
Page 2 – Five Roses – John Severin
Page 3 – Contents
Page 4 – Letters / Back Issues ad (#21-24) / Three Paperbacks ad
Page 6 – Photos That Have Been Cropped – John Severin
Page 11 – Get Back to Work Cards – Bill McCartney (Bill Ward)
Page 13 – Drive In Movie – John Severin

Page 16 – Cracked Space Helmets – John Severin
Page 18 – The Twist – John Severin
Page 21 – Hollywood's Fairy Tales – Oswaldo Laino
Page 22 – Joey Bishop An Up Coming Star – John Severin
Page 26 – If Different Cartoonists Had Painted the Mona Lisa – John Severin
Page 28 – Campers' Handbook – John Severin
Page 31 – Story of the Month (Hi, mom) – John Severin
Page 32 – Service-O-Mats of the Future – John Severin
Page 36 – Newspaper Mastheads
Page 38 – Cracked Proverb Stickers
Page 39 – New Gadgets for the Home
Page 41 – Those False Rumors About Cracked Magazine – John Severin / George Gladir
Page 46 – Horror House ad – John Severin
Page 47 – Do-it-Yourself Barometer – LePoer (John Severin)
Page 48 – Europe Prepares for the American Tourist
Page 50 – That Wonderful Year 1961 – Oswaldo Laino
Page 51 – Subscription ad
Back Cover – Chinese Paperback Book Cover – John Severin

**26, September 1962 (52 pages) (25c)** (The Severin record – 50 pages! He has drawn everything but the inside back cover subscription ad and a single page reprint by Bill Elder.)
Cover – Sylvester Sunglasses – John Severin
Page 2 – Bull Telephone System ad – Bill Elder (reprint from #11)
Page 3 – Contents
Page 4 – Letters / Back Issues ad (#21-24) / Three Paperbacks ad
Page 6 – Modern Products for Modern Redskins – John Severin
Page 10 – School for Monsters – Nireves (John Severin)
Page 15 – The Gradual Change in Men's Fashions – John Severin
Page 16 – Casey at the Clinic – Powers (John Severin)
Page 23 – Not-So-Well-Known Trademarks – John Severin
Page 25 – College Coloring Book – John Severin
Page 29 – Axis Sallies – John Severin
Page 32 – Art Lesson – John Severin
Page 35 – TV School – John Severin
Page 40 – Autobiographies by the Man in the Street – John Severin
Page 42 – A Cracked Guide to Hand Language – John Severin
Page 46 – Lands of Romance and Beautiful Women – John Severin
Page 50 – Horror House ad – John Severin
Page 51 – Subscription ad – Bill McCartney (Bill Ward)
Back Cover – Ristaction Air Conditioner – John Severin

**27, November 1962 (52 pages) (25c)**

Cover – 5th Anniworseary Issue – John Severin
Page 2 – Log Cabin Syrup ad – John Severin
Page 3 – Contents
Page 4 – Letters / Back Issues ad (#21-24) / Three Paperbacks ad
Page 6 – The Numbers Game – John Severin
Page 10 – Dear John Letters of History – John Severin
Page 12 – The Beach Balloon – John Severin
Page 13 – Who Will Replace Jack Paar? – John Severin
Page 16 – Story of the Month (Whoa, Bessie) – John Severin
Page 17 – Inside Teenage Russia – Bill McCartney (Bill Ward)
Page 22 – Custom Made Towels – John Severin
Page 24 – How Different T.V. Cowboys Get Their Man – John Severin
Page 27 – Navy-Rated Wife – John Severin
Page 32 – Have you Ever Noticed How Walking Advertisements Never Match the Man? – John Severin
Page 34 – Awards For Unsung Students – John Severin
Page 35 – If Madison Ave. Advertised the Twist – John Severin
Page 39 – New Designs for Business Cards – Oswaldo Laino
Page 40 – At the Art Gallery – J. Lewis (John Severin) / Jay Lynch (A very blatant Don Martin rip-off predating Martin's arrival at the magazine by 25 years!)
Page 42 – Television Commercials you Never Get to See – Bill McCartney (Bill Ward)
Page 43 – Typical Graduates – John Severin
Page 47 – Sensationalized Reference Books – John Severin
Page 49 – Horror House ad – John Severin
Page 50 – Lucky Panther Cigarette ad – John Severin
Page 51 – Subscription ad – John Severin
Back Cover – Subpoena and Parking Ticket

**28 (listed as #27 inside the front cover), February 1963 (52 pages) (25c)**

Cover – Raining Scarecrow – John Severin
Page 2 – Curvy Sewer Cognac ad – John Severin
Page 3 – Contents
Page 4 – Letters / Back Issues ad (#22-26) / Three Paperbacks ad
Page 6 – Trading Stamps – John Severin
Page 12 – Proverbs Can Wreck Your Life – LePoer (John Severin)
Page 14 – Headlines of Great Literature
Page 15 – Clan Clinkers – John Severin
Page 20 – Phone Services for Tots and Teens – John Severin
Page 25 – Ego Building TV Programs – Bill McCartney (Bill Ward)
Page 30 – The Old Lady and the Laundromat – Bill McCartney (Bill Ward)

Page 32 – Annoy Your Friends – John Severin
Page 35 – Ultra Realistic Dolls – Bill McCartney (Bill Ward)
Page 39 – Horror House ad – John Severin
Page 40 – Modern Coats of Arms – John Severin
Page 42 – Russian Record Albums – John Severin
Page 44 – Bank of America Travelers Checks ad – John Severin
Page 45 – Age Rage Ad Fad – John Severin
Page 51 – Subscription ad – John Severin
Back Cover – Important Notice

**29, May 1963 (52 pages) (25c)** (On sale date: March 5, 1963)
Cover – How Many Times Does *Cracked* Appear on the Cover? (The world may never know as the answer was never revealed, but see issue #359.) – John Severin
Page 2 – Friends of the Family ad – John Severin
Page 3 – Contents
Page 4 – Letters (Statement of Ownership: Average number of copies sold: 135,632) / Back Issues ad (#22-26) / Three Paperbacks ad
Page 6 – If All Civil Service Jobs Were Put on a Quota Basis – John Severin
Page 10 – A Glossary of Cracked Definitions – LePoer (John Severin)
Page 13 – Suspense Selling – Bill McCartney (Bill Ward)
Page 16 – If Colleges Advertised – John Severin
Page 22 – The Way They Should Have Filmed it – John Severin
Page 23 – Are you an In-Person? – John Powers (John Severin)
Page 26 – Mother Goose Confidential – John Severin
Page 28 – Background Music – John Severin
Page 32 – Brands for Famous People – John Severin
Page 34 – Real Official Detective – Bill McCartney (Bill Ward)
Page 38 – Of the Apes – Ned Kelly (John Severin) / Don Edwing
Page 39 – Getting There is All the Fun – LePoer (John Severin)
Page 42 – Cracked Silverware Patterns – John Severin
Page 44 – Horror House ad – John Severin
Page 45 – The Ugly American – John Severin
Page 50 – Cold Enough For Ya? – Ned Kelly (John Severin) / Don Edwing
Page 51 – Counting Contest ad / Subscription ad
Back Cover – Cracked Loiter Sign

**30, July 1963 (52 pages) (25c)**
Cover – Kennedy Hieroglyphics – John Severin (1st cover to feature the word "Mazagine.")
Page 2 – (dance studio captioned photo)
Page 3 – Contents

Page 4 – Letters (Statement of Ownership: Average number of copies sold: 145,438) / Back Issues ad (#22-26) / Three Paperbacks ad
Page 6 – Peace Corps in Reverse – Bill McCartney (Bill Ward)
Page 11 – The Machine Gun Nest – Ned Kelly (John Severin) / Don Edwing
Page 12 – Audience Participation Programs of the Future – John Severin
Page 17 – Sylvester's Hobby Corner – Bill McCartney (Bill Ward)
Page 19 – Montgomery Roebuck & Co. Mail Order Catalog – John Severin
Page 23 – The Chicken Killer – Bill McCartney (Bill Ward) / Jay Lynch (One of the most famous (and often reprinted) pieces in *Cracked* history. The original art was damaged and so was redrawn as a single page gag by Howard Nostrand when "reprinted" in #168.)
Page 25 – The Honest Boxer – Bill McCartney (Bill Ward)
Page 26 – This is a Recorded Announcement – Bill McCartney (Bill Ward)
Page 28 – The Stalk – Ned Kelly (John Severin) / Don Edwing
Page 29 – Relay Re-Runs – John Severin
Page 34 – Cracked Wind-Up Dolls – John Severin
Page 37 – Read the Fine Print – Bill McCartney (Bill Ward)
Page 42 – Horror House ad – John Severin
Page 43 – Dance Trend Graph – Bill McCartney (Bill Ward)
Page 44 – Cracked Bubble Gum Cards – John Severin
Page 50 – The Booby-Trapped Bomb – Bill McCartney (Bill Ward)
Page 51 – Subscription ad – John Severin
Back Cover – Cracked Beta Laten Evah Sign

**31, September 1963 (52 pages) (25c)**

Cover – Dropping the Liberty Bell – John Severin (One of the covers deemed "rejected" from the article used in #21.)
Page 2 – Kodiak ad – John Severin
Page 3 – Contents
Page 4 – Letters / Back Issues ad (#22-23, 25-27) / Three Paperbacks ad
Page 6 – Handufactured Products – John Severin
Page 10 – If the Old Masters Were Alive Today – Bill McCartney (Bill Ward)
Page 13 – Big-John is Coming – LePoer (John Severin)
Page 17 – Touchavision Radio Mirror – John Severin
Page 22 – Reunion – Pete Wyma
Page 23 – Modern Merchandise for Moneyed Mountaineers – John Severin
Page 26 – Monster Party! – John Severin (The article where the later *Cracked Monster Party* logo came from.)

Page 28 – Company – Ned Kelly (John Severin) / Don Edwing
Page 29 – The TV Commercial War – Al Durer (John Severin)
Page 34 – It All Depends Upon the Point of View – Pete Wyma
Page 36 – Horror House ad – John Severin
Page 37 – Specialized Retirement Cities – John Severin
Page 42 – Sound the Alarm – Ned Kelly (John Severin) / Don Edwing
Page 43 – If John Q. Public Hired a Press Agent – John Severin
Page 46 – The Dream Came True – (LePoer) John Severin
Page 50 – Cracked Fun Shoppe ad – John Severin
Page 51 – Subscription ad – John Severin
Back Cover – Eye Chart

**32, November 1963 (52 pages) (25c)**
Cover – Flyfishing – John Severin
Page 2 – Shoverollit ad – John Severin
Page 3 – Contents
Page 4 – Letters / Back Issues ad (#23, 25-27) / Three Paperbacks ad
Page 6 – Ads of Yore – Bill McCartney (Bill Ward)
Page 11 – The Rescue – John Severin / Don Edwing
Page 12 – The Evolution of Beauty Contests – John Severin
Page 15 – Hurry-Ups (house on fire) – John Severin
Page 16 – What I'd Like to be When I Grow up – John Severin
Page 19 – Inside Dope – Pete Wyma
Page 20 – Historical Scoops – John Severin
Page 22 – The Bully – John Severin
Page 23 – Cracked Future Antiques – Bill McCartney (Bill Ward)
Page 26 – Modern Chess Set – John Severin
Page 30 – The Duck Hunter – Bill McCartney (Bill Ward)
Page 32 – Letters from Bette
Page 34 – Cracked Fun Shoppe – John Severin
Page 35 – Getting the Gate in '68 – John Severin (This article, never reprinted, discusses what will happen to JFK in 1968 after the end of his second term. Ironically, the cover date of this issue is November 1963, the month JFK was assassinated.)
Page 40 – Horror House ad – John Severin
Page 41 – The Movie Monsters Strike – John Severin
Page 47 – The Horn – Bill McCartney (Bill Ward)
Page 49 – The American Space Base on Mars – John Severin
Page 51 – Subscription ad – John Severin
Back Cover – Cracked Invitation

**33, December 1963-January 1964 (52 pages) (25c)** (Cover says December, interior says January.)

Cover – Monk Painting Cracked Covers – John Severin
Page 2 – Lame ad – Bill McCartney (Bill Ward) Page 3 – Contents
Page 6 – Tarzan Goes Around the World in 80 Pictures – John Severin
Page 12 – Letters, We Have Letters – John Severin
Page 15 – Celebrity Credit Card Applications – John Severin
Page 20 – Shoot to Kill – John Severin
Page 21 – Newspaper Con Tests – Bill McCartney (Bill Ward)
Page 24 – G.I. Jr. – John Severin
Page 26 – Final Proof – John Severin / Don Edwing
Page 27 – Emotion Picture – John Severin
Page 30 – At Home with the First Family – John Severin (Another JFK article published during the President's untimely death.)
Page 32 – The Jumper – Bill McCartney (Bill Ward)
Page 33 – The Monster's Advertising Agency – John Severin
Page 39 – Cracked Fun Shoppe – John Severin
Page 40 – Trading Stamps Updated – Pete Wyma
Page 43 – Future Film Epics – John Severin
Page 47 – Encouragement – Don Orehek
Page 48 – Hurry-Ups (papa, papa) – John Severin
Page 50 – Horror House ad – John Severin
Page 51 – Subscription ad – Bill McCartney (Bill Ward)
Back Cover – This Side Up Sign

**34, February 1964 (52 pages) (25c)**

Cover – Steve Allen – John Severin
Page 2 – Cracked Famous Painting – John Severin
Page 3 – Contents
Page 4 – Letters / Back Issues ad (#24, 26-32) / Three Paperbacks ad
Page 6 – The Steve Allen Show! – John Severin
Page 12 – The Fairy Tale Follow Up – John Severin
Page 16 – The Pick-Up – John Severin
Page 17 – JFK Now and Then – John Severin (another JFK story appearing post-assassination.)
Page 20 – American Commercials in Foreign Lands – Bill McCartney (Bill Ward)
Page 22 – The Letters Celebrities Wrote to Santa Claus When They Were Kids
Page 25 – Cracked Rock 'n' Roll Museum – Bill McCartney (Bill Ward)
Page 28 – Hurry-Ups (daddy fell out) – Don Orehek
Page 29 – Millionaire Magazine – John Severin
Page 35 – Cracked Fun Shoppe ad – John Severin
Page 36 – Monster Sandwich-Board Men – John Severin
Page 38 – TV Medical Symbols

Page 42 – The Geisha House – Bill McCartney (Bill Ward)
Page 43 – Cracked Form Telegams (sic) – John Severin
Page 47 – Horror House ad – John Severin
Page 48 – Specialization Unlimited – Don Orehek
Page 50 – The Train Robber – Bill McCartney (Bill Ward)
Page 51 – Subscription ad – John Severin
Back Cover – Measles Come In Sign

**35, April 1964 (52 pages) (25c)**
Cover – Bullfighting Poster – John Severin
Page 2 – Top or Yo-Yo ad (real ad)
Page 3 – Contents
Page 4 – Letters / Back Issues ad (#27-34) / Three Paperbacks ad
Page 6 – Clay-Liston Fight – John Severin
Page 12 – The Cosa Nostra First Reader – Bill McCartney (Bill Ward)
Page 17 – Hurry-Ups (five dollar raise) – Don Orehek
Page 18 – Why Do Elephants Have Trunks? – John Severin
Page 21 – The Swordsman – Bill McCartney (Bill Ward)
Page 22 – Sylvester's Photo Album – John Severin
Page 26 – It All Depends on the Point of View – Bill McCartney (Bill Ward) (The first panel features JFK with glasses and a goatee added. Obviously, this was done to salvage the article, post-assassination.)
Page 28 – Their Dreams Almost Came True – Bill McCartney (Bill Ward)
Page 32 – The Sacrifice – John Severin
Page 33 – Cracked Fun Shoppe – John Severin
Page 34 – Notes – Don Orehek
Page 36 – The TV Strike – John Severin
Page 40 – Bullet Proof Car – John Severin
Page 41 – Horror House ad – John Severin
Page 42 – Personalized Wrist Watches! – John Severin
Page 44 – Board Her, Men! – Bill McCartney (Bill Ward)
Page 45 – The Big Wig Gig – Bill McCartney (Bill Ward)
Page 48 – McNasty's Great 3 Days Only Sale – Bill McCartney (Bill Ward)
Page 50 – Transylvania Life ad – John Severin
Page 51 – Subscription ad – John Severin
Back Cover – Cosa Nostra Sampler

**36, June 1964 (52 pages) (25c)**
Cover – Parachuting – John Severin
Page 2 – Tareyton Cigarette ad
Page 3 – Contents

Page 4 – Letters (Statement of ownership: Average number of copies sold: 138,463) (Photo of Steve Allen on his TV show with *Cracked* #34, probably the 1st televised appearance of *Cracked*.) / Back Issues ad (#27-34) / Three Paperbacks ad
Page 6 – Sylvester for President – John Severin (Sylvester is listed as being born in 1925, making him 39 years old. In subsequent reprints, his birth year is changed to 1929.)
Page 13 – Losers Can Be Choosers – John Severin
Page 17 – Transylvanian TV – Bill McCartney (Bill Ward)
Page 21 – That Wonderful Year 1032 BC – Bill McCartney (Bill Ward)
Page 22 – Cracked Takes a Look at Supermarkets – John Severin
Page 27 – Hurry-Ups (Sarge is pinned) – Bill McCartney (Bill Ward)
Page 28 – Don't Throw Away Anything! – John Severin
Page 30 – Easy, Exciting Ways to Earn Money in Beautiful Mexico – Al Jaffee (reprint from #6)
Page 33 – Hard-Luck Stories and How to Handle Them – Don Orehek
Page 34 – Cracked Fun Shoppe ad – John Severin
Page 35 – How to Understand Sports Officials' Signals – Bill McCartney (Bill Ward)
Page 41 – The Truth Behind the Press Agent's Items – Don Orehek
Page 44 – Fangmann's ad – John Severin
Page 45 – Civil War Facts – Jack Davis (reprint from #12)
Page 48 – Celebrities' License Plates – John Severin
Page 50 – The Bird House – John Severin
Page 51 – Subscription ad – Bill McCartney (Bill Ward)
Back Cover – Travel Stickers

**37, July 1964 (52 pages) (25c)**
Cover – The Beetles – John Severin
Page 2 – (Tip the waiters more)
Page 3 – Contents
Page 4 – Letters / Back Issues ad (#27-34) / Three Paperbacks ad
Page 6 – Cracked Looks at Dee-Jays – John Severin
Page 12 – Cracked Dee-Jay Hall of Fame – John Severin
Page 14 – A Guide to Modern Art – Bill McCartney (Bill Ward)
Page 19 – The Flower – Bob Zahn
Page 20 – Little League Everything – Bill McCartney (Bill Ward)
Page 22 – Black Magic – Bob Zahn
Page 23 – Cracked Fun Shoppe ad – John Severin
Page 24 – Cracked's Cracks – Don Orehek, Joe Kiernan, Bob Zahn, Vic Martin, Pete Wyma, John Severin
Page 26 – The Monster's Cracked Baseball Team – John Severin
Page 31 – Hurry-Ups (ship is sinking) – Bill McCartney (Bill Ward)

Page 32 – Illustrated Limericks – Jack Davis (reprint from #15)
Page 34 – Beatlemania – John Severin
Page 36 – Yoga – John Severin (reprint from #9)
Page 39 – Horror House ad – John Severin
Page 40 – Merged Comic Strips – Bill McCartney (Bill Ward)
Page 44 – Cracked World's Fair – John Severin
Page 50 – Recreation – Bob Zahn
Page 51 – Subscription ad – Bill McCartney (Bill Ward)
Back Cover – Beatle Wig Cut-Out and ad

**38, August 1964 (44 pages) (25c)** (Page count reduced back to 44 pages with this issue.)

Cover – Thumb Painting – John Severin
Page 2 – (hold your hand) Frankenstein photo
Page 3 – Contents
Page 4 – Letters / Three Paperbacks ad
Page 5 – Breakodent ad – John Severin
Page 6 – Throughout History with Home Movies – Ned Kelly (John Severin)
Page 12 – Water Shortage
Page 14 – The Lone Ranger
Page 15 – Hurry-Ups (last cigarette) – Bill McCartney (Bill Ward)
Page 18 – Everything of the Month Club
Page 20 – Hypnotism – Richard Doxsee (reprint from #6)
Page 23 – Help! Wanted – Garry Owen (John Severin)
Page 24 – A Visit with Crosby and Hope
Page 26 – A Visit to the Beach – LePoer (John Severin)
Page 28 – Land of the Free
Page 31 – Cracked Fun Shoppe ad – John Severin / Horror House ad – John Severin
Page 32 – Channel Femi-9 – John Severin
Page 38 – 4 Funny Ones
Page 39 – Cracked's Crack – Joe Kiernan, Don Orehek, Bob Zahn, Pete Wyma
Page 40 – Amateur Artists
Page 42 – Orders – John Severin
Page 43 – Back Issues ad (#29-36) / Subscription ad
Back Cover – Greetings from the Bronx Postcard

**39, September 1964 (44 pages) (25c)**

Cover – Western Gunfight – John Severin (1st appearance of the tragedy-tragedy shield.)
Page 2 – (area code) Pork Chop Hill photo
Page 3 – Contents

Page 4 – Letters / Three Paperbacks ad
Page 5 – Beastyrust ad – John Severin
Page 6 – The Skyfighters of World War 1 – John Severin
Page 11 – Surfing U.S.A. – Bill McCartney (Bill Ward)
Page 16 – 4 to Go
Page 17 – Cracked's Cracks – Vic Martin, Don Orehek, Jack Miller
Page 18 – The Art of Kissing – LePoer – John Severin
Page 21 – Monster Mirth
Page 22 – Judo – Jack Davis (reprint from #11)
Page 25 – The Moon Shot
Page 26 – Cracked Visits the N.Y. Mets – Charles Rodrigues
Page 28 – Rexell ad (reprint from #3)
Page 30 – The New Entertainer
Page 33 – Cracked Fun Shoppe ad – John Severin / Horror House ad – John Severin
Page 34 – Cannibal Chuckles – Charles Rodrigues
Page 35 – Vacation Guide to Outer Space – John Severin
Page 39 – Who'd She Expect…Richard Burton? – Bill McCartney (Bill Ward) (reprint from #4) (originally called "Who'd She Expect… Elvis?")
Page 40 – How the West was Lost
Page 42 – Hurry-Ups (mother will be here) – Bill McCartney (Bill Ward)
Page 43 – Back Issues ad (#29-36) / Subscription ad
Back Cover – No Hunting Sign

**40, November 1964 (44 pages) (25c)**
Cover – Eskimo on an Ice Cube – John Severin
Page 2 – (14-year-old girl) "West Side Story" photo
Page 3 – Contents
Page 4 – Letters / Three Paperbacks ad
Page 5 – American-Stanleyard ad
Page 6 – Social Nabobs of Boston U. – John Severin
Page 11 – Six is the Number
Page 12 – A Martian Writes Home from Earth – John Severin
Page 14 – Buggy – John Severin
Page 17 – Cracked's Cracks – Monroe Leung, T. Schock, Comagilao, Joe Kiernan, Don Edwing
Page 18 – Where Do We Go From Here? (reprint from #4)
Page 20 – The Big War
Page 22 – A Sunday at Coney Island – Bill McCartney (Bill Ward)
Page 24 – Cracked Takes a Look at the Transylvanian Teen Scene – John Severin

Page 29 – Picture This
Page 30 – Build This Beautiful Yacht – Bill Everett (reprint from #2)
Page 32 – Celebrity Baby Photos – John Severin
Page 34 – How I Saw Europe on Only 58c a Day – Bill McCartney (Bill Ward)
Page 37 – Way Out West! – Jack Davis (reprint from #11)
Page 39 – Cracked Fun Shoppe ad – John Severin / Horror House ad – John Severin
Page 40 – Charm Bracelets for Teens
Page 42 – The Frog Prince
Page 43 – Subscription ad / Back Issues ad (#31-38)
Back Cover – Don't Put Off Until Tomorrow What You Can Sign

**41, January 1965 (44 pages) (25c)**
Cover – Sylvester Flip Painting – John Severin
Page 2 – (I killed a lion) photo
Page 3 – Contents
Page 4 – Letters / Three Paperbacks ad
Page 5 – Ezoo ad – John Severin
Page 6 – Future Jet Set Fads – John Severin
Page 10 – The Public Links Golfer – Bill McCartney (Bill Ward)
Page 15 – Santa Claus is Comin' to Town – John Severin
Page 16 – Ad a Twist and it's New
Page 18 – Am I Really in Love? – John Severin (reprint from #11) (Originally called "How to Tell You're in Love.")
Page 20 – Personalized TV Sets – Bill McCartney (Bill Ward)
Page 23 – The Artist Selects his Model – John Severin
Page 24 – A Cracked Alphabet Book for Home Owners – John Severin
Page 28 – Cracked Fun Shoppe ad – John Severin / Horror House ad – John Severin
Page 29 – Still Smiles
Page 30 – Imaginary Fear and Complexes
Page 34 – Cracked's Cracks – Art Pottier, Don Edwing, Pete Wyma, Vic Martin
Page 35 – Bugged
Page 36 – Four for Fun
Page 37 – Bull Telephone System ad – John Severin
Page 38 – The Motel 40-Yard Line – John Severin
Page 42 – Hurry-Ups (fly in soup) – Bill McCartney (Bill Ward)
Page 43 – Subscription ad / Back Issues ad (#31-38)
Back Cover – Help Stamp Out Quicksand Sign

**42, March 1965 (44 pages) (25c)**

Cover - Sawing Down a Tree - John Severin
Page 2 - (hum a few bars) - War Movie photo
Page 3 - Contents
Page 4 - Letters / Three Paperbacks ad
Page 5 - Pesterfield Cigarette ad
Page 6 - Beatlezania - John Severin
Page 11 - Still Hanging in There
Page 12 - A Cracked Guide to Footwear - Bill McCartney (Bill Ward)
Page 14 - Animals in Advertising - John Severin
Page 18 - Dial 'A' for Africa - Bill McCartney (Bill Ward)
Page 19 - Farmer's Old Almanac - John Severin (reprint from #6)
Page 22 - Hut, Two, Tree, Four
Page 24 - Gamble Gambol - John Severin
Page 28 - Cracked Fun Shoppe ad - John Severin / Horror House ad - John Severin
Page 29 - Cracked's Cracks - John Severin, Don Orehek, Art Pottier, Joe Kiernan
Page 30 - Written Forms for all Occasions
Page 32 - Music Hath Charm - Bill McCartney (Bill Ward)
Page 33 - Great Scenes from Great Horror Movies - John Severin
Page 35 - Reel Laughs
Page 36 - Modern Mother Goose - Charles Rodrigues
Page 38 - Sticks and Stitches - John Severin
Page 42 - Shut-Ups (don't want to run) - John Severin
Page 43 - Subscription ad / Back Issues ad (#33-40)
Back Cover - Do Not Disturb Sign

**43, May 1965 (44 pages) (25c)**

Cover - Monster House - John Severin
Page 2 - (25c Toll Booth) car photo
Page 3 - Contents
Page 4 - Letters (Statement of Ownership: Average number of copies sold: 263,612) / Three Paperbacks ad
Page 5 - Fiendish Florist Telephone Delivery ad - John Severin
Page 6 - Tin Soldiers Brought Up-to-Date - John Severin
Page 10 - A Day in the Life of the Average Housewife - John Severin
Page 13 - Laugh Lines
Page 14 - Monsters in Everything - John Severin
Page 17 - Sing Along with Witch - John Severin
Page 18 - Push-Buttons Unlimited - Bill McCartney (Bill Ward)
Page 20 - Make up Your Own Story (reprint from #9)
Page 22 - Around the World in Hats

Page 24 – Childhood Games and Hobbies of Today's Famous Stars – John Severin
Page 27 – He's Really a Lone Ranger Now! – Bill Ward (reprint from #1) (Originally called "Why Doesn't This Ever Happen?.")
Page 28 – The Big Four
Page 29 – Cracked Fun Shoppe ad – John Severin / Horror House ad – John Severin
Page 30 – Do's and Don'ts (reprint from #8)
Page 32 – Cracked Cracks – Gene Myers, Ed Powers (John Severin), Art Pottier
Page 33 – Famous Scenes from Great Western Movies – John Severin (1st *Famous Scenes*)
Page 35 – Man's Best Friend? – Jack Davis (reprint from #11) (This was originally called "The Way That Movie Should've Ended.")
Page 36 – Monster Party – John Severin
Page 38 – Canned Music – Bill McCartney (Bill Ward)
Page 42 – Shut-Ups (baseball) – Bill McCartney (Bill Ward)
Page 43 – Subscription ad / Back Issues ad (#34-41)
Back Cover – If at First You Don't Succeed Sign

**44, July 1965 (44 pages) (25c)**

Cover – Cracked Newsstand – John Severin
Page 2 – (make sure he doesn't get away) sword photo
Page 3 – Contents
Page 4 – Letters / Three Paperbacks ad
Page 5 – Mexico – John Severin
Page 6 – Disconcerting Discourse on Discoteque Dances – John Severin
Page 10 – Still Smiling
Page 11 – Visible Objects to Come – John Severin
Page 14 – People Who Are Just Born Unlucky – Bill McCartney (Bill Ward)
Page 16 – Restaurants – Jack Davis (reprint from #11)
Page 18 – For Laughing Out Loud
Page 19 – Cracked Fun Shoppe ad – John Severin / Horror House ad – John Severin
Page 20 – If Famous Characters of Literature Were Alive Today – Bill McCartney (Bill Ward)
Page 23 – Great Scenes from Great World War I Movies – John Severin
Page 25 – 10-Day Posture Straightening Exercises – Bill McCartney (Bill Ward)
Page 27 – Cracked Cracks – John Severin, Art Pottier, Lennie Herman, Joe Kiernan, Pete Wyma
Page 28 – Impressing the Opposite Sex
Page 30 – New Books by Famous People

Page 33 – The Big Operators – Don Perlin
Page 34 – Boys and Girls Together
Page 36 – Cracked Visits the NY World's Fair
Page 38 – The Ed Sullivan Show – John Severin
Page 42 – Shut-Ups (Can I stop?) – Vic Martin
Page 43 – Subscription ad / Back Issues ad (#35-42)
Back Cover – Better Late Than Never Sign

**45, August 1965 (44 pages) (25c)**
Cover – Green Giant Island – John Severin
Page 2 – (8000 Box Tops) photo
Page 3 – Contents
Page 4 – Letters / Three Paperbacks ad
Page 5 – Panpm Airlines ad – Sigbjorn (John Severin)
Page 6 – Ultra Realistic Motor Motoring Sets – John Severin
Page 10 – What Do TV Characters Do After the Show is Over – Bill McCartney (Bill Ward)
Page 12 – Four Goodness Sakes
Page 13 – Sports Go Show Biz – Sigbjorn (John Severin)
Page 17 – Cracked Cracks – John Severin, Frank Baginski, Art Pottier, Lennie Herman
Page 18 – Movie Mirth Matinee
Page 19 – Cracked Fun Shoppe ad – John Severin / Horror House ad – John Severin
Page 20 – Architecture – Bill Elder (reprint from #12)
Page 22 – Status Symbols – Sigbjorn (John Severin)
Page 27 – Famous Scenes from Great Broadway Movies – Vic Martin
Page 29 – People Who Get on Our Nerves – John Severin (reprint from #16)
Page 32 – Daily Times-News-Sun-Post-Globe – Bill McCartney (Bill Ward)
Page 36 – Mighty Monster Laughs!!
Page 38 – Cracked Takes a Look at 1897 – Vic Martin
Page 39 – Report Cards – John Severin
Page 43 – Back Issues ad (#37-44) / Subscription ad
Back Cover – Insult Cards

**46, September 1965 (44 pages) (25c)**
Cover – All in Good Clean Fun – John Severin
Page 2 – (The Grass Needs Cutting) photo
Page 3 – Contents
Page 4 – Letters / Three Paperbacks ad
Page 5 – Gal-ixnay Cigarette ad – Bill McCartney (Bill Ward)
Page 6 – Rival TV Shows Cry U.N.C.L.E. – McCarthy (John Severin)

Page 10 – World War I – Bill McCartney (Bill Ward)
Page 14 – What Are the Celebrities of 1965 Doing Today in 1990? – John Severin / George Gladir (Ironically, this story predicts what will happen to The Beatles, with John Lennon predicted to be missing in 1990. Gladir was not happy to be so prophetic.)
Page 16 – Four Laughing Out Loud
Page 19 – Cracked Fun Shoppe ad – John Severin / Horror House ad – John Severin
Page 20 – Cracked Cracks – John Severin, Frank Baginski, Don Orehek
Page 21 – Sub Suburbia – Bill McCartney (Bill Ward)
Page 24 – The Gals are Here
Page 25 – Famous Scenes from Great Baseball Movies – Vic Martin
Page 27 – Charge it – John Severin (reprint from #10)
Page 30 – Right from the Horse's Mouth
Page 32 – Cracked's War on Poverty – Bill McCartney (Bill Ward)
Page 34 – Lose Weight by Exercising Right on your Job – John Severin
Page 36 – Rare Old Records
Page 38 – 3 Stories – Jerry Kirschen (reprint #15)
Page 39 – The Cult of Culture Snobbery – Bill McCartney (Bill Ward)
Page 42 – Shut-Ups (20 cents) – Rodrigliani (Charles Rodrigues)
Page 43 – Back Issues ad (#38-45) / Subscription ad
Back Cover – Psychedelic Eye Chart

**47, November 1965 (44 pages) (25c)**

Cover – Spies – John Severin
Page 2 – (Fish Diet) Monster photo
Page 3 – Contents
Page 4 – Letters / Three Paperbacks ad
Page 5 – Merry Old England Life ad
Page 6 – A Day in the Life of Soupy Sales TV's Fastest Shooting Star – Bill McCartney (Bill Ward)
Page 10 – Guide for Job Hunting on Madison Avenue – McCarton (John Severin)
Page 14 – Laugh it Up!
Page 15 – Cracked Cracks – Joe Kiernan, Ed Dahlin, Gene Myers, Lennie Herman, John Severin
Page 16 – Musical Strains for Brains – Bill McCartney (Bill Ward)
Page 19 – Cracked Fun Shoppe ad – John Severin / Horror House ad – John Severin
Page 20 – Vegas Vignettes
Page 22 – A Cracked Eye-View of Baseball – Bill McCartney (Bill Ward)
Page 24 – How I Rebuilt My Punk Lawn (reprint from #4)
Page 26 – Games, Hobbies and Sports

Page 28 – Thrills a Go-Go – Bob Schochet
Page 29 – Indorsements (sic) of the Future – McCarten (John Severin)
Page 32 – The Last Shot – Bob Zahn
Page 33 – Famous Scenes from Great "Dog Hero" Movies – Vic Martin
Page 35 – Towards Total Togetherness – Bill McCartney (Bill Ward)
Page 38 – All Weather Drive-In Movie – Jack Davis (reprint from #5)
Page 40 – It Never Happened But Someday it Might – Bill McCartney (Bill Ward)
Page 41 – Something to Smile About
Page 42 – Shut-Ups (drive so fast) – Vic Martin
Page 43 – Back Issues ad (#37-44) / Subscription ad
Back Cover – Cracked's Chinese Calendar

**48, December 1965 (44 pages) (25c)**

Cover – Which Hand has the Mirth and Merriment? – John Severin
Page 2 – (Barber Shop Quarter) Dave Clark 5
Page 3 – Contents
Page 4 – Letters / Three Paperbacks ad
Page 5 – Ravon Red ad – Bill McCartney (Bill Ward)
Page 6 – Politics Goes Show Biz – John Severin
Page 10 – Picket Signs of the Future – John Severin
Page 12 – Modern Cliff-Hanging Situations – Bill McCartney (Bill Ward)
Page 15 – Still Laughing
Page 16 – Throughout History with the Isolated Camera – John Severin
Page 20 – Snap Happy
Page 21 – Cracked Fun Shoppe ad – John Severin / Horror House ad – John Severin
Page 22 – Cracked Takes a Look at Skiing – Bill McCartney (Bill Ward)
Page 24 – How to Stop Smoking – Bill McCartney (Bill Ward)
Page 26 – The Banana Man – Jerry Kirschen (reprint from #15)
Page 27 – Cracked Cracks – Monroe Leong, Joe Kiernan, Frank Baginski, John Severin, Lennie Herman
Page 28 – School for T.V. Wrestlers – Sean Powers (John Severin)
Page 34 – Bottoms Up
Page 35 – Character Bumps – Joe Maneely (reprint from #5)
Page 36 – School Ties – Vic Martin
Page 38 – Billionaire – Bill McCartney (Bill Ward)
Page 41 – The Visitor in Africa – Bill McCartney (Bill Ward)
Page 42 – Shut-Ups (bottle of soda) – Vic Martin
Page 43 – Back Issues ad (#39-46) / Subscription ad
Back Cover – Danger! Beware of Stampeding Turtles – John Severin

**49, January 1966 (44 pages) (25c)**

Cover – Find the Mistakes on this Cover – John Severin
Page 2 – (Saber Tooth Tiger) Munsters photo
Page 3 – Contents
Page 4 – Letters / Three Paperbacks ad
Page 5 – Bunt's Catsup ad
Page 6 – TV Sports of Tomorrow – John Severin
Page 11 – Fun at Four!
Page 12 – Five Minutes Later – John Severin
Page 17 – Cracked Cracks – Lennie Herman, Art Pottier, John Severin
Page 18 – The Mystery of Palmistry – Bill McCartney (Bill Ward)
Page 21 – Famous Scenes from Great Artist-Type Movies – John Severin
Page 23 – Heart on Sleeve – Bill McCartney (Bill Ward) (reprint from #10)
Page 24 – Illustrated Slang – Chic Stone (reprint from #17)
Page 27 – This is a Laughing Matter
Page 28 – Stories of the Month – Angel Martinez (reprint from #17)
Page 29 – Rodeo Riders – Bill McCartney (Bill Ward)
Page 31 – Cracked Fun Shoppe ad – John Severin / Horror House ad – John Severin
Page 32 – Auto Improvements – John Severin
Page 34 – Back Issues ad (#42-48) / Subscription ad
Page 35 – Skydiving – Bill McCartney (Bill Ward)
Page 40 – Special Seats for Special Movies – John Severin
Page 42 – Shut-Ups (don't need haircut) – Vic Martin
Page 43 – Cover Mistakes Contest
Back Cover – Sylvester Wallet Photos – John Severin

**50, March 1966 (44 pages) (25c)**

Cover – Mini-Sylvester's Help Note – John Severin
Page 2 – Guess the Stars Contest
Page 3 – Contents
Page 4 – Letters (Statement of Ownership: Average number of copies sold: 266,338) / Three Paperbacks ad
Page 5 – Belnova Watch ad – John Severin
Page 6 – More Beatlezania – John Severin
Page 11 – Chinese Fortune Cookies
Page 12 – Monster Models from Every Day Life – Bill McCartney (Bill Ward)
Page 15 – Exclamation!!! – Don Perlin
Page 16 – Up-Dated Mechanical Banks – Sigbjorn (John Severin)
Page 20 – By the Numbers
Page 21 – It Happens Every Saturday Night! – Bob Schochet
Page 22 – Cracked Takes a Look at Basketball – Bill McCartney (Bill Ward)

Page 24 – The Joker's Wild – Bill McCartney (Bill Ward) (reprint from #5)
Page 25 – Cracked Cracks – Bob Schochet, Harreh, Monroe Leong, John Severin
Page 26 – The Comedy Trend on TV – Bill McCartney (Bill Ward)
Page 30 – Laughtime USA
Page 31 – Cracked Fun Shoppe ad – John Severin / Horror House ad – John Severin
Page 32 – The Origin of Nicknames (reprint from #3)
Page 34 – Cracked's Hall of Fame of Nut People
Page 36 – Cracked Rogue's Gallery (reprint from #5)
Page 38 – Future Automated Devices – Nireves (John Severin)
Page 40 – Shut-Ups (rocks) – Vic Martin
Page 41 – Back Issues ad (#42-49) / Subscription ad
Back Cover – A Comprehensive Guide to Longhair Chamber Music by Ringo Starr

**51, April 1966 (52 pages) (25c)**

Cover – In Case of Fire Break Glass – John Severin
Page 2 – (Remake Frankenstein) Beatles *A Hard Day's Night* photo
Page 3 – Contents
Page 4 – Letters / Three Paperbacks ad
Page 5 – 257 Country Music Hits ad – Vic Martin
Page 6 – Super Fan-Elan – John Severin
Page 10 – The Martian Report on Earth – Bill McCartney (Bill Ward)
Page 14 – Banks Unlimited or (Money Does Grow on Trees) – McCarty (John Severin)
Page 17 – Cracked's Do-it-Yourself Cartoons – John Severin
Page 19 – Caught in Traffic – J.T. Dennett
Page 20 – If the Comics Were Drawn by Famous Movie Directors – Bill McCartney (Bill Ward)
Page 24 – It All Depends Upon the Point of View – Bill McCartney (Bill Ward)
Page 26 – Story of the Month (I'm afraid) – Jack Davis (reprint from #11)
Page 27 – Famous Scenes from Great Football Movies – Vic Martin
Page 29 – Cracked Cracks – Don Orehek, Joe Kiernan, Art Pottier, George Kesner
Page 30 – The Silents Talk Back
Page 32 – Get Out the Vote! – John Severin
Page 33 – Back Issues ad (#43-50) / Subscription ad
Page 34 – Take the Giant Clod Test (reprint from #3?)
Page 36 – Look Befour You Laugh!
Page 37 – Cracked Fun Shoppe ad – John Severin / Horror House ad – John Severin

Page 38 – Flight 407 – Rory O'Moore (John Severin)
Page 42 – Shut-Ups (lookout man) – Charles Rodrigues
Page 43 – Find the Hidden Faces Contest!
Back Cover – Terror Trip! Game

**52, June 1966 (44 pages) (25c)**

Cover – Smythe at Sea! – John Severin
Page 2 – (Bull instead of turtle) bullfighting photo
Page 3 – Contents
Page 4 – Letters / Three Paperbacks ad
Page 5 – Squabb ad
Page 6 – The Flipsides! – O.O. Severin (John Severin) / George Gladir (*The Flipsides* was an animated cartoon produced by Krantz Films, the same producers of the 1967 *Spider-Man* cartoon series among other projects. Sylvester is one of the characters as a dimwitted janitor who is drawn with a large white shirt that covers his feet. It is believed to be an unsold series pilot, but has aired somewhere as I have seen it before.)
Page 10 – Four He's a Jolly Good Fellow!
Page 11 – Cracked Magazine Presents 65-Man Klonkball – Bill McCartney (Bill Ward) (One of the more blatant *Mad* rip-off pieces, totally similar to their "43-Man Squamish" article from *Mad* #95, June 1965.)
Page 14 – Russia Goes Madison Ave. – John Severin
Page 20 – Cracked's Fast Cut Out Comebacks – John Severin
Page 22 – Cracked Takes a Look at Spring Training – Bill McCartney (Bill Ward)
Page 24 – Teens All Over the TV Dial – John Severin
Page 27 – Cracked Cracks – John Severin, George Kesner, Joe Kiernan, Art Pottier
Page 28 – Cracked Trading Stamp Gift Catalog – Bill McCartney (Bill Ward)
Page 32 – We've Got the Laughs Right Here
Page 33 – Cracked Fun Shoppe ad – John Severin / Horror House ad – John Severin
Page 34 – Draw Your Own Conclusion – John Severin (reprint from #19)
Page 37 – Cracked Visits the Munsters
Page 38 – Ultra-Realistic Barbra & Ben Doll Accessories – Bill McCartney (Bill Ward)
Page 41 – The Bed of Nails – J.T. Dennett
Page 42 – Shut-Ups (duck call) – Vic Martin
Page 43 – Back Issues ad (#44-51) / Subscription ad
Back Cover – World's Greatest Deposit Bottle Returner Award

**53, July 1966 (44 pages) (25c)**

Cover – Super-Sylvester – O.O. Severin (John Severin)
Page 2 – Welcome to Marlboro Country – John Severin
Page 3 – Contents
Page 4 – Letters / Three Paperbacks ad
Page 5 – Troubleday Book ad
Page 6 – Dapperman! – O.O. Severin (John Severin) / George Gladir
Page 11 – Momrine ad / Three for the Price of One
Page 12 – What if There Had Been Guidance Counselors Throughout History? – O.O. Severin (John Severin)
Page 15 – A Little Off the Top! – BOJ
Page 16 – Take Me Out to the Old Cracked Ball Game – Charles Rodrigues
Page 18 – The Cracked Campaign Against Foreign Travel – Bill McCartney (Bill Ward) Page 22 – A Cracked Guide to College Reunion Conversation – O.O. Severin (John Severin)
Page 24 – Cracked Credit Cards – John Severin
Page 25 – Famous Scenes from Great Lawyer-Type Movies! – Vic Martin
Page 27 – Believe It-Nuts! – Jack Davis (Partial reprint from #13 with some omissions.)
Page 28 – The Cracked World of Children's TV Shows – Bill McCartney (Bill Ward)
Page 30 – Pill Dall Cigarette ad / Still Laughing it Up!
Page 31 – Cracked Fun Shoppe ad – John Severin / Horror House ad – John Severin
Page 32 – Special Clocks for Different Jobs – John Severin
Page 33 – Cracked Cracks – Jack O'Brien, Lennie Herman, Art Pottier, Joe Kiernan, Don Orehek
Page 34 – How a Rumor Gets Started – Al Jaffee (reprint from #7)
Page 36 – When the West Was Fun!
Page 38 – Products That Just Missed! – McCartin (John Severin)
Page 40 – Super Market Hospitals – Bill McCartney (Bill Ward)
Page 42 – Shut-Ups (Let's go home) – Charles Rodrigues
Page 43 – Back Issues ad (#45-52) / Subscriptions ad
Back Issues – Old, Old Record Labels

**54, August 1966 (44 pages) (30c)**

Cover – Monster Picnic – O.O. Severin (John Severin)
Page 2 – Big Baseball News Breaks in New York City
Page 3 – Contents
Page 4 – Charlie Weakling ad – Bill McCartney (Bill Ward)
Page 5 – When Teens Take Over Completely – O.O. Severin (John Severin)

Page 10 – Interior Decorating to Fit Your Job! – Bill McCartney (Bill Ward) (reprint from #23)
Page 12 – Sylvester, the Blaw Son of Glock – Charles Rodrigues
Page 14 – Four for the Laugh Set
Page 15 – The Sports Fan – Bill McCartney (Bill Ward)
Page 16 – Madison Ave. Word Game – John Severin
Page 20 – The Wide World of Laughs
Page 22 – Cracked Takes a Look at Night Clubs – Bill McCartney (Bill Ward)
Page 24 – O'Kreel's Once-in-a-Lifetime Sale – Bill McCartney (Bill Ward)
Page 26 – Reel Gone!
Page 27 – If Other Jobs Had the Pressures of Baseball – Bill McCartney (Bill Ward)
Page 30 – Cracked Cracks – Don Orehek, Lennie Herman, Jack O'Brien, Art Pottier, Pete Wyma
Page 31 – Cracked Fun Shoppe ad – John Severin / Horror House ad – John Severin
Page 32 – Develop a Sense of Humor – Carl Burgos (reprint from #9)
Page 34 – Cracked's 8 Great Ways to Beat the Heat – Vic Martin
Page 36 – Tipping (reprint from #10)
Page 38 – Welcome to the Strange World of Rodrigues – Charles Rodrigues
Page 39 – The Cracked Hollywood First Read – Bill McCartney (Bill Ward)
Page 42 – Shut-Ups (nice monkey) – Vic Martin
Page 43 – Subscription ad / Back Issues ad (#46-53)
Back Cover – Cracked Tickets

**55, September 1966 (44 pages) (30c)**
Cover – Hold this Cover up to the Light! – O.O. Severin (John Severin)
Page 2 – The Other Side of the Cover – John Severin
Page 3 – Contents
Page 4 – Letters / Three Paperbacks ad
Page 5 – Learn to Fix Color TV Sets ad
Page 6 – A Visit to Transylvania – Bill McCartney (Bill Ward)
Page 9 – Cracked's Footprint Forecourt of History – John Severin
Page 12 – Rock 'n' Rook Record Albums – J.T. Dennett
Page 14 – Four Film Swingers
Page 15 – The Day That Nothing Seemed to Go Right for the Ape Man – Fal Hoster (John Severin)
Page 18 – The "Strike Out" Strikes Back – Bill McCartney (Bill Ward)
Page 19 – Famous Scenes from Great Prison-Type Movies – Vic Martin
Page 21 – The Comparison Test – Vic Martin
Page 22 – Camp Kicey Doo-Bee – Bill McCartney (Bill Ward)
Page 24 – Redesigning Ads to Appeal to Children – John Severin

Page 28 – Cards to Get You of Jams – Charles Rodrigues
Page 30 – Cracked Cracks – Art Pottier, Lennie Herman, Jack O'Brien, George Kessner
Page 31 – Believe it or No! – Jack Davis (reprint from #11)
Page 32 – A Visit with Laurel and Hardy
Page 35 – 20th Century Coat-of-Arms – John Severin
Page 37 – Cracked Fun Shoppe ad – John Severin / Horror House ad – John Severin
Page 38 – If Wedding Cakes Really Symbolized Marriages – Bill McCartney (Bill Ward)
Page 40 – Screen Screams
Page 41 – The Terror Trip – BOJ
Page 42 – Shut-Ups (jump) – Rodrigliani (Charles Rodrigues)
Page 43 – Subscription ad / Back Issues ad (#47-54)
Back Cover – Bat Stickers

**56, November 1966 (44 pages) (30c)**
Cover – Highway Stripe – John Severin
Page 2 – Dean Martin photos
Page 3 – Contents
Page 4 – Letters / *Giant Cracked* #2 ad
Page 5 – Big Money in Imports! – Vic Martin
Page 6 – The Real Secrets Behind Agent 0007 – O.O. Severin (John Severin)
Page 10 – The Court Jester – Don Perlin
Page 11 – Future Late Show Programs – Bill McCartney (Bill Ward)
Page 14 – When Doctors Advertise! – Jack Davis, John Severin (reprint from #24)
Page 16 – Office Objects Laughs! – Bill McCartney (Bill Ward)
Page 18 – Reel Swingers!
Page 19 – Cracked Fun Shoppe ad – John Severin / Horror House ad – John Severin
Page 20 – Throw-Away Everything! – Bill McCartney (Bill Ward)
Page 23 – Famous Scenes from Great Monster Movies! – Vic Martin
Page 25 – Cracked Cracks – Bob Schochet, Jack O'Brien, Joe Kiernan, Art Pottier
Page 28 – The Yellow Page Rage – Bill McCartney (Bill Ward)
Page 30 – Dear John Letters of History – John Severin (reprint from #27)
Page 32 – Flicks that Click!
Page 33 – The TV Repairman Strikes Again! – Bob Schochet
Page 34 – Sports Smiles – John Severin
Page 36 – The Monsters Laugh it Up!
Page 38 – Hi-Fly-TV – John Severin

Page 41 – The Breaking Point! – Vic Martin
Page 42 – Shut-Ups! (tie clasps) – Rodrigliani (Charles Rodrigues)
Page 43 – Back Issues ad (#48-55) / Subscription ad
Back Cover – Dartboard Decision Maker

**57, December 1966 (44 pages) (30c)**

Cover – Pogo Sticks and Kangaroos – John Duillo
Page 2 – monster and Harold Lloyd photos
Page 3 – Contents
Page 4 – Letters / *Giant Cracked* #2 ad
Page 5 – Fleaber's School for Large Loot ad – Vic Martin
Page 6 – The Stones Keep Rollin! – John Severin
Page 10 – 4 Ever Funny
Page 11 – California Here I Went! – Bill McCartney (Bill Ward)
Page 14 – The War on Law – John Severin
Page 18 – Past, Present and Future Changes in Sports – John Severin (reprint from #24)
Page 21 – Cracked's Auto Safety Suggestions – Vic Martin
Page 25 – Cracked Cracks – Don Orehek, Jack O'Brien, Art Pottier, Lennie Herman
Page 26 – Cinema Chuckles
Page 27 – Cracked Fun Shoppe ad – John Severin / Horror House ad – John Severin
Page 28 – Photos That Have Been Cropped – John Severin (reprint from #25)
Page 32 – Celebrity Childhoods – William Hoest
Page 36 – Marvin of the Apes! – O.O. Severin (John Severin)
Page 39 – When it all Started (Ponce DeLeon ) – Jack Davis (reprint from #15)
Page 40 – Kings of Comedy
Page 42 – Shut-Ups (C-A-T) – Charles Rodrigues
Page 43 – Back Issues ad (#49-56) / Subscription ad
Back Cover – Fred's Steak House and Gas Station Menu

**58, February 1967 (44 pages) (30c)**

Cover – Hertz Tarzan – John Severin
Page 2 – (Raid, half the fun) photos
Page 3 – Contents
Page 4 – Letters / *Cracked Again* ad
Page 5 – Levenworth Mutual ad – John Severin (reprint from #19)
Page 6 – Vaughn-McCallum Roles of the Future – John Severin
Page 11 – Wonderful World of Wacky Laughs!
Page 12 – Cracked's G.I. Space Set – Bill Kresse

Page 14 – Updated Torture Devices for Catching the Witches of Today – John Severin
Page 17 – Five Fun Flicks!
Page 18 – Real Cracked Books – Vic Martin (reprint from #18)
Page 20 – Low Calorie Everything – Bill McCartney (Bill Ward)
Page 22 – "Camp" Comic Heroland – John Severin
Page 24 – How to Make Vehicles Safer – John Severin
Page 26 – When it all Ended (The Science Fiction Movie) – John Severin (reprint from #24)
Page 28 – Cracked Fun Shoppe ad – John Severin / Horror House ad – John Severin
Page 29 – Do-it-Yourself Captions – John Severin (reprint from #15)
Page 30 – Where the Action is!!!
Page 32 – Smiles from South of the Border – Oskar Blotta
Page 34 – The Flying Carpet – Golden
Page 35 – Camp is Champ – William Hoest
Page 38 – E.S.P. – Bill Kresse
Page 42 – Shut-Ups (AAEE-HOOEO!) – Nan Reik (Charles Rodrigues)
Page 43 – Back Issues ad (#50-57) / Subscription ad
Back Cover – Cool-School Stickers

**59, April 1967 (44 pages) (30c)**
Cover – Tiger Tamer – John Duillo
Page 2 – (Uncle Harry, manicure, brought the records) photos
Page 3 – Contents
Page 4 – Letters / *Cracked Again* ad
Page 5 – AT&TT ad – Vic Martin
Page 6 – Customized Career Cars – John Severin
Page 10 – The Swingers Set
Page 11 – The Ape Man in a Hurry
Page 13 – Cracked Looks at Old-Time Songs – Oswaldo Laino (reprint from #21)
Page 14 – Monsters in the News – John Severin
Page 16 – Super Heroes A-Round the World – William Hoest / George Gladir
Page 20 – If Picture Postcards Told the Truth! – John Severin
Page 22 – Cracked Takes a Look at Football – Vic Martin
Page 24 – Laurel and Hardy's Wacky World of Fun!
Page 26 – Blotta's Back Again! – Oskar Blotta
Page 27 – Room 5C – Sigbjorn (John Severin)
Page 31 – Four Smiles Only
Page 32 – Famous Scenes from Great Indian-Type Movies! – Vic Martin

Page 33 – Cracked Fun Shoppe ad – John Severin / Horror House ad – John Severin
Page 34 – The Hottest Questions in Basketball – Bill McCartney (Bill Ward)
Page 37 – If Colleges Advertised – John Severin
Page 42 – Shut-Ups! (erector set) – Arthur Knockwurst (Charles Rodrigues)
Page 43 – Back Issues ad (#51-58) / Subscription ad
Back Cover – Car Window Stickers

**60, May 1967 (44 pages) (30c)**
Cover – Danger – Look at Back Cover at Your Own Risk!
Page 2 – (Turtle, Fogging up) photos (one is from *The Reptile*)
Page 3 – Contents
Page 4 – Letters (Statement of Ownership: Average number of copies sold: 264,459) / Four Paperbacks ad
Page 5 – Draypuss Fund Inc. ad – Vic Martin
Page 6 – The Same Shows as Performed on TV & Radio – John Severin
Page 10 – A Tourist's Guide to Transylvania – Vic Martin
Page 15 – Shut-Ups (correct time) – Nelson Varicose (Charles Rodrigues)
Page 16 – Sonny & Cher Fashions Throughout History – O.O. Severin (John Severin)
Page 19 – Famous Scenes from Great Doctor Movies – Vic Martin
Page 20 – The Couples – John Severin
Page 22 – Dizzy Dissection of the Discotheque Disease! – Don Orehek
Page 24 – Super Hero Hall of Fame – O.O. Severin (John Severin) Page 28 – Lights Camera Action! – John Severin
Page 29 – Cracked Fun Shoppe ad – John Severin / Horror House ad – John Severin
Page 30 – A Glossary of Cracked Definitions – LePeor (John Severin) (reprint from #29)
Page 33 – Four Socko Smiles
Page 34 – Cracked's Intelligence Test (reprint from #15)
Page 37 – The Bard of Madison Avenue – John Langton
Page 39 – If Different Personalities Played Tarzan – John Severin
Page 43 – Back Issues ad (#52-59) / Subscription ad
Back Cover – Buy this Magazine…Or Else! – John Severin

**61, July 1967 (44 pages) (30c)**
Cover – Contents – John Severin (This is the first cover to state "Something Funny is Going on Here!)
Page 2 – (Simon Sez, discouraging, did you ever work) photos (one from *Wild Angels*)
Page 3 – Contents

Page 4 – Letters / Four Paperbacks ad
Page 5 – Snooper Academy ad – Bill McCartney (Bill Ward)
Page 6 – Movie Roles for Actors Who Plan to go into Politics! – John Severin
Page 10 – Take the Cracked Sports Test! – Bill McCartney (Bill Ward)
Page 12 – Gasoline Casinos – Don Orehek
Page 15 – Boy, Did you Get a Funny Number!
Page 16 – Specialized Buildings – Oskar Blotta
Page 19 – The Cigarette Commercial! – John Severin
Page 20 – Highway Signs by the Numbers!
Page 22 – A Cracked's-Eye View of Paris! – Bill Everett (reprint from #23)
Page 24 – Snide Guide to Camping – John Severin
Page 28 – The Ed Sullenpan Show! – John Langton
Page 29 – Cracked Fun Shoppe ad – John Severin / Horror House ad – John Severin
Page 30 – Great Lovers of Fiction – Oswaldo Laino (reprint from #21)
Page 32 – Ads and Animals!
Page 34 – Inflation – Bill McCartney (Bill Ward)
Page 37 – The Nuts are Here!
Page 38 – When Today's Animal Stars Begin to Fade! – William Hoest
Page 42 – Shut-Ups! (40) – Duke Mantee (Charles Rodrigues)
Page 43 – Subscription ad / Back Issues ad (#53-60)
Back Cover – Batty Buttons

**62, August 1967 (44 pages) (30c)**

Cover – Feamish's Mixed Nuts – O.O. Severin (John Severin)
Page 2 – (Formula didn't work, looking for trouble) photos (one from *For a Few Dollars More*)
Page 3 – Contents
Page 4 – Letters / Subscription ad
Page 5 – ATT&T ad
Page 6 – Der Black Und Blue Max – O.O. Severin (John Severin)
Page 10 – The Nutty Traffic Jam Pickle – Bill McCartney (Bill Ward)
Page 14 – Annoy Your Friends – John Severin (reprint from #28)
Page 17 – Make Mine Well Done! – John Langton
Page 18 – Hip Happenings
Page 19 – Future Specialized Banks – Arnoldo Franchioni
Page 22 – Mother Goose Confidential – John Severin (reprint from #29)
Page 24 – The Status Symbol Rat Race – O.O. Severin (John Severin)
Page 28 – Guns and Gags for Hire!
Page 30 – Merit Badges for Everyone – Tony Tallarico
Page 31 – Cracked Fun Shoppe ad – John Severin / Horror House ad – John Severin

Page 32 – Big Business of Little League – Tony Tallarico
Page 38 – TV Titles
Page 42 – Shut-Ups! (Running Deer) – Charles Rodrigues
Page 43 – Four Annuals (*Biggest* 1, 2; *Giant* 1, 2) / Four Paperbacks / Back Issues ad (#54 -61)
Back Cover – Travel Stickers – Tony Tallarico

**63, September 1967 (44 pages) (30c)**
Cover – Busted Hammer, Nails and Fingers – John Severin
Page 2 – (Albert, Jerry) photos
Page 3 – Contents
Page 4 – Letters / Subscription ad
Page 5 – Lame ad – Bill McCartney (Bill Ward)
Page 6 – Crime on Prime Time – Vic Martin
Page 10 – Look! Four Kooks!
Page 11 – The Emergency Landing – O.O. Severin (John Severin)
Page 14 – Famous Scenes from Great Jungle-Type Movies – Bwana Langton (John Langton)
Page 15 – A Cracked Look at Photography – O.O. Severin (John Severin)
Page 20 – Metropolis the Slave – Arnoldo Franchioni
Page 22 – Cracked Map – John Langton
Page 24 – Old Stars, Old Roles – William Hoest
Page 28 – Cracked Form Telegrams – John Severin (reprint from #34)
Page 31 – Cracked Fun Shoppe ad – John Severin / Horror House ad – John Severin
Page 32 – The Superiority of TV Over Movies – John O'Hara (John Severin)
Page 36 – Jungle Gems
Page 38 – Sylvester, the Baseball Fan! – John Langton
Page 39 – The Cracked Supermarket Primer – Don Orehek
Page 42 – Shut-Ups! (can't hold ladder) – Golden
Page 43 – Four Annuals (*Biggest* 1, 2; *Giant* 1, 2) / Four Paperbacks / Back Issues ad (#54-61)
Back Cover – Emergency Flap

**64, October 1967 (44 pages) (30c)**
Cover – Mountain Climbing – John Severin
Page 2 – "Honey Pot" photo
Page 3 – Contents
Page 4 – Letters / Subscription ad
Page 5 – Would Columbus Have Discovered America Etc.? – O.O. Severin (John Severin)
Page 10 – A Cracked Looks at Picture Phones – John Langton

Page 13 - Come and Get Me, Copper!
Page 14 - Take the Cracked Driving Test! - Tony Tallarico
Page 16 - Five Times Laughs
Page 17 - Air Cough-Cough Pollution - Bill McCartney (Bill Ward)
Page 20 - State Posters to Lure the Hippies - John Severin (Strangely, this article is signed "Elder" for Bill Elder, but it is obviously Severin's work.)
Page 22 - Prof. Whiffle-Bird Discovers a New Species - Tony Tallarico
Page 24 - Sylvester Meets the Mets - John Severin (This was written during a time when the New York Mets regularly were in last place. In just two short years, their fortunes would turn around and the Mets would go on to win the 1969 World Series.)
Page 28 - The Pirate Treasure Chest
Page 30 - The Jumper (reprint from #33)
Page 31 - If John Q. Public Hired a Press Agent - John Severin (reprint from #31)
Page 34 - Famous Scenes form Great World War I Aviation Movies!
Page 35 - Cracked Fun Shoppe ad - John Severin / Horror House ad - John Severin
Page 36 - The Condemned Man - John Severin
Page 37 - Specialized Trading Stamps Catalogs - Tony Tallarico
Page 42 - Shut-Ups! (can't stay up here) - Ellis Dee (Charles Rodrigues)
Page 43 - Three Annuals (*Biggest* 2; *Giant* 2, 3) / Four Paperbacks / Back Issues ad (#56-63)
Back Cover - Gorkel House - Tony Tallarico

**65, November 1967 (44 pages) (30c)**
Cover - Karate - John Severin
Page 2 - (107 days, two seconds, Gravy Train, Smokey) photos (one from *Satan Bug*)
Page 3 - Contents
Page 4 - Letters / Subscription ad
Page 5 - Pow U. - Tony Tallarico
Page 9 - Modern Tattoo Designs - Vic Martin
Page 12 - The Lone Rancher - O.O. Severin (John Severin)
Page 16 - Always a Rookie
Page 18 - T.V. Tally Ho Ho's
Page 19 - Ploys Against Noise - Vic Martin
Page 23 - The Dog House
Page 25 - Cracked's Do-it-Yourself Cartoons - John Severin (reprint from #51)
Page 27 - Get Out the Vote! - John Severin (reprint from #51)
Page 28 - 12 O'Clock High Jinks

Page 30 – A Note from the Teacher – Tony Tallarico
Page 32 – The Shade – Caracu
Page 33 – The Chicken Killer – Bill McCartney (Bill Ward) / Jay Lynch (reprint from #30)
Page 35 – Cracked Fun Shoppe ad – John Severin / Horror House ad – John Severin
Page 36 – Sunday Night Rating Battle – O.O. Severin (John Severin)
Page 40 – Bull Telephone System ad – John Severin (reprint from #41)
Page 42 – Shut-Ups (snowing) – Charles Rodrigues
Page 43 – Three Annuals (*Biggest* 2; *Giant* 2, 3) / Four Paperbacks / Back Issues ad (#56-63)
Back Cover – Ignore This Sign

**66, January 1968 (44 pages) (30c)**
Cover – Sylvester's Crystal Ball – John Severin
Page 2 – Four Annuals (*Biggest* 2; *Giant* 2, 3; *King-Sized* 1) / Three Paperbacks / Back Issues ad (#58-65)
Page 3 – Contents
Page 4 – Letters / Subscription ad
Page 5 – A Funny Thing Happened to Me on the Way to the Happening – O.O. Severin (John Severin)
Page 9 – When it all Started (blood pressure) – Jack Davis (reprint from #15)
Page 10 – What Might Happen if all Civil Service & Federal Employees Resorted to Work Slowdowns – Vic Martin (A mouse is depicted reading *Pow!* magazine.)
Page 14 – Graffiti – Tony Tallarico
Page 17 – The Conference – Lugoze
Page 18 – The Television Space Trend – Lugoze
Page 20 – New Highway Signs for the Speed Age – John Severin
Page 22 – Life's Dropouts are Getting Younger and Younger – Bill McCartney (Bill Ward)
Page 28 – Lights, Action, Camera!
Page 30 – The Garbage Can – Caracu
Page 31 – Tales for Tots – Don Orehek
Page 34 – Graphic Speech – John Langton
Page 36 – Cracked Fun Shoppe ad – John Severin / Horror House ad – John Severin
Page 37 – Super-Size Cigarettes – O.O. Severin (John Severin)
Page 41 – De Queers Rhinestone Co. ad – John Severin
Page 42 – Shut-Ups (five pounds of tea) – Charles Rodrigues
Page 43 – (hippies, Junior) photos (one from *Eight on the Lam*)
Back Cover – Bumper Sticker Bonus

**67, March 1968 (44 pages) (30c)**

Cover – Skiing – John Severin (The gag on this cartoon was originally done by Charles Addams for *New Yorker* magazine.)
Page 2 – Four Annuals (*Biggest* 2; *Giant* 2, 3; *King-Sized* 1) / Three Paperbacks / Back Issues ad (#58-65)
Page 3 – Contents
Page 4 – Letters / Subscription ad
Page 5 – Ocean ad – John Severin (reprint from #15)
Page 6 – The Establishment Goes Hippy – O.O. Severin (John Severin)
Page 10 – At the Barber Shop – Caracu
Page 11 – Annie Get Your Spacesuit – Lugoze
Page 19 – Blech Shampoo ad – LePoer (John Severin) (reprint from #21)
Page 20 – Laurel & Hardy Fun-o-Rama
Page 22 – Cracked Looks at an Outdoor Art Exhibit! – Walter Gastaldo
Page 24 – Take the Cracked Current Events Test – John Severin
Page 26 – Are you an Optimist or a Pessimist? – John Langton
Page 29 – Cracked Fun Shoppe ad – John Severin / Horror House ad – John Severin
Page 30 – Musical Strains for Brains – Bill McCartney (Bill Ward) (reprint from #47)
Page 33 – The Birthday Gift! – John Langton
Page 34 – Cracked Rides West!
Page 36 – Celebrity Christmas Wreaths
Page 38 – The Growing Complexity of Pro Football – Don Orehek
Page 42 – Shut-Ups! (big crowd) – Philip Garbage (Charles Rodrigues)
Page 43 – ("Keep Off the Grass") *The Good, The Bad & The Ugly* photo
Back Cover – This is an Unmarked Garbage Truck

**68, May 1968 (44 pages) (30c)**

Cover – Sylvesters on the Moon – John Severin
Page 2 – Four Annuals (*Biggest* 2; *Giant* 2, 3; *King-Sized* 1) / Three Paperbacks / Back Issues ad (#61-68)
Page 3 – Contents
Page 4 – Letters (Statement of Ownership: Average number of copies sold: 132,401) / Subscription ad
Page 5 – Super Composites – Lugoze
Page 7 – The Government Gambol in Gambling – O.O. Severin (John Severin)
Page 12 – More People We Can Do Without – John Langton
Page 14 – The Man with the Sign – Caracu
Page 15 – 4 Frantic Fun!
Page 16 – The Daily Atlantis – John Langton
Page 20 – Charm Bracelets for Celebrities – Arnoldo Franchioni

Page 22 – Cracked Examines All the Possibilities of Flying Saucers – Bill McCartney (Bill Ward)
Page 26 – Political Bubble Gum Cards – Bill McCartney (Bill Ward)
Page 28 – The Suicide – Caracu
Page 29 – The Day Kosygin Came to New York – Lugoze
Page 31 – The Fun Seekers!
Page 33 – Throughout History with the Isolated Camera – John Severin (reprint from #48)
Page 37 – Cracked Fun Shoppe ad – John Severin / Horror House ad – John Severin
Page 38 – The Trend to be Pally with Tin Pan Alley – Lugoze
Page 42 – Shut-Ups (rocks) – Vic Martin (reprint from #50)
Page 43 – ("Play bridge") Hollywood Bowl photo
Back Cover – Giant Miniature Posters – Tony Tallarico

**69, July 1968 (44 pages) (30c) (last 44-page issue)**
Cover – Two-Faced Sylvester – John Severin
Page 2 – Four Annuals (*Biggest* 2, 3; *Giant* 3; *King-Sized* 1) / Three Paperbacks / Back Issues ad (#61-68)
Page 3 – Contents
Page 4 – Letters / Subscription ad
Page 5 – The Growing Garbage Garble – John Severin
Page 9 – The Cracked Museum of Historical Trivia – Tony Tallarico
Page 12 – What Really Happens During the Filming of Television Commercials! – Arnoldo Franchioni
Page 16 – Foto Fun!
Page 17 – The Cracked TV Sports Primer – Bill McCartney (Bill Ward)
Page 21 – The Magician and the Man from the Audience! – Tony Tallarico
Page 22 – It Happened at the Cemetery – Caracu
Page 24 – Cracked's Gallery of Born Losers – Art Pottier
Page 26 – Future Automated Devices – Nireves (John Severin) (reprint from #50)
Page 30 – The Quick Quippers!
Page 31 – Black Thoughts – Caracu
Page 32 – If Comic Strip Characters Had to Face Simple But Realistic Problems! – John Severin
Page 35 – Cracked Fun Shoppe ad – John Severin / Horror House ad – John Severin
Page 36 – As the Trend Towards Violence Increases – Lugoze
Page 42 – Shut-Ups (Peanuts) – Ellsworth A. Sap (Charles Rodrigues)
Page 43 – (blue rattle, picket signs) photos (One from *The Court Jester*)
Back Cover – Crazy, Hip, Fun-Fad Bonus! – Tony Tallarico

**70, August 1968 (52 pages) (35c)** (Page count goes back up to 52 pages, but also price increases to 35c.)

Cover – Sylvester In Case of Fire – John Severin / Bill Lederle
Page 2 – Five Annuals (*Biggest* 2, 3; *Giant* 3; *King-Sized* 1, *Super* 1) / Three Paperbacks / Back Issues ad (#62-69)
Page 3 – Contents
Page 4 – Letters / Subscription ad
Page 5 – Snow Flake and the Seven Dwarfs – John Severin
Page 10 – The History of Early Flight – Tony Tallarico
Page 14 – The Celebrities' Flower Power – Lugoze
Page 16 – Dizzy Dialogue Ads We'll Soon Be Seeing – Lugoze
Page 18 – The Big Guns!
Page 20 – The Traffic Jam – Caracu
Page 21 – Truthful Ads They Wouldn't Print in Cracked – Lugoze
Page 26 – Cracked Visits a Skating Rink – John Langton
Page 28 – A Cracked Alphabet Book About Politicians – John Langton
Page 32 – Horror House ad – John Severin
Page 33 – How the Merger of Show Biz & Politics Will Affect Fan Magazines – Bill McCartney (Bill Ward)
Page 36 – Square Buttons for Squares
Page 38 – Lowering the Mental Level of TV Programs – John Severin
Page 42 – The Suntan – Caracu
Page 43 – The Pleasure is Ours!
Page 44 – Cracked Fun Shoppe ad – John Severin
Page 45 – N.Y.P.U. – Lugoze
Page 50 – Shut-Ups (haven't smoked) – Busby Berkley (Charles Rodrigues)
Page 51 – (racked with pain, 3 months) photos
Back Cover – Campaign Buttons 1968 – Tony Tallarico

**71, September 1968 (52 pages) (35c)**

Cover – Slippery Ink – John Severin
Page 2 – Five Annuals ad (*Biggest* 2, 3; *Giant* 3; *King-Sized* 1, *Super* 1)
Page 3 – Contents
Page 4 – Three Paperbacks ad / Letters / Subscription ad / Back Issues ad (#63-70)
Page 6 – Goryson's Gorillas – John Severin
Page 12 – The Cracked Guide for High Living Without Working – John Langton
Page 14 – The Charlie Chan Caper
Page 16 – Cracked's Think Tank Solutions
Page 21 – The Pick-Up – John Severin (reprint from #34)
Page 22 – The World's First Psychedelic Janitor – John Severin

Page 25 – A Swinging Good Time!
Page 26 – Cracked Visits a Doctor's Waiting Room – Arnoldo Franchioni
Page 28 – Take the Cracked History Test – John Langton
Page 30 – Cracked's Double-Take Signs
Page 32 – Horror House ad – John Severin
Page 33 – Cheeter, Tarzin's Faithful Chimp!
Page 36 – Up-Dated Mechanical Banks – Sigbjorn (John Severin) (reprint from #50)
Page 40 – Fields of Fun!
Page 43 – Cracked Fun Shoppe ad – John Severin
Page 44 – TV Protest Buttons – Tony Tallarico
Page 46 – The Day We Have Our First Female President – Bill McCartney (Bill Ward)
Page 50 – Shut-Ups (hang around) – Charles Rodrigues
Page 51 – (bein' fat, greasy kid stuff) photos
Back Cover – Cracked Business Cards! – Tony Tallarico

**72, October 1968 (52 pages) (35c)**
Cover – Sylvester for President – John Severin
Page 2 and 51 – No Darking After Park – Cracked Poster #6 (This is the 1st inside cover poster, but for mysterious reasons is referred to as "Cracked Poster #6")
Page 3 – Contents
Page 4 – Three Paperbacks ad / Letters / Subscription ad / Back Issues ad (#64-71)
Page 6 – Planets of the Creatures – John Severin
Page 12 – The Jazzy Jigsaw Jag – Tony Tallarico
Page 15 – Sports Oddities – Tony Tallarico
Page 16 – The Funnies in the Flicks!
Page 19 – Sylvester for President – John Severin (reprint from #36) (Sylvester's birth year has been changed from 1925 to 1929 in this and subsequent reprints.)
Page 26 – 11 Sure-Fire, Far-Out, Cool, New, Neat Ways to be Popular in College! – Joe Mead
Page 28 – Cracked Fun Shoppe ad – John Severin
Page 29 – How to Make Soccer Our National Pastime – John Langton
Page 31 – Six Annuals ad (*Biggest* 2, 3; *Giant* 3, 4; *King-Sized* 1, *Super* 1)
Page 32 – Cracked Switches on Popular Magic Tricks – Arnoldo Franchioni
Page 34 – Cracked Previews the New Groups – Vic Martin
Page 38 – Costume Party Type-Casting
Page 40 – Rent-a-Person – John Langton

Page 42 – Horror House ad – John Severin
Page 43 – Reel Gone! (reprint from #54)
Page 44 – A Modern Family Primer – Vic Martin
Page 50 – Shut-Ups (fear of dark rooms) – Charles Rodrigues
Back Cover – Tiny Tim Supports Sylvester P. Smythe for President (Tiny Tim photo)

**73, November 1968 (52 pages) (35c)**

Cover – Vegetable Soup – John Severin
Page 2 and 51 – Slow School – Cracked Poster #7
Page 3 – Contents
Page 4 – Three Paperbacks ad / Letters / Subscription ad / Back Issues ad (#65-72) – Jack Davis
Page 6 – Bonnie and Clyde! – O.O. Severin (John Severin)
Page 11 – Mini-Everything!! – Vic Martin
Page 14 – Four Fun Flicks!
Page 15 – The Hippies' Illustrated Dictionary – John Langton
Page 19 – Special Clocks for Different Jobs – John Severin
Page 20 – Rowan and Martin's Laugh-In – John Severin
Page 22 – Marx Brothers' Laff-In!
Page 25 – Six Annuals ad (*Biggest* 2, 3; *Giant* 3, 4; *King-Sized* 1, *Super* 1)
Page 26 – King of the Mafia – Art Pottier
Page 28 – Cracked Fun Shoppe ad – John Severin
Page 29 – French Foreign Legion – John Severin
Page 32 – Dear Sir!
Page 34 – Famous Scenes from Great Desert Island Movies – John Langton
Page 35 – A Picture is Worth 1,000 Lies – Lugoze
Page 39 – Protest Signs Unlimited – Joe Mead
Page 42 – The Day Bazman Almost Went Bats – John Severin
Page 44 – Horror House ad – John Severin
Page 45 – Cue Cards for Everyone – Bill McCartney (Bill Ward)
Page 50 – Shut-Ups! (stick-in-the-mud) – Vito Montigliani (Charles Rodrigues)
Back Cover – Goodnight, Dick! Goodnight, Chet! (Dan Rowan and Dick Martin photo)

**74, January 1969 (52 pages) (35c)**

Cover – Sardines – Nireves (John Severin)
Page 2 and 51 – Technical Difficulties – Cracked Poster #8
Page 3 – Contents
Page 4 – Three Paperbacks ad / Letters / Subscription ad / Back Issues ad (#66-73) – John Severin

Page 6 – Slums Can Be Made a Fun Thing! – John Severin
Page 10 – A Computer's Conception of Newspaper Headlines! – Lugoze
Page 13 – 5 Fun Grabbers
Page 14 – TV Scenes Worth Waiting For! – Lugoze
Page 18 – Stories of the Month The Psychiatrist – Vic Martin (reprint from #21)
Page 19 – Batzman Meets the Green Horned Bee! – M & O.O. Severin (Marie Severin, John Severin)
Page 25 – Seven Annuals ad (*Biggest* 2, 3; *Giant* 3, 4; *King-Sized* 1, 2; *Super* 1)
Page 26 – Cracked Takes You Back to the Year 1075 BC! – Bill McCartney (Bill Ward)
Page 28 – Nobody Knows I'm Chicken! – Art Pottier
Page 30 – The Monsters Laugh it Up! (reprint from #56)
Page 32 – What's in a Name? – Art Pottier
Page 34 – Horror House ad – John Severin
Page 35 – Go Fly a Kite – John Severin
Page 36 – The Luckless League – Lugoze
Page 38 – Cracked Fun Shoppe ad – John Severin
Page 39 – Dogs Magazine – John Severin
Page 47 – TV Commercials That are Wasted – John Langton
Page 50 – Shut-Ups (beans) – Charles Rodrigues
Back Cover – Optimists Anonymous (Pat Paulsen photo)

**75, March 1969 (52 pages) (35c)**
Cover – TV Orchestra – John Severin
Page 2 and 51 – Do Not Read This Sign – Cracked Poster #9
Page 3 – Contents
Page 4 – Three Paperbacks ad / Letters (Statement of Ownership: Average number of copies sold: 143,413) / Subscription ad / Back Issues ad (#67-74) – John Severin
Page 6 – Tiny Tim in Everything – John Severin
Page 9 – Reel Gone Goodies
Page 10 – The College Entrance Rat Race – John Langton
Page 14 – Simple Exercises for Simple People – Lugoze
Page 17 – Eight Annuals ad (*Biggest* 2, 3, 4; *Giant* 3, 4; *King-Sized* 1, 2; *Super* 1)
Page 18 – Cracked's Snappy Comebacks! – John Severin (Rip-off of Al Jaffee's *Snappy Answers to Stupid Questions* from *Mad.*)
Page 20 – The Day When the Under-30 Set Takes Over the Nation! – Joe Mead
Page 23 – The Marx Brothers Ride Again!
Page 24 – The Smythes – Losers Throughout History! – John Severin

Page 26 – Cracked Visits a Prison Yard – Lugoze
Page 28 – Future Commemorative Stamps – John Severin
Page 31 – Horror House ad – John Severin
Page 32 – Reducing the Violence in Movies – Lugoze
Page 36 – Cracked Fun Shoppe ad – John Severin
Page 37 – Sylvester P. Smythe Junior College Catalogue of Courses – John Langton
Page 42 – G.I. Laugh-In!
Page 44 – Randolph the Reindeer – John Severin
Page 46 – Family Albums of Celebrities – John Severin (reprint from #14)
Page 49 – The Evil Experiment! – John Langton
Page 50 – Shut-Ups (walking on air) – Vito Modigliani (Charles Rodrigues)
Back Cover – Goldie Hawn photo

**76, May 1969 (52 pages) (35c)**

Cover – "See Thru" Mirror Sandwich Board – John Severin
Page 2 and 51 – One Way – Cracked Poster #10
Page 3 – Contents
Page 4 – Three Paperbacks ad / Letters / Subscription ad / Back Issues ad (#68-75) – John Severin
Page 6 – When Other TV Shows Copy the Rowan & Martin Comedy Format – John Severin
Page 10 – Guess Who…? – Bill McCartney (Bill Ward)
Page 12 – Story of the Month (Whoa, Bessie) – John Severin (reprint from #27)
Page 13 – Rosemary's Baby Devlin – Lugoze
Page 16 – Why Does a Chicken Cross the Road? – Nellie Melba (Charles Rodrigues)
Page 17 – Eight Annuals ad (*Biggest* 2, 3, 4; *Giant* 3, 4; *King-Sized* 1, 2; *Super* 1)
Page 19 – The Completely Rebuilt Person – Vic Martin
Page 22 – A Kook Look at Sports
Page 24 – Cautionary Labels for Teenage Products – John Severin
Page 26 – Cracked Looks at Fishing – Vic Martin
Page 28 – Cracked Fun Shoppe ad – John Severin
Page 29 – 'Enry 'Iggins of Scotland Yard – John Severin (reprint from #5)
Page 32 – The Day Comic Strip Characters Got up on the Wrong Side of Bed – John Severin
Page 35 – Hudd & Dini (painted wall) – Vic Martin (1st *Hudd & Dini*)
Page 37 – Horror House ad – John Severin
Page 38 – The Cracked Travel Primer – Tony Tallarico
Page 42 – New Prizes for Breakfast Cereals – John Langton

Page 44 – Cracked Looks at Dating – Bill McCartney (Bill Ward) (This article bears a strong resemblance to Dave Berg's *Lighter Side* feature in *Mad*.)
Page 48 – Celebrity Cookbooks – John Severin
Page 50 – Shut-Ups (martini) – Cosi Van Tutti (Charles Rodrigues)
Back Cover – "See! Mom always did like him best!" (Tommy Smothers photo)

**77, July 1969 (52 pages) (35c)**
Cover – Sir Sylvester Newton Bonked by a "C" – John Severin
Page 2 and 51 – Fine, For Littering – Cracked Poster #11
Page 3 – Contents
Page 4 – *Cracked Again* ad / Letters / Subscription ad / Back Issues ad (#69-76) – Joe Maneely
Page 6 – Tall Story – John Severin
Page 11 – Hudd & Dini (missing key) – Vic Martin
Page 12 – Report Cards for Everybody – Lugoze
Page 14 – The Quickest Fun in the West
Page 17 – The Parakeet – John Severin
Page 18 – Drive-In Everything – John Langton
Page 20 – The Losingest Family in History! – John Severin
Page 23 – Eight Annuals ad (*Biggest* 2, 3, 4; *Giant* 3, 4; *King-Sized* 1, 2; *Super* 1)
Page 24 – A Cracked Look at Desert Islands – Lugoze
Page 26 – Cracked Visits a Restaurant –Vic Martin
Page 28 – "Whaddayacallits?" A New Cracked Game – Joe Mead
Page 31 – Cracked Fun Shoppe ad – John Severin (1st appearance of the *Cracked* Blow-Up Poster)
Page 32 – Phone Services for Tots and Teens – John Severin (reprint from #28)
Page 37 – Horror House ad – John Severin
Page 38 – The Dumb-Dumb People – Lugoze
Page 40 – Awards for School Kids – Bill McCartney (Bill Ward)
Page 44 – How to Become a Comedy Writer – John Severin
Page 46 – Oh, Those Oh-So-Long Lines – John Langton
Page 50 – Shut-Ups (Ladies first) – Rodrigliani (Charles Rodrigues)
Back Cover – Don Rickles Insult photo

**78, August 1969 (52 pages) (35c)**
Cover – Tossing the Christmas Tree – John Severin
Page 2 and 51 – U Turn Me On – Cracked Poster #12
Page 3 – Contents
Page 4 – *Cracked Again* ad / Letters / Subscription ad / Back Issues ad (#70-77) – Jack Davis

Page 6 – Bullet – John Severin
Page 11 – The Generation Gap!
Page 12 – Cracked's Crazy Comebacks – John Langton
Page 14 – Now They're Hi-Jacking Everything! – Vic Martin
Page 17 – Insult Cards for All Occasions – Bill McCartney (Bill Ward)
Page 20 – School for Baby Sitters – Vic Martin
Page 23 – Eight Annuals ad (*Biggest* 2, 3, 4; *Giant* 3, 4; *King-Sized* 1, 2; *Super* 1)
Page 24 – Sagebrush (various silent gags) – John Severin (1st *Sagebrush*)
Page 26 – Read Any Good Trees Lately? – John Severin
Page 28 – Cracked's Illustrated Quiz – Charles Rodrigues
Page 31 – Cracked Fun Shoppe ad – John Severin
Page 32 – Just What the Doctor Ordered
Page 34 – Yoga – John Severin (reprint from #9)
Page 37 – Horror House ad – John Severin
Page 38 – If Comic Strip Characters Had Summer Replacements – Lugoze
Page 42 – Cracked's Handy Guide to Self-Analysis – John Severin (reprint from #16)
Page 44 – Cracked Visits a Hollywood Motion Picture Studio – John Langton
Page 46 – Cracked Suggestions for Improving Mail Service – Bill McCartney (Bill Ward)
Page 50 – Shut-Ups (driving lesson) – Rodrigliani (Charles Rodrigues)
Back Cover – Oh, That Henny Youngman! – John Severin

**79, September 1969 (52 pages) (35c)**

Cover – Mechanical Horse and Indians – John Duillo
Page 2 and 51 – Important Notice – Cracked Poster #13
Page 3 – Contents
Page 4 – Back Issues ad (#71-78) / Letters / Subscription ad – John Severin
Page 6 – Help! I'm in the Pacific – Edvard Severin (John Severin) / Stu Schwartzberg
Page 11 – Chickie, the Fuzz
Page 12 – Old, Old Fashions for the New Generation – Johnny Langston
Page 14 – Fly Me to the Moon – Oskar Blotta
Page 17 – The Hippies' Coloring Book – Lugoze
Page 20 – How Madison Ave. Can Use Celebrities in Advertising – John Severin
Page 23 – Six Annuals ad (*Biggest* 4; *Giant* 4, 5; *King-Sized* 1, 2; *Super* 2)
Page 24 – That'll Be the Day! ($25,000) – John Langton (1st *That'll Be the Day!*)

Page 26 – Cracked Visits a U.S. Army Camp – Lugoze
Page 28 – Sagebrush (Sand! Sand!) – John Severin
Page 30 – The Girl and the Butterfly – Oskar Blotta
Page 31 – Cracked Fun Shoppe ad – John Severin
Page 32 – Destination Fun
Page 35 – The War on Law – John Severin (reprint from #57)
Page 39 – Horror House ad – John Severin
Page 40 – Medallions with a Message – Tony Tallarico
Page 43 – Hudd & Dini (Vacancy) – Vic Martin
Page 44 – How to Become a Writer of Westerns – John Severin
Page 46 – A Look at Correspondence Courses – John Langton
Page 50 – Shut-Ups (first men on moon) – Charles Rodrigues
Back Cover – Cracked's Ideal Couple Award for 1969 – *Laugh-In* photo

**80, October 1969 (52 pages) (35c)**
Cover – The Chicken or Sylvester – John Severin
Page 2 and 51 – Stamp Out Bald Peaches – Cracked Poster #14
Page 3 – Contents
Page 4 – Back Issues ad (#72-79) / Letters / Subscription ad – Jack Davis
Page 6 – Mission: Implausible – O.O. Severin (John Severin)
Page 12 – Are You a Dumb-Dumb? – Bill McCartney (Bill Ward)
Page 14 – What They Really Mean – Vic Martin
Page 15 – Everybody is Doing the Don Rickles Bit – Noel Severin (John Severin)
Page 18 – When Comic Strips Go Madison Avenue – Lugoze
Page 22 – The Man and the Beast – Oskar Blotta
Page 23 – Six Annuals ad (*Biggest* 4; *Giant* 4, 5; *King-Sized* 1, 2; *Super* 2)
Page 24 – Sagebrush (He sure hates rattlers) – John Severin
Page 26 – "Friends, Romans, Coutrymen, Lend Me Your Laughs!"
Page 28 – Cracked's Snide Guide to Motion Pictures – Bill McCartney (Bill Ward)
Page 30 – That'll Be the Day! – John Severin
Page 31 – Cracked Fun Shoppe ad – John Severin
Page 32 – The Cracked World of the Arts Primer – John Langton
Page 36 – Learning to Fly – John Severin
Page 41 – Horror House ad – John Severin
Page 42 – A Cracked Look at Typographical Errors – John Langton
Page 44 – Going Great Guns
Page 46 – Crime on Prime Time – Vic Martin (reprint from #63)
Page 50 – Shut-Ups (astronaut) – Charles Rodrigues
Back Cover – The National Geagraphic Magazine – John Severin (reprint from #13)

**81, November 1969 (52 pages) (35c)**

Cover – Fishing for Sylvester – John Severin
Page 2 and 51 – Panic Button – Cracked Poster #15
Page 3 – Contents
Page 4 – Back Issues ad (#73-80) / Letters / Subscription ad – Chic Stone
Page 6 – Churly – Vic Martin
Page 11 – Nutty Nicknames – John Langton
Page 14 – Commercializing the Moon – John Severin
Page 18 – How to Cool a Hot Problem! – Lugoze
Page 21 – Six Annuals ad (*Biggest* 4; *Giant* 4, 5; *King-Sized* 1, 2; *Super* 2)
Page 22 – Sagebrush (Z) – John Severin
Page 24 – Fun Under the Big Top!
Page 26 – Cracked Takes a Look at Night Clubs – Bill McCartney (Bill Ward) (reprint from #54)
Page 28 – More Whaddaya Callits – Joe Mead
Page 30 – Females Participating in All Sports – John Severin
Page 35 – Hudd & Dini (prison bars) – Vic Martin
Page 37 – Cracked Fun Shoppe ad – John Severin
Page 38 – "The Ex-Con Butler Did it in a Combat Zone!"
Page 40 – A Cracked Look at Dentists
Page 44 – That'll Be the Day! ($30 a week raise) – John Langton
Page 45 – Horror House ad – John Severin
Page 46 – Service-O-Mats of the Future – John Severin (reprint from #25)
Page 50 – Shut-Ups (cat dragged in) – Rodrigliani (Charles Rodrigues)
Back Cover – Freezca ad – John Severin

**82, January 1970 (52 pages) (35c)**

Cover – Sylvester's Newsstand Toothache – John Severin
Page 2 and 51 – Cracked's Super Socket – Cracked Poster #16
Page 3 – Contents
Page 4 – Back Issues ad (#74-81) / Letters / Subscription ad – John Severin
Page 6 – Ironslide – John Severin
Page 11 – The Cracked Guide for First Aid – Bob Taylor
Page 13 – Hudd & Dini (garbage cans) – Vic Martin
Page 14 – Daze & Knights
Page 16 – Deceiving Movie Titles – Lugoze
Page 19 – Six Annuals ad (*Biggest* 4; *Giant* 5; *King-Sized* 1, 2, 3; *Super* 2)
Page 20 – Don't Believe a Word of it – John Severin
Page 22 – Senior Citizen – Lugoze
Page 26 – Cracked Stars on the Moon – John Severin

Page 28 – Don Juan Lines That Just Don't Fit the Background – Joe Mead
Page 30 – Ship Shape
Page 32 – Handufactured Products – John Severin (reprint from #31)
Page 35 – Cracked Fun Shoppe ad – John Severin
Page 36 – Sagebrush (water) – John Severin
Page 38 – The Cracked Etiquette Quiz – John Langton
Page 40 – Trimming the Fat off the Budget – Bill McCartney (Bill Ward)
Page 44 – Horror House ad – John Severin
Page 45 – Nasty Neighbors – Caracu
Page 46 – Jogging Throughout History – John Severin
Page 50 – Shut-Ups (the water's fine) – Vincent Van Stop (Charles Rodrigues)
Back Cover – Leaving Hair ad – John Severin

**83, March 1970 (52 pages) (35c)**
Cover – Painting the Floor – John Severin
Page 2 and 51 – Hang-Out Tag Gag! – Cracked Poster #17
Page 3 – Contents
Page 4 – Back Issues ad (#75-82) / Letters (Statement of Ownership: Average number of copies sold: 137,676) / Subscription ad – John Severin
Page 6 – The Ghost and Mrs. Mire – John Severin
Page 11 – The Food People – Lugoze
Page 14 – Chip Shots
Page 17 – Six Annuals ad (*Biggest* 4; *Giant* 5; *King-Sized* 1, 2, 3; *Super* 2)
Page 18 – Sagebrush (fancy shooting) – John Severin
Page 20 – A Cracked Look at Supermarkets – Bill McCartney (Bill Ward)
Page 22 – Songs That Never Quite Made it – John Severin
Page 24 – Cracked Goes to Woodstock – John Severin
Page 26 – Adolt Education!
Page 27 – Ask a Silly Question, Get a – John Langton
Page 28 – Simulating the Thrills of Big-Time Sports at Home – Vic Martin
Page 33 – Cracked Fun Shoppe – John Severin
Page 34 – Guess the Question – Bob Taylor
Page 36 – The Dream Came True – LePoer (John Severin) (reprint from #31)
Page 40 – Ballad of the Squeaky Voiced Cowboy – Joe Mead
Page 43 – Horror House ad – John Severin
Page 44 – Astrological Horoscopes – John Severin

Page 49 – Hudd & Dini (mousetrap) – Vic Martin
Page 50 – Shut-Ups (deathly sick) – Charles Rodrigues
Back Cover – Join the Dodge Rebellion! – John Severin

**84, May 1970 (52 pages) (35c)**
Cover – Timber! – John Severin
Page 2 and 51 – "Turn-Off Poster!" – Cracked Poster #18 – Tony Tallarico
Page 3 – Contents
Page 4 – Letters / Back Issues ad (#76-83)
Page 6 – Ruin 222 – John Severin
Page 11 – Blind Date Phone Calls – Bob Taylor
Page 13 – W.C. Fields Laff-In
Page 14 – Fearless Forecasts for the Silly Seventies – John Severin
Page 17 – Six Annuals ad (*Biggest* 4, 5; *Giant* 5; *King-Sized* 1, 2, 3)
Page 18 – Specialized Record Albums – John Langton
Page 19 – Subscription ad – Bill McCartney (Bill Ward)
Page 20 – Frontier Dude Magazine – John Severin
Page 24 – Cracked Visits Washington, D.C. – John Severin
Page 26 – A Visit to Transylvania – Bill McCartney (Bill Ward) (reprint from #55)
Page 31 – Hudd & Dini (rodeo) – Vic Martin
Page 32 – The Growing Garbage Garble – John Severin (reprint from #69)
Page 36 – The Explorer, the Dog & the Bone – Oskar Blotta
Page 37 – Horror House ad – John Severin
Page 38 – Cracked Looks at Dining Out – Bill McCartney (Bill Ward)
Page 42 – Sagebrush (peace-pipe) – John Severin
Page 44 – Alice's Toy – Joe Mead
Page 45 – Cracked Fun Shoppe ad – John Severin
Page 46 – At Home with the Spiro T. Agnews – John Severin
Page 50 – Shut-Ups! (windshield wipers) – Rodrigliani (Charles Rodrigues)
Back Cover – Uncover America

**85, July 1970 (52 pages) (35c)**
Cover – Christening the Ship – John Severin
Page 2 and 51 – Copying Harms Your Vision – Cracked Poster #19 – Tony Tallarico
Page 3 – Contents
Page 4 – Letters / Back Issues ad (#77-84)
Page 6 – Krakaknuckle East of Hoboken! – John Severin
Page 11 – Hudd & Dini (boy scouts) – Vic Martin

Page 12 – Memorable Moments in Politics
Page 14 – Gadgets Go Hollywood – John Severin
Page 17 – Subscription ad – John Severin
Page 18 – Luck Is – Bob Taylor
Page 20 – Six Annuals ad (*Biggest* 4, 5; *Giant* 5; *King-Sized* 1, 2, 3)
Page 21 – The Status Symbol Rat Race – O.O. Severin (John Severin) (reprint from #62)
Page 25 – Medicinal Mirth
Page 26 – Tiny Tim's Wedding Reception – Vic Martin
Page 28 – The Frog Prince – John Severin
Page 29 – Cracked Magazine Presents 65-Man Klonkball – Bill McCartney (Bill Ward) (reprint from #52)
Page 32 – Sagebrush (Ah-Choo!) – John Severin
Page 34 – Cracked Looks at Television Viewers – Bill McCartney (Bill Ward)
Page 38 – The Painter's Fantasy – Oskar Blotta
Page 39 – Horror House ad – John Severin
Page 40 – Awards to Unsung Heroes – John Severin
Page 42 – Cracked's Travel Agency Tourist Attractions – John Langton (Johnny Langton is referred to as "John" from this point forward.)
Page 44 –First Prize, Man! – Joe Mead
Page 45 – Cracked Fun Shoppe ad – John Severin
Page 46 – Tom Jones – John Severin
Page 50 – Shut-Ups (long hair) – Modest Mussorgsky (Charles Rodrigues)
Back Cover – Cadillack – John Severin

**86, August 1970 (52 pages) (35c)**
Cover – Surfing Sylvester – John Severin
Page 2 and 51 – This Sign is Out of Order – Cracked Poster #20
Page 3 – Contents
Page 4 – Letters
Page 5 – Back Issues ad (#77-85)
Page 6 – It's a Weird, Weird, Weird, Weird, Weird World
Page 7 – Snappy Answers! – John Langton
Page 8 – Status Symbols for Dogs! – John Severin
Page 10 – The History of Inflation – Vic Martin
Page 12 – Cracked's Illustrated History – John Severin
Page 15 – More Crazy Comebacks – Warren Sattler
Page 16 – The Cornship of Oddie's Father – John Severin
Page 21 – Subscription ad – John Severin
Page 22 – Hudd & Dini (kite) – Vic Martin
Page 23 – Cracked's Fractured Nursery Rhymes

Page 24 – Cracked Looks at Hunting and Fishing – LePoer (John Severin)
Page 26 – Let's Travel Down Under…and Take a Cracked's-Eye View of Australia! – Bill McCartney (Bill Ward)
Page 28 – The Electric Shave – Oskar Blotta
Page 29 – Horror House ad – John Severin
Page 30 – Cracked Looks at Hospitals – Bill McCartney (Bill Ward)
Page 33 – Cracked's Time Capsule for the 1960s – Bill McCartney (Bill Ward)
Page 35 – Six Annuals ad (*Biggest* 4, 5; *Giant* 5; *King-Sized* 1, 2, 3)
Page 36 – Sagebrush (crossing the desert) – John Severin
Page 38 – When the Super-Jets Take Over – John Severin
Page 42 – Cracked Fun Shoppe ad – John Severin
Page 43 – Saturday Night in India – Oskar Blotta
Page 44 – How I Rebuilt My Punk Lawn (reprint from #4)
Page 46 – Goofed-Up Genes – Vic Martin
Page 48 – Consecutive Translation – Art Pottier
Page 50 – Shut-Ups (only girl) – Carlos Gerdel (Charles Rodrigues)
Back Cover – Excedruin ad – John Severin

**87, September 1970 (52 pages) (35c)** (Last issue distributed by Ace.)
Cover – Sweeping Up – John Severin
Page 2 and 51 – Warning! Reading This Sign May Affect – Cracked Poster
Page 3 – Contents
Page 4 – Letters / Subscription ad – John Severin
Page 6 – Butch Cavity and the Sundrenched Kid – John Severin
Page 11 – The Piggy Bank – Caracu
Page 12 – Cracked Looks at Telephones – Bill McCartney (Bill Ward)
Page 15 – The Man and the Bird – Oskar Blotta
Page 16 – The Fight Against Air & Water Pollution – John Severin
Page 20 – Sagebrush (hang on) – John Severin
Page 22 – When Prime Time Goes Gourmet – John Severin
Page 25 – Six Annuals ad (*Biggest* 4, 5; *Giant* 5; *King-Sized* 2, 3; *Super* 3)
Page 26 – Cracked Visits a Track Meet – Bill McCartney (Bill Ward)
Page 28 – Cracked's Fun and Puzzle Contests – Bob Taylor
Page 31 – Cracked Fun Shoppe ad – John Severin
Page 32 – Elvis Talks Salary (Like a Million!) – Vic Martin
Page 35 – Hudd & Dini (rocket) – Vic Martin
Page 36 – The Moon Ate a Big Pink Kumquat
Page 38 – Inflation – Bill McCartney (Bill Ward) (reprint from #61)
Page 41 – How to Make an "X" Movie Out of a Classic Film – Bob Taylor

Page 43 – Horror House ad – John Severin
Page 44 – Cracked's Record Reviews – John Langton
Page 46 – Specialized Parties That Fit a Magazine – John Severin
Page 50 – Shut-Ups (sports car) – Charles Rodrigues
Back Cover – Silver Spoon Magazine – John Severin

**88, October 1970 (52 pages) (35c)** (1st issue distributed by Dell.)
Cover – Life Guard – John Severin
Page 2 and 51 – (Hole in the Wall) – Cracked Poster – John Severin
Page 3 – Contents
Page 4 – Letters / Subscription ad – John Severin
Page 6 – Secretive Santa Victoria – John Severin
Page 11 – Hudd & Dini (D.D.T.) – Vic Martin
Page 12 – What Really Happened to General Custer – Larry Barth
Page 13 – Armpit Magazine – John Langton
Page 15 – The Blossoming Botany Business – Bill McCartney (Bill Ward)
Page 19 – Will Success Spoil the New York Mets? – John Severin
Page 22 – Armpit Magazine (part 2) – John Langton
Page 23 – Six Annuals ad (*Biggest* 4, 5; *Giant* 5; *King-Sized* 2, 3; *Super* 3)
Page 24 – Rare Olde Letters of History
Page 26 – Cracked Visits a Public Golf Course – Bill McCartney (Bill Ward)
Page 28 – "Make Me a Deal" – Bill McCartney (Bill Ward)
Page 31 – Cracked Fun Shoppe ad – John Severin
Page 32 – Laurel & Hardy Tell it Like it is!
Page 34 – What Are the Celebrities of 1970 Doing Today in the Year 2000? – John Severin
Page 38 – Sagebrush (stomping) – John Severin
Page 40 – Snide Guide to Camping – John Severin (reprint from #61)
Page 43 – Fruity Tunes – Vic Martin
Page 45 – Horror House ad – John Severin
Page 46 – The Selling of the Department of Defense – Bill McCartney (Bill Ward)
Page 50 – Shut-Ups! (exercise) – Pick and Pat (Charles Rodrigues)
Back Cover – Karate Magazine – John Severin

**89, November 1970 (52 pages) (35c)**
Cover – Shoes on the Wrong Feet – John Severin
Page 2 and 51 – I'm the Greatest – Cracked Poster
Page 3 – Contents
Page 4 – Letters / Subscription ad – John Severin
Page 6 – The Brainy Bunch – John Severin
Page 11 – Magnificent Mae West
Page 12 – If California Moved Into the Pacific – LePoer (John Severin)

Page 15 - Cracked Specialized Books of Etiquette - Bill McCartney (Bill Ward)
Page 19 - Paranoia News Magazine - John Langton
Page 22 - Lunch Time - Oskar Blotta
Page 23 - If Modern Personalities Had Written the Great Classics! - John Severin
Page 26 - If Other U.S. Wars Were as Controversial as the Vietnam War! - John Severin
Page 28 - If Dolphin's Day Every Comes! - John Severin
Page 31 - Six Annuals ad (*Biggest* 4, 5; *Giant* 5; *King-Sized* 2, 3; *Super* 3)
Page 32 - Baseball Hall of Shame - Bill McCartney (Bill Ward)
Page 35 - Horror House ad - John Severin
Page 36 - Sagebrush (what heat) - John Severin
Page 38 - Cracked Fun Shoppe ad - John Severin
Page 39 - Pow U. - Tony Tallarico (reprint from #65)
Page 43 - Hudd & Dini (Indu Magic) - Vic Martin
Page 44 - Television Roulette (*Mad* did this very same article at least twice before.)
Page 47 - If Everyday People Were Stand-Up Comics - John Langton
Page 50 - Shut-Ups! (exit slowly) - Charles Rodrigues
Back Cover - Ferd ad - John Severin

**90, January 1971 (52 pages) (35c)**

Cover - Counting Sylvesters - John Severin
Page 2 and 51 - Spiroman - Cracked Poster - John Severin
Page 3 - Contents
Page 4 - Letters / Subscription ad - John Severin
Page 6 - Mockus Smellby, M.D. - John Severin
Page 11 - The Revenge of the Bumble Bee - Bill McCartney (Bill Ward)
Page 12 - The Maxi-Mind-Midi Controversy! - Vic Martin
Page 15 - Cowsmoopolitan Magazine - John Severin
Page 19 - The Explorer and the Snowman - Oskar Blotta
Page 20 - Cracked Gets Greta Garbo to...Talk at Last!
Page 22 - Objects For Sale at a Hollywood Auction - John Severin
Page 25 - Tense Moments in Sports
Page 26 - Cracked Takes a Seat at Custer's Last Stand - Bill McCartney (Bill Ward)
Page 28 - Cracked Looks at Hotels - Bill McCartney (Bill Ward)
Page 31 - Miss America Contest! - John Severin
Page 34 - Cracked's Guess Who's the Sidekick Contest!
Page 36 - Horror House ad - John Severin
Page 37 - Initialists - Bill McCartney (Bill Ward)
Page 40 - The Cracked TV Sports Primer - Bill McCartney (Bill Ward)

(reprint from #69)
Page 43 – Cracked Fun Shoppe ad – John Severin
Page 44 – Sagebrush (filters) – John Severin
Page 46 – Underneath the Planet of the Apes – John Severin
Page 50 – Shut-Ups (good likeness) – Sigmund Froyd (Charles Rodrigues)
Back Cover – Aberican Bedical Association – John Severin

**91, March 1971 (52 pages) (35c)**
Cover – Fruit Salad Jackpot – John Severin
Page 2 and 51 – "Goodwill" – Cracked Poster
Page 3 – Contents
Page 4 – Letters / Subscription ad – John Severin
Page 6 – Airpot – John Severin
Page 11 – Nixon & Agnew in a Youth Bag – John Severin
Page 14 – Women's Lib Laughs – Charles Rodrigues
Page 17 – Popular Butterfingers Magazine – John Langton
Page 20 – You Know You're Rich When – Charles Rodrigues
Page 22 – How Hollywood Can Appeal to Today's Youth by Modernizing Old Movies – John Severin
Page 25 – Shaggies! – Larry Barth
Page 26 – "Farewell to the T.V. Cigarette People" – Bill McCartney (Bill Ward)
Page 28 – Talking Animals Take Over TV – John Severin
Page 31 – Horror House ad – John Severin
Page 32 – Sagebrush (buffalo stampede) – John Severin
Page 34 – Goldie Oldie Rock Yocks
Page 36 – Public-Spirited Ads – Bob Taylor
Page 39 – Cracked Fun Shoppe ad – John Severin
Page 40 – Sneaky TV Cigarette Commercials – John Severin
Page 42 – Cracked Looks at Another TV Commercial – Tony Tallarico
Page 43 – That'll Be the Day! (only $250) – John Langton
Page 44 – New Signs for Today!
Page 46 – When We All Move to Alaska – John Severin
Page 50 – Shut-Ups (true or false) – Sue Sioux (Charles Rodrigues)
Back Cover – Sellogg's Product 16 ad – John Severin

**92, May 1971 (52 pages) (35c)**
Cover – Spiro Agnew With Sylvester Watch – John Severin
Page 2 and 51 – Fly For Sale – Cracked Poster
Page 3 – Contents
Page 4 – Letters (Statement of Ownership: Average number of copies sold: 138,005) / Subscription ad – John Severin

Page 6 – The Yuch-hh Lawyers – John Severin
Page 11 – Give it Back to the Indians – John Severin
Page 15 – Hudd & Dini (garbage can magnets) – Vic Martin
Page 16 – Rollicking with Robert Redford
Page 18 – Coin Collecting Craze – John Langton
Page 21 – Six Annuals ad (*Biggest* 4, 5, 6; *Giant* 6; *King-Sized* 4; *Super* 3)
Page 22 – Famous Events as Seen on the Isolated Camera – John Severin
Page 26 – Cracked Looks at New York City – John Severin
Page 28 – New TV Tours By Other Stars – John Severin
Page 31 – Open the Door, Seymour! – Larry Barth
Page 32 – Cracked Previews the New Groups – Vic Martin (reprint from #72)
Page 35 – Horror House ad – John Severin
Page 36 – Getting There is Almost All the Fun!
Page 39 – Cracked Paste-On Tattoos – John Severin (reprint from #19)
Page 40 – New Gadgets for the Home (reprint from #25)
Page 43 – Cracked Fun Shoppe ad – John Severin
Page 44 – How Famous People Got Their Nicknames – LePoer (John Severin)
Page 46 – When the Woman's Lib Movement Spreads to the Comics! – John Severin
Page 50 – Shut-Ups (credit card) – Lefty Wright (Charles Rodrigues)
Back Cover – All Purpose Bumper Stickers for 1971

**93, July 1971 (52 pages) (35c)** (1st issue Bob Sproul published from Florida.)
Cover – Old Time Movie Stars – John Severin
Page 2 and 51 – W.C. Fields – Cracked Poster #21
Page 3 – Contents
Page 4 – Letters / Subscription ad – John Severin
Page 6 – Hi! I'm Johnny Cashew! – John Severin
Page 11 – Halls of Smaller Fame – Bill McCartney (Bill Ward)
Page 14 – Hudd & Dini (cannon) – Vic Martin
Page 15 – Cracked Fun Shoppe ad – John Severin
Page 16 – Snap! Crackle! Flop! – Vic Martin
Page 19 – Horror House ad – John Severin
Page 20 – Guess the Question – Bill McCartney (Bill Ward)
Page 22 – The Future Computerized of Sports – Bill McCartney (Bill Ward)
Page 24 – As Cracked Goes to the Race Track! – Bill McCartney (Bill Ward)
Page 26 – Six Annuals ad (*Biggest* 5, 6; *Giant* 6; *King-Sized* 4; *Super* 3, 4)
Page 27 – The Most Horrible Monster of All – Walt Lardner
Page 30 – Kings of Comedy (reprint from #57)

Page 32 – The Last of the Hollywood "B" Movies – Gray Morrow (reprint from #8) (originally titled "Pictures" not "Movies")
Page 35 – Great Scenes from Great Horror Movies – John Severin (reprint from #42)
Page 37 – Famous Scenes form Great World War I Aviation Movies! (reprint from #64)
Page 38 – The Big Guns! (reprint from #70)
Page 40 – A Visit with Laurel and Hardy (reprint from #55)
Page 42 – The Hollywoodization of Sopheeya Luring – Bill McCartney (Bill Ward) (reprint from #4)
Page 44 – Old Stars, Old Roles – William Hoest (reprint from #63)
Page 48 – Lights, Action, Camera! (reprint from #66)
Page 50 – Shut-Ups (drive-in movie) – Charles Rodrigues, Vic Martin
Back Cover – All Live! All Talking! Photos

**94, August 1971 (52 pages) (40c)**
Cover – Shadow Boxing – John Severin
Page 2 and 51 – This Poster Stolen From the FBI – Cracked Poster #22
Page 3 – Contents
Page 4 – Subscription ad / Letters
Page 5 – Loathe Story – John Severin
Page 10 – If the Help-Wanted Ads Mirrored Today's Inefficient Business World
Page 13 – Hudd & Dini (Agnew golfing) – Vic Martin
Page 14 – Exciting Games for Daredevils – Zackary Taylor (Bob Taylor)
Page 16 – Hiss the Villains
Page 20 – Some Cracked Franchises – Vic Martin
Page 23 – Horror House ad – John Severin
Page 23 – Sagebrush (extra precautions) – John Severin
Page 26 – Cracked Goes to the Hospital – John Severin
Page 28 – Sylvester Meets the Mets – John Severin (reprint from #64)
Page 32 – Famous Scenes from Great Jungle-Type Movies – Bwana Langton (John Langton) (reprint from #63)
Page 33 – Cracked Fun Shoppe ad – John Severin
Page 34 – Valentino Vibrations
Page 36 – What if They – John Severin
Page 40 – Take the Cracked Driving Test! – Tony Tallarico (reprint from #64)
Page 42 – If Famous People Had Listened to Their Mothers – John Severin
Page 45 – Five Annuals ad (*Biggest* 5, 6; *Giant* 6; *Super* 3, 4)
Page 46 – The Snowballing Callback of Defective Products – Bob Taylor
Page 50 – Shut-Ups (Can I sit) – Glenn Mukheryee (Charles Rodrigues)
Back Cover – Lily Tomlin photo

**95, September 1971 (52 pages) (40c)**

Cover – Raining Umbrella – John Severin (Cover is rip-off of cover of *Mad* #63.)
Page 2 and 51 – Keep America Beautiful – Cracked Poster – John Severin
Page 3 – Contents
Page 4 – Subscription ad / Letters
Page 5 – Ham 'n' Rye 'n's Daughter – John Severin
Page 10 – Cracked Looks at Mothers – Charles Rodrigues
Page 13 – Hudd & Dini (skeleton) – Vic Martin
Page 14 – Alice's Restaurant
Page 16 – Monster Greeting Cards – Don Orehek
Page 19 – Making the Old Songs Relevant
Page 20 – Great Scenes from Hollywood Movies if Shakespeare Had Written Them! – Bob Taylor
Page 23 – Famous Stars in Ads We'd Like to See
Page 26 – Cracked Goes to a Discotheque – Bill McCartney (Bill Ward)
Page 28 – Fhive for the Fhun it!
Page 29 – Cracked's "Silent Pages" Spot – Larry Barth
Page 31 – The Man & the Fly – Oskar Blotta
Page 32 – Horror House ad – John Severin
Page 33 – Letters We'll Really Be Looking For
Page 36 – Five Annuals ad (*Biggest* 5, 6; *Giant* 6; *Super* 3, 4)
Page 37 – One Morning in the Doctor's Office – Charles Rodrigues
Page 38 – Sports Smiles – John Severin (reprint from #56)
Page 40 – Heavy on the Horror, Please
Page 42 – The Smythes – Losers Throughout History! – John Severin (reprint from #75)
Page 44 – The Suicide – Caracu (reprint from #68)
Page 45 – Cracked Fun Shoppe ad – John Severin
Page 46 – Sincerely Yours, Sam Quarter – Bill McCartney (Bill Ward)
Page 50 – Shut-Ups (endless snow) – Sam Gross (Charles Rodrigues) (Charles Rodrigues commonly signed phony names to his *Shut-Ups* strips, but Sam Gross was an artist that Rodrigues admired and worked with for many years at the *National Lampoon*.)
Back Cover – Remember! Forest Fires Can Prevent Bears! – Russ Heath (reprint from #13)

**96, October 1971 (52 pages) (40c)**

Cover – Love it or Leave it – John Severin
Page 2 and 51 – Wanted Thumbprint – Cracked Poster #24 – John Severin
Page 3 – Contents
Page 4 – Letters / Subscription ad – John Severin
Page 6 – Today's Swinger is Tomorrow's Square – John Severin

Page 10 – Cracked Stereotypes – John Langton
Page 13 – When All Competition is Eliminated – John Severin Page 16 – Cracked Looks at Vacations – Bill McCartney (Bill Ward)
Page 19 – The Jockey – Caracu
Page 20 – Cracked Rides West! (reprint from #67)
Page 22 – Six Annuals ad (*Biggest* 5, 6; *Giant* 6, 7; *Super* 3, 4)
Page 23 – Success in Your Chosen Career – Bill McCartney (Bill Ward)
Page 26 – I Don't Care Who You Are – John Severin
Page 28 – The Growing Complexity of Pro Football – Don Orehek (reprint from #67)
Page 30 – If Comic Strip Heroes Had Hang-Ups Like the Rest of Us – Lugoze
Page 36 – Cracked Fun Shoppe ad – John Severin
Page 37 – Hudd & Dini (caveman) – Vic Martin
Page 38 – The Growing Cult of the Occult – Don Orehek
Page 41 – Horror House ad – John Severin
Page 42 – If T.V. Shows Were Combined to Make Hits – John Severin
Page 45 – Creating New Job Opportunities – John Severin
Page 48 – Keystone Komedy Kapers
Page 50 – Shut-Ups (king's dinner) – Julius Siezure (Charles Rodrigues)
Back Cover – Virginia Slums ad

**97, November 1971 (52 pages) (40c)**

Cover – Watering the Sidewalk Flower – John Severin
Page 2 and 51 – Ban Psychedelic Posters – Cracked Poster – John Severin
Page 3 – Contents
Page 4 – Letters / Subscription ad – John Severin
Page 6 – Escape from the Boredom of the Apes – John Severin
Page 11 – Four Annuals ad (*Biggest* 5, 6; *Giant* 7; King-Sized 5)
Page 12 – How to Tell If You Are An Adolescent – Howard Cruse
Page 14 – The Good Guys
Page 16 – Hudd & Dini (inflatable man) – Vic Martin
Page 17 – How the Airlines Can Save Money! – John Severin
Page 20 – The World's First Psychedelic Janitor – John Severin (reprint from #71)
Page 23 – The Awakening – John Severin
Page 24 – What to Do Until the TV Repairman Arrives – Don Orehek
Page 26 – A Cracked Look at the Beach – Don Orehek
Page 29 – Cracked Fun Shoppe ad – John Severin
Page 30 – Watermelon Jokes to End Them All! (Quite possibly the most politically incorrect feature to ever appear in *Cracked*.)
Page 32 – Footboxhockbasetennbasketgolfpoly – John Severin

Page 36 – Sagebrush (buffalo) – John Severin
Page 38 – The Cracked Annual Achievement Awards – Bill McCartney (Bill Ward)
Page 40 – Horrible Humor
Page 43 – New Celebrity Guitars – Vic Martin
Page 45 – Horror House ad – John Severin Page 46 – E.S.P. – Bill Kresse (reprint from #58)
Page 50 – Shut-Ups (spilled the beans) – Victor Modigliani (Charles Rodrigues)
Back Cover – Canadian Crud ad – John Severin

**98, January 1972 (52 pages) (40c)**
Cover – Cracking a Walnut – John Severin
Page 2 and 51 – Ignore Other Sign – Cracked Poster – John Severin
Page 3 – Contents
Page 4 – Letters / Subscription ad – John Severin
Page 6 – Those Old-Time Radio Serials or Ma Gherkins – She's Always in a Pickle – Vic Martin
Page 10 – You Know There's a Generation Gap When – Jared Lee
Page 12 – Mugging Minors
Page 13 – What People Would Do if they Banned Other Things Besides Cyclamates – John Severin
Page 16 – Horror House ad – John Severin
Page 17 – Training the Dog – Joe Mead
Page 18 – Cracked Looks at Dating – Bill McCartney (Bill Ward) (reprint from #76)
Page 22 – Ladie's Day
Page 23 – The Completely Rebuilt Person – Vic Martin (reprint from #76)
Page 26 – Cracked Looks at TV Commercials – Bill McCartney (Bill Ward)
Page 28 – How Wise are Wise Old Proverbs? – Vic Martin
Page 32 – Four Annuals ad (*Biggest* 5, 6; *Giant* 7; *King-Sized* 5)
Page 33 – Hudd & Dini (Vacancy) – Vic Martin (reprint from #79)
Page 34 – The Owlhoots
Page 36 – Sagebrush (aircraft carrier) – John Severin
Page 38 – The Waiter and the Customers – Vic Martin
Page 39 – What's it Going to Cost in 1980? – John Severin
Page 41 – Cracked Fun Shoppe ad – John Severin
Page 42 – The Dumb-Dumb People! – Lugoze (reprint from #77)
Page 44 – Monsterous Merriment
Page 46 – Los Angeles Balance – John Severin
Page 50 – Shut-Ups (unlimited talent) – Sam Gross Jr. (Charles Rodrigues)
Back Cover – Freezca ad – John Severin (reprint from #81)

**99, March 1972 (52 pages) (40c)**

Cover – We Are Not Mad – John Severin (1st Alfred E. Neuman cover)
Page 2 and 51 – Support Non Violence or We'll Kill Ya!!! – Cracked Poster – John Severin
Page 3 – Contents
Page 4 – Letters / Subscription ad
Page 5 – Will-Odd – John Severin
Page 11 – Four Annuals ad (*Biggest* 5, 6; *Giant* 7; *King-Sized* 5)
Page 12 – Telephone Madness – Jared Lee
Page 15 – Horror House ad – John Severin
Page 16 – The War on Law – John Severin (reprint from #57)
Page 20 – Armed Farces
Page 23 – The Cracked Supermarket Primer – Don Orehek (reprint from #63)
Page 26 – Nixon's Next Job – John Severin
Page 28 – Laurel & Hardy Fun-o-Rama (reprint from #67)
Page 30 – You Know You're Not a Kid Anymore When – Jared Lee
Page 32 – Sagebrush (Gulp!) – John Severin
Page 34 – Cracked Interviews the Hamburger King – John Severin (1st *Nanny Dickering Interview*)
Page 38 – Did You Ever Have One of Those Days? – Charles Rodrigues
Page 40 – Cracked Looks at Department Stores – Bob Taylor
Page 42 – Horror House ad – John Severin
Page 43 – Hudd & Dini (swimming pool) – Vic Martin
Page 44 – The Johnny Dick Griffson Show – John Severin
Page 49 – Reel Gone! (reprint from #54)
Page 50 – Shut-Ups (No cavities) – Sam Gross Jr. (Charles Rodrigues)
Back Cover – Find the Mistakes – John Severin

**100, May 1972 (52 pages) (40c)**

Cover – Genuine China – John Severin / Bob Sproul
Page 2 and 51 – Pollution – Cracked Poster
Page 3 – Contents
Page 4 – Letters (Statement of Ownership: Average number of copies sold: 133,997) / Subscription ad
Page 5 – O'Meagre Man – John Severin
Page 11 – The Monsters Laugh it Up! (reprint from #56)
Page 13 – Nixon, Chou Ho-Ho-Ho – Nireves (John Severin)
Page 16 – The History of Sports – Don Orehek
Page 19 – The Rescue? – Art Pottier
Page 20 – Horror House ad – John Severin
Page 21 – When Willard-Type Movies Take Over Hollywood – Nireves (John Severin)

Page 24 – '72 Political Pins – Jim Ivey
Page 27 – The Funnies in the Flicks! (reprint from #72)
Page 30 – The Hippies' Illustrated Dictionary – John Langton (reprint from #73)
Page 34 – Cracked Looks at the News – Jack Barrett
Page 36 – Five Annuals ad (*Biggest* 5, 6, 7; *Giant* 7; *King-Sized* 5)
Page 37 – Hudd & Dini (lifeguards) – Vic Martin
Page 38 – The New Mod Army – Bill McCartney (Bill Ward)
Page 42 – The Snell Test – John Langton
Page 43 – When Every One Called Him Dickie
Page 45 – Horror House ad – John Severin
Page 46 – The Day When the Under-30 Set Takes Over the Nation!
Page 49 – The Pick-Up – John Severin (reprint from #34)
Page 50 – Shut-Ups (snooping around) – Sam Gross Jr. (Charles Rodrigues)
Back Cover – The Discovery – Stu Schwartzberg

**101, July 1972 (52 pages) (40c)**

Cover – Smile/Frown Button – John Severin
Page 2 and 51 – Attention Very Important Notice – Cracked Poster #29
Page 3 – Contents
Page 4 – Letters / Subscription ad
Page 6 – Slums Can Be Made a Fun Thing! – John Severin (reprint from #74)
Page 10 – Silly Things We Do – John Severin
Page 12 – Destination Fun (reprint from #79)
Page 15 – Better Celebrity Dolls – John Severin
Page 18 – Somebody Wants You! – Jim Ivey
Page 20 – Non-Polluting Cars Auto Safety Devices – Jack Barrett
Page 24 – Cracked's Crazy Chuckles
Page 26 – Out of Ordre! – Cracked Poster #30
Page 28 – Cracked Fun Shoppe ad – John Severin
Page 29 – What the Government Intends to Do With Leftover Tax Dollars – John Severin
Page 32 – Hudd & Dini (sleeping Mexican) – Vic Martin
Page 33 – Females Participating in All Sports – John Severin (reprint from #81)
Page 38 – Horror House ad – John Severin
Page 39 – The Screamers (reprint from *For Monsters Only* #5)
Page 42 – With-it Nursery Rhymes – Bill McCartney (Bill Ward)
Page 44 – Five Annuals ad (*Biggest* 5, 6, 7; *Giant* 7; *King-Sized* 5)
Page 45 – Pop! Population Explosion – Jack Barrett / Ron Wiggins
Page 48 – If Famous Lines Were Said in Different Situations – John Severin
Page 50 – Shut Up and Get it Over With! – Jared Lee
Back Cover – Modern Slumlord Magazine – John Severin

**102, August 1972 (52 pages) (40c)**

Cover – Political Balloons – John Severin (Cover is rip-off of cover of *Mad* #122.)

Page 2 and 51 – If This Spot Turns Blue Evacuate Area Immediately – Cracked Poster #31

Page 3 – Contents

Page 4 – Letters / Subscription ad

Page 6 – The French Commotion – John Severin

Page 11 – Hudd & Dini (witches) – Vic Martin

Page 12 – The Big Big Guys!

Page 14 – Oops! Sorry! – Bruce Day

Page 16 – When Comic Strips Go Madison Avenue – Lugoze (reprint from #80)

Page 20 – The Cracked Camera

Page 23 – TV Commercials That are Wasted – John Langton (reprint from #74)

Page 26 – Bumper Sticker Cut-Outs

Page 28 – Horror House ad – John Severin

Page 29 – Nightmares – Vic Martin

Page 31 – Cracked Put-Ons – John Langton

Page 34 – Celebrity Waterbeds – Bill McCartney (Bill Ward)

Page 37 – Pix of the Flicks

Page 40 – Cracked Looks at Political Conventions – John Severin

Page 42 – Cracked Fun Shoppe ad – John Severin

Page 43 – TV's Defective Detectives – Jack Barrett

Page 47 – The Day Norman Told Off His Boss – Jack Barrett / Ron Wiggins

Page 48 – Fat is...Skinny is – Bob Taylor

Page 50 – Shut-Ups (hit a tree) – S. Gross Jr. (Charles Rodrigues)

Back Cover – Greetings from Brooklyn Postcard – John Severin (reprint from #38) (originally "Greetings from the Bronx")

**103, September 1972 (52 pages) (40c)**

Cover – Stepping on a Bug – O.O. Severin (John Severin)

Page 2 and 51 – Pop Art Telephone Poster – Cracked Poster

Page 3 – Contents

Page 4 – Letters / Subscription ad

Page 6 – Cracked Interviews the Toy King – O.O. Severin (John Severin)

Page 11 – The Class of 1932 – Bob Taylor

Page 14 – Three Terrific Teams

Page 17 – When Couple Act Take Over All of Showbiz – Jack Barrett

Page 20 – When Other TV Shows Copy the Rowan & Martin Comedy Format – John Severin (reprint from #76)

Page 23 – Hudd & Dini (octopus) – Vic Martin
Page 24 – The Cracked School of Applied Nuttiness – Jack Barrett
Page 26 – Cracked Looks at the Neighborhood Movie House – Vic Martin
Page 28 – Fight On!
Page 30 – Six Annuals ad (*Biggest* 6, 7; *Giant* 7, 8; *King-Sized* 5, *Super* 5)
Page 31 – Female Magazines of Tomorrow – Vic Martin
Page 35 – Horror House ad – John Severin
Page 36 – Inside George Wallace's Wallet (A rip-off on an older recurring *Mad* article called *Celebrity Wallets*)
Page 39 – Ten Tips on How to Become Rich – Vic Martin
Page 41 – It Happened on Main and First – Caracu
Page 43 – Wild and Wacky Westerns!
Page 44 – Cracked Fun Shoppe ad – John Severin
Page 45 – Would Columbus Have Discovered America Etc.? – O.O. Severin (John Severin) (reprint from #64)
Page 50 – Shut-Ups (winning tickets) – S. Gross Jr. (Charles Rodrigues)
Back Cover – Attention People Born 1952-1962

**104, October 1972 (52 pages) (40c)**

Cover – The Rodfather – O.O. Severino (John Severin) (This cover gag predates *Mad* #155's by two months. Both are based on *The Godfather* movie poster.)
Page 2 and 51 – Have Have You You Checked Checked Your Your Eyes Eyes For For Double Double Visions? Vision? – Cracked Poster
Page 3 – Contents
Page 4 – Letters / Subscription ad
Page 6 – The Rodfather – O.O. Severino (John Severin)
Page 12 – More Whaddaya Callits – Joe Mead (reprint from #81)
Page 14 – All At Sea
Page 17 – Nixon's Home Movies – Jack Barrett
Page 20 – Wedding Announcements We'd like to See
Page 22 – Commercializing the Moon – John Severin (reprint from #81)
Page 26 – Cracked Looks at a Big City Newspaper Office – Don Orehek
Page 28 – Safari So Good
Page 30 – Six Annuals ad (*Biggest* 6, 7; *Giant* 7, 8; *King-Sized* 5, *Super* 5)
Page 31 – Fat Magazine – Bob Taylor
Page 38 – Horror House ad – John Severin
Page 39 – Hudd & Dini (foot race) – Vic Martin
Page 40 – Sagebrush (KLOMK!) – John Severin
Page 42 – Wild Wheels
Page 44 – Cracked Fun Shoppe ad – John Severin

Page 45 – Cracked Interviews the Money King – Bob Taylor
Page 50 – Shut-Ups (innocent) – S. Gross (Charles Rodrigues)
Back Cover – Celebrity License Plates

**105, November 1972 (52 pages) (40c)**

Cover – Monster Movie – O.O. Severin (John Severin) / Bob Taylor
Page 2 and 51 – The World Will End On – Cracked Poster
Page 3 – Contents
Page 4 – Letters / Subscription ad
Page 6 – Zzzzpg – Zeverin (John Severin)
Page 10 – A Day at the Airport – Bernard Baily
Page 14 – Cracked's Guide to Bicycling – Bob Taylor
Page 18 – The Cracked Current Events Test – John Severin
Page 20 – Hudd & Dini (books) – Vic Martin
Page 21 – Hawk – John Severin
Page 25 – W.C. Fields Laff-In (reprint from #84)
Page 26 – Cracked Looks at a Dog Show – Don Orehek
Page 28 – Ask a Silly Question, Get a – John Langton (reprint from #83)
Page 29 – The Advantage of One-Man Elections – John Severin
Page 32 – Six Annuals ad (*Biggest* 6, 7; *Giant* 7, 8; *King-Sized* 6, *Super* 5)
Page 33 – Sagebrush (Mother Nature's secret) – John Severin
Page 34 – Laurel and Hardy's Wacky World of Fun! (reprint from #59)
Page 36 – Cracked Gives You the News-Makers – Vic Martin
Page 38 – Horror House ad – John Severin
Page 39 – Klotch – O.O. Severin (John Severin)
Page 44 – Cracked Fun Shoppe ad – John Severin
Page 45 – The Discount King – John Langton
Page 50 – Shut-Ups (magnifique) – S. Gross Jr. (Charles Rodrigues)
Back Cover – Historical Telegrams That Never Got There (reprint from #17)

**106, January 1973 (52 pages) (40c)**

Cover – I Want You to Buy This Magazine – James Montgomery Flaggione (John Severin) (Severin's head of Don Vito was used again on the cover of *Cracked* #124)
Page 2 and 51 – Godfather Poster – Cracked Poster – James Montgomery Flaggione (John Severin)
Page 3 – Contents
Page 4 – Letters / Subscription ad
Page 6 – The Yesterday Show – O.O. Severin (John Severin)
Page 11 – Psychologically Dangerous Toys – Vic Martin
Page 14 – Just Bumming Around! – Tony Tallarico
Page 15 – Advertising a Worthless Product – John Severin

Page 19 – Man's Best Friend – Bernard Baily
Page 22 – What Preceded Famous Events – Bill McCartney (Bill Ward)
Page 24 – Fields of Fun! (reprint from #71)
Page 26 – Are you a Hypochondriac? – John Langton
Page 28 – Rodrigues' Side Show – Charles Rodrigues
Page 31 – Six Annuals ad (*Biggest* 6, 7; *Giant* 7, 8; *King-Sized* 6, *Super* 5)
Page 32 – Super Star Mementos – John Severin
Page 36 – Cracked Fun Shoppe ad – John Severin
Page 37 – Sagebrush (Humbug!) – John Severin
Page 38 – "Friends, Romans, Countrymen, Lend Me Your Laughs!" (reprint from #80)
Page 40 – The Put-Downers – Vic Martin
Page 42 – Guest Appearances by the World's Top Humor Artists – Don Orehek (1st in a series profiling the artists of *Cracked*)
Page 44 – Horror House ad – John Severin
Page 45 – Cracked Interviews the Industrial King – John Langton
Page 50 – Shut-Ups (prison reforms) – Noah Sark (Charles Rodrigues)
Back Cover – Eden of the Future – John Severin

**107, March 1973 (52 pages) (40c)**
Cover – Voodoo Doll – John Severin (2nd Alfred E. Neuman cover)
Page 2 and 51 – America – Love it or Give it Back! – Cracked Poster
Page 3 – Contents
Page 4 – Letters / Subscription ad
Page 6 – The Candidaze – John Severin
Page 11 – Miss Weird – Bernard Baily
Page 14 – Rose Brawl Parade – Bob Taylor
Page 18 – Inside Henry Kissinger's Wallet – John Langton
Page 21 – Celebrities and Their Screen Idols – John Severin
Page 24 – Six Annuals ad (*Biggest* 6, 7; *Giant* 7, 8; *King-Sized* 6, *Super* 5)
Page 25 – Cracked Looks at World War I Sky Fighters – John Severin
Page 29 – The Pot-Rich Family – John Severin
Page 34 – Guest Appearances by the World's Top Humor Artists – Charles Rodrigues
Page 36 – Cracked Fun Shoppe – John Severin
Page 37 – Ads for Adolescents – Vic Martin
Page 41 – The First Dollar – Bernard Baily
Page 42 – Hudd & Dini (trampoline) – Vic Martin
Page 43 – Sagebrush (want to play a game?) – John Severin / Your (Ugh) Ancestors? (dragging) – Lo Linkert (1st appearance of *Your (Ugh) Ancestors?*)
Page 44 – Horror House ad – John Severin
Page 45 – Cracked Interviews the Gas King – John Langton

Page 50 – Shut-Ups (what he sees in her) – Norman Rockwell (Charles Rodrigues)
Back Cover – Build Your Own Hi-Fi Stereo System

**108, May 1973 (52 pages) (40c)**
Cover – Chicken Soap – John Severin (The inspiration for this cover was surely due to the *Wacky Packages* fad of 1973. A number or *Cracked*'s artists and writers also worked for Topps, the company that produced *Wacky Packages*, including Paul Laikin, Jay Lynch, John Pound, etc.)
Page 2 and 51 – Let Us Know if you Have Any Complaints – Cracked Poster
Page 3 – Contents
Page 4 – Letters (Statement of Ownership: Average number of copies sold: 148,750) / Subscription ad
Page 6 – Kansas City Bummer – Dick Wright
Page 10 – A Day at the Zoo – Charles Rodrigues
Page 13 – Cracked's Guide to Backpacking – John Severin
Page 18 – Vampires of the World – Bernard Baily
Page 22 – Five Annuals ad (*Biggest* 7, 8; *Giant* 8; *King-Sized* 5, 6)
Page 23 – How to Translate Travel Ads – Bob Taylor
Page 26 – Cracked Goes to Las Vegas – Don Orehek
Page 28 – If Archie Bunker Took Over the Leads in Other TV Series – John Severin
Page 32 – Cracked Fun Shoppe ad – John Severin
Page 33 – Orehek on Wry – Don Orehek
Page 36 – A Day in the Senate – Dick Wright
Page 39 – Lunch Time – Oskar Blotta (reprint from #89)
Page 40 – Famous Person's School Excuses
Page 42 – Horror House ad – John Severin
Page 43 – Cracked Interviews the Music King – John Langton
Page 48 – Hudd & Dini (saint bernard) – Vic Martin
Page 49 – Sagebrush (Hi! Hey!) – John Severin / Your (Ugh) Ancestors? (wheel ring) – Lo Linkert
Page 50 – Shut-Ups (I remember) – Charles Rodrigues
Back Cover – Chicken Soap label – John Severin

**109, July 1973 (52 pages) (40c)**
Cover – Time is Running Out! – John Severin
Page 2 and 51 – Help Fight Air Pollution – Cracked Poster
Page 3 – Contents
Page 4 – Lettuce from Our Readers (1st letters column with this name.) / Subscription ad

Page 6 – Dickie Von Dork Show – Nireves (John Severin)
Page 11 – The Last of the 'Desert Island' Cartoons! – Irit Kajiij Jr. (Charles Rodrigues)
Page 14 – Richard Nixon's Press Conference – Dick Wright
Page 18 – The World of Mr. Orehek – Don Orehek
Page 20 – A Cracked History of the Movies – Vic Martin
Page 24 – Cracked's Romantic Greeting Cards That Express Everything – John Langton
Page 26 – Cracked Looks at a Fender Bender – Don Orehek
Page 28 – Resort Brochure for Prison Living – John Langton
Page 32 – Sagebrush (buffalo stampede) – John Severin (reprint from #91)
Page 34 – Cracked Fun Shoppe ad – John Severin
Page 35 – Health Foods – Dick Wright
Page 38 – The Campaign to Use Less Power – Bernard Baily
Page 42 – Horror House ad – John Severin
Page 43 – Cracked Interviews the Auto King – John Severin
Page 44 – Five Annuals ad (*Biggest* 7, 8; *Giant* 8; *King-Sized* 5, 6)
Page 49 – Your (Ugh) Ancestors? (snow tire sale) – Lo Linkert / Hudd & Dini (guard disguise) – Vic Martin
Page 50 – Shut-Ups (plastic surgery) – Charles Rodrigues
Back Cover – Nader Raider Blasts Boss – Charles Rodrigues

**110, August 1973 (52 pages) (40c)**

Cover – Columbo – John Severin
Page 2 and 51 – Attention! For Service – Cracked Poster #54
Page 3 – Contents
Page 4 – Lettuce from Our Readers / Subscription ad
Page 6 – Columbore – John Severin
Page 11 – Upgrading the Female Image in Children's Books – Dick Wright
Page 14 – A Cracked History of Gambling – Bill Ward (This is first time that Bill Ward signed his real name at *Cracked*.)
Page 18 – Suggestions for Overcoming the School Crisis! – Bernard Baily
Page 22 – A Cracked Salute to Chicago – Russ Heath
Page 26 – Overheard on the Chicago Scene – Don Orehek
Page 28 – Horror House ad – John Severin
Page 29 – Cracked's Guide to Crime Prevention – Dick Wright
Page 33 – And the Defendant Answered – Bernard Baily
Page 34 – Cracked Fun Shoppe ad – John Severin
Page 35 – Rodrigues' Hospital-ity – Charles Rodrigues
Page 38 – If Other Civil Servants Tried to Hustle on the Side Like the Astronauts – Dick Wright

Page 42 – Cracked Interviews the Consumer King – Powers (John Severin)
Page 48 – Five Annuals ad (*Biggest* 7, 8; *Giant* 8; *King-Sized* 5, 6)
Page 49 – Sagebrush (here come food) – John Severin / Your (Ugh) Ancestors? (waterwheel) – Lo Linkert
Page 50 – Shut-Ups (bad luck to see bride) – Sam Gross Jr. (Charles Rodrigues)
Back Cover – Oh, No...Do We Have to Start All Over Again? – Charles Rodrigues

**111, September 1973 (52 pages) (40c)**

Cover – The Poseidon Adventure – John Severin
Page 2 and 51 – America's Most Sacred Cow – Cracked Poster
Page 3 – Contents
Page 4 – Lettuce from Our Readers / Subscription ad
Page 6 – The Perspirin' Adventure – John Severin
Page 11 – Cracked Fun Shoppe ad – John Severin
Page 12 – Cracked Looks at Drivers – Bill Ward
Page 16 – Cracked's Catchy First Lines For – Don Orehek
Page 18 – Black Movie Monsters – LePoer (John Severin)
Page 23 – Super Senses – Dick Wright
Page 26 – Cracked Looks at a Wedding Reception – Don Orehek
Page 28 – McClod – Nireves (John Severin)
Page 33 – How to Reduce Wedding Costs – John Langton
Page 37 – Trouble at the Reducing Clinic or The Weighty Problem – Bernard Baily / Joe Catalano
Page 41 – Cracked Guide to Acupuncture – Dick Wright
Page 44 – Horror House ad – John Severin
Page 45 – Cracked Interviews the Camp King – John Langton
Page 50 – Shut-Ups (SHA-LLALA-KOO) – Charles Rodrigues
Back Cover – I'm Emilio Fly Me to Cuba! – Charles Rodrigues

**112, October 1973 (52 pages) (40c)**

Cover – Kung Phew – John Severin
Page 2 and 51 – Help Stamp Out Tall Dogs – Cracked Poster
Page 3 – Contents
Page 4 – Lettuce from Our Readers / Subscription ad
Page 6 – Kung-Phew – John Severin
Page 11 – When Meat Becomes as Valuable as Money – John Langton
Page 15 – Cracked Fun Shoppe ad – John Severin
Page 16 – Specialized Magazines of the Future – Bill Ward
Page 18 – If the Government Labeled All Products as Hazardous – Bernard Baily
Page 22 – Cracked's New Look for the Post Office – Bill Ward

Page 26 – Boating – Don Orehek
Page 28 – Horror House ad – John Severin
Page 29 – How to Stretch Your Dollar Getting the Most While Spending Less – Vic Martin
Page 32 – Cracked Looks at An Apartment Building in the Big City – Bernard Baily
Page 34 – Dotty About Karate – Bill Ward
Page 38 – A Cracked Look at a Crowded Beach – Don Orehek
Page 40 – How Easily are you Embarrassed? – Vic Martin
Page 42 – Five Annuals ad (*Biggest* 8; *Collectors* 2; *Giant* 8; *King-Sized* 6; *Super* 6)
Page 43 – Cracked Interviews the Hospital King – John Severin
Page 48 – *Get Me Cracked* paperback ad / Stanley #68 (pollution) – Murray Ball (1st *Stanley*.)
Page 49 – Sagebrush (hey rock) – John Severin / Your (Ugh) Ancestors? (bar wheel) – Lo Linkert
Page 50 – Shut-Ups (fire escape) – Charles Rodrigues
Back Cover – Breakfast at the White House – Rumpelstiltskin (Charles Rodrigues)

**113, November 1973 (52 pages) (40c)**

Cover – Cover-Up Issue – John Severin
Page 2 and 51 – Do Not Read This Poster – Cracked Poster
Page 3 – Contents
Page 4 – Lettuce from Our Readers / Subscription ad
Page 6 – Dan Coyote-Man of La Rancha – John Severin
Page 12 – When Fat is in and Thin is Out – John Langton
Page 16 – Cracked's New Ways of Presenting the News – John Severin
Page 21 – Tarzan's Abdication – Bill Ward
Page 26 – Cracked Looks at a Doctor's Waiting Room – Don Orehek
Page 28 – How to Cover Up – John Severin
Page 32 – Reconstructing the Remains of 20th Century Civilization – Bill Ward
Page 37 – The Day America Runs Out of Gas – John Severin
Page 41 – Horror House ad – John Severin
Page 42 – Five Annuals ad (*Collectors* 2; *Giant* 8, 9; *King-Sized* 6; *Super* 6)
Page 43 – Cracked Interviews the TV King – John Severin
Page 48 – *Get Me Cracked* paperback ad / Stanley #124 (mankind) – Murray Ball
Page 49 – Sagebrush (Howdy Shage) – John Severin / Your (Ugh) Ancestors? (oil) – Lo Linkert
Page 50 – Shut-Ups (practice your violin) – Charles Rodrigues
Back Cover – Help Wanted – Charles Rodrigues

**114, January 1974 (52 pages) (40c)**

Cover – The Walled-Ins – John Severin
Page 2 and 51 – Important! Don't Waste Your Time – Cracked Poster
Page 3 – Contents
Page 4 – Lettuce from Our Readers / Subscription ad
Page 6 – The Walled-Ins – John Severin
Page 11 – A Cracked View of The Birds-Eye Crew – Bernard Baily / Bill Majeski
Page 15 – Fashion and the Hi-Heeled Platform Shoe – John Severin
Page 18 – The Cracked History of Music – John Langton
Page 22 – Personalized Checks – Vic Martin
Page 26 – Cracked Looks at Stock Car Racing – Don Orehek
Page 28 – If the Government Put a Tax on Our Sins – Bernard Baily
Page 32 – Cracked Fun Shoppe ad – John Severin
Page 33 – Accessories for the TV Football Freak – Bill Ward
Page 37 – Five Annuals ad (*Biggest* 8; *Collectors* 2; *Giant* 8; *King-Sized* 7; *Super* 6)
Page 38 – Cracked Goes to a Literary Cocktail Party – Don Orehek
Page 40 – Horror House ad – John Severin
Page 41 – Yellow Pearl – John Severin
Page 45 – The Information Clerk – Caracu
Page 46 – Sylvester's Silly Strips – Ye Hang Ups (Skrunch) – Nireves (John Severin) (1st *Ye Hang Ups*) / Your (Ugh) Ancestors? (stone TV) – Lo Linkert
Page 47 – Sagebrush (only the shadow knows) – John Severin / Sagebrush (Pikes Peak or Bust) – John Severin
Page 48 –*Get Me Cracked* paperback ad / Stanley (polluting our ocean) – Murray Ball
Page 49 – Shut-Ups (shoplifting) – Charles Rodrigues
Back Cover – Meet the White House Staff (L. Patrick Garfalo) – Robert Sproul Jr. (Charles Rodrigues)

**115, March 1974 (52 pages) (40c)**

Cover – M*U*S*H – John Severin
Page 2 and 51 – Color Blindness Test – Cracked Poster
Page 3 – Contents
Page 4 – Lettuce from Our Readers / Subscription ad
Page 6 – M*U*S*H (Dear Dad) – John Severin (1st of many, many, many *M*A*S*H* parodies.)
Page 11 – Cracked's Pollution Solution – Bill Ward
Page 15 – The Thrill of the Flying Chartered – Bernard Baily / Joe Catalano
Page 19 – Self-Praise in Government – John Severin
Page 22 – Programs for Non-Theatrical Events – John Langton

Page 26 - A Cracked Look at a Supermarket - John Severin
Page 28 - The Cracked Manual for Good Photography - John Langton
Page 33 - If We Didn't Have Hair - John Severin
Page 36 - Five Annuals ad (*Biggest* 8; *Collectors* 2; *Giant* 8; *King-Sized* 7; *Super* 6)
Page 37 - The Cracked Guide to Skiing - Bill Ward
Page 42 - Cracked Interviews the Liberation Queen - John Severin / Joe Catalano
Page 48 - *Get Me Cracked* paperback ad / Stanley (Blap!) - Murray Ball
Page 49 - Sagebrush (thinnin' hair) - John Severin / Ye Hang Ups #3 (He hates to drink alone) - John Severin
Page 50 - Shut-Ups (difficult time) - Charles Rodrigues
Back Cover - Meet the White House Staff (C. Gordon Jumpe) - Charles Rodrigues

**116, May 1974 (52 pages) (40c)**

Cover - Let's Make America Beautiful Again! - John Severin
Page 2 and 51 - Let's Make America Beautiful Again! - Cracked Poster
Page 3 - Contents
Page 4 - Lettuce from Our Readers (Statement of Ownership: Average number of copies sold: 203,330) / Subscription ad
Page 6 - Silly Jack - Nireves (John Severin)
Page 11 - If Real Life Were Like the Movies - Bill Ward
Page 14 - When America Runs Out of Electricity - Don Orehek
Page 17 - Five Annuals ad (*Biggest* 8; *Collectors* 2; *Giant* 8; *King-Sized* 7; *Super* 6)
Page 18 - The Hitler Nostalgia Craze - Bill Ward
Page 22 - Making Plain Ads Sensational - John Langton
Page 24 - A Cracked Look at a High School - Bill Ward
Page 27 - Cracked Fun Shoppe ad - John Severin
Page 28 - A Look at a UFO - Don Orehek
Page 30 - Celebrity Garage Sale - Bernard Baily
Page 34 - Cracked Interviews the Housing King - Sigbjorn (John Severin)
Page 39 - Horror House ad - John Severin
Page 40 - You Know Your Stars Are All Screwed Up When - Don Orehek
Page 42 - Laff and Let Die - O.O. Severin (John Severin)
Page 48 - *Get Me Cracked* paperback ad / Stanley (biggest spear) - Murray Ball
Page 49 - Sagebrush (nobody loves me) - John Severin / Ye Hang Ups (which way to the john) - Nireves (John Severin)
Page 50 - Shut-Ups (curtain about to go up) - Charles Rodrigues
Back Cover - Meet the White House Staff (Mrs. Olga Cog) - Charles Rodrigues

**117, July 1974 (52 pages) (40c)**

Cover – Cannon – John Severin
Page 2 and 51 – Always Be Sincere – Cracked Poster
Page 3 – Contents
Page 4 – Lettuce from Our Readers / Subscription ad
Page 6 – Canyon – John Severin
Page 11 – Cracked's Solution for Solving the Energy Crisis – Bill Ward
Page 16 – A Rodrigues Neighborhood – Charles Rodrigues
Page 18 – The Big City Versus the Small Town – Bernard Baily
Page 21 – The Seers Rubbish Catalog of Useless Items for 1974 – John Langton
Page 26 – A Cracked Look at a Chinese Restaurant – Don Orehek
Page 28 – Cracked's Sure-Fire Guide to Weight Control – Don Orehek
Page 32 – Five Annuals ad (*Biggest* 9; *Collectors* 2; *Giant* 8; *King-Sized* 7; *Super* 6)
Page 33 – Cracked Interviews the Advertising King – Bill Ward (1st *Nanny Dickering Interview* by Bill Ward.)
Page 38 – The Cracked History of Art – John Langton
Page 42 – High Plains Shifter – John Severin
Page 48 – *Get Me Cracked* paperback ad / Stanley (colony of ants) – Murray Ball
Page 49 – Sagebrush #25 (painting) – John Severin / Ye Hang Ups #4 (nice easy job) – Nireves (John Severin)
Page 50 – Shut-Ups (electronic calculator) – Charles Rodrigues
Back Cover – Cracked's Energy Saving Guide – Charles Rodrigues

**118, August 1974 (52 pages) (40c)**

Cover – The Stinger – John Severin
Page 2 and 51 – On This Spot On – Cracked Poster
Page 3 – Contents
Page 4 – Lettuce from Our Readers / Subscription ad
Page 6 – The Stinger – A. Shamed (John Severin)
Page 11 – Understanding Hi-Fidelity – John Langton
Page 15 – How Much Stress Can You Take? – Bill Ward
Page 18 – A Rodrigues Wedding Reception – Charles Rodrigues
Page 20 – *Get Me Cracked* paperback ad / Stanley (getting away from it all) – Murray Ball
Page 21 – Pet Plaza – Bill Ward
Page 26 – A Cracked Look at a Department Store – Don Orehek
Page 28 – Fighting Job Boredom – Bernard Baily
Page 32 – Martial Art Weapons and Techniques – Bill Ward

Page 35 – The Sappy Days – John Severin (1st *Happy Days* parody)
Page 40 – A Short Look at a Long Gas Line – Bill Ward
Page 42 – Cracked Interviews the College King – John Langton
Page 48 – Horror House ad – John Severin
Page 49 – Sagebrush #26 (invited a friend to lunch) – John Severin / Ye Hang Ups #26 (bong) – Nireves (John Severin)
Page 50 – Shut-Ups (Here's his picture) – Charles Rodrigues
Back Cover – Great Moments in Science 1934 – Charles Rodrigues (1st *Great Moments*)

**119, September 1974 (52 pages) (40c)**
Cover – Kung Fu – John Severin
Page 2 and 51 – Beware the Dog – Cracked Poster #119 (Numbering was changed to reflect the issue number as this really should be poster #63.)
Page 3 – Contents
Page 4 – Lettuce from Our Readers / Subscription ad
Page 6 – An Interview with David (Kung Fu) Carrotseed – John Severin
Page 12 – A Cracked Look at Little League Managers – Bill Ward
Page 15 – The Telephone Call – Charles Rodrigues
Page 16 – A Look at Typical Family Gathering – Don Orehek
Page 20 – How to Buy a New Car – Bernard Baily
Page 24 – How Today's Americans Might Have Answered the Polls of 200 Years Ago – Sururi Gumen
Page 26 – Cracked Looks at Camping – Don Orehek
Page 28 – New Methods Banks Can Use to Attract Customers – John Langton
Page 32 – Beserko! – John Severin
Page 38 – Six Annuals ad (*Biggest* 8; *Collectors* 2, 3; *Giant* 9; *King-Sized* 6; *Super* 7)
Page 39 – Cracked Do-it-Yourself Divorce – Don Orehek
Page 42 – The Effect of the Energy Crisis on the Entertainment World – John Severin
Page 47 – Binders and notebooks ad (real ad) (1st appearance of this ad. Product features covers of #98, 80, 105)
Page 48 – *Get Me Cracked* paperback ad / Stanley (mankind) – Murray Ball
Page 49 – Sagebrush #27 (reptiles are better) – John Severin / Ye Hang Ups #27 (fishing) – Nireves (John Severin)
Page 50 – Shut-Ups (deadbeats) – Charles Rodrigues
Back Cover – Great Moments in Art 1705 – Charles Rodrigues

**120, October 1974 (52 pages) (40c)** (On sale date July 16, 1974) (On sale dates are now listed in the previous issue and are mentioned here when known.)

Cover – The Six Billion Dollar Man! – John Severin
Page 2 and 51 – No Standing from Here to Corner – Cracked Poster #120
Page 3 – Contents
Page 4 – Lettuce from Our Readers / Subscription ad
Page 6 – The Six Billion Dollar Man – John Severin
Page 12 – What to Do with Your Obsolete Gas Guzzler – Bill Ward
Page 14 – The Cracked Guide to Tennis – Nat Ball (John Severin)
Page 19 – Policeman Magazine – Don Orehek
Page 23 – A Cracked Look at the Good Old Days? – John Langton
Page 26 – Cracked Looks at an Air Line Terminal – Don Orehek
Page 28 – More Cracked Solutions for Solving the Energy Crisis – John Langton
Page 32 – Are You a Loser? – Bernard Baily
Page 35 – The Inept-One Factor – John Severin
Page 40 – Pre-Historic News – Don Orehek
Page 42 – Cracked Interviews the Oil King – Bill Ward
Page 47 – Binders and notebooks ad
Page 48 –*Half-Cracked* and *Get Me Cracked* paperback ad / Stanley (look at that rain) – Murray Ball
Page 49 – Sagebrush #28 (reptiles were here) – John Severin / Ye Hang Ups #29 (toothache) – Nireves (John Severin)
Page 50 – Shut-Ups (grown man playing with a doll) – Charles Rodrigues
Back Cover – Who'd She Expect…Richard Burton? – Bill McCartney (Bill Ward) (reprint from #4)

**121, November 1974 (52 pages) (40c)** (On sale date August 20, 1974)

Cover – The Three Mascoteers – John Severin
Page 2 and 51 – Tear This Poster Down Immediately! – Cracked Poster #121
Page 3 – Contents
Page 4 – Lettuce from Our Readers / Subscription ad
Page 6 – Three Mascoteers – John Severin
Page 12 – The World of Kids – Don Orehek
Page 16 – Past Predictions of the Future – Sururi Gumen
Page 20 – The Eech 80's – John Severin
Page 22 – A History of Fashion – Bill Ward
Page 26 – Cracked Goes to a Weight Watcher's Meeting – Don Orehek

Page 28 – What are the Old TV & Movie Detectives Doing Today? – John Severin
Page 33 – Seven Annuals ad (*Biggest* 8; *Collectors* 2, 3; *Giant* 9, 10; *King-Sized* 6; *Super* 7)
Page 34 – Cracked's Charisma Test – John Langton
Page 36 – American Car-Daffy – Sururi Gumen
Page 42 – Cracked Interviews the Restaurant King – John Langton
Page 47 – Binders and notebooks ad
Page 48 – *Half-Cracked* and *Get Me Cracked* paperback ad / Stanley (breathing) – Murray Ball
Page 49 – Sagebrush #30 (look up in the sky) – C.E. Severin (Catherine Severin) / John Severin // Ye Hang Ups #30 (Houdini) – John Severin
Page 50 – Shut-Ups (ain't got no horses) – Charles Rodrigues
Back Cover – The Man and the Beast – Oskar Blotta (reprint from #80)

**122, January 1975 (52 pages) (50c)** (On sale date October 15, 1974)
Cover – Kojak and Serpico – John Severin
Page 2 and 51 – Attention! – Cracked Poster #122
Page 3 – Contents
Page 4 – Lettuce from Our Readers / Subscription ad
Page 6 – Beaujack – John Severin / Charles Rodrigues
Page 11 – Ridiculous Renting Spaces – Bill Ward
Page 14 – When the World Runs Out of Food – Sururi Gumen
Page 18 – A Cracked Look at Prizefighting – Don Orehek
Page 22 – Nostalgic Amusement Parks – Bill Ward
Page 26 – A Cracked Look at a Zoo – Don Orehek
Page 28 – Binders and notebooks ad
Page 29 – Chariots of the Clods? – John Severin
Page 32 – Cracked Methods of Staying Thin Forever – Bill Ward
Page 36 – Papion – John Severin
Page 42 – Seven Annuals ad (*Biggest* 8; *Collectors* 2, 3; *Giant* 9, 10; *King-Sized* 6; *Super* 7)
Page 43 – Cracked Interviews the Garbage King – Sururi Gumen
Page 48 – *Cracked Up*, *Half-Cracked* and *Get Me Cracked* paperback ad / Stanley #195 (fuel crisis) – Murray Ball
Page 49 – Sagebrush #29 (beware!) – C.E. Severin (Catherine Severin) / John Severin // Ye Hang Ups #28 (want to play a game?) – Nireves (John Severin)
Page 50 – Shut-Ups (new highway) – Charles Rodrigues
Back Cover – Great Moments in Medicine 1882 – Charles Rodrigues

**123, March 1975 (52 pages) (50c)** (On sale date December 17, 1974)
Cover – Planet of the Apes – John Severin
Page 2 – Binders and Notebooks ad
Page 3 – Contents
Page 4 – Lettuce from Our Readers (Statement of Ownership: Average number of copies sold: 366,800) / Subscription ad
Page 6 – Planet with the Apes – Harry Gibbons (John Severin)
Page 11 – How to Stay Warm Without Wasting Energy – Bill Ward
Page 14 – The Country Blues – John Langton
Page 18 – A Cracked Look at Golf – Bill Ward
Page 22 – How to Make Words Pictorial
Page 23 – If There Had Been Women's Lib Throughout History – Sururi Gumen
Page 26 – Cracked Goes to an Encounter Group Therapy Session – Don Orehek
Page 28 – The Cracked Bookstore ad – John Severin (real ad) (1st appearance of *The Cracked Bookstore* ad featuring many previous annuals and specials for sale. Also 1st appearance of the slogan "Order Now – Chaos Later" which I honestly never got as a kid.)
Page 29 – The Far-Out Four – Polly Titian (John Severin)
Page 34 – You Know It's Not Your Day When – Bill Ward
Page 37 – China Clown – Sururi Gumen
Page 43 – Cracked Interviews the Christmas King – Yul Tydde (John Severin)
Page 48 – *Cracked Up*, *Half-Cracked* and *Get Me Cracked* paperback ad / Stanley (check my traps) – Murray Ball
Page 49 – Sagebrush #31 (this is war) – John Severin / Ye Hang Ups #31 (Pierre) – Nireves (John Severin)
Page 50 – Shut-Ups (Tigers Bears) – Charles Rodrigues
Page 51 – If You're Cracked You're Happy! Iron-On – John Severin (1st *Iron-on*)
Back Cover – It Happened on Main and First – Caracu (reprint from #103)

**124, May 1975 (52 pages) (50c)** (On sale date January 28, 1975)
Cover – The Godfodder – John Severin (The head of Don Vito is cut and pasted from the cover of *Cracked* #106)
Page 2 and 51 – Important Message – Cracked Poster #124
Page 3 – Contents
Page 4 – Lettuce from Our Readers / Subscription ad
Page 6 – The Godfodder, Part XXIII – Seymour Redley (John Severin)
Page 12 – The Cracked History of Television – Bill Ward
Page 16 – What Will Super K Do When He Leaves the Government? – Sururi Gumen

Page 19 – Olympics for Non-Athletes – Bill Ward
Page 22 – How Past Events Might Have Been Reported with a Government-Controlled Press – Sururi Gumen
Page 26 – A Cracked Look at a Bowling Alley – Don Orehek
Page 28 – The Cracked World of Snow – Sururi Gumen
Page 32 – Magazine Covers from Planet of the Apes – John Severin
Page 34 – The Not So Great Gatsby – Sururi Gumen
Page 39 – The Ridiculous Things of Life – Bill Ward
Page 42 – The Cracked Bookstore ad – John Severin
Page 43 – Cracked Interviews the Newspaper King – Powers (John Severin)
Page 48 – *Cracked Up*, *Half-Cracked* and *Get Me Cracked* paperback ad / Stanley (I've invented money) – Murray Ball
Page 49 – Sagebrush #32 (Yahoo!) – John Severin / Ye Hang Ups #32 (no tipping) – Nireves (John Severin)
Page 50 – Shut-Ups (Helen doesn't mean anything) – Charles Rodrigues
Back Cover – The Man and the Mousey – Oskar Blotta

**125, July 1975 (52 pages) (50c)** (On sale date March 11, 1975)
Cover – Earthshake – John Severin
Page 2 and 51 – The World Will End Tomorrow – Cracked Poster #125
Page 3 – Contents
Page 4 – Lettuce from Our Readers / Cracked Iron-On ad / Subscription ad
Page 6 – Earthshake – Ty Dahlwave (John Severin)
Page 12 – If People Switched from One Profession to Another – John Langton
Page 16 – If Real Life Operated Like TV Quiz Shows – Don Orehek
Page 21 – Overlooked Disaster Movies – Bill Ward
Page 24 – Cat Gifts for Cats Who Have Everything – Mac Bush (Sururi Gumen)
Page 26 – A Cracked Look at a Garage Sale – Ron DeLay (John Severin)
Page 28 – The Cracked Bookstore ad – John Severin
Page 29 – The Cracked Guide to Golf – Bill Ward
Page 33 – Cracked Presents Future Insect Monster Movies – Sururi Gumen
Page 37 – Pell-Mell with Mel – Mort Uarrie (John Severin)
Page 42 – Binders and Notebooks ad
Page 43 – Cracked Interviews the Supermarket King – Sururi Gumen
Page 48 – *Your Cracked*, *Cracked Up*, *Half-Cracked* and *Get Me Cracked* paperback ad / Stanley (leggo my meat) – Murray Ball
Page 49 – Sagebrush #33 (traps all set for Winter) – John Severin / Ye Hang Ups #33 (Slam) – Nireves (John Severin)
Page 50 – Shut-Ups (KUH-RRRAK!) – Charles Rodrigues
Back Cover – The Stone Age – Oskar Blotta

**126, August 1975 (52 pages) (50c)** (On sale date April 22, 1975) (Last issue distributed by Dell.)

Cover – The Towering Infernal – John Severin
Page 2 and 51 – This Way Out – Cracked Poster #126
Page 3 – Contents
Page 4 – Lettuce from Our Readers / Cracked Iron-On ad / Subscription ad
Page 6 – The Towering Infernal – John Severin
Page 12 – The Cracked History of Boating? – Bill Ward
Page 15 – New T.V. Game Shows for Next Season – Artie Choake (John Severin)
Page 20 – The Cracked Bookstore ad – John Severin
Page 21 – Cracked Guide to Magic – Bill Ward
Page 24 – Discount Coupons of the Future – Bill Ward
Page 26 – Cracked Takes a Look at Spring Training – Bill McCartney (Bill Ward) (reprint from #52)
Page 28 – Murdering the Orient Express – John Severin
Page 34 – Products and Ads Designed for the Arab Market – Mac Bush (Sururi Gumen)
Page 38 – The Major Moose Show – John Severin
Page 42 – Binders and Notebooks ad
Page 43 – Cracked Interviews the Surveillance King – John Langton
Page 48 – *Your Cracked, Cracked Up, Half-Cracked* and *Get Me Cracked* paperback ad / Stanley #205 (it's frightening) – Murray Ball
Page 49 – Sagebrush #34 (Uh! Oh!) – John Severin / Ye Hang Ups #35 (four arms) – Nireves (John Severin)
Page 50 – Shut-Ups (good year) – Charles Rodrigues
Back Cover – Great Moments in Industry 1889 – Charles Rodrigues

**127, September 1975 (52 pages) (50c)** (On sale date June 10, 1975) (1st issue distributed by Select Magazines)

Cover – Star Trek – John Severin
Page 2 and 51 – Ignorance is Bliss – Cracked Poster #127
Page 3 – Contents
Page 4 – Lettuce from Our Readers / Subscription ad
Page 6 – Star Tracks – John Severin (1st *Star Trek* parody)
Page 11 – When the World Runs Out of Space – Makbush (Sururi Gumen)
Page 15 – If Other Industries Gave Rebates – Bill Ward
Page 17 – If Newspapers Carried Pictures to Match Their Headlines – John Severin
Page 20 – Monopo-Oil – John Langton
Page 23 – The Cracked Bookstore ad – John Severin

Page 24 – You Know You are a TV Addict When – Bill Ward
Page 26 – A Cracked Look at a Racetrack – Don Orehek
Page 28 – Airplot 1975 – Sururi Gumen
Page 34 – Cracked Traces a Spinoff – John Severin
Page 38 – The Cracked Guide to Self-Recognition – Bill Ward
Page 40 – A Teenager is – Don Orehek
Page 42 – Binders and Notebooks ad 2 (Covers of #97, 86, 93)
Page 43 – Cracked Interviews the Resort King – Bill Ward
Page 48 – *Your Cracked, Cracked Up, Half-Cracked* and *Get Me Cracked* paperback ad / Stanley (Ah nature) – Murray Ball
Page 49 – Sagebrush #35 (cactus flowers) – John Severin / Knights 'n' Daze #37 (Klang) – LePoer (John Severin)
Page 50 – Shut-Ups (manage our budget) – Charles Rodrigues
Back Cover – The Curious and the Modern Sculpture – Oskar Blotta

**128, October 1975 (52 pages) (50c)** (On sale date July 15, 1975)
Cover – Capone – John Severin
Page 2 and 51 – Don't Put Off For Tomorrow – Cracked Poster #128
Page 3 – Contents
Page 4 – Lettuce from Our Readers / Subscription ad – Bob Taylor
Page 6 – Capony – John Severin
Page 12 – If TV Characters Aged While Their Shows Stayed the Same – Sururi Gumen
Page 16 – The Cracked History of Medicine – Doe Torr (John Severin)
Page 20 – Some Cracked Tips for Whipping Inflation – Bill Ward
Page 24 – Little Known Facts of the American Revolution? – Makbush (Sururi Gumen)
Page 26 – Cracked Looks at a Summer Camp – Don Orehek
Page 29 – The Untold Story of How Betsy Ross Created the Flag
Page 32 – Binders and Notebooks ad 2
Page 33 – Disaster Movies You May Be Soon Seeing – John Severin
Page 36 – Summer is – John Langton
Page 38 – Police Lady – John Severin
Page 43 – Cracked Interviews the Stunt King – Sururi Gumen
Page 48 – *Your Cracked, Cracked Up, Half-Cracked* and *Cracked in the Saddle* paperback ad / Sliding Down the Family Tree – John Severin
Page 49 – Sagebrush #39 (thing on your back) – John Severin / Knights 'n' Daze #36 (hanging knight) – LePoer (John Severin) (1st *Knights 'n' Daze*)
Page 50 – Shut-Ups (provide a blindfold) – Charles Rodrigues
Back Cover – Great Moments in Journalism 1935 – Charles Rodrigues

**129, November 1975 (52 pages) (50c)** (On sale date August 19, 1975)
Cover – Jawz – John Severin
Page 2 and 51 – Avoid Shark Attacks – Cracked Poster #129
Page 3 – Contents
Page 4 – Lettuce from Our Readers / Subscription ad – Bob Taylor
Page 6 – Jawz – John Severin
Page 12 – How Colleges Can Attract New Students – Bill Ward
Page 16 – The Cracked Guide to Boating – Sailor Sam (John Severin)
Page 20 – Where are they Now? – Don Orehek
Page 22 – The Cracked World of Automobiles – R. Khivez (John Severin)
Page 26 – A Cracked Look at a Hamburger Franchise – Bill Ward
Page 28 – The Freaks of San Francisco – John Severin
Page 34 – Cracked Guide to Baseball – Bill Ward
Page 39 – The Specialized Bionic Man – John Severin
Page 42 – Binders and Notebooks ad 2
Page 43 – Cracked Interviews the Lemonade King – John Langton
Page 48 – *Your Cracked, Cracked Up, Half-Cracked* and *Cracked in the Saddle* paperback ad / Stanley (Erk! A snake!) – Murray Ball
Page 49 – Sagebrush #38 (rattler's territory) – John Severin / Ye Hang Ups #38 (ah-choo) – Nireves (John Severin)
Page 50 – Shut-Ups (black belt) – Charles Rodrigues
Back Cover – Great Moments in Cosmetics 1,000,000 B.C. – Mike Ricigliano

**130, January 1976 (52 pages) (50c)** (On sale date October 15, 1975)
Cover – Dyn-O-Mite – John Severin
Page 2 and 51 – Will All Those People 6' and Over Please Move – Cracked Poster #130
Page 3 – Contents
Page 4 – Lettuce from Our Readers / *Cracked in the Saddle* and *It's a Cracked World* paperback ad / Subscription ad
Page 6 – Good Tymes – John Severin (1st *Good Times* parody)
Page 11 – Cracked's Guide to Sharks – Don Orehek
Page 14 – The Non-People Population Explosion – Sururi Gumen
Page 18 – A Preview of Cracked's New TV Season – John Severin
Page 21 – The Monster – Sururi Gumen
Page 22 – Developing a New Product – Bill Ward
Page 26 – The TV Class Reunion of 1985 – Sururi Gumen
Page 28 – The French Commotion II – John Severin
Page 34 – Cracked Guide to Sky Diving – Sururi Gumen
Page 38 – The Cracked Bookstore ad – John Severin
Page 39 – The Cracked Guide to Plant Care – John Severin

Page 42 – Cracked's Cheaper Methods for Powering Automobiles – John Langton
Page 44 – Binders and Notebooks ad 2
Page 45 – Cracked Interviews the Sports King – John Severin
Page 50 – Shut-Ups (uncomfortable) – Charles Rodrigues
Back Cover – Great Moments in Aviation 1924 – rottenrigues (Charles Rodrigues)

**131, March 1976 (52 pages) (50c)** (On sale date December 16, 1975)
Cover – The Godfather Meets Jaws – John Severin
Page 2 and 51 – Attention! The End of the Line Begins Here – Cracked Poster #131
Page 3 – Contents
Page 4 – Lettuce from Our Readers (Statement of Ownership: Average number of copies sold: 413,481) / *Cracked in the Saddle* and *It's a Cracked World* paperback ad / Subscription ad
Page 6 – If Hit Movies Were Combined – John Severin (Alfred E. Neuman appearance) (1st *More Combined Movies*)
Page 12 – The Female Role in American History – Don Orehek
Page 16 – How a Big City Can Prevent Bankruptcy – LePoer (John Severin)
Page 20 – If TV Commercials Lasted 61 Seconds – Bill Ward
Page 23 – Celebrity Garbage – John Severin
Page 26 – Cracked Visits a Pro Football Locker Room – Bill Ward
Page 28 – Havaii 5-0 – John Severin
Page 33 – Rule Changes in Sports that Reflect the Real World – John Langton
Page 37 – The Loser – John Severin
Page 39 – The Cracked World of Movie Going – Sururi Gumen
Page 42 – You Know You're Nobody When – Bob Taylor
Page 44 – The Cracked Bookstore ad – John Severin
Page 45 – Cracked Interviews the Magic King – Bill Ward
Page 50 – Shut-Ups (It's a mirage) – Charles Rodrigues
Back Cover – Great Moments in History 1883 – Charles Rodrigues

**132, May 1976 (52 pages) (50c)** (On sale date January 27, 1976)
Cover – We Unmask Baretta – John Severin
Page 2 and 51 – Special Announcement Circle March 26th on Your Calendar at Once! – Cracked Poster #132
Page 3 – Contents
Page 4 – Lettuce from Our Readers / Subscription ad
Page 6 – Boretta – John Severin
Page 12 – Fill-in-the-Blank Form Letters and Cards for Every Occasion – Sururi Gumen

Page 15 – What Today's Programs Would Look Like if They Appeared in 2001 A.D. – John Severin
Page 18 – Cracked Exposes Detroit – Vic Martin
Page 22 – How Different Magazines and Newspapers Would Caption the Same Picture
Page 26 – Cracked Looks at a Typical Savings Bank – Don Orehek
Page 28 – Three Hours of the Condor – O.O. Severin (John Severin)
Page 34 – One Day in the Desert – Bill Ward
Page 35 – Postcard Collecting – Sururi Gumen
Page 39 – More Combined Movies "Dracula" and "Snow White and the Seven Dwarfs" – John Severin
Page 40 – The Cracked Guide to Hockey – John Severin
Page 44 – The Cracked Bookstore ad – John Severin
Page 45 – Cracked Interviews the Super Salesman King – Bill Ward
Page 50 – Shut-Ups (stopping the fight) – Charles Rodrigues
Back Cover – Great Moments in History 1656 – Charles Rodrigues

**133, July 1976 (52 pages) (50c)** (On sale date March 9, 1976)
Cover – Cracked Says Goodbye – John Severin (Fonzie from *Happy Days* makes the 1st of many cover appearances here.)
Page 2 and 51 – In Case of Emergency – Cracked Poster
Page 3 – Contents
Page 4 – Lettuce from Our Readers / *Cracked in the Saddle* and *It's a Cracked World* paperback ad / Subscription ad
Page 6 – Space: 1998 – Sururi Gumen
Page 12 – Cracked Frisbee Rating System – Bob Taylor
Page 15 – Why is it on T.V. You Never See – Bill Ward
Page 20 – New Items for the American Buycentennial – Bob Taylor
Page 23 – Winners & Losers – Vic Martin
Page 26 – A Cracked Look at a Tourist Welcome Center – John Severin
Page 28 – Welcome Back, Kutter – John Severin
Page 34 – One Evening in Old Mexico – Bob Taylor
Page 35 – Dreamy Acres – John Severin
Page 39 – More Combined Movies "My Fair Lady" & "King Kong" – John Severin
Page 40 – If Different National Products Became the World Money Standard – John Severin
Page 44 – Binders and Notebooks ad 2
Page 45 – Cracked Interviews the Used Car King – Bill Ward
Page 50 – Shut-Ups (flight show movies) – Charles Rodrigues
Back Cover – Great Moments in History 1976 – Mike Ricigliano

**134, August 1976 (52 pages) (50c)** (On sale date April 20, 1976)
Cover - The Fonze! - John Severin (This is quite possibly the best selling issue of *Cracked* ever.)
Page 2 and 51 - Hey-y-y (Fonze poster) - Cracked Poster #134 - John Severin
Page 3 - Contents
Page 4 - Lettuce from Our Readers / Subscription ad
Page 6 - Everything You've Ever Wanted to Know About "The Fonze" and More - John Severin
Page 12 - The Art of Ventriloquism - Bob Taylor
Page 16 - Satan's Campaign to Promote Hell - Makbush (Sururi Gumen)
Page 20 - One Afternoon in Japan - Sururi Gumen
Page 21 - The Academy Awards Show - John Severin
Page 26 - A Cracked Loko at Motocross - Bill Ward
Page 28 - Increasing Consumption in Order to Maintain Full Employment - LePoer (John Severin)
Page 32 - Realistic Toys and Games - Don Orehek (A rip-off of an article from *Crazy* #5.)
Page 35 - Tomorrow's Retirement Communities for the Now Generation - Bob Taylor
Page 39 - Barfsky and Clutch - John Severin
Page 44 - The Cracked Bookstore ad - John Severin
Page 45 - Cracked Interviews the Movie King - Bill Ward
Page 50 - Shut-Ups (good clean fight) - Mike Ricigliano
Back Cover - Great Moments in Politics 1949 - Charles Rodrigues

**135, September 1976 (52 pages) (50c)** (On sale date June 8, 1976)
Cover - The Bionic Woman - Nireves (John Severin)
Page 2 and 51 - The Bionic Couple - Cracked Poster #135 - Sigbjorn (John Severin)
Page 3 - Contents
Page 4 - Lettuce from Our Readers / Subscription ad
Page 6 - The Bionic Lady - John Severin
Page 12 - A Cracked Look at CB Radios - Bob Taylor
Page 16 - A Cracked Salute to the Olympics - Bill Ward
Page 21 - One Evening in a Fancy Restaurant - Bob Taylor
Page 22 - How America Won Her Independence - John Severin
Page 26 - A Cracked Look at an Airport Terminal - Bob Taylor
Page 28 - The Big Budget Epic vs. The Low Budget Quickie - John Severin
Page 32 - The Cracked Bookstore ad - John Severin
Page 33 - The Rock Craze Rolls On - John Langton

Page 36 – Fonzerella! – Sigbjorn (John Severin)
Page 41 – The Cracked Guide to Skateboarding – Don Orehek
Page 45 – Cracked Interviews the Political King – John Severin
Page 50 – Shut-Ups (the score's tied) – Mike Ricigliano
Back Cover – Great Moments in Inventions 1801 – Charles Rodrigues

**136, October 1976 (52 pages) (50c)** (On sale date July 13, 1976)
Cover – Laverne & Shirley – John Severin
Page 2 and 51 – Unemployment is Not Working! – Cracked Poster #136
Page 3 – Contents
Page 4 – Lettuce from Our Readers / Subscription ad
Page 6 – Leverne & Shirley (Thank you, whistle) – Sigbjorn (John Severin) (1st *Laverne and Shirley* parody)
Page 12 – The American Revolution as Seen Through British Eyes – Sururi Gumen
Page 15 – A Cracked History of the Bionic Man – Nireves (John Severin)
Page 19 – Cracked's Guide to Burglary Prevention – Vic Martin
Page 22 – One Day in Metropolitis – Don Orehek
Page 23 – Celebrities' Home Movies – John Severin
Page 26 – Cracked Goes to a Political Convention – Don Orehek
Page 28 – Cracked Guide to Surfing – John Severin
Page 33 – Reel Gone Goodies (reprint from #75)
Page 34 – The Fonz Throughout History – Don Orehek
Page 38 – The Bad News Bores – John Severin
Page 44 – The Cracked Bookstore ad – John Severin
Page 45 – Cracked Interviews the Olympic Training King – Bill Ward
Page 50 – Shut-Ups (let's go out dancing) – Mike Ricigliano
Back Cover – Great Moments in Science 495 B.C. – Mike Ricigliano

**137, November 1976 (52 pages) (50c)** (On sale date August 17, 1976)
Cover – The Sweathogs – John Severin
Page 2 – The Cracked Bookstore ad – John Severin
Page 3 – Contents
Page 4 – Lettuce from Our Readers / Subscription ad
Page 6 – How the Kotter Gang Spent Their Summer Vacation – John Severin
Page 12 – Another Combined Movie "Godzilla" vs. "The Towering Inferno" – Sururi Gumen
Page 13 – As the General, Young, and Restless Hospital Turns – Bill Ward

Page 18 – Cracked Methods for Repairing Your Car Inexpensively – Bill Dubay
Page 22 – The Problem The Richie Cunningham Solution The Fonz Solution – John Severin
Page 23 – If the American Revolution Happened Today – Don Orehek
Page 26 – A Cracked Look at a Wrestling Match – Bill Ward
Page 28 – Beach Blanket Party – John Severin
Page 33 – How to Make Baseball More Interesting – Bill Ward
Page 37 – W.C. Fields Laff-In (reprint from #84)
Page 38 – If the Fonze Guest Starred on Other Shows – Don Orehek
Page 42 – Cracked's Favorite TV Scenes from Last Season
Page 45 – Cracked Interviews the Art King – John Severin
Page 50 – Shut-Ups (can't hold out any longer) – Mike Ricigliano
Page 51 – I'm the Fonz on his Day Off! Iron-On – John Severin
Back Cover – Great Moments in History Ice Age – Mike Ricigliano

**138, December 1976 (52 pages) (50c)** (On sale date September 28, 1976)
Cover – Your TV Favorites – John Severin
Page 2 and 51 – $100,0.000 Rewarrd – Cracked Poster #138
Page 3 – Contents
Page 4 – Lettuce from Our Readers / *Cracked Collectors' Edition* #16 and *King-Sized Cracked* #10 ad / Subscription ad
Page 6 – Cracked Mazagine Presents the Great Nielson Airwave War – McTurk (John Severin) ("Nielson" should be spelled "Nielsen.")
Page 12 – A Cracked Look at America's Other Political Parties Running in November – Don Orehek
Page 15 – C.B. Mania – Bill Ward
Page 19 – The Magic Lamp – Don Orehek
Page 20 – Ford-Carter Fight – Howard Nostrand
Page 22 – How TV Shows Could be Killed Without Cancelling Them – John Severin
Page 26 – A Cracked Look at a Picnic Area – Bill Ward
Page 28 – Cracked's New Type Baseball Cards that Tell it Like it is – Howard Nostrand
Page 31 – Criminal She-Nanigans – John Severin
Page 35 – One Afternoon in a Local Stereo Store – Sururi Gumen
Page 36 – What Goes on in a Monster's Mind – Don Orehek
Page 39 – The Making of Silent Movie – McTurk (John Severin)
Page 44 – The Cracked Bookstore ad – John Severin
Page 45 – Cracked Interviews the Outdoor King – Bill Ward
Page 50 – Shut-Ups (Have a good time!) – Mike Ricigliano
Back Cover – Great Moments in Science 1699 – Mike Ricigliano

**139, January 1977 (52 pages) (50c)** (On sale date November 9, 1976)
Cover – We "Cop Out" on Barney Miller – John Severin
Page 2 and 51 – Warning!! The World Will End at 5:26PM!! – Cracked Poster #139
Page 3 – Contents
Page 4 – Lettuce from Our Readers / Subscription ad
Page 6 – Blarney Miller (my husband is missing) – John Severin (1st *Barney Miller* parody)
Page 12 – Evolution Revolution – Howard Nostrand
Page 15 – The Men Behind Kon – Bill Ward
Page 18 – "Going Out" Simulation Kits for Stay at Home People – Sean LePoer (John Severin)
Page 22 – Cowtown Gazette
Page 26 – A Cracked Look at an Unemployment Office – Don Orehek
Page 28 – Why Today Will Seem like the Good Old Days 20 Years from Now – Bill Ward (That's for sure!!!)
Page 32 – Cracked Looks at the World of Superdom – Don Orehek
Page 36 – The Check-Up – Don Orehek
Page 37 – The Wider World of Sports – John Severin
Page 42 – Behind Closed Doors – Don Orehek
Page 44 – One Extremely Foggy Night in Minnesota – Howard Nostrand
Page 45 – Cracked Interviews the Antique King – John Severin
Page 50 – Shut-Ups (set up camp) – Mike Ricigliano
Back Cover – Great Moments in Science 1600 – Mike Ricigliano

**140, March 1977 (52 pages) (50c)** (On sale date December 21, 1976)
Cover – We "Monkey" with King Kung – John Severin
Page 2 and 51 – King Kong – Cracked Poster #140 – John Severin
Page 3 – Contents
Page 4 – Lettuce from Our Readers (Statement of Ownership: Average number of copies sold: 441,245) / Subscription ad
Page 6 – King Kung – John Severin
Page 13 – The Cracked Guide to Hang Gliding – John Severin
Page 17 – The Mirage – Sururi Gumen
Page 18 – Randolph the Reindeer – John Severin (reprint from #75)
Page 20 – One Day in Los Angeles – Bill Ward
Page 21 – The Cracked Guide to Football – Howard Nostrand
Page 26 – A Cracked Look at a Newspaper – Don Orehek
Page 28 – If King Kong Made Guest Appearances on TV – Howard Nostrand
Page 32 – If the Fonz Became Bionic – John Severin
Page 36 – The Cracked Bookstore ad – John Severin
Page 37 – The Blue Night – John Severin

Page 43 - Guiness Book of Records - Howard Nostrand
Page 45 - Cracked Interviews the Traveling Carnival King - Bill Ward
Page 50 - Shut-Ups (outlawing handguns) - Mike Ricigliano
Back Cover - Great Moments in Gardening 1708 - Howard Nostrand

**141, May 1977 (52 pages) (50c)** (On sale date January 25, 1977)
Cover - We "Run-Down" Marathon Man - John Severin
Page 2 and 51 - End Alphabetical Discrimination Now!! - Cracked Poster #141
Page 3 - Contents
Page 4 - Lettuce from Our Readers / Subscription ad
Page 6 - Marathon Jam - John Severin
Page 12 - King Kong's Boyhood - Bill Ward
Page 16 - Video Games We'll Soon Be Seeing - Howard Nostrand
Page 19 - Cracked's New Learn-At-Home Schools - LePoer (John Severin)
Page 22 - Life's Big Losers - Bill Ward (Alfred E. Neuman appearance)
Page 26 - A Cracked Look at Plains, Georgia - Don Orehek
Page 28 - Redemption Coupons We'd Really Like to See - Howard Nostrand
Page 30 - The Search for Bigfoot - John Severin
Page 31 - The Cracked Guide to Bowling - Bill Dubay
Page 36 - Some Garage Sales We'd Like to See - Howard Nostrand
Page 38 - Churlie's Angels - John Severin (1st *Charlie's Angels* parody)
Page 44 - The Cracked Bookstore ad - John Severin
Page 45 - Cracked Interviews the Power Company King - Bill Ward
Page 50 - Shut-Ups (Abra-kadabra) - Mike Ricigliano
Back Cover - The Lonely Convict and the Pet - Oskar Blotta

**142, July 1977 (52 pages) (50c)** (On sale date March 8, 1977)
Cover - We Smash M*A*S*H - John Severin
Page 2 and 51 - Wanted King Kong - Cracked Poster #142
Page 3 - Contents
Page 4 - Lettuce from Our Readers / Subscription ad
Page 6 - M*U*S*H (millions of clocks) - John Severin (2nd *M*A*S*H* parody)
Page 12 - The Cracked Guide to Frizbee - Howard Nostrand
Page 16 - What Businesses Can Do With Leftover Items - Bill Ward
Page 18 - Redoing the Evening News - John Severin
Page 22 - You Know You're the Biggest Thing Around if - Howard Nostrand
Page 25 - One Day in a Washington, D.C. School - Sururi Gumen
Page 26 - A Cracked Look at an Amusement Area - Don Orehek
Page 28 - The Cracked Bookstore ad - John Severin

Page 29 – One Day at a Railroad Crossing – Howard Nostrand
Page 30 – How to Run Your Home Using No Electrical Power – Don Orehek
Page 33 – The Cracked Guide to Basketball – Howard Nostrand
Page 38 – One Date at a Time – John Severin
Page 44 – Late One Evening – Howard Nostrand
Page 45 – Cracked Interviews the Fad King – Bill Ward
Page 50 – Shut-Ups (put his footprints) – Mike Ricigliano
Back Cover – Great Moments in History 1,000,342 B.C. – Howard Nostrand

**143, August 1977 (52 pages) (50c)** (On sale date May 3, 1977)
Cover – We K.O. Rocky – John Severin
Page 2 and 51 – Down With the Colonel! – Cracked Poster #143
Page 3 – Contents
Page 4 – Lettuce from Our Readers / Subscription ad
Page 6 – Rockey – John Severin
Page 12 – If T.V. Commercials Were Honest – Warren Sattler
Page 16 – Specialty Signs for Specialty Stores – Bill Ward
Page 18 – Small is Beautiful – John Langton
Page 21 – Poems to Cry By
Page 24 – New Forms of Home Entertainment – Warren Sattler
Page 26 – A Cracked Look at the Circus – Bill Ward
Page 28 – Cracked's Specialized Greeting Cards – Don Orehek
Page 31 – Help Wanted – Bill Ward
Page 34 – Cracked Looks at the T-Shirt Craze – Howard Nostrand
Page 38 – Silver Streaked – Nireves (John Severin)
Page 44 – The Cracked Bookstore ad – John Severin
Page 45 – Cracked Interviews the Monster King – Bill Ward
Page 50 – Shut-Ups (My debts) – Mike Ricigliano
Back Cover – Great Moments in Dentistry 1755 – Howard Nostrand

**144, September 1977 (52 pages) (60c)** (On sale date June 7, 1977)
Cover – Happy Days – John Severin
Page 2 and 51 – Warning! Forget That You Saw This Poster – Cracked Poster #144
Page 3 – Contents
Page 4 – Lettuce from Our Readers / Subscription ad – John Severin
Page 6 – Happy Daze – John Severin (2nd *Happy Days* Parody)
Page 12 – Super Skateboard Stunts – Howard Nostrand
Page 16 – Ad Campaigns for Unwanted Products – Bill Ward
Page 20 – At An Afternoon Business Luncheon – Howard Nostrand
Page 21 – If Commercials Were Built Into TV Programs – John Severin

Page 26 – A Cracked Look at the Phone Company – Bill Ward
Insert – 18 Cracked Stickers – John Severin (full color insert)
Page 28 – Exposing the Con in Contests – Howard Nostrand
Page 32 – Digital Instruments of the Future – Warren Sattler
Page 35 – The Cracked History of Ecology – Bill Ward
Page 39 – Baad Baad Black Sheep – John Severin
Page 45 – Cracked Interviews the Pet Store King – Bill Ward
Page 50 – Shut-Ups (66…45…38) – Mike Ricigliano
Back Cover – Great Moments in Music 1,057,648 B.C. – Howard Nostrand

**145, October 1977 (52 pages) (60c)** (On sale date July 12, 1977)
Cover – Fonzie, Rocky, Laverne and Shirley – John Severin
Page 2 and 51 – Important Notice!!! This is Your Last Warning! – Cracked Poster #145
Page 3 – Contents
Page 4 – Lettuce from Our Readers / Subscription ad – John Severin
Page 6 – Leverne and Shurley (we have dates with men) – John Severin (2nd *Laverne and Shirley* parody)
Page 12 – The Cracked Guide to Babysitting – Bill Ward
Page 16 – A Cracked Look at Summer Camps – Howard Nostrand
Page 20 – Cottonin' to Carter! – John Severin
Page 25 – The Awakening – John Severin (reprint from #97)
Page 26 – A Cracked Look at a Skateboard Park – Sururi Gumen
Insert – 2 Cracked Postcards – Howard Nostrand
Page 28- The Cracked Guide to Soccer – Warren Sattler
Page 32 – An Afternoon at an Artist's Studio – Howard Nostrand
Page 33 – If Rockey Appeared in Other Movie and TV Spots – John Severin
Page 37 – The Cracked Bookstore ad – John Severin
Page 38 – Airplot '77 – Howard Nostrand
Page 45 – Cracked Interviews the Radio King – Bill Ward
Page 50 – Shut-Ups (I think I can K.O.) – Don Orehek
Back Cover – Great Moments in History 974 A.D. – Howard Nostrand

**146, November 1977 (52 pages) (60c)** (On sale date August 16, 1977)
Cover – Star Warz – John Severin (Another top-selling issue.)
Page 2 and 51 – Emergency Flap (reprint from #63 in new format)
Page 3 – Contents
Page 4 – Lettuce from Our Readers / Subscription ad
Page 6 – Star-Warz – O.O. Severin (John Severin) / Joe Catalano
Page 13 – The Cracked Guide to Canoeing – Warren Sattler
Page 17 – On Capitol Hill – Howard Nostrand

Page 18 – When the Country Runs Out of Water – Bill Ward
Page 22 – The Cracked Guide to Jogging – Howard Nostrand
Page 26 – Frustrationland – Bill Ward
Insert – 8 Cracked Cover Stickers – John Severin (reprints of #8, 12, 13, 17, 22, 23, 27, 28, 31, 40, 45, 53, 63, 65, 69, 70) (At the time, I thought this was the coolest insert ever.)
Page 28 – Fringe Benefits Athletes Will Soon Be Demanding – Howard Nostrand (John Severin) (Severin signs Nostrand signature as a joke.)
Page 31 – Crimedom's Mail Order Catalogue – Warren Sattler
Page 36 – The Great Airline War – Howard Nostrand (John Severin) (Severin did it here, too.)
Page 39 – The Deeep – Howard Nostrand (At last, the REAL Nostrand.)
Page 45 – Cracked Interviews the Insurance King – Bill Ward
Page 50 – Shut-Ups (Folkswagon Bunny) – Don Orehek
Back Cover – The Man and the Ink Spot – Oskar Blotta

**147, December 1977 (52 pages) (60c)** (On sale date September 27, 1977)
Cover – Sylvester Paints Himself – Powers (John Severin)
Page 2 and 51 – Formal Portrait of Sylvester P. Smythe – Cracked Poster – John Severin
Page 3 – Contents
Page 4 – Lettuce from Our Readers / Subscription ad
Page 6 – Star Warz II – O.O. Severin (John Severin)
Page 12 – Cracked's Amazing Calculator Readouts
Page 13 – The Cracked History of Art – Warren Sattler
Page 17 – Exercise Manual and Hot Dog Stunts for Super Heroes – Powers (John Severin)
Page 21 – A Gloomy Indian Story – Oskar Blotta
Page 22 – If Professional People Advertised – Howard Nostrand
Page 26 – A Cracked Look at New York City – Warren Sattler
Insert – 2 Cracked Postcards to Make Somebody Jealous – John Severin (Partial reprint from #38 in new format.)
Page 28 – The Cracked Bookstore ad – John Severin
Page 29 – Chatterbox Weekly Magazine
Page 35 – The Cracked Guide to Muscle Development – Howard Nostrand
Page 39 – Whaz' Happening? – Powers (John Severin)
Page 45 – Cracked Interviews the Writing King – Bill Ward
Page 50 – Shut-Ups (make up my mind) – Don Orehek
Back Cover – The Angry Elephant and Tarzan's Son – Oskar Blotta

**148, January 1978 (52 pages) (60c)** (On sale date November 8, 1977)
Cover – More Star Wars – Powers (John Severin) (Another top-selling issue.)
Page 2 and 51 – More Star Wars – Cracked Poster – Powers (John Severin)
Page 3 – Contents
Page 4 – Lettuce from Our Readers / Subscription ad – Warren Sattler
Page 6 – The Spy Who Snubbed Me – O.O. Severin (John Severin)
Page 12 – The Machine Mania Monopolizes the Movies – Warren Sattler
Page 15 – Cy-Threepiu & Arty-Ditto A Souvenir Photo Album of Their Visit to Earth – Cosa Nostrand (Howard Nostrand)
Page 19 – A Brochure from P.T.U. (Prime Time University) – Bill Ward
Page 22 – The "How to Insult" Manual – Powers (John Severin)
Page 26 – A Cracked Look at a Plant Store – Bill Ward
Page 28 – One Minute TV Shows of the Future – Howard Nostrand
Page 32 – The Cracked World of Toys and Games – Don Orehek
Page 36 – The 99,999 Mile Book – Warren Sattler
Page 40 – Cracked Interviews the Hobo King – Bill Ward
Page 45 – Star People Weekly and Creatures and Things Magazine – John Severin
Page 50 – Shut-Ups (best nap) – Don Orehek
Back Cover – Great Moments in Games 1,057,649 B.C. – Howard Nostrand

**149, March 1978 (52 pages) (60c)** (On sale date December 20, 1977)
Cover – Bionic Man in Star Wars – John Severin
Page 2 and 51 – Warning! Absolutely Nothing Will Be Tolerated! – Cracked Poster #149
Page 3 – Contents
Page 4 – Lettuce from Our Readers (Statement of Ownership: Average number of copies sold: 473,801 – The peak!)
Page 6 – The Six Billion Dollar Man vs. Dark Badar – O.O. Severin (John Severin)
Page 12 – Cracked's Specially Tailored Birth Announcements
Page 15 – Jerry Interviews the Stars – Howard Nostrand
Page 21 – One Afternoon at a Colorado Ski Competition – Sururi Gumen
Page 22 – Cracked Tips for Improving Home Movies – Warren Sattler
Page 26 – A Cracked Look at Santa's Workshop – Don Orehek
Page 28 – Subscription ad – Warren Sattler
Page 29 – If the Characters of Star Wars Appeared in Other Movies and TV Shows – Powers (John Severin)

Page 33 – If All Violence Were Eliminated from TV – Howard Nostrand
Page 36 – It's a Lot Worse in Buffalo – Warren Sattler
Page 39 – The Talking Blob – John Severin / Joe Catalano (1st *Talking Blob*)
Page 45 – Cracked Interviews the Wrestling King – Bill Ward
Page 50 – Shut-Ups (take it from the top) – Don Orehek
Back Cover – Great Moments in Auto Racing 1926 – Howard Nostrand

**150, May 1978 (52 pages) (60c)** (On sale date January 31, 1978)
Cover – Close Encounters of the Worst Kind! – John Severin
Page 2 and 51 – Top Secret – Cracked Poster #150
Page 3 – Contents
Page 4 – Lettuce from Our Readers
Page 5 – Subscription ad – Warren Sattler
Page 6 – Close Encounters of the Worst Kind – Michael Severin (John Severin)
Page 13 – The Cracked Guide to Paddleball – Warren Sattler
Page 17 – Cowtown U.S.A.
Page 22 – The Cracked World of Hospitals – Don Orehek
Page 26 – A Cracked Look at a Ski Lodge – Bill Ward
Page 28 – If the Carter Family Became TV Regulars – John Severin
Page 32 – Other "Self-Service" Businesses – Bruce Day
Page 35 – The Cracked Guide to Martial Arts – Sean Severin (John Severin)
Page 39 – Good Tymes – Howard Nostrand (2nd *Good Times* parody)
Page 45 – Cracked Interviews the Souvenir King – Bill Ward
Page 50 – Shut-Ups (Hollywood contract) – Don Orehek
Back Cover – Great Moments in Sports 1972 – Howard Nostrand

**151, July 1978 (52 pages) (60c)** (On sale date March 14, 1978)
Cover – Charlie's Angels – John Severin
Page 2 and 51 – Correct Time – Cracked Poster #151
Page 3 – Contents
Page 4 – Lettuce from Our Readers
Page 5 – Subscription ad – Warren Sattler
Page 6 – Churlie's Angels – C. Bynum (John Severin) (2nd *Charlie's Angels* parody)
Page 12 – How to Eat Better for Less Money – Warren Sattler
Page 16 – TV Guise Magazine
Page 22 – If Other Actors Played the Parts Made Famous by Somebody Else – John Severin

Page 26 – A Cracked Look at Old Jokes – Bill Ward
Page 28 – The Cracked World of Food – Don Orehek
Page 32 – Cracked's Detective Handbook – Bill Ward
Page 36 – Manufactured Products – John Severin
Page 39 – If Frankenstein's Monster Did Guest Appearances on T.V. – Howard Nostrand (Nostrand gives apologies to Jack Davis and draws an image of the Frankenstein monster similar to Davis' as sold in the back pages of Warren magazines. In the 50s, Nostrand did a number of horror comic book stories for Harvey Comics in a style similar to Davis' over at EC.)
Page 45 – Cracked Interviews the Airline King – Bill Ward
Page 50 – Shut-Ups (I like my new job) – Don Orehek
Back Cover – Great Moments in Horsemanship 456 A.D. – Howard Nostrand

**152, August 1978 (52 pages) (60c)** (On sale date April 25, 1978)
Cover – Star Wars has a Close Encounter – John Severin
Page 2 and 51 – The Poster is Condemned – Cracked Poster #152
Page 3 – Contents
Page 4 – Lettuce from Our Readers
Page 5 – Subscription ad – Warren Sattler
Page 6 – A Close Encounter with the Star Warz Gang – Howard Nostrand (John Severin)
Page 12 – Cracked's Method for Dealing with Traveling Salesman – Warren Sattler
Page 16 – Cracked's Inquiring Photographer Visits the Stars
Page 20 – Cracked Visits the "Proverbs and Familiar Sayings" Museum – John Severin
Page 23 – Sagebrush #51 (Injuns!) – John Severin / MF
Page 24 – A Cracked Look at a State Pen – Don Orehek
Page 28 – Super Hero Ads – Bruce Day
Page 30 – The Cracked Bookstore ad – John Severin
Page 31 – Honesty on the Tube – Howard Nostrand (John Severin)
Page 33 – Isn't it Rotten in School When – Warren Sattler
Page 36 – One Morning on John Severin's Drawing Board – John Severin
Page 38 – One Evening in the McDuffy Home – Warren Sattler
Page 39 – High Noonish – John Severin / Joe Catalano
Page 45 – Cracked Interviews the Skateboard King – Bill Ward
Page 50 – Shut-Ups (Who goes there?) – Don Orehek
Back Cover – Great Moments in Psychiatry 1227 – Howard Nostrand

**153, September 1978 (52 pages) (60c)** (On sale date June 6, 1978)
Cover – The Fonz Has a "Cool" Encounter – John Severin
Page 2 and 51 – Save Our Sharks – Cracked Poster #153
Page 3 – Contents
Page 4 – Lettuce from Our Readers
Page 5 – Subscription ad – Warren Sattler
Page 6 – The Happy Dazes' Close Encounters of the Third Kind – John Severin
Page 12 – If the "Family Hour" Extended Into Our Everyday Lives – Warren Sattler
Page 14 – Brother Billy as Prez – Howard Nostrand
Page 17 – Incurably Cracked
Page 20 – The Cracked Guide to Fishing – John Severin
Page 24 – A Cracked Look at House Pets – Don Orehek
Page 28 – The Cracked History of Humor – Bill Ward
Page 32 – Sagebrush #52 (Keep up with me) – John Severin / MF
Page 33 – The Cracked Almanac – Howard Nostrand
Page 38 – The Starry-Eyed Astronomers – Don Orehek
Page 39 – Enough is Enough! – John Severin
Page 45 – Cracked Interviews the Rock 'n' Roll King – Bill Ward
Page 50 – Shut-Ups (losing your hair) – Don Orehek
Back Cover – Great Moments in Medicine 30503 B.C. – Howard Nostrand

**154, October 1978 (52 pages) (60c)** (On sale date July 11, 1978)
Cover – Jawz Too! – John Severin
Page 2 – Do Not Remove This Screw! – Cracked Poster
Page 3 – Contents
Page 4 – Lettuce from Our Readers
Page 5 – Subscription ad – Warren Sattler
Page 6 – Jaws Too! – John Severin
Page 13 – Combination Sports of the Future – Bruce Day
Page 16 – Cloning: The Advantages and the Disadvantages – Howard Nostrand
Page 18 – The Cracked Lens (1st *Cracked Lens*)
Page 20 – When Businesses Start Going After the Over-65 Market – John Severin
Page 24 – The Cracked World of Travel – Don Orehek
Page 28 – You Know You're a Skateboard Freak When – Warren Sattler
Page 30 – Odd Jobs for Star Wars Stars – Howard Nostrand
Page 33 – Tyme Magazine
Page 39 – Family's Feud – Howard Nostrand
Page 45 – Cracked Interviews the Publicity King – Bill Ward

Page 50 – Shut-Ups (not going to forgive) – Don Orehek
Page 51 – Smile! You're On Candid Shark! Iron-On
Back Cover – Great Moments in War 1,000,007 B.C. – Howard Nostrand

**155, November 1978 (52 pages) (60c)** (On sale date August 15, 1978)
Cover – Various Stars Take a Dip – John Severin
Page 2 and 51 – Warning This Room Protected – Cracked Poster
Page 3 – Contents
Page 4 – Lettuce from Our Readers
Page 5 – Subscription ad – Warren Sattler
Page 6 – The Greatest Sequel Ever Made – John Severin / Joe Catalano
Page 13 – The Cracked Investigation of the UFO Phenomenon – Howard Nostrand
Page 16 – The Cracked World of Summer – Don Orehek
Page 20 – You Know You're in a Tacky Bank When – Warren Sattler
Page 22 – Cracked Puts the Bite on Dracula – Howard Nostrand
Page 26 – A Cracked Look at a Backyard Barbecue – Don Orehek
Insert – 2 Postcards – "Shark Bite" and "Star Warz" – John Severin
Page 28 – Vermin Fight Back – Warren Sattler
Page 30 – The Cracked Bookstore ad – John Severin
Page 31 – If UFO's Ever Do Land – Bill Ward
Page 34 – A Modern Parent vs. Traditional Parent – Warren Sattler
Page 38 – A Dog's Day Afternoon
Page 39 – Funniest Island – John Severin
Page 45 – Cracked Interviews the Garbage King – Bill Ward
Page 50 – Shut-Ups (I object) – Don Orehek
Back Cover – Great Moments in Sports 1837 – Howard Nostrand

**156, December 1978 (52 pages) (60c)** (On sale date September 26, 1978)
Cover – "Grease" is Great! – John Severin
Page 2 and 51 – Danger Radioactivity – Cracked Poster
Page 3 – Contents
Page 4 – Lettuce from Our Readers / Subscription ad
Page 6 – Greased! – John Severin
Page 13 – Fun City Olympics – Warren Sattler
Page 16 – Photoon (funniest looking person) (1st *Photoon*)
Page 17 – The Cracked Guide to Sailing – Bill Ward
Page 21 – Iffy U.F.O. Info Magazine – Howard Nostrand
Page 26 – The Cracked World of Appliances – Don Orehek
Page 30 – Cracked Products for Everyday Use – Warren Sattler
Page 32 – One Afternoon in the Park
Page 33 – More of The Cracked Lens

Page 35 – Popular Songs for Everyday Working People – Howard Nostrand
Page 39 – Three's Crummier – John Severin (1st *Three's Company* parody)
Page 45 – Cracked Interviews the Psychic King – Bill Ward
Page 50 – Shut-Ups (Squeaky's breaking out) – Don Orehek
Back Cover – Landing On Mars – Howard Nostrand / Murad Gumen

**157, January 1979 (52 pages) (60c)** (On sale date November 7, 1978)
Cover – Heaven Can Wait – John Severin
Page 2 – Due to Lack of Interest – Cracked Poster
Page 3 – Contents
Page 4 – Lettuce from Our Readers / Subscription ad
Page 6 – Heaven'll Wait – John Severin
Page 13 – Family Tree Pedicure – Bill Ward
Page 17 – Cracked Examines Telephone Answering Machines – Howard Nostrand
Page 20 – Bringing the Nile Style to the Potomac – Warren Sattler
Page 24 – Snappy Insults to Stupid Statements – Bill Ward
Page 26 – Great Books at Great Prices When You Join the Book-a-Month Club
Page 28 – You Like to Live Dangerously When – LePoer (John Severin)
Page 29 – Still More from The Cracked Lens
Page 32 – Cracked's I'm O.K. Test – Howard Nostrand
Page 35 – Photoon (I hate my body)
Page 36 – TV Contraptions We'll Soon Be Seeing – Val Mayerik
Page 39 – The Adventures of the Masked Bandito – John Severin
Page 45 – Cracked Interviews the Apartment King – Bill Ward
Page 50 – Shut-Ups (big game) – Don Orehek
Page 51 – Who's Perfect? Iron-On – John Severin
Back Cover – Happy-Daze Shut-Ups (I have a date) – Powers (John Severin)

**158, March 1979 (52 pages) (60c)** (On sale date December 19, 1978)
Cover – Mork and Mindy – John Severin
Page 2 and 51 – If at First You Don't Succeed – Cracked Poster
Page 3 – Contents
Page 4 – Lettuce from Our Readers (Statement of Ownership: Average number of copies sold: 463,085) / Subscription ad
Page 6 – Mork and Mindy – John Severin (1st of many, many, many *Mork and Mindy* parodies. Note that they didn't even bother coming up with a punny title.)
Page 12 – Cracked's Guide for Spotting Self-Lovers – Howard Nostrand

Page 14 – And Still More from The Cracked Lens
Page 17 – "The Villain" – Val Mayerik
Page 18 – A Cracked Look at Phobias – Warren Sattler
Page 22 – Special Interest and Digest Magazines – John Severin
Page 24 – Cracked's new Soon-to-be-a-Fad Diets – Don Orehek
Page 26 – Cracked Takes a Look at the Big Cats of the Big Top – Warren Sattler
Page 28 – Testimonial Ads, the Way They Should Be – Howard Nostrand
Page 30 – The Cracked Guide to Horseback Riding – Nireves (John Severin)
Page 34 – Your Dentist is Your Friend – Don Orehek
Page 36 – Phone Services of the Future – Warren Sattler
Page 38 – Nic Disposable ad
Page 39 – Lue Grunt – Noel Powers (John Severin)
Page 45 – Cracked Interviews the Health Nut King – Bill Ward
Page 50 – Shut-Ups (start off this auction) – Don Orehek
Back Cover – Great Moments in Hospitality 472 A.D. – Howard Nostrand

**159, May 1979 (52 pages) (60c)** (On sale date January 30, 1979)
Cover – Battlestar Galactica – John Severin
Page 2 and 51 – We're Experiencing Technical Difficulties – Cracked Poster #159
Page 3 – Contents
Page 4 – Lettuce from Our Readers / Subscription ad
Page 6 – Battlestar Garlictica – John Severin
Page 12 – Cracked Modernized Songs of Childhood – Bill Ward
Page 16 – A Cracked Look at Indirect Messages – Don Orehek
Page 18 – Sagebrush #50 (There's gold here) – John Severin
Page 19 – The Cracked Book of Games and Puzzles That Anyone Can Solve – Warren Sattler
Page 24 – Clone Ads of the Future – Samuel B. Whitehead
Page 26 – You Know You're in a Cracked Hospital When – Don Orehek
Page 29 – And Yet Still More from The Cracked Lens
Page 33 – The Scuba Diver – Howard Nostrand
Page 34 – The Cracked Handbook of Acting – Warren Sattler
Page 38 – Cracked's Absurd Album of More Appropriate Acronyms
Page 39 – M*U*S*H (Mail call!) – John Severin (3rd *M*A*S*H* parody)
Page 45 – Cracked Interviews the Saturday Morning Cartoon King – Bill Ward
Page 50 – Shut-Ups (best tattoo jobs) – Don Orehek
Back Cover – One Day in the Tropics – Val Mayerik

**160, July 1979 (52 pages) (60c)** (On sale date March 13, 1979)
Cover – A Man Can Fly? – John Severin
Page 2 and 51 – If This Spot Turns Blue Evacuate Area Immediately – Cracked Poster #31 (reprint from #102)
Page 3 – Contents
Page 4 – Lettuce from Our Readers / Subscription ad
Page 6 – Suped-Upman The Satire – Nireves (John Severin)
Page 13 – Cracked Looks at Racing – Samuel B. Whitehead
Page 17 – Airline Fares – Warren Sattler
Page 20 – And Yet Again Still More from The Cracked Lens
Page 22 – Cracked Guide to Roller Skating – Bill Ward
Page 26 – The Classified Ads of the Future – Howard Nostrand
Page 29 – Photoon (Haven't I seen you)
Page 30 – In Case of Emergency – Warren Sattler
Page 32 – The Layman's Guide to Hot and Cold Weather – Don Orehek
Page 35 – Cracked Presents Superheroes of the Future – Willy Orwonte (John Severin)
Page 38 – One Afternoon at a Stop Light – Howard Nostrand
Page 39 – Lyin Beat Magazine
Page 45 – Cracked Interviews the I.Q. King – Bill Ward
Page 50 – Shut-Ups (any other questions) – Don Orehek
Back Cover – Great Moments in Sports 1947 – Howard Nostrand

**161, August 1979 (52 pages) (60c)** (On sale date April 24, 1979)
Cover – Mork and Mindy and Gary Coleman – John Severin
Page 2 and 51 – Attention In the Interest of Fair Play – Cracked Poster
Page 3 – Contents
Page 4 – Lettuce from Our Readers / Subscription ad
Page 5 – The Further Adventures of Mork and Mindy – John Severin (2nd *Mork and Mindy* parody)
Page 12 – Last Words Before the Hang-Up – Sururi Gumen
Page 15 – Super Ms Magazine – Warren Sattler
Page 20 – And Yet Once Again Still More from The Cracked Lens
Page 24 – The Cracked World of Teenagers – Don Orehek
Page 28 – If Gary Coleman Played Other Parts – R. McGeddon (John Severin) (One story has Gary turn into the Hulk, a character John Severin drawn for many years for Marvel.)
Page 32 – Photoon (Peggy Steel)
Page 33 – Cracked Investigates I.F.O.'s – Samuel B. Whitehead
Page 37 – Pologloid No-Step ad
Page 38 – The Greatest TV Show Ever Made – John Severin
Page 45 – Cracked Interviews the Fashion King – Bill Ward

Page 50 – Shut-Ups (our little diet) – Don Orehek
Back Cover – Great Moments in Travel 1915 – Howard Nostrand

**162, September 1979 (52 pages) (60c)** (On sale date June 5, 1979)
Cover – Diff'rent Strokes – C.E. Severin (Catherine Severin) (This cover was done by John's 15-year-old daughter, Catherine when John was taken ill. Howard Nostrand was put on standby to do a cover, but Catherine came through.)
Page 2 and 51 – Do Not Read This Poster – Cracked Poster
Page 3 – Contents
Page 4 – Lettuce from Our Readers / Subscription ad
Page 6 – Diff'rent Strokes (Good morning, Mrs. Carrot) – John Severin (1st *Diff'rent Strokes* parody)
Page 12 – The Cracked Theory on the Relativity of Time – Howard Nostrand
Page 15 – The Cracked Fact Pack: Housing – Don Orehek
Page 20 – Sagebrush #53 (avalanche) – John Severin
Page 21 – And Yet Once Again Still Some More from The Cracked Lens
Page 26 – A Cracked Look at a Golf Course – Don Orehek
Page 28 – Products Designed for Overweight Americans – Warren Sattler
Page 32 – Cracked's Playful Ways to Make Work Fun – Sururi Gumen
Page 34 – A Typical College Registrar's Bulletin Board – Samuel B. Whitehead
Page 37 – Shylock Homes and the Case of the Lifted Locket – Moe Riarty (John Severin) / Joe Catalano
Page 44 – Marvin Manley Bodywrecking Club ad
Page 45 – Cracked Interviews the Psychiatric King – Bill Ward
Page 50 – Shut-Ups (drive away your customers) – Don Orehek
Back Cover – The Traffic Jam – Caracu (reprint from #70)

**163, October 1979 (52 pages) (75c)** (On sale date July 10, 1979)
Cover – Mork and Mindy on the Beach – John Severin
Page 2 and 51 – Fight Inflation at any Cost! – Cracked Poster #163
Page 3 – Contents
Page 4 – Lettuce from Our Readers / Official Reporter Cracked Magazine T-Shirt ad – John Severin (Bill Sproul appears in this ad.)
Page 6 – The Return of Mork and Mindy – John Severin (3rd *Mork and Mindy* parody)
Page 13 – Cracked's Inventory of Personal Spending Habits – Warren Sattler
Page 16 – And Yet Once Again Still Even Some More from The Cracked Lens

Page 20 – Colonel Jim Dandy's Guide to Good Manners for Discriminatin' Cowpokes 'n' Buckeroos – Samuel B. Whitehead
Page 24 – One Day in the North Woods – Howard Nostrand
Page 25 – Super People Magazine – Sururi Gumen
Insert – 2 Postcards – Bill McCartney (Bill Ward) / John Severin
Page 30 – How Adults Drive Kids Nuts – Warren Sattler
Page 32 – How to Improve Your...ah...ah...Memory – Howard Nostrand
Page 35 – When TV Goes Completely Sci Fi – Samuel B. Whitehead
Page 38 – Rock and Roll Your Eyeballs Out – John Severin
Page 45 – Cracked Interviews the Wedding King – Bill Ward
Page 50 – Shut-Ups (I LOVE a parade) – Don Orehek
Back Cover – Training the Dog – Samuel B. Whitehead

**164, November 1979 (52 pages) (75c)** (On sale date August 14, 1979)
Cover – Alien – Don't Look it's too Scary! – John Severin
Page 2 and 51 – The Way to Conserve Energy – Cracked Poster
Page 3 – Contents
Page 4 – Lettuce from Our Readers / Official Reporter Cracked Magazine T-Shirt ad – John Severin
Page 6 – Allien and How to Watch it – John Severin
Page 13 – When Gambling Becomes Legal in Everyday Life – Warren Sattler
Page 16 – The Cracked World of Ambition – Bill Ward
Page 20 – Auntie Dinger's ad
Page 21 – Cracked Tips for Economizing – Samuel B. Whitehead
Page 24 – The Cracked World of Marriage – Don Orehek
Page 28 – The Last of The Cracked Lens
Page 34 – You're Going a Little Too Far When – Sururi Gumen
Page 36 – Literal Interpretations of Baseball Expressions – LePoer (John Severin)
Page 38 – The Cracked World of Disco – Don Orehek
Page 42 – Ten Little Drivers – Warren Sattler
Page 44 – One Afternoon in a Plastic Surgeon's Office – Bill Ward
Page 45 – If Mork Appeared in Other TV Shows and Movies (Star Trek) – John Severin
Page 50 – Shut-Ups (pastrami on rye) – Don Orehek
Back Cover – Oh, Those Long Lines – Howard Nostrand

**165, December 1979 (52 pages) (75c)** (On sale date September 25, 1979)
Cover – Dracula – John Severin
Page 2 and 51 – Important Announcement – Cracked Poster #165
Page 3 – Contents

Page 4 – Lettuce from Our Readers / Official Reporter Cracked Magazine T-Shirt ad – John Severin
Page 6 – Drecula – John Severin
Page 13 – The Rhyme of the Thieving Sheik – John Langton
Page 17 – Photoon (Kitchie-kitchie coo!)
Page 18 – Gag Lines for Every Profession – Warren Sattler
Page 21 – Weather Forecasting Kit ad – Howard Nostrand
Page 22 – The Very Last of The Cracked Lens
Page 27 – You're Really Overdoing it a Little When – LePoer (John Severin)
Page 28 – The Cracked World of Lines – Don Orehek
Page 32 – Miracle Workers the World has Never Heard of ('Til Now) – Samuel B. Whitehead
Page 35 – Cracked's Guide to Understanding Your Pet – Sururi Gumen
Page 39 – Sport Sillystrated Magazine
Page 44 – Neveready Powercell ad
Page 45 – Cracked Interviews the Game Show King – Bill Ward
Page 50 – Shut-Ups (your eyes) – Don Orehek
Back Cover – One Night at the Garden – Howard Nostrand

**166, January 1980 (52 pages) (75c)** (On sale date November 6, 1979)
Cover – Laverne & Shirley with Lennie & Squiggy – John Severin
Page 2 and 51 – "You Too Can Be President" – Jimmy Carter Mask
Page 3 – Contents
Page 4 – Lettuce from Our Readers / Subscription ad
Page 6 – Leverne and Shurley (what do you want for dinner) – John Severin (3rd *Laverne and Shirley* parody)
Page 13 – The History of Advertising – Howard Nostrand
Page 17 – Positively the Very Last of The Cracked Lens
Page 22 – When Businesses Start Going After the Vampire Market – Warren Sattler
Page 26 – One Rustic Day Outside Tijuana, Mexico – John Severin
Page 27 – The Cracked Guide to Fortune Telling – Don Orehek
Page 31 – Specialized TV Stations for Different Interest Groups – Samuel B. Whitehead
Page 35 – Official Cracked Reporter T-Shirt ad
Page 36 – The Truth You'll Never Hear – Warren Sattler
Page 38 – Moonwrecker – Sururi Gumen
Page 45 – Cracked Interviews the Roller Disco King – Bill Ward
Page 50 – Shut-Ups (play like you never played) – Don Orehek
Back Cover – Great Moments in Hunting 999,999 B.C. – Howard Nostrand

**167, March 1980 (52 pages) (75c)** (On sale date December 18, 1979)
Cover – More Mork – John Severin
Page 2 and 51 – Warning the Earth is Tilting to the Right." – Cracked Poster #167
Page 3 – Contents
Page 4 – Lettuce from Our Readers (Statement of Ownership: Average number of copies sold: 434,946) / Subscription ad
Page 6 – If Mork Appeared in Other T.V. Shows and Movies (Fantasy Island) – John Severin
Page 12 – The Cracked History of the Automobile – Warren Sattler
Page 16 – Absolutely, Positively, the Very Last of The Cracked Lens
Page 20 – More Celebrity Nightmares – John Severin
Page 23 – The Cracked Fact Pack: Christmas Cards – Samuel B. Whitehead
Page 28 – Test Tube Products of the Future – Howard Nostrand
Page 30 – The Cracked Guide to Gymnastics – John Langton
Page 34 – Career Dreams That Came True – Sururi Gumen
Page 37 – Official Cracked Reporter T-Shirt ad
Page 38 – G.I. Donut Boys – John Severin
Page 45 – Cracked Interviews the Energy Conservation King – Bill Ward
Page 50 – Shut-Ups (married 25 years) – Don Orehek
Back Cover – The Beanstalk – Conky Nostrand (Howard Nostrand)

**168, May 1980 (52 pages) (75c)** (On sale date January 29, 1980)
Cover – More M*A*S*H – John Severin
Page 2 and 51 – Teachers Strike No School – Cracked Poster #168
Page 3 – Contents
Page 4 – Lettuce from Our Readers / Subscription ad
Page 6 – M*U*S*H (probably wondering why I called you) – John Severin (4th *M*A*S*H* parody)
Page 13 – How the Ads of Tomorrow Will Exploit the Energy Crisis – Howard Nostrand
Page 16 – How Madison Avenue Can Turn Anything Into a Great Selling Holiday Gift – Bill Ward
Page 19 – Absolutely, Positively the Very Last of Those Cracked Monsters
Page 22 – The Cracked Guide to Ice Skating – John Severin
Page 26 – A Cracked Look at a Health Spa – Don Orehek
Page 28 – Golf Oil Company ad
Page 29 – If Schools Patterned Themselves After TV – Samuel B. Whitehead
Page 33 – Official Cracked Reporter T-Shirt ad

Page 34 – How to Make Money in Your Spare Time – John Severin
Page 38 – Movie Posters We'll Soon Be Seeing
Page 44 – Cracked Interviews the Orkan King – Bill Ward
Page 50 – Shut-Ups (big struggle) – Don Orehek
Back Cover – The Chicken Killer – Howard Nostrand / Jay Lynch (redux of the same gag originally done by Bill Ward in issue #30.)

**169, July 1980 (52 pages) (75c)** (On sale date March 11, 1980)
Cover – We Wreck Star Trek – John Severin
Page 2 and 51 – Fine For Littering in This Area. – Cracked Poster #169
Page 3 – Contents
Page 4 – Lettuce from Our Readers / Subscription ad
Page 6 – Star Drek the Moving Picture – John Severin
Page 14 – The Coming Mini-Auto Age – John Langton
Page 18 – Cracked Handbook for Restaurant Owners – Warren Sattler
Page 22 – Absolutely, Positively, Unquestionably, the Very Last of The Cracked Lens
Page 26 – Cracked Goes to a Ski Mountain – Don Orehek
Page 28 – Cracked Predictions for the 1980's – Sururi Gumen
Page 32 – Photoon (Four score and seven years ago)
Page 33 – Famous Animal Celebrities – Nireves (John Severin)
Page 35 – College for Panhandlers – Don Orehek
Page 39 – The Billy Pluckett Story – John Severin
Page 44 – Cracked Interviews the Trekker King – Bill Ward
Page 50 – Shut-Ups (put out the dog) – Don Orehek
Back Cover – The Swordsman – Bill McCartney (Bill Ward) (reprint from #35)

**170, August 1980 (52 pages) (75c)** (On sale date April 22, 1980)
Cover – Dukes of Hazard Run Out of Gas! – John Severin
Page 2 and 51 – Important Notice – Cracked Poster #170
Page 3 – Contents
Page 4 – Lettuce from Our Readers / Subscription ad
Page 6 – The Not-So-Bright Shadow – John Severin
Page 13 – Cracked's Reasons to Be Cheerful – Warren Sattler
Page 17 – 4 Out of 5 Dentists Surveyed
Page 18 – Situations You Wish You Weren't In – Samuel B. Whitehead
Page 20 – What is a Fad Freak? – Sururi Gumen
Page 22 – Using Star Trek Logic and Technology to Solve Life's Everyday Problems – Don Orehek
Page 25 – Ye Hang Ups (mind closing the door) – C.E. Severin (Catherine Severin)
Page 26 – The Cracked World of Schooling – Bill Ward

Page 30 – Cracked's Random Samplings – Howard Nostrand
Page 34 – A Cracked Salute to New York City – Sururi Gumen
Page 39 – The Dorks of Hazzardous (kinda spongy Friday) – John Severin (1st *Dukes of Hazzard* parody)
Page 44 – Cracked Interviews the Nuclear Power King – Bill Ward
Page 50 – Shut-Ups (money and credit cards) – Don Orehek
Back Cover – Great Moments in Technology 1029 – Howard Nostrand

**171, September 1980 (52 pages) (75c)** (On sale date June 3, 1980)
Cover – More Diff'rent Strokes! – John Severin (Some consider this to be one of the most offensive *Cracked* covers with Sylvester in blackface.)
Page 2 – Three Mile Island Nuclear Plant – Cracked Poster #171
Page 3 – Contents
Page 4 – Lettuce from Our Readers / I'm a Perfect 10 Iron-On / Subscription ad
Page 6 – If Arnold Were Treated and Behaved Like a Real-Life Kid – John Severin
Page 11 – New Detectors of the Future – Don Orehek
Page 14 – The Medicine Man – John Langton
Page 17 – The Cracked Book of Running – Bill Ward
Page 22 – Absolutely, Undeniably, Positively, Unquestionably, the Very Last of The Cracked Lens
Page 25 – Ads from the Space Age – Warren Sattler
Page 30 – New Ideas for Phony "Optional Equipment" Car Dealers Can Gouge the Public With – Howard Nostrand
Page 32 – Company Mergers of the Future – Samuel B. Whitehead
Page 36 – Illustrated Idiotic Idioms
Page 38 – King Author and the Knights of the Reserved Table – John Severin
Page 44 – Cracked Interviews the Inflation Beating King – Bill Ward
Page 50 – Shut-Ups (worst case of bigamy) – Don Orehek
Page 51 – I'm a Perfect 10 Iron-On
Back Cover – Great Moments in Sports 1,217,003 B.C. – Conky Nostrand (Howard Nostrand)

**172, October 1980 (52 pages) (75c)** (On sale date July 8, 1980)
Cover – The Dukes Run Into Chips! – John Severin
Page 2 – 1st Annual Gala Jamboree Extravaganza – Cracked Poster
Page 3 – Contents
Page 4 – Lettuce from Our Readers / Official Reporter Cracked Magazine T-Shirt ad – John Severin
Page 6 – The Dorks of Hazzardous With Chipps to go – John Severin

Page 13 – Absolutely, Unquestionably, Positively, Undeniably, the Very, Very, Last of The Cracked Lens
Page 18 – If Women Really Want to Be Treated Equally – Don Orehek
Page 20 – Cracked Fantasies – Sururi Gumen
Page 23 – You're Not Going to Get Anywhere with Him/Her if – LePoer (John Severin)
Page 24 – What You're Really Thinking – Warren Sattler
Page 26 – Cracked Visits the Ol' Fishing Creek – Don Orehek
Page 28 – Cracked's All-Purpose, Time-Saving "Denial of Charges" Speech for Politicians – John Severin
Page 30 – The Cracked Penal Code – Warren Sattler
Page 32 – What "Help Wanted" Ads Say and What They Really Mean – Howard Nostrand
Page 35 – Loser Magazine – John Severin
Page 41 – Subscription ad – Warren Sattler
Page 42 – Cracked Songs from Outer Space – John Langton
Page 44 – Ye Hang Ups #3 (screams) – C.E. Severin (Catherine Severin)
Page 45 – Jimmy Carter's Telethon for Energy – Samuel B. Whitehead
Page 50 – Shut-Ups (Little Breeze) – Don Orehek
Page 51 – See Back of T-Shirt See Front of T-Shirt Iron-On
Back Cover – Great Moments in Technology 186 B.C. – Howard Nostrand

**173, November 1980 (52 pages) (75c)** (On sale date August 12, 1980)
Cover – Empire War – John Severin
Page 2 and 51 – Empire War – Cracked Poster – John Severin
Page 3 – Contents
Page 4 – Lettuce from Our Readers / Official Reporter Cracked Magazine T-Shirt ad – John Severin
Page 6 – The Empire Strikes Out – O.O. Severin (John Severin)
Page 13 – Cracked's New Sidewalk, Street and Playground Games – Warren Sattler
Page 17 – Ye Hang Ups #2 (castle) – C.E. Severin (Catherine Severin)
Page 18 – Cracked's Updated Punchlines to Some of the World's Oldest Jokes – Sururi Gumen
Page 21 – Absolutely, Unquestionably, Positively, Undeniably, the Very, Very, Last of The Cracked Lens (and we mean it this time!)
Page 26 – A Cracked Look at a Big City Office – Don Orehek
Page 28 – How the Government Can Cut Down on Spending – Warren Sattler
Page 32 – Cracked Facts – Bill Ward
Page 34 – The Cracked World of Vacations – Don Orehek
Page 38 – A Dozen Things Never to Do at the Beach – John Langton

Page 40 – Subscription ad – Warren Sattler
Page 41 – If Ronald Reagan Becomes President – Samuel B. Whitehead (he did)
Page 45 – Cracked Interviews the Multi-Cinema King – Bill Ward
Page 50 – Shut-Ups (flat tire) – Don Orehek
Back Cover – Great Moments in Aviation 1947 – Samuel B. Whitehead

**174, December 1980 (52 pages) (75c)** (On sale date September 23, 1980)
Cover – The Empire Strikes it Rich – John Severin
Page 2 and 51 – This Room Has Been Affected By the Energy Crisis! – Cracked Poster #174
Page 3 – Contents
Page 4 – Lettuce from Our Readers / Official Reporter Cracked Magazine T-Shirt ad – John Severin
Page 6 – Exploiting the Star Wars Figures to Their Fullest – John Severin
Page 12 – A Cracked Look at Dumb Investments – Warren Sattler
Page 15 – Absolutely, Unquestionably, Positively, Undeniably, the Very, Very, Last of The Cracked Lens (and we really mean it this time!)
Page 20 – The Cracked Question and Answer Guide to Racquetball – Don Orehek
Page 24 – How to Win a School Election – T. Severin (John Severin)
Page 28 – Future Ultra Realistic Electronic Games – Val Mayerik
Page 31 – Ye Hang Ups #4 (got a minute) – C.E. Severin (Catherine Severin)
Page 32 – Cracked's Little Known By-Laws – Don Orehek
Page 34 – Masters of Evil
Page 37 – You Won't Be Invited to Another Party When at Your Last Party – Warren Sattler
Page 39 – Real Incredible People – John Severin
Page 45 – Subscription ad – Warren Sattler
Page 46 – Cracked's Career Guide for Disc Jockeys – Bill Ward
Page 50 – Shut-Ups (my greatest work of art) – Don Orehek
Back Cover – The Man and the Beast – Oskar Blotta (reprint from #80)

**175, January 1981 (52 pages) (75c)** (On sale date November 4, 1980)
Cover – We Salute M*A*S*H – John Severin
Page 2 and 51 – To Conserve Energy – Cracked Poster
Page 3 – Contents
Page 4 – Lettuce from Our Readers / Official Reporter Cracked Magazine T-Shirt ad – John Severin
Page 6 – M*U*S*H (Colonel Potted) – John Severin (5th *M*A*S*H* parody)

Page 11 – The Cracked "Instant Status" Mail Order Catalog – Warren Sattler
Page 16 – If Our Currency Truly Reflected Our Economy – Samuel B. Whitehead
Page 19 – Ye Hang Ups (Elric) – C.E. Severin (Catherine Severin)
Page 20 – Absolutely, Unquestionably, Positively, Undeniably, the Very, Very, Last of The Cracked Lens (and we really mean it this time, for sure!)
Page 26 – Cracked Headlines
Page 28 – Every Cloud has a Silver Lining – John Severin
Page 31 – Profile of a Coward – Bill Ward
Page 34 – When the U.S. Adopts the Metric System – Warren Sattler
Page 36 – How the Politicians Kept Their Election Promises – Don Orehek
Page 39 – Subscription ad – Warren Sattler
Page 40 – Ideal Kid ad – Warren Sattler
Page 41 – How to be a Salesman – John Severin
Page 45 – Cracked Interviews the Time Saving King – Bill Ward
Page 50 – Shut-Ups (yellow-bellies) – Don Orehek
Back Cover – Great Moments in Sports 1967 – Warren Sattler

**176, March 1981 (52 pages) (75c)** (On sale date December 6, 1980)
Cover – We Lock-Up Barney Miller! – John Severin
Page 2 and 51 – This Wall is Closing in on You! – Cracked Poster
Page 3 – Contents
Page 4 – Lettuce from Our Readers (Statement of Ownership: Average number of copies sold: 388,863) / Official Reporter Cracked Magazine T-Shirt ad – John Severin
Page 6 – Blarney Miller (I want to report a crime) – John Severin (2nd *Barney Miller* parody)
Page 11 – Cracked's First (and Probably Last) Annual Soap Opera Awards – Warren Sattler
Page 15 – Absolutely, Unquestionably, Positively, Undeniably, the Very, Very, Last of The Cracked Lens (and we really, really mean it this time, for sure!)
Page 20 – The Cracked Handbook on Personal Grooming – Sururi Gumen
Page 23 – Morbad News
Page 28 – Cracked's Horoscopes for '81 – Val Mayerik
Page 32 – You Know You're Watching Too Much TV When – Don Orehek
Page 34 – How Magazines Will Attract New Subscribers in the Future – Samuel B. Whitehead

Page 37 – The Great Chicago Heist – John Severin
Page 45 – Cracked Interviews the Book Publishing King – Bill Ward
Page 50 – Shut-Ups (man trying to break down door) – Don Orehek
Back Cover – Great Moments in Sports 1958 – Warren Sattler

**177, May 1981 (52 pages) (75c)** (On sale date January 27, 1981)
Cover – We Get Hulked! – John Severin (3rd Alfred E. Neuman cover)
Page 2 and 51 – Hypnotism Poster – Cracked Poster
Page 3 – Contents
Page 4 – Lettuce from Our Readers / Official Reporter Cracked Magazine T-Shirt ad – John Severin
Page 6 – The Incredible Hunk – Sigbjorn (John Severin)
Page 11 – "Memorable Moments From Presidential History" – Val Mayerik
Page 15 – Absolutely, Unquestionably, Positively, Undeniably, the Very, Very, Last of The Cracked Lens (and we really, really mean it this time, for sure!) Part II
Page 19 – Dumb Questions That Don't Deserve an Answer – Don Orehek
Page 20 – Never Rent the Apartment if – Sururi Gumen
Page 22 – How to Interpret All Those Professional School Ads – Samuel B. Whitehead
Page 26 – If Professional Sports Were Played the Same Way as When We Were Kids – Val Mayerik
Page 29 – How to Get a Job – Bill Ward
Page 32 – Believe it or Not (East Pakistan) (1st *Believe it or Not*)
Page 35 – Ye Hang Ups (equal rights) – C.E. Severin (Catherine Severin)
Page 36 – How to Meet the Opposite Sex – John Langton
Page 40 – Those Little Things That Do Go Right – Warren Sattler
Page 43 – My Buddyguard – John Severin
Page 50 – Shut-Ups (Our son, the graduate) – Don Orehek
Back Cover – Great Moments in Dining 1953 – Warren Sattler

**178, July 1981 (52 pages) (75c)** (On sale date March 10, 1981)
Cover – We Get Hung-Up On Diff'rent Strokes! – John Severin
Page 2 and 51 – Cracked Automatic Digital Weather Forecaster – Cracked Poster #178
Page 3 – Contents
Page 4 – Lettuce from Our Readers / Subscription ad
Page 6 – Diff'rent Strokes (two cups of wheat germ) – John Severin (2nd *Diff'rent Strokes* parody)
Page 13 – More Believe it or Not (Syrians)
Page 15 – Why is it That – Don Orehek

Page 18 – The Cracked World of Staying in Shape – Bill Dubay
Page 21 – Cracked's Look at Superstitions – Warren Sattler
Page 24 – How You Picture a Business Operates and How it Really Does – Samuel B. Whitehead
Page 26 – Cracked Visits a Hollywood Movie Set – Sururi Gumen
Page 28 – The Cracked Movie – Nireves (John Severin) / Joe Catalano (1st *Cracked Movie*) (1st appearance of Robert C. Sproul as himself)
Page 35 – Absolutely, Unquestionably, Positively, Undeniably, the Very, Very, Last of The Cracked Lens (and we really, really mean it this time, for sure!) Part III
Page 38 – Other "No Frills" Items and Services – Don Orehek
Page 40 – Little Known Baby Pictures
Page 42 – If Newspapers Emphasized Good News – Samuel B. Whitehead
Page 45 – Cracked Interviews the Vacation King – Bill Ward
Page 50 – Shut-Ups (2 voice lessons) – Don Orehek
Back Cover – Great Moments in Communication 1383 – Warren Sattler

**179, August 1981 (52 pages) (90c)** (On sale date April 21, 1981) (Though it is not mentioned anywhere, the 1st *Spies and Saboteurs* by Mike Ricigliano appears around the margins of this issue.)
Cover – The Dukes! And Popeye! – John Severin
Page 2 and 51 – Giant UPC Code – Cracked Poster
Page 3 – Contents
Page 4 – Lettuce from Our Readers / Subscription ad
Page 5 – The Dorks of Hazzardous (Rub his roof) – John Severin (2nd *Dukes of Hazzard* parody)
Page 13 – Cracked's Unusual Gift Catalog
Page 16 – How to Make Baseball More Interesting – Bill Ward
Page 20 – It Isn't As Bad As It Sounds – John Langton
Page 22 – The Growing Garbage Problem and What to Do About it – Warren Sattler
Page 26 – Instant Epitaphs – Samuel B. Whitehead
Insert – Cracked's Insult Cards
Page 28 – Poopeye – Nireves (John Severin)
Page 35 – Absolutely, Unquestionably, Positively, Undeniably, the Very, Very, Last of The Cracked Lens (and we really, really mean it this time, for sure!) Part IV
Page 38 – How to Read Those Travel Ads – Samuel B. Whitehead
Page 40 – Cracked's Personality Profile Comparisons – Warren Sattler
Page 43 – Dangerous Barroom Encounters – John Severin
Page 45 – Cracked Interviews the Insurance King – Bill Ward (reprint from #146)

Page 50 – Shut-Ups (horn section) – Don Orehek
Back Cover – Great Moments in Technology 1,000,000 B.C. – Warren Sattler

**180, September 1981 (52 pages) (90c)** (On sale date June 2, 1981)
Cover and Back Cover – Win the "Mistakes on This Cover" Contest! – John Severin
Page 2 and 51 – The Cracked Public Service Eye Test – Cracked Poster #180
Page 3 – Contents
Page 4 – Lettuce from Our Readers / Subscription ad
Page 6 – The Incredible Shrunken Woman – John Severin
Page 13 – The Cracked World of Pets – Bill Dubay
Page 16 – When Hollywood Totally Takes Over Washington – Samuel B. Whitehead
Page 19 – "Find the Mistakes Contest!" – John Severin, Val Mayerik
Page 20 – You Know You're Unpopular if – Bill Ward
Page 22 – Cracked Ways of Conserving Water – Val Mayerik
Page 26 – A Cracked Look at the World's Worst "Knock Knock" Jokes – Don Orehek
Page 28 – Cracked's Sequels to Classic Movies – John Severin
Page 34 – Cracked's Unusual Gift Catalog Part II – John Severin
Page 36 – The Cracked World of Moving – Don Orehek
Page 40 – Press Mistakes! (avant-garde artist) – John Langton (1st *Press Mistakes!*)
Page 42 – Absolutely, Unquestionably, Positively, Undeniably, the Very, Very, Last of The Cracked Lens (and we really, really mean it this time, for sure!) Part V
Page 45 – Cracked Interviews the Comedy King – Bill Ward
Page 50 – Shut-Ups (supreme court) – Charles Rodrigues

**181, October 1981 (52 pages) (90c)** (On sale date July 7, 1981)
Cover – The Great American Hero – John Severin
Page 2 – The Cracked State-of-the-Nation Chart – Cracked Poster
Page 3 – Contents
Page 4 – Lettuce from Our Readers / Subscription ad
Page 6 – America's Greatest Hero – John Severin
Page 13 – The Cracked Book of Handy Hints – Don Orehek
Page 17 – Still More Believe it or Not (Warsaw, Poland)
Page 20 – What We'll Miss When the 80's Become the 'Good Old Days' – Samuel B. Whitehead
Page 23 – The JR Family Photo Album – John Severin
Page 26 – Cracked Word Play (Double Vision) (1st *Cracked Word Play*)

Page 28 – The Factors of Life – Samuel B. Whitehead
Page 35 – Absolutely, Unquestionably, Positively, Undeniably, the Very, Very, Last of The Cracked Lens (and we really, really mean it this time, for sure!) Part VI
Page 38 – The Cracked Guide to Golf – Warren Sattler
Page 42 – Jobs You Never Dreamed Someone Does – John Severin
Page 44 – In the Electronic Game Room – Sururi Gumen
Page 45 – Cracked Interviews the Video King – Bill Ward
Page 50 – Shut-Ups (To err is human) – Don Orehek
Page 51 – "Money Making" Iron-On
Back Cover – Great Moments in Entertainment 200 B.C. – Warren Sattler

**182, November 1981 (52 pages) (90c)** (On sale date August 11, 1981)
Cover – M*A*S*H Gets the Funny Business! – John Severin
Page 2 – Everyone Here Brings Happiness – Cracked Poster
Page 3 – Contents
Page 4 – Lettuce from Our Readers / Subscription ad – Bob Taylor
Page 6 – M*A*S*H*E*D – John Severin (6th *M*A*S*H* parody)
Page 12 – Dull vs. Exciting – Don Orehek
Page 15 – One Evening in a Posh Midwestern Restaurant – Sururi Gumen
Page 16 – Absolutely, Unquestionably, Positively, Undeniably, the Very, Very, Last of The Cracked Lens (and we really, really mean it this time, for sure!) Part VII
Page 19 – Crack Ups! Featuring Sagebrush (I'll ask this hombre) – John Severin
Page 20 – New Products to Make Kids Feel Even More Like Adults – Samuel B. Whitehead
Page 23 – Crack Ups! Featuring The Psychiatrists – Powers (John Severin)
Page 24 – The 15 Warning Signals of Hypochondria – Sururi Gumen
Page 26 – Cracked Word Play (Get Around to it)
Page 28 – The Ziggy Stardopple Handbook to Tennis – Val Mayerik
Page 33 – Ye Hang Ups #5 (lil' hug and kiss) – C.E. Severin (Catherine Severin)
Page 34 – How Modern Inventions Would Have Changed History – Samuel B. Whitehead
Page 36 – Aluce – John Severin
Page 42 – The J.R. Gift Catalog for the Super Rich – Warren Sattler
Page 45 – Cracked Interviews the Greeting Card King – Bill Ward
Page 50 – Shut-Ups (many horses ride) – Charles Rodrigues
Page 51 and Back Cover – "Cracked Paint" Iron-On – John Severin

**183, December 1981 (52 pages) (90c)** (On sale date September 22, 1981)
Cover – Raiders! (and Superman) – John Severin
Page 2 and 51 – The Cracked Import Eyechart – Cracked Poster #183
Page 3 – Contents
Page 4 – Lettuce from Our Readers / Subscription ad – Bob Taylor
Page 6 – Traitors of the Lost Ark – John Severin
Page 14 – It's Gonna Be One of Those Days – Don Orehek
Page 17 – Jock State University Bulletin – Warren Sattler
Page 20 – Absolutely, Unquestionably, Positively, Undeniably, the Very, Very, Last of The Cracked Lens (and we really, really mean it this time, for sure!) Part VIII
Page 23 – New Medical Maladies – Samuel B. Whitehead
Page 26 – Super Types in Ordinary Life – Warren Sattler
Page 30 – The Cracked World of Telephones – Don Orehek
Page 33 – What Christopher Reeve Will Be Like When He Gets Old – Samuel B. Whitehead (A sad story now since Reeve died young after being paralyzed after being thrown from a horse.)
Page 36 – The Cracked Movie II – Nireves (John Severin) / Joe Catalano
Page 43 – Believe it or Not Again
Page 45 – Cracked Interviews the T.V. Ratings King – Bill Ward
Page 50 – Shut-Ups (How do you address a king) – Charles Rodrigues
Back Cover – Great Moments in History 1561 – Warren Sattler

**184, January 1982 (52 pages) (90c)** (On sale date November 3, 1981)
Cover – We Kayo Diff'rent Strokes! – John Severin (Another arguably racist cover.)
Page 2 and 51 – The World's First Digital Wall Scale – Cracked Poster #184
Page 3 – Contents
Page 4 – Lettuce from Our Readers / Subscription ad – John Severin
Page 6 – Diff'rent Strokes (You can have the bathroom) – John Severin (3rd *Diff'rent Strokes* parody)
Page 12 – Absolutely, Unquestionably, Positively, Undeniably, the Very, Very, Last of The Cracked Lens (and we really, really mean it this time, for sure!) Part IX
Page 16 – How Dentist's Can Improve Business – Don Orehek
Page 18 – The Cracked Encyclopedia of Great Excuses! – Bull Dubay
Page 21 – Cracked Looks at Parent-Teacher Conferences – Sururi Gumen
Page 22 – The Cracked World of Video Games – Samuel B. Whitehead
Page 26 – Cracked Word Play (Upside Down Cake)
Page 28 – Sorry! Not This Time!!! – Don Orehek

Page 30 – Star Drek – The Last Hurrah? – John Severin / Joe Catalano (2nd *Star Trek* parody)
Page 37 – The Jay Walk – Sururi Gumen
Page 38 – Future At-Home Merchandising Parties – Warren Sattler
Page 40 – Cracked's Cartoon Showcase Featuring Bill Maul – Bill Maul (1st *Cartoon Showcase*)
Page 42 – Cracked T.V. Addict! – John Langton
Page 44 – Crack Ups! Featuring Sagebrush #1 (Hay Nah-Nah!) – John Severin
Page 45 – Cracked Interviews the Football Owner King – Bill Ward
Page 50 – Shut-Ups (Mad Doctors' Monsters!) – Charles Rodrigues
Back Cover – Great Moments in History 1656 – Charles Rodrigues (reprint from #132)

**185, March 1982 (52 pages) (90c)** (On sale date December 15, 1981)
Cover – The Dukes Bust Out! – John Severin
Page 2 and 51 – Join the Fight Against Metrics – Cracked Poster #185
Page 3 – Contents
Page 4 – Lettuce from Our Readers (Statement of Ownership: Average number of copies sold: 341,762) / Subscription ad – John Severin
Page 6 – The Dorks of Hazzardous (Uncle Fussy milking the cows) – John Severin (3rd *Dukes of Hazzard* parody)
Page 14 – More Press Mistakes! (Lady Diana) – John Langton
Page 16 – The Cracked Annoyance Barometer – Bill Ward
Page 19 – Absolutely, Unquestionably, Positively, Undeniably, the Very, Very, Last of The Cracked Lens (and we really, really mean it this time, for sure!) Part X
Page 24 – Cracked's Cartoon Showcase Featuring Jeff Keate (Don't open the umbrella) – Jeff Keate
Page 26 – A Cracked Look at an Airport Terminal – Bill Ward
Page 28 – The Cracked Manual of Modern Merchandising Methods – Warren Sattler
Page 31 – The Jabbersons – Samuel B. Whitehead
Page 37 – Crack Ups! Featuring The Child Psychiatrist – Powers (John Severin)
Page 38 – You're in Trouble If – John Langton
Page 40 – The Cracked History of Aviation – Bill Ward
Page 44 – Cracked Interviews the Cracked Mazagine King – Will Bored (John Severin) / Joe Catalano
Page 50 – Shut-Ups (writing a book) – Don Orehek
Back Cover – Great Moments in History 1,234,567 B.C. – Warren Sattler

**186, May 1982 (52 pages) (90c)** (On sale date January 26, 1982)
Cover – Blarney Miller! – John Severin
Page 2 and 51 – Door Mood Poster – Cracked Poster
Page 3 – Contents
Page 4 – Lettuce from Our Readers / Subscription ad – John Severin
Page 6 – Blarney Miller (Morning everyone) – John Severin (3rd *Barney Miller* parody)
Page 12 – Cracked's Predictions of the Future
Page 14 – If T.V. Commercials Were Forced to Tell the Truth – Samuel B. Whitehead
Page 18 – Cracked "You Know You're _________ When" – Don Orehek
Page 20 – Video Games of the Future – Warren Sattler
Page 23 – The Difference Between Upper Class & Middle Class – Warren Sattler
Page 26 – Cracked Look at Teacher Types – John Severin
Page 28 – Three'sa Company – Samuel B. Whitehead (2nd *Three's Company* parody)
Page 34 – Cracked's Cartoon Showcase Featuring Jeff Keate (I finally got Junior) – Jeff Keate
Page 36 – A Press Conference with Ronald Reagan – John Severin / Joe Catalano
Page 41 – Collision Courses (Air Traffic Controllers on Strike) – John Langton (1st *Collision Courses*)
Page 43 – Absolutely, Unquestionably, Positively, Undeniably, the Very, Very, Last of The Cracked Lens (and we really, really mean it this time, for sure!) Part XI
Page 44 – Cracked Interviews the Soap Opera King – Bill Ward
Page 50 – Shut-Ups (graduating class) – Charles Rodrigues
Back Cover – Great Moments in Education 486 B.C. – Warren Sattler

**187, July 1982 (52 pages) (90c)** (On sale date March 9, 1982)
Cover – Come With Us On a Wacky Love Boat Cruise! – John Severin
Page 2 and 51 – The Cracked Echo Poster – Cracked Poster
Page 3 – Contents
Page 4 – Lettuce from Our Readers / Subscription ad – John Severin
Page 6 – The Wildest and Weirdest Love Boat Cruise of Them All – John Severin
Page 12 – What They're Really Thinking When They Say – Bill Ward
Page 14 – A Good Date vs. A Bad Date – Frank Fitzgerald
Page 17 – More Believe it or Nots (Will Steele)
Page 20 – Collision Courses (Ban Guns) – John Langton
Page 21 – Video College – Warren Sattler
Page 25 – Ye Hang Ups #8 (Uh! Oh!) – C.E. Severin (Catherine Severin)

Page 26 – Cracked Word Play (Can't Keep a Straight Face)
Page 28 – The Cracked World of Relatives – Don Orehek
Page 32 – Absolutely, Unquestionably, Positively, Undeniably, the Very, Very, Last of The Cracked Lens (and we really, really mean it this time, for sure!) Part XII
Page 34 – Too Dumb For Comfort – Samuel B. Whitehead
Page 41 – More Celebrity Garbage – John Severin
Page 44 – Cracked Interviews the Ski Resort King – Bill Ward
Page 50 – Shut-Ups (wanted a two wheeler) – Don Orehek
Back Cover – Great Moments in Fashion 1857 – Warren Sattler

**188, August 1982 (52 pages) (90c)** (On sale date April 20, 1982)
Cover – How Many Times Does "Eva" Appear On This Cover? – John Severin
Page 2 and 51 – Public Park Rules – Cracked Poster #188
Page 3 – Contents
Page 4 – Lettuce from Our Readers
Page 5 – Video Game Contest ad / Subscription ad
Page 6 – The Falling Guy (Oh, Homer) – John Severin (1st *The Fall Guy* parody)
Page 13 – Collision Courses (Vote for Smith) – John Langton
Page 14 – How to Save the Banking Industry – Bill Ward
Page 18 – How Gullible Are You? – Ron Zalme
Page 21 – One Day in the Department Store – Mike Ricigliano
Page 22 – Talking Vending Machines – Sururi Gumen
Page 24 – Absolutely, Unquestionably, Positively, Undeniably, the Very, Very, Last of The Cracked Lens (and we really, really mean it this time, for sure!) Part XIII
Page 26 – T-Shirts We'll Never See Them Wearing! – John Langton
Page 28 – A Cracked Look at Household Chores – Samuel B. Whitehead
Page 31 – Kids, You Know You Really Have to Worry When – Don Orehek
Page 34 – More Believe it or Nots (Sunuva Beach)
Page 37 – Adults Following the Rules They Set For Children – Sururi Gumen
Page 38 – Stop Watches for a Contemporary Book of World Records – Arnoldo Franchioni
Page 42 – What's So Good About the World Today? – Warren Sattler
Page 44 – Cracked Interviews the Game Show King – Bill Ward (reprint from #165)
Page 50 – Shut-Ups (It takes a smart man) – Don Orehek
Back Cover – Great Moments in Transportation 1807 – Warren Sattler

**189, September 1982 (52 pages) ($1.00)** (On sale date June 1, 1982)
Cover – Happy Daze! – John Severin
Page 2 and 51 – Cracked's Exclusive 3-D Poster – Cracked Poster
Page 3 – Contents
Page 4 – Lettuce from Our Readers / Subscription ad
Page 6 – Happier Days – John Severin (3rd *Happy Days* parody)
Page 13 – The Translator & the Duel – Mike Ricigliano
Page 14 – How the Government Can Really Save Money – Don Orehek
Page 16 – Absolutely, Unquestionably, Positively, Undeniably, the Very, Very, Last of The Cracked Lens (and we really, really mean it this time, for sure!) Part XIV
Page 18 – The Cracked World of Teenage Dating – Warren Sattler
Page 22 – Cracked Spell Outs – Arnoldo Franchioni
Page 26 – More Press Mistakes! (Russians are noted) – John Langton
Page 28 – The Cracked Movie III – John Severin / Joe Catalano
Page 35 – Relief Is – Don Orehek
Page 38 – Great Moments in History (fishing)
Page 40 – Ye Hang Ups #9 (Hurry it up) – M.L. Severin (Margaret Severin)
Page 41 – The Spoiled Rotten Pet Catalogue – Sururi Gumen
Page 45 – Sagebrush (Howdy Shage) – John Severin (reprint from #113)
Page 46 – The Cracked World of Looking Good – Bill Ward
Page 50 – Shut-Ups (piece of my mind) – Don Orehek
Back Cover – Great Moments in Transportation XXXIII B.C. – Warren Sattler

**190, October 1982 (52 pages) ($1.00)** (On sale date July 6, 1982)
Cover – The End of M*A*S*H? – John Severin
Page 2 and 51 – Free! Take One! – Cracked Poster #190
Page 3 – Contents
Page 4 – Lettuce from Our Readers / Subscription ad
Page 6 – The Day M*A*S*H*E*D Almost Ended – John Severin (7th *M*A*S*H* parody)
Page 13 – If Authors Really Meant What They Said! – John Langton
Page 14 – Kids vs. Adults – Ron Zalme
Page 18 – Absolutely, Unquestionably, Positively, Undeniably, the Very, Very, Last of The Cracked Lens (and we really, really mean it this time, for sure!) Part XV
Page 20 – The Cracked Guide to Windsurfing – Bill Ward
Page 24 – New Uses for Televisions – Sururi Gumen
Page 26 – A Cracked Look at a Police Squad – Don Orehek
Page 28 – The Cracked Step-by-Step Guide for Growing Your Own Garden – Warren Sattler
Page 32 – Great Moments in History (Margie Rinn)

Page 35 – 1982 Catalog for Costumed Heroes – John Severin
Page 38 – Cracked's Cartoon Showcase Featuring Jeff Keate (camouflage experts) – Jeff Keate
Page 40 – Crack Ups! Featuring Sagebrush (keep on your toes) – John Severin
Page 41 – How Hot is it? – Don Orehek
Page 44 – Ye Hang Ups #10 (He can't be serious) – M.L. Severin (Margaret Severin)
Page 45 – Cracked Interviews the Special Effects King – Bill Ward
Page 50 – Shut-Ups (wrap it up) – Don Orehek
Back Cover – Great Moments in History 1924 – Warren Sattler

**191, November 1982 (52 pages) ($1.00)** (On sale date August 10, 1982)
Cover – Magnum P.I. – John Severin
Page 2 – Scratch 'n' Sniff Poster – Cracked Poster
Page 3 – Contents
Page 4 – Lettuce from Our Readers / Subscription ad – Bob Taylor
Page 6 – Magnumb Public Idiot – John Severin
Page 13 – Every Joke Ever Made – John Langton
Page 14 – If T.V. Warnings Appeared in Everyday Life – Don Orehek
Page 17 – Absolutely, Unquestionably, Positively, Undeniably, the Very, Very, Last of The Cracked Lens (and we really, really mean it this time, for sure!) Part XVI
Page 20 – A.C.R.O.N.Y.M.S. – Ron Zalme
Page 22 – Future All-Star TV Specials – Samuel B. Whitehead
Page 26 – Cracked's Cartoon Showcase Featuring Jeff Keate (Running Weasel) – Jeff Keate
Page 28 – Acnnie – John Severin
Page 36 – More Believe it or Nots (Timmy Burns)
Page 38 – The Cracked Soccer Question and Answer Booklet – Don Orehek
Page 42 – When All Businesses Go Automated – Sururi Gumen
Page 45 – Cracked Interviews the Useless Products King – Bill Ward
Page 50 – Shut-Ups (sit next to me) – Don Orehek
Page 51 – I Saw Rocky I, II, III, IV, V, VI Iron-On (What is funny is that there now have been six *Rocky* movies.)
Back Cover – Great Moments in History 30,000 B.C. – Warren Sattler

**192, January 1983 (52 pages) ($1.00)**
Cover – E.T. Pizza Delivery – John Severin (An example of John Severin's color blindness in action with all of the E.T.'s green instead of brown.)
Page 2 and 51 – Be Alert – Cracked Poster #192

Page 3 – Contents
Page 4 – Lettuce from Our Readers / Subscription ad – Bob Taylor
Page 6 – Heart to Heart – John Severin
Page 12 – Solutions to Everyday Frustrations – Don Orehek
Page 14 – More Believe it or Nots (Oxford University)
Page 17 – How Popular Are You? – Warren Sattler
Page 21 – Sagebrush (Abundant Bull) – John Severin
Page 22 – You Know You're Going Too Far When – Ron Zalme
Page 24 – True Facts They Never Teach You in School – Sururi Gumen
Page 26 – A Cracked Look at An Auto Repair Garage – Don Orehek
Page 28 – Absolutely, Unquestionably, Positively, Undeniably, the Very, Very, Last of The Cracked Lens (and we really, really mean it this time, for sure!) Part XVII
Page 32 – Retaliations to Dating Cliches – Sururi Gumen
Page 34 – Mod Fairy Tales (The Princess and the Frog) – C.E. Severin (Catherine Severin) (1st *Mod Fairy Tales*)
Page 35 – Rocky's Scrapbook – John Severin
Page 39 – Are You P.M. Magazine Material? – John Langton
Page 40 – It's a Sure Bet That – Warren Sattler
Page 43 – E.T.'s Report My Experiences on Earth – Don Orehek
Page 47 – Things We've Often Wondered About – Bill Ward
Page 50 – Shut-Ups (road to Las Vegas) – Don Orehek
Back Cover – Great Moments in The Art of Love 350,000 B.C. – Warren Sattler

**193, March 1983 (52 pages) ($1.00)** (On sale date December 14, 1982)
Cover – We Ride Knight Rider! – John Severin
Page 2 and 51 – No Hey! Get Out'a Here!! – Cracked Poster
Page 3 – Contents
Page 4 – Lettuce from Our Readers (Statement of Ownership: Average number of copies sold: 309,406) / Subscription ad – Bob Taylor
Page 6 – Knut Rider – John Severin
Page 13 – Newsweak Magazine
Page 18 – How the Football Moguls Expect to Make Up for All Those Lost Commercials – Don Orehek
Page 20 – The Very Rich and the Very Poor – Warren Sattler
Page 24 – The Pondering Plumber – Sururi Gumen
Page 25 – The Good Old Daze of the Automobile – John Severin
Page 29 – $trikes Illustrated Magazine – Ron Zalme
Page 33 – Mod Fairy Tales (Humpty Dumpty) – C.E. Severin (Catherine Severin)
Page 34 – A Cracked Look at Cable TV – Don Orehek

Page 38 - One Day at Tattoo School - Bill Ward
Page 39 - Ronald Reagan's Photo Album - John Severin
Page 42 - Absolutely, Unquestionably, Positively, Undeniably, the Very, Very, Last of The Cracked Lens (and we really, really mean it this time, for sure!) Part XVIII
Page 47 - Cracked Interviews the Elf King - Bill Ward
Page 50 - Shut-Ups (money out of the bank) - Don Orehek
Back Cover - Great Moments in Entertainment 1,432,600 B.C. - Warren Sattler

**194, May 1983 (52 pages) ($1.00)** (On sale date January 25, 1983)
Cover - M*A*S*H Says Goodbye - John Severin
Page 2 and 51 - Do Not Read This Poster - Cracked Poster
Page 3 - Contents
Page 4 - Lettuce from Our Readers / Subscription ad - Bob Taylor
Page 6 - Farewell M*A*S*H*E*D a Cracked Remembrance - John Severin (8th *M*A*S*H* parody)
Page 13 - Absolutely, Unquestionably, Positively, Undeniably, the Very, Very, Last of The Cracked Lens (and we really, really mean it this time, for sure!) Part XIX
Page 16 - How Come? - Sururi Gumen
Page 18 - Cracked's Employee of the Month Award - John Severin
Page 20 - Talking Cars - Warren Sattler
Page 24 - The Cracked World of Bad Habits - Don Orehek
Page 28 - An Owner and a Player Negotiating a Contract 1982 - Ron Zalme
Page 29 - Cracked Evolution Revolution - Mike Ricigliano
Page 32 - Robot Report Magazine - John Severin
Page 36 - Cracked's Video Cartoon Showcase - Jeff Keate
Page 38 - 3-D Horror Shows - Sururi Gumen
Page 41 - Who in the World Decided That - Arnoldo Franchioni
Page 44 - Great Moments in History (taffy pull)
Page 46 - What Today's Strips Would Look Like if They Were Drawn by Ronald Reagan - John Severin
Page 50 - Shut-Ups (pole-vaulting) - Don Orehek
Back Cover - Great Moments in Comedy 1391 - Mike Ricigliano

**195, July 1983 (52 pages) ($1.00)** (On sale date March 8, 1983)
Cover - E.T. Visits Diff'rent Strokes! - John Severin
Page 2 and 51 - Attention! An Unmarked Wallet - Cracked Poster #195
Page 3 - Contents
Page 4 - Lettuce from Our Readers / Official Cracked Fan Club ad - John Severin (1st appearance of The Official *Cracked* Fan Club.)

Page 6 – If EaTing Had Been Found By Arnuld – John Severin
Page 13 – Cracked Guide to Sky Diving – Sururi Gumen
Page 17 – The People's Courtroom – Bill Ward
Page 23 – When Men and Women Shop – Warren Sattler
Page 26 – A Cracked Look at a Supermarket – John Severin (reprint from #115)
Page 28 – The Cracked Movie IV – Nireves (John Severin) / Joe Catalano (1st appearance of Eva, Sylvester's girlfriend)
Page 36 – Absolutely, Unquestionably, Positively, Undeniably, the Very, Very, Last of The Cracked Lens (and we really, really mean it this time, for sure!) Part XX
Page 40 – How to Beat Those Video Game Players – Ron Zalme
Page 43 – Life in the 21st Century – John Langton
Page 45 – Cracked Interviews the Auto King – John Severin (reprint from #109)
Page 50 – Shut-Ups (aluminum siding) – Don Orehek
Back Cover – Sagebrush (Howdy, Cuchillo!) – John Severin

**196, August 1983 (52 pages) ($1.00)** (On sale date April 19, 1983)
Cover – The Dukes Meet Knight Rider – John Severin
Page 2 and 51 – The Cracked Ear Chart – Cracked Poster
Page 3 – Contents
Page 4 – Lettuce from Our Readers / Official Cracked Fan Club ad – John Severin
Page 6 – Knight Rider Meets The Dukes of Hazzardous – John Severin
Page 13 – Things You'll Never See – Warren Sattler
Page 15 – Gift Catalogue for Teen-Agers – Don Orehek
Page 19 – Read Between the Lines! – John Langton
Page 20 – Really Real People – Brian Buniak
Page 22 – Indicators in Our Lives We Could Really Use – Samuel B. Whitehead
Page 24 – "Going Out" Simulation Kits for Stay at Home People – Sean LePeor (John Severin) (reprint from #139)
Page 28 – The Ad War Heats Up – Sururi Gumen
Page 30 – "There's Good News and Bad News" – Warren Sattler
Page 32 – The Cracked Guide to Plant Care – John Severin (reprint from #130)
Page 35 – How to Have a Fun Time on Earth – Don Orehek
Page 40 – Cracked Predictions for the Not-Too-Distant Future
Page 43 – Tootsie Roll – John Severin
Page 50 – Shut-Ups (quick-acting remedy) – Don Orehek
Back Cover – The Truth About Pac-Man

**197, September 1983 (52 pages) ($1.00)** (On sale date May 31, 1983)
Cover – Bon Voyage Love Boat – John Severin
Page 2 and 51 – Historical Poster – Cracked Poster
Page 3 – Contents
Page 4 – Lettuce from Our Readers / Official Cracked Fan Club ad – John Severin
Page 6 – The A-a-aayy Team Takes a Ride on the Lovely Boat – John Severin
Page 13 – What Your Mother/Father Would Say – Don Orehek
Page 16 – If We Didn't Have Ears – Warren Sattler
Page 19 – More Believe it or Nots (Cid Still)
Page 23 – Cracked's Guide for Making Money in the 80's – John Severin
Page 26 – Real Kids Don't Eat Spinach – Warren Sattler
Page 30 – Creating Your Own Summer Jobs – Don Orehek
Page 32 – Cracked Interviews the Energy Conservation King – Bill Ward (reprint from #167)
Page 37 – How to Make Baseball More Interesting – Bill Ward (reprint from #137)
Page 41 – The Loser – John Severin (reprint from #131)
Page 44 – Simian & Simian – John Severin
Page 50 – Shut-Ups (bird imitations) – Don Orehek
Back Cover – Sagebrush #52 (Keep up with me) – John Severin / MF (reprint from #153)

**198, October 1983 (52 pages) ($1.00)** (On sale date July 5, 1983)
Cover – Jawz in 3-D! – John Severin
Page 2 and 51 – Important Notice!!! This is Your Last Warning! – Cracked Poster
Page 3 – Contents
Page 4 – Lettuce from Our Readers / Official Cracked Fan Club ad – John Severin
Page 6 – The Making of Jawz #23 – John Severin
Page 12 – What You'll Really Miss After you Graduate – Don Orehek
Page 16 – Word Play (Everything in its Place)
Page 17 – The Wider World of Sports – John Severin (reprint from #139)
Page 22 – One Day on Route 14 – Mike Ricigliano
Page 24 – Absolutely, Unquestionably, Positively, Undeniably, the Very, Very, Last of The Cracked Lens (and we really, really mean it this time, for sure!) Part XXI
Page 30 – Cracked's Early Warning Signs of "No Respect" – John Langton
Page 32 – Mrs. Kong Goes to Town – Sue Lyle

Page 33 – The True Story of The Lone Ranger – Brian Buniak
Page 36 – Cracked Interviews the Outdoor King – Bill Ward (reprint from #138)
Page 41 – Giant "Jaws" Contest
Page 43 – The Falling Guy (SPUDS!) – John Severin (2nd *The Fall Guy* parody)
Page 50 – Shut-Ups (one more quarter) – Don Orehek
Back Cover – Sagebrush (can't hold on) – John Severin (reprint from *Cracked Collectors' Edition* #5)

**199, November 1983 (52 pages) ($1.00)** (On sale date August 9, 1983)
Cover – Jed Eye Returns! – John Severin
Page 2 and 51 – Do Not Straighten This Poster! – Cracked Poster #199
Page 3 – Contents
Page 4 – Lettuce from Our Readers / Official Cracked Fan Club ad – John Severin
Page 6 – Returns of the Jed Eye – John Severin
Page 14 – Past, Present and Future Changes in Sports – Don Orehek
Page 18 – Signs That It's a Computer Age – Warren Sattler
Page 20 – One Evening in a Fancy Restaurant – Bob Taylor (reprint from #135)
Page 22 – The Cracked Guide to Kite Flying – Bill Ward
Page 25 – Increasing Consumption in Order to Maintain Full Employment – LePoer (John Severin) (reprint from #134)
Page 30 – You Know You're a Real Monster if – Brian Buniak
Page 31 – The Cracked Fix-It Yourself Manual – Bill Ward
Page 35 – Absolutely, Unquestionably, Positively, Undeniably, the Very, Very, Last of The Cracked Lens (and we really, really mean it this time, for sure!) Part XXII
Page 39 – How is it That? – Warren Sattler
Page 42 – Misleading Movie and TV Titles – Don Orehek
Page 44 – One Day in Metropolitis – Don Orehek (reprint from #136)
Page 45 – Cracked Interviews the Newspaper King – Powers (John Severin) (reprint from #124)
Page 50 – Shut-Ups (man cannot live on bread) – Don Orehek
Back Cover – The Stone Age – Oskar Blotta (reprint from #125)

**200, December 1983 (52 pages) ($1.00)** (On sale date September 20, 1983)
Cover – War Games – John Severin (4th Alfred E. Neuman cover)
Page 2 and 51 – Pobody's Nerfect – Cracked Poster #200
Page 3 – Contents
Page 4 – Lettuce from Our Readers / Official Cracked Fan Club ad – John Severin

Page 6 – War Gains – John Severin
Page 13 – The Cracked Guide to Hobbies – Warren Sattler
Page 17 – How to Buy a New Car – John Severin
Page 20 – Help Wanted – Bill Ward (reprint from #143)
Page 23 – When All of Television Goes 3-D – John Severin
Page 26 – Accessories That Duplicate the Thrills of Arcade Playing Right in the Home – Don Orehek
Page 28 – Absolutely, Unquestionably, Positively, Undeniably, the Very, Very, Last of The Cracked Lens (and we mean it this time!) (reprint from #173)
Page 33 – The Cracked Guide to Hockey – Bill Ward
Page 37 – Can You Pass the Teen-Age Drivers Test? – Warren Sattler
Page 40 – How Past Events Might Have Been Reported with a Government-Controlled Press – Sururi Gumen (reprint from #124)
Page 44 – You Know It's Gonna Be "One of Dem Days" When – Frank Matera
Page 46 – Cracked Interviews Star Warts Creator George Lucre – John Severin
Page 50 – Shut-Ups (Pate de Fois Gros) – Don Orehek
Back Cover – Sagebrush (Mother Nature's secret) – John Severin (reprint from #105)

**201, January 1984 (52 pages) ($1.00)** (On sale date November 1, 1983)
Cover – We Attack the A-Team – John Severin
Page 2 and 51 – State Environmental Commission – Cracked Poster #201
Page 3 – Contents
Page 4 – Lettuce from Our Readers / Official Cracked Fan Club ad – John Severin
Page 6 – The A-a-ayy Team (Excuse me officer) – John Severin (1st *A-Team* parody)
Page 13 – The Cracked Guide to Bicycle Motocross – Don Orehek
Page 17 – Cracked Hold-Ups! (don't feel like cooking) – Sururi Gumen (1st *Cracked Hold-Ups!*)
Page 19 – Why is There a Difference in Your Parents and Other Kids' Parents? – Warren Sattler
Page 22 – Don't You Feel Stupid – Fran Matera
Page 24 – A Cracked Look at Home Computers – Warren Sattler
Page 28 – Word Play (Curtain Going Up)
Page 30 – The Alien – Brian Buniak
Page 31 – And Yet Once Again Still More from The Cracked Lens (reprint from #161)
Page 35 – Tree's Company – John Severin (3rd *Three's Company* parody)

Page 42 – New Tamper-Resistant Packaging – Sururi Gumen
Page 44 – You Know You're Skinny When – Warren Sattler
Page 45 – Cracked Interviews the Pet Store King – Bill Ward (reprint from #144)
Page 50 – Shut-Ups (start off this auction) – Don Orehek (reprint from #158)
Back Cover – Sagebrush (see the preacher) – John Severin

**202, March 1984 (52 pages) ($1.00)** (On sale date December 13, 1983)
Cover – This is Total Madness! – John Severin (5th Alfred E. Neuman cover)
Page 2 and 51 – Important! Don't Waste Your Time – Cracked Poster
Page 3 – Contents
Page 4 – Lettuce from Our Readers (Statement of Ownership: Average number of copies sold: 272,581) / Official Cracked Fan Club ad – John Severin
Page 6 – The Day Mr. Smyth Saved Knut Rider – John Severin
Page 13 – Cracked Hold-Ups! (fat of the land) – Sururi Gumen
Page 15 – When the World Runs Out of Space – Makbush (Sururi Gumen) (reprint from #127)
Page 18 – Products That Just Missed! – McCartin (John Severin) (reprint from #53)
Page 20 – The Cracked World of Owning Your Own Phone – Don Orehek
Page 23 – One Afternoon at a Company Picnic – Don Orehek (Doing his best Don Martin imitation.)
Page 24 – You Know You're Boring When – Bill Ward
Page 26 – Word Play (Days are Numbered)
Page 28 – Another Side of Life – John Severin (Doing his best Dave Berg imitation.)
Page 32 – Absolutely, Unquestionably, Positively, Undeniably, the Very, Very, Last of The Cracked Lens (and we really, really mean it this time, for sure!) Part XXIII
Page 35 – Family Ties – Vance Rodewalt (1st *Family Ties* parody)
Page 42 – Don't You Feel Stupid – Fran Matera (1st *Don't You Feel Stupid*)
Page 44 – Hudd & Dini (laundry truck) – John Langton (Doing his best Vic Martin imitation.)
Page 45 – Cracked Interviews the Stunt King – Sururi Gumen (reprint from #128)
Page 50 – Shut-Ups (TV over in the corner) – Don Orehek
Back Cover – One Evening at Home – Don Orehek (Doing his best Don Martin imitation again.)

**203, May 1984 (52 pages) ($1.00)** (On sale date January 24, 1984)
Cover – We Take on the A-Team – John Severin
Page 2 and 51 – Do Not Enter! This Room Has Been Condemned – Cracked Poster #203
Page 3 – Contents
Page 4 – Lettuce from Our Readers / Official Cracked Fan Club ad – John Severin
Page 6 – The A-a-ayy Team (Excuse me, waitress) – John Severin (2nd *A-Team* parody)
Page 13 – Cracked Guide to Winter Sports – Warren Sattler
Page 17 – Cracked Hold-Ups! (horoscope) – Sururi Gumen
Page 19 – How the Ads of Tomorrow Will Exploit the Energy Crisis – Howard Nostrand (reprint from #168)
Page 22 – Don't You Feel Stupid – Fran Matera
Page 24 – The Cracked History of the Automobile – Warren Sattler (reprint from #167)
Page 28 – Word Play (Water Fall)
Page 30 – Things You Should Have Done – Walt Lardner
Page 34 – AfterM*U*S*H – O.O. Severin (John Severin)
Page 41 – The Cracked Humor Quiz – Vic Martin
Page 45 – Cracked Interviews the 3-D King – Bill Ward
Page 50 – Shut-Ups (Checkmate!!) – Don Orehek
Back Cover – One Afternoon in the Big City – Warren Sattler

**204, July 1984 (52 pages) ($1.00)** (On sale date March 6, 1984)
Cover – "What's Wrong with This Cover?" Contest – John Severin
Page 2 and 51 – The Cracked Eye Chart – Cracked Poster #204
Page 3 – Contents
Page 4 – Lettuce from Our Readers / Official Cracked Fan Club ad – John Severin
Page 6 – Magdumb P.I. – O.O. Severin (John Severin)
Page 13 – Cracked Hold-Ups! (pressure on the cooler) – Sururi Gumen
Page 15 – The Cracked Guide to Basketball – Howard Nostrand (reprint from #142)
Page 20 – The A-Team Way of Doing Things – O.O. Severin (John Severin)
Page 23 – "What's Wrong with The Cover?" Contest
Page 24 – Word Play (Go Broke)
Page 26 – Don't You Hate it at the Movies – Sururi Gumen
Page 28 – The More Things Change the More They Stay the Same – Warren Sattler
Page 32 – Absolutely, Unquestionably, Positively, Undeniably, the Very, Very, Last of The Cracked Lens (and we really, really mean it this time, for sure!) Part XXIV

Page 36 – Alaffin's Magic Lamp – Fran Matera
Page 37 – The Gary Coleman Workout Book for Kids – John Severin
Page 42 – Cat Gifts for Cats Who Have Everything – Mac Bush (Sururi Gumen) (reprint from #125)
Page 44 – Hudd & Dini (gorilla) – John Langton (Doing his best Vic Martin imitation.)
Page 45 – Cracked Interviews the Olympic Training King – Bill Ward (reprint from #136)
Page 50 – Shut-Ups (cable, let's get it installed) – Don Orehek
Back Cover – Great Moments in Safety 2001 B.C. – Warren Sattler

**205, August 1984 (52 pages) ($1.00)** (On sale date April 17, 1984)
Cover – We Knock-Out Webster! – John Severin
Page 2 and 51 – In Case of Emergency Break Glass – Cracked Poster – John Severin
Page 3 – Contents
Page 4 – Lettuce from Our Readers / Official Cracked Fan Club ad – John Severin
Page 6 – Webfoot – O.O. Severin (John Severin)
Page 13 – How to Eat Better for Less Money – Warren Sattler (reprint from #151)
Page 17 – Cracked Hold-Ups! (official time) – Sururi Gumen
Page 19 – The Cracked Guide to Jogging – Howard Nostrand (reprint from #146)
Page 23 – Hudd & Dini (shark) – John Langton
Page 24 – If TV Shows Were Combined – John Severin
Page 29 – Godzilla Tours Washington D.C. – Sururi Gumen
Page 30 – Video Nightmares – Don Orehek
Page 34 – The Three Moosekateers – John Severin
Page 41 – The Cracked Home Computer I.Q. Test
Page 45 – Cracked Interviews the Rock 'n' Roll King – Bill Ward (reprint from #153)
Page 50 – Shut-Ups (missing a great show) – Don Orehek
Back Cover – Great Moments in War 1,000,007 B.C. – Howard Nostrand (reprint from #154)

**206, September 1984 (52 pages) ($1.00)** (On sale date May 29, 1984)
Cover – Michael Jackson Meets Mr. T! – John Severin
Page 2 and 51 – Everybody Makes Makes Mistakes – Cracked Poster #206
Page 3 – Contents
Page 4 – Lettuce from Our Readers / Official Cracked Fan Club ad – John Severin

Page 6 – The A-a-a-y-y Team (Let's go men) – John Severin (3rd *A-Team* parody)
Page 13 – Cracked Hold-Ups! (Comrade Mishkin) – Sururi Gumen, Don Orehek
Page 15 – Cracked Looks at Computers – Warren Sattler
Page 19 – Cracked Presents Future Insect Monster Movies – Sururi Gumen (reprint from #125)
Page 22 – Hudd & Dini (swimming pool) – Vic Martin (reprint from #99)
Page 23 – Snide Guide to Camping – John Severin (reprint from #61)
Page 26 – Word Play (Nothing but the Truth)
Page 28 – The ABC's of Video – Warren Sattler
Page 32 – One Late Afternoon in a Butcher Shop – Sururi Gumen
Page 33 – If Kids Took Over Completely – Vance Rodewalt
Page 36 – Absolutely, Unquestionably, Positively, Undeniably, the Very, Very, Last of The Cracked Lens (and we really, really mean it this time, for sure!) Part XXV
Page 40 – The Cracked World of Music – Don Orehek
Page 44 – More Press Mistakes! (reserved seats) – John Langton
Page 45 – Cracked Interviews the Hamburger King – John Severin (reprint from #99)
Page 50 – Shut-Ups (such a dump) – Don Orehek
Back Cover – Great Moments in Politics 1949 – Charles Rodrigues (reprint from #134)

**207, October 1984 (52 pages) ($1.00)** (On sale date July 3, 1984)
Cover – We Salute Michael Jackson – John Severin
Page 2 and 51 – I (heart) the Jackson 5 – Cracked Poster #207
Page 3 – Contents
Page 4 – Lettuce from Our Readers / Official Cracked Fan Club ad – John Severin
Page 6 – If Michael Jackson had Starred in – John Severin
Page 12 – Absolutely, Unquestionably, Positively, Undeniably, the Very, Very, Last of The Cracked Lens (and we really, really mean it this time, for sure!) Part XXVI
Page 16 – The '84 Olympics go Commercial – Warren Sattler
Page 19 – Cracked Hold-Ups! (Nine Lives Louie) – Sururi Gumen
Page 21 – The Cracked Guide to Swimming – Don Orehek
Page 25 – Hudd & Dini (soap guns) – John Langton
Page 26 – Cracked's Topsy-Turvy Video Game Puzzle Page – Warren Sattler
Page 28 – A Cracked Look at Summer Camps – Howard Nostrand (reprint from #145)

Page 32 – Talking Everything – Sururi Gumen
Page 34 – One Fine Day at the Bowling Alley – Warren Sattler
Page 35 – The Making of Thriller
Page 41 – The Wish – Brian Buniak
Page 42 – Cracked's Surefire Excuse Kits – Warren Sattler
Page 45 – Cracked Interviews the Lemonade King – John Langton (reprint from #129)
Page 50 – Shut-Ups (stuck on this job) – Don Orehek
Back Cover – Great Moments in Sports 304,787 B.C. – Vance Rodewalt

**208, November 1984 (52 pages) ($1.00)** (On sale date August 7, 1984)
Cover – We Cut-Up Indiana Jones! – John Severin
Page 2 and 51 – How to Avoid Confusion! – Cracked Poster
Page 3 – Contents
Page 4 – Lettuce from Our Readers / Official Cracked Fan Club ad – Don Orehek
Page 6 – Indianapolis Bones and the Temple of Gloom – John Severin
Page 13 – A Cracked Catalog of Summer Survival Gear – Warren Sattler
Page 16 – The Miss Match – Don Orehek
Page 17 – Absolutely, Unquestionably, Positively, Undeniably, the Very, Very, Last of The Cracked Lens (and we really, really mean it this time, for sure!) Part XXVII
Page 21 – The Cracked Guide to Boating – Sailor Sam (John Severin) (reprint from #129)
Page 25 – Another Cracked Look at a Video Arcade – Sururi Gumen
Page 28 – The Difference Between the 1st Date and 2nd Date – Fran Matera
Page 32 – Cracked Products for Everyday Use – Warren Sattler (reprint from #156)
Page 34 – The Camp Gotchamoney News
Page 38 – Rodrigues' Side Show – Charles Rodrigues (reprint from #106)
Page 41 – Cracked Hold-Ups! (population explosion) – Sururi Gumen
Page 43 – The Falling Guy (get this *Cracked* satire rolling) – John Severin (3rd *The Fall Guy* parody)
Page 50 – Shut-Ups (Michael Jackson) – Don Orehek
Back Cover – Great Moments in Inventions 1952 – Vance Rodewalt

**209, January 1985 (52 pages) ($1.25)** (On sale date October 30, 1984)
Cover – We Turn On Music Videos and Gremlins – John Severin
Page 2 and 51 – Official Location Map – Cracked Poster
Page 3 – Contents
Page 4 – Lettuce from Our Readers / Subscription ad – John Severin / Sliding Down the Family Tree – John Severin (reprint from #128)

Page 6 – Grumblins – John Severin
Page 13 – Cracked Looks at Archeology – Warren Sattler
Page 17 – Ye Hang Ups (Autumn again) – O.O. Severin (John Severin)
Page 18 – Absolutely, Unquestionably, Positively, Undeniably, the Very, Very, Last of The Cracked Lens (and we really, really mean it this time, for sure!) Part XXVIII
Page 23 – Showbiz-Type Election Ads – John Severin
Page 26 – Cracked Blasts Nasa – Don Orehek
Page 28 – If Famous Lines Were Said in Different Situations – John Severin (reprint from #101)
Page 30 – What Athletes Do on the Off Season – Warren Sattler
Page 33 – Throughout History with the Real Gremlins – John Severin
Page 35 – How Schools Can Save Money – Don Orehek
Page 38 – Star Drek III: The Search for Spook – John Severin
Page 45 – Cracked Interviews the Music Video King – Vance Rodewalt
Page 50 – Shut-Ups (forbidden volcano) – Don Orehek
Back Cover – Great Moments in Sports 1972 – Howard Nostrand (reprint from #150)

**210, March 1985 (52 pages) ($1.25)** (On sale date December 11, 1984)
Cover – The A-Team Goes Non-Violent! – John Severin
Page 2 and 51 – Danger Danger Danger – Cracked Poster
Page 3 – Contents
Page 4 – Lettuce from Our Readers (Statement of Ownership: Average number of copies sold: 238,595) / Subscription ad – John Severin
Page 6 – If the A-a-ayy Team Was Made Less Violent – John Severin
Page 13 – Absolutely, Unquestionably, Positively, Undeniably, the Very, Very, Last of The Cracked Lens (and we really, really mean it this time, for sure!) Part XXIX
Page 16 – Don't You Hate it on Your Birthday – Don Orehek
Page 18 – Career Guide for Obnoxious Kids – Warren Sattler
Page 21 – Frontier Dude Magazine – John Severin (reprint from #84)
Page 26 – Word Play (Room for One More)
Page 28 – You Know You're an MTV Freak When – Bill Powers (John Severin)
Page 30 – Randolph the Reindeer – John Severin (reprint from #75)
Page 32 – You Know You've Got Big Problems When – Warren Sattler
Page 34 – Translating Technical Talk – Don Orehek
Page 37 – The Cracked Money Diet – LePoer (John Severin)
Page 40 – Sagebrush (Abundant Bull) – John Severin (reprint from #192)
Page 41 – The Cracked TV Watchers Guide to Small Screen Etiquette – Warren Sattler

Page 46 – Sell it Back! – Warren Sattler
Page 47 – Things That Annoy Us the Most – John Severin
Page 50 – Shut-Ups (haven't had this much fun) – Don Orehek
Back Cover – Hudd & Dini (R/C racer) – Don Orehek (Doing his best Vic Martin imitation.)

**211, May 1985 (52 pages) ($1.25)**
Cover – Special Crime Busters Issue!! – John Severin
Page 2 and 51 – Remember National Students Day – Cracked Poster
Page 3 – Contents
Page 4 – Lettuce from Our Readers / Subscription ad – John Severin
Page 6 – The Cracked Movie V – John Severin / Joe Catalano
Page 13 – Absolutely, Unquestionably, Positively, Undeniably, the Very, Very, Last of The Cracked Lens (and we really, really mean it this time, for sure!) Part XXX
Page 17 – Products for Pampered Pets – Don Orehek
Page 20 – A Cracked Catalog of Equipment & Supplies for Weathering Winter – John Severin
Page 23 – Kitchenland – Rurik Tyler
Page 26 – Rock Music Word Play
Page 28 – You Know You're a Super Type – Warren Sattler
Page 30 – If Different National Products Became the World Money Standard – John Severin (reprint from #133)
Page 34 – A Cracked Western You'll Never See – John Severin
Page 35 – Cracked's Little Known Trivia Facts
Page 38 – Sagebrush (Sand! Sand!) – John Severin (reprint from #79)
Page 40 – The Charming India Fire Department – Warren Sattler
Page 41 – Cracked Interviews the Break Dancing King – Vance Rodewalt
Page 46 – If the Whole World Turned Fat – Clyde S. Dale (John Severin)
Page 50 – Shut-Ups (It's a masterpiece) – Don Orehek
Back Cover – Hudd & Dini (potato sacks) – Don Orehek

**212, July 1985 (52 pages) ($1.25)** (Last Major Magazines issue and last issue with Robert C. Sproul involvement, closing 27 years of faithful service, the longest publisher tenure on *Cracked*.)
Cover – Magnum P.I. Trick Mirror – John Severin (Rip-off of Jack Davis' cover on #16)
Page 2 and 51 – Remember National Students Day – Cracked Poster
Page 3 – Contents
Page 4 – Lettuce from Our Readers / Subscription ad – John Severin
Page 6 – Simple & Simple – John Severin

Page 13 - TV Cable Guide Magazine
Page 18 - Your Money's Worth - Walt Lardner
Page 19 - Kids, Toys, and Future Careers - Rurik Tyler
Page 22 - Magazines That Tried to Copy Cracked, But Failed - M.E. Tate (John Severin)
Page 26 - Wishful Thinking - Bob Taylor
Page 28 - The True Meaning of Art - Rurik Tyler
Page 29 - VCR Home Movie Accessories Catalog - Warren Sattler
Page 32 - What's Good and Not so Good About Bigfoot - John Severin
Page 34 - Expanding the Use of Picture Signs - John Langton
Page 37 - If Television Censors Had Their Way - John Severin
Page 41 - The Silly Cosbey Show - John Severin (1st *Cosby Show* parody)
Page 44 - The Pond - Walt Lardner
Page 45 - Cracked Interviews the Technical School King - Bob Taylor
Page 50 - Shut-Ups (Monday morning paper) - Don Orehek
Back Cover - A Scuplture's Studio - Walt Lardner

**213, August 1985 (52 pages) ($1.25)** (1st Larken Communications issue and the 1st issue without any new John Severin art.) (Paul Laikin returns as Editor.)

Cover - Great Big Monster Issue - Murad Gumen
Page 2 and 51 - Keep America Beautiful - Cracked Sign (Now called *Cracked Sign.*)
Page 3 - Contents
Page 4 - Lettuce from Our Readers / Subscription ad - John Severin
Page 6 - Old Movie Monster Films Updated for Today - Kent Gamble
Page 10 - If the Boy George Craze Spreads Everywhere - John Reiner
Page 12 - Cracked Ways to Make Ends Meet - Charles Nicholas
Page 14 - Cracked's More Practical Tranzformer-type Toys - Bill Burke
Page 17 - A Cracked Look at TV Commercials You'll Never Get to See - Bill Burke
Page 20 - Hee-Man, Mister of the Universe - Walter Brogan
Page 22 - Absent-Minded Answers to Simple-Stated Statements - Vic Martin
Page 24 - Fancy Work Titles and the Actual Jobs - Charles Nicholas
Page 26 - Cracked's Billion Dollar Game - Tony Tallarico
Page 28 - Establishment-type Comedians - Aron Laikin
Page 31 - Video Nut Magazine - Arnoldo Franchioni
Page 38 - Newly-Created Jobs for Today's Modern Age - Bill Burke
Page 40 - Headlines We'd Like to See
Page 42 - When Computers Take Over Everywhere - Bob Gillespie
Page 45 - Cracked Commercial No. 482 - Walter Brogan

Page 46 – Cracked Visits a New Youth Cult – Murad Gumen
Page 50 – Shut-Ups (here's my plan) – Bill Burke
Back Cover – Great Moments in Discover 1839 – Murad Gumen

**214, September 1985 (52 pages) ($1.25)** (Last Larken Communications issue and the last distributed by Select Magazines.)

Cover – This Issue Really Swings – Aron Laikin (Cover is a rip-off of *Crazy* #41.)
Page 2 and 51 – Watch Out for School Children – Cracked Sign
Page 3 – Contents
Page 4 – Lettuce from Our Readers / Cracked Hat ad / Subscription ad – Bill Burke
Page 6 – Hollywood Version of Nursery Rhymes – John Reiner
Page 11 – If (with Apologies to Rudyard Kipling) (The old Paul Laikin standby article that saw print in practically every other black and white humor magazine that Paul worked.)
Page 12 – Updating Old Kids' Games to Fit Today's Youth – Charles Nicholas
Page 14 – Specialized Diets for Different Kinds of People – Cuz (This looks suspiciously like an older *Sick* article updated to become a *Cracked* article that Mort Todd mentioned, due to its poor paste-up job.)
Page 16 – Movie Monsters Based on Video Games – Walter Brogan
Page 19 – Mother Magazine – Arnoldo Franchioni
Page 26 – A Cracked Look at a College Campus – Al Scaduto
Page 28 – Foreign Versions of American Toys – John Langton
Page 30 – First it was Montezuma's Revenge, Now We're Getting – Bernie Cootner
Page 32 – Saturday Morning TV Cartoon Shows We Want to See – Tony Tallarico
Page 36 – Designer Jeans with Other Celebrity Labels – Tony Tallarico
Page 38 – Son of The Cracked Lens
Page 40 – You Know You're a Real Optimist When – Vic Martin
Page 42 – Cracked Puzzle Page (1st *Cracked Puzzle Page*)
Page 44 – Bubblegum Joke Contest – Aron Laikin
Page 45 – Cracked Interviews the Travel Agency King – Bill Burke
Page 50 – Shut-Ups (really dig my job) – Bill Burke
Back Cover – Great Moments in History 1775 – Aron Laikin

**215, October 1985 (52 pages) ($1.25)** (1st Globe Communications issue distributed by Globe.)

Cover – We Sock it to Wrestling! – Aron Laikin
Page 2 and 51 – Please Ring the Bell – Cracked Sign

Page 3 – Contents
Page 4 – Letters – John Severin / Subscription ad – Jack Davis
Page 6 – Wrestlin' T 'n' T – Bill Burke
Page 11 – How Come? – Vic Martin (1st *How Come?*)
Page 12 – The Trend Toward More Specialized Sports Magazines – John Langton
Page 14 – Ideas for Other Seat-Belt Laws – Al Scaduto
Page 16 – Hee-Man Meets Mr. Tee, Man! – John Reiner
Page 19 – Stupor-Hero Fanzine – Walter Brogan
Page 25 – Hudd & Dini (ice cream) – Vic Martin (Vic Martin's return to *Hudd & Dini.*)
Page 26 – Celebrity Balloons – Tony Tallarico (1st *Celebrity Balloons*)
Page 28 – Talking Computer Devices of Tomorrow – Cuz
Page 30 – Who's Who in the Classroom – John Reiner
Page 32 – Absolutely, Unquestionably, Positively, Undeniably, the Very, Very, Last of The Cracked Lens (and we really, really mean it this time, for sure!) Part XXVIII (Title reprint from #209; otherwise it's new material.)
Page 35 – Beverly Hills Slop – Kent Gamble
Page 40 – What is Cracked? Funny You Should Ask. Cracked is – Al Scaduto
Page 42 – Cracked Back Issue Riot!! ad
Page 44 – Stupor-Hero Joke Contest – Aron Laikin
Page 45 – Cracked Interviews the Wrestling King – Bill Ward (reprint from #149)
Page 50 – Wrasslin' Shut-Ups (wear that mask) – Mort Todd
Back Cover – Great Moments in History 1775 – Aron Laikin

**216, November 1985 (52 pages) ($1.25)** (On sale date August 6, 1985)
Cover – Unicorn – Aron Laikin
Page 2 and 51 – Help Stamp Out Literacy – Cracked Poster
Page 3 – Contents
Page 4 – Letters – John Severin / Subscription ad – John Severin
Page 6 – Miami Nice – John Reiner
Page 11 – When Theatre Owners Advertise Other Things Besides the Movie – Walter Brogan
Page 14 – Future Uses of Video
Page 16 – Summer Jobs for Movie Monsters – Kent Gamble
Page 18 – If the Unicorn Horn Was on Other Animals – John Langton
Page 20 – Unicorn Horn Contest – Aron Laikin
Page 21 – The Final Episode of Comic Strips – Tony Tallarico
Page 24 – Cracked Puzzle Page
Page 26 – A Cracked Look at the Circus – Al Scaduto

Page 28 – Telling the Truth in the New Regional-Type Magazines – Walter Brogan
Page 30 – Absolutely, Unquestionably, Positively, Undeniably, the Very, Very, Last of The Cracked Lens (and if we don't mean it, we should be struck deaaaddd)
Page 33 – How Come? – Vic Martin
Page 34 – Look Out for Them Household Hazzards! – Eric Cartier / Michael Weitz
Page 36 – Aren't You Nervous When – Dan Clowes / Michael Weitz (1st Dan Clowes artwork)
Page 38 – The Aliens are Here!! – Tom Short
Page 40 – Hudd & Dini (hospital bed) – Vic Martin
Page 41 – A Cracked Look at 007! – O.O. Severin (John Severin) / Mort Todd
Page 44 – Robot Wars (Krash!) – Mort Todd (1st *Robot Wars*)
Page 45 – TV Word Plays
Page 45 – Cracked Interviews the Low-Budget Movie King – Bill Burke
Page 50 – Shut-Ups (mop the floor) – Bill Burke
Back Cover – Unicorn Horn – Aron Laikin

**217, January 1986 (52 pages) ($1.25)** (On sale date October 29, 1985)
Cover – We Zap Halley's Comet – Aron Laikin
Page 2 and 51 – Only Buy Products Made in America – Cracked Hangup
Page 3 – Contents
Page 4 – Letters – John Severin / Subscription ad – John Severin
Page 6 – Rambo First Blood Part II – Kent Gamble
Page 11 – Robot Wars (Hehz Hehz Hawz) – Mort Todd
Page 12 – How Different Mags Will Cover Halley's Comet – Mort Todd / George Gladir
Page 14 – Alien TV! – John Severin / Gene Perone, Mort Todd
Page 19 – Sylvester's Corner The Artist – Kevin Sacco
Page 20 – Positive Thinking is – Warren Sattler
Page 23 – Sports Word Plays
Page 24 – The Commercialization of X.T. – Rick Altergott / George Gladir
Page 26 – Halley's Comet as Seen By Different Celebrities – Tony Tallarico
Page 28 – Cracked Max III Beyond Blunderdome! – Bob Fingerman
Page 32 – Cracked Visits a Midnight Monster Picnic – Al Scaduto
Page 34 – Advertising on Postage Stamps – Arnoldo Franchioni
Page 36 – Absolutely, Unquestionably, Positively, Undeniably, the Very, Very, Last of The Cracked Lens (and we really, really mean it this time, for sure!) Part XIV (Title reprint from #189; otherwise it's new material.)

Page 39 – Ye Hang Ups (rioting again) – John Severin
Page 40 – Cracked Interviews Frankenstein, the Movie Monster King – Bill Burke
Page 44 – Cracked Tranzformers Contest Results – Mort Todd
Page 45 – The Cozby Kids Meet the A-Teem – John Reiner
Page 50 – Shut-Ups (little off the top) – Don Orehek
Back Cover – Sylvester Mask – Aron Laikin

**218, March 1986 (52 pages) ($1.25)** (Mike Ricigliano's *Spies and Saboteurs* returns with this issue.) (Last issue edited by Paul Laikin.)
Cover – Rocky IV – John Severin
Page 2 and 51 – This is a Chain Letter Sign – Cracked Sign
Page 3 – Contents
Page 4 – Letters – John Severin / Subscription ad
Page 6 – Box Office Future – John Severin / Joe Catalano, Mort Todd
Page 12 – Cracked Look at Super-Zeros! – Mort Todd / Tom Bacas
Page 15 – Sports Strikes for '86! – Tom Short
Page 18 – Am I Normal? – Dan Clowes / Joe Catalano
Page 21 – Robot Wars (heh heh bbbzzz) – Steve Ditko / Mort Todd (1st Steve Ditko artwork)
Page 22 – When the World Runs Out of Water! – Eric Cartier / George Gladir
Page 25 – Laughing Matter – Hark Abner / Tom Bacas
Page 26 – More Celebrity Balloons – Tony Tallarico
Page 28 – G.I. Joke "A Real American Nut!" – Bob Fingerman (1st *G.I. Joke*)
Page 32 – Don't You Feel Stupid
Page 34 – How Come Sylvester Gets So Much Space in Cracked – Cuz
Page 37 – Hudd & Dini (get your picture) – Vic Martin
Page 38 – More Cracked is – Arnoldo Franchioni
Page 40 – Unreceived Xmas Gifts
Page 42 – Absolutely, Unquestionably, Positively, Undeniably, the Very, Very, Last of The Cracked Lens (and if we don't mean it, we should be struck deaaaddd) (Title reprint from #216, otherwise it's new material.)
Page 44 – Sylvester's Corner The Painting – Kevin Sacco
Page 45 – Christmas Joke Contest – Aron Laikin (Image rip-off from *Crazy* #16)
Page 46 – Cracked Interviews Santa Claus, The Christmas King – Bill Burke
Page 50 – Shut-Ups (don't want to visit Grandma) – Don Orehek
Back Cover – Kiss Sylvester Under the Mistletoe – Aron Laikin

**219, May 1986 (52 pages) ($1.25)** (1st issue edited by Mort Todd aka Michael Delle-Femine.)

Cover – Action Packed Laugh Riot Special!! – John Severin / Mort Todd
Page 2 and 51 – Sylvester P, Smythe is Rambozo! – Cracked Movie Poster – Bob Fingerman
Page 3 – Contents
Page 4 – Letters – John Severin / Subscription ad
Page 6 – Arnold Fluffernutter Commandope – Bob Fingerman / Mort Todd
Page 11 – A Fish Story – Milton Knight
Page 12 – Sylvester P. Smythe's Cracked Pleasure Dome – Eric Cartier / George Gladir
Page 15 – Cracked Hold-Ups! (Mia Optik)
Page 17 – Sylvester's Photo Album – John Severin (reprint from #35)
Page 21 – The Cracked Lens (I can't stop it) (Starting the series over.)
Page 24 – Read 'em & Rate 'em! – Frank Caruso
Page 26 – Cracked Look at Godzilla! – Bill Wray / Joe Catalano
Page 29 – Ye Hang Ups #77 (small serving) – John Severin
Page 30 – Mr. Rockey's Neighb'hood! – John Reiner / Mark Lewis
Page 32 – Bad Professionals! – Tom Bacas
Page 35 – Rockey: 2001 – John Severin / Eel O'Brian (Mort Todd)
Page 39 – Robot Wars (Whirrrrrrrr) – Steve Ditko / Mort Todd
Page 40 – Word Plays (Shipwreck)
Page 41 – Celebrities Pump Iron! – Tom Short
Page 44 – Hudd & Dini (pool) – Vic Martin
Page 45 – Cracked Interviews with the Gangster King! – Walter Brogan / Joe Catalano
Page 50 – Cracked Shut-Ups (driving in the country) – Bill McCartney (Bill Ward) (reprint from #9)
Back Cover – Sagebrush (can't hold on) – John Severin (reprint from *Cracked Collectors' Edition* #5)

**220, July 1986 (52 pages) ($1.25)** (Flip-book issue)

Cover and Back Cover – Non Violence Special (April Fool!) – Nireves (John Severin)
Page 2 and 2 – Hole in the wall – Cracked Poster – John Severin
Page 3 and 3 – Contents
Page 4 – Merlin Calling Collect! – Stan Goldberg / Mike Esposito
Page 5 – Cracked Interviews Dick Clog the Blooper & Practical Joke King – John Severin / Mort Todd
Page 10 – Tricks Are For Kids! – Milton Knight
Page 11 – Letters / Square Egg Maker ad / Subscription ad

Page 13 – Werd Plaiz
Page 14 – Let the Punishment Fit the Crime!! – Dan Clowes / Peter Bagge
Page 16 – Rockey IV – Bob Fingerman / Mort Todd
Page 21 – The High Lama – Eric Cartier / Tom Bacas
Page 22 – Hazardous to Your Health! – Al Scaduto
Page 24 – Hudd & Dini (mermaid) – Vic Martin
Page 25 – Shut-Ups (going to hurt me) – Don Orehek
Page 26 – Robot Wars (Swoosh) – Steve Ditko / Mort Todd (Now flip the magazine over.)
Page 4 – Man's First Attempts to Harness the Power of Electricity – Bill Wray / Mat Jacobs
Page 5 – Death Wishy-Washy 3! – Bob Fingerman
Page 9 – Rock 'n' Roll Losers! – Tom Short
Page 11 – What's the Beef? – John Reiner / Joe Catalano
Page 15 – Hudd & Dini (net) – Vic Martin
Page 16 – Great Moments of the Future!
Page 18 – Cracked Look at Young Schlock Holmes! – Walter Brogan / Joe Catalano
Page 22 – Get Off it Already! – Frank Caruso
Page 24 – Sylvester: Supermarket Stock Boy – Al Scaduto
Page 25 – Shut-Ups (brown leather bag) – Don Orehek

**221, August 1986 (52 pages) ($1.25)**
Cover – Poltergeist Goes Psycho! – John Severin / Mort Todd
Page 2 – Subscription ad
Page 3 – Contents
Page 4 – Painting the Town – John Severin / Roger Brown
Page 5 – Rock, Rattle & Moan! – Bob Fingerman
Page 11 – Real Life Horror! – Milton Knight
Page 12 – Don Orehek's Horrible Humor – Don Orehek
Page 14 – Hudd & Dini (CLICK!) – Vic Martin
Page 15 – Monstrous Practical Jokes! – John Severin / Hilary Zatz
Page 17 – The Lovesick Connection – Frank Caruso
Page 20 – Horror Tales for the 80s – Shawn Kerri
Page 23 – Robot Wars (grrrrr) – Steve Ditko / Mort Todd
Page 24 – The Cracked List of Stupid Things That Only Kids Like! – Bill Wray / Peter Bagge
Page 26 – Polter-Psycho-Geist – John Reiner / Mortimer Post, Mort Todd
Page 31 – Letters
Page 32 – Cryptic Commercials – Frank Caruso
Page 34 – Cracked Horror Lens – Randy Epley

Page 36 – Gorbachev in America! – John Severin / Moe McMahon (Marian McMahon)
Page 39 – The Uggly Family (give this bone) – Stosh Gillespie (Dan Clowes) / Eel O'Brian (Mort Todd) (2nd appearance of *The Uggly Family*; 1st was in *Extra Special Cracked* #9)
Page 40 – Monster Combination Movies – Walter Brogan / Jim Wheelock
Page 42 – Don't Even Start!! – Al Scaduto
Page 45 – Cracked Interviews Stephen Kink the Horror King! – Stan Goldberg, Mike Esposito / Joe Catalano
Page 50 – Shut-Ups (holding up the works) – Don Orehek
Page 51 – Cracked X-15 Survival Knife – Bob Fingerman
Back Cover – Dee Sylvester – Bill Wray (1st *Sylvester Celebrity Poster*)

**222, September 1986 (52 pages) ($1.25)**
Cover – Handprints in Cement – John Severin
Page 2 – Subscription ad – John Severin
Page 3 – Contents
Page 4 – One Knight at the Statue of Liberty – Milton Knight
Page 5 – Cracked Movie VI: A New Beginning – John Severin / Joe Catalano
Page 10 – The Cracked World of Vic Martin – Vic Martin
Page 13 – Sylvester's Corner The Rubber Duck – Kevin Sacco
Page 14 – Messed up by Modern Times! – Bob Fingerman
Page 20 – Rock 'n' Roll Word Plays – Rick Parker / Mark Dressler
Page 22 – New Cracked Dances! – Al Scaduto
Page 24 – Cracked Sports Profile – Tom Short
Page 27 – Squeeeal of Fortune!! – John Reiner / Joe Catalano
Page 31 – Before Heimlich! – Vic Martin
Page 32 – Celebrity Phobias! – Frank Caruso
Page 34 – The 1st Annual Cracked Lens Worst Movie Awards – Randy Epley
Page 36 – Letters
Page 37 – Cracked Interviews Steven Spielberg, the Movie King! – Stan Goldberg, Mike Esposito / Joe Catalano
Page 41 – The Transdeformers vs Boltron – Steve Ditko / Mort Todd, John Arcudi
Page 44 – Hudd & Dini (zebra) – Vic Martin
Page 45 – The Moldin Girls – Marie Severin / Stu Schwartzberg
Page 50 – Shut-Ups (heavyweight champ) – Don Orehek
Page 51 – Leaving Hair ad – John Severin (reprint from #82)
Back Cover – Sylvester P. Reagan – Bill Wray

**223, October 1986 (52 pages) ($1.25)**

Cover - Sylvester, the Statue of Liberty - Bill Wray
Page 2 - *Cracked Digest* #1 ad
Page 3 - Contents
Page 4 - Once Upon a Time - Milton Knight / Mat Jacobs
Page 5 - Cracked Interviews the Vice Kings - Rob Orzechowski / Joe Catalano
Page 9 - Hudd & Dini (Tunnel of Love) - Vic Martin
Page 10 - Movie Mystery Credits - Thyme Foxpound (John Severin) / E. Nelson Bridwell
Page 12 - Cracked Loot at the Statue of Liberty - Wally Brogan / Joe Catalano
Page 15 - Subscription ad - John Severin
Page 16 - Cracked Looks at Dating - Bill McCartney (Bill Ward) (reprint from #76)
Page 18 - The Cracked Lens - Randy Epley
Page 22 - Ronald Reagan's Photo Album - John Severin (reprint from #193)
Page 25 - Another Knight at the Statue of Liberty - Milton Knight
Page 26 - Real Competition! - Shawn Kerri
Page 28 - Robot Wars (giant destroy-bots on their way here) - Steve Ditko / Mort Todd
Page 29 - Letters (Statement of Ownership: Average number of copies sold: 190,100)
Page 32 - The Unsung Sports Heroes! - Cliff Mott
Page 34 - Ms. Liberty as Influenced By - Bo Badman (Rurik Tyler)
Page 37 - Rasslin' Rowdies Magazine - John Severin / George Gladir
Page 41 - Hurry-Ups! (perfect compliment) - Rick Altergott
Page 42 - Feeble Foresights - Frank Caruso
Page 44 - ZZ Slop vs. the Space Pirates - Bob Fingerman (This is the article that got Fingerman fired for supposedly having Satanic messages.)
Page 50 - Shut-Ups (don't deserve to die) - Don Orehek
Page 51 - Big Foot Expedition - Vic Martin
Back Cover - Sgt. S. Laughter - Bill Wray

**224, November 1986 (52 pages) ($1.25)** (On sale date July 24, 1986)

Cover - Sylvester Springsteen - Bill Wray
Page 2 - The Chicken Killer - Howard Nostrand / Jay Lynch (reprint from #168)
Page 3 - Contents
Page 4 - Shut-Ups (new Walkman) - Don Orehek
Page 5 - The Cosby Show - John Severin (2nd *Cosby Show* parody)

Page 10 – Cracked Top Hits – Frank Caruso
Page 12 – Count Dracula …2086 A.D. – John Severin / George Gladir
Page 13 – The Uggly Family (Whatcha got there) – Stosh Gillespie (Dan Clowes) / Eel O'Brian (Mort Todd)
Page 16 – Commercial Dilemma – Milton Knight
Page 17 – Ninjerk Magazine – Walter Brogan
Page 22 – Rock Celebrity Childhoods – John Severin / George Gladir
Page 24 – The Lifecycle of a Rock 'n' Roll Song! – Pete Friedrich, Lloyd Dangle
Page 26 – What's On Their Minds? – Bill Wray / Peter Bagge (1st *What's On Their Minds?*)
Page 27 – Cracked Interviews the T.V. Ratings King – Bill Ward (reprint from #183)
Page 32 – Blech Shampoo ad – LePoer (John Severin) (reprint from #21)
Page 33 – Letters
Page 35 – Cracked World of Rock
Page 38 – You Know It's a Crummy Date When – Don Orehek / Joe Catalano
Page 40 – The First Annual Cracked Music Awards! – Tom Short
Page 43 – Garbage Dump Pop Stars (Paul Shaver) (1st *Garbage Dump Pop Stars*)
Page 46 – Hands Across America – Bill Wray / Stu Schwartzberg
Page 50 – Shut-Ups (sound of heavy metal) – Don Orehek
Page 51 – Great Moments in Travel 1915 – Howard Nostrand (reprint from #161)
Back Cover – Sylly Idol – Bill Wray

**225, January 1987 (52 pages) ($1.25)**

Cover and Back Cover – G.I. Joke, Stallone and Schwarzenegger – Bill Wray
Page 2 – Sylvester P. Stalloon – Bill Wray
Page 3 – Contents
Page 4 – Cobrat – Bill Wray / Mort Todd
Page 10 – You Know You're a VCR Freak if – Al Scaduto / George Gladir
Page 12 – Cracked Action-Adventure Hero Sandwiches! – Milton Knight / Hilary Zatz
Page 15 – U.S.A. Superforce – John Severin / E. Nelson Bridwell
Page 20 – The Cracked Lens! (Really, Fred!) – Randy Epley
Page 23 – Canine the Barbarian (the most savage barbarian) – Gary Fields (2nd appearance of *Canine the Barbarian*; 1st was in *Super Cracked* #32)

Page 26 – A Day in the Life of the Uggly Family Game – Stosh Gillespie (Dan Clowes) / Eel O'Brian (Mort Todd)
Page 28 – Letters / Cracked Pen Pals
Page 30 – Rock 'n' Roll Fairy Tales! – Frank Caruso
Page 32 – Ron Rover – Rick Altergott / Dan Knotts
Page 35 – Cracked Interviews the Doll Queen – Rob Orzechowski / Mortimer Post
Page 39 – G.I. Joke in Peace, Love & Harmony – Shawn Kerri
Page 44 – Robot Wars (boom box) – Steve Ditko / Mort Todd
Page 45 – Big Deal
Page 50 – Shut-Ups (little off the top) – Don Orehek (reprint from #217)
Page 51 – Subscription ad – John Severin

**226, March 1987 (52 pages) ($1.25)** (On sale date mid-December 1986)
Cover – 29th Anniversary Special!! – John Severin
Page 2 – Evolution of Smythe – Bill Wray
Page 3 – Contents
Page 4 – Shut-Ups (pumpkin pie) – Don Orehek
Page 5 – Familiar Ties – John Severin / Joe Catalano (2nd *Family Ties* parody)
Page 10 – What's On Their Minds? (TV) – Bill Wray / Peter Bagge
Page 11 – Blundercats – Steve Ditko / Mike Carlin
Page 16 – Hudd & Dini (street rock king) – Vic Martin
Page 17 – Cracked Milestones! – Bob Fingerman / George Gladir
Page 20 – Hurry-Ups – Rick Altergott / Charlie Schneider
Page 21 – Alieens – Bill Wray / Joe Catalano, Mort Todd
Page 26 – Tour of the Cracked Magazine Offices! – John Severin / Joe Catalano, Michael Delle-Femine
Page 28 – You Know You're a Robot – Brad Joyce / George Gladir
Page 30 – Letters
Page 31 – Cracked Interviews Broke Shields the Glamour Queen! – Rob Orzechowski / Moe McMahon (Marian McMahon)
Page 35 – Cracked Pen Pals / Win One of 10 Free Cracked Subscriptions
Page 36 – Subscription ad – John Severin / (Statement of Ownership: Average number of copies sold: 197,047)
Page 37 – Goonlighting – Bob Fingerman / Stu Schwartzberg
Page 42 – How Time Has Changed the Comedians! – Frank Caruso
Page 44 – 29th Anniversary Edition Who's Who
Page 45 – Tardzan the Apish Man – John Clayton (John Severin) / Joe Catalano, Mort Todd
Page 50 – Shut-Ups (Fourth of July) – Don Orehek

Page 51 – The Uggly Family Poster – Stosh Gillespie (Dan Clowes) / Eel O'Brian (Mort Todd)
Back Cover – Santa Smythe – Bill Wray

**227, April 1987 (52 pages) ($1.25)**
Cover – We Heat Up the Cold War! – John Severin
Page 2 – Comrade Klein – Bill Wray
Page 3 – Contents
Page 4 – Cracked Around the World! / Subscription ad
Page 5 – Communist Broadcasting System's New TV Lineup! – Ivan Severinovitch (John Severin)
Page 10 – Russian One-Shots (Miss Moscow) – Mike Ricigliano (1st *One-Shots*)
Page 12 – Better Off Red! – Bo Badmananoff (Rurik Tyler)
Page 15 – The Transinformers vs the Defecticons! – Steve Ditko
Page 17 – Ronnie at the Bat! – Walter Broganoff (Walter Brogan)
Page 20 – Barbski and Kenov in Capitalist Cut-Ups
Page 22 – Hurry-Ups! (File, file, file!)
Page 23 – Searski Katalogue
Page 26 – All-New Soviet Car Window Signs
Page 28 – Russian Commie Strips! – Gary Fieldsky (Gary Fields) / Pyoter Cicconewicz
Page 30 – The Dougy Dougan Letters – Mike Carlin
Page 32 – Ronnie-Gorb
Page 36 – Hudd & Dini (You are now leaving Russia) – Vic Martinov (Vic Martin)
Page 37 – Life in Amerika Magazine – O.O. Severin (John Severin)
Page 40 – Russian Word Plays!
Page 42 – A Red-White-and-Blueprint for Unspying an Amerikan Hotel Room!
Page 44 – Lifestyles of the Decadent and Opulent – Bob Fingermanski (Bob Fingerman)
Page 46 – Cracked Interviews the Commie Commissar! – Bob Orzechowski
Page 50 – The Soviet Shut-Ups (beautiful clear night) – Don Orehek
Page 51 – Great Moments in History 1656 – Charles Rodrigues (reprint from #132)
Back Cover – Mikhail P. Gorbasmythe – Bill Wray

**228, July 1987 (52 pages) ($1.35)**
Cover – Star Trek IV – John Severin
Page 2 – Shut-Ups (get my hands on) – Don Orehek / Mort Todd
Page 3 – Contents

Page 4 – Some Rescue – Mike Ricigliano
Page 5 – Eeeeekualizer – O.O. Severin (John Severin) / Joe Catalano
Page 9 – 'Puter Kids – Bob Fingerman / Peter Bagge
Page 10 – You Know You're a Rad Biker When – Brad Joyce / George Gladir
Page 12 – Hurry-Ups (Neutral Zone) – Rick Altergott
Page 13 – Star Drek IV: The Voyage Back Home to the Future! – Bill Wray / Mort Todd (This was the parody that Bill Wray brought in without doing the backgrounds, so Mort Todd had to complete them.)
Page 18 – Gross is Great – Stosh Gillespie (Dan Clowes) / Eel O'Brian (Mort Todd)
Page 20 – R.A.L.F. Real Alien Life Form – Walter Brogan / Joe Catalano
Page 23 – Letters / Cracked Checklist
Page 25 – Cracked Guide to Guitars! – John Severin / Charles E. Hall
Page 29 – Cracked Pen Pals – Mike Ricigliano
Page 30 – Cracked Lens? (That's weird) – Randy Epley
Page 32 – Pee-Yoo's Playhovel – Bob Fingerman
Page 36 – Their Dreams Almost Came True! – Al Scaduto / Skene Catling
Page 38 – Really Cracked Celebrity Lens!
Page 40 – Future Crocodile Dundee Movies – Gray Morrow / George Gladir
Page 43 – One-Shots (Run for it!) – Mike Ricigliano
Page 45 – Cracked Interviews Max Headache – Rob Orzechowski / Ellis O'Brien
Page 49 – Put Your Best Foot Back! – Mike Ricigliano
Page 50 – Shut-Ups (light you are on your feet) – Don Orehek
Page 51 – Hudd & Dini (wrestling) – Vic Martin
Back Cover – Bill Cosbsmythe – Bill Wray

**229, August 1987 (52 pages) ($1.35)** (On sale date April 20, 1987)
Cover – For Monsters Only! – John Severin
Page 2 – *Super Cracked* #1 ad
Page 3 – Contents
Page 4 – Monster One-Shots (Alien dental floss) – Mike Ricigliano / Roger Brown
Page 5 – Transylvanian TV – John Severin
Page 10 – Don Orehek's Horrible Humor II: A New Beginning! – Don Orehek
Page 12 – Cracked Monster Lens! (Was somebody already sitting) – Randy Epley
Page 14 – G.I. Joke Super-Macho Coloring Book – Shawn Kerri

Page 17 – Fright Court – Bob Fingerman / Joe Catalano
Page 21 – Monstrous Hurry-Ups! (sweetest cherries) – Rick Altergott / Charles Schneider
Page 22 – Uggly Family in "Meet the Trashformers" – Stosh Gillespie (Dan Clowes) / Eel O'Brian (Mort Todd)
Page 26 – Cracked Super Party! – John Severin / Jerry De Fuccio
Page 28 – Letters
Page 29 – Cracked Ugly Oracles #1 Psychic Psycho! – Bo Badman (Rurik Tyler) (1st *Ugly Oracles*)
Page 31 – Your Little Brother Really is a Monster When – Walter Brogan / Joe Catalano
Page 34 – Monster Babie's Horror Tales – Bill Wray
Page 37 – Monster Pets – John Severin / Moe McMahon (Marian McMahon)
Page 38 – Slippery When Wet – Walter Brogan
Page 39 – Fangorier Magazine – Gray Morrow / George Gladir
Page 42 – Monsters Get Teed Off! – Rob Orzechowski / George Gladir
Page 44 – Fadballs – Rick Parker / Pete Ciccone
Page 45 – Cracked Pen Pals / Cracked Coming Attractions
Page 46 – Cracked Interviews the Grossout King! – Rob Orzechowski / Joe Catalano
Page 50 – Shut-Ups (contact lenses) – Don Orehek
Page 51 – Nanny's Pin Up Page – Skene Catling
Back Cover – Sylvester P. Alf – Bill Wray

**230, September 1987 (52 pages) ($1.35)** (On sale date June 2, 1987)
Cover – Unnaturally Cracked – John Severin
Page 2 – Subscription ad – Don Orehek
Page 3 – Contents
Page 4 – A Weighty Matter! – Walter Brogan
Page 5 – The Creation of a Hit TV Show! – John Severin / Peter Bagge
Page 9 – Unnaturally Cracked Examiner Magazine – Al Scaduto / Richard Dominick
Page 11 – Letters / Cracked Coming Attractions
Page 13 – On the Beach! – Mike Ricigliano / Roger Brown
Page 14 – Growing Painful – Walter Brogan / Joe Catalano
Page 18 – Cracked Reader's Poll and Free Subscription Winners!
Page 19 – Designer Genes – Bob Fingerman / George Gladir
Page 22 – Cracked's 10 Most Unwanted List – Bill Wray
Page 24 – One-Shots (stiltwalking) – Mike Ricigliano / Roger Brown
Page 26 – The Wheel of Fortune for Summer Jobs! – Bo Badman (Rurik Tyler)
Page 28 – Hudd & Dini (Cracked Annual Monster Party) – Vic Martin

Page 30 – The Minute After the Meineke Commercial! – Don Orehek / Jerry De Fuccio
Page 31 – Murder, She Wrot – Marie Severin / Stu Schwartzberg
Page 35 – Cracked Lens (anti-perspirant)
Page 37 – What's On Their Minds? (Rambo) – Bill Wray / Peter Bagge
Page 38 – The Beginning of Fire! – Mike Ricigliano / Roger Brown
Page 39 – The Donkees – John Severin / Charles E. Hall, Mort Todd
Page 44 – Cracked Lottery Nuts! – Al Scaduto
Page 46 – Cracked Interviews Gummi the Clayboy King! – Rob Orzechowski / Gary Fields
Page 49 – Hudd & Dini (peace pipe) – Vic Martin
Page 50 – Shut-Ups (favorite breakfast) – Don Orehek
Page 51 – Great Moments in History (Boston Tea Party) – John Severin
Back Cover – Sylvelvis Presley Smythe – Bill Wray

**231, October 1987 (52 pages) ($1.35)** (On sale date early July, 1987)
Cover – Hollywood's Biggest Squares – Bob Fingerman / Mort Todd
Page 2 – *Cracked Collectors' Edition* #72 and *Cracked Digest* #5 ad
Page 3 – Contents
Page 4 – The Boat Ride – Mike Ricigliano / Roger Brown
Page 5 – Hollyweird Squares! – Rob Orzechowski / Moe McMahon (Marian McMahon), Mort Todd
Page 9 – Cracked Lens (cup of coffee) – Randy Epley
Page 12 – Nothing New Under, Around or Beyond the Sun! – Tom Short
Page 15 – The Haircut – Mike Ricigliano / Roger Brown
Page 16 – The Cracked Video Revolution! – Vic Martin / George Gladir
Page 19 – A Night Out with Siskel & Ebert – Bob Fingerman / David Kaminsky
Page 20 – Canine the Barkbarian (hasty exit) – Gary Fields
Page 22 – Cracked Rock Video Cliches! – Frank Caruso / Joey Cavalieri
Page 25 – Cracked Pen Pals – John Severin
Page 26 – Form & Function: Rad Bikes! – Bo Badman (Rurik Tyler) (1st *Form & Function*)
Page 28 – Robot Horror Story (what's that?) – Steve Ditko
Page 29 – Letters / Cracked Coming Attractions
Page 31 – A Grizzly Escape! – Mike Ricigliano / Roger Brown
Page 32 – Hudd & Dini (kangaroo) – Vic Martin
Page 33 – Jeoparty! – John Severin / Joe Catalano
Page 35 – Rock and Roll Mutations! – Bob Fingerman / Hilary Zatz
Page 38 – One-Shots (Darth Vader) – Mike Ricigliano
Page 40 – Cracked Game Show Lens – Randy Epley
Page 41 – Imperfect Strangers! – Walter Brogan / Joe Catalano

Page 45 – One-Shots (Andre the Giant) – Mike Ricigliano / Roger Brown
Page 47 – Cracked Interviews Vainna White! – John Severin / Moe McMahon (Marian McMahon)
Page 50 – Shut-Ups (Eagle has landed) – Don Orehek
Page 51 – Subscription ad – Don Orehek
Back Cover – Goonlighting – Bill Wray

**232, November 1987 (52 pages) ($1.35)**
Cover – TV Cliff Hangers! – John Severin / Mort Todd
Page 2 – What's On Their Minds? (conductor) – Bill Wray / Peter Bagge
Page 3 – Contents
Page 4 – The Grip – Mike Ricigliano / Roger Brown
Page 5 – Cracked Interviews Bill Cozby! – Rob Orzechowski / Joe Catalano
Page 9 – Stoopy Dum – Milton Knight
Page 10 – The Final Episodes of Soured Sitcoms! – Frank Caruso
Page 12 – Cracked Birds! – Alba Ballard / Kevin McMahon
Page 15 – Magnumb R.I.P – John Severin / Robert Loren Fleming
Page 19 – Melbin and the Uggly Family in Dragnut – Stosh Gillespie (Dan Clowes) / Eel O'Brian (Mort Todd)
Page 23 – Garbage Pail Kids Movie Poster ad
Page 24 – A Visit to Ralf's Home Planet! – Walter Brogan / Joe Catalano
Page 26 – Mmmax Headache All Over the World! – John Severin
Page 28 – Late Nut with David Letterhead!
Page 32 – Spies and Saboteurs Activity Pages! – Mike Ricigliano
Page 34 – Replacements for Dieann on Jeers! – Walter Brogan / Joe Catalano
Page 38 – New Jobs for Vanna! – John Severin / Joe Catalano
Page 40 – Star Drek: The Next De-Generation – Bo Badman (Rurik Tyler)
Page 44 – Letters / Coming Attractions – John Severin (1st appearance of the Sylvester P. Smythe plush doll.) (Photo of Pee-Wee Herman on Joan Rivers' *Late Show* with *Cracked.*)
Page 46 – Cracked Interviews Michael J. Foxy – Rob Orzechowski / Joe Catalano
Page 50 – Shut-Ups (garbage disposal) – Don Orehek
Page 51 – Sylvester the Bird! – Alba Ballard, Bill Wray
Back Cover – Garbage Ail Kid (Cracked Creep) – Bob Fingerman

**233, January 1988 (52 pages) ($1.35)** (On sale date December 1987)
Cover – Movie Mania! – John Severin / Mort Todd
Page 2 – Ye Hang Ups (cell with a good view) – John Severin

Page 3 – Contents
Page 4 – One Day in Russia – Mike Ricigliano / Roger Brown
Page 5 – Untouchy Bulls! – John Severin / Mort Todd
Page 10 – Winfrah Oprey! – Bill Wray / Peter Bagge
Page 14 – Bon Jovi vs. Bruce! – Frank Caruso
Page 16 – .007 Devices that Bombed! – Rob Orzechowski / Eel O'Brian (Mort Todd)
Page 19 – InyerFace – Bob Fingerman
Page 23 – Progress of a Cracked Technophile! – John Severin / Peter Bagge
Page 25 – Premedator – William York Wray (Bill Wray) / Robert Loren Fleming
Page 30 – Beverly Hills Slop II – Walter Brogan / Joe Catalano
Page 35 – How the Movies Wrecked Supedupman – Rick Altergott / Mort Todd
Page 39 – Cracked Pen Pals / 1988 Cracked T-Shirt ad – John Severin
Page 40 – RoboCop Out – Mark Pacella / John Arcudi
Page 43 – Subscription ad – Bob Fingerman / Sylvester P. Smythe Doll ad
Page 44 – Letters
Page 46 – Cracked Busts Out With Th' Rap Kings – Bob Fingerman
Page 50 – Shut-Ups (cook a pizza) – Don Orehek
Page 51 – Cracked Crew – Bob Fingerman
Back Cover – Sylvester Pee-Wee Smythe – Bill Wray

**234, March 1988 (52 pages) ($1.35)**

Cover – We Smash Sledge Hammer! – John Severin, Don Martin (1st Don Martin art in *Cracked*)
Page 2 – The Uggly Family (Why are we having dinner) – Stosh Gillespie (Dan Clowes) / Eel O'Brian (Mort Todd)
Page 3 – Contents
Page 4 – Don Martin's The Kick-Off! – Don Martin
Page 5 – Sludge Hammer! – Rick Altergott
Page 9 – Cyborgs Unlimited – John Severin / George Gladir
Page 12 – What Stores Do For Christmas! – Don Orehek / Joe Catalano
Page 14 – One-Shots Look at Sports – Mike Ricigliano / Roger Brown
Page 16 – Battyman – Rick Altergott / Charles E. Hall
Page 20 – The Short-Lived Reformation of Ebenezer Scrooge – Al Scaduto
Page 21 – Nightlife with Ked Toppel – Frank Caruso / Steve Skeates
Page 23 – Miner Mistake – Mike Ricigliano / Roger Brown
Page 24 – The Uggly Family Uglystoppers Textbook – Stosh Gillespie (Dan Clowes) / Eel O'Brian (Mort Todd)

Page 28 – Cracked Star Cars! – John Severin / Cliff Mott
Page 31 – Letters (David Letterman photo with *Cracked* #232)
Page 32 – Subscription ad – Don Martin / Sylvester P. Smythe Doll ad / 1988 Cracked T-Shirt ad – John Severin
Page 33 – Don Martin's The Half-Time Show! – Don Martin
Page 34 – SuperSylvester the Cracked Crusader! The Legend – John Severin / Mort Todd
Page 38 – Form & Function (skateboards) – Bo Badman (Rurik Tyler)
Page 40 – Don Martin's Things That Irritate You the Most! – Don Martin
Page 42 – Cracked Movie Carol! – Walter Brogan / Stu Schwartzberg
Page 45 – Cracked Look at Frankenstein – Cliff Mott / John Arcudi
Page 47 – Cracked Interviews Clint Beastwood – Rob Orzechowski / Joe Catalano
Page 50 – Shut-Ups (Roman nose) – Don Orehek
Page 51 – Stain-It! – Milton Knight
Back Cover – Syl Jon Bon Jovial – Bill Wray

**235, May 1988 (52 pages) ($1.35)**

Cover – Don Martin is Cracked – Don Martin
Page 2 – Suds MacFrenzie – John Severin / Jerry De Fuccio
Page 3 – Contents
Page 4 – Don Martin's One Fine Evening in Transylvania – Don Martin
Page 5 – A Deficient World – Rick Altergott / Joe Catalano
Page 9 – Sagebrush (gettin' fed-up) – John Severin
Page 10 – Cracked Mirrors – Vic Martin
Page 13 – Perry Mazin The Case of the Guilty Client – Bill Wray / Robert Loren Fleming
Page 16 – One-Shots (fried chicken) – Mike Ricigliano / Roger Brown
Page 18 – Constitutional Crisis! – John Severin / George Gladir
Page 19 – Cracked Ugly Oracles #2 Mama Meany – Bo Badman (Rurik Tyler)
Page 21 – A Public Disservice – Milton Knight
Page 22 – Bummers! – Dick Ayers / Moe McMahon (Marian McMahon)
Page 24 – Letters / Subscription ad – John Severin
Page 26 – Don Martin's One Especially Fine Day this Winter – Don Martin
Page 27 – The Uggly Family Recipe No. 1 Dump Cake – Stosh Gillespie (Dan Clowes) / Eel O'Brian (Mort Todd)
Page 28 – Sylvester P. Smythe Doll ad / 1988 Cracked T-Shirt ad – John Severin / (Statement of Ownership: Average number of copies sold: 182,654)

Page 29 – Supedupman's 50th Birthday! – John Severin / George Gladir
Page 33 – Yo Yo – Mike Ricigliano / Roger Brown
Page 34 – Railroad Crossing – Mike Ricigliano / Roger Brown
Page 35 – Star Drek The Next Cancellation – Bo Badman (Rurik Tyler)
Page 39 – The Phrenologist! – Al Scaduto / Paul Proch, Charles Kaufman
Page 40 – Polly! – Bill Wray / Peter Bagge
Page 44 – The Rock Stars Speak! – Bob Fingerman / Peter Bagge
Page 46 – Don Martin's One Fine Mid-Afternoon – Don Martin
Page 47 – Cracked Interviews R.A.L.F. – Rob Orzechowski / Joe Catalano
Page 50 – Hurry-Ups! (sit tight) – Rick Altergott
Page 51 – Canine the Barkbarian (exotic an' heroic adventures) – Gary Fields
Back Cover – S. Polly Darton – Bill Wray

**236, July 1988 (52 pages) ($1.35)**
Cover – Schwarzenegger & Stallone Cracked Movie – John Severin
Page 2 – One-Shots (Jet-Pak) – Mike Ricigliano / Roger Brown
Page 3 – Contents
Page 4 – Don Martin's The Evolution of the Movie Kiss! – Don Martin
Page 6 – Leonard Part 6 – Rick Altergott / Joe Catalano
Page 10 – You Know You're a Couch Potato When – Bud Jones / Gary Fields
Page 12 – It's Back and Badder than Every Cracked Lens! – Randy Epley
Page 15 – My Two Duds! – Walter Brogan / Joe Catalano
Page 18 – One-Shots (Superman) – Mike Ricigliano / Roger Brown
Page 20 – Toilet Zone – Bob Fingerman / Steve Skeates
Page 22 – Rangey Loner – John Severin
Page 27 – Don Martin's One Electrifying Morning at the State Pen – Don Martin
Page 28 – Letters / Cracked Coming Attractions
Page 29 – Hudd & Dini (football) – Vic Martin
Page 30 – YuckTales – Gary Fields / John Arcudi
Page 33 – Sylvester P. Smythe Doll ad / 1988 Cracked T-Shirt ad – John Severin / subscription ad
Page 34 – The Stake-Out – John Severin
Page 35 – Forgotten Funnies! – Gary Fields
Page 37 – The Job – Mike Ricigliano / Roger Brown
Page 38 – Ye Hang Ups (knees are killing me) – John Severin
Page 40 – One Knight at the White House – Milton Knight
Page 41 – Gigglin's Island – Bill Wray
Page 46 – Don Martin's Monday Morning, Rather Early! – Don Martin

Page 47 – Teen-Age Movie Monsters – Rob Orzechowski / George Gladir
Page 50 – Shut-Ups (li'l twit) – Don Orehek
Page 51 – Two Heads Are Better Than – John Severin
Back Cover – Arnie Sylvesternegger – Bill Wray

**237, August 1988 (52 pages) ($1.49)**

Cover – 30th Anniversary Celebration – John Severin, Don Martin / Mort Todd
Page 2 and 51 – 30th Anniversary Celebration – Cracked Poster – John Severin
Page 3 – Contents
Page 4 – Don Martin's One Evening on the Sleazy Side of Town – Don Martin
Page 5 – False Rumors About Cracked – John Severin / George Gladir
Page 8 – Radzilla – Mike Ricigliano / Roger Brown
Page 9 – Cracked Fold-Up! – Bo Badman (Rurik Tyler)
Page 10 – Cracked Olympic Lens! – Randy Epley
Page 11 – Press and Jerk – Al Scaduto
Page 12 – Ron Rover – Rick Altergott / Dan Knotts
Page 16 – One-Shots (surfing torpedo) – Mike Ricigliano / Roger Brown
Page 18 – Cracked Olympic Lens II! – Randy Epley
Page 19 – Couch Potato Catalog – Vic Martin / George Gladir
Page 22 – Canine the Barkbarian (Tee hee!) – Gary Fields
Page 23 – The Uggly Family Go to the Olympics! – Stosh Gillespie (Dan Clowes) / Eel O'Brian (Mort Todd)
Page 26 – Ye Hang Ups (fat little guy) – John Severin
Page 28 – Don Martin's One Sunday in the Country – Don Martin
Page 29 – Letters / Cracked Coming Attractions
Page 30 – 30 Years of Cracked Convention ad / Don Martin T-Shirts ad – Don Martin
Page 31 – Robocops and Roborobbers – John Severin / John Arcudi
Page 34 – Form & Function Looks at Little League Gear! – Bo Badman (Rurik Tyler)
Page 36 – History of Cracked – Don Orehek / Darren Auck, John Arcudi
Page 39 – Hudd & Dini (wishing well) – Vic Martin
Page 41 – Head of the Klass – Walter Brogan / Joe Catalano
Page 44 – Cracked Olympic Lens III! – Randy Epley
Page 45 – Olympic One-Shots (medals) – Mike Ricigliano / Roger Brown
Page 46 – Don Martin's One Fine Afternoon Next Week – Don Martin
Page 47 – The Sabotage Handbook – Mike Ricigliano

Page 50 – Shut-Ups (soaring over the city) – Don Orehek
Back Cover – Subscription ad – John Severin (reprint from #66)

**238, September 1988 (52 pages) ($1.49)**
Cover – Rambozo III – John Severin
Page 2 – Don Martin's See Sickness – Don Martin
Page 3 – Contents
Page 4 – If Rambo Fought Other Wars! – John Severin / George Gladir
Page 7 – Viva Las Vegas! – Bill Wray
Page 8 – One-Shots Looks at the Olympics – Mike Ricigliano / Roger Brown
Page 10 – What Rock Stars Were Like as Children – Rob Orzechowski / Joe Catalano
Page 12 – Things That You Can Do to Scare You to Heck! – Walter Brogan / Richard Dominick
Page 13 – Cracked Ugly Oracles #3 Clair & Voyant – Bo Badman (Rurik Tyler)
Page 15 – What's the Score? – Al Scaduto
Page 16 – G.I. Joke Gets Totally Thrashed! – Shawn Kerri
Page 21 – A Photo History of Cracked – Randy Epley
Page 24 – Rambo III Poster Book ad / 1988 Cracked T-Shirt ad – John Severin
Page 25 – Don Martin's One Fine Day in the Great Outdoors – Don Martin
Page 26 – Cracked 30th Anniversary Party! – John Severin / Joe Catalano (Severin draws himself, Catalano, Mort Todd and a number of celebrities.)
Page 28 – Lunch Break! – Mike Ricigliano / Roger Brown
Page 29 – Letters (Don Martin photo)
Page 31 – Didja Notice on Star Trek? – Gray Morrow / Douglas Martin
Page 33 – Vernon Swallowing's Friend – Jeremy Banx
Page 34 – Cracked Form & Function Looks at the Summer Olympics! – Bo Badman (Rurik Tyler)
Page 36 – Ye Hang Ups (I hate this place!) – John Severin
Page 38 – Subscription ad – Jack Davis / Cracked Top 5 (1st *Cracked Top 5*) / Cracked Coming Attractions – John Severin
Page 39 – The Cracked List of What's Hot and What's Not – Gary Fields
Page 41 – Jeers II – Walter Brogan / Joe Catalano (2nd *Cheers* parody)
Page 44 – Olympic One-Shots (Alfred E. Neuman appearance) – Mike Ricigliano / Roger Brown
Page 45 – Don Martin's One Fine African Afternoon – Don Martin
Page 47 – Cracked Interviews Rambozo! – Rob Orzechowski / Joe Catalano

Page 50 – Shut-Ups (can't seem to make out) – Don Orehek
Page 51 – Hudd & Dini (totem poles) – Vic Martin
Back Cover – Jerko, the Enersmyther! – Bill Wray

**239, October 1988 (52 pages) ($1.49)** (On sale date Early July 1988)
Cover – We Squeeze Beetlejuice – John Severin
Page 2 – A Cracked Look at Robin Hood – Walter Brogan
Page 3 – Contents
Page 4 – Don Martin's One Day at the Ad Agency – Don Martin
Page 5 – Spittlejuice – John Severin / Mort Todd
Page 9 – Wonderland Revisited – Brad Joyce / George Gladir
Page 10 – Suds McFrenzie – Gary Fields
Page 11 – Monster Olympic One-Shots – Mike Ricigliano / Roger Brown
Page 13 – Hudd & Dini (flying carpet taxi) – Vic Martin
Page 14 – A Cracked Look at Robin Hood – Walter Brogan / John Arcudi
Page 18 – Martyred with Children – Rob Orzechowski / Murad Gumen
Page 21 – Orehek's Horrible Humor III: A New Beginning! – Don Orehek (Don Orehek photo)
Page 24 – Subscription ad – Jack Davis / 1988 Cracked T-Shirt ad – John Severin
Page 25 – Handbook for Scaring People! – Bo Badman (Rurik Tyler) / George Gladir
Page 29 – Wow! (we give you) (1st *Wow!*) – Pat Boyette
Page 30 – 50/50 – Bill Wray / Peter Bagge
Page 32 – Ye Hang Ups (What a beautiful morning!) – John Severin
Page 37 – Letters (Mark Baratto photo) / Cracked Top 5 / Cracked Coming Attractions
Page 39 – Trasher! Magazine – Brad Joyce / Bo Badman (Rurik Tyler)
Page 43 – Blunder Years – Walter Brogan / Joe Catalano
Page 46 – Don Martin's Adjustments – Don Martin
Page 47 – Cracked Interviews Mike Dyson the Boxing King! – Rob Orzechowski
Page 50 – Shut-Ups (well-preserved mummy) – Don Orehek
Page 51 – The Spy and Saboteur Reunion Photo – Mike Ricigliano
Back Cover – Mike P. Smyson – Bill Wray

**240, November 1988 (52 pages) ($1.49)**
Cover – "I realize you won the dart game" – Don Martin
Page 2 – Spaced Out – Al Scaduto
Page 3 – Contents
Page 4 – Don Martin's One Fine Day in a Learning Lab – Don Martin
Page 5 – Cracked Coloring Pages – Vic Martin

Page 8 – Shut-Ups (li'l cream puss) – Don Orehek
Page 9 – Weird Fun with the Uggly Family – Stosh Gillespie (Dan Clowes) / Eel O'Brian (Mort Todd)
Page 10 – Pre-Hystericals – Gary Fields
Page 11 – Dull House – Walter Brogan / Vic Bianco (Lou Silverstone)
Page 15 – Quentin Plasma's Life-Form – Jeremy Banx
Page 16 – Form & Function Looks at Scuba Gear – Bo Badman (Rurik Tyler)
Page 18 – The Ninja – Mike Ricigliano / Roger Brown
Page 19 – Ye Hang Ups (The moon is full) – John Severin
Page 21 – Letters / Cracked Top 5 / Cracked Coming Attractions
Page 23 – How the West Was Lost – Gary Fields / Randy Epley
Page 25 – The First Proposal – Henry Boltinoff
Page 26 – Freddy's Celebrity Nightmares! – John Severin / Tony Frank (Lou Silverstone)
Page 28 – Don Martin's One Menza-Menza Day in October – Don Martin
Page 29 – Garbage Dump Pop Stars (Linda Roundsnout)
Page 32 – Wow! (sensational) – Pat Boyette
Page 33 – One-Shots (Guide to Picking Out the Fakes) – Mike Ricigliano / Roger Brown
Page 35 – Subscription ad – Jack Davis / 1988 Cracked T-Shirt ad – John Severin
Page 36 – Butting Heads – Mike Ricigliano / Roger Brown
Page 37 – If – John Severin / John Arcudi (See note on issue #214)
Page 38 – When Old Age Finally Hits Monsterdom – Vic Martin / George Gladir
Page 41 – Canine the Barkbarian (Canine has heard rumors) – Gary Fields
Page 43 – Tales My Unca Gran'pa Told Me – Stosh Gillespie (Dan Clowes) / Eel O'Brian (Mort Todd)
Page 44 – Lifesize Saboteurs – Mike Ricigliano
Page 46 – Cracked Rock Star Cars! – John Severin / Cliff Mott
Page 49 – Don Martin's One Sunny Mid-Day in the Sahara – Don Martin
Page 50 – Shut-Ups (wish you hadn't brought animals) – Don Orehek
Page 51 – Fantasy? – Pat Boyette
Back Cover – Crackedile Dummee – Bill Wray

**241, December 1988 (52 pages) ($1.49)**
Cover – Who'd Like to Kill Roger Wabbit – John Severin
Page 2 – Friday the 12$^{th}$ – Pat Boyette
Page 3 – Contents
Page 4 – The Kongquerer – Henry Boltinoff

Page 5 – Rambozo III – Walter Brogan / Joe Catalano
Page 9 – Ye Hang Ups (The Wall!!) – John Severin
Page 11 – Pig – Rob Orzechowski / Tony Frank (Lou Silverstone)
Page 16 – Subscription ad / Cracked cap ad / 30th Anniversary Cracked T-Shirt – John Severin (Same shirt as the 1988 T-Shirt.)
Page 17 – Red Meat – Rick Altergott / Vic Bianco (Lou Silverstone)
Page 22 – Giddyup! – Pat Boyette
Page 23 – Cracked Party Pix! (Photos of John Severin, Don Martin, Don Orehek, Rick Altergott, Peter Bagge, Dan Clowes, Bebe Buell, Michael Delle-Femine (Mort Todd), Cliff Mott, Walter Brogan, Dan Knotts, Vic Martin, Bill Wray, George Gladir, Randy Epley, Joe Catalano, Charles E. Hall at the *Cracked* 30th Anniversary Party.)
Page 25 – Cracked Armor! – Al Scaduto
Page 26 – Don Martin Does Quasimodo – Don Martin
Page 29 – Colors Coloring Book – Walter Brogan / Tony Frank (Lou Silverstone)
Page 32 – Crackadile Dandee, Too! – Gray Morrow / Tony Frank (Lou Silverstone)
Page 37 – Gruesome Gags – Henry Boltinoff
Page 38 – If Morton Downey, Jr. was President! – Frank Caruso / Tony Frank (Lou Silverstone)
Page 41 – Monster Vote Getters – John Severin / George Gladir
Page 44 – Who Framed Roger Wabbit / Wawwy Bwogan (Walter Brogan) / Rich Kriegel (Lou Silverstone)
Page 50 – Rock and Roll Shut-Ups (3000 people) – Don Orehek / Charles E. Hall
Page 51 – The Art of Graffiti – Al Scaduto
Back Cover – Sylly Harry – Bill Wray

**242, January 1989 (52 pages) ($1.49)**

Cover – And the Winner: Who Cares? – Walter Brogan / Mort Todd
Page 2 – Hudd & Dini (rainbow) – Vic Martin
Page 3 – Contents
Page 4 – Don Martin's Late One Night in a Large Midwestern Prison – Don Martin
Page 5 – Cracked Movie VIII – John Severin / Joe Catalano
Page 9 – Wow! (ecogeographic reflections) – Pat Boyette
Page 10 – Noid's Raisin Hell! – Frank Caruso / Eel O'Brian (Mort Todd)
Page 11 – Examining Those TV Political Ads with the Hidden Camera! – Al Scaduto / George Gladir
Page 14 – One-Shots (Biff Masters) – Mike Ricigliano / Roger Brown
Page 16 – 21 Dump Street – Rob Orzechowski / Joe Catalano
Page 20 – Don Martin's One Fine Evening in Manhattan – Don Martin

Page 21 - More Cracked List of What's Hot and What's Not - Gary Fields
Page 23 - The Dead Fool - Peter McDonnell / Tony Frank (Lou Silverstone)
Page 27 - It Came to Pass - Jeremy Banx
Page 28 - Cracked Letters / Coming Cracked Attractions
Page 29 - Ye Hang Ups (Lice! Fleas!) - O.O. Severin (John Severin)
Page 31 - Slumming in America - Walter Brogan / Tony Frank (Lou Silverstone)
Page 36 - Spy and Saboteur Paper Airplanes Pilots - Mike Ricigliano
Page 37 - Cracked Look at Flying - Dick Ayers / Moe McMahon (Marian McMahon)
Page 40 - Double Scare! - Frank Caruso / Joe Catalano
Page 44 - Don Martin's One Terribly Hot Day Last Summer - Don Martin
Page 45 - Cracked Interviews Edward Kroch The Big Apple Mayor! - Bill Ward / Tony Frank (Lou Silverstone)
Page 50 - Shut-Ups (wonderful to sleep) - Don Orehek
Page 51 - Sylvesteroger Rabbit - Bill Wray
Back Cover - Subscription ad - John Severin (reprint from #66)

**243, March 1989 (52 pages) ($1.49)**

Cover - Santa Skateboarder - John Severin / Mort Todd
Page 2 - The Emergency - Mike Ricigliano / Roger Brown
Page 3 - Contents
Page 4 - Don Martin's One Fine Day in a Pet Shop - Don Martin
Page 5 - Young Bums - Rick Altergott
Page 9 - Jolly Jolly Jolly - Pat Boyette
Page 10 - Mervin Mohair's Power! - Jeremy Banx
Page 11 - Screwge - Wally Dickens Brogan (Walter Brogan) / Vic Bianco (Lou Silverstone)
Page 15 - Cracked Hot Stove League Baseball Cards! - John Severin / George Gladir
Page 18 - Things a Hero's Mom Could Never Get Used To! - Kurt Schaffenberger
Page 20 - Arctic Antic - Henry Boltinoff
Page 21 - The Zillionaire Starring the Uggly Family - Stosh Gillespie (Dan Clowes)
Page 25 - Super Hurry-Ups! (Sure is romantic) - Rick Altergott
Page 26 - Form & Function Scopes Out Santa! - Bo Badman (Rurik Tyler)
Page 28 - Canine the Barkbarian (Eh? What is it?) - Gary Fields
Page 29 - From Bad to Worse - Mike Ricigliano / Roger Brown

Page 31 – The Icy Reception! – Dick Ayers
Page 32 – X-Mess the Movie – Bill Wray, Tony Salmons / Robert Loren Fleming
Page 35 – In Santa Ty – John Severin
Page 36 – Cracked Letters (Mort Todd, Jason Hervey photos) / On Sale Soon
Page 37 – Sly Stallone's Greatest Xmas Hits!
Page 38 – Remotely Controlled – Frank Caruso / Joe Catalano
Page 41 – Hazards of: Being a Superhero – Mike Ricigliano / Roger Brown (1st *Hazards of:*)
Page 43 – 1989 – Pat Boyette
Page 44 – Don Martin's Life Can Be So Embarrassing! – Don Martin
Page 45 – It's a Wonderful Laff – Peter McDonnell / Tony Frank (Lou Silverstone)
Page 50 – Shut-Ups (watered down drinks) – Don Orehek
Page 51 – Subscription / Hat / T-Shirt / Sylvester Doll ad – John Severin (reprint from #113)
Back Cover – Aerosmythe – Bill Wray

**244, May 1989 (52 pages) ($1.49)** (On sale date February 1989)
Cover – Take Your Picture with Elvis – Don Martin (This was an all-Elvis issue. The ironic thing was, that Elvis apparently was a *Cracked* fan, according to Jay Lynch.)
Page 2 – Elvis Hurry-Ups (that Elvis) – Rick Altergott
Page 3 – Contents
Page 4 – Don Martin's One Fine Day at the Nuclear Test Site! – Don Martin
Page 5 – Cracked Interviews Elvis the King – John Severin / Rich Kriegel (Lou Silverstone)
Page 8 – Elvis What's Hot and What's Not – Gary Fields
Page 9 – Grossanne – Walter Brogan / Rich Kriegel (Lou Silverstone)
Page 13 – It's Him! It's Elvis! He's Alive! – Pat Boyette
Page 14 – Elvis Paper Doll Pages – Rob Orzechowski / George Gladir
Page 16 – La Bumba – Rick Altergott / Terry Gentile
Page 20 – Tonite Only: Cracked Form and Function Presents: Elvis Impersonator Gear – Bo Badman (Rurik Tyler)
Page 22 – Mister Bignose (invisible) – Jeremy Banx
Page 23 – The Elvis Parsley Story – Bill Wray, John Severin / Tony Frank (Lou Silverstone)
Page 27 – Don Martin's One Fine Day on the Art Freen Show! – Don Martin
Page 28 – The Uggly Family in "Elvis, You're a Janitor?" – Stosh Gillespie (Dan Clowes)

Page 31 – Cracked Letters (Jeremy Banx and Bebe Buell & the Gargoyles photos.) (Bebe also portrayed Nanny Dickering and was a *Playboy* model and is the mother of actress Liv Tyler, whose father is Aerosmith's Steve Tyler, of which Buell had a brief relationship, at least one long enough to consummate and bear a child.) / Cracked Coming Attractions
Page 33 – The Health Nut – Henry Boltinoff
Page 34 – Elvis Bubble Gum Cards – Pat Redding / Joe Catalano
Page 36 – Dead/Live Rock Star – John Severin / Charles E. Hall
Page 37 – Ailing Nation – Walter Brogan / Vic Bianco (Lou Silverstone)
Page 41 – The Greenhouse Effect – John Severin / George Gladir
Page 44 – A Day in the Life of Elvis' Greatest Fan! – Rob Orzechowski / Joe Catalano
Page 46 – Don Martin's One Fine Evening at the Castle! – Don Martin
Page 47 – Cracked Interviews Yoko Ohno – Bill Ward
Page 50 – Shut-Ups (we saw Elvis) – Don Orehek
Page 51 – Cop Some Cracked Laundry ad
Back Cover – Sylvester P. Lennon – Bill Wray

**245, July 1989 (52 pages) ($1.49)** (On sale date early March 1989)
Cover – We Take a Shot at 'Toons – John Severin / Mort Todd
Page 2 – Who'll Maim Roger Wabbit – Skene Catling
Page 3 – Contents
Page 4 – Don Martin's One Morning in the Biology Lab! – Don Martin
Page 5 – Pla'Toons – Walt Disbroganey (Walter Brogan) / Matthew Sweney
Page 8 – It's Those Ghastly Toothpaste People! – Jeremy Banx
Page 9 – Freddie the Menace – Gary Fields
Page 11 – Where are they Now? – Bill Wray
Page 12 – Things You Don't See – Mike Ricigliano / Roger Brown
Page 14 – Comic Strip Oddities! – John Severin / George Gladir
Page 16 – Tarius the Planet – Henry Boltinoff
Page 17 – Toon Town Babylon – Bill Wray / Eel O'Brian (Mort Todd)
Page 21 – Stars' Wars – Pat Boyette
Page 23 – Twits – Walter Brogan
Page 27 – Don Martin's One Fine Day at the Psychiatrist's Office! – Don Martin
Page 28 – Ye Hang Ups (We never go out) – John Severin
Page 29 – Letters / Cracked Coming Attractions / Cracked Top Ten
Page 31 – Spy and Saboteur Mini Flip-Action Funnies – Mike Ricigliano
Page 33 – Cracked Sunday Comics – Gary Fields / John Arcudi
Page 37 – Jeraldo Revoltin's Guide to Be an Expert at Trash TV – Rob Orzechowski / Joe Catalano

Page 40 – Comic Character Evolution! – Bo Badman (Rurik Tyler)
Page 42 – Mister Bignose (butterflies) – Jeremy Banx
Page 43 – Acme Manual for Nabbing Road Runners! – Walter Brogan / George Gladir
Page 46 – Don Martin's One Tedious Afternoon at the Courthouse! – Don Martin
Page 47 – Cracked Interviews Roger Wabbit – John Severin / Vic Bianco (Lou Silverstone)
Page 50 – Shut-Ups (who does the dishes) – Don Orehek
Page 51 – Cracked Subs and Stuff ad
Back Cover – Gunsyl P. Rosmythe – Bill Wray

**246, August 1989 (52 pages) ($1.49)** (On sale date late April 1989)
Cover – Special Last Issue!! – John Severin / Mort Todd
Page 2 – Cracked presents the Aftermath of the Dinosaurs Attack Cards! – Bo Badman (Rurik Tyler)
Page 3 – Contents
Page 4 – Don Martin's One Bright and Sunny Day! – Don Martin
Page 5 – The Coming Environmental Crisis! – John Severin / George Gladir
Page 9 – The Ward World of Sports (Burp Beer) – Bill Ward (1st *The Ward World of Sports*)
Page 11 – The Final Episodes of Fantasy Shows – Rick Altergott
Page 16 – Reason for Living – Mike Ricigliano
Page 17 – Goon with the Wind: 1990 – Walter Brogan / Rich Kriegel (Lou Silverstone)
Page 21 – Playbot Magazine – Bill Wray / John Arcudi
Page 26 – Form and Function Looks at the Roach! – Bo Badman (Rurik Tyler)
Page 28 – Don Martin's One Fine Day Down on the Farm – Don Martin
Page 29 – Travel Ads Before and After – John Severin / Charles E. Hall
Page 32 – The Amazing Prophecies of Nostradoomus – Walter Brogan / Charles E. Hall
Page 34 – Bomb Shelters of the Rich & Famous! – Bo Badman (Rurik Tyler)
Page 36 – Cracked Letters / Coming Distractions! (Raunch Hands photo)
Page 37 – Monsters Get Off on Ecological Disasters! – Vic Martin / George Gladir
Page 40 – Catastrophes (Estate for Sale) – Pat Boyette
Page 41 – On the Beach the Day After with Dr. Strangelove or How I Learned to Live with and Love Roaches – Wally Kubrogan (Walter Brogan) / Rich Kriegel (Lou Silverstone)

Page 45 – Torture in Baseball Terms – Henry Boltinoff
Page 46 – Cracked Survival Primer – LePoer (John Severin) / Vic Bianco (Lou Silverstone)
Page 50 – Don Martin's One Summer's Day in the Big City – Don Martin
Page 51 – Shut-Ups (Happy Birthday, Muckey!) – Don Orehek
Back Cover – P. Sylvester Quayle – Bill Wray

**247, September 1989 (52 pages) ($1.49)** (On sale date June 1989)
Cover – See the Chef – Don Martin
Page 2 – Peter Pan Reads a Bedtime Story – Mike Ricigliano / Roger Brown
Page 3 – Contents
Page 4 – Sherlock Holmes vs Jack the Ripper – John Severin / Tony Frank (Lou Silverstone)
Page 9 – Don Martin's One Summer's Day in Bayonne – Don Martin
Page 10 – The Ward World of Sports (forgot your contacts) – Bill Ward
Page 11 – Great Moments in History Not in History Books – Henry Boltinoff
Page 12 – Star Drek the Next Generation – Mike Ricigliano / Roger Brown
Page 13 – Hudd & Dini (crocodile) – Vic Martin
Page 15 – Guillotine Gags! – Don Orehek / George Gladir Page 19 – Subscription ad – John Severin
Page 20 – Having a Wonderful Time – Henry Boltinoff
Page 21 – Shut-Ups (shell fragment) – Don Orehek
Page 22 – Fairy Tale Characters – Mike Ricigliano / Roger Brown
Page 25 and 33 – Cracked Letters / Cracked Coming Attractions (Berkeley Breathed letter) (Mort Todd with Archie and Betty photo)
Page 26 – Don Martin's One Partly Cloudy Day Downtown – Don Martin
Page 27 – Skata Curb (Skateboard Keyboard) – Phillips Studios (1st *Skata Curb*)
Page 28 – Whiners & Losers who Draw Badly! – Rob Orzechowski / Peter Bagge
Page 31 – Lover's Lane – Henry Boltinoff
Page 32 – A Sad Day in Megalopolis – Bill Wray / George Gladir
Page 34 – The Ward World of Sports (umpire was as blind) – Bill Ward
Page 35 – The Musketeers – Mike Ricigliano / Roger Brown
Page 36 – Confessions of a Party Dog – Gary Fields
Page 38 – A Crummy Affair – Frank Caruso / Joe Catalano
Page 41 – Pow! – Pat Boyette

Page 42 – Beam Us Up, Scotty! – Mike Ricigliano / Roger Brown
Page 43 – Columbum – Walter Brogan / Tony Frank (Lou Silverstone)
Page 47 – Separate Sections at the Ballpark! – Bill Ward
Page 49 – Don Martin's One Balmy Day on a Desert Island – Don Martin
Page 50 – Shut-Ups (a bit more progress) – Don Orehek
Page 51 – *Cracked Monster Party* #6 and *Monsters Attack!* #1 ad
Back Cover – Sylattolah – Bill Wray

**248, October 1989 (52 pages) ($1.49)**

Cover – Cracked Goes Batty – Rurik Tyler / Mort Todd
Page 2 – Cracked Interviews Rabid the Wonder Boy! – Skene Catling
Page 3 – Contents
Page 4 – Batman to the Rescue – Mike Ricigliano / Roger Brown
Page 5 – Harried...with Children – Rob Orzechowski / Rich Kriegel (Lou Silverstone)
Page 9 – Batty-Weapons that Didn't Quite Make it to the Utility Belt! – John Severin / George Gladir
Page 12 – The Cracked Lens Presents the Bat-Photo Scrapbook!
Page 14 – The F.B.I. Ten Most Wanted Saboteurs – Mike Ricigliano
Page 15 – Hudd & Dini (Batman) – Vic Martin
Page 17 – Dinosaurs of Rock Attack! – Pat Redding / Pete Ciccone
Page 20 – Comic Con Confidential! – John Severin / George Gladir
Page 22 – Batman What's Hot and What's Not – Gary Fields
Page 23 – Geez...What Cushy Job Being Badtman – Pat Boyette
Page 25 – Cracked Letters / On Sale Soon! (Mort Todd photo) (Don Martin's *Nutheads* comic strip pictured)
Page 26 – Cracked Form & Function The Batty-Wing – Rurik Tyler
Page 28 – Don Martin Presents the Sounds of Battyman! – Don Martin
Page 31 – A Cracked Look at Batman – Mike Ricigliano / Roger Brown
Page 33 – Skata Curb (Motorized Skateboard) – Phillips Studios
Page 34 – What if Bruise Payne Didn't Become Battyman?! – Ron Wagner / George Gladir
Page 38 – Them Battyman Sequels We're Sure to See! – John Severin / George Gladir
Page 41 – Wiseass – Walter Brogan / Vic Bianco (Lou Silverstone)
Page 46 – Cracked Interview with Rabid the Wonder Boy! – John Severin / Rich Kriegel (Lou Silverstone)
Page 50 – Shut-Ups (crummy issue of *Cracked*) – Don Orehek
Page 51 – Varoom! – Vic Martin
Back Cover – The Jerker – Bill Wray

**249, November 1989 (52 pages) ($1.49)**

Cover - Batman, Ghostbusters, Indiana Jones - John Severin / Mort Todd

Page 2 - Hudd & Dini (genie) - Vic Martin

Page 3 - Contents

Page 4 - The Spy & Saboteur Activity Page Part II The Sequel - Mike Ricigliano

Page 6 - Bat$man - John Severin / Mort Todd (Alfred E. Neuman appearance)

Page 14 - Don Martin's One Fine Day in Your Typical Cave Dwelling - Don Martin

Page 16 - Remote Controls We'll Soon Be Seeing! - Gray Morrow / George Gladir Page 20 - Ripper's Believe it or Bail! (No Skateboarding) - Phillips Studios (1st *Ripper's Believe it or Bail!*)

Page 21 - Woodstock - Don Orehek / Vic Bianco (Lou Silverstone)

Page 25 - The Water Hole - Henry Boltinoff

Page 26 - Cracked Ghostbuggers Gear - Rurik Tyler

Page 27 - Cracked Toon Videos - Gary Fields

Page 29 - The Guest Dusters - Pat Boyette

Page 33 - Cracked Arena Rock Show! - John Severin / Charles E. Hall

Page 37 - The Mystic - Henry Boltinoff

Page 38 - Sylvester P. Smythe's 60's Scrapbook! - Rob Orzechowski / Charles E. Hall

Page 40 - 1-900-Cracked - Rurik Tyler

Page 42 - 100 Degrees in the Sun - Henry Boltinoff

Page 43 - One-Shots Looks at Animals - Mike Ricigliano / Roger Brown

Page 45 - Indiana Bones and the Loot Crusade - Walter Brogan / Tony Frank (Lou Silverstone)

Page 50 - Ghostbugger Shut-Ups (Class 5 apparitions) - Rurik Tyler

Page 51 - Goin' Up the Country - Frank Caruso

Back Cover - Sylimer - Bill Wray

**250, December 1989 (52 pages) ($1.49)** (On sale date September 29, 1989)

Cover - 250 Issues 32 Years of Visual Satire - John Severin / Mort Todd

Page 2 - Don Martin's Calling All Hands - Don Martin

Page 3 - Contents

Page 4 - Cracked Looks at Baseball Trading Cards - John Severin / George Gladir

Page 8 - Hudd & Dini (Vic Martin) - Vic Martin (Martin draws Severin, Don Martin, Cliff Mott, Mort Todd, Mike Ricigliano and himself.)

Page 10 - Ghostbuggers II - Walter Brogan / Vic Bianco (Lou Silverstone)

Page 15 – One Day in Chinese Acupuncture Hospital – Don Orehek
Page 17 – The Sabotron! – Mike Ricigliano
Page 18 – Ripper's Believe it or Bail! (skateboard jewelry) – Phillips Studios
Page 19 – Don Martin's One Dat in the Dawn of Civilization – Don Martin
Page 20 – Shut-Ups (wanted an early American dwelling) – Don Orehek
Page 21 – Tales from the Creep – Bill Wray / Archie Falbo (John Arcudi) (This is the infamous story assigned to Bill Wray when he wanted to improve his art at *Cracked* in order to impress *Mad* so that he could get hired there. It features a parody of *Tales from the Crypt* with a caricature of William M. Gaines.)
Page 25 – Ye Hang Ups (I hope you don't mind) – John Severin
Page 26 – Form & Function Looks at the New Bat Gear! – Rurik Tyler
Page 28 – One-Shots! (mine blasting) – Mike Ricigliano / Roger Brown
Page 30 – Ward Weird of Sports! (McEnroe) – Bill Ward
Page 31 – Subscription ad – John Severin
Page 32 – Hazards of: (Dating) – Mike Ricigliano / Roger Brown
Page 34 – Ye Hang Ups (I'd like to help your aunt) – John Severin
Page 35 – Oh, My Aching Back! – Henry Boltinoff
Page 36 – High Adventures – Pat Boyette
Page 38 – Medical One-Shots – Mike Ricigliano / Roger Brown
Page 40 – Superswine – Gary Fields
Page 41 – Shut-Ups (found a roach) – Don Orehek
Page 42 – Cracked Rock 'n' Roll Museum! – John Severin / George Gladir
Page 44 – Tarius the Planet – Henry Boltinoff
Page 45 – Hudd & Dini and Ye Hang Ups – Vic Martin, John Severin
Page 46 – Cracked Interviews the Jerker – Walter Brogan / Rich Kriegel (Lou Silverstone)
Page 50 – Don Martin's One Evening in Greenwich Village – Don Martin
Page 51 – Transylvanian Summertime – Vic Martin
Back Cover – Great Moments in History 1314 – Mike Ricigliano

**251, January 1990 (52 pages) ($1.49)** (On sale date November 2, 1989)
Cover – Welcome to the 1990s! – John Severin / Mort Todd
Page 2 and 51 – Formal Sylvester P. Smythe Portrait – John Severin
Page 3 – Contents
Page 4 – Don Martin's Quasimodo at the Doctor's Office – Don Martin
Page 5 – Cracked Guide to Customized Skateboards – John Severin / George Gladir

Page 8 – Ill-Legal Weapons – Walter Brogan / Vic Bianco (Lou Silverstone)
Page 14 – Unknown Facts About the California Raisins – Rurik Tyler
Page 16 – Spy and Saboteur in The Peace Treaty – Mike Ricigliano
Page 17 – The Crackedtile – Rob Orzechowski
Page 18 – Metyluna Mutant Smythe – Rob Orzechowski
Page 19 – Dr. Fu Mansmythe – Rob Orzechowski
Page 20 – Sylvo Hatton "The Crackeder" – Rob Orzechowski
Page 21 – Drawing the Line – Rurik Tyler
Page 22 – Orehek Gags! – Don Orehek
Page 24 – Just Folks – Pat Boyette
Page 25 – Sign of the Times – Henry Boltinoff
Page 26 – Ripper's Believe it or Bail! (Longest Railslide!) – Phillips Studios
Page 27 – Don Martin's The Warsaw Snake Charmer – Don Martin
Page 28 – Random Funnies (upset) – Mike Ricigliano / Roger Brown
Page 30 – Hudd & Dini (snake charmers) – Vic Martin
Page 31 – Monster Kids – Gary Fields
Page 32 – Be Prepared! – Henry Boltinoff
Page 33 – Taking it Literally – Mike Ricigliano / Roger Brown
Page 35 – Ye Hang Ups (Guards!) – John Severin
Page 38 – Come On-Enuf Awready! – Pat Boyette
Page 40 – Shut-Ups (he was a loving) – Don Orehek
Page 41 – Freddy Krocker Food Company – Rurik Tyler
Page 44 – Honey, I Stunk the Kids! – Walter Brogan / Charles E. Hall
Page 50 – Don Martin's The Warsaw Werewolf – Don Martin
Back Cover – Smythe Character (Mammal Killers ad) – Bill Wray

**252, March 1990 (52 pages) ($1.49)**
Cover – Run Away Humor – John Severin / Mort Todd
Page 2 – Dorkitos ad – Walter Brogan
Page 3 – Contents
Page 4 – Don Martin's One Fine Day in Nantucket – Don Martin
Page 5 – The Abyssmal – John Severin / Terry Gentile
Page 9 – Spy and Saboteur in The Library – Mike Ricigliano
Page 10 – The Ward World of Sports (inexplainable face) – Bill Ward
Page 11 – America's Least Wanted – Rob Orzechowski / Matt Sweney
Page 14 – Cracked Dinosaur True or Fossil Quiz? – Rurik Tyler
Page 17 – Shut-Ups (autobiography) – Don Orehek
Page 18 – Hudd & Dini (Cracked Christmas Party) – Vic Martin
Page 20 – At the Heavy Metal Concert – Mike Ricigliano
Page 21 – Star Drek V The Finite Frontier – Rick Altergott / Tony Frank (Lou Silverstone)

Page 26 – Don Martin's One Fine Day at the Amusement Park – Don Martin
Page 27 – Aiming Gun Ads at Specific Groups – John Severin / George Gladir
Page 30 – Court Room Capers – Don Orehek
Page 32 – Vampire Gags – Gary Fields
Page 35 – Ye Hang Ups (starting to resent) – John Severin
Page 36 – The Inspection – Mike Ricigliano / Roger Brown
Page 37 – Vic Martin's Monsters on Parade! – Vic Martin
Page 40 – Star Trek Funnies – Mike Ricigliano / Roger Brown
Page 42 – Cracked Multi-Mini-Plex – Walter Brogan / Linc Pershad
Page 45 – Don Martin's One August Day in the Nursing Home – Don Martin
Page 46 – Cracked Interviews the Fast Food King – Bill Ward / Charles E. Hall
Page 50 – Shut-Ups (liver, bacon and onions) – Don Orehek
Page 51 – Ye Hang Ups (feed her cats) – John Severin
Back Cover – Rotting Bones Steel Wheel Chair Tour – Bill Wray

**253, May 1990 (52 pages) ($1.49)**

Cover – Back to the Future with Bill & Ted! – John Severin
Page 2 – Nanny Dickering Goes Hollywood! – Skene Catling
Page 3 – Contents
Page 4 – Don Martin's One Fine Day in Florence – Don Martin
Page 5 – More Freak Outs from Back in the Future! – John Severin / George Gladir
Page 9 – The Two-Hundred-Dollar-a-Day Bum – Don Orehek
Page 10 – Ailing Nation – Walter Brogan / Archie Falbo (John Arcudi)
Page 14 – Man Invents the Wheel – Mike Ricigliano
Page 15 – Skateboards of the World! – Pete Fitzgerald / Charles E. Hall
Page 19 – Sagebrush (Sorry about this load) – John Severin
Page 20 – My Stupid Identity Supedupboy – Pete McDonnell
Page 22 – Nanny in Hollywood – Skene Catling
Page 26 – Don Martin's Early One Morning in the City – Don Martin
Page 27 – Japanese Entertainment Take Overs – Severino San (John Severin) / Gladir San (George Gladir)
Page 30 – Lack Brain – Walter Brogan / Charles E. Hall
Page 35 – The Human Mind! – Pat Boyette
Page 37 – Road Sign – Mike Ricigliano / Roger Brown
Page 38 – The Ward World of Sports (Thank goodness) – Bill Ward
Page 39 – How the Future has Changed – Gray Morrow / Charles E. Hall
Page 43 – Ye Hang Ups (get no break) – John Severin

Page 44 – Bull & Tad's Excrement Adventure – Rick Altergott
Page 49 – Don Martin's Early One Morning – Don Martin
Page 50 – Shut-Ups (two hours) – Don Orehek
Page 51 – TV Guise Pee-Wee Herman Cover – Rurik Tyler
Back Cover – Sylbastian P. Bach – Bill Wray

**254, July 1990 (52 pages) ($1.75)**
Cover – Should We Kill Sylvester? – John Severin
Page 2 – Ye Hang Ups (New Kids on the Block) – John Severin
Page 3 – Contents
Page 4 – Don Martin's One Hot Muggy Day in the Jungle – Don Martin
Page 5 – Cracked to the Future Part II – John Severin / Tony Frank (Lou Silverstone)
Page 10 – Numskulls in the News – Basil Wolverton (New to *Cracked.*)
Page 11 – The Bunisher – Gary Fields
Page 13 – The Ward World of Sports (State used to wave) – Bill Ward
Page 14 – Sabotage in the 1990's – Mike Ricigliano
Page 16 – Critic's Corner – Pat Boyette
Page 17 – Cracked Mini-TV Tube – Pete McDonnell / Vic Bianco (Lou Silverstone)
Page 21 – TV Sets for Watching Specific TV Shows! – John Severin / Charles E. Hall
Page 25 – Meet the People – Basil Wolverton (New to *Cracked.*)
Page 26 – Don Martin's One Fine Day Whilst Walking – Don Martin
Page 27 – Doggie Hoser M.D. – Walter Brogan / Tony Frank (Lou Silverstone)
Page 31 – Cracked Phone Number ad – John Severin
Page 34 – Cracked Mirrors II – Vic Martin
Page 37 – Sagebrush (Okay! Okay!) – John Severin
Page 38 – Cracked Letters / Call the Cracked Hotline! Ad / Cracked Coming Distractions / Black Cracked T-Shirt / Severin Cracked T-Shirt / Cracked Hat / Sylvester Doll / Subscription ad
Page 40 – Ghastly Garageful – Basil Wolverton (New to *Cracked.*)
Page 41 – Harlem Nughts – Walter Brogan / Vic Bianco (Lou Silverstone)
Page 46 – Don Martin's One Fine Day in Holland – Don Martin
Page 47 – Big Foots – Gary Fields
Page 48 – Baby One-Shots – Mike Ricigliano / Roger Brown
Page 50 – Shut-Ups (perfect vacation spot) – Don Orehek
Page 51 – Hudd & Dini (witch doctor) – Vic Martin
Back Cover – Sylvester as Noriega – Bob Orzechowski

**255, August 1990 (52 pages) ($1.75)** (On sale date May 1990)
Cover – Teenage Mutant Ninja Cracked – John Severin / Mort Todd
Page 2 – Dear Hearts and Gentle People! – Pat Boyette
Page 3 – Contents
Page 4 – Don Martin's One Fine Evening in Jersey City – Don Martin
Page 5 – Cracked Mini-Movie Theatre! – Walter Brogan / Tony Frank (Lou Silverstone)
Page 8 – Spy & Saboteur in Steel Cage Match – Mike Ricigliano
Page 9 – More Cigarette Ads Aimed at Specific Groups! – John Severin / George Gladir
Page 12 – Famous Funny Animals – Gary Fields
Page 13 – Good News and Bad News for Teenage Mutated Ninjerk Turdles – Rurik Tyler
Page 16 – The Comic Book Restorer – John Severin / George Gladir
Page 17 – Paint Gunner Magazine – Pete Fitzgerald / Matt Sweney
Page 21 – I.M.A. Gravs Earthling Zoo – Gene Colan
Page 25 – Random Funnies (having a sale) – Mike Ricigliano / Roger Brown
Page 26 – Don Martin's One Fine Tuesday Afternoon…or Was it Wednesday? – Don Martin
Page 27 – Teenage Mutated Ninjerk Turdles Unfit Role Models for Our Children! – Rurik Tyler
Page 28 – Hazards of: (saying the wrong thing) – Mike Ricigliano / Roger Brown
Page 30 – Cracked Classroom TV Scream – John Severin / George Gladir
Page 33 – Morons from Mars – Stephen DeStefano (1st *Morons from Mars*)
Page 34 – Shoe Biz is Going Show Biz! – Bill Ward / George Gladir
Page 37 – Ye Hang Ups (underarm deodorant) – John Severin
Page 38 – Cracked Letters / Call the Cracked Hotline! Ad / Black Cracked T-Shirt / Severin Cracked T-Shirt / Cracked Hat / Sylvester Doll / Subscription ad (Ken Wahl photo)
Page 40 – Strange Places for Cellular Phones – Mike Ricigliano / Roger Brown
Page 42 – Kojerk – Walter Brogan / Tony Frank (Lou Silverstone)
Page 46 – Don Martin's One Fine Day in the Outback – Don Martin
Page 47 – Cracked Interviews Howeird Stern – Rob Orzechowski / Terry Gentile (Alfred E. Neuman appearance)
Page 50 – Shut-Ups (sleeping in tonight) – Don Orehek
Page 51 – Great Moments in Fashion Ice Age – Mike Ricigliano
Back Cover – Cracked Mutant Turtle Soup Cut-Up! – Rurik Tyler

**256, September 1990 (52 pages) ($1.75)**

Cover – Exclusive Comics Movie/TV Club – John Severin / Mort Todd
Page 2 – Subscription ad (reprint from #66)
Page 3 – Contents
Page 4 – Don Martin's One Fine Morning in the Himalayas – Don Martin
Page 5 – New Villains for Future Dick Tracy Movies – John Severin / George Gladir
Page 9 – Hudd & Dini (Space Shuttle Grounds) – Vic Martin
Page 11 – The Hunt for Rad Crackedober – Walter Brogan / Tony Frank (Lou Silverstone)
Page 16 – The Ward World of Sports (that's ridiculous) – Bill Ward
Page 17 – Video Games & Equipment of the Future IV! – Pete Fitzgerald / George Gladir
Page 21 – Canine Meets the King – Gary Fields
Page 22 – Ye Hang Ups (Surf's up!) – John Severin
Page 23 – Yippie Ti-Yo! – Pat Boyette
Page 24 – Letters / Cracked Hotline / Coming Cracked Attractions
Page 26 – Don Martin's Fisherman's Tale – Don Martin
Page 27 – Toon-Age Mutant Ninjerk Turtles – John Severin / Tony Frank (Lou Silverstone)
Page 33 – Spy and Saboteur at Echo Canyon – Mike Ricigliano
Page 34 – Cracked Science-Fiction Museum – Vic Martin
Page 35 – Yertle the Mutant Ninja Turtle! – Gary Fields
Page 39 – Celebrity Garbage – Kurt Schaffenberger / George Gladir
Page 43 – New Kids Hate Mail to Cracked
Page 44 – Proper Etiquette for Everyday Living – Mike Ricigliano / Roger Brown
Page 46 – Warren Beatty Meets the Real Dick Tracy! – John Severin / George Gladir
Page 50 – Don Martin's One Rather Dull Saturday Evening – Don Martin
Page 51 – Shut-Ups (wrong man) – Don Orehek
Back Cover – Donyld P. Strump – Rob Orzechowski, John Severin

**257, October 1990 (52 pages) ($1.75)** (Last issue edited by Mort Todd aka Michael Delle-Femine.)

Cover – Most Wanted – John Severin / Mort Todd
Page 2 – Don Martin's One Fine Day in Sarasota – Don Martin
Page 3 – Contents
Page 4 – Great Moments in Police Technology 1931 – Mike Ricigliano
Page 5 – America's Crummiest Home Videos – Vic Martin / Charles E. Hall

Page 9 – Well, La De Da! – Pat Boyette
Page 10 – A Day Training at Seaworld – Mike Ricigliano / Roger Brown
Page 11 – You Know You're a Monster if – Gene Colan / George Gladir
Page 14 – Rejected Cracked Covers – John Severin / George Gladir
Page 16 – How Governments Work – Mike Ricigliano / Roger Brown
Page 18 – Darn Orehek – Don Orehek
Page 19 – The Ward World of Sports (play yer divots) – Bill Ward
Page 20 – Dan Quayle & Friends Coloring Book! – Walter Brogan / Lou Silverstone
Page 24 – You Know You're a New Kids on the Blockhead if – Vic Martin / George Gladir
Page 26 – Don Martin's One Fine Morning a Million Years Ago – Don Martin
Page 27 – The Simplesons – Gary Fields / Rich Kriegel (Lou Silverstone)
Page 31 – The Art of Plastic Surgery – Vic Martin
Page 32 – The Button – Gary Fields
Page 33 – The Exercist – Henry Boltinoff
Page 34 – Things You Hate So Much – Mike Ricigliano / Roger Brown
Page 36 – Don Martin's One Dark Night in Fonebone Memorial Park – Don Martin
Page 37 – Morons from Mars (Yes! Nitwits) – Stephen DeStefano
Page 38 – Gosh All Hemlock! – Pat Boyette
Page 40 – Canine the Barkbarian (The end is near!) – Gary Fields
Page 41 – Ye Hang Ups (Sob! Moan!) – John Severin
Page 42 – Superhero Long-Shots – Mike Ricigliano / Roger Brown
Page 45 – Battyman (Where's Dr. Freeze) – Rick Altergott
Page 50 – Shut-Ups (101 Gourmet Ways Cookbook) – Don Orehek
Page 51 – Subscription ad (reprint from #66)
Back Cover – Sylly Smythenegger – Rob Orzechowski, John Severin

**258, November 1990 (52 pages) ($1.75)** (1st issue edited by Lou Silverstone and Jerry De Fuccio)
Cover – Exclusive Simpsons Interview – John Severin
Page 2 – Shut-Ups (slow down) – Don Orehek
Page 3 – Contents
Page 4 – Dink Trazy – Walter Brogan
Page 10 – Cracked Interviews The Simpersons – Gary Fielding (Gary Fields) / Lou Silverstoning (Lou Silverstone)
Page 13 – The 7 Deadly Sins – Phillips Studios
Page 16 – Spy and Saboteur in Outer Space – Mike Ricigliano
Page 17 – Letters
Page 18 – Don Martin's Dork Tracy – Don Martin
Page 23 – Battle of the Tattoo Artists – Mike Ricigliano

Page 24 - Form & Function Q & A Looks at Robo Cop - Rurik Tyler
Page 26 - Totally Recalled - Walter Brogan
Page 31 - Cracked History of Skateboarding - Ron Wagner
Page 34 - Animal One-Shots - Mike Ricigliano / Roger Brown
Page 36 - The Last Issues of Popular Comic Books - Pete Fitzgerald / George Gladir
Page 40 - Still More Dick Tracy Bad Guys - John Severin
Page 42 - Cracked's Uses for Used Computers - Mike Ricigliano / Roger Brown
Page 44 - Cracked to the Future Part III - John Severin / Tony Frank (Lou Silverstone)
Page 50 - Shut-Ups (Dick, what's your pleasure) - Don Orehek
Page 51 - Flatsyl P. Topsmythe - Rob Orzechowski, John Severin
Back Cover - Tinoctin ad - John Severin

**259, December 1990 (52 pages) ($1.75)**
Cover - We Kick the New Kids off the Block - Don Martin
Page 2 and 51 - The Great T-Shirts Rip-Off - Gary Fields
Page 3 - Contents
Page 4 - Tried Hard - John Severin
Page 11 - Don Martin's One Fine Day on Duncan Avenue - Don Martin
Page 12 - Cracked Interviews New Kids on the Block - Gary Fields
Page 13 - Cracked Interviews Donald Trumpet - Gary Fields
Page 16 - Smooth Character Camels You'll Never See - Ron Wagner
Page 18 - Robocop Ramblings - John Severin
Page 22 - Fairy Tales for the 1990s! - Mike Ricigliano / Roger Brown
Page 25 - Don Martin's One Leisurely Evening in the Jungle - Don Martin
Page 26 - Get the New Kids Off the Block - Pete Fitzgerald
Page 28 - Days of Plunder - Walter Brogan
Page 34 - Cracked Trading Cards for Less Glamorous Professions - Pete Fitzgerald
Page 36 - Shut-Ups (swig of my wife's coffee) - Don Orehek
Page 37 - Spy and Saboteur go Dancin' - Mike Ricigliano
Page 38 - Cracked Mini-Movie Theatre - Walter Brogan
Page 41 - Don Martin's Early One Morning in Surgery - Don Martin
Page 42 - Robocop-Out, Too! - Frank Borth
Page 48 - Vacationland U.S.A. - Pat Redding
Back Cover - Andrew Smythe Clay - Rob Orzechowski, John Severin

**260, January 1991 (52 pages) ($1.75)**

Cover – Cracked Celebrates Spider Appreciation Month! – John Severin / Scott Thaler
Page 2 – Stars and Gripes Forever – Rurik Tyler
Page 3 – Contents
Page 4 – Don Martin's On the Arachnophobia Set – Don Martin
Page 5 – The Confusing Spider-Dude – Frank Borth / Jerry De Fuccio, Lou Silverstone
Page 12 – The Scoreboard Kid – John Severin
Page 16 – Mattlocch – Walter Brogan
Page 21 – Subscription ad – Bill Elder
Page 25 – Don Martin's Crime-Thwarters Handbook – Don Martin
Page 26 – Send in the Cowabunglers! – Frank Borth / Ronnie Nathan
Page 28 – Smurphy Brown – John Severin / Vic Bianco (Lou Silverstone)
Page 33 – Shut-Ups (SLOOP-SUP) – Don Orehek
Page 34 – The Web of Overexposure – Rurik Tyler / Howie Mitchell
Page 36 – The Arsenico Gall Show – Gary Fields / Lou Silverstone
Page 39 – Arachnomania – Mike Ricigliano
Page 41 – When All TV Reflects the Simpson Influence – John Severin / George Gladir
Page 44 – Don Martin's One Fine Day at the Beach – Don Martin
Page 45 – Dork, Man! – Walter Brogan
Page 51 – Arsylio Hall – Rob Orzechowski, John Severin
Back Cover – Who is Dorkman? – John Severin

**261, March 1991 (52 pages) ($1.75)**

Cover – Hulk Hogan's Head – Don Martin
Page 2 and 51 – The Twin Geaks Game – Mike Ricigliano
Page 3 – Contents
Page 4 – Memphis Bull! – John Severin
Page 10 – Mother Goose Goes to Court – Gary Fields / Ronnie Nathan
Page 13 – Orehek's Cracked Look at Wrestling – Don Orehek
Page 16 – Transylvania's Funniest Home Videos – John Severin / Jack Harris
Page 21 – *Cracked Collectors' Edition* #86 ad – John Severin, Mike Ricigliano
Page 22 – Roadside Historical Markers – Frank Borth / Howie Mitchell
Page 25 – Shut-Ups (pull them offside) – Don Orehek
Page 26 – Cracked Highways for Tourists – Mike Ricigliano / Howie Mitchell
Page 28 – Flip Flop – Rurik Tyler / George Gladir
Page 30 – Goodfelons – Walter Brogan / Vic Bianco (Lou Silverstone)

Page 36 – A Cracked Look at Santa's Problems – Don Orehek
Page 38 – Don Martin's Wrestling – Don Martin
Page 43 – Spies and Saboteurs Hit the Mats – Mike Ricigliano
Page 44 – Future Turtlemania Product Tie-Ins – John Severin / George Gladir
Page 47 – Cracked's New Magazines for the New America – Pete Fitzgerald / Howie Mitchell
Page 49 – Twin Geaks Game Suspect Cards – Mike Ricigliano
Back Cover – Only 39 More to Go Until Our 300th Issue – Jack Rickard

**262, May 1991 (52 pages) ($1.75)**
Cover – Rocky and Home Alone – John Severin
Page 2 – It's the Non-Biodegradables or Us! – John Severin / Jerry De Fuccio
Page 3 – Contents
Page 4 – Homeboy Alone – John Severin
Page 11 – Don Martin's One Fine Evening at Emmy Lou's – Don Martin
Page 12 – Cracked Helpful Hints for Shooting Snappier Snapshots – Vic Martin
Page 16 – Big Race on the Mississippi – Mike Ricigliano
Page 18 – The Shlocky Horror Picture Show – Walter Brogan
Page 23 – TV Moms Go to War! – Rurik Tyler
Page 26 – The Perils of Edward Scissorhands – Rurik Tyler
Page 28 – Cracked Mental Implant Fantasies – Pete Fitzgerald / George Gladir
Page 31 – To the Victors – Mike Ricigliano
Page 32 – Still More Cracked List of What's Hot and Not – Gary Fields
Page 34 – Milli Vanilli Answer Their Critics – Rurik Tyler
Page 36 – Don Martin's One Dark and Rainy Night of West Market Street – Don Martin
Page 37 – Orehek at Large in a Tacky Department Store – Don Orehek
Page 40 – Subscription ad – Jack Davis
Page 41 – Spies and Saboteurs Hit the Mob – Mike Ricigliano
Page 42 – Sockey V – Walter Brogan
Page 49 – Shut-Ups (two cowpokes) – Don Orehek
Page 50 – Don Martin's One Fine Day on the Great American Plains – Don Martin
Page 51 – Jungle Rot – Frank Borth / Scott Thaler
Back Cover – Rocky V – Walter Brogan / Lou Silverstone

**263, July 1991 (52 pages) ($1.75)**

Cover – We Go Down the Drain with the Mutant Ninja Turtles – John Severin
Page 2 – A Dignified Evening at the Strongarm Social & Unity Club – Mike Ricigliano / Jerry De Fuccio
Page 3 – Contents
Page 4 – The Clodfather – Walter Brogan
Page 11 – Don Martin's One Fine Day in the Park – Don Martin
Page 12 – Celebrity Guest Appearances on TV – Rurik Tyler – George Gladir
Page 14 – Cracked Interviews Teenage Mutant Ninja Turdles – Gary Fields / Lou Silverstone
Page 18 – Some Things Never Change – John Severin / George Gladir
Page 21 – Once and For All – Mike Ricigliano
Page 22 – Cracked Mini-Movie Multiplex – Rurik Tyler, Frank Borth / Steve Strangio, Tony Frank (Lou Silverstone)
Page 26 – The Drawbacks of Being the Famous Ninja Turtles – Rurik Tyler
Page 28 – Orehek at Large in a Grade School – Don Orehek Page 31 – Don Martin's One Fine Day in the Andes – Don Martin
Page 33 – Cracked's Guide to Good Eating – Pete Fitzgerald / Howie Mitchell
Page 35 – A Cracked Eye View of the Gulf – Rurik Tyler
Page 37 – How the Other Half Lives – Mike Ricigliano
Page 38 – Cracked Letters (Don Martin photo)
Page 40 – Kindergarten Pap – John Severin / Vic Bianco (Lou Silverstone)
Page 47 – Totally Turtle! – Mike Ricigliano
Page 50 – Home Alone Goes Public – Don Orehek
Page 51 – Subscription ad – Rurik Tyler
Back Cover – Anygizer ad – John Severin / Scott Thaler

**264, August 1991 (52 pages) ($1.75)**

Cover – We Crack Vanilla Ice – Don Martin
Page 2 – Don Martin's Jacques Cousteau in his Submarine – Don Martin
Page 3 – Contents
Page 4 – King Ralf – Walter Brogan / Lou Silverstone
Page 10 – The Non-Celebrity Workout Video – Pete Fitzgerald / Paul Giles
Page 12 – The Melanie Joy is Missing – John Severin / Jerry De Fuccio
Page 16 – Werewolves Were Affected by Other Types of Moons – Rurik Tyler

Page 18 – How the Glitch Sold a Crisis! – Gary Fields / Ronnie Nathan
Page 21 – Don Martin's Early One Morning in the Jungle – Don Martin
Page 22 – It's the Long-Awaited Cracked Shut-Ups Contest! – Don Orehek
Page 23 – Shut-Ups (supposed to laugh) – Don Orehek
Page 24 – Doctor Ricig – Mike Ricigliano
Page 25 – Cracked Letters
Page 26 – See the Hammer to the Ice – Rurik Tyler / Ronnie Nathan
Page 28 – Spies and Saboteurs Hit the Superheroes – Mike Ricigliano / Jerry De Fuccio
Page 31 – The Further Adventures of Gas-Man – Mike Ricigliano
Page 32 – Super Heavies – Pete Fitzgerald / Steve Strangio
Page 34 – A Cracked Look at Future Specialized Camps – Frank Borth / Tony Frank (Lou Silverstone)
Page 37 – Don Martin's Later on in the Evening – Don Martin
Page 38 – Just How Fast is the Flash? – Rurik Tyler
Page 40 – If I Won the Lottery – Mike Ricigliano
Page 43 – Orehek at Large on a Field Day at the Zoo – Don Orehek  Page 46 – The Vanilla Ice Cream Story The Man, his Music, the Legend – John Severin / Vic Bianco (Lou Silverstone)
Page 50 – Would You Buy a Used Tank (or Even a New One) from This Man? – Don Orehek
Page 51 – Subscription ad – Rurik Tyler
Back Cover – The Dud Bowl – John Severin / Jerry De Fuccio

**265, September 1991 (52 pages) ($1.75)**
Cover – We Knock Off Robin Hood – John Severin
Page 2 – Norman Schwarzkopfenegger – Mike Ricigliano
Page 3 – Contents
Page 4 – The Toonage Mutant Ninja Turdles II – John Severin / Vic Bianco (Lou Silverstone)
Page 11 – The New and Sometimes Improved Robin Hood – Mike Ricigliano
Page 14 – Cracked's Joy of Sports – Pete Fitzgerald / Fred Sahner
Page 17 – National Pooch Press & Tabby Tattler – Vic Martin / George Gladir
Page 21 – Don Martin's One Sunny Day on the Great American Desert – Don Martin
Page 22 – Toontown Movie Posters – Gary Fields
Page 24 – What Saddam Said on TV and What he Said Off Camera – Don Orehek
Page 26 – Stormin' Norman – Rurik Tyler / Ronnie Nathan
Page 28 – Spies and Saboteurs Hit Baseball – Mike Ricigliano

Page 31 – Don Martin's Frog Prince 1991 – Don Martin
Page 32 – What is a Bummer Summer Vacation? – Frank Borth
Page 34 – If You Had the Flash's Power – Pete Fitzgerald / Roger Brown
Page 35 – Orehek at Large Goin' Bowling – Don Orehek
Page 38 – U.S. Arsenal Munitions Catalog 1996 – Frank Borth
Page 39 – Slamming the Doors – Rurik Tyler / Ronnie Nathan
Page 42 – Don Martin's One Grey Day in the City – Don Martin
Page 43 – Familiar Patter – Walter Brogan / Lou Silverstone
Page 48 – Letters / *Cracked Blockbuster* #5, *Cracked Monster Party* #13, *Cracked Summer Special* #1 ad
Page 50 – Sports Fan's Dream – John Severin / Rich Kriegel (Lou Silverstone)
Page 51 – Subscription ad – Frank Borth
Back Cover – One Afternoon in Sherwood Forest – Walter Brogan / Lou Silverstone

**266, October 1991 (52 pages) ($1.75)**

Cover – We Terminate Schwarzenegger – John Severin
Page 2 and 51 – Gallery of Ghastly Ghoulies – Mike Ricigliano / May Sakami
Page 3 – Contents
Page 4 – Cracked's College President of the Year – Walter Brogan / Lou Silverstone
Page 8 – Superman's Bachelor Party! – Mike Ricigliano / Jerry De Fuccio
Page 10 – Cracked Work Songs for Today's Monotonous Jobs Songbook – Frank Borth / Howie Mitchell
Page 14 – The New Fast Food Restaurants – John Severin / Fred Sahner
Page 16 – Spies and Saboteurs at the Beach – Mike Ricigliano
Page 19 – Orehek at Large Goes to a Rock Concert – Don Orehek
Page 22 – Script Your Own Steven Seagul Movie – John Severin / Tony Frank (Lou Silverstone)
Page 26 – Our Lady of Garbage – Rurik Tyler / Ronnie Nathan
Page 28 – Another Collection of Cracked Baseball Cards – Pete Fitzgerald / Fred Sahner
Page 31 – Cracked Hold-Ups! – (three point goal) Don Orehek Page 33 – Roasting Mother Goose (Star Light) – Vic Martin / Lyle Roberts Kain (1st *Roasting Mother Goose*)
Page 34 – Don Martin's Robin Hood – Don Martin
Page 39 – Fairy Tale Characters Where Are They Now? – Rurik Tyler / Steve Strangio
Page 42 – One Afternoon in Jersey City – Don Orehek Page 43 – Arnold Schwartzburger Film Festival – Walter Brogan

Page 48 – Letters – Mike Ricigliano
Page 50 – Subscription ad – Rurik Tyler
Back Cover – The Day the Paulsbury Doughboy's Oven Overheated! – John Severin / Scott Thaler

**267, November 1991 (52 pages) ($1.75)**
Cover – We Toon Out Toons – Walter Brogan
Page 2 and 51 – Toon In! – Gary Fields
Page 3 – Contents
Page 4 – Robbing Hood Prance of Thieves – Walter Brogan / Lou Silverstone
Page 11 – Don Martin's One Afternoon in New York City – Don Martin
Page 12 – Cartoondom Confidential – Gary Fields
Page 14 – Cracked's Plan for Converting Weapons for Civilian Use – John Severin / Fred Sahner
Page 17 – Bart's Catalogue for Conniving Underachievers – Frank Borth
Page 20 – Don Martin's One Fine Day at the Race Track – Don Martin
Page 21 – Spies & Saboteurs Hit the Toons – Mike Ricigliano
Page 25 – Subscription ad – Rurik Tyler
Page 26 – R-Rated Ads for Family Films – Gary Fields / Evelyn Gabai
Page 28 – You Know You're Courting "Big" Trouble When – Don Orehek
Page 30 – Cracked's Joy of Working – Pete Fitzgerald / Steve Strangio
Page 33 – Don Martin's One Day at the Cro-Magnon Inventor's Club – Don Martin
Page 35 – Wrestling Hype for Boring Sports – Rurik Tyler / Bill Ignizio
Page 38 – Roasting Mother Goose (Little Jack Horner) – Vic Martin
Page 39 – Hackdraft – John Severin / Tony Frank (Lou Silverstone)
Page 45 – Letters to the Editors – Mike Ricigliano
Page 47 – Announcing the Winner of the Greatest Shut-Up in Captivity – Don Orehek
Page 48 – Ye Hang Ups (Oh No NO!) – John Severin
Page 49 – Other Impact Tests – Mike Ricigliano / Jerry De Fuccio
Back Cover – They Didn't Know When to Say "When"! – John Severin / Lou Silverstone

**268, December 1991 (52 pages) ($1.75)**
Cover – We Total Bill and Ted! – John Severin
Page 2 – Roasting Mother Goose (Jack and Jill) – Vic Martin / Bob Kain
Page 3 – Contents – Mike Ricigliano
Page 4 – The Crocketeer – John Severin / Lou Silverstone
Page 11 – Don Martin's One Hot Afternoon in the Jungle – Don Martin

Page 12 – Really Scary Creatures from Everyday Life! – Gary Fields / Bill Ignizio
Page 14 – Up Close and Personal with the Rocketeer – Mike Ricigliano
Page 17 – Orehek at Large at a Comedy Club – Don Orehek / Steve Strangio
Page 20 – Cracked's Comparative Guide to Learning Institutions – Pete Fitzgerald / Steve Strangio
Page 24 – It Wasn't So Long Ago When – John Severin / Bill Ignizio
Page 26 – The Advantages of Being The Rocketeer – Rurik Tyler / George Gladir
Page 28 – Cracked Horses Around – Arnoldo Franchioni
Page 30 – Germinator 2: Judgment Daze – Walter Brogan / Tony Frank (Lou Silverstone)
Page 37 – The Little Dread Schoolhouse – Lee Chenell
Page 38 – The Robocop Crime-Fighters Catalogue – Frank Borth
Page 41 – Rocketeen! – Mike Ricigliano / Jerry De Fuccio
Page 42 – Letters
Page 43 – Subscription ad – Rurik Tyler
Page 44 – Don Martin's Bird-Watching Couple – Don Martin
Page 45 – Bill & Ted's Big Budget Journey – John Severin / Vic Bianco (Lou Silverstone)
Page 50 – Don Martin's Parting Shot A Rocketeer Outtake – Don Martin
Page 51 – The Society for the Preservation of Eardrums – Rurik Tyler / Jerry De Fuccio
Back Cover – Vanity Bare – Rurik Tyler / Hall (In #269 it was explained that even though this cover was in the works first, *Spy* beat *Cracked* to the newsstand with this same joke.)

**269, January 1992 (52 pages) ($1.75)**
Cover – We Slam Dunk Air Jordan – John Severin, Mike Ricigliano
Page 2 – A TV Commercial You'll Never See (Milk) – Walter Brogan / Spark
Page 3 – Contents – Mike Ricigliano
Page 4 – The Naked Bun 2½ The Smell of Beer – Walter Brogan
Page 11 – Don Martin's One Fine Day at the Museum – Don Martin
Page 12 – A Cracked Numbtendo Video Game Shopping Mall Adventure – Pete Fitzgerald / Steve Strangio
Page 15 – Francho's Ark – Arnoldo Franchioni
Page 19 – Spies and Saboteurs Hit the Hoops – Mike Ricigliano
Page 22 – Where They Should Have Been Born! – Don Orehek
Page 24 – Viering Off (Beginner's Chopsticks) – Gary Fields / Jed Vier (1st *Viering Off*)
Page 26 – And the Winner is #23, a Whole Lot of Bull! – Rurik Tyler

Page 28 – Cracked Contest and Reader Survey – Mike Ricigliano
Page 30 – Nickelodown Tonight's Feature Mr. Id – John Severin / Tommy Uno
Page 33 – Don Martin's One Fine Morning at the Dermatologist – Don Martin
Page 34 – Super Couple's Housewarming Party – Mike Ricigliano / Jerry De Fuccio
Page 37 – Don't Ya Hate – Gary Fields
Page 39 – Orehek at Large Back to School – Don Orehek / Suzy Orehek
Page 42 – Letters to the Editor – Mike Ricigliano (George Gladir photo)
Page 44 – Roasting Mother Goose (Little Tommy Tucker) – Vic Martin / Lyle Roberts Kain
Page 45 – Hot Snots! – John Severin / Tony Frank (Lou Silverstone)
Page 50 – Don Martin's One Afternoon in Arithmetic Class – Don Martin
Page 51 – The Rocketeer Goes One-on-One with Air Jordan – Mike Ricigliano
Back Cover – Sports Integrated Magazine – John Severin / Lou Silverstone

**270, March 1992 (52 pages) ($1.75)**
Cover – We Flunk Beverly Hills 90210 – John Severin
Page 2 – *Cracked Collectors' Edition* #90 and *Cracked Monster Party* #15 ad
Page 3 – Contents – Mike Ricigliano
Page 4 – Barferly Hills-911 – John Severin / Lou Silverstone
Page 10 – Don Martin's Late One Night in the City – Don Martin
Page 12 – Cracked Movie Video Rentals – Frank Borth, Walter Brogan / Steve Strangio
Page 15 – The Daredevil – Mike Ricigliano
Page 16 – Orehek at Large Touring a Horror House – Don Orehek
Page 18 – Everyday Neuroses – Rurik Tyler / Steve Strangio
Page 21 – Lifestyles of the Rich and Famous Toons – Walter Brogan / Steve Strangio
Page 24 – Transylvanian Breakfast Cereals – Gary Fields
Page 26 – The Night After Christmas – Rurik Tyler / May Sakami
Page 28 – Some New Celebrity Haircuts We'd Like to See – Don Orehek / John Fahs
Page 31 – Ghastly Ghoulies of the Gridiron – Mike Ricigliano
Page 34 – Viering Off (Ye Olde Barber Shoppe) – Gary Fields / Jed Vier
Page 36 – Modern-Day Creatures We Could Do Without – Pete Fitzgerald / Spark
Page 38 – Cracked's 1-900 Telephone Numbers – Vic Martin

Page 40 – Cracked Guide to Behavior in Public Places – John Severin / Fred Sahner
Page 42 – Letters to the Editors – Mike Ricigliano / Subscription ad – Bill Elder
Page 44 – Blood Kicker – Walter Brogan / Tony Frank (Lou Silverstone)
Page 50 – Don Martin's Parting Shot One Afternoon at the South Pacific Hilton Lounge – Don Martin
Page 51 – Desert Storm Chess Set – John Severin / House
Back Cover – Leevi's ad – Rurik Tyler / Lou Silverstone

**271, May 1992 (52 pages) ($1.75)**
Cover – We Torch the Olympics – Don Martin, Mike Ricigliano
Page 2 – The Saboteur Family Tree – Mike Ricigliano
Page 3 – Contents – Mike Ricigliano
Page 4 – Star Wreck The Next Degeneration – John Severin / Lou Silverstone
Page 11 – Don Martin's Winter Olympics – Don Martin
Page 14 – Orehek at Large at a High School Graduation – Don Orehek / Steve Strangio
Page 16 – Viering Off (Sleeping Beauty) – Gary Fields / Jed Vier
Page 18 – Cracked Senator of the Year – Walter Brogan / Lou Silverstone
Page 22 – Cracked's New, Revamped (and Lots More Interesting) Olympic Events – Mike Ricigliano
Page 25 – The Candidate – John Severin
Page 26 – Throw Out the Clowns – Rurik Tyler / Bill Ignizio
Page 28 – Some of my Best Friends are Monsters! – Arnoldo Franchioni
Page 30 – The Cracked Vidiot Musick Awards – Pete Fitzgerald / Paul Castiglia
Page 34 – Spies and Saboteurs Hit the Winter Olympics Part I – Mike Ricigliano
Page 35 – Cracked Collectors – Don Orehek / George Gladir
Page 38 – Letters to the Editors – Mike Ricigliano / *Cracked Collectors' Edition* #90 ad
Page 40 – The Replacement Shows – John Severin / Steve Strangio
Page 43 – Spies and Saboteurs Hit the Winter Olympics Part II – Mike Ricigliano
Page 44 – The Addled Family – Walter Brogan / Vic Bianco (Lou Silverstone)
Page 50 – Don Martin's Parting Shot (Floydoit) – Don Martin
Page 51 – Subscription ad – Mike Ricigliano
Back Cover – Skinny Book of the Month Club – Rurik Tyler / Lou Silverstone

**272, July 1992 (52 pages) ($1.75)** (Last issue with Jerry De Fuccio as Co-Editor with Lou Silverstone.)

Cover - We Pan Hook - John Severin
Page 2 - *Cracked Monster Party* #16 ad
Page 3 - Contents - Mike Ricigliano
Page 4 - Shnook - John Severin / Lou Silverstone
Page 11 - Don Martin's One Fine Day in the Desert with Only a Stick - Don Martin
Page 13 - When They Were Kids - Don Orehek / Tony Rubino
Page 16 - Spies and Saboteurs Hit Ice Hockey - Mike Ricigliano
Page 18 - Cracked's Fantastic Facts - Walter Brogan / Bill Ignizio
Page 20 - Cracked on Safari - Arnoldo Franchioni
Page 22 - Presents for Hard to Please Monsters - John Severin
Page 25 - Shut-Ups (There's a seat) - Don Orehek / Gayle-Adams Pierpont
Page 26 - Beyond Beauty and the Beast - Mike Ricigliano
Page 28 - New Muppets! - Pete Fitzgerald / Rob Weske
Page 31 - Slayboy Magazine - John Severin / George Gladir
Page 35 - Michael Jackson Strang-R-Us - Rurik Tyler
Page 38 - Letters to the Editors - Mike Ricigliano / Subscription ad - Mike Ricigliano
Page 40 - Don Martin's The Incredible Hulk's Dog - Don Martin
Page 41 - The Appropriate and Inappropriate Captain Hook - Mike Ricigliano
Page 44 - Star Wrek VI The Uninspired Conclusion - Walter Brogan / Tony Frank (Lou Silverstone)
Page 50 - Don Martin's Parting Shot One Fine Evening at Home - Don Martin
Page 51 - They've Fallen and They Can't Get Up! - Mike Ricigliano
Back Cover - Bitterfinger ad - Gary Fields / Lou Silverstone

**273, August 1992 (52 pages) ($1.75)** (1[st] issue with Andy Simmons as Co-Editor with Lou Silverstone.)

Cover - Wayne's World - John Severin
Page 2 - *Cracked Collectors' Edition* #91 ad
Page 3 - Contents - Mike Ricigliano
Page 4 - Wayne's Hurled - John Severin / Lou Silverstone
Page 9 - Don Martin's An Evening in the Big City - Don Martin
Page 10 - Candidates We'd Like to See Run Against President Bush - Don Orehek / Robert Ignizio
Page 12 - Magazines for the Psychologically Disturbed - Pete Fitzgerald / Lenore Skenazy
Page 15 - Spies and Saboteurs Hit TV - Mike Ricigliano

Page 18 – Book Reports of the Rich and Famous – John Severin / Lenore Skenazy
Page 20 – Viering Off (Billy the Squid) – Gary Fields / Jed Vier
Page 21 – Don Martin's Lost Again on the Great American Desert – Don Martin
Page 23 – Cracked's Big City Gift Catalog – Frank Borth / Scott Franklin
Page 26 – Plastic Surgery of the Cartoon Stars – Mike Ricigliano / Jerry De Fuccio
Page 28 – Letters to the Editors – Mike Ricigliano (Howard Stern, John Melendez, Jackie Martling, Cliff Mott, Lou Silverstone, Walter Brogan photos.)
Page 30 – Some Improvement – Walter Brogan / Tony Frank (Lou Silverstone)
Page 36 – The Fast Food Wars! – Gary Fields / Paul Castiglia
Page 39 – Cracked Hold-Ups! (now belong) – Don Orehek
Page 41 – The Cracked List Top Nine Most Useless College Courses – Mike Ricigliano (1st *The Cracked List*)
Page 42 – Next Years' "Real Life" Shows – John Severin / Steve Glaser
Page 44 – Subscription ad – John Severin
Page 45 – The Ham That Rocks the Cradle – Walter Brogan / Tony Frank (Lou Silverstone) Page 50 – Don Martin's Parting Shot One Fine Day in the Sierre Madre Bicycle Shop – Don Martin
Page 51 – A TV Commercial You'll Never See (Klog's Totally) – John Severin / Spark
Back Cover – BusinessWeak Magazine – Rurik Tyler / Lou Silverstone

**274, September 1992 (52 pages) ($1.75)**

Cover – Batman, Penguin and Catwoman – John Severin
Page 2 – Nicoduct ad – Tom Grimes / Andy Simmons
Page 3 – Contents – Mike Ricigliano
Page 4 – The Batzman Tapes – John Severin / Lou Silverstone
Page 9 – The Family Gathering of Doom – Pete Fitzgerald / Steve Strangio
Page 12 – Another Serving of Transylvanian Breakfast Cereals – Gary Fields / Randy Epley
Page 15 – Don Martin's Batman – Don Martin
Page 18 – Daredevils, Stuntmen and Stand-Ins – Arnoldo Franchioni
Page 21 – White Men Can't Dunk!! – Walter Brogan / Link Pershad
Page 26 – Spies and Saboteurs Hit an Amusement Park – Mike Ricigliano
Page 28 – Letters to the Editors – Mike Ricigliano / *Cracked Blockbuster* #6 and *Cracked Monster Party* #17 ad / Subscription ad – Rurik Tyler

Page 30 – The Fuzzy Image Catalogue – John Severin / Lance Contrucci
Page 33 – Are We in a Recession? It All Depends on Who You Are! – Don Orehek / Lou Silverstone
Page 35 – Batastrophes! – Mike Ricigliano
Page 37 – Things are Gonna Get a Lot Worse Before They Get Better! – John Severin / George Gladir
Page 40 – The Cracked Guide to Determine if Someone Has Mailed You a Bomb – Frank Borth / Robert Hess
Page 42 – Some Rhymes of the Times – Rurik Tyler / Lenore Skenazy
Page 44 – Another Batastrophe – Mike Ricigliano
Page 45 – My Cousin Whiny – Walter Brogan / Vic Bianco (Lou Silverstone)
Page 50 – Don Martin's Parting Shot One Afternoon in Gotham – Don Martin
Page 51 – Politically Incorrect Sequels to "White Men Can't Jump" – John Severin
Back Cover – The Straw-Man Writes a Book – Jeff Wong / Lou Silverstone

**275, October 1992 (52 pages) ($1.75)**
Cover – Lethal Weapon 3½ – John Severin
Page 2 – *Cracked Summer Special* #2 and *Cracked Collectors' Edition* #92 ad
Page 3 – Contents – Mike Ricigliano
Page 4 – Backwash / Viering Off (Mount Rushmore) – Mike Ricigliano, Jed Vier (1st *Backwash*)
Page 6 – Ill-Legal Weapon 3½ - Walter Brogan / Lou Silverstone
Page 11 – Don Martin's One Fine Sunday in the Back Yard – Don Martin
Page 12 – Cutting Edge! – John Severin / Jeffery Wilson
Page 14 – Cracked's Strategems and Weapons for Everyday Hostilities – Arnoldo Franchioni
Page 16 – Pet Movie Remakes – Pete Fitzgerald / Lenore Skenazy
Page 19 – More Interesting, Livelier Summer Olympics! – Mike Ricigliano
Page 22 – Cracked's Killer Card Manufacturer of the Year – John Severin / Rich Kriegel (Lou Silverstone)
Page 26 – What a Riot! – Bruce Bolinger / Steve Strangio
Page 28 – Don Martin's One Summer's Day in Dakota – Don Martin
Page 29 – Megasuperultramania Magazine – Rurik Tyler / Steve Strangio
Page 34 – How Cartoon Characters are Coping with the Recession – Gary Fields / Andy Simmons

Page 36 – Shut-Ups (we're being watched) – Don Orehek / Gayle Adams-Pierpont
Page 37 – Money-Ball: The New Baseball – John Severin / Andy Simmons
Page 41 – Spies and Saboteurs Hit the Olympics – Mike Ricigliano
Page 42 – Famous Sandboxes Through History – Frank Borth / Bob Weske
Page 44 – The Cracked Top Ten List Least Popular Ballpark Promotional Dates – Mike Ricigliano
Page 45 – Subscription ad – Rurik Tyler
Page 46 – Kooch – Walter Brogan / Lance Contrucci
Page 50 – Don Martin's Parting Shot Early One Evening in the Suburbs – Don Martin
Page 51 – The Lim-Bo Rock! – Mike Ricigliano
Back Cover – Magic Goes Up for Yet Another Uncontested Lay-Up – Jeff Wong / BDR

**276, November 1992 (52 pages) ($1.75)**
Cover – We Sink Super Soakers! – Nireves (John Severin)
Page 2 – Save the Aliens – Rurik Tyler
Page 3 – Contents – Mike Ricigliano
Page 4 – Backwash / Viering Off (We made it down here) – Mike Ricigliano, Jed Vier
Page 6 – Battyman Return? – Walter Brogan / Lou Silverstone
Page 12 – Don Martin's Alien 3 – Don Martin
Page 14 – Snacks That Time Forgot – John Severin / Lenore Skenazy
Page 17 – Why/When – Don Orehek / Joseph O'Brien
Page 19 – Soak-Mart – Mike Ricigliano (blue color added)
Page 22 – Roasting Mother Goose (Little Boy Blue) – Vic Martin
Page 23 – The Crash Test Dummies Test Other Products – Tim Grimes / Eric Goldberg, Mark Howard
Page 26 – Spies and Saboteurs Hit a Political Convention – Mike Ricigliano
Page 28 – The Exam for the Presidency of the United States – Gary Fields / John Street
Page 32 – Cracked's Roadkill Bingo – Rurik Tyler
Page 34 – Olympic Events Based on Everyday Stuff? – Walter Brogan
Page 36 – The Illiterati – Bruce Bolinger / Andy Simmons
Page 40 – The Cracked Student Profile – Pete Fitzgerald / Steve Strangio
Page 42 – Cracked Conspiracy Theories – Rob Orzechowski / Daniel O'Keefe
Page 44 – Subscription ad
Page 45 – Alienated 3 – John Severin / Tony Frank (Lou Silverstone)

Page 50 – Don Martin's Parting Shot On the Alien Set Take Three – Don Martin
Page 51 – *Cracked Super* #6 ad
Back Cover – Great Moments in Education 2021 – Jeff Wong

**277, December 1992 (52 pages) ($1.75)**
Cover – The Real American Gladiators – John Severin
Page 2 – *Cracked Collectors' Edition* #93 ad
Page 3 – Contents – Mike Ricigliano
Page 4 – Backwash / Viering Off (rubber lances) – Mike Ricigliano, Jed Vier
Page 6 – Universal Shlocker – Walter Brogan / Rich Kriegel (Lou Silverstone)
Page 12 – Don Martin's The Quasimodo Family Through History – Don Martin
Page 14 – Nun's the Word! – Rurik Tyler / Andrew Osborne
Page 16 – Hello, Columbus! – Arnoldo Franchioni
Page 19 – How Things Work…Sort Of – John Severin / Lance Contrucci
Page 23 – Rule the School! – Pete Fitzgerald / Steve Strangio
Page 25 – Subscription ad
Page 26 – Spies and Saboteurs Hit American Gladiators – Mike Ricigliano
Page 28 – Cracked Prison Greeting Cards – Bruce Bolinger / Patric Abedin
Page 30 – Don Martin's One Depressing Night in the City – Don Martin
Page 31 – Cracked's Plan to Help Our Schools – Don Orehek / George Gladir
Page 34 – The Further Adventures of Pinocchio – Mike Ricigliano
Page 36 – Instant Talk Show – Jeff Wong / Lenore Skenazy
Page 38 – Don Martin's Parting Shot The New Shoppe on Main Street – Don Martin
Page 39 – Stop Reading!
Cover – Prez Beat Magazine
Page 2 – Prez Spirit ad
Page 3 – Prez Beat's Inside Scoop
Page 4 – Prez Beat Quiz Time
Page 5 – Would They Ever Have Been Elected President? – John Severin / George Gladir
Page 8 – Dan Quayle's Career Opportunities – Jim Bennett / Eric Goldberg, Mark Howard
Page 10 – Sickly Minutes – Walter Brogan / Lou Silverstone

**278, January 1993 (52 pages) ($1.75)**

Cover – Home Alone 2½ Zit Happens! – John Severin
Page 2 – Don Martin's One Fine Day in the Andes – Don Martin
Page 3 – Contents – Mike Ricigliano
Page 4 – Backwash / Viering Off (Cannibal Entrepreneurs) – Mike Ricigliano, Jed Vier
Page 5 – Gunforgiven – Walter Brogan / Lou Silverstone
Page 12 – Don Martin's Early One Morning at the Bus Station – Don Martin
Page 13 – When Government Regulations Apply to the Wild Kingdom! – Don Orehek / Dan Birtcher
Page 16 – Our Real Keyboard For Rock Star Wannabes! – Bruce Bolinger / Dan Birtcher
Page 18 – Who Else is Home Alone? – Jim Bennett / Spark
Page 20 – The Cracked Top 11 List Columbus's Disappointing Discoveries – Mike Ricigliano / Daniel O'Keefe
Page 21 – Cracked Kiss 'n' Tales – Arnoldo Franchioni
Page 23 – Zit Happens! Starring Macaulay Culkin – Rurik Tyler / Andy Simmons
Page 26 – The Saboteur "Home Alone" Home Protection System – Mike Ricigliano
Page 28 – Einstein's Other Theories of Relativity – Frank Borth / Larry Macloud
Page 30 – Shut-Ups (for your muffler) – Don Orehek / Lou Silverstone
Page 31 – Replacement Shows – John Severin / Steve Strangio
Page 34 – Cracked's Kid-Vid Clearance – Gary Fields
Page 36 – Warning Labels for People – Pete Fitzgerald / Eric Goldberg, Mark Howard
Page 38 – Celebrity Answering Machines – Jeff Wong / David Boone
Page 40 – Subscription ad – Rurik Tyler
Page 41 – Monster Football League – Mike Ricigliano
Page 45 – Smelrose Place – John Severin / Vic Bianco (Lou Silverstone)
Page 50 – Don Martin's Parting Shot Bride of Frankenstein – Don Martin
Page 51 – Jim Bum ad – John Severin / Cliff Mott
Back Cover – Axl Rose Finally Finishes a Concert – Jeff Wong

**279, March 1993 (52 pages) ($1.75)**

Cover – We Bust Madonna for Indecent Overexposure! – John Severin
Page 2 – The Uncanny Malcolm X, Man – Jim Lee Williams
Page 3 – Contents – Mike Ricigliano
Page 4 – Backwash / Viering Off (Protest Evolution) – Mike Ricigliano, Jed Vier

Page 6 - Don Martin's One Fine Day in Dr. Frankenstein's Laboratory - Don Martin
Page 7 - Under Sludge - Walter Brogan / Lou Silverstone (red color added)
Page 11 - One Incredibly Obnoxious Guy's Cheap Movie Giveaways Warehouse - Tom Grimes, Rurik Tyler
Page 14 - The Continuing Adventures of Aladdin - Mike Ricigliano
Page 16 - The Mighty Dorks - Pete Fitzgerald
Page 17 - Proper Football Safety Techniques - Rurik Tyler / Andy Simmons
Page 20 - The Crusty Spoon Placemat - Bruce Bolinger / Lenore Skenazy (red color added)
Page 22 - Self Help Books for Pre-Schoolers - John Severin / Lenore Skenazy
Page 24 - Cracked's Guide to Enjoying the Great Outdoors - Don Orehek / Fred Sahner
Page 26 - Spies and Saboteurs Hit the Shopping Mall - Mike Ricigliano
Page 28 - Cracked's Personalized Remotes - Terry Colon
Page 31 - Goodies for Transylvanian Gourmets! - Rob Orzechowski / Gayle Adams-Pierpont (red color added)
Page 34 - Subscription ad (red color added)
Page 35 - Madonna's Top 86 (Give or Take 79) New Year's Resolutions - Mike Ricigliano
Page 36 - Our First Annual Hell of a Time! - Jim Bennett / Andy Simmons
Page 38 - The List of the Mosthokum - John Severin / Rich Kriegel (Lou Silverstone)
Page 43 - Yo, Santa! - Arnoldo Franchioni (red color added)
Page 44 - Sparky's Dog House Placemat - Bruce Bolinger / Lenore Skenazy (red color added)
Page 46 - Other Magazine Covers Madonna Will Be Appearing On - Rurik Tyler / Chick Chasen
Page 48 - Dangerous Toys - Ron Barrett
Page 50 - Don Martin's Another Find Day in Dr. Frankenstein's Laboratory - Don Martin
Page 51 - Dead Fred's Discount Funeral Shack! - Rurik Tyler
Back Cover - Cracked Presents the Real Mighty Ducks - Walter Brogan

**280, May 1993 (52 pages) ($1.75)**

Cover - Special Swimsuit Issue - Don Martin
Page 2 - Looose Leevi's - Tom Grimes / Steve Strangio
Page 3 - Contents - Mike Ricigliano
Page 4 - Backwash - Mike Ricigliano, Jed Vier

Page 6 – Don Martin's Swimsuit Beauties Around the World – Don Martin
Page 8 – Homeboy Alone, Too – Walter Brogan / Lou Silverstone
Page 14 – Cats Are People Too! – P.C. Vey
Page 15 – Test Your First Aid Knowledge! – John Severin / Rob Petrie
Page 18 – The Cracked Family Reunion Dinner Games – Bruce Bolinger / Andrew Osborne
Page 20 – Cracked's Swimsuit Model I.Q. Test – Mike Ricigliano
Page 22 – Kenny the Cockroach's Toy Tenement Sale! – Frank Borth / Scott Franklin
Page 26 – Spies and Saboteurs Hit a Water Theme Park – Mike Ricigliano
Page 28 – Castle Dracula – Rurik Tyler / George Gladir
Page 30 – The Wit and Wisdom of the Fisherman – John Severin / Lenore Skenazy
Page 32 – This Valentine's Day Cracked Says it with Flowers – Arnoldo Franchioni
Page 33 – Jobs Video Games Will Prepare You For – Pete Fitzgerald / Paul Giles
Page 35 – Cracked Animal Species That Didn't Quite Make it – Bruce Bolinger / Donald Neiswinger
Page 38 – White House Yard Sale – Jim Bennett / Bob Silverstone
Page 40 – After-School Job Opportunities – Ron Barrett
Page 42 – The Cracked List 13 Ways to Know You've Had Enough of Winter – Mike Ricigliano / Andy Simmons
Page 43 – Cashing in on the Man of Steel – Rurik Tyler / Eric Goldberg, Mark Howard
Page 45 – Subscription ad
Page 46 – Aquatic Leap – John Severin / Eric Goldberg, Mark Howard
Page 50 – Don Martin's Parting Shot One Summer's Day in the Suburbs – Don Martin
Page 51 – *Cracked Collectors' Edition* #94 ad
Back Cover – Take Number 593 of Robin Williams Trying to Get Out of Aladdin's Lamp – Jeff Wong / Cliff Mott

**281, July 1993 (52 pages) ($1.75)**

Cover – Teenage Mutant Ninja Sushi – John Severin
Page 2 – The Frog Prince of Buckingham Palace – Jim Bennett
Page 3 – Contents – Mike Ricigliano
Page 4 – Backwash – Mike Ricigliano, Jed Vier
Page 6 – The Cracked List 13 Alternatives for Bungee Jumpers – Mike Ricigliano / Dan Birtcher
Page 7 – Teenage Mutant Ninjerk Turdles III The Sacred Sequel of Dumbness – Walter Brogan / Andy Simmons (green color added)

Page 11 – Don Martin's Health Care USA – Don Martin
Page 13 – History Time Line – Mark Martin / Jeff Wilson
Page 16 – The Monkey Quotient – Bruce Bolinger / Arnie Bernstein
Page 20 – Bumper Stickers We're Stuck With
Page 22 – Vey Out – P.C. Vey
Page 23 – Gangland Land America's First Urban Decay Theme Park – Don Orehek / Bill Frenzer
Page 26 – Spies and Saboteurs Hit Madison Square Garden – Mike Ricigliano
Page 28 – The Cracked Movie Awards – Rurik Tyler / Steve Strangio
Page 31 – Subscription ad (green color added)
Page 32 – If There Was Truth in Advertising – Gary Fields / Gayle Adams-Pierpont (green color added)
Page 34 – A Few Odd Men – John Severin / Lou Silverstone
Page 40 – Little-Known Insurance Policies – Bruce Bolinger / Craig Farrell
Page 43 – *Cracked Monster Party* #20 ad (green color added)
Page 44 – Teenage Mutant Ninja Turtles in Japan – Mike Ricigliano (green color added)
Page 46 – Get Smarty – Walter Brogan / Tony Frank (Lou Silverstone)
Page 50 – Don Martin's Parting Shot One Fine Day in Surgery – Don Martin
Page 51 – Charles Barkley vs. Godzilla Part XVII – John Severin / Rob Weske
Back Cover – The Losers Congratulate the Winners – Jeff Wong

**282, August 1993 (52 pages) ($1.75)**

Cover – A Farewell Toast to Cheers – John Severin
Page 2 – *Cracked Spaced Out* #1 ad
Page 3 – Contents – Mike Ricigliano
Page 4 – Backwash – Mike Ricigliano / Randy Epley, David Boone, Steve Strangio, Andy Lamberti, Jed Vier, Terry Colon, Andy Simmons, Daniel O'Keefe
Page 6 – Beers – John Severin / Andy Simmons (3rd *Cheers* parody)
Page 11 – Don Martin's One Grey Day Last Winter – Don Martin
Page 12 – Slimeco Chemical and Food Industries Presents Genetically Enhanced Food for the 90's – Bruce Bolinger / Joseph O'Brien
Page 14 – Banned Children's Books – Gary Fields / David Boone
Page 16 – TV Gameshows Through History – Pete Fitzgerald / Rob Weske
Page 18 – Evilrock Magazine – Jeff Wong / Steve Strangio
Page 24 – First Cat – The Adventures of Socks Clinton – Don Orehek
Page 26 – Spies and Saboteurs Hit the Ballpark – Mike Ricigliano

Page 28 – Subscription ad
Page 29 – Don Martin's One Fine Day at the Fire Station – Don Martin
Page 30 – Great Views from Your Typical Airline Coach Seat – John Severin / Jim Bauer
Page 32 – The Cracked List 13 Things to Expect During the NBA Playoffs – Mike Ricigliano
Page 33 – Cracked's Truly Atrocious Trading Cards – Rurik Tyler / Dan Birtcher
Page 36 – Lifesize Shaquille O'Neal Poster
Page 38 – Don Martin's One Sunday Afternoon on TV – Don Martin
Page 39 – Victor's Secret Catalogue – Bruce Bolinger / Steve Strangio
Page 42 – Movies From Hell – Jim Bennett / Andrew Osborne
Page 44 – Groundhog Daze – Walter Brogan / Lou Silverstone
Page 50 – Don Martin's Parting Shot One Fine Morning at the Hospital – Don Martin
Page 51 – The Special on Aisle 9 – Bruce Bolinger
Back Cover – Marky Mark Bears All – Jeff Wong

**283, September 1993 (52 pages) ($1.75)**

Cover – Jurassick Park – John Severin
Page 2 – *Cracked Super* #7 and *Cracked Monster Party* #21 ad
Page 3 – Contents – Mike Ricigliano
Page 4 – Backwash – Dan Birtcher, David Boone, Terry Colon, Daniel O'Keefe, Mike Ricigliano, Andy Simmons, Steve Strangio, Jed Vier
Page 6 – Jurassick Park – Walter Brogan / Lou Silverstone
Page 13 – Don Martin's One Fine Day in the South Pacific – Don Martin
Page 14 – Easy-to-Read EKG Readings For – John Severin / Rob Weske
Page 16 – Jurassic Park's Dinosaur Experiments Gone Bad! – Pete Fitzgerald / Mike Ricigliano
Page 18 – The Cracked List 14 Tipoffs That You're Dating Princess Di – Mike Ricigliano / Dan Birtcher
Page 19 – The Sophisti-Kids Go To Camp Elegance – Jeff Bennett
Page 21 – A Visit to Jurassic Park – Don Orehek / Rob Weske
Page 22 – Landmark Remodeling – Terry Colon
Page 26 – Spies and Saboteurs Hit Jurassic Park – Mike Ricigliano
Page 28 – Newly-Discovered Greek Theater Masks! – John Severin / Dan Birtcher
Page 30 – Don Martin's One Fine Day at South and Main – Don Martin
Page 31 – Superchumps – Rurik Tyler, Gary Fields / Steve Strangio
Page 37 – That Not-So-Championship Season – Mike Ricigliano
Page 40 – Charlie Brown Specials for the 90's – Gary Fields / Craig Farrell

Page 42 – The Complete Cracked Guide to the Industrial Arts – Bruce Bolinger / Dan Birtcher
Page 44 – Subscription ad
Page 45 – Martian – John Severin / Andrew Osborne
Page 50 – Don Martin's Parting Shot Early One Morning in Calcutta – Don Martin
Page 51 – Stan Lee's Press-On Nails – John Severin / Gene Perone
Back Cover – The Auditions for "Jurassic Park" – Jeff Wong

**284, October 1993 (52 pages) ($1.75)**
Cover – Year of the Brat! – John Severin
Page 2 – Don Martin's The Mural Painter – Don Martin
Page 3 – Contents – Mike Ricigliano
Page 4 – Backwash – Terry Colon, Randy Epley, Daniel O'Keefe, Mike Ricigliano, Andy Simmons, Jed Vier, Jeff Wilson
Page 6 – Blossomed – Walter Brogan / Steve Strangio
Page 11 – Don Martin's One Summer Day at the Mall – Don Martin
Page 12 – Grunge is Really Getting Out of Hand When – Jeff Wong / Gene Perone
Page 14 – Barney: The Missing Episodes – Rob Orzechowski / Eric Goldberg, Mark Howard
Page 16 – Tomorrow's High-Tech Gadgets for Couch-Potato Sports Fans – John Severin / George Gladir
Page 19 – Parents! Can't Live With 'em, Can't Live Without 'em – P.C. Vey
Page 20 – The Family Profile – Pete Fitzgerald / Steve Strangio
Page 22 – A Cracked Interview with a Minor-League Manager – Bruce Bolinger / Randy Epley
Page 25 – Subscription ad
Page 26 – Spies and Saboteurs Hit Summer Camp – Mike Ricigliano
Page 28 – Shut-Ups (book report) – Don Orehek / Gayle Adams-Pierpont
Page 29 – Mr. Wilson's Revenge – Gary Fields / Eric Goldberg, Mark Howard
Page 32 – Why is it That the Same People Who – Walter Brogan / Rich Kriegel (Lou Silverstone)
Page 34 – The Cracked List 10 Conservation Tips – Mike Ricigliano
Page 35 – Beverly Hills High School Yearbook – Jim Bennett
Page 40 – Sani-Strips – Ron Barrett
Page 42 – The 1st Annual Cracked NFL All-Dough Team – Mike Ricigliano
Page 44 – If We Had Designer Labels on Everything – Bruce Bolinger
Page 45 – Bart Goes to the Movies – John Severin

Page 50 – Don Martin's One Fine Evening in the Jungle – Don Martin
Page 51 – *Cracked Collectors' Edition* #96 and *Cracked Summer Special* #3 ad
Back Cover – Great Moments in Baseball 1998 – Jeff Wong

**285, November 1993 (52 pages) ($1.75)**
Cover – Squashed Action Hero – John Severin
Page 2 – *Cracked Spaced Out* #2 ad
Page 3 – Contents – Mike Ricigliano
Page 4 – Backwash – Terry Colon, Randy Epley, Mike Mikula, Daniel O'Keefe, Mike Ricigliano, Andy Simmons, Jed Vier, Jeff Wilson
Page 6 – Lost Action Hero – Walter Brogan / Lou Silverstone
Page 11 – Don Martin's One Fine Morning on the "Jurassic Park" Set – Don Martin
Page 13 – Modern Clowns
Page 16 – Pez Dispensers That Didn't Quite Make it – John Severin / Eric Goldberg, Mark Howard
Page 18 – Coupons! Coupons! Coupons! – Bruce Bolinger / Steve Strangio
Page 20 – The Cracked List 14 Versions of "Last Action Hero" That Would've Been Better – Mike Ricigliano / Link Pershad
Page 21 – Cracked Fantasy Camps – Don Orehek / Mike Sacks
Page 24 – How Has Success Changed the Dinosaurs of "Jurassic Park"? – Jeff Wong / Missy Wheathins
Page 26 – Spies and Saboteurs Hit the Cineplex – Mike Ricigliano
Page 28 – Hot Snots1 Part 2 – John Severin / Tony Frank (Lou Silverstone)
Page 32 – Don Martin's Dinosaur Quest: North Pole – Don Martin
Page 33 – When 90's Headlines Catch Up with Comic Strips – Gary Fields / Mike Mikula
Page 36 – Cracked's Summertime Word Problem – Pete Fitzgerald / Judd Stomp
Page 38 – Subscription ad – Rurik Tyler
Page 39 – Barney Has a Snack – Don Orehek / Rob Weske
Page 40 – Cracked's Creative Concepts for Jump-Starting the Economy – Mike Ricigliano
Page 43 – In the Dog-House – P.C. Vey
Page 44 – The Back Room of the Hall of Fame – Bruce Bolinger / Andy Simmons
Page 46 – Cliffhangout – John Severin / Rich Kriegel (Lou Silverstone)
Page 50 – Don Martin's Parting Shot Jurassic Park III One Fine Day in June, 1993 – Don Martin

Page 51 – A Sunday Afternoon in Jurassic Trailer Park – Rurik Tyler / Cliff Mott
Back Cover – Conan the Comedian is Victorious in the Talk Show Wars – Jeff Wong

**286, December 1993 (52 pages) ($1.75)**
Cover – Feed Willy – John Severin
Page 2 – *Cracked Collectors' Edition* #97 ad
Page 3 – Contents – Mike Ricigliano
Page 4 – Backwash – Terry Colon, Randy Epley, Daniel O'Keefe, Mike Ricigliano, Andy Simmons, Jed Vier, Jeff Wilson
Page 6 – In the Line That Fired – John Severin / Lou Silverstone
Page 11 – Don Martin's One Fine Day in the Slammer (17th Century Style) – Don Martin
Page 12 – If More Holidays Were Combined – Bruce Bolinger / Judd Stomp
Page 14 – If Romance Writers Wrote – Rurik Tyler / Jeff Wilson
Page 17 – Your High School Reunion – Pete Fitzgerald / Patric Abedin
Page 20 – Modern-Day Neuroses – Walter Brogan / Spark
Page 22 – The Cracked List Warning Signs That Socks Clinton Has Too Much Influence in Washington – Mike Ricigliano
Page 23 – Unlikely Celebrity Product Endorsements – Jim Bennett / Eric Goldberg, Mark Howard, Mike Mikula
Page 26 – Spies and Saboteurs Hit School – Mike Ricigliano
Page 28 – Famous Last Laughs – Don Orehek / Andrew Osborne
Page 30 – Don Martin's Early One Morning in the Himilayas – Don Martin
Page 31 – Rookie of the Weird – Walter Brogan / Andy Simmons
Page 36 – Comic Book Heroes – Bruce Bolinger / Dan DeBruin
Page 38 – Ill Literacy – Arnoldo Franchioni
Page 39 – Monster Sports Card Collector's Guide – Mike Ricigliano
Page 42 – You Know the Clear Products Trend Has Gone Too Far When – John Severin / Dan Birtcher
Page 44 – Subscription ad – Rurik Tyler
Page 45 – Shut-Ups (I hope dis noize) – Don Orehek / Eric Goldberg, Mark Howard
Page 46 – Feed Whaley – Jeff Wong / Vic Bianco (Lou Silverstone)
Page 50 – Don Martin's Parting Shot Another Fine Sunday, Driving in the Country – Don Martin
Page 51 – The Infirmed – Jim Bennett
Back Cover – Clint and Abe Take in a Show – Jeff Wong

**287, January 1994 (52 pages) ($1.75)**

Cover – We Salute TV Violence! – John Severin
Page 2 – *Cracked Monster Party* #23 and *Cracked Spaced Out* #3 ad – Walter Brogan
Page 3 – Contents – Mike Ricigliano
Page 4 – Backwash – Terry Colon, Randy Epley, Daniel O'Keefe, Mike Ricigliano, Andy Simmons, Jed Vier, Jeff Wilson
Page 6 – Skeevis and Butt-Face Check Out the Tube! – Walter Brogan / Andrew Osborne
Page 11 – Two American Tourists in a Saskatchewan Restaurant – Don Orehek / Judd Stomp
Page 12 – Miniature Golf from Hell!! – Ron Barrett
Page 14 – Lunch Boxes that Never Caught On! – John Severin / Rob Weske
Page 16 – Television Warnings – Jim Bennett / Eric Goldberg, Mark Howard
Page 19 – A Guide to Canada Our 51st State – Bruce Bolinger / Andy Simmons
Page 23 – Don Martin's One Fine Day at the Beach in Newfoundland – Don Martin
Page 24 – Drawnout Crime Scenes – Arnoldo Franchioni
Page 26 – Spies and Sab's Hit the Thanksgiving Parade – Mike Ricigliano
Page 28 – Subscription ad – Rurik Tyler
Page 29 – America's Most Daunted – Rurik Tyler / Judd Stomp
Page 34 – Don Martin's Soap Capsules – Don Martin
Page 36 – Cracked's Saturday Morning TV Review – Walter Brogan / Judd Stomp
Page 38 – Royal Canadian Shut-Ups (La Forge) – Don Orehek / Eric Goldberg, Mark Howard
Page 39 – Mamie van Pierre de la Beliveau's Guide to Ice Hockey Etiquette – Mike Ricigliano
Page 42 – Numbtendo's Megaplex Mania – Pete Fitzgerald / Steve Strangio
Page 44 – The Phewww-gitive – John Severin / Lou Silverstone
Page 50 – The Cracked List 12 Possible Replacements for "Studs" – Mike Ricigliano
Page 51 – The Thanksgiving Day Parade: The Morning After – Arnoldo Franchioni
Back Cover – A Really Grimm Fairy Tale The Pied Piper of Encino – Jeff Wong

**288, March 1994 (52 pages) ($1.75)**

Cover – Bruce Wayne's World – Walter Brogan
Page 2 – *Cracked Monster Party* #23 and *Cracked Spaced Out* #3 ad – John Severin (reprint from #243)

Page 3 – Contents – Mike Ricigliano
Page 4 – Backwash – Eric Bohlen, Terry Colon, Randy Epley, Daniel O'Keefe, Mike Ricigliano, Fred Sahner, Andy Simmons
Page 6 – Bruce Waine's World – John Severin / Lou Silverstone
Page 12 – New Weather Vanes You Might Have Missed! – Pete Fitzgerald / Dan Birtcher
Page 14 – Video Piracy Warnings that Might Actually Work – Walter Brogan / David Allikas
Page 17 – Hillary's Health Care Plan – Gray Morrow / Randy Epley
Page 20 – Desperate Cigarette Ad Campaigns! – Ron Devue (John Severin) – Scott Franklin, Rick Rodgers
Page 22 – Ho-Ho Hollywood! – Arnoldo Franchioni
Page 23 – The Nielsen Ratings for Everyday Life! – Gary Fields / Dan Birtcher
Page 26 – Spies and Sabs Hit the NFL Game – Mike Ricigliano (1st "Spies and Sabs Hit")
Page 28 – It's the Smell that Sells – Lee Chenelle / Andrew Osborne
Page 30 – Subscription ad
Page 31 – The Cracked Travel Guidebook – Bruce Bolinger / Judd Stomp Page 35 – Cracked's Christmas Quiz – Mike Ricigliano / Eric Bohlen
Page 37 – Christmas Gifts for the Dog on Your Shopping List – Jim Bennett / Eric Bohlen
Page 40 – Cracked Goodies – Gary Fields / Rob Weske
Page 42 – Tabloids Through History – Bruce Bolinger / David Levesque
Page 44 – More Shakespearean Shut-Ups (Damn Spot!) – Don Orehek / Dan Birtcher
Page 45 – The Fresh Prance of Bel Air – Walter Brogan / Lance Contrucci
Page 50 – The Cracked List 14 Signs of a Weak Economic Recovery – Mike Ricigliano
Page 51 – Immoral Kombat – Rurik Tyler / Steve Strangio
Back Cover – Christmas in Bosnia – Jeff Wong

**289, May 1994 (52 pages) ($1.75)**

Cover – We Devour The Three Musketeers – John Severin
Page 2 – *Cracked Collectors' Edition* #98 ad Page 3 – Contents – Mike Ricigliano
Page 4 – Backwash – Randy Epley, Greg Grabianski, Mike Ricigliano, Andy Simmons, Steve Strangio, Jed Veir, Terry Colon
Page 6 – Schmatz Dysentery Presents: The Three Muske-Twits – Walter Brogan / Andy Simmons
Page 11 – The Big Bird and the Little Old Lady – Arnoldo Franchioni

Page 12 – Lawsuits for Everyday Annoyances – Tom Grimes / Scott Franklin (photos of Lou Silverstone and Walter Brogan among others)
Page 14 – Fast Food Tray Liners that Never Worked Out – Gary Fields / Rob Weske
Page 17 – Voila! – A. Blinken (John Severin) / Andy Simmons
Page 21 – Hyper Image Homeboy Goodz for Hangin' in Da 'Hood – Todd James / Barry Zeger
Page 24 – Addams Family Valentines – Jeff Wong / Scott Franklin
Page 26 – Spies and Sabs Hit the Winter Olympics – Mike Ricigliano
Page 28 – Subscription ad – John Severin (reprint from *Cracked Collectors' Edition* #88)
Page 29 – Cracked's Sneaker Manufacturer of the Year – Walter Brogan / Lou Silverstone
Page 33 – Cracked Tattoons – Mike Ricigliano
Page 36 – New Rules of Thumb! – Pete Fitzgerald / Daniel Birtcher
Page 38 – Bizarre Business Cards We Hope We Never See – Terry Colon
Page 40 – Shut-Ups (I can do no moore!) – Don Orehek / Eric Goldberg, Mark Howard
Page 41 – Hollywoodworld Resort – Bruce Bolinger / Rob Weske
Page 45 – Kops – John Severin / Greg Grabianski
Page 50 – The Cracked List Bad Roadside Signs to See While in Traffic – Mike Ricigliano
Page 51 – Marlburrow ad – John Severin / Judd Stomp
Back Cover – Cracked's Great Moments in Science (Look Professor) – Jeff Wong / Rob Weske

**290, July 1994 (52 pages) ($1.75)**

Cover – We Shred Mighty Moron Power Rangers – John Severin
Page 2 – *Cracked Spaced Out* #4 and *Cracked Monster Party* #24 ad – Greg Grabianski Page 3 – Contents – Mike Ricigliano
Page 4 – Backwash – Eric Bohlen, Greg Grabianski, Fred Sahner, Andy Simmons, Jed Veir, Terry Colon, Mike Ricigliano
Page 6 – The Mighty-Moron Chowder Rangers – John Severin / Greg Grabianski
Page 12 – Where They Got the Genes to Splice Barney – Pete Fitzgerald / Mike Mikula
Page 14 – What if Everyone Talked Like a Race Car Driver? – Bruce Bolinger / Eric Bohlen
Page 16 – Saturday Morning Cartoon Shut-Ups (Don't shoot me!) – Don Orehek / Eric Goldberg, Mark Howard
Page 17 – Crush People's Heads – The Morty Lee Way – Tom Grimes / Eric Goldberg, Mark Howard (Walter Brogan photo)
Page 21 – Curses for Our Time – Ron Barrett

Page 24 – Yahoo Wild West – Arnoldo Franchioni
Page 26 – Spies and Sabs Hit a Health Club – Mike Ricigliano
Page 28 – Subscription ad – John Severin (reprint from *Cracked Collectors' Edition* #88)
Page 29 – Mrs. Doubtful – Walter Brogan / Andy Simmons
Page 34 – Cracked Colognes – Jim Bennett / Jeff Wilson, Randy Epley, Judd Stomp
Page 36 – The NCMMM Basketball Tournament! – Mike Ricigliano
Page 38 – The Animal Kingdom Gets Tattooed – Bruce Bolinger / Lenore Skenazy
Page 41 – Just Plane Stupid – Terry Colon
Page 44 – Sin-filled – Walter Brogan / Lou Silverstone
Page 50 – The Cracked List 10 Most Unpopular Tropical Island Activities at Club Med – Mike Ricigliano / Greg Grabianski
Page 51 – Commemorative Plate Rejects – Rurik Tyler / Andy Lamberti
Back Cover – Cracked's Great Moments in Advertising Deception – Jeff Wong

**291, August 1994 (52 pages) ($1.75)**
Cover – Mortal Combat 3 The Spinal Chapter – John Severin
Page 2 – You Drink Milk and It Shows ad – Ron Barrett
Page 3 – Contents – Mike Ricigliano
Page 4 – Backwash – Eric Bohlen, Randy Epley, Greg Grabianski, Andrew Hansen, Darren Johnson, Mike Ricigliano, Andy Simmons, Scott Woof, Barry Zeger, Terry Colon
Page 6 – Ass Ventoro, Pest Detective & On Shaky Ground – Walter Brogan / Lou Silverstone
Page 11 – Saturday Morning Commercial Shut-Ups (Rice Krispies) – Don Orehek / Eric Goldberg, Mark Howard
Page 12 – Custom Coffin Catalog – Ron Barrett
Page 14 – Virtual-Reality Games We Won't Be So Quick to Try – Pete Fitzgerald / Greg Grabianski
Page 16 – How Clinton's Programs Have Affected Mother Goose – Gary Fields / Dan Birtcher
Page 19 – The Pentagon's Latest Weapons – John Severin / Dan Birtcher
Page 24 – When an Owner Sez…He Really Means – Bruce Bolinger / Lou Silverstone
Page 26 – Spies and Sabs Hit the Video Arcade – Mike Ricigliano
Page 28 – Lifestyles of the Rich and Violent – Rurik Tyler / Judd Stomp
Page 32 – Crackedheads! – Arnoldo Franchioni (1st *Crackedheads*)
Page 34 – Why/When – Don Orehek / Joseph O'Brien
Page 36 – Subscription ad – John Severin (reprint from *Cracked Collectors' Edition* #88)

Page 37 – Sneak Preview of Christmas Toys – Rurik Tyler / Judd Stomp
Page 40 – Cracked Rates the New Thrill-Ride Roller Coasters – Mike Ricigliano
Page 42 – Cracked's Guide to Subspecies of Everyday Imbeciles and Idiots – Walter Brogan / Barry Zeger
Page 44 – Shut-Ups (call a doctor) – Don Orehek
Page 45 – Grossanne: the Second Helping – John Severin / Greg Grabianski
Page 50 – The Cracked List 47 Future Sequels to "Saved By the Bell – The College Years" – Mike Ricigliano
Page 51 – *Cracked Collectors' Edition* #99 ad
Back Cover – The Michael Jordan Paper Doll – Jeff Wong

**292, September 1994 (52 pages) ($1.75)**
Cover – Meet the Real Flintstones – John Severin
Page 2 – *Cracked Blockbuster* #8 ad
Page 3 – Contents – Mike Ricigliano
Page 4 – Backwash – Eric Bohlen, Randy Epley, Mike Ricigliano, Lou Silverstone, Andy Simmons, Jed Vier, Terry Colon
Page 6 – The Finkstones – Walter Brogan / Lou Silverstone
Page 12 – The License Exam – Don Orehek / Greg Grabianski
Page 13 – The Beaver Newspaper – Ron Barrett
Page 16 – New Dance Steps for Urban Street Survival – Rurik Tyler / Barry Zeger
Page 18 – The Cracked Institute of Entomology Summertime Insect Identification Chart – Mike Ricigliano
Page 20 – Celebrity Robots – John Severin / Rob Weske
Page 23 – Rob Weske's Interpreting Cave Drawings – Bruce Bolinger / Rob Weske
Page 26 – Spies and Sabs Hit the World Cup – Mike Ricigliano
Page 28 – Modern Music Endorsements – Jeff Wong / Buddy Flip Page 30 – What if Comic Strips Featured Guest Stars? – Gary Fields / Ed Subitzky
Page 33 – Cracked Movie Awards – Walter Brogan / Randy Epley
Page 36 – The Animal Rights Debate – Randy Jones / Lenore Skenazy
Page 38 – The Hunter – Don Orehek / Rob Weske
Page 39 – Full of it House – John Severin / Greg Grabianski
Page 44 – The Cracked List 11 Baseball Mascots that Didn't Work Out – Mike Ricigliano
Back Cover – Sports Illustrated for Klods Magazine – Rurik Tyler

**293, October 1994 (52 pages) ($1.75)**

Cover - We Dump on the Lion King - Walter Brogan
Page 2 - *Cracked Collectors' Edition* #100 and *Cracked Summer Special* #4 ad - John Severin (reprint from #86)
Page 3 - Contents - Mike Ricigliano
Page 4 - Backwash - Randy Epley, William Faulkner, Ernest Hemingway, Mike Ricigliano, William Shakespeare, Lou Silverstone, Norman Mailer, Andy Simmons, F. Scott Fitzgerald, Jeff Whelan, Pablo Picasso, Terry Colon, Rembrandt
Page 6 - City Suckers II - John Severin / Andy Simmons
Page 12 - Cracked's Practical Joke Items for Emergency Workers - Gary Fields / Scott Franklin
Page 14 - Life's a Beach! - Mike Ricigliano (blue color added)
Page 16 - Cracked's Guide to Specialized Summer Camps! - John Severin / Rob Weske
Page 20 - Advertising Fantasy vs. Everyday Reality - Pete Fitzgerald / Barry Zeger
Page 22 - A TV Scene We're Dying to See - Jeff Wong
Page 23 - What's Really in Those Cigarettes? - Bruce Bolinger / Lenore Skenazy
Page 26 - Spies and Saboteurs Hit the Jungle! - Mike Ricigliano
Page 28 - Yahoo Wild West Part II - Arnoldo Franchioni
Page 30 - Subscription ad (blue color added)
Page 31 - NYPD Blue Moon - Walter Brogan / Lou Silverstone (blue color added)
Page 36 - Lease Agreements for Melrose Place - Jeff Wong / Mike Mikula
Page 38 - Water Parks of the Damned! - Ron Barrett (blue color added)
Page 40 - The Lion King Returns to his Kingdom - Don Orehek / Rob Weske
Page 41 - Cracked Visits America's Grossest Kid - Bruce Bolinger / Barry Zeger
Page 44 - The Monster Home Shopping Channel - Rob Orzechowski / Craig Farrell
Page 46 - "The Lion King" Promotional Blitz - Walter Brogan / Greg Grabianski
Page 50 - The Cracked List 19 Ways to Be a Tough Guy - Mike Ricigliano
Page 51 - One Day Out West - Arnoldo Franchioni
Back Cover - A TV Commercial You'll Never See! (UT&T) - John Severin / R. Rhine

**294, November 1994 (52 pages) ($1.75)**

Cover – We Speed Back to School – John Severin
Page 2 – How to Detect Counterfeit Trading Cards – Gray Morrow
Page 3 – Contents – Mike Ricigliano
Page 4 – Backwash – Dan Birtcher, Randy Epley, Lou Silverstone, Andy Simmons, Jeff Wilson, Terry Colon, Mike Ricigliano
Page 6 – The Loin King – Walter Brogan
Page 12 – Where's Oswaldo? – Rurik Tyler / David Boone
Page 14 – Rules and Regulations Regarding the Mask – Mike Ricigliano
Page 16 – Discovery: Inside the Pharaoh's Tomb – Don Orehek / Rob Weske
Page 17 – Fashion Pages for Teachers (and Other School Types) – Chris Bartlett / Greg Grabianski
Page 20 – Rich Suburban Schools vs. Poor Suburban Schools – John Severin / Andy Simmons
Page 25 – The Boulder and the Sword – Arnoldo Franchioni
Page 27 – Spies and Saboteurs Hit the Rodeo – Mike Ricigliano
Page 28 – Peed – Walter Brogan / Lou Silverstone
Page 32 – Whitewater Testimony for Dummies – Bruce Bolinger / Dan Birtcher
Page 34 – Clothing Ideas for the 90's – Don Orehek / Mike Mikula
Page 35 – The Big Book of Cracked Birthday Ideas! – Gary Fields / Lenore Skenazy
Page 39 – New Automobile Safety Accessories for '95 – Bruce Bolinger / Danny DeBruin
Page 42 – Classroom Turmoil Accessories – Todd James / Greg Grabianski
Page 44 – The Mask Goes to the Cineplex – John Severin / Greg Grabianski, Missy Wheathins
Page 50 – The Cracked List – 10 Bad Signs – Mike Ricigliano
Page 51 – Subscription ad
Back Cover – Cracked's Great Moments in Education Kermit the Frog Goes Back to School – Jeff Wong / Rob Weske

**295, December 1994 (52 pages) ($1.95)**

Cover – America's #1 TV Show: The Simpson – Sgt. Pluposki, LAPD
Page 2 – *Cracked Collectors' Edition* #101 ad
Page 3 – Contents – Mike Ricigliano
Page 4 – Backwash – David Boone, Randy Epley, Andy Simmons, Terry Colon, Mike Ricigliano
Page 6 – True Spies – Walter Brogan
Page 13 – On the Beach – Arnoldo Franchioni
Page 14 – Prehistoric Cocktail Party – Bruce Bolinger / Lenore Skenazy

Page 16 – Famous Missed Phone Calls that Changed History – Pete Fitzgerald / Mike Mikula
Page 18 – Dee-Fenses – Don Orehek / Paul Giles
Page 19 – Baseball Stadia for the 90's – Terry Colon
Page 23 – Politically Incorrect Kids Games for the 90's – John Severin / Barry Zeger
Page 26 – Spies and Saboteurs Hit a Television Studio – Mike Ricigliano
Page 28 – Bad Professionals – Randy Jones / Randy Epley
Page 30 – Subscription ad
Page 31 – Angels in the Sapfield – John Severin / Andy Simmons
Page 36 – Lion-Sized Problems Faced by a Lion King – Mike Ricigliano
Page 38 – In the Park – Arnoldo Franchioni
Page 40 – Cracked's "How-To" Video Clearance – Bruce Bolinger / Scott Franklin
Page 42 – Movie Product Tie-Ins – Rurik Tyler / Michael Kaufman
Page 44 – The Simpson – Don Orehek / Greg Grabianski
Page 50 – The Cracked List 10 Toy Ideas That Didn't Make it – Mike Ricigliano / Michael Kaufman
Page 51 – Da Diss Dat Made Chester a Gangster – Alan Kupperberg / Barry Zeger
Back Cover – Forrest Gump Chocolates – Jeff Wong / Tom Grimes

**296, January 1995 (52 pages) ($1.95)**

Cover – We Phase Out Star Trek Generations! – John Severin
Page 2 – *Cracked Monster Party* #27 ad
Page 3 – Contents – Mike Ricigliano
Page 4 – Backwash – Carson Demmans, Randy Epley, Michael Kaufman, Andy Simmons, Rick Sprague, Steve Strangio, Terry Colon, Mike Ricigliano
Page 6 – Star Wreck Degenerations – John Severin / Lou Silverstone
Page 13 – Catchy Jingles for Unpleasant Yet Necessary Products – Bruce Bolinger / Barry Zeger
Page 16 – MFL Hall of Fame – Mike Ricigliano
Page 18 – The Water Skier – Don Orehek / Rob Weske
Page 19 – The NBA Bam Rulebook – Rurik Tyler / Steve Strangio
Page 24 – So You Wanna Be a Blues Singer – Pete Fitzgerald / Lenore Skenazy
Page 26 – Spies and Sabs Hit an Airport Terminal – Mike Ricigliano
Page 28 – Awkward Moments for Limbs to Fall Off (Archie Bunker) – Gray Morrow / Ricky Sprague (1st *Awkward Moments for Limbs to Fall Off*)
Page 29 – Cracked Health and Beauty Ads – John Severin / Steve Strangio

Page 33 – Subscription ad – Rurik Tyler
Page 34 – If America Really was Policeman to the World! – Gary Fields / Dan Birtcher
Page 36 – The Forrest Gump Scrapbook – Randy Jones / Mike Mikula
Page 38 – More Horrors from the Cracked Pen of Don Orehek – Don Orehek
Page 39 – Trojan Horse Designs that Didn't Quite Make it – Terry Colon
Page 43 – Clearly a President Deranged – Walter Brogan / Tony Frank (Lou Silverstone)
Page 50 – The Cracked List 10 Ways to Turn the President Into an Average Joe – Mike Ricigliano / I. Dillon
Page 51 – The Cracked "Lose Weight Permanently" Diet Pyramid – Gary Fields / Brian Glass
Back Cover – Frankenstein's Creature – Bruce Bolinger / Missy Wheathins

**297, March 1995 (52 pages) ($1.95)**
Cover – We Pave Over Street Fighter – John Severin
Page 2 – Country Hits from Death Row – Rurik Tyler / Lenore Skenazy
Page 3 – Contents – Mike Ricigliano
Page 4 – Backwash – Randy Epley, James Giordano, Lou Silverstone, Andy Simmons, Rick Sprague, Steve Strangio, Terry Colon, Mike Ricigliano
Page 6 – Meat-Fighter – John Severin
Page 11 – The Cracked List Top 11 Cracked Magazine New Year's Resolutions for 1995 – Mike Ricigliano
Page 12 – New NFL Rules – Bruce Bolinger
Page 14 – O.J. Industries United Liability Company – Terry Colon
Page 17 – Hollywood Sports Fantasy vs. Everyday Reality – Walter Brogan / Barry Zeger
Page 19 – Jean Claude Van Damme: Serious Actor? – Don Orehek / Rob Weske
Page 20 – A Christmas Poem: The Month Before Christmas! – Gary Fields / Eric Bohlen
Page 22 – When the Power Rangers' Format Spreads to Other TV Shows – John Severin / Greg Grabianski
Page 26 – Spies and Sabs Hit the Toy Store – Mike Ricigliano
Page 28 – Cracked Signs – Pete Fitzgerald / David Boone
Page 30 – Crackedheads – Arnoldo Franchioni
Page 31 – Least Popular Frozen Dinner Coupons – Chris Bartlett / David Boone
Page 34 – If TV is So Influential How Come – Randy Jones / David Connor
Page 36 – Frozen – Walter Brogan / Greg Grabianski

Page 41 – Awkward Moments for Limbs to Fall Off (Quit spraying) – Gray Morrow / Ricky Sprague
Page 42 – Nobody Said Life was Fair – Don Orehek / Lou Silverstone
Page 44 – The Amazingly Clairvoyant Ricig's Predictions for 1995 – Mike Ricigliano
Page 46 – Subscription ad – John Severin (reprint from *Cracked Collectors' Edition* #88)
Back Cover – Fighter Beat Magazine – Walter Brogan

**298, May 1995 (52 pages) ($1.95)**
Cover – Our 2nd Annual Swimsuit Issue! – Don Martin (Last Don Martin work for *Cracked*.)
Page 2 – *Cracked Super* #9 ad
Page 3 – Contents – Mike Ricigliano (red color added)
Page 4 – Backwash – Eric Bohlen, Randy Epley, James Giordano, Greg Grabianski, Todd Jackson, Andy Simmons, Steve Strangio, Terry Colon, Mike Ricigliano
Page 6 – Chunior – Walter Brogan / Lou Silverstone
Page 10 – If Other Magazines Had Swimsuit Issues...Like Cracked – Bruce Bolinger / Barry Zeger
Page 12 – One Day at Richie Rich's House – Don Orehek / Rob Weske
Page 13 – The Winter Exhibition at the Buffalo Museum of Art – John Severin / Mike Ricigliano
Page 16 – Fans Strike Back! – Mike Ricigliano
Page 18 – Retchie Retch – Don Orehek / Lou Silverstone
Page 23 – Cracked Valentine's Day Cards – Randy Jones / Randy Epley (red color added)
Page 25 – How the Gingrinch Stole Congress! – Gary Fields / Lenore Skenazy (red color added)
Page 29 – Subscription ad – Rurik Tyler (red color added)
Page 30 – Spies and Saboteurs Hit a Swimsuit Issue Photo Shoot – Mike Ricigliano
Page 32 – Eternal Penpals Associates – Rob Orzechowski
Page 33 – The Spring Break Problem / Solution Book of Inventions – John Severin / Rob Weske
Page 36 – If TV Cops Worked on the O.J. Case! – Walter Brogan / Lou Silverstone
Page 42 – Dumb and Dumber – Rurik Tyler / Randy Epley
Page 44 – Real Life Nature Tapes – Pete Fitzgerald / Aimee Keillor
Page 46 – The Cracked List 13 Alternative Ways to Execute Someone on a Talk Show – Mike Ricigliano / David Connor
Page 47 – The Santa Clod – John Severin / Andy Simmons (red color added)

Page 51 – I Want to Make Money! – Tom Grimes / William Garvin
Back Cover – Great Moments in Motherhood Arnie and Child – Jeff Wong

**299, July 1995 (52 pages) ($1.95)**
Cover – Dumb and Dumber – John Severin
Page 2 – *Cracked Monster Party* #28 ad
Page 3 – Contents – Mike Ricigliano
Page 4 – Backwash – Terry Colon, Mike Ricigliano
Page 6 – Duh-mb and Duh-mber – Walter Brogan / Lou Silverstone
Page 12 – Unusual Sports Camera Angles – Rurik Tyler / Rob Weske
Page 14 – Awkward Moments for Limbs to Fall Off (first day at a new school) – Gray Morrow / Ricky Sprague
Page 15 – In Yo' Face! – Bruce Bolinger / Barry Zeger
Page 18 – The Chinese Restaurant Zodiac Placement – Randy Jones / Wolfgang Steiner
Page 20 – Rules for Making Soccer Less Boring – John Severin / Rob Weske
Page 24 – Give-Away Items That Would Really Make Money for Businesses – Pete Fitzgerald / Greg Grabianski, Aimee Keillor
Page 26 – Spies and Saboteurs Hit the Academy Awards – Mike Ricigliano
Page 28 – Subscription ad – John Severin (reprint from #68)
Page 29 – Ye Olde Transport Catalogue – Terry Colon
Page 32 – The Story of the Marooned Sailor – Todd James / Henry Demond
Page 34 – One of Those Obnoxious PBS Pledge Drives – Bruce Bolinger / Ricky Sprague
Page 39 – Monster Basketball Association MBA – Mike Ricigliano
Page 42 – Poorly Crafted Commercials – Jeff Wong / Mike Stevenson
Page 44 – Who's the Most Important Person of the 20th Century? – Pete Fitzgerald
Page 45 – Bore Meets World – John Severin / Greg Grabianski
Page 50 – The Cracked List 12 Signs That You're a Dummy – Mike Ricigliano
Page 51 – Magazine, the New Fragrance – Tom Grimes / Greg Grabianski
Back Cover – The Dumb and Dumber Guide to Sure-Fire Dating Success – Randy Jones / Rob Weske

**300, August 1995 (52 pages) ($1.95)**
Cover – We Doom the Brady Bunch – John Severin
Page 2 – *Cracked Collectors' Edition* #103 ad – John Severin (reprint from *Cracked Collectors' Edition* #90)
Page 3 – Contents – Mike Ricigliano
Page 4 – Backwash – Dan Birtcher, Randy Epley, James Giordano, Andy Lamberti, Andy Simmons, Terry Colon, Mike Ricigliano, Jed Vier

Page 6 - The Barfy Bunch - Walter Brogan (John Severin) / Tony Frank (Lou Silverstone) (Strangely, the artwork is credited to Walter Brogan, but it is obviously John Severin.)
Page 12 - What the "M" in MTV Really Stands For - Danny Hellman / Greg Grabianski
Page 14 - Do We Really Need - Walter Brogan / Barry Zeger
Page 16 - Training Your Dog the Morty Stinkmuller Way - Bruce Bolinger / Andy Simmons
Page 20 - Letterboxed Comics!!! - Gary Fields / Michael Gilbert
Page 23 - Dr. Phlogg's Pog Catalog - Mike Ricigliano
Page 26 - Spies and Saboteurs Hit the Indianapolis 500 - Mike Ricigliano
Page 28 - Subscription ad - John Severin (reprint from *Cracked Collectors' Edition* #88)
Page 29 - Doom and Doomer - Rurik Tyler / Todd Jackson, Andy Simmons
Page 34 - Baseball Strike Cards - Don Orehek / Ricky Sprague, Steve Strangio
Page 36 - When Stupidity Takes Over TV - Bruce Bolinger / Lou Silverstone
Page 40 - Where the Money We Spend on Things Really Goes! - Terry Colon / Dan Birtcher
Page 42 - The Newt Fall Season - Sin E (John Severin)
Page 44 - Shut-Ups (Hey, Bro) - Don Orehek / Eric Goldberg, Mark Howard
Page 45 - Loser and Cluck The New Adventures of Stuporman - Walter Brogan / Andrew Osborne
Page 50 - The Cracked List 10 Superheroes and Their Not-So-Super Day Jobs - Mike Ricigliano
Page 51 - Lawn Styles of the Rich and Famous - Terry Colon
Back Cover - John Madden Free Agency Football - Jeff Wong / Missy Wheathins

**301, September 1995 (52 pages) ($1.95)**
Cover - We Riddle Batman…Forever! - John Severin
Page 2 - *Cracked Monster Party* #29 and *Cracked Blockbuster* #9 ad
Page 3 - Contents - Mike Ricigliano
Page 4 - Backwash - Eric Bohlen, Randy Epley, James Giordano, Andy Lamberti, Steve Strangio, Terry Colon, Mike Ricigliano, Jed Vier
Page 6 - Batty, Man, Forever - Walter Brogan / Lou Silverstone
Page 13 - Scientific Principles That Every Kid Knows - Pete Fitzgerald / Darren Johnson
Page 16 - Mighty Moviestar Power Rangers - Mike Ricigliano

Page 18 – Shut-Ups (bird-watching) – Don Orehek / Greg Grabianski
Page 19 – The Cracked Family Travel Map 1995 – Bruce Bolinger / Greg Grabianski
Page 23 – Secrets of Batman Revealed – John Severin / Dan Birtcher
Page 26 – Spies and Saboteurs Hit School Prom – Mike Ricigliano
Page 28 – The Jerk Formerly Known As – Jack Intosh / Rob Lizarraga
Page 30 – Cracked Gallery of Fun Products You Can't Live Without – Bruce Bolinger
Page 31 – SamePro Magazine – Rurik Tyler / Eric Goldberg, Mark Howard, Odd Todd
Page 38 – Subscription ad
Page 39 – Secret Cheers – Randy Jones / Lenore Skenazy
Page 42 – Whyizzit? – Walter Brogan / Rob Weske
Page 44 – More Cracked Fun Products You Can't Live Without – Bruce Bolinger
Page 45 – Gross Under Fire – John Severin / Greg Grabianski
Page 50 – The Cracked List Top 10 New Michael Jordan Abilities (Since His Return to the NBA) – Mike Ricigliano
Page 51 – "B"-Movies of Cartoon Characters! – John Severin / Rob Weske
Back Cover – Cracked's Woman of the Year – Tom Grimes / Barry Zeger

**302, October 1995 (52 pages) ($1.95)**

Cover – We Gump Up the Works On Apollo 13 – John Severin
Page 2 – *Cracked Collectors' Edition* #104 and *Cracked Summer Special* #5 ad
Page 3 – Contents – Mike Ricigliano
Page 4 – Backwash – Randy Epley, James Giordano, Todd Jackson, Andy Simmons, Steve Strangio, Rob Weske, Terry Colon, Mike Ricigliano, Jed Vier
Page 6 – Apollogy 13 – John Severin / Lou Silverstone
Page 12 – Dictionary of Disgusting Phrases – Randy Jones / Barry Zeger, Sue Zeger
Page 14 – Family Mob Values – Arnoldo Franchioni
Page 15 – The Beginner's Guide to Roller Hockey – Mike Ricigliano
Page 20 – Summer Movie Shut-Ups (secret identity of Batman) – Don Orehek / Eric Goldberg, Mark Howard
Page 21 – The Lost Batman Villains Files – Pete Fitzgerald / Rob Weske
Page 24 – No Noose is Good Noose – Rurik Tyler
Page 26 – Spies and Saboteurs Hit the Seashore – Mike Ricigliano
Page 28 – Cracked's Militia Man of the Year – Bruce Bolinger / Lou Silverstone

Page 33 – Summer Camp The Board Game! – John Severin / Rob Weske
Page 36 – New Dance Steps for the Year 2000!!! – Arnoldo Franchioni
Page 38 – Subscription ad – John Severin (reprint from *Cracked Collectors' Edition* #88)
Page 39 – 101 Bad Occupations – Gary Fields / Michael Sachs
Page 43 – Art Dog – Randy Jones
Page 44 – Battyman and Friends Go to the Movies – Walter Brogan / Andy Simmons, Rob Weske
Page 50 – The Cracked List 11 Baseball Promo Nights (To Help Bring the Fans Back to the Ballpark) – Mike Ricigliano
Page 51 – The Flower – Gary Fields / Ricky Sprague
Back Cover – Ito Judge Dread – Jeff Wong

**303, November 1995 (52 pages) ($1.95)**
Cover – Our Violence & Gore-O Issue! – John Severin
Page 2 – The Riddler Gets the Point! – Walter Brogan
Page 3 – Contents – Mike Ricigliano
Page 4 – Backwash – Randy Epley, Todd Jackson, Tim Padovano, Lou Silverstone, Andy Simmons, Terry Colon, Mike Ricigliano, Jed Vier
Page 6 – Moron Kombat – John Severin / Andy Simmons
Page 13 – When History Gets the Disney Treatment – Don Orehek / Rob Weske
Page 16 – Cracked Bell's New Phone Services – Pete Fitzgerald / Eric Goldberg, Mark Howard
Page 18 – The Cracked Guide to Professional Jargon – Randy Jones / Lenore Skenazy
Page 20 – At the Opera – Bruce Bolinger / Greg Grabianski
Page 21 – The Second Time Around for Commercial Pitchmen – Walter Brogan / Eric Goldberg, Mark Howard
Page 24 – Rapper Rap Sheets – Todd James / Barry Zeger
Page 26 – Spies and Saboteurs Hit NFL Training Camp – Mike Ricigliano
Page 28 – Subscription ad – John Severin (reprint from #68)
Page 29 – The Lyons Township Imbecile – Tom Grimes / Greg Grabianski
Page 34 – A Look at Some Less Popular Snow Globes – John Severin / Scott Franklin
Page 36 – They Try Doing Cracked's Extreme Sports – Mike Ricigliano
Page 39 – When the Anti-Violence Trend Takes Over in Hollywood – Rurik Tyler / Vic Bianco (Lou Silverstone)
Page 42 – The Techno-Geek Geeks – Bruce Bolinger / Mike Mikula
Page 44 – Tried Hard With Violence – Walter Brogan / Lou Silverstone

Page 50 – The Cracked List 10 Second String Mortal Kombat II Fighters – Mike Ricigliano
Page 51 – Tragic The Trial – Rurik Tyler
Back Cover – Field & Scream Magazine – Jeff Wong

**304, December 1995 (52 pages) ($1.99)**
Cover – Our Violence & Gore-O Issue! – John Severin
Page 2 – *Cracked Collectors' Edition* #105 ad
Page 3 – Contents – Mike Ricigliano
Page 4 – Backwash – Tom Blumenfeld, Eric Bohlen, James Giordano, Greg Grabianski , Andy Simmons, Ricky Sprague, Terry Colon, Mike Ricigliano, Jed Vier
Page 6 – Daddy-Long Legs-Man – Alan Kupperberg / Andy Simmons
Page 12 – Truth in Adages – Bruce Bolinger / Lenore Skenazy
Page 14 – Sesame Street Then & Sesame Street Now – Walter Brogan / Rob Weske
Page 17 – The Bloody Ryan Smashmouth NFL Playbook – Mike Ricigliano
Page 21 – Creative Casting Ideas for Future Hollywood Remakes and Sequels – Gunnar Johnson
Page 24 – The New Fortified White House – Jim Hunt
Page 26 – Spies and Saboteurs Hit State Fair! – Mike Ricigliano
Page 28 – Shut-Ups (Gordy) – Don Orehek / Eric Goldberg, Mark Howard
Page 29 – Cuteness – John Severin / Lou Silverstone
Page 34 – Cracked's Complete Guide to Piercing – Terry Colon
Page 37 – Subscription ad – John Severin (reprint from *Cracked Collectors' Edition* #88)
Page 38 – Article – Tom Grimes / Ricky Sprague
Page 40 – Doomed III Hell Up in High School – Pete Fitzgerald / Eric Goldberg, Mark Howard
Page 43 – Tennis, Anyone? – J. Kelly
Page 44 – Friendzy – Walter Brogan / Greg Grabianski
Page 50 – The Cracked List 12 Reasons to Buy the New, Totally "Green" Cracked – Mike Ricigliano
Page 51 – Under Siege The Cookbook for the Harried Chef! – Jeff Wong
Back Cover – Breast Milk What a Surprise! – Officer Smythe, LAPD

**305, January 1996 (52 pages) ($1.99)**
Cover – Cracked Stinks Up Ace Ventura II – Jeff Wong
Page 2 – *Cracked Monster Party* #31 ad
Page 3 – Contents – Mike Ricigliano
Page 4 – Backwash – Eric Bohlen, Randy Epley, Greg Grabianski, Andrew Hansen, Andy Simmons, Terry Colon, Mike Ricigliano, Jed Vier

Page 6 – Ass Venturda: When Nature Fails – Walter Brogan / Lou Silverstone
Page 13 – Recipes from Celebrity Cookbooks – Tom Grimes / Ricky Sprague
Page 16 – The Cracked Teacher Creature Chart – Mike Ricigliano
Page 18 – The Unorganized Militia's Top Secret Entrance Exam! – John Severin / Dan Birtcher
Page 21 – Gramps and the Flies – J. Kelly
Page 22 – Superhero Services Guide – Brian Buniak / Steve Strangio
Page 25 – A Cracked Look at the X-Files – Bruce Bolinger / Rob Weske
Page 26 – Spies and Saboteurs Hit the Rock and Roll Hall of Fame – Mike Ricigliano
Page 28 – Cracked Ponders Death – Frank Cummings / Coyote J. Calhoun
Page 30 – Subscription ad
Page 31 – A to Z Chips We'd Really Like to See! – Jim Hunt / Dan Birtcher
Page 34 – Rock and Roll or Pro Wrestling – Bruce Bolinger / Terry Colon
Page 36 – 007's Latest Supercool Spy Gadgets – Pete Fitzgerald / Barry Zeger
Page 39 – Aphorisms from Round the World – Randy Jones / Lenore Skenazy
Page 42 – Urban Obstacle Course – Arnoldo Franchioni
Page 44 – Back to School Shut-Ups (orderly fashion) – Don Orehek / Eric Goldberg, Mark Howard
Page 45 – Schlep by Schlep – John Severin / Greg Grabianski
Page 50 – The Cracked List Top 11 Signs You're in a Bad Tanning Salon – Mike Ricigliano / Tom Carr
Page 51 – The New Crime Magazines – Rurik Tyler / Lenore Skenazy
Back Cover – Won't You Please Help Jerry's Kids? – Walter Brogan / Greg Grabianski

**306, March 1996 (52 pages) ($1.99)**

Cover – We Nuke Toy Story! – John Severin
Page 2 – Meet the McPoops – J. Kelly
Page 3 – Contents – Mike Ricigliano
Page 4 – Backwash – Coyote J. Calhoun, Darren Johnson, Lou Silverstone, Andy Simmons, Ricky Sprague, Terry Colon, Mike Ricigliano, Jed Vier
Page 6 – Oy, Whatta Story – John Severin / Andy Simmons
Page 12 – Reindeer Games – Randy Jones / Michael O'Rourke
Page 14 – Cracked Looks at Schools in the '90's – Walter Brogan / Vic Bianco (Lou Silverstone)

Page 16 – The Sky Divers – Bruce Bolinger / Rob Weske
Page 17 – Bizarre Combos! – Gary Fields / Michael Sacks
Page 21 – Shut-Ups (brand new) – Don Orehek / Randy Epley
Page 22 – What if Every Game Was Like Jumanji? – Pete Fitzgerald / Todd Jackson
Page 24 – Without _________, We'd Never – Frank Cummings / Mike Mikula
Page 26 – Spies and Saboteurs Hit a New Year's Party – Mike Ricigliano
Page 28 – Subscription ad
Page 29 – Winter TV Replacement Shows – John Severin / Scott Franklin
Page 32 – The Case of the Seven Dead Dwarfs – Don Orehek / Barry Zeger
Page 34 – A Cracked Peek at Monday Night Football – Bruce Bolinger / Rob Weske
Page 38 – Cracked Superhero Makeovers – Mike Ricigliano
Page 40 – Why the Angel Sits Atop Our Christmas Tree – Gary Fields / Eric Bohlen
Page 42 – One Day on the Mean Streets – Don Orehek / Rob Weske
Page 43 – 007 – Plasticeye – Walter Brogan / Lou Silverstone
Page 50 – The Cracked List 12 Dysfunctional Toys for Dysfunctional Kids – Mike Ricigliano / William Raschendorfer
Page 51 – Santa: North Pole Ninja – Rurik Tyler
Back Cover – O.J. Crew – Tom Grimes

**307, May 1996 (52 pages) ($1.99)**
Cover – A Dizzying Look at the Mask – John Severin
Page 2 – *Cracked Super* #11 ad
Page 3 – Contents – Mike Ricigliano
Page 4 – Backwash – Eric Bohlen, Randy Epley, James Giordano , Todd Jackson, Andy Simmons, Jeff Wilson, Terry Colon, Mike Ricigliano, Jed Vier
Page 6 – The Dumb & Dumber Mask Meets Ace Ventura – Walter Brogan / Lou Silverstone
Page 11 – One Night in a Cave – Don Orehek / Rob Weske
Page 12 – Resume Embellishment for Kids – Pete Fitzgerald / Patric Abedin
Page 14 – The Official Guide to Snowboarding – John Severin / Greg Grabianski
Page 18 – Specialized "In Case Of..." Boxes for Everyday Situations – Bruce Bolinger / Rob Weske
Page 20 – Other Dead Musicians the Beatles Could Make New Recordings With – Gunnar Johnson

Page 24 – Cracked Lawsuits – Randy Jones / Mark Morelli
Page 26 – Spies and Saboteurs Hit Gym Class – Mike Ricigliano
Page 27 – Free Stuff! (*Cracked* Reader Survey) – Mike Ricigliano
Page 28 – Comic Book vs. Comic Strip Crossover Battles! – Alan Kupperberg / Judd Stomp
Page 33 – Patient Complaints About Witch Doctors – Frank Cummings / Coyote J. Calhoun
Page 34 – Cracked's Plan to Balance the Federal Budget in One Year – Terry Colon
Page 36 – Subscription ad – Rurik Tyler
Page 37 – Monster Hockey League All-Star Game Official Souvenir Program – Mike Ricigliano
Page 40 – Season's Highlights – Mike Ricigliano
Page 42 – Bosnian School-Yard Taunts – Frank Cummings / Coyote J. Calhoun
Page 44 – One Day in the Police Station – Don Orehek / Rob Weske
Page 45 – Hanging With Mr. Pooper – John Severin / Greg Grabianski
Page 50 – The Cracked List America's 10 Deadliest Amusement Park Rides – Mike Ricigliano
Page 51 – McPoop's Best Friend – J. Kelly
Back Cover – Updated Board Games – Gary Fields / Rob Weske

**308, July 1996 (52 pages) ($1.99)**

Cover – We Slash Killer Instinct – John Severin
Page 2 – *Cracked Monster Party* #32 ad
Page 3 – Contents – Mike Ricigliano
Page 4 – Backwash – Dan Birtcher, Eric Bohlen, Randy Epley, Craig Farrell, Michael Sacks, Terry Colon, Mike Ricigliano, Jed Vier
Page 6 – Wrecker Texas Mangler – Walter Brogan / Lou Silverstone
Page 12 – You Certainly Ain't No Computer Genius When – Gary Fields / R.J. Reiley, C.L. Walker
Page 14 – Dinner For Two and Dessert – Don Orehek / Rob Weske
Page 15 – ESPN 3 – Mike Ricigliano
Page 18 – School Prayers Everybody Can Use – Bruce Bolinger / John Fahs
Page 20 – Hybrids of the Human Race: An Evolutionary Study – Pete Fitzgerald / Rob Weske
Page 23 – The Toys Not in Toy Story Catalogue – Brian Buniak / Ricky Sprague
Page 26 – Spies and Saboteurs Hit Spring Training – Mike Ricigliano
Page 28 – New Diseases Caused by Video Games – Frank Cummings / Eric Goldberg, Mark Howard
Page 30 – Subscription ad – John Severin (reprint from *Cracked Collectors' Edition* #88)

Page 31 – Killer Stinky Instruction Booklet – Rurik Tyler / Steve Strangio
Page 36 – Lesser Known Mergers of Small Companies – Terry Colon / Ricky Sprague
Page 38 – Mister and Myth – J. Kelly
Page 39 – Times They Sure Are a Changing – Walter Brogan / Tony Frank (Lou Silverstone)
Page 42 – Words of Wisdumb – Bruce Bolinger
Page 44 – More Crackedheads (trashcanhead, brushhead) – Arnoldo Franchioni
Page 45 – Jumonkey – John Severin / Andy Simmons
Page 50 – The Cracked List 11 Oscar Categories We Don't Hear About – Mike Ricigliano / Todd Jackson
Page 51 – Absolut Drunk – Tom Grimes
Back Cover – Coffin Stickers – Frank Cummings

**309, August 1996 (52 pages) ($1.99)**
Cover – Our Alien Autopsy of 3rd Rock From the Sun – John Severin
Page 2 – Dysfunctional Greeting Cards for All Occasions – Bruce Bolinger / Craig Farrell, Stephanie Fairchild
Page 3 – Contents – Mike Ricigliano
Page 4 – Backwash – R.J. Reiley, Andy Simmons, Mike Stevenson, Rob Weske, Sue Zeger, Terry Colon, Mike Ricigliano, Jed Vier
Page 6 – Tired Crock Far From Fun – John Severin / Greg Grabianski
Page 11 – Ouch – Gary Fields
Page 12 – Sports Relocation Map – Mike Ricigliano
Page 14 – What Really Happens When – Bruce Bolinger / Ed Subitzky
Page 17 – Animated Characters Booted from Disney Movies – Walter Brogan / Joseph Reiter
Page 20 – Guide to Handwriting Analysis – Ricky Sprague
Page 22 – When This Character Crossover Trend Gets Out of Control! – Frank Cummings / Judd Stomp
Page 26 – Spies and Saboteurs Hit Graduation! – Mike Ricigliano
Page 28 – Siskel and Ebert: Away From the Movies – Brian Buniak / Mike Stevenson
Page 30 – The Fitness Fanatic! – Don Orehek / Curato Lo
Page 31 – Rejected Yearbook Pages! – John Severin / Greg Grabianski
Page 36 – Cracked's Real-Life Video Arcade – Arnoldo Franchioni
Page 38 – Burp – Gary Fields
Page 39 – Cracked Sports Awards – Randy Jones / Terry Colon
Page 42 – Commonly Undiagnosed Health Club Injuries – Pete Fitzgerald / Mike Mikula

Page 44 - Broken Eardrums - Walter Brogan / Lou Silverstone
Page 50 - The Cracked List The 11 Least Popular High School Mascots - Mike Ricigliano / Kerry Soper
Page 51 - Subscription ad - John Severin (reprint from #125)
Back Cover - The Western Union Commercial (The Way We'd Like to See it) - Rurik Tyler / Greg Grabianski

**310, September 1996 (52 pages) ($1.99)**
Cover - We Blow Up Mission: Impossible! - John Severin
Page 2 - *Cracked Blockbuster* #10 and *Cracked Monster Party* #33 ad
Page 3 - Contents - Mike Ricigliano
Page 4 - Backwash - Eric Bohlen, Randy Epley, Andy Simmons, Rob Weske, Terry Colon, Mike Ricigliano, Jed Vier
Page 6 - Mish Mosh: Implausible - Walter Brogan / Lou Silverstone
Page 13 - McPoop: The Stinker on the Links - J. Kelly
Page 14 - Mating Calls for the Rich and Lonely - Randy Jones / Lenore Skenazy
Page 16 - Crazy Tony's Novelty and Joke Prom-a-Rama - Mike Ricigliano
Page 18 - Pubescent Olympics World Records - Bruce Bolinger
Page 21 - The Clod Scout Handbook - John Severin / Randy Epley
Page 26 - Spies and Saboteurs Hit a National Park - Mike Ricigliano
Page 28 - Hey, It Was Only 20 Minutes Ago - Todd James / R.J. Reiley, C.L. Walker
Page 30 - Quack - Gary Fields
Page 31 - Booby's World - Walter Brogan / Lou Silverstone
Page 35 - The Swimming Hole - Rurik Tyler / Rob Weske
Page 36 - Dirty Jokes From Other Galaxies - Pete Fitzgerald / Ed Subitzky
Page 38 - Superheroes Fly Over the Hill! - Brian Buniak / Dan Birtcher
Page 41 - Man vs. Shark - Don Orehek / Rob Weske
Page 42 - Gymnastic Events We Won't Be Seeing at the Olympics - Terry Colon / Ricky Sprague
Page 44 - Subscription ad - John Severin (reprint from #44)
Page 45 - Try Hard - Frank Cummings, Walter Brogan / Andy Simmons
Page 50 - The Cracked List The Top 10 Least Mentioned Baseball Stats - Mike Ricigliano
Page 51 - One Day in the Maternity Ward - Bruce Bolinger / Greg Grabianski
Back Cover - Pippi Longfilters - Frank Cummings / John Fahs

**311, October 1996 (52 pages) ($1.99)**

Cover – We Soak in Depends Day – John Severin
Page 2 – *Cracked Collectors' Edition* #108 and *Cracked Summer Special* #6 ad – John Severin (reprint from #88)
Page 3 – Contents – Mike Ricigliano
Page 4 – Backwash – Randy Epley, Andy Lamberti, Andy Simmons, Lou Silverstone, Briley Webb, Terry Colon, Mike Ricigliano, Jed Vier
Page 6 – In Depends Day – Walter Brogan / Lou Silverstone
Page 12 – Great Moments in Aviations – Pete Fitzgerald / Judd Stomp
Page 14 – Cliff's Other Notes – Bruce Bolinger / Dan Birtcher
Page 16 – Summer Movie Shut-Ups (It's Flipper!) – Don Orehek / Eric Goldberg, Mark Howard
Page 17 – Movie Merchandise That Never Quite Caught On! – Frank Cummings / Barry Dutter
Page 20 – McPoop's Dilemma – J. Kelly
Page 21 – The Fanny – John Severin / Greg Grabianski
Page 26 – Spies and Saboteurs Hit a Cruise Ship – Mike Ricigliano
Page 28 – Miranda Rights for Everyday Living – Randy Jones / Ed Subitzky
Page 30 – Lord of the Rings – Pete Fitzgerald / Curtis Roquemore
Page 31 – The Unstable Guy – Frank Cummings / Andy Simmons, Rob Weske
Page 36 – Job Changes Caused by Downsizing – Don Orehek / Fred Sahner
Page 38 – Cracked Animal Ailments – Bruce Bolinger / Eric Goldberg, Mark Howard
Page 40 – The Cracked List The 10 Most Common Olympic Injuries – Mike Ricigliano / Ginger Stomp
Back Cover – The Official Unofficial Guide to the Summer Olympics – Jeff Wong, Gary Fields, Rurik Tyler, Mike Ricigliano / Greg Grabianski
Page 41 – Subscription ad

**312, November 1996 (52 pages) ($1.99)**

Cover – Back to School Issue! – John Severin
Page 2 – *Cracked Monster Party* #34 ad
Page 3 – Contents – Mike Ricigliano
Page 4 – Backwash – Barry Dutter, Randy Epley, Todd Jackson, Andy Simmons, Rob Weske, Terry Colon, Mike Ricigliano, Jed Vier
Page 6 – Twisted – Walter Brogan / Lou Silverstone
Page 12 – Secret Work Rules – Pete Fitzgerald / Fred Sahner
Page 14 – The Lonely Guy – Don Orehek / Rob Weske

Page 15 – Outhouse Rock! – Gary Fields / Barry Zeger
Page 19 – The Appropriate and Inappropriate Hunchback of Notre Dame – Mike Ricigliano (red color added)
Page 22 – The Airline Emergency Card – Rurik Tyler, Alan Kupperberg / Randy Epley
Page 26 – Spies and Sabs Hit the Golf Course – Mike Ricigliano (red color added)
Page 28 – Subscription ad – John Severin (reprint from #160) (red color added)
Page 29 – Cracked's American Hand Signing – Bruce Bolinger
Page 30 – If You're Teacher Corrected Graffiti – Todd James / Barry Dutter (red color added)
Page 32 – The Real Handbook of School Decorum – Frank Cummings / Greg Grabianski (red color added)
Page 36 – Scenes Left on the Cutting Room Floor (and with Good Reason) The Fan – Walter Brogan / Rich Kriegel (Lou Silverstone)
Page 38 – Items on These Pages Are Actual Size – Jim Hunt, Tom Grimes / Rob Lizarraga
Page 41 – Summer Shut-Ups (Woooo…woooo!!) – Don Orehek / Eric Goldberg, Mark Howard
Page 42 – Proper Tantrum-Throwing Techniques for all Sports – The Albert Belle Way – Bruce Bolinger / Andy Simmons
Page 44 – The Butt-y Professor – John Severin / Andy Simmons
Page 50 – The Cracked List 8 Little Known Records for This Summer Olympics – Mike Ricigliano / Ginger Stomp
Page 51 – Graduation Day at Lumberjack Academy – Randy Jones / Greg Grabianski
Back Cover – Now Appearing: Albert Belle – Jeff Wong

**313, December 1996 (52 pages) ($1.99)**

Cover – We Trap Rugrats & Nickelodeon – Walter Brogan
Page 2 – *Cracked Collectors' Edition* #109 ad
Page 3 – Contents – Mike Ricigliano
Page 4 – Backwash – Eric Bohlen, Randy Epley, Andy Lamberti, Andy Simmons, Ricky Sprague, Terry Colon, Mike Ricigliano, Jed Vier
Page 6 – Nickelodious! – Walter Brogan / Greg Grabianski
Page 12 – Tori Smelling's Guide to Chic Acne Style – Pete Fitzgerald / Barry Zeger
Page 14 – Student Council Campaign Trail – Bruce Bolinger / Todd Jackson
Page 17 – Extreme Gym Class – Mike Ricigliano
Page 20 – Political Shut-Ups (not enough to go around) – Don Orehek / Eric Goldberg, Mark Howard

Page 21 – Cracked Cineplex – John Severin / Rob Weske
Page 25 – Know Your Boogers – J. Kelly
Page 26 – Spies and Saboteurs Hit the Zoo – Mike Ricigliano
Page 28 – Dog Greet Dog Greeting Cards – Bruce Bolinger / Lenore Skenazy
Page 30 – Subscription ad – John Severin (reprint from *Cracked Collectors' Edition* #88)
Page 31 – A Cracked Investigative Report Smoking – Walter Brogan / Lou Silverstone
Page 36 – Madonna's Material Tot Catalogue – Earl Whooton / Lenore Skenazy
Page 38 – The Peep Show – Arnoldo Franchioni / Greg Grabianski
Page 39 – Puberty The Board Game – Frank Cummings / Rob Weske
Page 42 – C.R.A.P, Cracked Readers Answer Poll – Gary Fields / Joseph O'Brien
Page 44 – Erase Her – John Severin / Tony Frank (Lou Silverstone)
Page 50 – The Cracked List Top 10 Unofficial Police Signals – Mike Ricigliano / Wolfgang Steiner
Page 51 – Make Yourself a Halloween Costume – Gary Fields / Mike Lotter
Back Cover – Dole and Clinton Vie for the Youth Vote – Jeff Wong

**314, January 1997 (52 pages) ($1.99)**
Cover – We Assimilate Star Trek First Contact – John Severin
Page 2 – *Cracked Monster Party* #35 ad – Walter Brogan
Page 3 – Contents – Mike Ricigliano
Page 4 – Backwash – Eric Bohlen, Andy Simmons, Ricky Sprague, Steve Strangio, Terry Colon, Mike Ricigliano, Jed Vier
Page 6 – Star Drek: First Contact – Walter Brogan / Lou Silverstone
Insert – Subscription Card – Walter Brogan / Mike Ricigliano
Page 12 – Surgery for Slackers – Pete Fitzgerald / Mark Morelli
Page 14 – McPoop's New Fall Sneezin' – J. Kelly
Page 15 – Cracked's Holiday Travel Guide – Bruce Bolinger / Greg Grabianski
Page 19 – The Shaqarena – Rurik Tyler / Barry Zeger
Page 20 – Rejected Kids Meals – John Severin / Rob Weske
Page 23 – Cool School Dude Duds Fashions – Walter Brogan / Barry Zeger, Greg Grabianski Page 26 – Spies and Sabs Hit a High School Science Fair – Mike Ricigliano
Page 28 – For Better Orca Worse – Don Orehek / Mike Lotter
Page 29 – Ultimate Bleeding – Rurik Tyler / Steve Strangio
Page 34 – Hey, You Wanted Front Row So Don't Complain If – Frank Cummings / Mike Lotter

Page 36 - The Stupid Idiot's Guide to Watching Football - Mike Ricigliano
Page 40 - Police Line-Ups Around the World (and Beyond) - Terry Colon
Page 42 - Subscription ad
Insert - Subscription Card - Walter Brogan / Mike Ricigliano
Page 43 - Bungled All the Way - John Severin / Andy Simmons, Lou Silverstone
Page 50 - The Cracked List Top 9 Mysteries That Don't Need Investigating On the X-Files - Mike Ricigliano
Page 51 - Feece's Miniatures ad - Frank Cummings
Back Cover - Space Jam - Tom Grimes, Gary Fields

**315, March 1997 (52 pages) ($1.99)**
Cover - Beavis & Butt-Head Do Hollywood! - Walter Brogan
Page 2 - Cartoon Makeovers - Gary Fields / Mike Ricigliano
Insert - Subscription Card - John Severin / Mike Ricigliano
Page 3 - Contents - Mike Ricigliano
Page 4 - Backwash - Eric Bohlen, Jenny Jordan, Andy Lamberti, Mike Lotter, Terry Colon, Mike Ricigliano, Jed Vier
Page 6 - Beaver & Putz-Head Dupe America - Walter Brogan / Judd Stomp
Page 12 - Other Restaurant Eating Sections - John Severin / Ginger Stomp
Page 14 - Catch of the Day - Don Orehek / Fred Curatolo
Page 15 - Cracked's Extreme Board Games - Mike Ricigliano
Page 18 - The Cruella De Vile Disobedience School - Frank Cummings / Andy Simmons
Page 20 - How to Draw Superhero Comic Books - Alan Kupperberg / Greg Grabianski, Ricky Sprague
Page 24 - Unique Suicide Techniques - Oskar Blotta / Luciano Blotta
Page 26 - Spies and Sabs Hit Santa's Workshop - Mike Ricigliano
Page 28 - Subscription ad - John Severin (reprint from #44)
Page 29 - The Officer Dingleberry Method of Preventing Carjacking - Bruce Bolinger / Ricky Sprague
Page 32 - Cracked Predicts - Pete Fitzgerald / Barry Dutter
Page 34 - Burp - Gary Fields
Page 35 - Updating Classic Toys for the 90's - Tom Grimes, Rurik Tyler / Barry Dutter
Page 38 - The Xmas Eye Exam - Arnoldo Franchioni
Page 39 - L.L. Dweeb Technowear - Kerry Soper
Page 42 - The Dennis Rodman Assertiveness Training Course - Walter Brogan / Ricky Sprague

Page 44 – Mars Bars Attacks – John Severin / Lou Silverstone
Page 50 – The Cracked List 10 Daytime TV Talk Show Guests They'll Soon Be Resorting To – Mike Ricigliano / Dan Birtcher
Insert – Subscription Card – Walter Brogan / Mike Ricigliano
Page 51 – Crapbisco Christmas Cookies – Frank Cummings / Rob Weske
Back Cover – The Special Collectors Sports Cup Series – Rurik Tyler, Tom Grimes

**316, May 1997 (52 pages) ($1.99)**
Cover – We Slime Goosebumps – John Severin
Page 2 – *Cracked Super* #13 ad
Insert – Subscription Card – John Severin / Mike Ricigliano
Page 3 – Contents – Mike Ricigliano
Page 4 – Backwash – Barry Dutter, Randy Epley, Andy Lamberti, Ellen Lynch, Ricky Sprague, Steve Strangio, Terry Colon, Mike Ricigliano, Jed Vier
Page 6 – Goosedumps – John Severin / Greg Grabianski
Page 12 – When Women Act Like Men – Randy Jones / Ginger Stomp
Page 14 – Cracked Monster Swimsuit Issue – Mike Ricigliano
Page 18 – Bad Hobbies – Gary Fields / Michael Sacks
Page 19 – Beverly Hills Sumo – Bruce Bolinger
Page 22 – Hi-Tech High: The High School of the Future – John Severin / Rob Weske
Page 26 – Spies and Sabs Hit the Star Wars Bar – Mike Ricigliano
Page 28 – Word for Windows – The '97 Version – Terry Colon / John Fahs
Page 30 – Subscription ad – John Severin (reprint from *Cracked Collectors' Edition* #88)
Page 31 – Textbooks That Today's Kids Can Understand – Earl Whooton / Greg Grabianski
Page 36 – Soccer Time? – Arnoldo Franchioni
Page 38 – One Afternoon in the Jungle – Don Orehek / E. Vosquez
Page 39 – The True Supermodel Workout Video – Frank Cummings / Greg Grabianski
Page 42 – What's Going on in Your Dog's Tiny, Little Peabrain When He Does These Silly Things He Does? – Bruce Bolinger / Ricky Sprague
Page 44 – Sin City – Walter Brogan / Lou Silverstone
Page 50 – The Cracked List 10 Versions of "Goosebumps" That Would Be An Improvement – Mike Ricigliano
Insert – Subscription Card – John Severin / Mike Ricigliano
Page 51 – The Man and the Strange Bug – Oskar Blotta
Back Cover – Valentine's Day Cards – Randy Jones

**317, July 1997 (52 pages) ($1.99)**

Cover – We Shoot Down Sabrina the Teenage Witch – John Severin
Page 2 – *Cracked Monster Party* #36 ad – John Severin (reprint from #199)
Page 3 – Contents – Mike Ricigliano
Page 4 – Backwash – Andy Lamberti, Ellen Lynch, Ricky Sprague, Briley Webb, Terry Colon, Mike Ricigliano, Jed Vier
Page 6 – Duhbrina the Teenage Witch – Walter Brogan / Lou Silverstone
Page 11 – The Michael Jackson Baby Book – Rurik Tyler / Clandy Silverson
Page 14 – More Baseball Rule Changes – Mike Ricigliano
Page 16 – Dinner Plans at Sea – Don Orehek / Rob Weske
Page 17 – Cracked's Driving Exam – Pete Fitzgerald / Bob Brabant
Page 21 – Which is the Bigger Disaster – Bruce Bolinger / Greg Grabianski
Page 24 – Brutally Honest Fortune Cookies – Randy Jones / Lenore Skenazy
Page 26 – Spies and Sabs Hit Spring Break! – Mike Ricigliano
Page 28 – Subscription ad
Page 29 – The Real Private Farts – Walter Brogan / Lou Silverstone
Page 34 – The New Cracked School – Arnoldo Franchioni
Page 36 – The Natural Examineder – Don Orehek / Eric Bohlen
Page 38 – Internet Sites That Hardly Anybody Visits – Frank Cummings / Greg Grabianski
Page 42 – Rednecks Or Poor White Trash? – Bruce Bolinger / Joseph Reiter
Page 44 – More Bad Hobbies – Gary Fields / Michael Sacks
Page 45 – Lawyer, Lawyer – Nireves (John Severin)
Page 50 – The Cracked List 10 Really Bad Class Field Trips – Mike Ricigliano
Page 51 – The Tickle Me Elmo Rip-Offs – Frank Cummings
Back Cover – Lois Discovers a Flaw in Superman's New Powers – Alan Kupperberg

**318, August 1997 (52 pages) ($1.99)**

Cover – We Expose the X-Files! – Jeff Wong
Page 2 – *Cracked Collectors' Edition* #111 and *Cracked Blockbuster* #11 ad
Page 3 – Contents – Mike Ricigliano
Page 4 – Backwash – Randy Epley, Todd Jackson, Ellen Lynch, Steve Strangio, Briley Webb, Terry Colon, Mike Ricigliano, Jed Vier
Page 6 – The Ecchhh Files – Walter Brogan / Lou Silverstone
Page 12 – The Rules for Losers! – Pete Fitzgerald / Ricky Sprague

Page 14 – Planet Hollywood Once They Become Desperate for Memorabilia – Bruce Bolinger / Greg Grabianski
Page 16 – Cracked's Guide to Hockey Equipment – John Severin / Dan Birtcher
Page 21 – The Fishing Hole – Don Orehek / Rob Weske
Page 22 – The Cracked List of Lies – Donald Hornbeck
Page 25 – Bowling Pinhead – Arnoldo Franchioni / Ricky Sprague
Page 26 – Spies and Sabs Hit Miniature Golf – Mike Ricigliano
Page 28 – One Day At the Cinema – Don Orehek / Rob Weske
Page 29 – Clodsby – John Severin / Greg Grabianski
Page 34 – The Howard Stern Family Tree – Mike Ricigliano
Page 36 – Scientific Phenomena Concerning Warner Brothers Cartoons 101 – Walter Brogan / Barry Zeger
Page 39 – Roller Coaster Mania – Terry Colon
Page 42 – A Cracked Look at Little League – Rob Orzechowski
Page 44 – The Cracked List 11 Ways Celebrities Know Their Star is Fading – Mike Ricigliano / Barry Dutter
Page 45 – Subscription ad – John Severin (reprint from #44)
Back Cover – Sp-yawn – Alan Kupperberg / Barry Zeger

**319, September 1997 (52 pages) ($1.99)**
Cover – The Lost Hurl Jurasick Puke – John Severin
Page 2 – True Tales of Romantic Love – Todd James / Kit Lively
Page 3 – Contents – Mike Ricigliano
Page 4 – Backwash – Ellen Lynch, Andy Lamberti, Terry Colon, Mike Ricigliano, Jed Vier
Page 6 – The Loot World Jurassick Park – John Severin / Lou Silverstone
Page 12 – Self-Hurt Books – Randy Jones / Oliver Fultz
Page 14 – The Wishing Well – Bruce Bolinger / Kit Lively
Page 15 – Cloning: Cloning: How How I I Made Made Miss Miss Dolly Dolly – Ron Barrett
Page 18 – Famous Last Words – Walter Brogan / Barry Zeger
Page 20 – Morphing – Donald Hornbeck
Page 23 – The Whining – Rurik Tyler / Rich Kriegel (Lou Silverstone)
Page 26 – Spies and Sabs Hit the Museum of Natural History – Mike Ricigliano
Page 28 – The Moose Hunters – Don Orehek / Rob Weske
Page 29 – Professor Swizzlestik's Guide to Getting At Least a "D" on Your Term Paper – Tom Grimes / August Swizzlestik
Page 32 – Phone Menus We'd Rather Not Hear – Pete Fitzgerald / Mike Lotter
Page 34 – The Drone Corny Show – Walter Brogan / Greg Grabianski
Page 39 – Clone Zone – Mike Ricigliano

Page 42 – Unpopular Advertisements – Rurik Tyler / David Conner
Page 44 – Subscription ad – John Severin (reprint from #285)
Page 45 – Jumble 2 Jumble – Frank Cummings / Andy Simmons
Page 50 – The Cracked List 12 Obnoxious Things to Do During Graduation – Mike Ricigliano / Todd Jackson
Page 51 – Customized Checks for Criminals! – John Severin / Ricky Sprague
Back Cover – In a Stunning Upset, The Raptors Devour the Bulls – Jeff Wong

**320, October 1997 (52 pages) ($1.99)**

Cover – Chillin' With B-B-Batman & R-R-Robin – John Severin
Page 2 – *Cracked Monster Party* #37 ad
Page 3 – Contents – Mike Ricigliano
Page 4 – Backwash – Carson Demmans, Randy Epley, Kit Lively, Ellen Lynch, Bob Rafal, Terry Colon, Mike Ricigliano, Jed Vier
Page 6 – Barfman & Slobbin' – Walter Brogan / Andy Simmons
Page 13 – A Gypsy's Tale – Don Orehek / Kit Lively
Page 14 – Cracked Visits a Modern Hospital – Frank Cummings / Fred Sahner
Page 16 – Leech Lake Camp – Ron Barrett
Page 20 – Mother Goosebumps – Gary Fields / Dan Birtcher
Page 23 – The Cracked Guide to Beanie Babies – Rurik Tyler / Greg Grabianski
Page 26 – Spies and Saboteurs Hit Gotham City – Mike Ricigliano
Page 28 – Subscription ad – Rurik Tyler
Page 29 – The Worst Real-Life TV Show Producer – Bruce Bolinger / Todd Jackson
Page 33 – Tanks, But No Tanks – Terry Colon
Page 36 – A Cracked Look at Soccer Moms – Arnoldo Franchioni / Rob Weske
Page 38 – Sandy Shortt's Basics of Beach Volleyball – Mike Ricigliano / Scott Jackson
Page 42 – If Hercules Had Been Born in America – Gary Fields / Dan Birtcher
Page 44 – Dog's Best Friend – Don Orehek / Kit Lively
Page 45 – Aycaramba – John Severin / Lou Silverstone
Page 50 – The Cracked List Signs Your Folks Hate Your Guts! – Mike Ricigliano / Andy Lamberti
Page 51 – A Stork's Tale – Gary Fields / Kit Lively
Back Cover – Wacdonalds' Unhappy Meals Featuring Teenie Meanie Babies – Rurik Tyler / Greg Grabianski

**321, November 1997 (52 pages) ($1.99)**

Cover – We Tee Off On Tiger Woods! – Jeff Wong
Page 2 – *Cracked Super* #14 ad
Page 3 – Contents – Mike Ricigliano
Page 4 – Backwash – Kit Lively, Ellen Lynch, Ricky Sprague, Terry Colon, Mike Ricigliano, Jed Vier
Page 6 – Air Farce One – Walter Brogan / Lou Silverstone
Page 12 – Occupational Hazard – Randy Jones / Mike Lotter
Page 14 – Drive-Thru Dunderhead – Gary Fields / Ricky Sprague
Page 15 – New York Yecchees Game Day Program and Scorecard – Mike Ricigliano
Page 19 – Batgirl's Super Rules – Pete Fitzgerald / Todd Jackson
Page 22 – Other Celebrity Name Brand Products – Sven Forkbeard (Gunnar Johnson)
Page 26 – Spies and Sabs Hit An Alien Attack – Mike Ricigliano
Page 28 – Subscription ad – John Severin (reprint from *Cracked Collectors' Edition* #88)
Page 29 – The Tiger Woods Phenomenon – Frank Cummings / Ricky Sprague
Page 34 – Cracked Clip (Vice Girls) – Cliff Mott / Barry Zeger (1st *Cracked Clip*)
Page 36 – Other Mythological Creatures Left Out of Hercules – Pete Fitzgerald / Steve Strangio
Page 38 – Diary of a Tamgotchi Owner – Bruce Bolinger / Mike Lotter
Page 42 – Polite Ways Animals Break-Up! – Walter Brogan / Lenore Skenazy
Page 44 – Cracked Fractured History D-Day The Invasion of Normandy – Don Orehek / Vic Bianco (Lou Silverstone)
Page 45 – Die Hard 27: The Fifth Element – John Severin / Andy Simmons
Page 50 – The Cracked List 11 Failed Baby Products – Mike Ricigliano / Thomas Williams
Page 51 – The Little Miss Fetus Beauty Pageant – Randy Jones / Ginger Stomp
Back Cover – Cracked's Video Blow Out Sale! – Rurik Tyler

**322, December 1997 (52 pages) ($1.99)**

Cover – Holy Men in Black – John Severin
Page 2 – *Cracked Collectors' Edition* #113 ad – Jeff Wong
Page 3 – Contents – Mike Ricigliano
Page 4 – Backwash – Eric Bohlen, Katey Dash, Randy Epley, Kit Lively, Terry Colon, Mike Ricigliano, Jed Vier
Page 6 – Con Job – Walter Brogan / Lou Silverstone

Page 13 – Nature Calls – Oskar Blotta / Luciano Blotta
Page 14 – Caveman Technology Advances! – John Severin / Ricky Sprague
Page 16 – Everything You Wanted to Know About Cocaine But Were Too Stupid to Ask – Bruce Bolinger / Lou Silverstone
Page 17 – Burnout High's After-School Activities – Mike Ricigliano
Page 20 – Somber Toddler's Book Club – Rurik Tyler / Lenore Skenazy, Oliver Fultz
Page 22 – Men in Black Manual – Frank Cummings / Andy Simmons
Page 26 – Spies and Sabs Hit a Family Amusement Center – Mike Ricigliano
Page 28 – The Upside and Downside of Future Inventions – Gary Fields / Dan Fiorella
Page 30 – Subscription ad – Walter Brogan
Page 31 – Field & Streaming Blood Magazine – John Severin / Greg Grabianski
Page 37 – Another Gypsy's Tale – Don Orehek / Carson Demmans
Page 38 – You Think You Got it Bad? – Oskar Blotta / Luciano Blotta
Page 40 – When Gay-Themed TV Shows Get Completely Out of Hand – Harold Bluetooth (Gunnar Johnson)
Page 44 – Why It's a Bad Idea to Hire Zombie Workers – Todd James / Kit Lively
Page 45 – Boffy the Vampy Slayer – Walter Brogan / Greg Grabianski
Page 50 – The Cracked List Top 11 New Pilots That Didn't Make the New Fall Schedule – Mike Ricigliano
Page 51 – Make Yourself a Cracked Halloween Costume – Bruce Bolinger / Mike Lotter
Back Cover – Cracked Clip (Handsome) Frank Cummings / Barry Zeger

**323, January 1998 (52 pages) ($1.99)**

Cover – We Operate on E.R.! Alien Regurgitation – Frank Cummings, Tom Grimes
Page 2 – *Cracked Monster Party* #38 ad – Walter Brogan
Page 3 – Contents – Mike Ricigliano
Page 4 – Backwash – Randy Epley, Eric Goldberg, Greg Grabianski, Mark Howard, Kit Lively, Ellen Lynch, Terry Colon
Page 6 – Alien Repetition – John Severin / Lou Silverstone
Page 12 – May I Help You? – Randy Jones / Mike Lotter
Page 14 – Law Ads Found in the Yellow Pages – Alan Kupperberg / Randy Epley
Page 16 – One Day in Geppetto's Yard – Gary Fields / J. Enrique Vasquez

Page 17 – Sylvester P. Smythe – The Man, The Mystery, The Janitor – Mike Ricigliano
Page 20 – A Cracked Look at the Pyramids – Bruce Bolinger / Rob Weske
Page 24 – How Referrees Signal a Penalty – Tom Grimes / Dan Birtcher
Page 26 – Spies and Sabs Hit a Pep Rally – Mike Ricigliano
Page 28 – Subscription ad
Page 29 – If the Pilgrims Landed in America Today – Frank Cummings / Andy Simmons
Page 33 – A Visit to the Doctor – Oskar Blotta / Luciano Blotta
Page 34 – Shoot / Don't Shoot!!! – Pete Fitzgerald / Mike Lotter
Page 36 – If Advertisers Rewrote Great Works of Literature – John Severin / John Samony
Page 38 – The Flier Sneakers – Don Orehek / Rob Weske
Page 39 – Stalag High: School for Brats – Bruce Bolinger / Andy Simmons
Page 42 – Upside / Downside of Movie Going – Todd James / Dan Fiorella
Page 44 – D'er – Walter Brogan / Steve Strangio, Eric Goldberg, Mark Howard
Page 50 – The Cracked List 10 Things That Don't Mix – Mike Ricigliano
Page 51 – Fed X-Men – John Severin
Back Cover – Fix-O-Dent and Forget It! – Rurik Tyler / Mike Lotter

**324, March 1998 (52 pages) ($1.99)**

Cover – Beaver and Butt-Face Do the Real Real World We Turn Off Our MTV – Walter Brogan, Associated Press
Page 2 – Be All You Can Be. You Can Do it in the Army – John Severin
Page 3 – Contents – Mike Ricigliano
Page 4 – Backwash – Eric Bohlen, Katey Dash, Barry Dutter, Greg Grabianski, Mike Lotter, Rob Weske, Terry Colon
Page 6 – Cracked Takes a Look at MTV! – Frank Cummings / Judd Stomp, Katey Dash
Page 11 – Movie Ideas Before They Got Them Right! – Randy Jones / Dan Fiorella
Page 14 – Rudolph Rednose, the Reindeer – Walter Brogan / Lou Silverstone
Page 16 – Aggressive Advertising – Don Orehek / Mike Lotter
Page 17 – Reality-Based Toys – Rurik Tyler, Tom Grimes / R.J. Reiley, C.L. Walker, Joseph O'Brien
Page 21 – A Charlie Brown Politically Correct Holiday Season – Walter Brogan / Mike Lotter
Page 22 – Cracked Clip "You'll Be Buying it" by Fluff Lady – Todd James / Mark Gomez
Page 23 – Sports World Tamagotchis – Pete Fitzgerald / Dan Birtcher

Page 26 – Spies and Sabs Hit a Christmas Tree Farm – Mike Ricigliano
Page 28 – The Little Boy Drummer – Walter Brogan / Rich Kriegel (Lou Silverstone)
Page 29 – Chelsea Clinton's Freshman Notebook – Kerry Soper / Todd Jackson, Jason Eaton, Ian Lendler, Chris Boznos (Excerpt from book)
Page 33 – If Beavis and Butt-Head Were in Classic Christmas Films – Gary Fields / Judd Stomp
Page 36 – Cracked's 1998 Calendar Concepts That Didn't Quite Make it – Mike Ricigliano
Page 38 – A Christmas Tale – Don Orehek / Rob Weske
Page 39 – Diary of the Last Draft Pick – Bruce Bolinger / Todd Jackson
Page 42 – How the Grinch Downsized Christmas – Walter Brogan / Mike Lotter
Page 44 – Gourde O' Th' Bungle – John Severin / Lou Silverstone
Page 50 – The Cracked List Top 10 Predictions for 1998 – Mike Ricigliano
Page 51 – Christmas in Bosnia – Jeff Wong
Back Cover – The MIR Space Station! – Rurik Tyler, Tom Grimes

**325, May 1998 (52 pages) ($1.99)**

Cover – Celebrating 40 Titannically Disastrous Years! – John Severin
Page 2 – Cracked Winter Olympics Pins – Mike Ricigliano
Page 3 – Contents – Mike Ricigliano
Page 4 – Backwash – Katey Dash, Randy Epley, Barry Dutter, Greg Grabianski, Mike Lotter, Rob Weske, Terry Colon, Mike Ricigliano, Jed Vier
Page 6 – Tipanic! – John Severin / Andy Simmons
Page 12 – Tell Us Sylvester's Middle Name and Win $1,000,000! –Mike Ricigliano, John Severin (I actually won this contest and received one of the 40 *Cracked* flying saucers!)
Page 14 – Cracked Clip Jamiroquack Video Insanity – Cliff Mott / Barry Zeger
Page 15 – Not-So-Superhero Temps – Pete Fitzgerald / Jill Hamilton
Page 18 – Fashion and Cosmetic Make-Overs for the Animal Kingdom – Gunnar Johnson
Page 23 – Salesman's Tale – Don Orehek / Carson Demmans
Page 24 – Other Things That Make You Scream – Pete Fitzgerald / Barry Zeger
Page 26 – Spies and Sabs Hit the Nagano, Japan Winter Olympics – Mike Ricigliano
Page 28 – Subscription ad – John Severin (reprint from *Cracked Collectors' Edition* #97)

Page 29 – Oh, Henry & His Six Wives the Cartoon – Walter Brogan / Lou Silverstone
Page 34 – Embarrassing White House Documents – Bruce Bolinger / Ricky Sprague
Page 36 – A Look Back at 40 Years of Cracked with Founding Editor Morty Shlub – Frank Cummings / Andy Simmons
Page 40 – Mob Family Values – Arnoldo Franchioni
Page 41 – Cracked Collectors Corner – John Severin / Ricky Sprague
Page 44 – True Morons Never Die – Walter Brogan / Lou Silverstone
Page 50 – The Cracked List 11 Exhibition Sports That Didn't Quite Make the 1998 Winter Olympics – Mike Ricigliano / Rob Weske
Page 51 – *Cracked Collectors' Edition* #114 ad
Back Cover – Sports Illustrated for Klods Annual Swimsuit Edition – Jeff Wong

**326, July 1998 (52 pages) ($1.99)**
Cover – We 'Toon Out! – Nireves (John Severin)
Page 2 – *Cracked Super* #15 ad
Page 3 – Contents – Mike Ricigliano
Page 4 – Backwash – Katey Dash, Randy Epley, Dan Fiorella, Ricky Sprague, Terry Colon, Jay Sharkey
Page 6 – King of the Ill – Frank Cummings / Todd Jackson
Page 11 – Cracked Clip Pariah Scary "Money" – Cliff Mott / Barry Zeger
Page 12 – The Newest Baseball Expansion Teams – Bruce Bolinger / Mike Morse
Page 14 – The Clone Classifieds – Pete Fitzgerald / R.J. Reiley, C.L. Walker
Page 16 – A TV Commercial We'd Pay to See (American Express) – Walter Brogan / Tony Frank (Lou Silverstone)
Page 17 – If the Simpsons Starred in a TV Drama – Don Orehek / Lou Silverstone, Andy Simmons, Todd Jackson
Page 20 – Joe Camel Replacement Ads Sure to Keep Kids Smoking! – John Severin / Dan Birtcher
Page 24 – Totally Rad Stickers for Senior Citizens – Todd James / R.J. Reiley, C.L. Walker
Page 26 – Spies and Sabs Hit the Westminster Dog Show – Mike Ricigliano
Page 28 – Subscription ad – John Severin (reprint from *Cracked Collectors' Edition* #88)
Page 29 – Shlubber – Walter Brogan / Lou Silverstone
Page 35 – Shut-Ups (This is Amazing) – Don Orehek / Joseph O'Brien
Page 36 – "Vintage" Stores – Bruce Bolinger / Chris Gennusa

Page 38 – The Latrell Sprewell Sports Camp for Hotheads – Mike Ricigliano
Page 42 – Cracked Paper Airlines! – Rurik Tyler / Eb Subitzky
Page 45 – Mouth Park – Gary Fields / Greg Grabianski
Page 50 – The Cracked List 10 Promises We'd Like to See the Promise-Keepers Keep – Mike Ricigliano / Kerry Jones
Page 51 – Sing & Snore Ernie Rip-Offs – Frank Cummings / Greg Grabianski
Back Cover – Mr. Beanie Babies – Gunnar Johnson / Sherry Johnson

**327, August 1998 (52 pages) ($1.99)**
Cover – The End of Seinfeld! – Walter Brogan
Page 2 – *Cracked Collectors' Edition* #115 ad
Page 3 – Contents – Mike Ricigliano
Page 4 – Backwash – Katey Dash, Dan Fiorella, Ricky Sprague, Thomas Williams, Terry Colon, Jay Sharkey
Page 6 – Seinfeld Retrospective – Walter Brogan / Lou Silverstone
Page 12 – I'm Horny Bill – Gary Fields / Sue Zeger, Barry Zeger
Page 14 – De-Evolutionary Charts – Randy Jones / Mike Morse
Page 17 – Garbagefellas – Don Orehek / Mike Lotter
Page 18 – How Seinfeld Should End – Gunnar Johnson
Page 20 – The Cracked Guide to Photography – John Severin / Mike Lotter
Page 24 – Spell it Out! – Frank Cummings / Nick Beef
Page 26 – Spies and Sabs Hit a Mall Food Court – Mike Ricigliano
Page 28 – Subscription ad – John Severin (reprint from #44)
Page 29 – Twisted Kid's Meal Toys – Gregg Theakston / Phil Rockstone
Page 32 – Real-Life Plop-Up Video – John Severin / Mike Lotter
Page 34 – Cracked's Spring Fashion Preview – Mike Ricigliano
Page 37 – The Cracked Guide to Disney World 2000 – Bruce Bolinger / Dan Birtcher
Page 41 – True Tales of Romantic Love – Todd James / Kit Lively
Page 42 – Super Stores We Really Don't Need! – Gary Fields / R.J. Riley, C.L. Walker
Page 44 – Losers in Space – John Severin / Andy Simmons
Page 50 – The Cracked List Upcoming Pro Sports Public Relations Events – Mike Ricigliano / Dennis Spurling
Page 51 – The Anatomy of a Slob – J. Kelly
Back Cover – I Want You for White House Intern – Jeff Wong

**328, September 1998 (52 pages) ($1.99)**
Cover – We Play Footsie with Godzilla – Rurik Tyler
Page 2 – *Cracked Blockbuster* #12 ad
Page 3 – Contents – Mike Ricigliano

Page 4 – Backwash – Katey Dash, Ricky Sprague, Rob Weske, Thomas Williams, Terry Colon
Page 6 – Clodzilla – Walter Brogan / Lou Silverstone
Page 12 – The X-Files Paranoia Quiz – Pete Fitzgerald / David Standish, Willie Standish
Page 14 – The Fetic Pharaoh – Don Orehek / John Schmitz
Page 15 – History's Least Successful Proto Humans – Terry Colon
Page 18 – If Ordinary People Acted Like Professional Athletes – Tom Grimes / Andy Simmons
Page 20 – The Ice Cream Parlor – Don Orehek / Kit Lively
Page 21 – What Makes You Think You Can Learn Bowling! – John Severin / Ricky Sprague
Page 25 – Still More Bad Hobbies – Gary Fields / Michael Sacks
Page 26 – Spies and Sabs Hit a State-of-the-Art Movieplex – Mike Ricigliano
Page 28 – Subscription ad – John Severin (reprint from #26)
Page 29 – Modern Immaturity Magazine – Gunnar Johnson
Page 34 – It's Going to Be a Bad Prom When – Randy Jones / Joseph O'Brien
Page 36 – Cracked Rules for Bad Manners – Bruce Bolinger / Stu Vivetchek, Ricky Sprague
Page 40 – Buffy the Vampire Slayer's Dating Tips – Walter Brogan / Mike Morse
Page 42 – A Cracked Look at a Fast-Food Restaurant – Frank Cummings / Rob Weske
Page 44 – The Winner of the Sylvester Middle Name Contest – Mike Ricigliano, John Severin (The winning entry was "Phooey.")
Page 45 – Tortured By An Angel – John Severin / Greg Grabianski
Page 50 – The Cracked List Top 9 Dysfunctional Family Toys – Mike Ricigliano / Andy Lamberti
Page 51 – Hate Songs – Tom Grimes / Randy Epley
Back Cover – A Line Up at N.Y.P.D. Blue – Jeff Wong

**329, October 1998 (52 pages) ($1.99)**

Cover – Leonardo DeCapitated – Jeff Wong
Page 2 – *Cracked Collectors' Edition* #116 and *Cracked Summer Special* #8 ad – John Severin (reprint from #86)
Page 3 – Contents – Mike Ricigliano
Page 4 – Backwash – Dan Fiorella, Gunnar Johnson, Ricky Sprague, David Standish, Terry Colon
Page 6 – Doctor Poolittle – John Severin /Andy Simmons
Page 11 – The Cracked 4-Step Self-Motivation Tape – Don Orehek / Mike Lotter

Page 12 – Kids With Careers – Pete Fitzgerald / Mike Morse
Page 14 – Toys of the Third Reich – Rurik Tyler / R.J. Reiley, C.L. Walker
Page 17 – Paid Too Much / Paid Too Little – Walter Brogan / Nina Love
Page 18 – The Cracked Marine Biological Chart for Beach Species – Mike Ricigliano
Page 20 – Other Big-Time Hollywood Productions of Classic TV Shows – Gunnar Johnson
Page 24 – The Bargain Budget Thrifty Discount Big Lot Close-Out Value Wholesale Liquidator's Store Weekly Sale! – Pete Fitzgerald / Randy Epley
Page 26 – Spies and Sabs Hit The Park! – Mike Ricigliano
Page 28 – Subscription ad Cover – Tom Grimes, John Severin, Walter Brogan / Nathaniel Cardonsky (reprint from *Cracked Collectors' Edition* #104)
Page 29 – Cracked Interviews Leonardo – Bruce Bolinger / Lou Silverstone
Page 34 – Saturday Morning Cartoons That Never Quite Caught On – Gary Fields / Kerry Soper
Page 36 – Off the Hook – Don Orehek / Rob Weske
Page 37 – Cracked's Guide to Hiking! – Pete Fitzgerald / Ricky Sprague
Page 41 – Cracked's Summer Camp Survival Catalogue – Bruce Bolinger / Rob Weske
Page 44 – The Hustler – Walter Brogan / John Schmitz
Page 45 – Dawson's Geeks – Frank Cummings / Greg Grabianski
Page 50 – The Cracked List Top 9 Leonard DiCaprio Pickup Lines – Mike Ricigliano
Page 51 – An Earrie Tale – Oskar Blotta / Luciano Blotta
Back Cover – EMCI ad – Gunnar Johnson

**330, November 1998 (52 pages) ($2.25)** (Much color is added from this issue on.)
Cover – Jerry Springer "Cartoon Confessions" – John Severin
Page 2 – *Cracked Monster Party* #41 ad – Rob Orzechowski
Insert – Subscription Card – Walter Brogan / Mike Ricigliano
Page 3 – What's Inside Cracked / Idiotorial – Mike Ricigliano (full color) (1st *What's Inside Cracked / Idiotorial*)
Page 4 – Backwash – Nick Beef, Katey Dash, Barry Dutter, Kit Lively, Cliff Mott, Terry Colon (full color)
Page 6 – Crappy Cracked Greeting Cards – Bruce Bolinger (full color)
Page 8 – Behind the Scenes of Comic Book SFX! – Alan Kupperberg / Ricky Sprague (full color)
Page 11 – Extreme Ideas for Everyday Activities – Todd James / Mike Morse

Page 12 – Suspicious Ads – John Severin / Denny Spurling
Page 14 – Warnings for the Terminally Cool – Pete Fitzgerald / Mike Morse
Page 16 – One Brutally Hot Day in Bombay – Don Orehek / Rob Weske
Page 17 – Make Baseball More Like Football – Mike Ricigliano
Page 20 – The Wrong Can – Ian Baker
Page 21 – Dr. Dolittle's First Aid for Animals – Bruce Bolinger / Mike Lotter
Page 25 – One Summer Day in the Park – Don Orehek / Rob Weske
Page 26 – Spies and Sabs Hit the Boardwalk – Mike Ricigliano
Page 28 – Gangster or Gangsta Do You Know the Difference? – Randy Jones / Jay Oakes
Page 30 – Cracked's Guide to TV Talk Shows – Frank Cummings / Greg Grabianski
Page 34 – Pondering the Great Questions of the Day – Mark Poutenis / Joe Newkirk
Page 36 – Breaking the Code: Your Uncle's Magic Tricks Exploded! Starring the Masked Uncle – John Severin / Dan Fiorella
Page 40 – Deadiquette A Guide to Bad Manners for the Dead – Rob Orzechowski
Page 42 – Subscription ad – Frank Borth
Page 43 – Small Soldiers Left on the Cutting Room Floor – Tom Grimes, Rurik Tyler / Katey Dash (full color)
Page 46 – If the Simpsons Were Guests on the Jerry Springer Show – Gary Fields / Greg Grabianski (full color)
Page 50 – The Cracked List 10 Ideas Whose Time Never Came – Mike Ricigliano / Dan Fiorella (full color)
Insert – Subscription Card – Mike Ricigliano
Page 51 – National Rifle Association ad – Alan Kupperberg / R.J. Reiley
Back Cover – When Fox Stars Attack! – Gunnar Johnson

**331, December 1998 (52 pages) ($2.25)**
Cover – We Pass Water, Boy! – Jeff Wong
Page 2 – *Cracked Collectors' Edition* #117 ad
Insert – Subscription Card – Walter Brogan / Mike Ricigliano
Page 3 – What's Inside Cracked / Idiotorial – Mike Ricigliano (full color)
Page 4 – Backwash – Katey Dash, Randy Epley, Dan Fiorella, Dan Lee, Ricky Sprague, Terry Colon, Jay Sharkey (full color)
Page 6 – Maddening NFL '99 – Frank Cummings / Ricky Sprague (full color)
Page 11 – That's News to Us! – Don Orehek / Mike Lotter
Page 12 – America's Weirdest Restaurants – Randy Jones / Mike Morse

Page 14 – True, Man (It's a Snow Job) – Walter Brogan / Lou Silverstone
Page 19 – Maternity Ward 10 – Ian Baker
Page 20 – Canes and Walkers for Oldsters On the Go – Ron Barrett
Page 22 – Cracked Looks at the Sport Utility Vehicle Craze – John Severin / Greg Grabianski
Page 26 – Spies and Sabs Hit a Telethon – Mike Ricigliano
Page 28 – Charlton Heston's Ten Commandments of the NRA – Gunnar Johnson
Page 30 – Good Idea…Now Take it a Step Further – Don Orehek / Mike Lotter
Page 31 – The Waterbug – John Severin / Andy Simmons
Page 36 – Road Rage Accessories Catalog – Bruce Bolinger / Greg Grabianski
Page 38 – Kurt Cobain Memorial High School – Mike Ricigliano
Page 42 – Subscription ad – John Severin (reprint from *Cracked Collectors' Edition* #106)
Page 43 – Ty Beanie Babies We'll Soon Be Seeing Everywhere – Rurik Tyler / Josh Cohen (full color)
Page 46 – Mulame – Walter Brogan / Greg Grabianski (full color)
Page 50 – The Cracked List Top 10 Least Scary Halloween Costumes – Mike Ricigliano (full color)
Insert – Subscription Card – Mike Ricigliano
Page 51 – Cracked Video Sale Bonanza! – Gary Fields / Dan Fiorella
Back Cover – ABC ad - Chris Gennusa

**332, January 1999 (68 pages) ($2.99)** (Double-size issue)
Cover – We Squash Ants – John Severin
Page 2 – The Outer Space Rescue – Oskar Blotta
Insert – Subscription Card – Walter Brogan / Mike Ricigliano
Page 3 – What's Inside Cracked / Idiotorial – Mike Ricigliano (full color)
Page 4 – Backwash – Josh Cohen, Katey Dash, Dan Lee, Kit Lively, Terry Colon, Jay Sharkey (full color)
Page 6 – I'm a Geddon – Walter Brogan / Tony Frank (Lou Silverstone) (full color)
Page 11 – Stuttering John's Historical Interviews (Honest Abe Lincoln) – John Halpern / Mike Morse (1st *Stuttering John's Historical Interviews*)
Page 12 – The First Kiddie Casino – Bruce Bolinger / Mike Morse
Page 14 – Classifieds You Really Shouldn't Answer – Randy Jones / R.J. Reiley
Page 17 – Complaints From the North Pole – Frank Cummings / Coyote J. Calhoun

Page 18 – Less Throw-Time, More Showtime! – Ron Barrett
Page 20 – The Cracked Multi-Plex – John Severin / Greg Grabianski
Page 27 – General Schwarzpatton's Paintball Manual – Mike Ricigliano (full color)
Page 30 – It's a Wonderful Bug's Life – Rurik Tyler / Rich Kreigel (full color) Page 34 – Spies and Sabs Hit an Ant Farm – Mike Ricigliano (green color added)
Page 36 – Specialized Holiday Gift Baskets – Rurik Tyler / Rob Weske (full color)
Page 38 – If All Products Were Modeled After the Swiss Army Knife – Pete Fitzgerald / Chris Gennusa, Katey Dash (red color added)
Page 40 – Mistletoe – Gary Fields / Kit Lively (green and red color added)
Page 41 – TV Guideth Magazine – John Severin / C.L. Walker, Karl Tiedeman, R.J. Reiley (full color)
Page 46 – Proposed NASA Missions – Terry Colon / John Cohen
Page 48 – A Cracked Fairy Tale – Don Orehek / Rob Weske
Page 49 – Jujubee Jury Rate Heaving Private Ryan – Walter Brogan / Lou Silverstone
Page 56 – You Spent How Much On That Movie?!? – Pete Fitzgerald /. Henry Faulkner
Page 58 – When All Magazines Publish Special Editions Just For Kids – Gunnar Johnson / Anthony Zampano
Page 60 – Aint'z – Frank Cummings / Andy Simmons (full color)
Page 65 – Subscription ad – Walter Brogan (reprint from #279) (full color)
Page 66 – The Cracked List Top 10 Plays Banned in the NFL – Mike Ricigliano (full color)
Insert – Subscription Card – Mike Ricigliano
Page 67 – Corporate Sponsors Rename Our National Parks – John Severin / Greg Grabianski
Back Cover – Macho 33 – Tom Gieseke

**333, March 1999 (52 pages) ($2.25)**

Cover – Annual Swimsuit Issue – Rurik Tyler, Tom Grimes
Page 2 – *Cracked Super* #16 ad
Insert – Subscription Card – Walter Brogan / Mike Ricigliano
Page 3 – What's Inside Cracked / Idiotorial – Mike Ricigliano (full color)
Page 4 – Backwash – Katey Dash, Barry Dutter, Randy Epley, Dan Fiorella, Dan Lee, Mike Morse, Terry Colon, Jay Sharkey, Gunnar Johnson (full color) (Greg Grabianski and Sergio Aragonés photo)
Page 6 – Cracked Swimsuit Edition Fun & Frolic in South Park, Colorado – Rurik Tyler, Tom Grimes / Greg Grabianski (full color)

Page 11 – A Very Special Drinking & Driving Episode of Home Improvement – Walter Brogan / Greg Grabianski
Page 12 – Job Opportunities for Genetic Mutations – John Severin / Mike Morse
Page 14 – When the Famous Join the Everyday Workforce – Jeff Wong / John Samony
Page 16 – A Valentine's Day True Tale of Romantic Love – Todd James / Kit Lively
Page 17 – The Cracked Spring Training Preview – Mike Ricigliano
Page 21 – The Clothes-Out Sale – Don Orehek / Linc Pershad
Page 22 – When All Organizations Offer Their Own Visa Cards – Gunnar Johnson
Page 24 – Good Expression, Bad Timing – Bruce Bolinger / Mike Morse
Page 26 – Spies and Sabs Hit a Winter Carnival – Mike Ricigliano
Page 28 – Stuttering John's Historical Interviews (Mahatma Ghandi) – John Halpern / Mike Morse
Page 29 – Moldy Joe Dung – John Severin / Rich Kriegel (Lou Silverstone)
Page 34 – Upside/Downside of Cyberspace – Todd James / Dan Fiorella
Page 36 – Cracked's Driver's Ed. Class – Frank Cummings / Dan Fiorella
Page 40 – Horror Scopes – Rob Orzechowski / Steve Strangio Page 42 – Subscription ad – Walter Brogan
Page 43 – The Fresh Prince of Egypt – Walter Brogan /.Lou Silverstone (full color)
Page 48 – Saint Patrick's Day Do's & Don'ts! – Randy Jones / R.J. Reiley (full color)
Page 50 – The Cracked List 11 Ways the British Monarchy Can Improve Its Image – Mike Ricigliano / Dan Birtcher (full color)
Insert – Subscription Card – Terry Colon, Mike Ricigliano
Page 51 – Lee Press-On Teeth – Tom Grimes / John Bregoli
Back Cover – Shred This! – Bruce Bolinger / Greg Grabianski

**334, May 1999 (52 pages) ($2.25)**
Cover – WWF vs. WCW – John Severin
Page 2 – *Cracked Monster Party* #43 ad
Page 3 – What's Inside Cracked / Idiotorial – Mike Ricigliano (full color)
Page 4 – Backwash – Katey Dash, Randy Epley, Gunnar Johnson, Kit Lively, Thomas Williams, Terry Colon (full color)
Page 6 – Cracked's Academy Awards for Wrestlers – Walter Brogan / Lou Silverstone (full color) Page 11 – Stuttering John's Historical Interviews (Nostradamus) – John Halpern / Mike Morse

Page 12 – Cracked Guide to Wrestling Fans – Bruce Bolinger / Steve Strangio
Page 14 – Doodle Pads Through History – Ron Barrett
Page 18 – Cracked's Guide to Braces – John Severin / Dan Fiorella, Jackie Rose
Page 21 – The Fake-ulty – Frank Cummings / Andy Simmons
Page 25 – Suplex Marks the Spot – Don Orehek / Katey Dash
Page 26 – Spies and Sabs Hit a Computer Superstore – Mike Ricigliano
Page 28 – When the Jesse "The Body" Ventura Trend Takes Over Washington – Gunnar Johnson
Page 30 – The Furby Phenomenon – Pete Fitzgerald / Greg Grabianski
Page 33 – MWF Monster Wrestling Federation – Mike Ricigliano
Page 36 – Putz Adumbs – Walter Brogan / Lou Silverstone
Page 40 – Musical Goulash! – Cliff Mott / Jay Oakes
Page 42 – Subscription ad – John Severin (reprint from *Cracked Blockbuster* #10)
Page 43 – Don Archie – Gary Fields / R.J. Reiley (full color)
Page 47 – Cut Out a Can of Whoop Ass – Cliff Mott / Todd Jackson (full color)
Page 48 – Changes to the Currency We'd Really Like to See – Rurik Tyler / Dan Birtcher (full color)
Page 50 – The Cracked List 9 Ways Life in Minnesota Will Change with Jesse "The Body" Ventura as Governor – Mike Ricigliano / Greg Grabianski (full color)
Page 51 – NBA Sham 99 – Frank Cummings, Tom Grimes
Back Cover – Get Ready to Thumble! – Jeff Wong

**335, July 1999 (52 pages) ($2.25)**

Cover – The Mummy Unwraps Lara Croft – Rurik Tyler
Page 2 – *Cracked Collectors' Edition* #119 ad
Page 3 – What's Inside Cracked / Idiotorial – Mike Ricigliano (full color)
Page 4 – Backwash – Katey Dash, Barry Dutter, Randy Epley, Dan Fiorella, Kit Lively, Rob Weske, Terry Colon, Gunnar Johnson (full color)
Page 6 – Cracked's Quickee Guide to Mummification – Mike Ricigliano (full color)
Page 8 – What to Expect When All Corporations Merge – Gunnar Johnson / Sherry Johnson (full color)
Page 10 – The Cat in the Hat Strikes Back – Gary Fields / Dan Fiorella (full color)
Page 11 – Party of Hives – John Severin / Greg Grabianski
Page 17 – Stuttering John's Historical Interviews (Leonardo Da Vinci) – John Halpern / Mike Morse

Page 18 – Some Ridiculously "Safe" Products – Pete Fitzgerald / Ricky Sprague
Page 20 – The Not-So-Idle Rich – Bruce Bolinger / Dan Fiorella
Page 22 – Unusual Chess Moves – Ian Baker
Page 23 – CDs That Today's Aging Pop Stars Will Be Releasing When They Get Really Old – Gunnar Johnson
Page 26 – Spies and Sabs Hit a Softball Game – Mike Ricigliano
Page 28 – Subscription ad – Rurik Tyler
Page 29 – The Sunnydale Scythe – Frank Cummings / Ricky Sprague Page 33 – The Dummy – Walter Brogan / Andy Simmons
Page 38 – Essays From Recent College Applications – Ricky Sprague
Page 40 – Even More Ridiculously "Safe" Products – Pete Fitzgerald / Ricky Sprague
Page 42 – One Miserable Day in Bombay – Oskar Blotta
Page 43 – The Latest Tomb Raider Games – Frank Cummings / Lou Motson (full color)
Page 47 – The 1999 Steroid Games – Randy Jones / Josh Cohen (full color)
Page 50 – Cracked List Top 12 Mothers From Hell – Mike Ricigliano (full color)
Page 51 – Little Sneezers – Tom Gieseke / Martin Heeley
Back Cover – Nickelodeon ad – Jorge Pacheco, Tom Grimes

**336, August 1999 (52 pages) ($2.25)**

Cover – Phantom Menace Exposed! – John Severin
Page 2 – *Cracked Blockbuster* #13 ad
Page 3 – What's Inside Cracked / Idiotorial – Mike Ricigliano (full color)
Page 4 – Backwash – Katey Dash, Barry Dutter, Dan Fiorella, Martin Heeley, Gunnar Johnson, Kit Lively, Nancy Lombardo, Terry Colon (full color)
Page 6 – A Cracked Behind-the-Scenes Look at The Phantom Menace – Walter Brogan / Lou Silverstone (full color)
Page 11 – Stuttering John's Historical Interviews (Napoleon) – John Halpern / Mike Morse
Page 12 – When the Y2K Bug Wreaks Havoc! – Randy Jones / Mike Morse
Page 14 – Letters of Complaint Thru History – Bruce Bolinger / R.J. Reiley, C.L. Walker Page 17 – The Cracked Graduation Evaluation – Mike Ricigliano
Page 20 – Supermodel Shut-Ups (I'm a perfect size!) – Don Orehek / Eric Goldberg, Mark Howard
Page 21 – Everybody Loathes Raymundane – John Severin / Greg Grabianski

Page 26 – Spies and Sabs His the Mummy's Tomb – Mike Ricigliano
Page 28 – Game Shows to Play With Your Grandparents – Todd James / Dan Lee
Page 30 – The Body Language Dictionary – Randy Jones / Professor Nincompoop, Rob Weske, Mike Lotter
Page 34 – Combinventions! – John Severin / Mike Morse
Page 36 – Push Down the Stairs, LTD – Ian Baker
Page 37 – ODDtv – Walter Brogan / Lou Silverstone
Page 42 – Subscription ad – Tom Grimes (reprint from *Cracked Monster Party* #36)
Page 43 – Tattooine Suns – Frank Cummings / Steve Strangio, Lou Motson (full color)
Page 47 – VH1 Before They Were Star Wars Stars! – Gunnar Johnson / Jay Oakes (full color)
Page 48 – If I Had a Superhero – Pete Fitzgerald, Tom Grimes / Dan Lee (full color)
Page 50 – The Cracked List 8 Ways to Make This a Special Fathers Day – Mike Ricigliano (full color)
Page 51 – Z&Z's ad – Frank Cummings, Courtland Richards, Charlie Lovelady
Back Cover – Star Bores Epic-Dud1 Poster – Jeff Wong

**337, September 1999 (52 pages) ($2.25)**

Cover – We Horse Around With Wild Wild West! – Jeff Wong
Page 2 – *Cracked Summer Special* #9, *Cracked Monster Party* #44 and *Cracked Collectors' Edition* #120 ad
Page 3 – What's Inside Cracked / Idiotorial – Mike Ricigliano (full color)
Page 4 – Backwash – Katey Dash, Carson Demmans, Randy Epley, Todd Jackson, Kit Lively, Terry Colon (full color)
Page 6 – TheWild Wild Mess – Walter Brogan / Lou Silverstone (full color)
Page 11 – The Dictionary of Sports Injuries & Diseases – Randy Jones / Rob Weske, Martin Heeley
Page 14 – Spot the Corporate Logos – Pete Fitzgerald / Greg Grabianski
Page 16 – Stuttering John's Historical Interviews (Babe Ruth) – John Halpern / Mike Morse
Page 17 – Government Regulations Through the Ages – John Severin / Jessie Shimon
Page 21 – A Peek Inside Austin Powers' Scrapbook – Gunnar Johnson
Page 24 – Sports Equipment Breakthroughs – Bruce Bolinger / Mike Morse
Page 26 – Spies and Sabs Hit The Wild Wild West – Mike Ricigliano

Page 28 – The Really Wild Wild West – Don Orehek / Lou Motson
Page 29 – Muscular Pinhead Magazine – John Severin / Greg Grabianski
Page 34 – WNBA – Mike Ricigliano
Page 37 – Shamed By the Smell – The New Pains-in-the-Class – Walter Brogan / Mike Morse
Page 42 – Subscription ad – John Severin (reprint from #90)
Page 43 – Nature Guide for Campers – Ron Barrett (full color)
Page 46 – Children's Classics Grown-Up – Gary Fields / Dan Fiorella (full color)
Page 50 – The Cracked List 8 Wild Gadgets – Mike Ricigliano (full color)
Page 51 – Austin Powers – Gunnar Johnson
Back Cover – Tae Boba Workout – Eric Snodgrass, Jonathan Skaines, Matt Martelli / Todd Jackson

**338, October 1999 (52 pages) ($2.25)**
Cover – Special Taping of Backstreet Boys – John Severin
Page 2 – Chia Pest Chia Back & Crack – Aimee Keillor, Rurik Tyler, Tom Grimes
Page 3 – What's Inside Cracked / Idiotorial – Mike Ricigliano (full color)
Page 4 – Backwash – Katey Dash, Randy Epley, Kit Lively, Nancy Lombardo, Jay Oakes, Steve Strangio, Terry Colon (full color)
Page 6 – The Cracked Guide to Boy Groups – Frank Cummings / Greg Grabianski (full color)
Page 10 – Tarzzzzzan – Walter Brogan / Linc Pershad (full color)
Page 11 – Cracked Pharmaceuticals
Page 13 – The Tatooine 500 – Bruce Bolinger / Rob Weske
Page 16 – Total Request Lovin' the Ego Stroke-a – Cliff Mott / Barry Zeger
Page 18 – Stuttering John's Historical Interviews (Jesus Christ) – John Halpern / Mike Morse
Page 19 – Big Duddy at the Cineplex – Walter Brogan / Tony Frank (Lou Silverstone), Katey Dash
Page 25 – You're a Worthwhile Individual, Churlish Brawn! – Gary Fields / Ricky Sprague
Page 26 – Spies and Sabs Hit a Teen Heartthrob Concert – Mike Ricigliano
Page 28 – Textbooks You Can Really Use – Rurik Tyler / Mike Morse
Page 31 – "Big Boomer's" NFL Fan Pre-Season Camp – Mike Ricigliano
Page 34 – New Ripped From the Pages of the Sports Section…a Hundred Years From Now – Pete Fitzgerald / Martin Heeley

Page 38 – Boomtique.com – Tom Grimes / Mike Morse
Page 42 – Subscription ad – John Severin (reprint from *Cracked Blockbuster* #5)
Page 43 – Ravenous in the Stone Age – Oskar Blotta (full color)
Page 44 – Snore Wars Epic-Dud 1 The Phantom Cuteness – John Severin / Lou Silverstone (full color)
Page 50 – The Cracked List 8 Ways to Sneak Into An R-Rated Movie – Mike Ricigliano / Lou Motson (full color)
Page 51 – This Locker Protected By Fang! – Tom Gieseke
Back Cover – La Tower Recordas – Jeff Wong

**339, November 1999 (52 pages) ($2.25)**
Cover – They're So Cute You'll Want to Puke-Mon – Rurik Tyler
Page 2 – *Cracked Collectors' Edition* #121 ad
Page 3 – What's Inside Cracked / Idiotorial – Mike Ricigliano (full color)
Page 4 – Backwash – Katey Dash, Barry Dutter, Randy Epley, Dan Fiorella, Andy Lamberti, Dan Lee, Kit Lively, Nancy Lombardo, Terry Colon (full color)
Page 6 – Everything You Never Wanted to Know About Pokemon – Gary Fields / Steve Strangio, Dan Fiorella (full color)
Page 11 – Animorons – Bruce Bolinger / Dan Fiorella
Page 14 – The New Softer and Kinder Ads – John Severin / Dennis Spurling
Page 16 – How to Get Rich Quick With Ebay – Steve Casino, Steve Fink, Chris Spensely
Page 19 – American Lie – Walter Brogan / Andy Simmons
Page 23 – A Hair in the Nose – Oskar Blotta
Page 24 – Cracked Guide to the Millenium Computer Crash – Bruce Bolinger / Dan Fiorella
Page 26 – Spies and Sabs Hit a Halloween Costume – Mike Ricigliano
Page 28 – The Cliques of Outback High – John Severin / Dan Lee, Todd Jackson
Page 33 – Umpire Outfitters Catalog – Terry Colon
Page 36 – True "Tails" of Romantic Love – Don Orehek / Kit Lively
Page 37 – The Lazy Kids' Guide to Raking Leaves – Mike Ricigliano
Page 40 – "The New Defectables" – Pete Fitzgerald / R.J. Reiley, C.L. Walker
Page 42 – Subscription ad – John Severin, Rurik Tyler, Jeff Wong (reprint from #66, 335, 337)
Page 43 – Tarzan – Walter Brogan / Lou Silverstone (full color)
Page 48 – Hot Toy Timeline – Rurik Tyler / Dan Fiorella (full color)
Page 50 – The Cracked List 8 After School Detention Punishments – Mike Ricigliano / Kit Lively (full color)

Page 51 - Cracked's Notorious Nosepickers Guide - Bruce Bolinger / Martin Heeley
Back Cover - Cartoon Nutwork Presents The Flopstones - Don Orehek / Greg Grabianski

**340, December 1999 (52 pages) ($2.25)**
Cover - We Crack-Up Futurama - Gary Fields
Page 2 - *Cracked Monster Party* #45 ad
Insert - Subscription Card - Jeff Wong / Mike Ricigliano
Page 3 - What's Inside Cracked / Idiotorial - Mike Ricigliano (full color)
Page 4 - Backwash - Dan Fiorella, Andy Lamberti, Dan Lee, Kit Lively, Steve Strangio, Terry Colon (full color)
Page 6 - Futuredrama - John Severin / Greg Grabianski (full color)
Page 11 - Stuttering John's Historical Interviews (The First Man) - John Halpern / Mike Morse
Page 12 - The Future Ain't What It's Cracked Up to Be - Terry Colon
Page 14 - Soccer Star - Pete Fitzgerald / Claire Brucker
Page 16 - Bilking Blanks' Tae Bore - Tom Grimes / Mike Morse
Page 18 - The Choke's On You - Ian Baker
Page 19 - Preparing for the SAT - Alan Kupperberg / R.J. Reiley, Dan Fiorella
Page 24 - Ian Baker's Cartoons From Another Galaxy or: They Come in Peace - Ian Baker
Page 26 - Spies and Sabs Hit a Football Locker Room - Mike Ricigliano
Page 28 - What Would You Do If You Ran the Thanksgiving Parade? - Bruce Bolinger / Jay Oakes
Page 30 - Duh-dley Duh-Right - Walter Brogan / Lou Silverstone Page 34 - The Future Ain't What It's Cracked Up to Be, Again - Terry Colon
Page 36 - The Next Don - Don Orehek / Mike Lotter
Page 37 - Lazyman's Guide to Thanksgiving - Mike Ricigliano
Page 40 - Six Cents - John Severin / Tony Frank (Lou Silverstone)
Page 42 - Subscription ad - Jeff Wong, Rurik Tyler, John Severin (reprint from #335, 337, 338)
Page 43 - Scratcher Magazine - Steve Casino (full color)
Page 47 - Ron McDonald - Pete Fitzgerald / Barry Zeger, Sue Zeger (full color)
Page 48 - Sharks 2000 - Randy Jones / R.J. Reiley, C.L. Walker (full color)
Page 50 - The Cracked List Ten Failed First Attempts - Mike Ricigliano / Thomas Williams (full color)
Insert - Subscription Card - Walter Brogan / Mike Ricigliano

Page 51 – The Berenstain Bears Get Relocated – Gary Fields / Dan Fiorella
Back Cover – Divine Interventsion – Kent Kennedy

**341, January 2000 (52 pages) ($2.25)**

Cover – Toy Story 2 A Disarming Love Story – John Severin (7th Alfred E. Neuman cover)
Page 2 – Worst Promotional Characters – Frank Cummings / Mike Morse
Page 3 – What's Inside Cracked / Idiotorial – Mike Ricigliano (full color)
Page 4 – Backwash – Katey Dash, Eric Goldberg, Mark Howard, Todd Jackson, Kit Lively, Steve Strangio, Rob Weske, Terry Colon (full color)
Page 6 – Toy Borey, Too – John Severin / Lou Silverstone (full color)
Insert – Subscription Card – Walter Brogan / Mike Ricigliano
Page 11 – Cracked Stocking Stuffer – Pete Fitzgerald / R.J. Reiley
Page 12 – Fat is Phat on TV! – Randy Jones / Mike Morse
Page 14 – Interactive Urinal Cakes – Kent Kennedy
Page 16 – Hook, Line & Sink-err – Pete Fitzgerald / Mike Lotter
Page 17 – Monster Christmas – Mike Ricigliano
Page 22 – Cracked History of Humor – Frank Cummings / R.J. Reiley, Karl Tiedeman, Dan Fiorella
Page 26 – Spies and Sabs Hit Times Square – Mike Ricigliano
Page 28 – Uncouth Christmas Carols – Gary Fields / Barry Zeger, Sue Zeger
Page 30 – Do-It-Yourself "Behind the Music" – Bruce Bolinger / Mike Morse
Page 33 – One Christmas Eve On Death Row – Don Orehek / Rob Weske
Page 34 – Galaxy Queasy – Walter Brogan / Andy Simmons
Page 40 – Pop Stars on Broadway – Jeff Wong / Mike Morse
Page 42 – Subscription ad – John Severin (reprint from #26)
Insert – Subscription Card – Terry Colon / Mike Ricigliano
Page 43 – Guide to Dreamcast's New Realistic Video Games – Rurik Tyler / Josh Cohen (full color)
Page 46 – Biography Presents Barbie To Hell and Back – Gunnar Johnson (full color)
Page 50 – The Cracked List 8 New Year's Resolutions of the Rich and Famous – Mike Ricigliano / Lou Motson (full color)
Page 51 – American Goth-ick – Jeff Wong
Back Cover – Fetus Gap – John Halpern / Henry Faulkner

**342, March 2000 (52 pages) ($2.25)**

Cover - The Toon Issue! - John Severin (Severin's last cover for *Cracked*.)

Page 2 - *Cracked Super* #17 ad

Page 3 - What's Inside Cracked / Idiotorial - Mike Ricigliano (full color)

Page 4 - Backwash - Katey Dash, Randy Epley, Dan Fiorella, Kit Lively, Mike Morse, Terry Colon (full color)

Page 6 - Pukemon the First Movie - Frank Cummings / Andy Simmons (full color)

Page 11 - Valentine Cards For Your Loathed Ones - Bruce Bolinger / Randy Epley

Page 13 - Car Games For Snow-Stranded Travelers - Randy Jones / Michael Sachs

Page 16 - Other Cross-Over Attempts By Music Stars - Gunnar Johnson, Tom Murphy / Jay Oakes

Page 19 - The Bicentennial Man - Walter Brogan / Lou Silverstone

Page 25 - A Push in the Right Direction - Rob Orzechowski / Kit Lively

Page 26 - Spies and Sabs Hit a Ski Resort - Mike Ricigliano

Page 28 - It's All the (Road) Rage - Don Orehek / Rob Weske

Page 29 - OK-Mart - Alan Kupperberg / Dan Fiorella, Randy Epley

Page 33 - At the Movies, Didja Ever Notice That - Walter Brogan / R.J. Reiley

Page 36 - Darnugly & Greed - John Severin / Greg Grabianski

Page 41 - The Cracked List 7 Lousy Replacement Shows for 7 Lousy Shows - Mike Ricigliano / Katey Dash

Page 42 - Subscription ad - John Severin (reprint from #265)

Back Cover - Toon People Magazine - Gary Fields, Pete Fitzgerald, Jorge Pacheco, Rurik Tyler / Mike Morse, Lou Motson, R.J. Reiley, Karl Tiedemann (full color)

**343, May 2000 (52 pages) ($2.25)** (Last issue edited by Lou Silverstone and Andy Simmons.)

Cover - We Clean Up Wrestling! - Jeff Wong

Page 2 - *Cracked Monster Party* #46 ad

Page 3 - What's Inside Cracked / Idiotorial - Mike Ricigliano (full color) (Cartoon tribute by Ricigliano about Don Martin who passed away in 2000.)

Page 4 - Backwash - Katey Dash, Carson Demmans, Randy Epley, Dan Fiorella, Kit Lively, Mike Morse, Jorge Pacheco, Cliff Mott (full color)

Page 6 - A Cracked Interview With Mr. Socko - Walter Brogan (full color)

Page 11 – One Crappy Day in the Ozarks – Don Orehek / Kit Lively
Page 12 – Roller Coasters – John Severin / Dan Fiorella
Page 14 – The Sports Fans Essentials Catalog – Pete Fitzgerald / Mike Morse
Page 17 – Cigarettes For Pets – Bruce Bolinger / Martin Heeley
Page 20 – When Wrestling Takes on TV! – Cliff Mott / Barry Dutter
Page 22 – Who Wants to Behead a Millionaire? – John Severin / Greg Grabianski
Page 26 – Spies and Saboteurs Hit the Final Four – Mike Ricigliano
Page 28 – Creative Suicide Techniques – Oskar Blotta
Page 30 – Bowling Bummer – Gary Fields / Ricky Sprague
Page 31 – If Oscars Were Awarded to Everyone – Bruce Bolinger / Dan Fiorella
Page 34 – Sorry My Bad – Kent Kennedy
Page 36 – A Commercial We'd Like to Make – Don Orehek / Katey Dash
Page 37 – Pokemon Gone Wild! – Mike Ricigliano
Page 40 – X-Treme Sports Coming Soon to ESPN3 – Frank Cummings / Coyote J. Calhoun
Page 42 – Subscription ad – John Severin (reprint from *Cracked Blockbuster* #5)
Page 43 – Short Attention-Span Video Club! (full color)
Page 44 – Upside / Downside of Easter – Gary Fields / Dan Fiorella (full color)
Page 46 – Quack III – Frank Cummings / Andy Simmons, Todd Jackson (full color)
Page 50 – The Cracked List 7 Other Awards for Films – Mike Ricigliano / Katey Dash (full color)
Page 51 – Post Global Warming Snowglobes – Rurik Tyler, Tom Grimes
Back Cover – Oscar Migraine Munchables! – Tom Grimes / Martin Heeley

**344, June 2000 (52 pages) ($2.95)** (1st issue edited by Dick Kulpa. 1st monthly issue. Numbering changed.)

Cover – We Spear Britney and Jennifer! – Dick Kulpa / Nelson Dewey
Inside Front Cover – Britney's Sphere's – Kent Kennedy
Page 1 – Inside Cracked (full color)
Page 2 – Announcing…The New and Improved Cracked / Backwash (full color)
Page 4 – Malcontents in the Middle – Frank Cummings / Andy Simmons (full color)
Page 8 – Roasting Mother Goose (Old Mother Goose) – Vic Martin (full color)

Page 10 – Life in the Year 1900 vs. Life in the Year 2000 – Walter Brogan / Barry Dutter
Page 12 – Marshmallow Law – John Severin / Greg Grabianski
Page 18 – A Handy Guide to Hands – Kent Kennedy
Page 20 – UFO – Dick Kulpa
Page 21 – Shut-Ups! (Push! Push!) – Don Orehek / Joe O'Brien
Page 22 – Recreational Sports for the Undead – Cliff Mott
Page 24 – Spies and Sabs Hit a Nudist Colony – Mike Ricigliano
Page 26 – God-Hilla! – Tom Richmond
Page 32 – Peek@You! I See You – Kent Kennedy
Page 34 – Designer Pots – Rurik Tyler, Dick Kulpa / Mike Morse
Page 36 – "Stewed a Little" – Walter Brogan / Lou Silverstone Page 41 – Indoor Adventures Magazine – Ron Barrett (full color)
Page 44 – When the Post Office Starts Selling Really Popular Stamps – Gunnar Johnson (full color)
Page 46 – Teen Magazines Through the Ages – Gunnar Johnson (full color)
Page 48 – Let's Make Books More Like Web Sites – Howard Cruse (full color)
Inside Back Cover – Spoof Daddy! – Bobbie Bender / Dick Kulpa
Back Cover – Bad Marketing Ideas – Tom Milutinovic

**345, July 2000 (52 pages) ($2.95)**

Cover – We Stick it to Scream 3 – Dick Kulpa, Bruce Bolinger / Nelson Dewey
Inside Front Cover – Who Wants to – Gunnar Johnson
Page 1 – Inside Cracked (full color)
Page 2 – Scram 3 – Frank Cummings / Andy Simmons (full color)
Page 7 – Magazines You Won' See! – Bobbie Bender / Gunnar Johnson, Tom Murphy (full color)
Page 9 – Joe Studd Screens His Calls – Rurik Tyler / Barry Studder (Barry Dutter) (1st *Joe Studd*)
Page 10 – The Tom Green Family Tree – Frank Cummings / Mike Morse
Page 13 – Cracked Magazine Driving Test! – Walter Brogan / Barry Dutter
Page 16 – How Regis Philbin Can Save TV – John Severin / Barry Dutter, Bobbie Bender, Peet Janes
Page 18 – School Dazed! – Nelson Dewey / Barry Dutter
Page 20 – Mr. Precious Goes Fishing! – Ed Steckley (1st *Mr. Precious*)
Page 21 – On Steee-Riiike!!! – Nelson Dewey / Mike Morse
Page 24 – Cracked Looks at Surgeons! – Dick Kulpa
Page 26 – Fuggeddaboudits (these shoes go okay) – Don Orehek / Barry Dutter

Page 27 – Tony Soprano Answers Your Questions About the Mafia – Mike Ricigliano / Mike Morse
Page 30 – Rapper in the Crapper – Bruce Bolinger / Bobbie Bender
Page 32 – The Stupranos – Tom Richmond / Jim Batts
Page 37 – Cracked's School for Bullies! – Bruce Bolinger / KC Tiedeman, R.J. Reiley
Page 41 – Godfather Knows Best! – Don Orehek / Barry Dutter (full color)
Page 42 – Cable Kids' Channel Least Popular Movies – Gary Fields / Randy Epley (full color) Page 46 – It's a Cracked Cracked Cracked Cracked World! / Guest Idiotorial / Wise-Crackeds / Chalk Board – David Cooney (full color) (1st *It's a Cracked Cracked Cracked Cracked World!*)
Page 48 – One Day at the Office! – Steph Ramsay / Barry Dutter (full color) Inside Back Cover – The Big Cheese – Kent Kennedy
Back Cover – Modern-Day Dude Ranch – Mike Ricigliano / Barry Dutter

**346, August 2000 (52 pages) ($2.95)**

Cover – X-Men Movies / We Stuff Bullwinkle & Rocky! – Tom Richmond, Dick Kulpa, Frank Cummings, Ed Steckley
Inside Front Cover and Inside Back Cover – The Excrement Bonus Mini-Poster – John Severin / Barry Dutter
Page 1 – Inside Cracked
Page 2 – Rocker and Bullwanker – Frank Cummings / Bobbie Bender
Page 7 – The Advantages of Being a Circus Clown – Frank Cummings / Coyote J. Calhoun
Page 8 – World's Most Hated Man Gets Help From Mother Teresa's Ghost! – Dick Kulpa (1st *Simpy Dumpkins, World's Most Hated Man*)
Page 9 – Fantasy Baseball Magazine – Mike Ricigliano
Page 13 – Mr. Precious Goes "MeeeYowch!!!!" – Ed Steckley
Page 15 – Popular Pukes – Rick Parker
Page 17 – OverseXedMen – Nadeau / Ensign (full color)
Page 18 – EXcreMENt! – Tom Richmond / Barry Dutter (full color)
Page 24 – Spies and Sabs Hit the X-Men – Mike Ricigliano (full color)
Page 26 – Cracked Magazine Re-Presents "The Fall of Rogue!" – Walter Brogan / Greg Grabianski (originally called "Stan Leak Presents: "The Fall of Rogue!") (reprint from *Cracked Super* #8) (full color)
Page 30 – X-Funnies – Gary Fields / Barry Dutter (full color)
Page 33 – Rock, Scissors, Paper – Mike Ricigliano
Page 34 – She's Alive! A Cracked Look at the Statue of Liberty…Sure to Crack You Up! – Ed Steckley / Stephen Barrington

Page 36 – Phreaks & Fogies – Steph Ramsay / Scott Wood
Page 39 – Famous Last Words – Bruce Bolinger
Page 40 – Gross Pickup Lines That Don't Work! – Pete Fitzgerald / Dave Polski
Page 42 – It's a Cracked Cracked Cracked Cracked World! (Mark Goddard photo) / We "Crack" Up a Comic Convention! – Suzie Estridge / Meet Peet Janes: Cracked Magazine's Managing Editor / But Cracked / Mutants That Didn't Make it...The Rejex-Men! / Crackups – Dick Kulpa / Barry Dutter / Chalk Board – David Cooney
Page 44 – Mission Improbable: 2 – Walter Brogan / Andy Simmons
Page 48 – Cleaned-Up Rap Lyrics – Bruce Bolinger / Bobbie Bender
Back Cover – *Cracked Collectors' Edition* #124 ad

**347, September 2000 (52 pages) ($2.95)**
Cover – A Cracked Peek at 6 Summer Movies! – Dick Kulpa, Tom Richmond
Inside Front Cover – The Walk – Gary Fields / Suzie Estridge
Page 1 – Inside Cracked (full color)
Page 2 – Battyfield Earth – Frank Cummings / Andy Simmons (full color)
Page 6 – Cracked's CD Box Sets We Can Do Without! – Gunnar Johnson, Tom Murphy / Rob Weske (full color)
Page 8 – Can You Spot the Difference? – Art Bouthillier (full color) Page 9 – Cracked Multiplex – Steph Ramsay / Barry Dutter (1st *Cecil, the Cracked Movie Critic*)
Page 10 – Me, Myself & Ireek – Walter Brogan / Barry Dutter
Page 12 – The Patridiot – John Severin / Peet Janes
Page 14 – Graft – Dick Ayers / Robbie Bender
Page 16 – Done in 60 Seconds! – Dick Kulpa / Suzie Estridge
Page 18 – Rappin' Country – Bruce Bolinger / Bobbie Bender
Page 20 – This Does Not Compute! – Don Orehek / Nelson Dewey, Barry Dutter
Page 21 – Is There Anyone Who Likes the World's Most Hated Man? – Dick Kulpa / Bobbie Bender
Page 22 – Kids' Books That Never Made it To Print – Steph Ramsay / Craig Massey
Page 24 – Phamous Pharts – Rick Parker / Martin Heeley
Page 26 – Who's Who at the Multiplex Theatre – Randy Jones / Dan Fiorella
Page 28 – After Lunch on Ward "F" – Bruce Bolinger
Page 29 – Mr. Precious Gets the Point! – Ed Steckley
Page 31 – Cracked-onyms – Pete Fitzgerald / Bobbie Bender

Page 34 – Gladidiot! – Tom Richmond / Barry Dutter
Page 39 – Pierce Pressure – Mike Ricigliano
Page 40 – Summer Shut-Ups! (burgers don't burn) – Rich Hedden / Peet Janes
Page 41 – Ye Middle Ages Yellow Pages – Gunnar Johnson, Tom Murphy / Sherry Johnson (full color) Page 44 – If Boring Magazines Were More Like the Tabloids! – Gunnar Johnson / Dan Fiorella
Page 46 – It's a Cracked Cracked Cracked Cracked World! / Artist John Severin: The Granddaddy of Cracked! – John Severin / Barry Dutter / But Cracked / Crackups – Dick Kulpa / Barry Dutter / Chalk Board – David Cooney (full color)
Page 48 – Tuesday at Burger Bob's – Art Bouthillier (full color)
Inside Back Cover – Warning Labels for Idiots – Tom Milutinovic / Denny Spurling
Back Cover – Cracked Celebrity Graffiti – Steph Ramsay / Andy Lamberti

**348, October 2000 (52 pages) ($2.95)**

Cover – Cracked Goes Back to (S)kool! – Steph Ramsay
Inside Front Cover – So Sad It's Mondays ad – Gunnar Johnson / Damon Schnurr
Page 1 – Inside Cracked (full color)
Page 2 – One Particularly Boring Saturday Afternoon – Art Bouthillier (full color)
Page 3 – Out of Place Cowboys – John Severin / Bobbie Bender (full color) Page 7 – Meet Simpy Dumpkins, the World's Most Hated Man! (A bug!) – Dick Kulpa (full color) Page 8 – It's a Cracked Cracked Cracked Cracked World! / But Cracked / Yo! Butch! – Dick Kulpa (1st *Yo! Butch!*) / Chalk Bored – David Cooney (full color)
Page 9 – High School Horror Movies! – Ick Parker (Rick Parker) / Rancid Epley (Randy Epley)
Page 13 – One Fine Fall Day – Bruce Bolinger
Page 14 – Regular Jobs ...For Former Circus Performers – Mike Kazaleh / Chad Elliot
Page 16 – Celebrity Cars! – Nelson Dewey / Bobbie Bender
Page 18 – A Day in the Life of a Deer Tick – Keith Knight / David Conner
Page 20 – Peanutz – Gary Fields / Martin Heeley
Page 21 – The Shady Peeps – Bruce Bolinger / Bobbie Bender
Page 23 – Tight-azz – Dick Ayers, Dick Kulpa / Andy Simmons, Barry Dutter

Page 27 – Shut-Ups! (What are you complaining about) – Mike Ricigliano / Randy Epley
Page 28 – If School Was Cool! – Pete Fitzgerald / Barry Dutter
Page 32 – Mr. Precious Goes to the Zoo! – Ed Steckley
Page 33 – Top Ten Thrillingest Thrill Rides – Mike Ricigliano / Peet Janes
Page 36 – One Dog Day Afternoon – Kent Kennedy
Page 37 – Snot on the Menu – Grant Meihm / Martin Heeley
Page 38 – The Upside & Downside of Going Back to School! – Randy Jones / Dan Fiorella
Page 40 – To E…Or Not to E! – Mike Ricigliano
Page 41 – The Butty Professor 2: The Plumps! – Frank Cummings / Barry Dutter (full color) Page 46 – The Cracked List of Easy & Hard – Gunnar Johnson (full color)
Inside Back Cover – Can You Spot the Differences? (beach) – Art Bouthillier
Back Cover – *Cracked Collectors' Edition* #124 ad

**349, November 2000 (52 pages) ($2.95)**
Cover – Fall T.V. Spoof-tacular! – Kent Kennedy, Dick Kulpa, Rich Hedden, Ed Steckley, Rurik Tyler
Inside Front Cover – Meet Simpy Dumpkins, the World's Most Hated Man! (Time to check e-mail!) – Dick Kulpa (full color)
Page 1 – Inside Cracked (full color)
Page 2 – Cracked Charities That Need Your Support! – Ian Baker / David Connor (full color)
Page 4 – The Simpranos – Rich Hedden / Barry Dutter (full color)
Page 9 – Mr. Precious (Aww!! Sweet kitty!) – Ed Steckley Page 10 – Stale Prince – Ed Steckley / Barry Dutter
Page 12 – Pro Sports Public Relations Disasters! – Steve Smith / Denny Spurling
Page 14 – How to Buy Cracked – Rick Parker / Barry Dutter
Page 15 – Off the Hook – Don Orehek / Rob Weske (reprint from #329)
Page 16 – Saturday Morning Cartoons That Never Quite Caught On – Gary Fields / Kerry Soper (reprint from #329)
Page 18 – Comic Book vs. Comic Strip Crossover Battles! – Alan Kupperberg / Judd Stomp (reprint from #307)
Page 22 – New Specialty Cable Channels – Grant Meihm / Martin Heeley
Page 24 – When Sitcoms Go Ape! – Ed Steckley / Chris Painter
Page 26 – New TV Shows We'd Like to See – Rick Parker / Steve Strangio
Page 29 – "Must Flee" TV – Walter Brogan, Dick Kulpa, Steph Ramsay / Dan Fiorella

Page 32 – Toon Town Babylon – Bill Wray / Eel O'Brian (Mort Todd) (reprint from #245)
Page 36 – But On the Other Hand – John Severin / Barry Dutter
Page 38 – Real Life Impossible Missions! – Gary Fields / Barry Dutter
Page 40 – Shut-Ups! (remote is broken) – Dick Kulpa / Mulder Gere
Page 41 – Video Games: Final Fantasy vs. Painful Reality – Rurik Tyler / Damon Schnurr (full color) Page 42 – It's a Cracked Cracked Cracked Cracked World! / Meet Cracked's Crack Writer Bashful Barry Dutter – John Severin, Steph Ramsay / But Cracked / Yo! Butch! – Dick Kulpa / Chalk Bored – David Cooney (full color)
Page 46 – South Park Cards – Kent Kennedy
Inside Back Cover – Can You Spot the Differences? (Desk Sergeant) – Art Bouthillier
Back Cover – Cracked.com ad (1st Cracked.com ad)

**350, December 2000 (52 pages) ($2.95)**

Cover – We Flip Our Lid – Dick Kulpa
Inside Front Cover – Meet Simpy Dumpkins, the World's Most Hated Man! (a real head for football) – Dick Kulpa (full color)
Page 1 – Inside Cracked (full color)
Page 2 – It's a Cracked Cracked Cracked Cracked World! / "Easy Ed" Steckley Kills a Cat a Month! – Ed Steckley / Cracked Celebrity Personal Ads – Barry Dutter / But Cracked – Jonathan Grey, Tom Richmond / Yo! Butch! – Dick Kulpa / Chalk Bored – David Cooney (full color)
Page 4 – Scoopy-Poo and the Blare Witch Too! – Dick Kulpa / Barry Dutter (full color)
Page 8 – Hot-Tubbin' With a Babe! – Art Bouthillier (full color)
Page 9 – Mr. Precious Gets Lost! – Ed Steckley / Barry Dutter
Page 10 – Breaking the Mechanics Code – Mike Ricigliano / Mike Morse
Page 13 – The Girl Next Door – Rick Parker
Page 14 – Take a Turd for the Worse – Charles Filius / Bobbie Bender
Page 16 – Paper Training – Al Scaduto
Page 17 – Haunted Home Shopping Club – Rob Orzechowski / Barry Dutter
Page 20 – New Actors for the X-Files – Ed Steckley / Barry Dutter
Page 23 – Shut-Ups (ghost costume) – Dick Kulpa / John Salerno
Page 25 – From the Cracked Lens! (Do you like 'em)
Page 27 – It's the Great Punkin, Churlie Braun! – Gary Fields (reprint from *Cracked Monster Party* #7)
Page 29 – Martin's Screams – Vic Martin (reprint from *For Monsters Only* #2)

Page 30 – In a Perfect World – Steve Kurth / Barry Dutter
Page 32 – Desperate Times – Chris Eliopoulos
Page 35 – Shut-Ups (happiest day) – Don Orehek (reprint from *Cracked Monster Party* #11)
Page 36 – Ghost Story Club – Dick Kulpa / Allan Zullo
Page 39 – You Know You're a Loser When – Frank Cummings
Page 41 – Redneck Computer Hacker – Rick Parker (full color)
Page 42 – That 70s Craze! – Steph Ramsay / Bobbie Bender (full color)
Page 46 – One Day on the Enterprise – Dick Kulpa / Barry Dutter (full color) Page 47 – Sometimes it Sneaks Up On Ya – Art Bouthillier (full color)
Page 48 – Cracked.com ad
Inside Back Cover – Falling Rock Zone – John Severin / Daryl Butler
Back Cover – The Nare Witch Project – Dick Kulpa, Suzie Estridge / Barry Dutter

**351, January 2001 (52 pages) ($2.95)**
Cover – The Grinch Steals X-Mas From the 'Hood! – Ed Steckley
Inside Front Cover – Simpy Dumpkins, the World's Most Hated Man! (sinking ship) – Dick Kulpa (full color)
Page 1 – Inside Cracked (full color)
Page 2 – The Grunch Who Repossessed Christmas – Rich Hedden / Barry Dutter (full color)
Page 6 – It's a Cracked Cracked Cracked Cracked World! / Guess Who's "Cummings" to Dinner – Frank Cummings / Cracked Message Boards / But Cracked (full color)
Page 8 – Wedgie Boy! – Steph Ramsay / Barry Dutter (full color) (1st *Wedgie Boy*)
Page 9 – A "Precious" Gift – Ed Steckley
Page 10 – Cracked Lens (lay off the hot sauce)
Page 12 – The Yo-Yo Champion – Art Bouthillier
Page 13 – Off the Cave Wall – Steph Ramsay / Barry Dutter
Page 14 – The Totally Honest TV Guide – Gunnar Johnson
Page 16 – It's Practically Magic – Kent Kennedy
Page 17 – Brainpan & Cheesy (cold outside) – Gary Fields (1st *Brainpan & Cheesy*)
Page 18 – What Parents Say, What Parents Mean – Mike Kazaleh / Bobbie Bender
Page 21 – Can You Spot the Differences? (Popcorn) – Art Bouthillier
Page 22 – If Santa Lived Like the Rest of Us! – Charles Filius
Page 23 – Why It's Great to Be a Dog – Gary Fields
Page 24 – Christmas Toys for the New Millennium! – Charles Filius / Ted Ratburry

Page 26 – When Being with the Obese is a Blessing! – Mike Ricigliano / Bobbie Bender
Page 28 – Redneck Rock – Charles Filius
Page 29 – Cracked Shut-Ups (Europe) – Bill McCartney (Bill Ward) (reprint from #2)
Page 30 – When DNA Testing is Done on All Historical Figures – Gunnar Johnson
Page 32 – The $64,000,000 Cracked-Pot Question – John Severin (reprint from #1)
Page 34 – A Bad Day for the "Whassup" Dude – Martin Heeley
Page 35 – Simpy Dumpkins: The World's Most Hated Man! (toilet) – Dick Kulpa
Page 36 – A Cracked Look at the Secret Lives of Shopping Carts! – Charles Filius / Stephen Barrington
Page 38 – Caractors – Dick Kulpa
Page 39 – It's Practically Magic Part II – Kent Kennedy
Page 40 – The Painter's Fantasy – Oskar Blotta (reprint from #85)
Page 41 – Charlie's Hotties – Frank Cummings / Barry Dutter (full color)
Page 45 – The Tox-Sick Avenger! – Dick Kulpa / Barry Dutter (full color)
Inside Back Cover – One Super Day at the Gorge – Art Bouthillier
Back Cover – Cracked.com ad

**352, February 2001 (52 pages) ($2.95)**

Cover – Survivor Plus…We Cast Off Castaway! – Ed Steckley
Inside Front Cover – Meet Simpy Dumpkins, the World's Most Hated Man! (ambulance) – Dick Kulpa (full color)
Page 1 – Inside Cracked (full color)
Page 2 – Cracked Survivor! – Dick Kulpa / Barry Dutter (full color)
Page 8 – Wedgie Boy! – Steph Ramsay / Barry Dutter (full color)
Page 9 – Mr. Precious Hits Broadway! – Ed Steckley
Page 10 – Apt. 4F – Kutsky & Trisania
Page 11 – Hapless Hound – Gary Fields
Page 12 – Now We Are True-ly Cracked! – Daryl Cagle
Page 14 – Klugg! – Rich Hedden / Barry Dutter (1st *Klugg!*)
Page 15 – 2 Hungry Kats! – Gary Fields
Page 16 – Subscription ad – John Severin (reprint from #9)
Page 17 – Suppositories Can Kill You – Art Bouthillier
Page 18 – The Last Mile – Don Orehek
Page 20 – Lame But Easy Science Projects – Kent Kennedy
Page 22 – New Uses For Old People! – Charles Filius / Chad Elliott
Page 24 – College…The Best of Times, The Worst of Times – Charles Filius / Chad Elliott

Page 26 – Cussed Away! – Ed Steckley
Page 30 – Cracked Gross-Outs – Bruce Bolinger / Andy Lamberti
Page 32 – Off On the Wrong Foot! – Bill McCartney (Bill Ward) (reprint from #3) (originally called, "A Case of Mistaken Identity")
Page 33 – An Autopedia – Nelson Dewey
Page 36 – Crack-Ups! – Charles Filius
Page 37 – Survivor Shut-Ups (wanted a thigh) – Mike Ricigliano / John Salerno Page 38 – Practical Jokes in Sports – Mike Kazaleh / Bobbie Bender
Page 40 – Can You Spot the Differences? (News Break) – Art Bouthillier
Page 41 – The Incredible Shrinking Friends – Frank Cummings / Barry Dutter (full color)
Page 45 – Cracked Fake-Out Coupons! (full color)
Page 46 – It's a Cracked Cracked Cracked Cracked World! / Some of the Greatest Artists of All Time Have Drawn for Cracked Magazine! – Jack Davis / But Cracked / Meet Artist Kent "K-Toons" Kennedy – Kent Kennedy / Yo! Butch! / Cracked New Year's Resolutions / Next Issue / Non-Corrections! (full color)
Page 48 – Warning Labels for Idiots – Tom Milutinovic / Denny Spurling (full color)
Inside Back Cover – One Dandy Stroll in the Park – Art Bouthillier
Back Cover – Cracked.com ad

**353, March 2001 (52 pages) ($2.95)**
Cover – Pika-Nose – Dick Kulpa
Inside Front Cover – Simpy Dumpkins Tells the Story of His Birth! – Dick Kulpa (full color)
Page 1 – Inside Cracked – Dick Kulpa (full color)
Page 2 – EXcreMENt! – Tom Richmond / Barry Dutter (reprint from #346) (full color)
Page 8 – The Big Bad Wolf's Secret Weapon! – Santiago Cornejo (full color)
Page 9 – A (Really!) Precious Valentine! – Ed Steckley
Page 10 – Movie Prequels We'd Like to See! – Frank Cummings / Barry Dutter
Page 14 – Perfect Jobs for the Elderly! – Bruce Bolinger / Bobbie Bender
Page 16 – New Jobs for Bill Clinton – Noel Anderson / Barry Dutter
Page 18 – The Burglar – Don Orehek / Barry Dutter
Page 19 – Another Klugg Moment in History – Rich Hedden / Barry Dutter
Page 20 – The Real Truth Over Those False Rumors About Cracked Magazine – John Severin / George Gladir (reprint from #25) (originally called, "Those False Rumors About Cracked Magazine")

Page 24 – Cracked Crashes the Antiques Road Show! – Martin Heeley
Page 26 – Rite of Passage – Mike Kazaleh / Dan Fiorella, Barry Dutter
Page 28 – Joe Studd in Escape From the Cell! – Gary Fields / Barry Dutter
Page 29 – Pokemon Gone Wild! – Mike Ricigliano (reprint from #343, not #342 as it says in the issue)
Page 32 – Harry PotBelly – Wayne Novelli / Barry Dutter
Page 33 – One Day at a Florida Marine World Theme Park – Don Orehek / Barry Dutter
Page 34 – What's My IQ? – Kent Kennedy / Denny Spurling
Page 36 – The Year in Rap! – Steve Kurth / Barry Dutter, Dick Kulpa
Page 39 – Backwash / Yo Butch! – Dick Kulpa / But Cracked – Dick Kulpa
Page 40 – Subscription ad – Bill McCartney (Bill Ward) (reprint from #8)
Page 41 – Other Celebrity Name-Brand Products – Gunnar Johnson (full color) Page 46 – Trying to Figure This Pokeman Phenomenon Out? We at Cracked Are Too! – Gary Fields / Steve Strangio, Dan Fiorella (reprint from #339) (originally called, "Everything You Never Wanted to Know About Pokemon) (full color)
Page 48 – Cracked.com ad
Inside Back Cover – Phone Sounds Like – Art Bouthillier
Back Cover – It's Not Easy Being a Big Bad Wolf! – Santiago Cornejo

**354, April 2001 (52 pages) ($2.95)**
Cover – We Rap Eminem! – Dick Kulpa
Inside Front Cover – Back Issues ad (#346, 347, 348, 349, 350, 351, 352)
Page 1 – Inside Cracked (full color)
Page 2 – Dork Angel – Frank Cummings / Barry Dutter (full color)
Page 7 – The Great White Dope! – Dick Kulpa / Barry Dutter (full color)
Page 9 – Mr. Precious: No Pussyfootin' Around Here! – Ed Steckley
Page 10 – Non-Violent Super Heroes! – Chuck Frazier / Barry Dutter
Page 12 – Shut-Ups (I'll find you) – John Severin (reprint from #13, not #25 as it says in the issue)
Page 13 – Superhero Trading Cards You'll Never See! – Grant Meihm / Barry Dutter
Page 16 – Rapper in the Crapper – Bruce Bolinger / Bobbie Bender (reprint from #345)
Page 18 – Joe Studd in The Legend of Joe Studd! – Gary Fields / Barry Dutter
Page 19 – Replacement TV Shows We'd Like to See – Bruce Bolinger / Steve Strangio

Page 22 – Believe it or Nuts!! – Jack Davis (reprint from #13, not #25 as it says in the issue)
Page 23 – Cracked Cliques! – Mike Kazaleh / Dan Fiorella
Page 26 – World's Most Hated Man Meets the World's "Baddest" Rapper! – Dick Kulpa
Page 27 – Cracked 'Toons of the Year – Jack Davis (reprint from #13, not #25 as it says in the issue) (originally called "Cartoons of the Year")
Page 29 – Klugg Epochs in History – Rich Hedden / Barry Dutter
Page 30 – Freezing People – Jack Davis (reprint from #13, not #25 as it says in the issue)
Page 32 – You Know You've Been Listening to Too Much Howard Stern, When – Rob Orzechowski / Barry Dutter
Page 35 – Celebrity Dogs! – Chuck Frazier / Barry Dutter
Page 38 – "How Things Really Began – Not! (First World War) – John Severin (reprint from #13, not #25 as it says in the issue) (originally called, "When it all Started")
Page 39 – Subscription ad – Jack Davis (reprint from #13, not #25 as it says in the issue)
Page 40 – Superhero Shut-Ups! (Stuporman) – Mike Ricigliano
Page 41 – Wedgie Boy! (Go get 'em) – Steph Ramsay / Dick Kulpa (full color)
Page 45 – One Day at Bennie's Burrito Hut – Art Bouthillier (full color)
Page 46 – Strange But "True"-ly Cracked! – Daryl Cagle (full color)
Page 48 – Backwash / But Cracked / Yo Butch! – Dick Kulpa / Glick Glidewell – Kane Lynch (full color)
Inside Back Cover – Cracked.com ad
Back Cover – All in a Day's Work! – Santiago Cornejo

**355, May 2001 (52 pages) ($2.99)** (Last monthly issue)
Cover – Digi-Mon Are Taking Over! – Rick Parker
Inside Front Cover – Cracked.com ad
Page 1 – Inside Cracked (full color)
Page 2 – Cannibal! – Frank Cummings / Barry Dutter (full color)
Page 6 – Backwash / Websites We'd Love to See! / Meet Cracked's Resident Rapper: Noel Anderson! / But Cracked / Glick Glidewell – Kene Lynch / She's the Hottest Mascot You'll Ever Need! Meet "Miss Cracked!" / Yo! Butch! – Dick Kulpa / Fender Benders (full color)
Page 8 – Cracked Signs ad – Dick Kulpa (full color)
Page 9 – Cracked's Latest Yarn About Mr. Precious – Ed Steckley
Page 10 – The Soapranos – Walter Brogan / Lou Silverstone
Page 14 – Sim-sations! – Steve Kurth / Dan Fiorella
Page 16 – Cracked DVDs! – Noel Anderson / Dan Fiorella

Page 18 – Computer Crack-Ups! – Mike Kazaleh / Barry Dutter
Page 21 – Klugg Epochs in History – Rich Hedden
Page 22 – Chip Hacker Compter Nerd – Gary Fields / Barry Dutter
Page 23 – Computer Shut-Ups (I'm here for my date) – Mike Ricigliano / John Salerno
Page 24 – Internet Dating Warning Signs!! – Rick Parker / Michael Eury
Page 26 – TV: Then & Now – Bruce Bolinger / Barry Dutter
Page 29 – Subscription ad – John Severin (reprint from #34)
Page 30 – These Will "True"-ly Crack You Up! – Daryl Cagle
Page 32 – Cracked Shut-Ups (driving in the country) – Bill McCartney (Bill Ward) (reprint from #9)
Page 33 – Joe Studd (Wassup, Joe) – Gary Fields / Barry Dutter
Page 34 – Star Dreck: Voyeur – Chuck Frazier / Charlie Bihler
Page 40 – Viceboy Cigarette ad – John Severin (reprint from #9)
Page 41 – Digi-Money – Dick Kulpa / Barry Dutter (full color)
Page 45 – Stupid Teen Magazine – Gunnar Johnson (full color)
Page 48 – Dining at the Taco Emporium – Art Bouthillier (full color)
Inside Back Cover – Back Issues ad (#346, 347, 348, 349, 350, 351, 352)
Back Cover – One Good Turn Deserves Another – Santiago Cornejo

**356, July 2001 (52 pages) ($2.99)**

Cover – Rock Music Issue! – Chuck Frazier
Inside Front Cover – Back Issues ad (#346, 347, 348, 349, 350, 351, 352)
Page 1 – Inside Cracked (full color)
Page 2 – Gross-ie and the Pussycats – Frank Cummings / Barry Dutter (full color)
Page 6 – One Drunk Helping Another – Art Bouthillier (full color)
Page 7 – Cracked.com ad
Page 8 – Backwash (Jonathan Harris photo) / Cracked Movie Awards / Next Issue (Issue #357 is promoted as coming out in the next month, but it literally came out an entire year later.) (full color)
Page 9 – Mr. Precious Takes a Bath! – Ed Steckley Page 10 – Cracked Rap – Noel Anderson / Trudy Tereba
Page 12 – New Jobs for Rock Stars – Chuck Frazier / Bobbie Bender, Barbie Dunder
Page 15 – Musical Shut-Ups (Puffy Combs) – Mike Ricigliano / John Salerno
Page 16 – But Cracked – Chuck Frazier, Bill Ward / Yo! Butch! – Dick Kulpa
Page 18 – Joe Studd (You come here a lot?) – Mike Kazaleh / Barry Dutter
Page 19 – Know Your Boogers – J. Kelly (reprint from #313)
Page 20 – New Wrestling Leagues! – Bruce Bolinger / Steve

Strangio Page 22 – How We Cracked Howard Stern's Radio Show! – Dick Kulpa

Page 24 – The History of Rock Starring Klugg – Rich Hedden / Barry Dutter

Page 26 – Cracked's Style Do's & Dont's – Mike Kazaleh / James Oakes, Barry Dutter

Page 28 – Develop a Sense of Humor – Carl Burgos (reprint from #9)

Page 30 – You Know You're Really Sick, When – Rick Parker / Kevin Kwak

Page 33 – Unbearable – Ed Steckley / Barry Dutter

Page 37 – Sylvester (you spilled my bottled water) – Tayyar Ozkan / Brady Blaine

Page 38 – These Will "True"-ly Crack You Up! – Daryl Cagle

Page 40 – Subscription ad (reprint from #25)

Page 41 – La Tower Recordas – Jeff Wong (reprint from #338) (full color)

Page 42 – The Cracked Guide to Boy Groups – Frank Cummings / Greg Grabianski (reprint from #338) (full color)

Page 46 – When More Celebrities Get Their Own Magazines – Gunnar Johnson (full color)

Inside Back Cover – Cracked Sign ad – Dick Kulpa

Back Cover – Preacher Says the Magic Word! – Santiago Cornejo

**357, July 2002 (52 pages) ($2.99)** (1[st] issue in a year.)

Cover – Toon Wars! – Rick Parker

Inside Front Cover – Barry Dutter's *Shy Guy's Guide to Dating* ad

Page 1 – Inside Cracked (full color)

Page 2 – Loon Raider – Frank Cummings / Barry Dutter (full color)

Page 6 – A Cracked Review! Silly CD's – Dave Berns, Jay Lynch, John Pound / Rudy Panucci, Dick Kulpa (full color)

Page 8 – The Naked Tooth – Art Bouthillier (full color)

Page 9 – Mr. Precious Catches Arachnaphobia – Ed Steckley Page 10 – New Jobs for Celebs! – Chuck Frazier / Bobbie Bender, Barbie Dunder

Page 13 – Backwash – Dutter Nonsense – Barry Dutter / Read Why Cracked-heads Love Artist Chuck Frazier's Work – Chuck Frazier / Animation Poll

Page 14 – But Cracked (Lisa Pepitone Photo) / Letter of the Month / Yo! Butch! – Dick Kulpa

Page 17 – Joe Studd in "I've Got You Under My Skin!" – Mike Kazaleh / Barry Dutter

Page 18 – True-ly Entertaining Toons, Sure to Crack You Up! – Daryl Cagle

Page 20 – The Family Ruckus – Martin Heeley
Page 22 – Top 10 'Toons of All Time! / Double Eagle & Co. – Dick Kulpa
Page 24 – Meekest Link – Chuck Frazier / Barry Dutter
Page 29 – Pukey McSpew Gets a Dog! – Martin Heeley (1st *Pukey McSpew*)
Page 30 – Extreme Gameshows – Rob Orzechowski / Steve Strangio
Page 32 – Cracked Sick Flicks – Waynodraino Designs
Page 34 – King of All Wedgies – Dave Berris
Page 37 – One Day at the Cracked Offices – Tayyar Ozkan / Brady Blaine
Page 38 – Everything You Ever Wanted to Know About…Homer Simpson – Max Power / Double Eagle & Co. – Dick Kulpa / Cracked's Jr. Editor of the Month!
Page 40 – Klugg Badrock Blues – Rich Hedden / Barry Dutter
Page 41 – Toon Wars: U.S. vs. Japan! – Mike Kazaleh / Barry Dutter (full color)
Page 45 – Newsjunkie – Dave Berns (full color)
Page 47 – Back Issues ad (#343, 346, 347, 348, 349, 350, 351, 352, 353, 355, 356)
Page 48 – Cracked Drawing the Line Meet the Cracked Man Behind Cracked – Dick Kulpa / Double Eagle & Co. – Dick Kulpa
Inside Back Cover – Cracked Lithograph ad – Zina Saunders, Jay Lynch, John Severin (new, with reprint from #71)
Back Cover – Simpy Dumpkin's The World's (Second) Most Hated Man! (New *Cracked* T-shirt) – Dick Kulpa

**358, September 2002 (52 pages) ($2.99)**

Cover – Summer Movie Spectacular! – Chuck Frazier
Inside Front Cover – Back Issues ad (#343, 346, 347, 348, 349, 350, 351, 352, 353, 355, 356, 357)
Page 1 – Idiotorial – Dick Kulpa / What's Inside / This Month's Junior Editor (full color)
Page 2 – Amazing Sissy-Man – Dick Ayers / Barry Dutter, Dick Kulpa (full color)
Page 8 – Pukey McSpew Chews Gum – Martin Heeley (full color)
Page 9 – Li'l Klugg in "One Bad Apple" – Rich Hedden
Page 10 – Updating Kids Books for the New Millennium! – Kent Kennedy Page 13 – Style Do's & Don't's – Mike Kazaleh / Jay Oaks
Page 14 – What's So Great About Friends? – Frank Cummings / Barry Dutter
Page 16 – Sports Rule Changes We'd Like to See – Jeff Austin / Denny Spurling

Page 18 – Joe Studd (Morning, Joe) – Mike Kazaleh / Barry Dutter
Page 19 – One Day at Cracked Magazine – Tayar Ozkari / Bobbie Bender, Dave Berns
Page 22 – But Cracked / Yo! Butch! – Dick Kulpa
Page 23 – Double Eagle & Co. – Dick Kulpa
Page 24 – Hurl Harbor – Ed Steckley / Barry Dutter
Page 30 – Embarrassing Moments for Super Heroes – Dick Ayers, Dick Kulpa / Chad Elliott
Page 32 – Good Girls & Bad Boys – Pete Fitzgerald / Bobbie Bender
Page 34 – Backwash / Artist Mike Kazaleh is All He's Cracked Up to Be! – Mike Kazaleh / Dutter Nonsense – Barry Dutter
Page 35 – Pukey McSpew Gets a Cat – Martin Heeley
Page 36 – When Other Musicians Start Acting Like Gangsta Rappers – Chuck Frazier / Barry Dutter
Page 39 – Buy-Buy-Buy! – Noel Anderson / Trudy Tereba
Page 40 – Hollywood Shut-Ups (strange new breed of spider) – Dave Berns / Troy Hickman
Page 41 – The Way to a Man's Heart – Santiago Cornejo (full color) Page 42 – If Cracked Ran the T.V. Networks – Gunnar Johnson (full color) Page 44 – Cracked Lithograph ad – Zina Saunders, Jay Lynch, Basil Gogos (new, with reprint from #71) (full color)
Page 45 – Star Snores Episode II Send in the Clones – Dave Berns / Barry Dutter (full color) Page 48 – Zero Temptation Island – Gunnar Johnson (full color) Inside Back Cover – Barry Dutter's *Shy Guy's Guide to Dating* ad
Back Cover – Cracked America T-Shirts ad

**359, February 2003 (52 pages) ($3.50)**
Cover – Insane Cracked Posse Raps Eminem! – Chuck Frazier
Inside Front Cover – Santa Flaws! – Santiago Cornejo
Page 1 – Inside Cracked Megazine (full color)
Page 2 – "Crackedass" – Ben Jones, Ray Morelli / Jonathan Lenin (full color)
Page 5 – Bad News vs Good News – Huw Evans (full color)
Page 8 – Lines Are Hell – Santiago Cornejo (full color)
Page 9 – Cracked Mascot Sylvester P. Smythe "Quittin' Time!" – Tayyar Ozkan
Page 10 – Shut Up MTV! – Dave Berns / Troy Hickman
Page 11 – Joe Studd in "The Magic Words" – Michael Neno / Barry Dutter
Page 12 – Ghost Story Club – Claude St. Aubin, Dick Kulpa / Allan Zullo

Page 15 – Backwash Cracked Kulpa Meets "Crazy" Ed / Dutter Nonsense – Barry Dutter
Page 16 – Where the Hell is Osama? – Noel Anderson / Scott Gosar
Page 18 – Magazines for Dogs! – Gunnar Johnson
Page 20 – Scenes We'll Never See On The Anna Nicole Show – Kevin Karsteins / Scott Gosar
Page 22 – 8 Simple Rules for Dating a Middle-Aged Nerd – Derrick Wyatt / Wil Radcliffe
Page 24 – Hate Mile! – Kevin Tuma / Barry Dutter
Page 27 – Pukey McSpew Reads a Book – Martin Heeley Page 28 – The World's Most Frightening Fan Club Presidents – Eric Kirchberg / Bernie Soul
Page 30 – Yo! Butch! Insane Clown Posse: Mad Mom Wants Band Banned! – Butch Byteme / Dick Kulpa
Page 31 – Cracked Designer Mailboxes – Kent Kennedy Page 32 – New Theme Restaurants We'd Like to See! – Jay Chuppe / Barry Dutter
Page 34 – Joe Studd in "The Only Girl" – Michael Neno / Barry Dutter
Page 35 – 007 versus XXX – Eric Kirchberg / Barry Dutter
Page 36 – Never Cheat a Cheater – Art Bouthillier
Page 37 – But Cracked / Letter of the Month (The answer to "How Many Times Does *Cracked* Appear on the Cover?" Contest from *Cracked* #29, is 4103 (or is it 4104)? (Sarah Douglas photo)
Page 39 – Cracked Customer Care Survey
Page 40 – Welcome to the Mega Mall! (full color)
Page 42 – YYY – Dave Berns / Barry Dutter (full color)
Page 46 – When the Movies Have Corporate Sponsors! – Gunnar Johnson, Dave Berns / Barry Dutter (full color) Page 48 – Life's a Beach! – Santiago Cornejo (full color)
Inside Back Cover – The Cracked Lens Does (in) Comic Conventions
Back Cover – Barry Dutter's *Shy Guy's Guide to Dating* ad

**360, May 2003 (52 pages) ($3.50)**

Cover – We Swat Harry Potter – Tom Fleming
Inside Front Cover – Silly CDs ad
Page 1 – Inside Cracked Megazine (full color)
Page 2 – Hogwart's Confidential – Ben Jones / Jonathan Lenin, Garry Messick (full color)
Page 4 – Got Milk (Elsie D. Cow) – Kent Kennedy (full color)
Page 5 – Mr. Precious in "Family Dinner" – Todd Casey / Barry Dutter (full color)
Page 6 – The Silliness Continues! – Jay Lynch, John Pound / Elizabeth Semple (full color)

Page 8 – Simpy Dumpkins World's Most Hated Man (Dang – Everyone still hates me) – Dick Kulpa (full color)
Page 9 – Here Comes Peter Cottontail – Kent Kennedy
Page 10 – Will Success Spoil Spongebomb Squarepegs – Dave Berns / Troy Hickman
Page 12 – Simon Searches Pop Music History for the Ultimate American Idol – Chuck Frazier
Page 13 – Why Doesn't This Ever Happen? – Bill Ward (reprint from #1)
Page 14 – The Top Ten Simpsons Episodes Ever! – John Severin / Barry Dutter (new, with reprint from #330)
Page 16 – Commercial Mascots Gone Bad – Ray Morelli / Wil Radcliffe
Page 18 – Ghost Story Club! – Dick Kulpa / Allan Zullo
Page 20 – Cracked Mascot Sylvester P. Smythe "A Dog's World" – Tayyar Ozkan / Brady Blaine
Page 21 – The Perfect Spam Recipient! – Huw Evans
Page 22 – Reality Game Show Shut-Ups! ($50,000) – Andy Ristiano / Bernie Soul, Barry Dutter
Page 23 – Backwash Cracked Turns 45! Dutter Nonsense – Barry Dutter
Page 24 – Lord, Not the Rings The Two Tired – Troy Hickman, Dave Berns / Scott Dalrymple
Page 29 – Cracked Magazine Annual Syllie Awards – Kevin Karstens / Barry Dutter
Page 30 – Today's Top Celebrities Star in Yesterday's Favorites – Chuck Frazier / Will Radcliffe
Page 32 – The Up and Downside of Modern Living – Shawn Brailey / Dan Fiorella
Page 34 – Kent Kennedy's Cracked Gags – Kent Kennedy
Page 35 – Klugg The First HMO – Rich Hedden
Page 36 – But Cracked (Dick Kulpa photo) / Yo! Butch! – Dick Kulpa
Page 38 – Joe Studd (Whatever happened with that girl) – Mike Kazaleh / Barry Dutter
Page 39 – Keep Those Letters Coming! / Barry Wants Your Drawings! / Subscription ad
Page 40 – Welcome to the Mega Mall! (full color)
Page 41 – Buy Another Day – Ed Steckley / Barry Dutter (full color)
Page 46 – A Few Things Superheroes Would Never Do! – Dave Berns / Dan Fiorella
Page 48 – The Cracked Lens (Barry Zito, Jamie Farr, Bob Levy, Artie Lange, K.C. Armstrong, Insane Clown Posse, Scott Gosar photos)
Inside Back Cover – Barry Dutter's *Shy Guy's Guide to Dating* ad
Back Cover – Frat Life at Hogwart's Academy – Derrick Wyatt / Jonathan Lenin, Garry Messick

**361, September 2003 (52 pages) ($3.50)**

Cover – Reality TV Issue! – Jason Seiler
Inside Front Cover – Chip Hacker in That's No Virus – That's My Wife! – Ray Morelli / Barry Dutter
Page 1 – Inside Cracked Megazine (full color)
Page 2 – Cracked Magazine Answers That Age-Old Question: What is Rock n' Roll? – Jason Seiler / Scott Gosar (full color)
Page 4 – The Lighter Side of Sci-Fi – Tye Bourdony (full color)
Page 5 – Mr. Precious in "A Place in the Shade" – Todd Casey (full color)
Page 6 – Reality Shows We'd Like to See! – Ben Jones / Barry Dutter (full color)
Page 9 – In the Bad Old Days – Kevin Tuma / Scott Gosar
Page 12 – Yao-Za! – Shawn Brailey / Jonathan Lenin
Page 14 – Ruin & Stumpy? – Wil Branca / Troy Hickman
Page 16 – Glumps "Delusions of Saddam Hussein" Figurine ad – Ross
Page 17 – Simpy Dumpkins & Sylvester P. Smythe in: Idle Americans – Noel Anderson / Barry Dutter
Page 18 – Bling Bling Ding-a-Lings – Dave Berns / Bernie Soul
Page 20 – Celebrity Frankenfoods! – Derrick Wyatt / Huw Evans
Page 22 – Joe Studd (We've gone over these figures) – Mike Kazaleh / Barry Dutter
Page 23 – Klugg in Feeding Frenzy – Rich Hedden
Page 24 – Busty the Franchise Slayer – Jason Robinson / Travis Kramer
Page 27 – Backwash The Many Faces of Jason Seiler! – Jason Seiler / Cracked Salutes: CCC Promotions
Page 28 – Ghost Story Club! – Dick Kulpa / Allan Zullo
Page 30 – Horror Movies That Would Really Scare People! – Huw Evans
Page 32 – Marvel Goes to the Movies – Chris Caldwell / Barry Dutter / Comics Invade the Movies! – Barry Dutter
Page 34 – If "I Love Lucy" Did Reality TV – Angelo Torres (reprint from #10) (originally called "Casual Format")
Page 35 – Kent Kennedy's Cracked Gags – Kent Kennedy
Page 36 – But Cracked (Dick Kulpa photo) / Yo! Butch! – Dick Kulpa
Page 39 – Question Authority Shut-Ups! (my fellow Americans) – Chris Caldwell / Gary Messick
Page 40 – It's a Super Sale at the Mega Mall (full color)
Page 42 – Yugi Uh-Oh! $ell$ Out! – Dave Berns / Troy Hickman (full color) Page 44 – Devildawg – Bradford Hess / Barry Dutter (full color) Inside Back Cover – The Cracked Lens (Lou Ferrigno, Raven, Dick Kulpa, Barry Dutter, Scott Gosar photos)
Back Cover – Barry Dutter's *Shy Guy's Guide to Dating* ad

**362, April 2004 (52 pages) ($2.95)** (Cover price reduces.) (Note: "Magazine")

Cover – Recall Freak-All – Jason Seiler, John Severin, Mike Ricigliano (new, with reprint from *Cracked Collectors' Edition* #76)
Inside Front Cover – Dreamcon ad
Page 1 – Inside Cracked (full color)
Page 2 – What Up With That? – Jay Chuppe / Don Fiorella (full color)
Page 4 – The Mumbler! – Huw Evans (full color)
Page 6 – Mr. Precious in: School Daze – Todd Casey / Scott Gosar (full color)
Page 7 – The "Cracked-ables" – Ray Morelli / John Samony, Scott Gosar (full color)
Page 9 – Backwash Marten Jallad & Scott Gosar: 2 Heads Are Better Than 1 – Marten Jallad, Jason Seiler, Dick Kulpa (Dick Kulpa photo)
Page 10 – Cracked Separates Men From Boys! – Kent Gamble / Scott Gosar
Page 12 – Joe Studd (meet my mom) – Mike Kazaleh / Barry Dutter / Our 1st Annual Cracked Mutilation Competition
Page 13 – Celeb Recipes – Mike Morse
Page 15 – T.V. Through a Cracked Screen! – Anthony Owsley
Page 16 – The Last People on Earth You'd Ever Want to Be! – Jason Seiler / Scott Gosar
Page 18 – Chip Hacker in "Reality Bites" – Ben Boling / Barry Dutter
Page 19 – It'll Be a Cold Day in Hell, When – Ben Boling / Scott Gosar
Page 20 – Subscription ad (Glen Campbell photo)
Page 21 – Who Do You Think You're Fooling? – Dave Newton / Huw Evans
Page 22 – But Cracked / Letters of the Month! / Yo! Butch! – Dick Kulpa
Page 24 – Buy American or It's 'Bye, America! – Billy Genius
Page 26 – Cracked Gross Gags!
Page 27 – If Michael Jackson had Starred in – John Severin (reprint from #207)
Page 33 – They Never Seem to Mention – Huw Evans
Page 35 – Rapper Remakes of Hollywood Blockbusters! – Dave Berns / Matthew Pellowski
Page 37 – Cracked Shut-Ups! (bountiful feast) – Noel Anderson / Scott Gosar
Page 38 – 10 Reasons Why Arnold Should Be Recalled! – Dick Kulpa / Carson Demmans, Scott Gosar, Evelyn A.R. Gabai
Page 40 – Chalk Bored – Terry Copeland
Page 41 – Hot Back Issue Sale! (#343, 346, 347, 348, 349, 350, 355, 357, 358, 360, 361) (full color)

Page 42 – The Sulk – Steve Stanley / Barry Dutter (full color)
Page 46 – Cracked Hits the Jackpot With These Gambling Gems! – Santiago Cornejo (full color)
Page 48 – The Date – Ben Boling / Steve Herold (full color)
Inside Back Cover – Cracked Lens – Scott Gosar (Julie Newmar, Dan Aykroyd, Adam West, Dick Kulpa photos)
Back Cover – Cracked Lens (Cracked Challenge) – Dick Kulpa

**363, July 2004 (52 pages) ($2.95)** (Note: "Magazine")
Cover – Rock Music Issue! – Kent Gamble
Inside Front Cover – Cracked Lens (Lorenzo Lamas, Virginia Hey, Robert Englund, Dick Kulpa, Erin Gray photos)
Page 1 – Inside Cracked (full color)
Page 2 – Martha Stewpid: Prisoner of Good Taste – Anne Timmons / John Lustig (full color)
Page 4 – Personalized Greeting Cards for Music Celebs – Huw Evans (full color)
Page 6 – Mr. Precious: "Collar My World" – Todd Casey / Evelyn A.R.Gabai (full color)
Page 8 – Chip Hacker in "Spam for Pam" – Ben Boling / Barry Dutter (full color)
Page 9 – Shut-Ups! (50 cent) – Noel Anderson / Scott Gosar
Page 10 – A Cracked Loot at the Last 14 Grammy Winners – Joe Calchi / Neal Angel
Page 12 – Beatles Tunes for Our Loony Times! – Kent Gamble / Scott Gosar
Page 15 – The Confessional – Mike Arnold
Page 16 – Game Shows – David Alvarez, Dick Kulpa / Dan Fiorella
Page 18 – Pukey Goes Kara-icky! – Martin Heeley
Page 19 – Cracked Interviews the King of Pop Music Management – Noel Anderson
Page 22 – But Cracked (Dick Kulpa photo) / Yo! Butch! – Dick Kulpa
Page 24 – Cracked Tourist Destinations (for the Not-So-Discriminating Traveler) – Dave Newton / Carson Demmans
Page 26 – Something Fishy Going on Here! – Marten Jallad / Comic Conventions ad
Page 27 – Pop Stars in Space! – Mike Morse
Page 30 – If Jessica Simpson "Did" History! – Randy Martinez / Scott Gosar
Page 32 – Webitorial
Page 33 – New Celebrity Guitars – Vic Martin (reprint from #97)
Page 35 – Gawdzilla Gets His Just Desserts – Rich Hedden
Page 36 – More Shut-Ups! (endorsement deal) – Noel Anderson / Scott Gosar

Page 37 – A Leg Up On the Competition! – Rasheed Humphrey
Page 38 – Retired at 35! – Billy Genius / Jim Stewart
Page 40 – Subscription ad – John Severin (reprint from *Cracked Blockbuster* #5)
Page 41 – Hot Back Issue Sale! (#343, 346, 347, 348, 349, 350, 355, 357, 360, 361, 362) (full color)
Page 42 – Pinheads of the Caribbean The Curse of the Bleak Hurl – Kevin Tuma / Scott Gosar (full color)
Page 48 – Backwash Cover Artist Kent Gamble Uncovered – Kent Gamble / Cheap Trick photo) / Artist Rasheed "Rush" Humphrey Cracks Cracked (Rasheed Humphrey photo)
Inside Back Cover – Dreamcon ad
Back Cover – Nothing But the Tooth – Santiago Cornejo

**364, September 2004 (52 pages) ($2.95)** (Note: "Magazine")
Cover – We Trump "The Donald" – Michael D'Antuono
Inside Front Cover – Nogglestones ad – Ernie Colon / Wil Radcliffe
Page 1 – Inside Cracked Cheap Trick's Rick Nielsen "Cracked's" New Publisher (full color)
Page 2 – For What Folks Are Paid, is it Any Wonder – Dave Newton / Neal Angel (full color)
Page 4 – Mr. Precious How Our Tax Dollars Are Spent – Mike Arnold / Evelyn A.R. Gabai (full color)
Page 5 – Chump-Mahal – Austin Janowsky / Mitch Hyman (full color)
Page 8 – Chip Hacker Make Over! – Ben Boling / Marten Jallad (full color)
Page 9 – Crack-ing the Code – Rasheed Humphrey
Page 10 – McSlang for Future McDictionaries – Kent Gamble / Scott Gosar
Page 12 – Trump Golf – June Brigman, Roy Richardsen / Dan Fiorella
Page 15 – "Worst in Show" – Ben Boling / Scott Gosar
Page 16 – Cracked Predictions for the 2004/2005 School Year
Page 18 – Cracked-fil-a – Anthony Owsley
Page 19 – Xtreme Changes to Classic Sports – Billy Genius / Steve Strangio
Page 24 – People to Avoid at the Hospital – Mike Arnold
Page 26 – "Omarosa" – Michael D'Antuono / Scott Gosar
Page 27 – Food For Thought – Kent Kennedy / Steve Herold
Page 28 – Cracked Visits a Modern Hospital – Frank Cummings / Fred Sahner
Page 30 – Hands Off! – Don Orehek / Kit Lively (reprint from #320, not #319 as it says in the issue) (originally called, "A Gypsy's Tale")
Page 31 – Mother of All Shut-Up Jokes – Marten Jallad

Page 32 – But Cracked (Dick Kulpa, Debbie Rochon photos) / Yo! Butch! – Dick Kulpa
Page 34 – If It Weren't For – Mike Arnold / Scott Gosar
Page 37 – Shut-Ups! (you're a sissy) – Noel Anderson / Scott Gosar
Page 38 – "Queer Eye" Makeovers Gone Horribly Wrong! – Tim Toolen / Steve Strangio
Page 40 – Subscription ad – Dick Kulpa
Page 41 – Hot Back Issue Sale! (#343, 346, 348, 349, 350, 355, 357, 360, 361, 362, 363) (full color)
Page 42 – If Cartoon Characters Existed in the Real World – Micah Harmon / Wil Radcliffe (full color)
Page 44 – Why it Sux to be Donald Trump – Mike Morse (full color)
Page 45 – Fright Night at the Laff Haus – Ben Boling / Steve Herold (full color)
Page 46 – How Would We Explain Earth to an Alien?!? – Huw Evans (full color) Page 48 – Backwash Meet Funnyman Huw Evans – Huw Evans (Blue Öyster Cult photo)
Inside Back Cover – Van Bushing ad (George W. Bush photo)
Back Cover – Look Who's Cracked (Steven Tyler, Rick Nielsen photos)

**365, November 2004 (52 pages) ($2.95)** (Last issue of the original series.)
Cover – Unwanted by Intelligent, Informed American Voters – Kelly Freas
Inside Front Cover – Somedays it Just Doesn't Pay to Be a Sponge! – Santiago Cornejo
Page 1 – Inside Cracked / Idiotorial (full color)
Page 2 – All-New 2004 Garbage Pol Kids – Jim Hunt / Mike Arnold (full color)
Page 3 – Mr. Precious The Great Debate – Mike Arnold /.Scott Gosar (full color)
Page 5 – Sideshow Freaks and Performers Where Are They Now? – Huw Evans (full color)
Page 8 – Chip Hacker Hack-Proof Computer – Ben Boling / Jim Stewart (full color) Page 9 – Kerry – Kent Gamble / Scott Gosar
Page 14 – 7 Embarrassments of the Ancient World – R. Martinez
Page 16 – "Potty" Line – Rasheed Humphrey Page 17 – Too Pretentious – Anthony Owsley
Page 18 – A Peek Inside the Personal Date Book of George W. Bush / John Kerry – Gunnar Johnson Page 20 – Presidential Shut-Ups! (Bush / Reagan) – Rasheed Humphrey / Scott Gosar
Page 21 – Orlando Collection Convention ad
Page 22 – Prophetical Political Poetics – Neil Shapiro / Scott Gosar
Page 24 – The Ten Commandments of Michael Moore – Gunnar Johnson

Page 26 - Rock Bottom Foreign TV Programs You'll Never See Here!
Page 28 - Bubba Meets Cracked! - Jesse Hanson / Mitch Hyman
Page 33 - Olympic Games Just for NYC! - Billy Genius / Mike Morse
Page 36 - If History's Greatest Speeches Were Delivered by Dubya Bush - Kevin Tuma / Neal Levin
Page 38 - Presidential Party Gags!!!
Page 39 - More Presidential Shut-Ups! (Clinton / Lincoln) - Rasheed Humphrey / Scott Gosar
Page 40 - Subscription ad - John Severin (reprint from "Cracked Collectors' Edition #106)
Page 41 - Hot Back Issue Sale! (#343, 346, 348, 349, 350, 357, 360, 361, 362, 363, 364) (full color)
Page 42 - 2004 Election Olympics - Mike Arnold (full color)
Page 44 - The Anatomy of a Slob - J. Kelly (reprint from #327) (full color)
Page 45 - Sty Weenie Babies - Rurik Tyler / Josh Cohen (reprint from #331) (originally called, "Ty Beanie Babies We'll Soon Be Seeing Everywhere") (full color)
Page 48 Backwash - Dick Kulpa / Shut Up, Michael Moore - Alex Zima (full color)
Inside Back Cover - Cracked Lens - Scott Gosar (Maury Povich, Kevin Nealon, Jesse Ventura, Jim McMahon, Brett Hull, Matt Williams, Donald Trump photos)
Back Cover - I Want You for White House Intern - Jeff Wong (reprint from #327)

**01, September / October 2006 (84 pages) ($3.99) (First issue of new series. Issues are now full color and a totally different format with very little artwork.)**

Cover - The 44-Year-Old Virgin? (Tom Cruise photo)
Page 2 - Drambuie ad
Page 3 - Cracked.com ad
Page 4 - Contents
Page 6 - Editor's Letter - John Czop / Monty Sarhan
Page 7 - Contributors
Page 8 - Letters
Page 9 - Busanity ad - Nick Felton / Kurt Metzger
Page 10 - Cracked Den
Page 13 - Celeb Scoop!
Page 15 - Great Moments in History 1985 - Richard Weinstein
Page 16 - Paris Hilton Sex Contract - Brian Sack
Page 17 - Match.gov - Alan Cross, Paul Fourie
Page 18 - Boobs
Page 19 - Wisecracks - Michael Ian Black

Page 20 – Mexican Boys: Surprisingly Expensive – Jay Pinkerton
Page 22 – Are You Naked?
Page 23 – Spy Scope! – Michael Kupperman
Page 24 – Let's Roll! – Todd Levin
Page 26 – Don't Tread On Me! - Maddox
Insert – Subscription Card
Insert – Cracked Survey
Page 27 – Quit Horsin' Around – George Pickens
Page 28 – About Face! – Brian Sack
Page 30 – The Rooks! – Aaron Lange
Page 33 – Mission: Enlistable – Jonathan Yevin Page 36 – The Next Super Power – John DeVore
Page 39 – The 2006 Douchebag Comprehensive Guide – Holly Schlesinger, Shauna Cagan
Page 42 – Periodic Table of the 1980s
Page 44 – Fastman! – Steve Sloan, Chris Eisert / Jay Pinkerston, Peter Lynn
Page 46 – Britney Xpress ad – Alan Cross, Paul Fourie
Page 47 – ESPN Magazine
Page 56 – 2007 Comedy Writing Competition
Page 57 – But Seriously – Jason Seiler (Jason is the first holdover artist from the old *Cracked*.)
Page 58 – Mencia in Hell – Justin Droms
Insert – Subscription ad
Page 59 – Ready For Prime Time – Darren Kane
Page 60 – Inoperable Humor – Michael J. Nelson
Page 62 – Million Dollar Daily – Justin Borucki
Page 66 – Canada Laughs Back – Jason Seiler / Jeff Felshman
Page 69 – SNL Primer – Justin Droms
Page 70 – Laugh Audit: Bill Murray
Page 72 – Mouths of the South – Rich Markey
Page 75 – Reviews
Page 79 – Crowd Pleaser Isla Fisher
Page 80 – Cracked Mall
Page 82 – Last Crack Dennis Miller
Page 83 – Subscription ad
Back Cover – RCA ad

**02, November / December 2006 (84 pages) ($3.99)**
Cover – Mel Gibson's Guide to Hanukkah (Mel Gibson photo)
Page 2 – National Lampoon Comedy Countdown Show ad (Funny that *National Lampoon* is taking out a real ad in *Cracked*.)
Page 3 – Cracked.com ad Page 4 – Contents

Page 72 – Prime Time at the D.I. – Justin Droms
Page 75 – Reviews
Page 79 – Funny Girl Amy Smart
Page 80 – Cracked Mall
Page 82 – Last Crack Steven Wright
Page 83 – Spousal Abuse ad
Back Cover – Cracked.com Subscription ad

**03, January / February 2007 (84 pages) ($3.99) (Last issue ever! )**
Cover – Celeb Adoption (Paris Hilton photo)
Page 2 – Prank the Monkey ad
Page 3 – Cracked.com ad
Page 4 – Contents
Page 6 – Editor's Letter – John Severin / Monty Sarhan (Severin's only new artwork for the new *Cracked*.)
Page 7 – Contributors
Page 8 – Inbox
Page 9 – Larry Holmes Grillmaster X-L ad
Page 10 – Cracked Den
Page 12 – Celeb Scoop!
Page 15 – Great Moments in History 1940
Page 16 – Smoldering Pistol
Page 18 – Drunkio ad / Baby Disguises ad / Ravens-B-Gone ad
Page 19 – Wisecracks – Michael Ian Black
Page 20 – Spring Movie Preview – Cody Johnston, Jordan Posner
Page 22 – Are You On Fire? – Tim Kochenderfer
Page 23 – New Sex Foods – Maddox
Page 24 – Taking Care of Your Pet Lohan – Wayne Gladstone
Page 26 – Would You Like a Bag? – Aaron Lange
Insert – Subscription ad
Page 27 – Socrates Moves to the Neighborhood
Page 28 – Supervillain Science Projects – John Czop / Dale Dobson
Page 30 – So You've Regained Consciousness – Jay Pinkerton
Page 31 – The Adventures of Estiman – John Czop / Scott Bassett, Eben Weiss
Page 32 – Everything You Need to Know About Pirates – Fenris
Page 33 – 2007 Comedy Writing Competition ad
Page 34 – It's a Lock! – Jack O'Brien, Sean McGrane, DJ Gallo, Jake Bell
Page 38 – Madonna & Child – 14
Page 42 – Smirnoff Ice ad
Page 44 – Marketing Consultant for the Homeless – Sir John Hargrave
Page 48 – Sex-Off!

Page 50 – Rogues Gallery A Fastman! Adventure – Steve Sloan, Chris Eisert / Jay Pinkerton, Peter Lynn
Page 53 – The New Yorker magazine – Richard Weinstein, Keiron Dwyer
Page 58 – Cracked.com ad
Insert – Subscription ad
Page 59 – But Seriously
Page 60 – Scot Armstrong Takes Us Back to School – Justin Borucki / Jesse Falcon
Page 63 – Ready for Prime Time Rich Vos – Justin Droms
Page 64 – Funny Films – Michael J. Nelson
Page 66 – Great Night with Conan O'Brien – Victor Varnado
Page 68 – Romantic Comedies – Chris Sims
Page 70 – White Faces & Red Noses – Peter Lynn
Page 72 – More Information Than You Require – Max Burbank
Page 75 – Reviews
Page 79 – Funny Girl Elizabeth Banks
Page 80 – Cracked Mall
Page 82 – Last Crack Mitch Hedberg
Page 83 – Council for Indian Adoption ad
Back Cover – Cracked.com Subscription ad

***The Biggest Greatest Cracked Annual*, 1965 (92 pages) (50c)**
Cover – TV Stars Balancing Act – John Severin (new)
Page 2 – (Bleep Bleep) *Castle of Frankenstein* photo (new)
Page 3 – Contents
Page 4 – Cracked Takes a Look at the Transylvanian Teen Scene – John Severin (reprint from #40)
Page 9 – Buggy – John Severin (reprint from #40)
Page 12 – The New Entertainer (reprint from #39)
Page 15 – The Fairy Tale Follow Up – John Severin (reprint from #34)
Page 18 – Picture This (reprint from #40)
Page 19 – Surfing U.S.A. – Bill McCartney (Bill Ward) (reprint from #39)
Page 24 – The Evolution of Beauty Contests – John Severin (reprint from #32)
Page 27 – Cannibal Chuckles – Charles Rodrigues (reprint from #39)
Page 28 – Modern Merchandise for Moneyed Mountaineers – John Severin (reprint from #31)
Page 31 – The Moon Shot (reprint from #39)
Page 32 – Charm Bracelets for Teens (reprint from #40)
Page 34 – Land of the Free (reprint from #38)

Page 37 – Hurry-Ups (last cigarette) – Bill McCartney (Bill Ward) (reprint from #38)
Page 38 – The Movie Monsters Strike – John Severin (reprint from #32)
Page 44 – Social Nabobs of Boston U. – John Severin (reprint from #40)
Page 49 – Way Out West! – Jack Davis (reprint from #11)
Page 51 – Vacation Guide to Outer Space – John Severin (reprint from #39)
Page 55 – The Train Robber – Bill McCartney (Bill Ward) (reprint from #34)
Page 56 – Celebrity Baby Photos – John Severin (reprint from #40)
Page 58 – Build This Beautiful Yacht – Bill Everett (reprint from #2)
Page 60 – Hurry-Ups (daddy fell out) – Don Orehek (reprint from #34)
Page 61 – The Skyfighters of World War 1 – John Severin (reprint from #39)
Page 66 – Where Do We Go From Here? (reprint from #4)
Page 68 – 4 to Go (reprint from #39)
Page 69 – Judo – Jack Davis (reprint from #11)
Page 72 – The Frog Prince (reprint from #40)
Page 73 – Cracked Cracks – Joe Kiernan, Don Orehek, Bob Zahn, Pete Wyma (reprint from #38)
Page 74 – 4 Funny Ones (reprint from #38)
Page 75 – A.P.E. Comic Book – John Severin, Bill McCartney (Bill Ward), Don Orehek, Vic Martin (full color insert) (new)
Page 91 – Beastyrust ad – John Severin (reprint from #39)
Back Cover – Gloom Toothpaste ad (reprint from #8)

***The Second Biggest Greatest Cracked Annual*, 1966 (92 pages) (50c)**
Cover – Sylvester's Court – John Severin (new)
Page 2 – Pesterfield Cigarette ad (reprint from #42)
Page 3 – Contents
Page 4 – Real Official Detective – Bill McCartney (Bill Ward) (reprint from #29)
Page 8 – Tin Soldiers Brought Up-to-Date – John Severin (reprint from #43)
Page 10 – He's Really a Lone Ranger Now! – Bill Ward (reprint from #1)
Page 13 – Reel Laughs (reprint from #42)
Page 14 – If All Civil Service Jobs Were Put on a Quota Basis – John Severin (reprint from #29)
Page 16 – Man's Best Friend? – Jack Davis (reprint from #11) (this was originally called "The Way That Movie Should've Ended")
Page 19 – Getting There is All the Fun – LePoer (John Severin) (reprint from #29)

Page 22 – Great Inventions in History – Oswaldo Laino (reprint from #24)
Page 23 – Newspaper Con Tests – Bill McCartney (Bill Ward) (reprint from #33)
Page 26 – Hut, Two, Tree, Four (reprint from #42)
Page 28 – Shut-Ups (don't want to run) – John Severin (reprint from #42)
Page 29 – The Gradual Change in Men's Fashions – John Severin (reprint from #26)
Page 32 – Which One is a Banker? Ad – John Severin (reprint from #23)
Page 33 – Inside Teenage Russia – Bill McCartney (Bill Ward) (reprint from #27)
Page 37 – Famous Quotations – Vic Martin (reprint from #23) (originally called "Famous Quotations Shut-Ups")
Page 38 – Childhood Games and Hobbies of Today's Famous Stars – John Severin (reprint from #43)
Page 41 – Awards For Unsung Students – John Severin (reprint from #27)
Page 42 – Make up Your Own Story (reprint from #9)
Page 44 – The Tipsy Mother Goose – John Severin (reprint from #23)
Page 49 – The Way They Should Have Filmed it – John Severin (reprint from #29)
Page 50 – If the Old Masters Were Alive Today – Bill McCartney (Bill Ward) (reprint from #31)
Page 53 – Specialized Retirement Cities – John Severin (reprint from #31)
Page 58 – Do's and Don'ts (reprint from #8)
Page 60 – Illustrated Slang – Bill McCartney (Bill Ward) (reprint from #23)
Page 61 – Axis Sallies – John Severin (reprint from #26)
Page 64 – Progressive Child Psychology – John Severin (reprint from #23)
Page 66 – If Madison Avenue Advertised Crime – John Severin (reprint from #24)
Page 71 – Advance of Civilization – John Severin (reprint from #24)
Page 73 – Hurry-Ups (daddy fell out) – Don Orehek (reprint from #34)
Page 74 – The Sacrifice – John Severin (reprint from #35)
Page 75 – Cracked's Fab Grab Bag of Instant Laughs! – Vic Martin (new)
Page 91 – Television Commercials you Never Get to See – Bill McCartney (Bill Ward) (reprint from #27)
Back Cover – Cracked Playing Cards – Jack Davis (reprint from #16)

***The Third Biggest Greatest Cracked Annual*, 1967 (92 pages) (50c)**

Cover – Sylvester-in-the-Box – O.O. Severin (John Severin) (new)
Page 2 – Four Annuals (*Biggest* 2; *Giant* 2, 3; *King-Sized* 1) / Three Paperbacks / Back Issues ad (#58-65)
Page 3 – Contents
Page 4 – Rival TV Shows Cry U.N.C.L.E. – McCarthy (John Severin) (reprint from #46)
Page 6 – If Famous Characters of Literature Were Alive Today – Bill McCartney (Bill Ward) (reprint from #44)
Page 11 – A Day in the Life of the Average Housewife – John Severin (reprint from #43)
Page 14 – First Impressions – Bill McCartney (Bill Ward) (reprint from #9)
Page 16 – How the West was Lost (reprint from #39)
Page 18 – Gal-ixnay Cigarette ad – Bill McCartney (Bill Ward) (reprint from #46)
Page 19 – Famous Scenes from Great "Dog Hero" Movies – Vic Martin (reprint from #47)
Page 21 – Visible Objects to Come – John Severin (reprint from #44)
Page 24 – Report Cards – John Severin (reprint from #45)
Page 28 – Right from the Horse's Mouth (reprint from #46)
Page 30 – Merry Old England Life ad (reprint from #47)
Page 31 – Indorsements (sic) of the Future – McCarten (John Severin) (reprint from #47)
Page 34 – Recreation – Bob Zahn (reprint from #37)
Page 35 – Sub Suburbia – Bill McCartney (Bill Ward) (reprint from #46)
Page 38 – Animals in Advertising – John Severin (reprint from #42)
Page 42 – A Martian Writes Home from Earth – John Severin (reprint from #40)
Page 44 – Four for Fun (reprint from #41)
Page 45 – Great Scenes from Great World War I Movies – John Severin (reprint from #44)
Page 47 – Santa Claus is Comin' to Town – John Severin (reprint from #41)
Page 48 – Cracked's War on Poverty – Bill McCartney (Bill Ward) (reprint from #46)
Page 50 – Around the World in Hats (reprint from #43)
Page 52 – People Who Are Just Born Unlucky – Bill McCartney (Bill Ward) (reprint from #44)
Page 54 – Status Symbols – Sigbjorn (John Severin) (reprint from #45)
Page 59 – Famous Scenes from Great Artist-Type Movies – John Severin (reprint from #49)
Page 61 – Ezoo ad – John Severin (reprint from #41)

Page 62 – Cracked Looks at Dee-Jays – John Severin (reprint from #37)
Page 68 – The Mystery of Palmistry – Bill McCartney (Bill Ward) (reprint from #49)
Page 71 – Laugh Lines (reprint from #43)
Page 72 – It Never Happened…But Someday It Might! – Bill McCartney (Bill Ward) (reprint from #8)
Page 73 – Cracked Fun Shoppe ad – John Severin / Horror House ad – John Severin
Page 74 – Hurry-Ups (ship is sinking) – Bill McCartney (Bill Ward) (reprint from #37)
Page 75 – Jig-Saw Puzzle – John Severin (reprint from #14)
Page 91 – (Raid, half the fun) photos (reprint from #58)
Back Cover – Subpoena and Parking Ticket (reprint from #27)

***The Fourth Biggest Greatest Cracked Annual*, 1968 (92 pages) (50c)**
Cover – Laugh-In – John Severin
Page 2 – Seven Annuals (*Biggest* 2, 3; *Giant* 3, 4; *King-Sized* 1, 2; *Super* 1) / Three Paperbacks / Back Issues ad (#67-74)
Page 3 – Contents
Page 4 – Five Minutes Later – John Severin (reprint from #49)
Page 9 – Hi-Fly-TV – John Severin (reprint from #56)
Page 12 – Low Calorie Everything – Bill McCartney (Bill Ward) (reprint from #58)
Page 14 – Ivery Soap ad – John Severin (reprint from #17)
Page 15 – The Ride of Paul Revere – John Severin (reprint from #20)
Page 17 – Four Socko Smiles (reprint from #60)
Page 18 – Take Me Out to the Old Cracked Ball Game – Charles Rodrigues (reprint from #53)
Page 20 – More Things We Shoulda Done – John Severin (reprint from #23)
Page 22 – Peace Corps in Reverse – Bill McCartney (Bill Ward) (reprint from #30)
Page 27 – Fine Art Captions – Jack Davis (reprint from #17)
Page 30 – Modern Mother Goose – Charles Rodrigues (reprint from #42) Page 32 – The Real Secrets Behind Agent 0007 – O.O. Severin (John Severin) (reprint from #56)
Page 36 – Interior Decorating to Fit Your Job – Jerry Kirschen (reprint from #18)
Page 38 – Kings of Comedy (reprint from #57)
Page 40 – Imaginary Fears and Complexes (reprint from #7)
Page 44 – *Cracked* Takes a Look at Football – Vic Martin (reprint from #59)

Page 46 – Updated Torture Devices for Catching the Witches of Today – John Severin (reprint from #58) (Dates in the article were changed from 1567 and 1967 to 1569 and 1969.)
Page 49 – Four Smiles Only (reprint from #59)
Page 50 – Cutt'r Sank ad – John Severin (reprint from #22)
Page 51 – Trading Stamps – John Severin (reprint from #28)
Page 56 – Special Seats for Special Movies – John Severin (reprint from #49)
Page 58 – A Visit with Laurel and Hardy (reprint from #55)
Page 60 – Stories of the Month (My problem, Doctor) – Vic Martin (reprint from #19)
Page 61 – Saturday Night Dance – Joe Maneely (reprint from #4)
Page 64 – The Machine Gun Nest – Ned Kelly (John Severin) / Don Edwing (reprint from #30)
Page 65 – Cracked Fun Shoppe ad – John Severin
Page 66 – A Cracked Guide to College Reunion Conversation – O.O. Severin (John Severin) (reprint from #53)
Page 68 – The Flying Carpet – Golden (reprint from #58)
Page 69 – Horror House ad – John Severin
Page 70 – If the Comics Were Drawn by Famous Movie Directors – Bill McCartney (Bill Ward) (reprint from #51)
Page 74 – Shut-Ups (send me in) – Bill McCartney (Bill Ward) (reprint from #3)
Page 75 – Boysplay – John Severin, John Langton, George Gladir, Vic Martin (Updated and revised from #24.) (full color insert)
Page 91 – Viceboy Cigarette ad – John Severin (reprint from #9)
Back Cover – Dartboard Decision Maker (reprint from #56)

***The Fifth Biggest Greatest Cracked Annual*, 1969 (92 pages) (50c)**
Cover – Sylvester, Court Jester – John Severin (new)
Page 2 – Six Annuals (*Biggest* 4; *Giant* 5; *King-Sized* 1, 2, 3; *Super* 2) / Back Issues ad (#76-83)
Page 3 – Contents
Page 4 – The Same Shows as Performed on TV & Radio – John Severin (reprint from #60)
Page 8 – Stories of the Month – Angel Martinez (reprint from #17)
Page 9 – Future Specialized Banks – Arnoldo Franchioni (reprint from #62)
Page 12 – Wacky Inventions – Joe Sinnott (reprint from *Zany* #2)
Page 14 – 12 O'Clock High Jinks (reprint from #65)
Page 16 – Charlie Weakling ad – Bill McCartney (Bill Ward) (reprint from #54)

Page 17 – How to Prepare a Job Resume (reprint from #19)
Page 20 – A Tourist's Guide to Transylvania – Vic Martin (reprint from #60)
Page 25 – Get Out the Vote! – John Severin (reprint from #51)
Page 26 – Take the Cracked Sports Test! – Bill McCartney (Bill Ward) (reprint from #61)
Page 28 – Photos That Have Been Cropped – John Severin (reprint from #25)
Page 32 – The Breaking Point! – Vic Martin (reprint from #56) (Whoops #1! This article was reprinted in reverse!!)
Page 33 – Five Times Laughs (reprint from #64)
Page 34 – Mother Goose Confidential – John Severin (reprint from #29)
Page 37 – Background Music – John Severin (reprint from #29)
Page 40 – Merged Comic Strips – Bill McCartney (Bill Ward) (reprint from #37)
Page 44 – Dizzy Dissection of the Discotheque Disease! – Don Orehek (reprint from #60)
Page 46 – The Art of Kissing – LePoer – John Severin (reprint from #39)
Page 49 – Sensationalized Reference Books – John Severin (reprint from #27) (The telephone directory was updated to 1970.)
Page 51 – Reel Swingers! (reprint from #56) (Whoops #2! This article was printed upside down!!)
Page 52 – Madison Ave. Word Game – John Severin (reprint from #54)
Page 56 – Horror House ad – John Severin
Page 57 – The Emergency Landing – O.O. Severin (John Severin) (reprint from #63)
Page 60 – Try This Cracked 5-Day Diet (reprint from #4)
Page 62 – Sea Haunt – Jack Davis (reprint from #14)
Page 66 – Cracked's Hall of Fame of Nut People (reprint from #50)
Page 68 – Cracked Fun Shoppe ad – John Severin
Page 69 – Would Columbus Have Discovered America Etc.? – O.O. Severin (John Severin) (reprint from #64)
Page 74 – Shut-Ups! (tie clasps) – Rodrigliani (Charles Rodrigues) (reprint from #56)
Page 75 – Your Official Cracked Holiday & Appointment Calendar for 1970 – John Severin (new)
Page 91 – Blech Shampoo ad – LePoer (John Severin) (reprint from #21)
Back Cover – Dry Paint Sign (new)

***The Sixth Biggest Greatest Cracked Annual*, 1970 (92 pages) (50c)**

Cover – Yancy's Appalachian Flukes – John Severin
Page 2 – Six Annuals ad (*Biggest* 4, 5; *Giant* 6; *King-Sized* 2, 4; *Super* 3)
Page 3 – Contents
Page 4 – Bonnie and Clyde! – O.O. Severin (John Severin) (reprint from #73)
Page 9 – Modern Tattoo Designs – Vic Martin (reprint from #65)
Page 12 – The Charlie Chan Caper (reprint from #71)
Page 14 – Bull Telephone System ad – John Severin (reprint from #41)
Page 15 – The Chicken Killer – Bill McCartney (Bill Ward) / Jay Lynch (reprint from #30)
Page 17 – Future Automated Devices – Nireves (John Severin) (reprint from #50)
Page 19 – Something to Smile About (reprint from #47)
Page 20 – Cheeter, Tarzin's Faithful Chimp! (reprint from #71)
Page 25 – Celebrity Childhoods – William Hoest (reprint from #57)
Page 29 – The Quick Quippers! (reprint from #69)
Page 30 – It All Depends Upon the Point of View – Bill McCartney (Bill Ward) (reprint from #51)
Page 32 – What Really Happens During the Filming of Television Commercials! – Arnoldo Franchioni (reprint from #69)
Page 36 – Cracked Looks at an Outdoor Art Exhibit! – Walter Gastaldo (reprint from #67)
Page 38 – Annie Get Your Spacesuit – Lugoze (reprint from #67)
Page 46 – Cracked's Think Tank Solutions (reprint from #71)
Page 51 – Cracked Fun Shoppe ad – John Severin
Page 52 – The Funnies in the Flicks! (reprint from #72)
Page 55 – Super Fan-Elan – John Severin (reprint from #51)
Page 59 – Horror House ad – John Severin
Page 60 – Past, Present and Future Changes in Sports – John Severin (reprint from #24)
Page 63 – Truthful Ads They Wouldn't Print in Cracked – Lugoze (reprint from #70)
Page 68 – Marx Brothers' Laff-In! (reprint from #73)
Page 71 – The Shade – Caracu (reprint from #65)
Page 72 – Celebrity Christmas Wreaths (reprint from #67)
Page 74 – Shut-Ups (lookout man) – Charles Rodrigues (reprint from #51)
Page 75 – The Spiro Agnew Coloring Book – Don Orehek (new)
Page 91 – 257 Country Music Hits ad – Vic Martin (reprint from #51)
Back Cover – Cracked's Chinese Calendar (reprint from #47) (The date on the calendar was changed from 1965 to 1971 on this reprint.)

***The Seventh Biggest Greatest Cracked Annual*, 1971 (84 pages) (60c)**

Cover - Sylvester on Sylvester's Nose - John Severin
Page 2 - Four Annuals ad (*Biggest* 5, 6; *Giant* 7; *King-Sized* 5)
Page 3 - Contents
Page 4 - Help! I'm in the Pacific - Edvard Severin (John Severin) / Stu Schwartzberg (reprint from #79)
Page 9 - Foto Fun! (reprint from #69)
Page 10 - The History of Early Flight - Tony Tallarico (reprint from #70)
Page 14 - Report Cards for Everybody - Lugoze (reprint from #77)
Page 16 - Cracked Suggestions for Improving Mail Service - Bill McCartney (Bill Ward) (reprint from #78)
Page 20 - The Traffic Jam - Caracu (reprint from #70)
Page 21 - The Quickest Fun in the West (reprint from #77)
Page 24 - A Cracked Alphabet Book About Politicians - John Langton (reprint from #70)
Page 28 - Reel Gone Goodies (reprint from #75)
Page 29 - Yoga - John Severin (reprint from #9)
Page 32 - The Cracked Guide for High Living Without Working - John Langton (reprint from #71)
Page 34 - Oh, Those Oh-So-Long Lines - John Langton (reprint from #77)
Page 38 - Chickie, the Fuzz (reprint from #79)
Page 39 - Why People Move to the Suburbs - Jack Davis (reprint from #14)
Page 43 - Sagebrush (Sand! Sand!) - John Severin (reprint from #79)
Page 45 - Horror House ad - John Severin
Page 46 - Cracked Visits a Skating Rink - John Langton (reprint from #70)
Page 48 - Dear Sir! (reprint from #73)
Page 50 - Cracked Visits a U.S. Army Camp - Lugoze (reprint from #79)
Page 52 - Cracked Fun Shoppe ad - John Severin
Page 53 - Hudd & Dini (painted wall) - Vic Martin (reprint from #76)
Page 55 - Awards for School Kids - Bill McCartney (Bill Ward) (reprint from #77)
Page 59 - The Luckless League - Lugoze (reprint from #74)
Page 61 - Throughout History with the Isolated Camera - John Severin (reprint from #48)
Page 64 - New Prizes for Breakfast Cereals - John Langton (reprint from #76)
Page 66 - Shut-Ups (driving lesson) - Charles Rodrigues (reprint from #78)
Page 67 - Fly Me Model Plane Kit
Page 83 - (blue rattle, picket signs) photos (One from *The Court Jester*) (reprint from #69)
Back Cover - This is an Unmarked Garbage Truck (reprint from #67)

***The Eighth Biggest Greatest Cracked Annual*, 1972 (84 pages) (60c)**

Cover – Thumb Painting – John Severin (reprint from #38)
Page 2 – Six Annuals ad (*Biggest* 6, 7; *Giant* 7, 8; *King-Sized* 6; *Super* 5)
Page 3 – Contents
Page 4 – The Brainy Bunch – John Severin (reprint from #89)
Page 9 – Nasty Neighbors – Caracu (reprint from #82)
Page 10 – Snide Guide to Camping – John Severin (reprint from #61)
Page 13 – Women's Lib Laughs – Charles Rodrigues (reprint from #91)
Page 16 – If Dolphin's Day Every Comes! – John Severin (reprint from #89)
Page 19 – "Make Me a Deal" – Bill McCartney (Bill Ward) (reprint from #88)
Page 22 – Sagebrush (Ah-Choo!) – John Severin (reprint from #85)
Page 24 – The War on Law – John Severin (reprint from #57)
Page 28 – Cracked Looks at Hotels – Bill McCartney (Bill Ward) (reprint from #90)
Page 31 – The Birthday Gift! – John Langton (reprint from #67)
Page 32 – Cracked Looks at New York City – John Severin (reprint from #92)
Page 34 – Senior Citizen – Lugoze (reprint from #82)
Page 38 – You Know You're Rich When – Charles Rodrigues (reprint from #91)
Page 40 – Give it Back to the Indians – John Severin (reprint from #92)
Page 44 – Horror House ad – John Severin
Page 45 – Inflation – Bill McCartney (Bill Ward) (reprint from #61)
Page 48 – When the Woman's Lib Movement Spreads to the Comics! – John Severin (reprint from #92)
Page 52 – Hudd & Dini (boy scouts) – Vic Martin (reprint from #85)
Page 53 – The Blossoming Botany Business – Bill McCartney (Bill Ward) (reprint from #88)
Page 57 – Open the Door, Seymour! – Larry Barth (reprint from #92)
Page 58 – Goldie Oldie Rock Yocks (reprint from #91)
Page 60 – Cracked Fun Shoppe ad – John Severin
Page 61 – The Cracked Museum of Historical Trivia – Tony Tallarico (reprint from #69)
Page 64 – Public Spirited Ads – Bob Taylor (reprint from #91)
Page 66 – Shut-Ups! (exit slowly) – Charles Rodrigues (reprint from #89)
Page 67 – Your Own Personal Cracked Events Calendar for 1973 (revised reprint from *Biggest Greatest Cracked* #5)
Page 83 – Laurel & Hardy photos (new)
Back Cover – Virginia Slums ad (reprint from #96)

***The Ninth Biggest Greatest Cracked Annual*, 1973 (84 pages) (75c)**

Cover - Feamish's Mixed Nuts - O.O. Severin (John Severin) (reprint from #62)
Page 2 - Cracked Fun Shoppe ad - John Severin
Page 3 - Contents
Page 4 - TV's Defective Detectives - Jack Barrett (reprint from #102)
Page 8 - How Hollywood Can Appeal to Today's Youth by Modernizing Old Movies - John Severin (reprint from #91)
Page 11 - Miss America Contest! - John Severin (reprint from #90)
Page 14 - Cracked Looks at Dining Out - Bill McCartney (Bill Ward) (reprint from #84)
Page 18 - If Famous People Had Listened to Their Mothers - John Severin (reprint from #94)
Page 21 - The Selling of the Department of Defense - Bill McCartney (Bill Ward) (reprint from #88)
Page 25 - Shaggies! - Larry Barth (reprint from #91)
Page 26 - What to Do Until the TV Repairman Arrives - Don Orehek (reprint from #97)
Page 28 - Nixon's Next Job - John Severin (reprint from #99)
Page 30 - Cracked Looks at TV Commercials - Bill McCartney (Bill Ward) (reprint from #98)
Page 32 - Sagebrush (Gulp!) - John Severin (reprint from #99)
Page 34 - The New Mod Army - Bill McCartney (Bill Ward) (reprint from #100)
Page 38 - The Screamers (reprint from *For Monsters Only* #5)
Page 41 - Alice's Toy - Joe Mead (reprint from #84)
Page 42 - Cracked Goes to a Discotheque - Bill McCartney (Bill Ward) (reprint from #95)
Page 44 - Are You a Dumb-Dumb? - Bill McCartney (Bill Ward) (reprint from #80)
Page 46 - Status Symbols for Dogs! - John Severin (reprint from #86)
Page 48 - If Famous Lines Were Said in Different Situations - John Severin (reprint from #101)
Page 50 - I Don't Care Who You Are - John Severin (reprint from #96)
Page 52 - Telephone Madness - Jared Lee (reprint from #99)
Page 54 - Rare Olde Letters of History (reprint from #88)
Page 56 - Oops! Sorry! - Bruce Day (reprint from #102)
Page 58 - Watermelon Jokes to End Them All! (reprint from #97)
Page 60 - Hudd & Dini (lifeguards) - Vic Martin (reprint from #100)
Page 61 - Frontier Dude Magazine - John Severin (reprint from #84)
Page 66 - Shut-Ups (Can I sit) - Glenn Mukheryee (Charles Rodrigues) (reprint from #94)

Page 67 – The Cracked Puzzle Book – John Langton (new)
Page 83 – Five Annuals ad (*Biggest* 8; *Collectors* 2; *Giant* 8; *King-Sized* 7; *Super* 6)
Back Cover – Canadian Crud ad – John Severin (reprint from #97)

***The Tenth Biggest Greatest Cracked Annual*, 1974 (84 pages) (75c)**
Cover – Tiger Tamer – John Duillo (reprint from #59)
Page 2 – Binders and notebooks ad
Page 3 – Contents
Page 4 – Loathe Story – John Severin (reprint from #94)
Page 9 – Simulating the Thrills of Big-Time Sports at Home – Vic Martin (reprint from #83)
Page 12 – It All Depends on the Point of View – Bill McCartney (Bill Ward) (reprint from #35)
Page 14 – Cracked Examines All the Possibilities of Flying Saucers – Bill McCartney (Bill Ward) (reprint from #68)
Page 18 – Are you a Hypochondriac? – John Langton (reprint from #106)
Page 20 – Man's Best Friend – Bernard Baily (reprint from #106)
Page 23 – A Picture is Worth 1,000 Lies – Lugoze (reprint from #73)
Page 26 – Lowering the Mental Level of TV Programs – John Severin (reprint from #70)
Page 30 – Luck Is – Bob Taylor (reprint from #85)
Page 32 – Room 5C – Sigbjorn (John Severin) (reprint from #59)
Page 36 – As Cracked Goes to the Race Track! – Bill McCartney (Bill Ward) (reprint from #93)
Page 38 – Dear John Letters of History – John Severin (reprint from #27)
Page 40 – Creating New Job Opportunities – John Severin (reprint from #96)
Page 43 – The Rescue? – Art Pottier (reprint from #100)
Page 44 – Cracked Looks at a Dog Show – Don Orehek (reprint from #105)
Page 46 – A Cracked Look at Dentists (reprint from #81)
Page 50 – Mini-Everything!! – Vic Martin (reprint from #73)
Page 52 – Slums Can Be Made a Fun Thing! – John Severin (reprint from #74)
Page 56 – One Morning in the Doctor's Office – Charles Rodrigues (reprint from #95)
Page 58 – Nightmares – Vic Martin (reprint from #102)
Page 60 – Hudd & Dini (garbage can magnets) – Vic Martin (reprint from #92)

Page 61 – The Discount King – John Langton (reprint from #105)
Page 66 – Big Money in Imports! – Vic Martin (reprint from #56)
Page 67 – 8 Posters (reprints from #72, 73, 74, 87, 99, 101, 104, 105)
Page 83 – The Cracked Bookstore ad – John Severin
Back Cover – Karate Magazine – John Severin (reprint from #88)

***The Eleventh Biggest Greatest Cracked Annual*, 1975 (84 pages) ($1.00)**
Cover – Sylvester's Newsstand Toothache – John Severin (reprint from #82)
Page 2 – The Cracked Bookstore ad – John Severin
Page 3 – Contents
Page 4 – The Walled-Ins – John Severin (reprint from #114)
Page 9 – The Explorer, the Dog & the Bone – Oskar Blotta (reprint from #84)
Page 10 – A Day in the Senate – Dick Wright (reprint from #108)
Page 13 – How to Cover Up – John Severin (reprint from #113)
Page 17 – Rodrigues' Hospital-ity – Charles Rodrigues (reprint from #110)
Page 20 – Cracked Looks at Hotels – Bill McCartney (Bill Ward) (reprint from #90)
Page 23 – How the Airlines Can Save Money! – John Severin (reprint from #97)
Page 26 – Cracked Looks at a Big City Newspaper Office – Don Orehek (reprint from #104)
Page 28 – Columbore – John Severin (reprint from #110)
Page 33 – Training the Dog – Joe Mead (reprint from #98)
Page 34 – The Cracked TV Sports Primer – Bill McCartney (Bill Ward) (reprint from #69)
Page 37 – Cowsmoopolitan Magazine – John Severin (reprint from #90)
Page 41 – Cracked Looks at World War I Sky Fighters – John Severin (reprint from #107)
Page 45 – At the Barber Shop – Caracu (reprint from #67)
Page 46 – You Know You're Not a Kid Anymore When – Jared Lee (reprint from #99)
Page 48 – Footboxhockbasetennbasketgolfpoly – John Severin (reprint from #97)
Page 52 – Television Roulette (reprint from #89)
Page 55 – Zzzzpg – Zeverin (John Severin) (reprint from #105)
Page 59 – Cracked Interviews the Auto King – John Severin (reprint from #109)
Page 64 – Orehek on Wry – Don Orehek (reprint from #108)

Page 66 – Shut-Ups (SHA-LLALA-KOO) – Charles Rodrigues (reprint from #111)
Page 67 – The Cracked Puzzler of Puzzle Books – Jack Davis, Bob Taylor (new)
Page 83 – Binders and Notebooks ad 2
Back Cover – The National Geagraphic Magazine – John Severin (reprint from #13)

***The Twelfth Biggest Greatest Cracked Annual*, 1976 (84 pages) ($1.00)**
Cover – Sylvesters on the Moon – John Severin (reprint from #68)
Page 2 – The Cracked Bookstore ad – John Severin
Page 3 – Contents
Page 4 – The Inept-One Factor – John Severin (reprint from #120)
Page 9 – The Cracked Guide to Skiing – Bill Ward (reprint from #115)
Page 14 – When it all Ended (The Science Fiction Movie) – John Severin (reprint from #24)
Page 15 – When Fat is in and Thin is Out – John Langton (reprint from #113)
Page 19 – A Cracked View of The Birds-Eye Crew – Bernard Baily / Bill Majeski
Page 23 – The Day America Runs Out of Gas – John Severin (reprint from #113)
Page 27 – The Flying Carpet – Golden (reprint from #58)
Page 28 – Graphic Speech – John Langton (reprint from #66)
Page 30 – As the Trend Towards Violence Increases – Lugoze (reprint from #69)
Page 36 – Cracked Looks at Camping – Don Orehek (reprint from #119)
Page 38 – 4 Frantic Fun! (reprint from #68)
Page 39 – Fashion and the Hi-Heeled Platform Shoe – John Severin (reprint from #114)
Page 42 – The Hitler Nostalgia Craze – Bill Ward (reprint from #116)
Page 46 – Smiles from South of the Border – Oskar Blotta (reprint from #58)
Page 48 – Cracked Looks at a Fender Bender – Don Orehek (reprint from #109)
Page 50 – Inside Henry Kissinger's Wallet – John Langton (reprint from #107)
Page 52 – Modern Tattoo Designs – Vic Martin (reprint from #65)
Page 56 – A Cracked Gallery of New Artists – Oswaldo Laino, John Severin (reprint from #21)
Page 60 – The Little World of Don Swanson (chinning hanger) – Don Swanson (reprint from #20)

Page 61 – Cracked Interviews the College King – John Langton (reprint from #118)
Page 66 – Hip Shut-Ups (I'm floatin') – John Severin (reprint from #11)
Page 67 – Cracked Big Ape Game – Sururi Gumen
Page 83 – "Friends, Romans, Countrymen, Lend Me Your Laughs!" (reprint from #80)
Back Cover – Great Moments in Art – Charles Rodrigues (reprint from #119)

***The 13th Biggest Greatest Cracked Annual*, 1978 (84 pages) ($1.00) (For some reason, there was no *Biggest Greatest Cracked* published in 1977.)**
Cover – The Chicken or Sylvester – John Severin (reprint from #80)
Page 2 – The Cracked Bookstore ad – John Severin
Page 3 – Contents
Page 4 – How the Kotter Gang Spent Their Summer Vacation – John Severin (reprint from #137)
Page 10 – The Day Comic Strip Characters Got up on the Wrong Side of Bed – John Severin (reprint from #76)
Page 13 – Future Late Show Programs – Bill McCartney (Bill Ward) (reprint from #56)
Page 16 – The French Commotion – John Severin (reprint from #102)
Page 22 – Postcard Collecting – Sururi Gumen (reprint from #132)
Page 26 – Russian Magazines – Bill Elder (reprint from #13)
Page 28 – Public-Spirited Ads – Bob Taylor (reprint from #91)
Page 30 – Blind Date Phone Calls – Bob Taylor (reprint from #84)
Page 33 – More Combined Movies "Dracula" and "Snow White and the Seven Dwarfs" – John Severin (reprint from #132)
Page 34 – How Different Magazines and Newspapers Would Caption the Same Picture (reprint from #132)
Page 38 – Take Me Out to the Old Cracked Ball Game – Charles Rodrigues (reprint from #53)
Page 40 – Wedding Announcements We'd like to See (reprint from #104)
Page 42 – Developing a New Product – Bill Ward (reprint from #130)
Page 46 – Cracked Rides West! (reprint from #67)
Page 48 – A Cracked Look at a Tourist Welcome Center – John Severin (reprint from #133)
Page 50 – Cracked Frisbee Rating System – Bob Taylor (reprint from #133)
Page 53 – Famous Scenes from Great "Dog Hero" Movies – Vic Martin (reprint from #47)
Page 55 – The Day Norman Told Off His Boss – Jack Barrett / Ron Wiggins (reprint from #102)

Page 56 – Cracked Looks at Television Viewers – Bill McCartney (Bill Ward) (reprint from #85)
Page 60 – Recreation – Bob Zahn (reprint from #37)
Page 61 – Cracked Interviews the Sports King – John Severin (reprint from #130)
Page 66 – It Shouldn't Happen to a Dog – LePoer (John Severin) (reprint from #4)
Page 67 – Paperback Book Covers – John Severin
Page 83 – Bull Telephone System ad – John Severin (reprint from #41)
Back Cover – Great Moments in History 1976 – Mike Ricigliano (reprint from #133)

***The 14th Biggest Greatest Cracked Annual*, Fall 1979 (84 pages) ($1.25)**
Cover – Slippery Ink – John Severin (reprint from #71)
Page 2 – The Cracked Bookstore ad – John Severin
Page 3 – Contents
Page 4 – Fonzerella! – Sigbjorn (John Severin) (reprint from #135)
Page 9 – Satan's Campaign to Promote Hell – Makbush (Sururi Gumen) (reprint from #134)
Page 13 – The Cracked Guide to Football – Howard Nostrand (reprint from #140)
Page 18 – Life's Big Losers – Bill Ward (Alfred E. Neuman appearance) (reprint from #141)
Page 22 – Increasing Consumption in Order to Maintain Full Employment – LePoer (John Severin) (reprint from #134)
Page 26 – Cracked Looks at the T-Shirt Craze – Howard Nostrand (reprint from #143)
Page 30 – Cracked's Specialized Greeting Cards – Don Orehek (reprint from #143)
Page 33 – When Every One Called Him Dickie (reprint from #100)
Page 35 – The New Mod Army – Bill McCartney (Bill Ward) (reprint from #100)
Page 39 – Great Scenes from Hollywood Movies if Shakespeare Had Written Them! – Bob Taylor (reprint from #95)
Page 42 – The Johnny Dick Griffson Show – John Severin (reprint from #99)
Page 47 – Cracked Put-Ons – John Langton (reprint from #102)
Page 50 – Laurel and Hardy's Wacky World of Fun! (reprint from #59)
Page 52 – Super Senses – Dick Wright (reprint from #111)
Page 55 – Baad Baad Black Sheep – John Severin (reprint from #144)
Page 61 – Cracked Interviews the Fad King – Bill Ward (reprint from #142)

Page 66 – Sagebrush (hey rock) – John Severin / Your (Ugh) Ancestors? (bar wheel) – Lo Linkert (reprint from #112)
Page 67 – Do-it-Yourself Newspapers (revised reprint from *Giant Cracked* #1)
Page 83 – On Capitol Hill – Howard Nostrand (reprint from #146)
Back Cover – Freezca ad – John Severin (reprint from #81)

***The 15th Biggest Greatest Cracked Special,*** **Fall 1980 (68 pages) ($1.25)**
Cover – The Empire Strikes Back – Samuel B. Whitehead
Page 2 – The Cracked Bookstore ad – John Severin
Page 3 – Contents
Page 4 – The Empire Strikes Out Again – Samuel B. Whitehead (new)
Page 8 – Cy-Threepiu & Arty-Ditto A Souvenir Photo Album of Their Visit to Earth – Cosa Nostrand (Howard Nostrand) (reprint from #148)
Page 12 – If the Characters of Star Wars Appeared in Other Movies and TV Shows – Powers (John Severin) (reprint from #149)
Page 16 – Close Encounters of the Worst Kind – Michael Severin (John Severin) (reprint from #150)
Page 23 – If UFO's Ever Do Land – Bill Ward (reprint from #155)
Page 26 – Odd Jobs for Star Wars Stars – Howard Nostrand (reprint from #154)
Page 29 – Hudd & Dini (rocket) – Vic Martin (reprint from #87)
Page 30 – A Close Encounter with the Star Warz Gang – Howard Nostrand (John Severin) (reprint from #152)
Page 36 – The Classified Ads of the Future – Howard Nostrand (reprint from #160)
Page 39 – Iffy U.F.O. Info Magazine – Howard Nostrand (reprint from #156)
Page 44 – Subscription ad – Warren Sattler
Page 45 – Star Warz II – O.O. Severin (John Severin) (reprint from #147)
Page 51 – The War of the Empires Game – John Severin
Page 65 – I'm Darth Vader On My Day Off! Iron-On
Page 67 – Official Cracked Reporter T-Shirt ad
Back Cover – More Star Wars – Cracked Poster – Powers (John Severin) (reprint from #148)

***The 16th Biggest Greatest Cracked Annual,*** **Fall 1981 (84 pages) ($1.25)**
Cover – Fish Eating Bait – John Severin
Page 2 – Contents
Page 3 – Cracked Non-Electronic Electronic Game Game – Mike Ricigliano, John Severin (new)
Page 19 – The Cracked Bookstore ad – John Severin

Page 20 – Diff'rent Strokes (Good morning, Mrs. Carrot) – John Severin (reprint from #162)
Page 26 – You Know You are a TV Addict When – Bill Ward (reprint from #127)
Page 28 – Past Predictions of the Future – Sururi Gumen (reprint from #121)
Page 32 – Cracked Examines Telephone Answering Machines – Howard Nostrand (reprint from #157)
Page 35 – The Seers Rubbish Catalog of Useless Items for 1974 – John Langton (reprint from #117)
Page 40 – In Case of Emergency – Warren Sattler (reprint from #160)
Page 42 – Cracked Products for Everyday Use – Warren Sattler (reprint from #156)
Page 44 – Star Tracks – John Severin (reprint from #127)
Page 49 – If Real Life Were Like the Movies – Bill Ward (reprint from #116)
Page 52 – The Cracked Manual for Good Photography – John Langton (reprint from #115)
Page 57 – The Cracked Guide to Hockey – John Severin (reprint from #132)
Page 61 – The Country Blues – John Langton (reprint from #123)
Page 65 – A Preview of Cracked's New TV Season – John Severin (reprint from #130)
Page 68 – You Know It's Not Your Day When – Bill Ward (reprint from #123)
Page 71 – Cracked Interviews the Supermarket King – Sururi Gumen (reprint from #125)
Page 76 – Shut-Ups (black belt) – Charles Rodrigues (reprint from #129)
Page 77 – Cracked Fishing Game Kit – Don Orehek (new)
Page 83 – Hudd & Dini (caveman) – Vic Martin (reprint from #96)
Back Cover – Great Moments in Medicine 30503 B.C. – Howard Nostrand (reprint from #153)

***The 17th Biggest Greatest Cracked Annual*, Fall 1982 (84 pages) ($1.50)**

Cover – We K.O. Rocky – John Severin (reprint from #143)
Page 2 – Contents
Page 3 – Cracked Games and Puzzles That Almost Anyone Can Solve Vol. III – Don Orehek (new)
Page 19 – Rockey – John Severin (reprint from #143)

Page 25 – At An Afternoon Business Luncheon – Howard Nostrand (reprint from #144)
Page 26 – Cracked Tips for Improving Home Movies – Warren Sattler (reprint from #149)
Page 30 – A Cracked Look at Prizefighting – Don Orehek (reprint from #122)
Page 34 – Illustrated Idiotic Idioms (reprint from #171)
Page 36 – The Cracked Guide to Babysitting – Bill Ward (reprint from #145)
Page 40 – Exposing the Con in Contests – Howard Nostrand (reprint from #144)
Page 44 – Cracked Goes to a Weight Watcher's Meeting – Don Orehek (reprint from #121)
Page 46 – If Rockey Appeared in Other Movie and TV Spots – John Severin (reprint from #145)
Page 50 – The Big City Versus the Small Town – Bernard Baily (reprint from #117)
Page 53 – Golf Oil Company ad (reprint from #169)
Page 54 – If Newspapers Carried Pictures to Match Their Headlines – John Severin (reprint from #127)
Page 57 – An Afternoon at an Artist's Studio – Howard Nostrand (reprint from #145)
Page 58 – The Medicine Man – John Langton (reprint from #171)
Page 61 – Cracked Interviews the Trekker King – Bill Ward (reprint from #169)
Page 66 – Photoon (Four score and seven years ago) (reprint from #169)
Page 67 – 3 Iron-Ons (new)
Page 73 – 5 Posters (1 new, rest reprints from #124, 155, 163, 165)
Page 83 – The Cracked Bookstore ad – John Severin
Back Cover – One Night at the Garden – Howard Nostrand (reprint from #165)

***The 18th Biggest Greatest Cracked Annual,* Fall 1983 (84 pages) ($1.75)**

Cover – Raining Umbrella – John Severin (reprint from #95)
Page 2 – Contents
Page 3 – The Cracked Trivia Game (new)
Page 4 – The Cracked Bookstore ad – John Severin
Page 20 – Three's Crummier – John Severin (reprint from #156)
Page 26 – If T.V. Commercials Were Honest – Warren Sattler (reprint from #143)
Page 30 – Cracked's Guide to Sharks – Don Orehek (reprint from #130)
Page 33 – The Flying Carpet – Golden (reprint from #58)

Page 34 – Prof. Whiffle-Bird Discovers a New Species – Tony Tallarico (reprint from #64)
Page 36 – Cracked Looks at Hunting and Fishing – LePoer (John Severin) (reprint from #86)
Page 38 – Believe it or Not (reprint from #177)
Page 41 – Hudd & Dini (rocket) – Vic Martin (reprint from #87)
Page 42 – If California Moved Into the Pacific – LePoer (John Severin) (reprint from #89)
Page 44 – The Cracked History of Humor – Bill Ward (reprint from #153)
Page 48 – Phone Services of the Future – Warren Sattler (reprint from #158)
Page 50 – Shut-Ups (the water's fine) – Vincent Van Stop (Charles Rodrigues) (reprint from #82)
Page 51 – 4 Iron-Ons (1 new, reprints from #157, 172, 181), 1 small poster (new), Fly Me Model Plane Kit (partial reprint from *Biggest Greatest Cracked* #7), 8 Super-Size Posters (reprints from #96, 101, 118, 125, 127, 128, 131, 144) (reprint from *Giant Cracked Fun-Kit* #22)
Page 83 – The Electric Shave – Oskar Blotta (reprint from #86)
Back Cover – Gorkel House – Tony Tallarico (reprint from #64)

***The 19th Biggest Greatest Cracked Annual*, Fall 1984 (84 pages) ($1.75)**
Cover – The Dukes Bust Out! – John Severin (reprint from #185)
Page 2 – Contents
Page 3 – Cracked's Shut-Ups Game – John Severin, Charles Rodrigues, Bill Ward (reprint from *Giant Cracked Fun-Kit* #29)
Page 19 – The Dorks of Hazzardous (Uncle Fussy milking the cows) – John Severin (reprint from #185)
Page 27 – Cracked's Reasons to Be Cheerful – Warren Sattler (reprint from #170)
Page 31 – Absolutely, Unquestionably, Positively, Undeniably, the Very, Very, Last of The Cracked Lens (and we really mean it this time!) (reprint from #174)
Page 36 – The Cracked Handbook on Personal Grooming – Sururi Gumen (reprint from #176)
Page 39 – The Cracked Book of Running – Bill Ward (reprint from #171)
Page 44 – How to Read Those Travel Ads – Samuel B. Whitehead (reprint from #179)
Page 46 – The Cracked World of Teenage Dating – Warren Sattler (reprint from #189)

Page 50 - More Press Mistakes! (Russians are noted) - John Langton (reprint from #189)
Page 52 - Crack Ups! Featuring Sagebrush (I'll ask this hombre) - John Severin (reprint from #182)
Page 53 - The Cracked Question and Answer Guide to Racquetball - Don Orehek (reprint from #174)
Page 57 - Cracked Interviews the Vacation King - Bill Ward (reprint from #178)
Page 62 - What You're Really Thinking - Warren Sattler (reprint from #172)
Page 64 - A Dozen Things Never to Do at the Beach - John Langton (reprint from #173)
Page 66 - The Jay Walk - Sururi Gumen (reprint from #184)
Page 67 - 8 Posters (reprints from #154, 157, 159, 164, 167, 168, 169, 172) (reprint from *Giant Cracked Fun-Kit* #32)
Page 83 - Get Out the Vote! - John Severin (reprint from #51)
Back Cover - Great Moments in Fashion 1857 - Warren Sattler (reprint from #187)

***The 20th Biggest Greatest Cracked Annual,* Fall 1985 (84 pages) ($2.00)**
Cover - Monster Fight - John Severin (reprint from *For Monsters Only* #2)
Page 2 - Contents
Page 3 - Cracked Record Labels (new)
Page 11 - Cracked Shut-Ups Cards (new)
Page 19 - The A-a-ayy Team (Excuse me, waitress) - O.O. Severin (John Severin) (reprint from #203)
Page 26 - The Cracked World of Schooling - Bill Ward (reprint from #170)
Page 30 - Video Nightmares - Don Orehek (reprint from #205)
Page 34 - Cracked Looks at Computers - Warren Sattler (reprint from #206)
Page 38 - The Ad War Heats Up - Sururi Gumen (reprint from #196)
Page 40 - Cracked T.V. Addict! - John Langton (reprint from #184)
Page 42 - A Cracked Look at a Health Spa - Don Orehek (reprint from #168)
Page 44 - Adults Following the Rules They Set For Children - Sururi Gumen (reprint from #188)
Page 45 - Poopeye - Nireves (John Severin) (reprint from #179)
Page 52 - The Cracked Guide to Kite Flying - Bill Ward (reprint from #199)
Page 56 - Talking Cars - Warren Sattler (reprint from #194)

Page 60 – How to Get a Job – Bill Ward (reprint from #177)
Page 63 – Why is There a Difference in Your Parents and Other Kids' Parents? – Warren Sattler (reprint from #201)
Page 66 – Heart to Heart – John Severin (reprint from #192)
Page 72 – The Cracked World of Relatives – Don Orehek (reprint from #187)
Page 76 – True Facts They Never Teach You in School – Sururi Gumen (reprint from #192)
Page 78 – Cracked Interviews the Nuclear Power King – Bill Ward (reprint from #169)
Page 82 – Shut-Ups (TV over in the corner) – Don Orehek (reprint from #202)
Page 83 – Auntie Dinger's ad (reprint from #164)
Back Cover – Cool-School Stickers (reprint from #58)

***Biggest Greatest Cracked* #21, Fall 1986 (84 pages) ($2.00)**
Cover – Four-Eyed Sylvester – John Severin (reprint from #24)
Page 2 – Log Cabin Syrup ad – John Severin (reprint from #27)
Page 3 – Contents
Page 4 – Their Dreams Almost Came True – Bill McCartney (Bill Ward) (reprint from #35)
Page 8 – T.V. Tally Ho Ho's (reprint from #65)
Page 9 – Cracked's Do-it-Yourself Cartoons – John Severin (reprint from #51)
Page 11 – Hudd & Dini (prison bars) – Vic Martin (reprint from #81)
Page 13 – One Date at a Time – John Severin (reprint from #142)
Page 19 – Incurably Cracked (reprint from #153)
Page 22 – The Six Billion Dollar Man – John Severin (reprint from #120)
Page 28 – Believe it or Nuts!! – Jack Davis (reprint from #13)
Page 29 – The Sports Fan – Bill McCartney (Bill Ward) (reprint from #54)
Page 30 – The Empire Strikes Out – O.O. Severin (John Severin) (reprint from #173)
Page 37 – Cracked Interviews the Housing King – Sigbjorn (John Severin) (reprint from #116)
Page 42 – Shut-Ups (Folkswagon Bunny) – Don Orehek (reprint from #146)
Page 43 – Why People Move to the Suburbs – Jack Davis (reprint from #14)
Page 47 – Modern Merchandise for Moneyed Mountaineers – John Severin (reprint from #31)

Page 50 – And Still More from The Cracked Lens (reprint from #158)
Page 53 – The Pot-Rich Family – John Severin (reprint from #107)
Page 58 – More Things We Shoulda Done – John Severin (reprint from #23)
Page 60 – There's One in Every Crowd – John Severin (reprint from #23)
Page 62 – Drecula – John Severin (reprint from #165)
Page 69 – Sagebrush #50 (There's gold here) – John Severin (reprint from #159)
Page 70 – Handshakes – John Severin (reprint from #11)
Page 72 – Modern Art – John Severin (reprint from #9)
Page 74 – The Nightmares of Monsters – Bill McCartney (Bill Ward) (reprint from *For Monsters Only* #5)
Page 76 – Robot Wars (Krash!) – Mort Todd (reprint from #216)
Page 77 – Cracked Interviews the Antique King – John Severin (reprint from #139)
Page 82 – Shut-Ups (make up my mind) – Don Orehek (reprint from #147)
Page 83 – An Afternoon at an Artist's Studio – Howard Nostrand (reprint from #145)
Back Cover – Remember! Forest Fires Can Prevent Bears! – Russ Heath (reprint from #13)

***Cracked Blockbuster* #1, Summer 1987 (100 pages) ($2.75)**
Cover – Earthshake – John Severin (reprint from #125)
Page 2 – Dial 'A' for Africa – Bill McCartney (Bill Ward) (reprint from #42)
Page 3 – Contents
Page 4 – Cracked's Employee of the Month Award – John Severin (reprint from #194)
Page 6 – A Press Conference with Ronald Reagan – John Severin / Joe Catalano (reprint from #186)
Page 11 – Cracked Guide to Roller Skating – Bill Ward (reprint from #160)
Page 15 – How to Win a School Election – T. Severin (John Severin) (reprint from #174)
Page 19 – The Cracked Book of Games and Puzzles That Anyone Can Solve – Warren Sattler (reprint from #159)
Page 24 – The Truth You'll Never Hear – Warren Sattler (reprint from #166)
Page 26 – How to Buy a New Car – John Severin (reprint from #200)

Page 29 – The Cracked Question and Answer Guide to Racquetball – Don Orehek (reprint from #174)
Page 33 – Profile of a Coward – Bill Ward (reprint from #175)
Page 36 – The Classified Ads of the Future – Howard Nostrand (reprint from #160)
Page 39 – The Cracked Guide to Fortune Telling – Don Orehek (reprint from #166)
Page 43 – Fly Me Model Plane Kit (reprint from *Biggest Greatest Cracked* #7)
Page 59 – Absolutely, Unquestionably, Positively, Undeniably, the Very, Very, Last of The Cracked Lens (and we really mean it this time, for sure!) (reprint from #175)
Page 65 – A Cracked Look at the Good Old Days? – John Langton (reprint from #120)
Page 68 – A Cracked Look at an Airport Terminal – Bill Ward (reprint from #185)
Page 70 – How Popular Are You? – Warren Sattler (reprint from #192)
Page 74 – Cracked's Cartoon Showcase Featuring Jeff Keate (Don't open the umbrella) – Jeff Keate (reprint from #185)
Page 76 – The Cracked Guide to Babysitting – Bill Ward (reprint from #145)
Page 80 – You Know You're Going Too Far When – Ron Zalme (reprint from #192)
Page 82 – How Wise are Wise Old Proverbs? – Vic Martin (reprint from #98)
Page 86 – What They're Really Thinking When They Say – Bill Ward (reprint from #187)
Page 88 – A Good Date vs. A Bad Date – Frank Fitzgerald (reprint from #187)
Page 90 – Farmer's Old Almanac – John Severin (reprint from #6)
Page 93 – One Day at a Railroad Crossing – Howard Nostrand (reprint from #142)
Page 94 – Cracked Looks at a Typical Savings Bank – Don Orehek (reprint from #132)
Page 96 – Fill-in-the-Blank Form Letters and Cards for Every Occasion – Sururi Gumen (reprint from #132)
Page 98 – Shut-Ups (wanted a two wheeler) – Don Orehek (reprint from #187)
Page 99 – The Explorer, the Dog & the Bone – Oskar Blotta (reprint from #84)
Back Cover – Painting the Floor – John Severin (reprint from #83)

***Cracked Blockbuster* #2, Summer 1988 (100 pages) ($2.75)**

Cover – The Talking Blob – John Severin (new)

Page 2 – Contents

Page 3 – The Talking Blob – John Severin / Joe Catalano (reprint from #149)

Page 9 – High Noonish – John Severin / Joe Catalano (reprint from #152)

Page 15 – The Greatest Sequel Ever Made – John Severin / Joe Catalano (reprint from #155)

Page 22 – Shylock Homes and the Case of the Lifted Locket – Moe Riarty (John Severin) / Joe Catalano (reprint from #162)

Page 29 – King Author and the Knights of the Reserved Table – John Severin (reprint from #171)

Page 36 – The Cracked Movie – Nireves (John Severin) / Joe Catalano (reprint from #178)

Page 43 – The Cracked Movie II – Nireves (John Severin) / Joe Catalano (reprint from #183)

Page 50 – Star Drek – The Last Hurrah? – John Severin / Joe Catalano (reprint from #184)

Page 57 – Cracked Interviews the Cracked Mazagine King – Will Bored (John Severin) / Joe Catalano (reprint from #185)

Page 63 – A Press Conference with Ronald Reagan – John Severin / Joe Catalano (reprint from #186)

Page 68 – The Cracked Movie III – John Severin / Joe Catalano (reprint from #189)

Page 75 – The Cracked Movie IV – Nireves (John Severin) / Joe Catalano (reprint from #195)

Page 83 – The Cracked Movie V – John Severin / Joe Catalano (reprint from #211)

Page 89 – Cracked Movie VI: A New Beginning – John Severin / Joe Catalano (reprint from #222)

Page 94 – Tardzan the Apish Man – John Clayton (John Severin) / Joe Catalano, Mort Todd (reprint from #226)

Page 99 – Sagebrush #25 (painting) – John Severin (reprint from #117) / Ye Hang Ups #28 (want to play a game?) – John Severin (reprint from #122)

Back Cover – Cover – Handprints in Cement – John Severin (reprint from #222)

***Cracked Blockbuster* #3, Summer 1989 (100 pages) ($2.75)**

Cover – Surfing Sylvester – John Severin (reprint from #86)

Page 2 – One Night at the Garden – Howard Nostrand (reprint from #165)

Page 3 – Contents

Page 4 – Hudd & Dini (trampoline) – Vic Martin (reprint from #107)

Page 5 – Vacation Guide to Outer Space – John Severin (reprint from #39)
Page 9 – The Visitor in Africa – Bill McCartney (Bill Ward) (reprint from #48)
Page 10 – Snide Guide to Camping – John Severin (reprint from #61)
Page 13 – Surfing U.S.A. – Bill McCartney (Bill Ward) (reprint from #39)
Page 18 – The Emergency Landing – O.O. Severin (John Severin) (reprint from #63)
Page 21 – How I Saw Europe on Only 58c a Day – Bill McCartney (Bill Ward) (reprint from #40)
Page 24 – A Cracked's-Eye View of Paris! – Bill Everett (reprint from #23)
Page 26 – A Martian Writes Home from Earth – John Severin (reprint from #40)
Page 27 – Shut-Ups (drive so fast) – Vic Martin (reprint from #47)
Page 29 – Take the Cracked Sports Test! – Bill McCartney (Bill Ward) (reprint from #61)
Page 31 – Sagebrush (stomping) – John Severin (reprint from #88)
Page 32 – When the Super-Jets Take Over – John Severin (reprint from #86)
Page 36 – Ancient Egypt (reprint from #4)
Page 38 – Cracked Looks at Fishing – Vic Martin (reprint from #76)
Page 40 – Airpot – John Severin (reprint from #91)
Page 45 – Simulating the Thrills of Big-Time Sports at Home – Vic Martin (reprint from #83)
Page 48 – Cracked Looks at Vacations – Bill McCartney (Bill Ward) (reprint from #96)
Page 50 – How the Airlines Can Save Money! – John Severin (reprint from #97)
Page 54 – Let's Travel Down Under…and Take a Cracked's-Eye View of Australia! – Bill McCartney (Bill Ward) (reprint from #86)
Page 56 – The Put-Downers – Vic Martin (reprint from #106)
Page 58 – When We All Move to Alaska – John Severin (reprint from #91)
Page 62 – Cracked Looks at Hotels – Bill McCartney (Bill Ward) (reprint from #90)
Page 65 – Hudd & Dini (garbage can magnets) – Vic Martin (reprint from #92)
Page 66 – State Posters to Lure the Hippies – John Severin (reprint from #64)
Page 68 – You Know You're Not a Kid Anymore When – Jared Lee (reprint from #99)

Page 70 – Footboxhockbasetennbasketgolfpoly – John Severin (reprint from #97)
Page 74 – A Cracked Salute to Chicago – Russ Heath (reprint from #110)
Page 78 – Cracked's Guide to Backpacking – John Severin (reprint from #108)
Page 83 – The Last of the 'Desert Island' Cartoons! – Irit Kajiij Jr. (Charles Rodrigues) (reprint from #109)
Page 86 – A Cracked Look at a Tourist Welcome Center – John Severin (reprint from #133)
Page 88 – A Cracked Look at a Skateboard Park – Sururi Gumen (reprint from #145)
Page 90 – Cracked Frisbee Rating System – Bob Taylor (reprint from #133)
Page 93 – Cracked Interviews the Vacation King – Bill Ward (reprint from #178)
Page 98 – Cracked Shut-Ups (send me in) – Bill McCartney (Bill Ward) (reprint from #3)
Page 99 – Great Moments in Sports 304,787 B.C. – Vance Rodewalt (reprint from #207)
Back Cover – Greetings from Brooklyn Postcard – John Severin (reprint from #38)

***Cracked Blockbuster* #4, Summer 1990 (100 pages) ($3.50)**

Cover – New Kids on the Blockbuster – Pete Fitzgerald (new)
Page 2 and 99 – New Kids on the Chopping Blockbuster Poster – Pete Fitzgerald (new)
Page 3 – Contents
Page 4 – Black Day at Cwub MTVee (new)
Page 9 – Cracked Rock 'n' Roll Museum – Bill McCartney (Bill Ward) (reprint from #34)
Page 12 – Beatlemania – John Severin (reprint from #37)
Page 14 – Rock Celebrity Childhoods – John Severin / George Gladir (reprint from #24)
Page 16 – ZZ Slop vs. the Space Pirates – Bob Fingerman (reprint from #223)
Page 22 – Cracked Goes to Woodstock – John Severin (reprint from #83)
Page 24 – The Stones Keep Rollin! – John Severin (reprint from #57)
Page 28 – Popular Songs Shut-Ups (smile umbrella) – Bill McCartney (Bill Ward) (reprint from #22)
Page 29 – Carmen – John Severin (reprint from #9)

Page 32 – What Are the Celebrities of 1965 Doing Today in 1990? – John Severin / George Gladir (reprint from #46)
Page 36 – Popular Songs for Everyday Working People – Howard Nostrand (reprint from #156)
Page 40 – Greased! – John Severin (reprint from #156)
Page 47 – Garbage Dump Pop Stars (Paul Shaver) (reprint from #224)
Page 50 – The Rock Stars Speak! – Bob Fingerman / Peter Bagge (reprint from #235)
Insert – Landing On Mars – Howard Nostrand / Murad Gumen (reprint from #156)
Insert – New Kids on the Blockbuster Poster – Pete Fitzgerald (new)
Insert – One Night at the Garden – Howard Nostrand (reprint from #165)
Page 52 – Beatlezania – John Severin (reprint from #42)
Page 57 – Celebrity Song Sheet for Celebrities (reprint from #10)
Page 59 – Canned Music – Bill McCartney (Bill Ward) (reprint from #43)
Page 63 – The Donkees – John Severin / Charles E. Hall, Mort Todd (reprint from #230)
Page 68 – The Cracked World of Music – Don Orehek (reprint from #206)
Page 72 – More Beatlezania – John Severin (reprint from #50)
Page 77 – Touchavision Radio Mirror – John Severin (reprint from #31)
Page 81 – Cracked World of Rock (reprint from #224)
Page 84 – Cracked's Career Guide for Disc Jockeys – Bill Ward (reprint from #174)
Page 88 – Cracked Rock Star Cars! – John Severin / Cliff Mott (reprint from #240)
Page 91 – Fashion and the Hi-Heeled Platform Shoe – John Severin (reprint from #114)
Page 94 – Cracked Busts Out With Th' Rap Kings – Bob Fingerman (reprint from #233)
Page 98 – Shut-Ups (sound of heavy metal) – Don Orehek (reprint from #224)
Back Cover – Sylvelvis Presley Smythe – Bill Wray (reprint from #230)

***Cracked Rockbuster* #5, Summer 1991 (100 pages) ($3.50)**
Cover – Smythe Gone Wild – John Severin, Mike Ricigliano (new)
Page 2 and 99 – New Kids on the Chopping Blockbuster Poster – Pete Fitzgerald (reprint from *Cracked Blockbuster* #4)
Page 3 – Contents
Page 4 – Box Office Future – John Severin / Joe Catalano, Mort Todd (reprint from #218)

Page 10 – Cracked to the Future Part II – John Severin / Tony Frank (Lou Silverstone) (reprint from #254)
Page 15 – Cracked to the Future Part III – John Severin / Tony Frank (Lou Silverstone) (reprint from #258)
Page 21 – Cracked Interviews the Rock 'n' Roll King – Bill Ward (reprint from #153)
Page 26 – Cracked Rock Star Cars! – John Severin / Cliff Mott (reprint from #240)
Page 29 – The Elvis Parsley Story – Bill Wray, John Severin / Tony Frank (Lou Silverstone) (reprint from #244)
Page 33 – The First Annual Cracked Music Awards! – Tom Short (reprint from #224)
Page 36 – Rock 'n' Roll Fairy Tales! – Frank Caruso (reprint from #225)
Page 38 – Understanding Hi-Fidelity – John Langton (reprint from #118)
Page 42 – New Cracked Dances! – Al Scaduto (reprint from #222)
Page 44 – You Know You're an MTV Freak When – Bill Powers (John Severin) (reprint from #210)
Page 46 – La Bumba – Rick Altergott / Terry Gentile (reprint from #244)
Page 50 – Tonite Only: Cracked Form and Function Presents: Elvis Impersonator Gear – Bo Badman (Rurik Tyler) (reprint from #244)
Page 52 – Lyin Beat Magazine (reprint from #160)
Page 58 – Cracked Rock 'n' Roll Museum! – John Severin / George Gladir (reprint from #250)
Page 60 – What Rock Stars Were Like as Children – Rob Orzechowski / Joe Catalano (reprint from #238)
Page 62 – Elvis What's Hot and What's Not – Gary Fields (reprint from #244)
Page 63 – Cracked Interviews Elvis the King – John Severin / Rich Kriegel (Lou Silverstone) (reprint from #244)
Page 66 – The Rock Stars Speak! – Bob Fingerman / Peter Bagge (reprint from #235)
Page 68 – Hands Across America – Bill Wray / Stu Schwartzberg (reprint from #224)
Page 71 – The Rock Craze Rolls On – John Langton (reprint from #135)
Page 74 – Cracked Interviews the Music King – John Langton (reprint from #108)
Page 79 – Cracked Rock Video Cliches! – Frank Caruso / Joey Cavalieri (reprint from #231)
Page 82 – Elvis Bubble Gum Cards – Pat Redding / Joe Catalano (reprint from #244)

Page 84 – Rock and Roll Your Eyeballs Out – John Severin (reprint from #163)
Page 90 – Cracked Interviews Yoko Ohno – Bill Ward (reprint from #244)
Page 93 – Bon Jovi vs. Bruce! – Frank Caruso (reprint from #233)
Page 95 – Rock and Roll Shut-Ups (3000 people) – Don Orehek / Charles E. Hall (reprint from #241)
Page 96 – Rock 'n' Roll Losers! – Tom Short (reprint from #220)
Page 98 – Subscription ad – Frank Borth
Back Cover – Leaving Hair ad – John Severin (reprint from #82)

***Cracked Blockbuster* #6, Summer 1992 (100 pages) ($2.95)**
Cover – Yo, There's Waldo! – John Severin (new)
Page 2 and 99 – The Great T-Shirts Rip-Off – Gary Fields (reprint from #259)
Page 3 – Contents – Mike Ricigliano
Page 4 – The Confusing Spider-Dude – Frank Borth / Jerry De Fuccio, Lou Silverstone (reprint from #260)
Page 11 – What You'll Really Miss After you Graduate – Don Orehek (reprint from #198)
Page 14 – Before Heimlich! – Vic Martin (reprint from #222)
Page 15 – Couch Potato Catalog – Vic Martin / George Gladir (reprint from #237)
Page 18 – The Cracked Penal Code – Warren Sattler (reprint from #172)
Page 20 – Non-Polluting Cars Auto Safety Devices – Jack Barrett (reprint from #101)
Page 24 – Handufactured Products – John Severin (reprint from #31)
Page 27 – Sagebrush (Howdy Shage) – John Severin (reprint from #113)
Page 28 – Adults Following the Rules They Set For Children – Sururi Gumen (reprint from #188)
Page 29 – The Cracked Guide to Skateboarding – Don Orehek (reprint from #134)
Page 33 – Trasher! Magazine – Brad Joyce / Bo Badman (Rurik Tyler) (reprint from #239)
Page 37 – Cracked History of Skateboarding – Ron Wagner (reprint from #258)
Page 40 – Form & Function (skateboards) – Bo Badman (Rurik Tyler) (reprint from #234)
Page 42 – A Cracked Look at a Skateboard Park – Sururi Gumen (reprint from #145)
Page 44 – Super Skateboard Stunts – Howard Nostrand (reprint from #144)
Page 48 – You Know You're a Skateboard Freak When – Warren Sattler (reprint from #154)

Page 50 – The Job – Mike Ricigliano / Roger Brown (reprint from #236)
Insert – The Spy and Saboteur Reunion Photo – Mike Ricigliano (reprint from #239)
Insert – Where's Weirdo Poster – Rurik Tyler (full color, glossy) (new)
Insert – Who is Dorkman? – John Severin (reprint from #260)
Page 51 – Dork, Man! – Walter Brogan (reprint from #260)
Page 57 – A Typical College Registrar's Bulletin Board – Samuel B. Whitehead (reprint from #162)
Page 60 – Stop Watches for a Contemporary Book of World Records – Arnoldo Franchioni (reprint from #188)
Page 64 – The Cracked World of Schooling – Bill Ward (reprint from #170)
Page 68 – The Grip – Mike Ricigliano / Roger Brown (reprint from #232)
Page 69 – Mother Magazine – Arnoldo Franchioni (reprint from #214)
Page 76 – Replacements for Dieann on Jeers! – Walter Brogan / Joe Catalano (reprint from #232)
Page 80 – One Day in Africa – Mike Ricigliano / Roger Brown (new)
Page 81 – G.I. Joke Gets Totally Thrashed! – Shawn Kerri (reprint from #238)
Page 86 – Kids vs. Adults – Ron Zalme (reprint from #190)
Page 90 – Shut-Ups (piece of my mind) – Don Orehek (reprint from #189)
Page 91 – Chariots of the Clods? – John Severin (reprint from #122)
Page 94 – Females Participating in All Sports – John Severin (reprint from #81)
Page 98 – Subscription ad – Mike Ricigliano
Back Cover – Painting the Floor – John Severin (reprint from #83)

***Cracked Blockbuster* #7, Winter 1993 (100 pages) ($2.95)**
Cover – Summer Movie Spectacular! – Walter Brogan (new)
Page 2 – *Cracked Spaced Out* #2 ad
Page 3 – Contents – Mike Ricigliano
Page 4 and 50 – Cracked Quiz – John Severin (new, with reprint from #93)
Page 5 – Arnie Goes to the Movies – Bruce Bolinger / Andy Simmons (new)
Page 10 – Cracked's Snide Guide to Motion Pictures – Bill McCartney (Bill Ward) (reprint from #80)
Page 12 – Goon with the Wind: 1990 – Walter Brogan / Rich Kriegel (Lou Silverstone) (reprint from #246)
Page 16 – The Big Budget Epic vs. The Low Budget Quickie – John Severin (reprint from #135)

Page 20 – American Car-Daffy – Sururi Gumen (reprint from #121)
Page 26 – The Cracked World of Movie Going – Sururi Gumen (reprint from #131)
Page 29 – The Perspirin' Adventure – John Severin (reprint from #111)
Page 34 – Messed up by Modern Times! – Bob Fingerman (reprint from #222)
Page 40 – Japanese Entertainment Take Overs – Severino San (John Severin) / Gladir San (George Gladir) (reprint from #253)
Page 43 – Tried Hard – John Severin (reprint from #259)
Insert – Cracked Dinosaur Chart – Mike Ricigliano (full color, glossy) (new)
Page 51 – The Rest of the Garbage (new)
Page 52 – Cracked Examines Telephone Answering Machines – Howard Nostrand (reprint from #157)
Page 55 – The Cracked Almanac – Howard Nostrand (reprint from #153)
Page 60 – One-Shots (stiltwalking) – Mike Ricigliano / Roger Brown (reprint from #230)
Page 62 – How to Eat Better for Less Money – Warren Sattler (reprint from #151)
Page 66 – Fringe Benefits Athletes Will Soon Be Demanding – Howard Nostrand (John Severin) (reprint from #146)
Page 69 – Subscription ad
Page 70 – A Cracked Look at Summer Camps – Howard Nostrand (reprint from #145)
Page 74 – Frustrationland – Bill Ward (reprint from #146)
Page 76 – A Cracked Look at House Pets – Don Orehek (reprint from #153)
Page 80 – Special Interest and Digest Magazines – John Severin (reprint from #158)
Page 82 – The Cracked History of Humor – Bill Ward (reprint from #153)
Page 86 – Cracked Lottery Nuts! – Al Scaduto (reprint from #230)
Page 88 – And Yet Still More from The Cracked Lens (reprint from #159)
Page 92 – Cracked's new Soon-to-be-a-Fad Diets – Don Orehek (reprint from #158)
Page 94 – The Cracked Guide to Babysitting – Bill Ward (reprint from #145)
Page 98 – Shut-Ups (wish you hadn't brought animals) – Don Orehek (reprint from #240)
Page 99 – Evolution of Smythe – Bill Wray (reprint from #226)
Back Cover – Help Wanted – Charles Rodrigues (reprint from #113)

***Cracked Blockbuster Sci-Fi Special* #8, Summer 1994 (68 pages) ($2.95) (Issue is polybagged with a 16"x 21" full color, glossy poster featuring *Cracked Data Unplugged* by Rurik Tyler.)**

Cover - The Next Next Generation - Jeff Wong (new)
Page 2 - Leaving Hair ad - John Severin (reprint from #82)
Page 3 - Contents - Mike Ricigliano
Page 4 - Sci-Fi Section (Godzilla photo) (new)
Page 5 - Star Drek The Last Degradation - Walter Brogan / Steve Strangio (new)
Page 9 - The American Space Base on Mars - John Severin (reprint from #32)
Page 11 - Nothing New Under, Around or Beyond the Sun! - Tom Short (reprint from #231)
Page 14 - Interplanetary Magazines - Bill Everett (reprint from #8)
Page 16 - Star Drek: The Next De-Generation - Bo Badman (Rurik Tyler) (reprint from #232)
Page 19 - Star People Weekly and Creatures and Things Magazine - John Severin (reprint from #148)
Page 24 - Star Trek Funnies - Mike Ricigliano / Roger Brown (reprint from #252)
Page 26 - Star Wreck The Next Degeneration - John Severin / Lou Silverstone (reprint from #271)
Page 33 - Orehek's Cracked Look at Wrestling - Don Orehek (reprint from #261)
Page 36 - The Last of the Hollywood "B" Pictures - Gray Morrow (reprint from #8)
Page 39 - Winfrah Oprey! - Bill Wray / Peter Bagge (reprint from #233)
Page 43 - The Translator & the Duel - Mike Ricigliano (reprint from #189)
Page 44 - Ms. Liberty as Influenced By - Bo Badman (Rurik Tyler) (reprint from #223)
Page 47 - Cracked Hold-Ups! (Nine Lives Louie) - Sururi Gumen (reprint from #207)
Page 49 - Cracked's Guide to Crime Prevention - Dick Wright (reprint from #110)
Page 53 - And Yet Once Again Still Some More from The Cracked Lens (reprint from #162)
Page 58 - Spies and Saboteurs Hit the Winter Olympics Part I - Mike Ricigliano (reprint from #271)
Page 59 - Spies and Saboteurs Hit the Winter Olympics Part II - Mike Ricigliano (reprint from #271)
Page 60 - Hackdraft - John Severin / Tony Frank (Lou Silverstone) (reprint from #267)

Page 66 – Shut-Ups (garbage disposal) – Don Orehek (reprint from #232)
Page 67 – Subscription ad – Frank Borth
Back Cover – The Chicken Killer – Howard Nostrand / Jay Lynch (reprint from #168)

***Cracked Blockbuster* #9, Summer 1995 (68 pages) ($2.95) (Issue is polybagged with six random of 50 possible *Cracked* Phloggs.)**
Cover – Phloggs – John Severin (new)
Page 2 and 67 – Cracked Phloggs Checklist Poster (new)
Page 3 – Contents – Mike Ricigliano
Page 4 – The Phlogg Scrapbook! (new)
Page 5 – How to Play with Phloggs – Pete Fitzgerald (new)
Page 8 – Kooch – Walter Brogan / Lance Contrucci (reprint from #275)
Page 12 – Random Funnies (upset) – Mike Ricigliano / Roger Brown (reprint from #251)
Page 14 – Cracked's Roadkill Bingo – Rurik Tyler (reprint from #276)
Page 16 – Shut-Ups (two cowpokes) – Don Orehek (reprint from #262)
Page 17 – The Greenhouse Effect – John Severin / George Gladir (reprint from #244)
Page 20 – Medical One-Shots – Mike Ricigliano / Roger Brown (reprint from #250)
Page 22 – Kindergarten Pap – John Severin / Vic Bianco (Lou Silverstone) (reprint from #263)
Page 29 – Orehek at Large Goin' Bowling – Don Orehek (reprint from #265)
Page 32 – What is a Bummer Summer Vacation? – Frank Borth (reprint from #265)
Page 34 – Sports Fan's Dream – John Severin / Rich Kriegel (Lou Silverstone) (reprint from #265)
Page 35 – Michael Jackson Strang-R-Us – Rurik Tyler (reprint from #272)
Page 38 – The Clodfather – Walter Brogan (reprint from #263)
Page 45 – New Muppets! – Pete Fitzgerald / Rob Weske (reprint from #272)
Page 48 – One Day in Chinese Acupuncture Hospital – Don Orehek (reprint from #250)
Page 50 – Strange Places for Cellular Phones – Mike Ricigliano / Roger Brown (reprint from #255)
Page 52 – Shut-Ups (swig of my wife's coffee) – Don Orehek (reprint from #259)
Page 53 – TV Moms Go to War! – Rurik Tyler (reprint from #262)

Page 56 – Man Invents the Wheel – Mike Ricigliano (reprint from #253)
Page 57 – Skateboards of the World! – Pete Fitzgerald / Charles E. Hall (reprint from #253)
Page 61 – A Day in the Life of Elvis' Greatest Fan! – Rob Orzechowski / Joe Catalano (reprint from #244)
Page 63 – Nickelodown Tonight's Feature Mr. Id – John Severin / Tommy Uno (reprint from #169)
Page 66 – Subscription ad
Back Cover – The Day the Paulsbury Doughboy's Oven Overheated! – John Severin / Scott Thaler (reprint from #266)

***Cracked Blockbuster* #10, Summer 1996 (84 pages) ($2.95)**
Cover – Wrestling Special – John Severin (new)
Page 2 – *Cracked Monster Party* #33 ad
Page 3 – Contents – Mike Ricigliano
Page 4 – We Terminate Schwarzenegger – John Severin (reprint from #266)
Page 5 – Under Sludge – Walter Brogan / Lou Silverstone (reprint from #279)
Page 8 – Rambozo: Worst Blood II – Kent Gamble (reprint from #217)
Page 14 – Universal Shlocker – Walter Brogan / Rich Kriegel (Lou Silverstone) (reprint from #277)
Page 20 – A Cracked Look at 007! – O.O. Severin (John Severin) / Mort Todd (reprint from #216)
Page 23 – Arnold Schwartzburger Film Festival – Walter Brogan (reprint from #266)
Page 28 – When All TV Reflects the Simpson Influence – John Severin / George Gladir (reprint from #260)
Page 31 – Cracked Helpful Hints for Shooting Snappier Snapshots – Vic Martin (reprint from #262)
Page 35 – Sylvester for President – John Severin (reprint from #36)
Page 40 – Form & Function Looks at Scuba Gear – Bo Badman (Rurik Tyler) (reprint from #240)
Page 42 – Sissy Boy! (new)
Insert – Bulk Hoagie vs. Mucho Man Poster – Frank Cummings (full color, glossy) (new)
Insert – Stink vs. The Undiestaker – Jeff Wong (full color, glossy) (new)
Page 43 – Megasuperultramania Magazine – Rurik Tyler / Steve Strangio (reprint from #275)

Page 48 – Spies and Saboteurs Hit the Mats – Mike Ricigliano (reprint from #261)
Page 49 – Orehek's Cracked Look at Wrestling – Don Orehek (reprint from #261)
Page 52 – Sports Oddities (Fullback Arnold) – Jack Davis (reprint from #15)
Page 53 – Sticks and Stitches – John Severin (reprint from #42)
Page 57 – Shut-Ups (pull them offside) – Don Orehek (reprint from #261)
Page 58 – Spies and Saboteurs Hit American Gladiators – Mike Ricigliano (reprint from #277)
Page 60 – A Cracked Look at a Wrestling Match – Bill Ward (reprint from #137)
Page 62 – Females Participating in All Sports – John Severin (reprint from #81)
Page 67 – The Cracked List 13 Alternatives for Bungee Jumpers – Mike Ricigliano / Dan Birtcher (reprint from #281)
Page 68 – Combination Sports of the Future – Bruce Day (reprint from #154)
Page 71 – Sports Oddities (Hank Luckeezi) – Jack Davis (reprint from #15)
Page 72 – Spies and Saboteurs Hit Madison Square Garden – Mike Ricigliano (reprint from #281)
Page 74 – Mission: Implausible – O.O. Severin (John Severin) (reprint from #80)
Page 80 – Company Names – Al Jaffee (reprint from #7)
Page 82 – Subscription ad – John Severin (reprint from #260)
Page 83 – Great Moments in History 1314 – Mike Ricigliano (reprint from #250)
Back Cover – The Frog Prince of Buckingham Palace – Jim Bennett (reprint from #281)

***Cracked Blockbuster* #11, Summer 1997 (84 pages) ($2.95)**

Cover – Our Phat Music Issue! – Frank Cummings (new)
Page 2 – Country Hits from Death Row – Rurik Tyler / Lenore Skenazy (reprint from #297)
Page 3 – Contents – Mike Ricigliano
Page 4 – Really Bad Rock Bands – Kerry Soper (new)
Page 6 – Greased! – John Severin (reprint from #156)
Page 13 – Michael Jackson Strang-R-Us – Rurik Tyler (reprint from #272)
Page 16 – Our Real Keyboard For Rock Star Wannabes! – Bruce Bolinger / Dan Birtcher (reprint from #278)

Page 18 – Modern Music Endorsements – Jeff Wong / Buddy Flip (reprint from #292)
Page 20 – At the Heavy Metal Concert – Mike Ricigliano (reprint from #252)
Page 21 – The Elvis Parsley Story – Bill Wray, John Severin / Tony Frank (Lou Silverstone) (reprint from #244)
Page 25 – Hyper Image Homeboy Goodz for Hangin' in Da 'Hood – Todd James / Barry Zeger (reprint from #289)
Page 28 – The Rock Stars Speak! – Bob Fingerman / Peter Bagge (reprint from #235)
Page 30 – What the "M" in MTV Really Stands For – Danny Hellman / Greg Grabianski (reprint from #300)
Page 32 – Cracked Interviews the Rock 'n' Roll King – Bill Ward (reprint from #153)
Page 37 – Orehek at Large Goes to a Rock Concert – Don Orehek (reprint from #266)
Page 40 – Spies and Saboteurs Hit the Rock and Roll Hall of Fame – Mike Ricigliano (reprint from #305)
Page 42 and Insert – Unbelievably Sneaky Fake-Out Covers!!! – Mike Ricigliano, Rurik Tyler (full color, glossy) (new and reprint from *Cracked Summer Special* #4)
Page 43 – How to Get Your CD Out of the Damn Package! – Bruce Bolinger / Andy Simmons (new)
Page 44 – La Bumba – Rick Altergott / Terry Gentile (reprint from #244)
Page 48 – Our Lady of Garbage – Rurik Tyler / Ronnie Nathan (reprint from #266)
Page 50 – Rock and Roll or Pro Wrestling – Bruce Bolinger / Terry Colon (reprint from #305)
Page 52 – Understanding Hi-Fidelity – John Langton (reprint from #118)
Page 55 – Cracked Rock Video Cliches! – Frank Caruso / Joey Cavalieri (reprint from #231)
Page 58 – Grunge is Really Getting Out of Hand When – Jeff Wong / Gene Perone (reprint from #284)
Page 60 – Rapper Rap Sheets – Todd James / Barry Zeger (reprint from #303)
Page 62 – The Vanilla Ice Cream Story The Man, his Music, the Legend – John Severin / Vic Bianco (Lou Silverstone) (reprint from #264)
Page 66 – Other Magazine Covers Madonna Will Be Appearing On – Rurik Tyler / Chick Chasen (reprint from #279)
Page 68 – More Beatlezania – John Severin (reprint from #50)

Page 73 – Woodstock – Don Orehek / Vic Bianco (Lou Silverstone) (reprint from #249)
Page 77 – 20/21 Interviews Hard Rock's Superstars – Walter Brogan / Greg Grabianski (reprint from *Cracked Summer Special* #4)
Page 82 – Rock and Roll Shut-Ups (3000 people) – Don Orehek / Charles E. Hall (reprint from #241)
Page 83 – Subscription ad – John Severin (reprint from *Cracked Blockbuster* #5)
Back Cover – Marky Mark Bears All – Jeff Wong (reprint from #282)

***Cracked Blockbuster* #12, Summer 1998 (84 pages) ($2.99)**
Cover – Godzilla's N.Y. Vacation – Frank Cummings (new)
Page 2 – Charles Barkley vs. Godzilla Part XVII – John Severin / Rob Weske (reprint from #281)
Page 3 – Contents – Mike Ricigliano
Page 4 – E.Z. Meets Clodzilla – Rob Orzechowski (reprint from *Cracked Monster Party* #12)
Page 9 – The New and Sometimes Improved Robin Hood – Mike Ricigliano (reprint from #265)
Page 12 – Without _________, We'd Never – Frank Cummings / Mike Mikula (reprint from #306)
Page 14 – Cracked's Sneaker Manufacturer of the Year – Walter Brogan / Lou Silverstone (reprint from #289)
Page 18 – Cracked Look at Godzilla! – Bill Wray / Joe Catalano (reprint from #219)
Page 20 – Old Movie Monster Films Updated for Today – Kent Gamble (reprint from #213)
Page 25 – Cracked Guide to Customized Skateboards – John Severin / George Gladir (reprint from #251)
Page 28 – Germinator 2: Judgment Daze – Walter Brogan / Tony Frank (Lou Silverstone) (reprint from #268)
Page 35 – Baseball Stadia for the 90's – Terry Colon (reprint from #295)
Page 39 – The Monster – Sururi Gumen (reprint from #130)
Page 40 – Cracked Trading Cards for Less Glamorous Professions – Pete Fitzgerald (reprint from #259)
Page 43 – Ye Hang Ups (get no break) – John Severin (reprint from #253)
Insert – Know Your Godzilla Poster – Frank Cummings (full color, glossy) (new)
Insert – Godzilla Poster – Bruce Bolinger (full color, glossy) (new)
Page 43 – Godzilla's Greetings from New York City! – Mike Ricigliano (new)
Page 47 – Hollywoodworld Resort – Bruce Bolinger / Rob Weske (reprint from #289)

Page 51 – Ye Hang Ups #3 (screams) – C.E. Severin (Catherine Severin) (reprint from #172)
Page 52 – Encino Man's College Scrapbook – Don Orehek / Steve Strangio (reprint from *Cracked Monster Party* #19)
Page 54 – Magnumb Public Idiot – John Severin (reprint from #191)
Page 61 – Hyper Image Homeboy Goodz for Hangin' in Da 'Hood – Todd James / Barry Zeger (reprint from #289)
Page 64 – Proper Etiquette for Everyday Living – Mike Ricigliano / Roger Brown (reprint from #256)
Page 66 – "The Lion King" Promotional Blitz – Walter Brogan / Greg Grabianski (reprint from #293)
Page 70 – Celebrity Answering Machines – Jeff Wong / David Boone (reprint from #278)
Page 72 – Spy & Saboteur in Steel Cage Match – Mike Ricigliano (reprint from #255)
Page 73 – When They Were Kids – Don Orehek / Tony Rubino (reprint from #272)
Page 76 – The Mask Goes to the Cineplex – John Severin / Greg Grabianski, Missy Wheathins (reprint from #294)
Page 82 – Shut-Ups (There's a seat) – Don Orehek / Gayle-Adams Pierpont (reprint from #272)
Page 83 – Subscription ad – Frank Borth
Back Cover – Cracked's Great Moments in Science (Look Professor) – Jeff Wong / Rob Weske (reprint from #289)

***Cracked Blockbuster* #13, Summer 1999 (84 pages) ($2.99)**
Cover – We Flip-Off the South Park Movie – Rurik Tyler (new)
Page 2 – Marlburrow ad – John Severin / Judd Stomp (reprint from #289)
Page 3 – Contents – Mike Ricigliano
Page 4 – Script Your Own South Park Movie – Gary Fields / Tony Frank (Lou Silverstone) (new)
Page 7 – Kindergarten Pap – John Severin / Vic Bianco (Lou Silverstone) (reprint from #263)
Page 14 – The Sophisti-Kids Go To Camp Elegance – Jeff Bennett (reprint from #283)
Page 16 – The Inspection – Mike Ricigliano / Roger Brown (reprint from #252)
Page 17 – Victor's Secret Catalogue – Bruce Bolinger / Steve Strangio (reprint from #282)
Page 20 – Charlie Brown Specials for the 90's – Gary Fields / Craig Farrell (reprint from #283)
Page 22 – The Scoreboard Kid – John Severin (reprint from #260)

Page 26 – Homeboy Alone, Too – Walter Brogan / Lou Silverstone (reprint from #280)
Page 32 – Arachnomania – Mike Ricigliano (reprint from #260)
Page 34 – Test Your First Aid Knowledge! – John Severin / Rob Petrie (reprint from #280)
Page 37 – Cracked's Truly Atrocious Trading Cards – Rurik Tyler / Dan Birtcher (reprint from #282)
Page 40 – Spies and Saboteurs Hit the Ballpark – Mike Ricigliano (reprint from #282)
Page 42 – Flipbook Instructions (new)
Insert – 4 South Park Flipbooks – Rurik Tyler, Frank Cummings (full color, card stock) (new)
Page 43 – Shut-Ups (wanted an early American dwelling) – Don Orehek (reprint from #250)
Page 44 – Tried Hard – John Severin (reprint from #259)
Page 51 – A Cracked Look at Future Specialized Camps – Frank Borth / Tony Frank (Lou Silverstone) (reprint from #264)
Page 54 – The Complete Cracked Guide to the Industrial Arts – Bruce Bolinger / Dan Birtcher (reprint from #283)
Page 56 – Hazards of: (Dating) – Mike Ricigliano / Roger Brown (reprint from #250)
Page 58 – Hot Snots! – John Severin / Tony Frank (Lou Silverstone) (reprint from #269)
Page 63 – Spies and Saboteurs Hit the Hoops – Mike Ricigliano (reprint from #269)
Page 66 – Cracked's Detective Handbook – Bill Ward (reprint from #151)
Page 70 – First Cat – The Adventures of Socks Clinton – Don Orehek (reprint from #282)
Page 72 – Cracked Looks at Baseball Trading Cards – John Severin / George Gladir (reprint from #250)
Page 76 – Great Moments in Police Technology 1931 – Mike Ricigliano (reprint from #257)
Page 77 – Lost Action Hero – Walter Brogan / Lou Silverstone (reprint from #285)
Page 82 – Subscription ad – John Severin (reprint from *Cracked Blockbuster* #5)
Page 83 – Commemorative Plate Rejects – Rurik Tyler / Andy Lamberti (reprint from #290)
Back Cover – The Michael Jordan Paper Doll – Jeff Wong (reprint from #291)

***Cracked Classics* (*The 3-D Zone* #19), 1989 (36 pages) ($2.50) (All reprinted features are in 3-D.)**

Cover – Sylvester in 3-D – Bill Wray (new)
Page 2 – Introduction – Michael Delle-Femine (Mort Todd) (new)
Insert – 3-D glasses frames
Page 3 – Cracked Interviews the Magic King – Bill Ward (reprint from #131)
Page 8 – A Beatnik Goes to a Party – Jack Davis (reprint from #12)
Page 10 – Robot Wars (heh heh bbbzzz) – Steve Ditko / Mort Todd (reprint from #218)
Page 11 – A Cracked History of the Movies – Vic Martin (reprint from #109)
Page 15 – Man's Best Friend? – Jack Davis (reprint from #11)
Page 16 – Interplanetary Magazines – Bill Everett (reprint from #8)
Page 18 – Late One Evening – Howard Nostrand (reprint from #142)
Page 19 – Gunsmokes – Russ Heath (reprint from #1)
Page 22 – Psychological Predictions – Bill Elder (reprint from #6)
Page 24 – The Uggly Family Uglystoppers Textbook – Stosh Gillespie (Dan Clowes) / Eel O'Brian (Mort Todd) (reprint from #234)
Page 28 – The Talking Blob – John Severin / Joe Catalano (reprint from #149)
Page 34 – Cracked Space Shut-Ups! (most beautiful girl) – Bill McCartney (Bill Ward) (reprint from #8)
Insert – 3-D glasses earpieces
Page 35 – Basil Wolverton drawing (reprint from #10)
Back Cover – Sylvester in 3-D in reverse – Bill Wray (new)

***Cracked Shut-Ups* #1, 1971 (52 pages) (50c) (*Cracked Collectors' Edition* #1)**

Cover – Four-Eyed Sylvester – John Severin (reprint from #24 with bandage added)
Page 2 – Shut-Ups! (Running Deer) – Charles Rodrigues (reprint from #62)
Page 3 – Contents
Page 4 – Popular Songs Shut-Ups (smile umbrella) – Bill McCartney (Bill Ward) (reprint from #22)
Page 6 – Shut-Ups (duck call) – Vic Martin (reprint from #52)
Page 7 – Shut-Ups (C-A-T) – Charles Rodrigues (reprint from #57)
Page 8 – Shut-Ups (snowing) – Charles Rodrigues (reprint from #65)
Page 9 – Cracked Shut-Ups (Bwanna Jim) – Bill McCartney (Bill Ward) (reprint from #6)
Page 10 – Shut-Ups (astronaut) – Charles Rodrigues (reprint from #80)
Page 11 – Shut-Ups (first men on moon) – Charles Rodrigues (reprint from #79)

Page 12 – Shut-Ups (five pounds of tea) – Charles Rodrigues (reprint from #66)
Page 13 – Shut-Ups (king's dinner) – Julius Siezure (Charles Rodrigues) (reprint from #96)
Page 14 – Shut-Ups (nice monkey) – Vic Martin (reprint from #54) and various reprints by Charles Rodrigues
Page 16 – Shut-Ups (rocks) – Vic Martin (reprint from #50)
Page 17 – Shut-Ups (Peanuts) – Ellsworth A. Sap (Charles Rodrigues) (reprint from #69)
Page 18 – Shut-Ups (haven't smoked) – Busby Berkley (Charles Rodrigues) (reprint from #70)
Page 19 – Shut-Ups (spilled the beans) – Vito Modigliani (Charles Rodrigues) (reprint from #97)
Page 20 – Shut-Ups (walking on air) – Vito Modigliani (Charles Rodrigues) (reprint from #75)
Page 21 – Shut-Ups (martini) – Cosi Van Tutti (Charles Rodrigues) (reprint from #76)
Page 22 – Shut-Ups (Ladies first) – Rodrigliani (Charles Rodrigues) (reprint from #77)
Page 23 – Shut-Ups (driving lesson) – Rodrigliani (Charles Rodrigues) (reprint from #78)
Page 24 – Shut-Ups (cat dragged in) – Rodrigliani (Charles Rodrigues) (reprint from #81)
Page 25 – Shut-Ups (the water's fine) – Vincent Van Stop (Charles Rodrigues) (reprint from #82)
Page 26 – Shut-Ups! (windshield wipers) – Rodrigliani (Charles Rodrigues) (reprint from #84)
Page 27 – Shut-Ups (endless snow) – Sam Gross (Charles Rodrigues) (reprint from #95)
Page 28 – Shut-Ups (long hair) – Modest Mussorgsky (Charles Rodrigues) (reprint from #85)
Page 29 – Shut-Ups! (can't stay up here) – Ellis Dee (Charles Rodrigues) (reprint from #64)
Page 30 – Shut-Ups! (can't hold ladder) – Golden (reprint from #63)
Page 31 – Shut-Ups! (40) – Duke Mantee (Charles Rodrigues) (reprint from #61)
Page 32 – Shut-Ups (AAEE-HOOEO!) – Nan Reik (Charles Rodrigues) (reprint from #58)
Page 33 – Shut-Ups (big crowd) – Philip Garbage (Charles Rodrigues) (reprint from #67)
Page 34 – Shut-Ups (hang around) – Charles Rodrigues (reprint from #71)

Page 35 – Shut-Ups (fear of dark rooms) – Charles Rodrigues (reprint from #72)
Page 36 – Shut-Ups (lookout man) – Charles Rodrigues (reprint from #51)
Page 37 – Shut-Ups (correct time) – Nelson Varicose (Charles Rodrigues) (reprint from #60)
Page 38 – Shut-Ups (credit card) – Lefty Wright (Charles Rodrigues) (reprint from #92)
Page 39 – Shut-Ups (drive-in movie) – Charles Rodrigues, Vic Martin (reprint from #93)
Page 40 – Shut-Ups (Can I sit) – Glenn Mukheryee (Charles Rodrigues) (reprint from #94)
Page 41 – Shut-Ups! (exercise) – Pick and Pat (Charles Rodrigues) (reprint from #88)
Page 42 – Shut-Ups! (exit slowly) – Charles Rodrigues (reprint from #89)
Page 43 – Shut-Ups (good likeness) – Sigmund Froyd (Charles Rodrigues) (reprint from #90)
Page 44 – Shut-Ups (true or false) – Sue Sioux (Charles Rodrigues) (reprint from #91)
Page 45 – Shut-Ups! (tie clasps) – Rodrigliani (Charles Rodrigues) (reprint from #56)
Page 46 – Television Shut-Ups (cashier's check) – John Severin (reprint from #21)
Page 47 – Cracked Space Shut-Ups! (most beautiful girl) – Bill McCartney (Bill Ward) (reprint from #8)
Page 48 – Cracked Shut-Ups (diamond ring) – Bill McCartney (Bill Ward) (reprint from #5)
Page 49 – Shut-Ups (only girl) – Carlos Gerdel (Charles Rodrigues) (reprint from #86)
Page 50 – Famous Quotations Shut-Ups (Don't give up the ship) – Vic Martin (reprint from #23)
Page 51 – Shut-Ups (sports car) – Charles Rodrigues (reprint from #87)
Back Cover – Shut-Ups (I'll find you) – John Severin (reprint from #13)

***Cracked Shut-Ups* #2, 1972 (52 pages) (50c) (*Cracked Collectors' Edition* #2)**

Cover – Sardines – Nireves (John Severin) (reprint from #74 and partial reprint #17)
Page 2 – Six Annuals ad (*Biggest* 6, 7; *Giant* 7, 8; *King-Sized* 5; *Super* 5)
Page 3 – Contents
Page 4 – Cracked Shut-Ups (driving in the country) – Bill McCartney (Bill Ward) (reprint from #9)

Page 5 – Cracked Shut-Ups (Europe) – Bill McCartney (Bill Ward) (reprint from #2)
Page 6 – Famous Proverb Shut-Ups (small packages) – John Severin (reprint from #15)
Page 8 – Madison Avenue Shut-Ups (no cavities) – Vic Martin (reprint from #20)
Page 10 – Shut-Ups (hit a tree) – S. Gross Jr. (Charles Rodrigues) (reprint from #102)
Page 11 – Hurry-Ups (Sarge is pinned) – Bill McCartney (Bill Ward) (reprint from #36)
Page 12 – Hurry-Ups (papa, papa) – John Severin (reprint from #33)
Page 13 – Shut-Ups (winning tickets) – S. Gross Jr. (Charles Rodrigues) (reprint from #103)
Page 14 – Hurry-Ups (daddy fell out) – Don Orehek (reprint from #34)
Page 15 – Cracked Shut-Ups (daddy run) – Al Jaffee (reprint from #5)
Page 16 – Hurry-Ups (house on fire) – John Severin (reprint from #32)
Page 17 – Cracked's Snappy Comebacks! – John Severin (reprint from #75)
Page 19 – Rare Olde Shut-Upf – Jack Davis (reprint from #16)
Page 20 – Orders – John Severin (reprint from #38)
Page 21 – Hip Shut-Ups (I'm floatin') – John Severin (reprint from #11) (originally called "Bop Shut-Ups")
Page 22 – Six Annuals ad (Biggest 6, 7; Giant 7, 8; King-Sized 5; Super 5)
Page 23 – Shut-Ups! (stick-in-the-mud) – Vito Montigliani (Charles Rodrigues) (reprint from #73)
Page 24 – Celebrity Shut-Ups (shampoo) – John Severin (reprint from #14)
Page 26 – Russian Shut-Ups (Russia) – Bill McCartney (Bill Ward) (reprint from #12)
Page 27 – Hurry-Ups (five dollar raise) – Don Orehek (reprint from #35)
Page 28 – Famous Scenes from Great Desert Island Movies – John Langton (reprint from #73)
Page 29 – Cracked Shut-Ups (beastly hot) – Bill McCartney (Bill Ward) (reprint from #7)
Page 30 – Shut-Ups (20 cents) – Rodrigliani (Charles Rodrigues) (reprint from #46)
Page 31 – Shut-Ups (don't want to run) – John Severin (reprint from #42)
Page 32 – Hurry-Ups (fly in soup) – Bill McCartney (Bill Ward) (reprint from #41)
Page 33 – Shut-Ups! (erector set) – Arthur Knockwurst (Charles Rodrigues) (reprint from #59)

Page 34 – Hurry-Ups (last cigarette) – Bill McCartney (Bill Ward) (reprint from #38)
Page 35 – Shut-Ups (Can I Stop?) – Vic Martin (reprint from #44)
Page 36 – Horror House ad – John Severin
Page 37 – Shut-Ups (innocent) – S. Gross (Charles Rodrigues) (reprint from #104)
Page 38 – Shakespearean Shut-Ups (Romeo) – John Severin (reprint from #17)
Page 40 – Black Magic – Bob Zahn (reprint from #37)
Page 41 – Hurry-Ups (ship is sinking) – Bill McCartney (Bill Ward) (reprint from #37)
Page 42 – Cracked Fun Shoppe ad – John Severin
Page 43 – Shut-Ups (No cavities) – Sam Gross Jr. (Charles Rodrigues) (reprint from #99)
Page 44 – Shut-Ups (don't need haircut) – Vic Martin (reprint from #49)
Page 45 – Shut-Ups (drive so fast) – Vic Martin (reprint from #47)
Page 46 – Fine Art Shut-Ups (lopsided hat) – John Severin (reprint from #19)
Page 47 – Shut-Ups (bottle of soda) – Vic Martin (reprint from #48)
Page 48 – Shut-Ups (baseball) – Bill McCartney (Bill Ward) (reprint from #43)
Page 49 – Shut-Ups (snooping around) – Sam Gross Jr. (Charles Rodrigues) (reprint from #100)
Page 50 – Shut Up and Get it Over With! – Jared Lee (reprint from #101)
Page 51 – Shut-Ups (jump) – Rodrigliani (Charles Rodrigues) (reprint from #55)
Back Cover – Shut-Ups (unlimited talent) – Sam Gross Jr. (Charles Rodrigues) (reprint from #98)

***Cracked Special* #3 (*Cracked Goes to the Movies*), 1973 (52 pages) (50c) (*Cracked Collectors' Edition* #3)**

Cover – Western Gunfight – John Severin (reprint from #39)
Page 2 – Welcome to Marlboro Country – John Severin (reprint from #53)
Page 3 – Contents
Page 4 – The Moon Ate a Big Pink Kumquat (reprint from #87)
Page 6 – Fun Under the Big Top! (reprint from #81)
Page 8 – "The Ex-Con Butler Did it in a Combat Zone!" (reprint from #81)
Page 10 – Going Great Guns (reprint from #80)
Page 14 – Just What the Doctor Ordered (reprint from #78)
Page 16 – The Cracked Camera (reprint from #102)

Page 19 – Cracked Fun Shoppe ad – John Severin
Page 20 – Ship Shape (reprint from #82)
Page 22 – Horror House ad – John Severin
Page 23 – Ship Shape (reprint from #83)
Page 26 – Fight On! (reprint from #103)
Page 28 – Laurel & Hardy Tell it Like it is! (reprint from #88)
Page 30 – Three Terrific Teams (reprint from #103)
Page 34 – Cracked Gets Greta Garbo to…Talk at Last! (reprint from #90)
Page 36 – Wild and Wacky Westerns! (reprint from #103)
Page 38 – Valentino Vibrations (reprint from #94)
Page 40 – Hiss the Villains (reprint from #94)
Page 44 – Wild Wheels (reprint from #104)
Page 46 – Safari So Good (reprint from #104)
Page 48 – Getting There is Almost All the Fun! (reprint from #92)
Page 51 – Five Annuals ad (*Biggest* 8; *Collectors* 2; *Giant* 8; *King-Sized* 7; *Super* 6)
Back Cover – Sellogg's Product 16 ad – John Severin (reprint from #91)

***Cracked Collectors' Edition* #4 (*Those Cracked Monsters*), 1974 (52 pages) (50c)**

Cover – Monster Picnic – O.O. Severin (John Severin) (reprint from #54)
Page 2 – (Raid, half the fun) photos (reprint from #58)
Page 3 – Contents
Page 4 – Chilling Chuckles (reprint from *For Monsters Only* #10)
Page 6 – Horrible Humor (reprint from #97)
Page 9 – Great Scenes from Great Horror Movies – John Severin (reprint from #42)
Page 11 – Killer-Dillers! (reprint from *For Monsters Only* #9)
Page 12 – The Biggies Break it Up! (reprint from *For Monsters Only* #10)
Page 14 – Quick Quiz (two guys went on the wagon) (reprint from *For Monsters Only* #10)
Page 16 – Horror Hee-Haw (reprint from *For Monsters Only* #10)
Page 18 – The Painter's Fantasy – Oskar Blotta (reprint from #85)
Page 19 – The Big Things Do Their Thing! (reprint from *For Monsters Only* #9)
Page 21 – The Condemned Man – John Severin (reprint from #64)
Page 22 – Fiendish for Fun! (reprint from *For Monsters Only* #10)
Page 24 – Heavy on the Horror, Please (reprint from #95)
Page 26 – Cracked Fun Shoppe ad – John Severin
Page 27 – Let's Meet the Ladies (reprint from *For Monsters Only* #9)
Page 29 – Hudd & Dini (skeleton) – Vic Martin (reprint from #95)
Page 30 – The Bed of Nails – J.T. Dennett (reprint from #52)

Page 31 – A Little Off the Top! – BOJ (reprint from #53)
Page 32 – Monster Laughs!!! (reprint from *For Monsters Only* #9)
Page 33 – More Fiendish Delights (reprint from *For Monsters Only* #9)
Page 34 – Make Mine Well Done! – John Langton (reprint from #62)
Page 35 – The Monsters Laugh it Up! (reprint from #56)
Page 37 – Horror House ad – John Severin
Page 38 – Monsterous Merriment (reprint from #98)
Page 40 – The Terror Trip – BOJ (reprint from #55)
Page 41 – The Wacky Weirdos (reprint from *For Monsters Only* #6)
Page 43 – The Most Horrible Monster of All – Walt Lardner (reprint from #93)
Page 44 – Mad Mirth Makers! (reprint from *For Monsters Only* #10)
Page 46 – The Evil Experiment! – John Langton (reprint from #75)
Page 47 – The Howls Are Here! (reprint from *For Monsters Only* #9)
Page 48 – Howl Makers (reprint from *For Monsters Only* #10)
Page 50 – Orders – John Severin (reprint from #38)
Page 51 – Five Annuals ad (*Biggest* 9; *Collectors* 2; *Giant* 8; *King-Sized* 7; *Super* 6)
Back Cover – (scalp treatments) photo (reprint from *For Monsters Only* #10)

***Cracked Collectors' Edition* #5 (*Cracked Goes West*), 1974 (52 pages) (50c)**
Cover – Mechanical Horse and Indians – John Duillo (reprint from #79)
Page 2 – Six Annuals ad (*Biggest* 8; *Collectors* 2, 3; *Giant* 9; *King-Sized* 6; *Super* 7)
Page 3 – Contents
Page 4 – Fields of Fun! (reprint from #71)
Page 7 – The Train Robber – Bill McCartney (Bill Ward) (reprint from #34)
Page 8 – Cracked Rides West! (reprint from #67)
Page 10 – The Quickest Fun in the West (reprint from #77)
Page 13 – What Really Happened to General Custer – Larry Barth (reprint from #88)
Page 14 – Have Gun Won't Travel – Bill McCartney (Bill Ward) (reprint from #5)
Page 17 – Sagebrush (can't hold on) – John Severin (new)
Page 18 – When the West Was Fun! (reprint from #53)
Page 20 – The Owlhoots (reprint from #98)
Page 22 – The Last Shot – Bob Zahn (reprint from #47)
Page 23 – Big-John is Coming – LePoer (John Severin) (reprint from #31)
Page 27 – ("Keep Off the Grass") *The Good, The Bad & The Ugly* photo (reprint from #67)
Page 28 – Cracked Fun Shoppe ad – John Severin

Page 29 – Bat Masteyson – Jack Davis (reprint from #13)
Page 33 – The Good Guys (reprint from #97)
Page 35 – The Way They Should Have Filmed it – John Severin (reprint from #29)
Page 36 – Sagebrush (peace-pipe) – John Severin (reprint from #84)
Page 38 – Right from the Horse's Mouth (reprint from #46)
Page 40 – Rodeo Riders – Bill McCartney (Bill Ward) (reprint from #49)
Page 44 – Horror House ad – John Severin
Page 45 – How to Become a Writer of Westerns – John Severin (reprint from #79)
Page 47 – The Lone Ranger (reprint from #38)
Page 49 – How the West was Lost (reprint from #39)
Page 50 – Story of the Month (Whoa, Bessie) – John Severin (reprint from #27)
Page 51 – Binders and notebooks ad
Back Cover – Ferd ad – John Severin (reprint from #89)

***Cracked Collectors' Edition* #6 (*The Cracked Gangster Gallery*), 1974 (52 pages) (50c)**

Cover – Gangsters – John Severin
Page 2 – Seven Annuals ad (*Biggest* 8; *Collectors* 2, 3; *Giant* 9, 10; *King-Sized* 6; *Super* 7)
Page 3 – Contents
Page 6 – The Rodfather – O.O. Severino (John Severin) (reprint from #104)
Page 10 – The Big Guns! (reprint from #70)
Page 12 – Bullet Proof Car – John Severin (reprint from #35)
Page 13 – Crime on Prime Time – Vic Martin (reprint from #63)
Page 17 – Famous Scenes from Great Prison-Type Movies – Vic Martin (reprint from #55)
Page 19 – Chickie, the Fuzz (reprint from #79)
Page 20 – Hudd & Dini (caveman) – Vic Martin (reprint from #96)
Page 21 – Bullet – John Severin (reprint from #78)
Page 26 – King of the Mafia – Art Pottier (reprint from #73)
Page 28 – Guns and Gags for Hire! (reprint from #62)
Page 30 – The Joker's Wild – Bill McCartney (Bill Ward) (reprint from #5)
Page 31 – Bonnie and Clyde! – O.O. Severin (John Severin) (reprint from #73)
Page 36 – Notes – Don Orehek (reprint from #35)
Page 38 – Sincerely Yours, Sam Quarter – Bill McCartney (Bill Ward) (reprint from #95)
Page 42 – The Cosa Nostra First Reader – Bill McCartney (Bill Ward) (reprint from #35)

Page 47 – Come and Get Me, Copper! (reprint from #64)
Page 48 – The Charlie Chan Caper (reprint from #71)
Page 50 – Music Hath Charm – Bill McCartney (Bill Ward) (reprint from #42)
Page 51 – Binders and notebooks ad
Back Cover – Join the Dodge Rebellion! – John Severin (reprint from #83)

***Cracked Collectors' Edition* #7 (*The Cracked T.V. Screen*), 1974 (52 pages) (50c)**

Cover – TV Orchestra – John Severin (reprint from #75)
Page 2 – Seven Annuals ad (*Biggest* 8; *Collectors* 2, 3; *Giant* 9, 10; *King-Sized* 6; *Super* 7)
Page 3 – Contents
Page 4 – Mission: Implausible – O.O. Severin (John Severin) (reprint from #80)
Page 10 – TV Titles (reprint from #62)
Page 14 – Ironslide – John Severin (reprint from #82)
Page 19 – Future Late Show Programs – Bill McCartney (Bill Ward) (reprint from #56)
Page 22 – The Pot-Rich Family – John Severin (reprint from #107)
Page 27 – TV Commercials That are Wasted – John Langton (reprint from #74)
Page 30 – N.Y.P.U. – Lugoze (reprint from #70)
Page 35 – Hi-Fly-TV – John Severin (reprint from #56)
Page 38 – The TV Space Trend – Lugoze (reprint from #66)
Page 42 – "Make Me a Deal" – Bill McCartney (Bill Ward) (reprint from #88)
Page 44 – McClod – Nireves (John Severin) (reprint from #111)
Page 50 – Cracked Visits the Munsters (reprint from #52)
Page 51 – Binders and notebooks ad
Back Cover – Excedruin ad – John Severin (reprint from #86)

***Cracked Collectors' Edition* #8 (*Cracked Goes to the Movies Again*), 1975 (52 pages) (50c)**

Cover – Old Time Movie Stars – John Severin (reprint from #93)
Page 2 – The Cracked Bookstore ad – John Severin
Page 3 – Contents
Page 4 – Lights, Action, Camera! (reprint from #66)
Page 6 – Four for the Laugh Set (reprint from #54)
Page 7 – Five Fun Flicks! (reprint from #58)
Page 8 – Something to Smile About (reprint from #47)
Page 9 – Four Film Swingers (reprint from #55)

Page 10 – Hut, Two, Tree, Four (reprint from #42)
Page 12 – Movie Mirth Matinee (reprint from #45)
Page 13 – Screen Screams (reprint from #55)
Page 14 – Four Smiles Only (reprint from #59)
Page 15 – Look! Four Kooks! (reprint from #63)
Page 16 – Boys and Girls Together (reprint from #44)
Page 18 – Look Befour You Laugh! (reprint from #51)
Page 19 – Cinema Chuckles (reprint from #57)
Page 20 – Armed Farces (reprint from #99)
Page 23 – The Fun Seekers! (reprint from #68)
Page 24 – The Swingers Set (reprint from #59)
Page 25 – Boy, Did you Get a Funny Number! (reprint from #61)
Page 26 – Reel Gone! (reprint from #54)
Page 27 – Wonderful World of Wacky Laughs! (reprint from #58)
Page 28 – Four Socko Smiles (reprint from #60)
Page 29 – The Screamers (reprint from *For Monsters Only* #5)
Page 32 – Five Times Laughs (reprint from #64)
Page 33 – Reel Swingers! (reprint from #56)
Page 34 – Where the Action is!!! (reprint from #58)
Page 36 – Four for Fun (reprint from #41)
Page 37 – Laugh Lines (reprint from #43)
Page 38 – Alice's Restaurant (reprint from #95)
Page 40 – The Quick Quippers! (reprint from #69)
Page 41 – Bottoms Up (reprint from #48)
Page 42 – 12 O'Clock High Jinks (reprint from #65)
Page 44 – Cracked's Crazy Chuckles (reprint from #101)
Page 46 – Four Goodness Sakes (reprint from #45)
Page 47 – The Generation Gap! (reprint from #78)
Page 48 – "Friends, Romans, Countrymen, Lend Me Your Laughs!" (reprint from #80)
Page 50 – Ladie's Day (reprint from #98)
Page 51 – Binders and Notebooks ad
Back Cover – (Formula didn't work, looking for trouble) photos (one from *For a Few Dollars More*) (reprint from #62)

***Cracked Collectors' Edition* #9 (*Cracked Strikes it Rich with Sagebrush*), 1975 (52 pages) (50c) (1st *Collectors' Edition* with predominantly new material. Full page is new unless part of page is listed as reprint below.)**

Cover – Sagebrush Strikes it Rich – John Severin
Page 2 – The Cracked Bookstore ad – John Severin
Page 3 – Contents
Page 4 – Sagebrush (can't hold on) – John Severin (reprint from *Cracked Collectors' Edition* #5)

Page 6 – Sagebrush (heavy pack) – John Severin
Page 7 – Sagebrush (see them a-tumblin' down) – John Severin
Page 8 – Sagebrush (think we can make it) – John Severin
Page 9 – Sagebrush (a rattler!) – John Severin
Page 10 – Sagebrush #25 (painting) – John Severin (reprint from #117)
Page 11 – Sagebrush (FOOD!) – John Severin
Page 12 – Sagebrush (Rattle! Rattle!) – John Severin
Page 13 – Sagebrush (barrel cactus) – John Severin
Page 14 – Sagebrush (wide open spaces) – John Severin
Page 15 – Sagebrush (nobody loves me) – John Severin (reprint from #116)
Page 16 – Sagebrush (sunsets) – John Severin / Sagebrush (Hi! Hey!) – John Severin (reprint from #108)
Page 17 – Sagebrush (hey rock) – John Severin (reprint from #112) / Sagebrush (dadburned rattler) – John Severin
Page 18 – Sagebrush (life in Indian country) / Sagebrush (only the shadow knows) – John Severin (reprint from #114)
Page 19 – Sagebrush (want to play a game?) – John Severin (reprint from #107) / Sagebrush (RAP) – John Severin
Page 20 – Sagebrush (buffalo stampede) – John Severin (reprint from #91) / Sagebrush (KLOMK!) – John Severin (reprint from #104)
Page 21 – Sagebrush (disguise yourself) – John Severin
Page 22 – Sagebrush (here come food) – John Severin (reprint from #110) / Sagebrush (gold is) – John Severin
Page 23 – Sagebrush (twenty years of prospecting) – John Severin
Page 24 – Sagebrush (turtle living) – John Severin
Page 25 – Sagebrush (YIPE!) – John Severin
Page 26 – (wild west gags) – John Severin (originally called "OKKO Corral") (partial reprint from #4)
Page 28 – Sagebrush (KOFF!) – John Severin
Page 29 – Sagebrush (stomping) – John Severin (reprint from #88) / Sagebrush (overturned turtle) – John Severin
Page 30 – Sagebrush (150 degrees today) – John Severin
Page 31 – Sagebrush (THUMP!) – John Severin
Page 32 – Sagebrush (SHMUNCH!) – John Severin
Page 33 – Sagebrush (whatcha want) – John Severin
Page 34 – Sagebrush (primitive arrows) – John Severin
Page 35 – Sagebrush (look good with a pipe) – John Severin
Page 36 – Sagebrush (PFOOF!) – John Severin
Page 37 – Sagebrush (Lil' Bear sends message) – John Severin
Page 38 – Sagebrush (crossing the desert) – John Severin (reprint from #86)
Page 39 – Sagebrush #26 (invited a friend to lunch) – John Severin (reprint from #118)

Page 40 – Sagebrush (hiding behind that rock) – John Severin
Page 41 – Sagebrush (what a set-up) – John Severin
Page 42 – Sagebrush (got my lunch) – John Severin
Page 43 – Sagebrush (fancy shooting) – John Severin (reprint from #83)
Page 44 – Sagebrush (Happy Anniversary) – John Severin
Page 45 – Sagebrush (Howdy Shage) – John Severin (reprint from #113)
Page 46 – Sagebrush (thinnin' hair) – John Severin (reprint from #115)
Page 47 – Sagebrush (BOM-BIDDY) – John Severin
Page 48 – Sagebrush (such a bad character) – John Severin
Page 49 – Sagebrush (bubble-nose) – John Severin
Page 50 – *Your Cracked, Cracked Up, Half-Cracked* and *Get Me Cracked* paperback ad / Sagebrush (Pikes Peak or Bust) – John Severin (reprint from #114)
Page 51 – Binders and Notebooks ad
Back Cover – The Discovery – Stu Schwartzberg (reprint from #100)

***Cracked Collectors' Edition* #10 (*The Cracked Manual of Put-Downs*), 1975 (52 pages) (50c)**

Cover – Sylvester, Court Jester – John Severin (reprint from *Biggest Greatest Cracked* #5)
Page 2 – Binders and Notebooks ad
Page 3 – Contents
Page 4 – Everybody is Doing the Don Rickles Bit – Noel Severin (John Severin) (reprint from #80)
Page 7 – Cracked's Snappy Comebacks! – John Severin (reprint from #75)
Page 9 – That'll Be the Day! (only $250) – John Langton (reprint from #91)
Page 10 – How to Cool a Hot Problem! – Lugoze (reprint from #81)
Page 13 – The Day Norman Told Off His Boss – Jack Barrett / Ron Wiggins (reprint from #102)
Page 14 – Cracked's Crazy Comebacks – John Langton (reprint from #78)
Page 16 – Don't Believe a Word of it – John Severin (reprint from #82)
Page 18 – Silly Things We Do – John Severin (reprint from #101)
Page 20 – Rate Your Personality – LePoer (John Severin) (reprint from #12)
Page 22 – More Things We Shoulda Done – John Severin (reprint from #23)
Page 24 – That'll Be the Day! ($25,000) – John Langton (reprint from #79)
Page 26 – Cracked's Fast Cut Out Comebacks – John Severin (reprint from #52)
Page 28 – Cracked's Romantic Greeting Cards That Express Everything – John Langton (reprint from #109)

Page 30 – Are you an Optimist or a Pessimist? – John Langton (reprint from #67)
Page 33 – That'll Be the Day! – John Severin (reprint from #80)
Page 34 – If Everyday People Were Stand-Up Comics – John Langton (reprint from #89)
Page 35 – The Waiter and the Customers – Vic Martin (reprint from #98)
Page 36 – Cracked Looks at Mothers – Charles Rodrigues (reprint from #95)
Page 39 – The Breaking Point! – Vic Martin (reprint from #56)
Page 40 – Blind Date Phone Calls – Bob Taylor (reprint from #84)
Page 42 – More People We Can Do Without – John Langton (reprint from #68)
Page 44 – More Whaddaya Callits – Joe Mead (reprint from #81)
Page 46 – What They Really Mean – Vic Martin (reprint from #80)
Page 47 – Annoy Your Friends – John Severin (reprint from #28)
Page 50 – Shut-Ups (plastic surgery) – Charles Rodrigues (reprint from #109)
Page 51 – The Cracked Bookstore ad – John Severin
Back Cover – Don Rickles Insult photo (reprint from #77)

***Cracked Collectors' Edition* #11 (*Cracked World of Advertising*), 1975 (52 pages) (50c)**
Cover – "See Thru" Mirror Sandwich Board – John Severin (reprint from #76)
Page 2 – Binders and Notebooks ad 2
Page 3 – Contents
Page 4 – On-the-Spot Test Commercials – John Severin (reprint from #21)
Page 8 – Public-Spirited Ads – Bob Taylor (reprint from #91)
Page 11 – AT&TT ad – Vic Martin (reprint from #59)
Page 12 – When Comic Strips Go Madison Avenue – Lugoze (reprint from #80)
Page 16 – Cautionary Labels for Teenage Products – John Severin (reprint from #76)
Page 18 – Ads and Animals! (reprint from #61)
Page 20 – Sneaky TV Cigarette Commercials – John Severin (reprint from #91)
Page 22 – Ocean ad – John Severin (reprint from #15)
Page 23 – If the Help-Wanted Ads Mirrored Today's Inefficient Business World (reprint from #94)
Page 26 – Products That Just Missed! – McCartin (John Severin) (reprint from #53)

Page 28 – Madison Ave. Word Game – John Severin (reprint from #54)
Page 32 – Draypuss Fund Inc. ad – Vic Martin (reprint from #60)
Page 33 – Truthful Ads They Wouldn't Print in Cracked – Lugoze (reprint from #70)
Page 36 – Shoverollit ad – John Severin (reprint from #32)
Page 37 – Ads for Adolescents – Vic Martin (reprint from #107)
Page 41 – Montgomery Roebuck & Co. Mail Order Catalog – John Severin (reprint from #30)
Page 44 – Advertising a Worthless Product – John Severin (reprint from #106)
Page 49 – Charlie Weakling ad – Bill McCartney (Bill Ward) (reprint from #54)
Page 50 – Bull Telephone System ad – John Severin (reprint from #41)
Page 51 – The Cracked Bookstore ad – John Severin
Back Cover – Freezca ad – John Severin (reprint from #81)

***Cracked Collectors' Edition* #12 (*Cracked Goes to the Movies*), 1975 (52 pages) (50c)**

Cover – Sardines – Nireves (John Severin) (reprint from #74)
Page 2 and 51 – Godfather Poster – Cracked Poster – James Montgomery Flaggione (John Severin)
Page 3 – Contents
Page 4 – The Perspirin' Adventure – John Severin (reprint from #111)
Page 9 – Nixon's Home Movies – Jack Barrett (reprint from #104)
Page 12 – Laurel and Hardy's Wacky World of Fun! (reprint from #59)
Page 14 – Dan Coyote-Man of La Rancha – John Severin (reprint from #113)
Page 20 – Keystone Komedy Kapers (reprint from #96)
Page 22 – Kansas City Bummer – Dick Wright (reprint from #108)
Page 26 – Cracked Looks at the Neighborhood Movie House – Vic Martin (reprint from #103)
Page 28 – Ham 'n' Rye 'n's Daughter – John Severin (reprint from #95)
Page 32 – When Willard-Type Movies Take Over Hollywood – Nireves (John Severin) (reprint from #100)
Page 36 – The Last of the Hollywood "B" Pictures – Gray Morrow (reprint from #8)
Page 39 – Famous Scenes from Great Desert Island Movies – John Langton (reprint from #73)
Page 40 – The Hollywoodization of Sopheeya Luring – Bill McCartney (Bill Ward) (reprint from #4)
Page 42 – The Funnies in the Flicks! (reprint from #72)
Page 45 – Klotch – O.O. Severin (John Severin) (reprint from #105)

Page 50 – Famous Scenes form Great World War I Aviation Movies! (reprint from #64)
Back Cover – (Raid, half the fun) photos (reprint from #58)

***Cracked Collectors' Edition* #13 (*Cracked Makes History Humorous*), 1976 (52 pages) (50c)**
Cover – Dropping the Liberty Bell – John Severin (reprint from #31)
Page 2 and 51 – America – Love it or Give it Back! – Cracked Poster (reprint from #107)
Page 3 – Contents
Page 4 – Cracked's Illustrated History – John Severin (reprint from #86)
Page 7 – Cracked's Footprint Forecourt of History – John Severin (reprint from #55)
Page 10 – How the West was Lost (reprint from #39)
Page 12 – How Today's Americans Might Have Answered the Polls of 200 Years Ago – Sururi Gumen (reprint from #119)
Page 14 – Jogging Throughout History – John Severin (reprint from #82)
Page 18 – What Preceded Famous Events – Bill McCartney (Bill Ward) (reprint from #106)
Page 20 – The History of Inflation – Vic Martin (reprint from #86)
Page 22 – Armed Farces (reprint from #99)
Page 24 – Cracked's Time Capsule for the 1960s – Bill McCartney (Bill Ward) (reprint from #86)
Page 26 – If Other U.S. Wars Were as Controversial as the Vietnam War! – John Severin (reprint from #89)
Page 28 – 12 O'Clock High Jinks (reprint from #65)
Page 30 – Great War Heroes – Jack Davis (reprint from #15)
Page 32 – What if There Had Been Guidance Counselors Throughout History? – O.O. Severin (John Severin) (reprint from #53)
Page 35 – More Armed Farces (reprint from #99)
Page 36 – Cracked Takes You Back to When it all Started (blood pressure) – Jack Davis (reprint from #15)
Page 37 – The Cracked Museum of Historical Trivia – Tony Tallarico (reprint from #69)
Page 40 – Rare Olde Letters of History (reprint from #88)
Page 42 – Take the Cracked History Test – John Langton (reprint from #71)
Page 44 – The Smythes – Losers Throughout History! – John Severin (reprint from #75)
Page 46 – Reconstructing the Remains of 20th Century Civilization – Bill Ward (reprint from #113)
Back Cover – Historical Telegrams That Never Got There (reprint from #17)

***Cracked Collectors' Edition* #14 (*More from the Cracked TV Screen*), 1976 (52 pages) (50c)**

Cover – M*U*S*H – John Severin (reprint from #115)
Page 2 – The Cracked Bookstore ad – John Severin
Page 3 – Contents
Page 4 – The Sappy Days – John Severin (reprint from #118)
Page 9 – Accessories for the TV Football Freak – Bill Ward (reprint from #114)
Page 13 – An Interview with David (Kung Fu) Carrotseed – John Severin (reprint from #119)
Page 19 – What to Do Until the TV Repairman Arrives – Don Orehek (reprint from #97)
Page 21 – The Yesterday Show – O.O. Severin (John Severin) (reprint from #106)
Page 26 – Cracked Looks at TV Commercials – Bill McCartney (Bill Ward) (reprint from #98)
Page 28 – Three Terrific Teams (reprint from #103)
Page 31 – Canyon – John Severin (reprint from #117)
Page 36 – If Comic Strip Characters Had Summer Replacements – Lugoze (reprint from #78)
Page 40 – Cracked Looks at Television Viewers – Bill McCartney (Bill Ward) (reprint from #85)
Page 44 – The Charlie Chan Caper (reprint from #71)
Page 46 – Cracked Interviews the TV King – John Severin (reprint from #113)
Page 51 – Mugging Minors (reprint from #98)
Back Cover – Fonzie photo (new)

***Cracked Collectors' Edition* #15 (*Shut-Ups Plus Hang-Ups Plus Hudd & Dini*), 1976 (52 pages) (50c)**

Cover – Slippery Ink – John Severin (reprint from #71)
Page 2 – The Cracked Bookstore ad – John Severin
Page 3 – Contents
Page 4 – Shut-Ups (new highway) – Charles Rodrigues (reprint from #122)
Page 5 – Shut-Ups (Helen doesn't mean anything) – Charles Rodrigues (reprint from #124)
Page 6 – Hudd & Dini (Indu Magic) – Vic Martin (reprint from #89)
Page 7 – Shut-Ups (manage our budget) – Charles Rodrigues (reprint from #127)
Page 8 – Shut-Ups (king's dinner) – Julius Siezure (Charles Rodrigues) (reprint from #96)
Page 9 – Hudd & Dini (garbage cans) – Vic Martin (reprint from #82)

Page 10 – Ye Hang Ups #3 (He hates to drink alone) – John Severin (reprint from #115) / Ye Hang Ups (which way to the john) – Nireves (John Severin) (reprint from #116)
Page 11 – Shut-Ups (difficult time) – Charles Rodrigues (reprint from #115)
Page 12 – Hudd & Dini (swimming pool) – Vic Martin (reprint from #99)
Page 13 – Shut-Ups (grown man playing with a doll) – Charles Rodrigues (reprint from #120)
Page 14 – Shut-Ups (good likeness) – Sigmund Froyd (Charles Rodrigues) (reprint from #90)
Page 15 – Hudd & Dini (missing key) – Vic Martin (reprint from #77)
Page 16 – Shut-Ups (electronic calculator) – Charles Rodrigues (reprint from #117)
Page 17 – Ye Hang Ups #4 (nice easy job) – Nireves (John Severin) (reprint from #117) / Ye Hang Ups #26 (bong) – Nireves (John Severin) (reprint from #118)
Page 18 – Hudd & Dini (sleeping Mexican) – Vic Martin (reprint from #101)
Page 19 – Shut-Ups (Here's his picture) – Charles Rodrigues (reprint from #118)
Page 20 – Shut-Ups (ain't got no horses) – Charles Rodrigues (reprint from #121)
Page 21 – Hudd & Dini (octopus) – Vic Martin (reprint from #103)
Page 22 – Ye Hang Ups #27 (fishing) – Nireves (John Severin) (reprint from #119) /
Ye Hang Ups #29 (toothache) – Nireves (John Severin) (reprint from #120)
Page 23 – Hudd & Dini (mousetrap) – Vic Martin (reprint from #83)
Page 24 – Shut-Ups (good year) – Charles Rodrigues (reprint from #126)
Page 25 – Hudd & Dini (witches) – Vic Martin (reprint from #102)
Page 26 – Shut-Ups (deadbeats) – Charles Rodrigues (reprint from #119)
Page 27 – Shut-Ups (bad luck to see bride) – Sam Gross Jr. (Charles Rodrigues) (reprint from #110)
Page 28 – Shut-Ups (credit card) – Lefty Wright (Charles Rodrigues) (reprint from #92)
Page 29 – Shut-Ups (astronaut) – Charles Rodrigues (reprint from #80)
Page 30 – Hudd & Dini (boy scouts) – Vic Martin (reprint from #85)
Page 31 – Shut-Ups! (windshield wipers) – Rodrigliani (Charles Rodrigues) (reprint from #84)
Page 32 – Ye Hang Ups #30 (Houdini) – John Severin (reprint from #121) / Ye Hang Ups (catch!) – John Severin (reprint from #122)

Page 33 – Hudd & Dini (kite) – Vic Martin (reprint from #86)
Page 34 – Shut-Ups! (exercise) – Pick and Pat (Charles Rodrigues) (reprint from #88)
Page 35 – Shut-Ups (KUH-RRRAK!) – Charles Rodrigues (reprint from #125)
Page 36 – Ye Hang Ups #33 (Slam) – Nireves (John Severin) (reprint from #125) / Ye Hang Ups #35 (four arms) – Nireves (John Severin) (reprint from #126)
Page 37 – Shut-Ups (long hair) – Modest Mussorgsky (Charles Rodrigues) (reprint from #85)
Page 38 – Hudd & Dini (D.D.T.) – Vic Martin (reprint from #88)
Page 39 – Shut-Ups (I remember) – Charles Rodrigues (reprint from #108)
Page 40 – Hudd & Dini (books) – Vic Martin (reprint from #105)
Page 41 and 44 – Shut-Ups (shoplifting) – Charles Rodrigues (reprint from #114)
Page 42 – Shut-Ups (practice your violin) – Charles Rodrigues (reprint from #113)
Page 43 – Ye Hang Ups #32 (no tipping) – Nireves (John Severin) (reprint from #124) / Ye Hang Ups #31 (Pierre) – Nireves (John Severin) (reprint from #123)
Page 44 – Hudd & Dini (skeleton) – Vic Martin (reprint from #95)
Page 46 – Hudd & Dini (inflatable man) – Vic Martin (reprint from #97)
Page 47 – Shut-Ups! (tie clasps) – Rodrigliani (Charles Rodrigues) (reprint from #56)
Page 48 – Ye Hang Ups #38 (ah-choo) – Nireves (John Severin) (reprint from #129) / Hudd & Dini (guard disguise) – Vic Martin (reprint from #109)
Page 49 – Shut-Ups (snooping around) – Sam Gross Jr. (Charles Rodrigues) (reprint from #100)
Page 50 – Shut-Ups (fire escape) – Charles Rodrigues (reprint from #112)
Page 51 – Hudd & Dini (Vacancy) – Vic Martin (reprint from #79)
Back Cover – Shut-Ups (curtain about to go up) – Charles Rodrigues (reprint from #116)

***Cracked Collectors' Edition* #16 (*Fonz for President!*), 1976 (52 pages) (60c) (Another issue with predominantly new material.)**

Cover – Fonz for President! – John Severin
Page 2 and 51 – Arthur Fonzarelli for President – Cracked Poster
Page 3 – Contents
Page 4 – Lettuce to the Fonz

Page 6 – Fonzie's Presidential Platform – John Severin
Page 13 – Fonzie's Financial Statement and Holdings – John Severin
Page 16 – Fonzie's Cabinet
Page 26 – A Cracked Look at Arnold's Drive-In – Sururi Gumen
Page 28 – Fonz Campaign Buttons – John Severin
Page 30 – The Cracked Bookstore ad – John Severin
Page 31 – Selected Pages from Fonzie's Diary
Page 34 – Wild Wheels (reprint from #104)
Page 36 – Sylvester for President – John Severin (reprint from #36)
Page 40 – Letters from the Fonz and his Ancestors to Famous People Throughout History – John Severin
Page 44 – Fonzie's Supporters
Page 48 – Fonzie's New Declaration of Independence
Page 50 – Cool-Its (take me out) – Mike Ricigliano
Back Cover – The Committee to Elect Arthur Fonzarelli

***Cracked Collectors' Edition* #17 (*Those Cracked Monsters*), 1977 (52 pages) (50c)**

Cover – Monster Movie – O.O. Severin (John Severin) (reprint from #105 and partial reprint from #140)
Page 2 – The Cracked Bookstore ad – John Severin
Page 3 – Contents
Page 4 – Planets of the Creatures - John Severin (reprint from #72)
Page 18 – The Big Ones Scream Again! (reprint from *For Monsters Only* #6)
Page 13 – The Birthday Gift! – John Langton (reprint from #67)
Page 14 – The Wacky Weirdos Howl Again! (reprint from *For Monsters Only* #5)
Page 16 – The Stone Age – Oscar Blotta (reprint from *For Monsters Only* #5)
Page 18 – Girls and Ghouls (reprint from *For Monsters Only* #3)
Page 19 – Son of Monster Mirth!!! (reprint from *For Monsters Only* #3)
Page 20 – The Greatest Monster Battle of all Time! – John Severin (reprint from *For Monsters Only* #2)
Page 22 – The Chiller-Dillers Swing Again! (reprint from *For Monsters Only* #6)
Page 23 – Gags To Howl About (reprint from *For Monsters Only* #6)
Page 24 – The Desert Island Guest – John Severin (reprint from *For Monsters Only* #3)
Page 25 – Big Things are Happening! (reprint from *For Monsters Only* #7)
Page 26 – Monster Party – John Severin (reprint from #43)
Page 28 – Screams from Land and Sea!(reprint from *For Monsters Only* #8)

Page 30 – Boys and Ghouls Together! (reprint from *For Monsters Only* #4)
Page 31 – McCartney's Mighty Monsters – Bill McCartney (Bill Ward) (reprint from *For Monsters Only* #5)
Page 32 – Just Good Fiends! (reprint from *For Monsters Only* #7)
Page 33 – Shoot to Kill – John Severin (reprint from #33)
Page 34 – A MonStar is Reborn – John Severin / George Gladir (reprint from *For Monsters Only* #1)
Page 40 – The Wild Weirdos' Scream-In! (reprint from *For Monsters Only* #7)
Page 42 – Monster Phrases – Vic Martin (reprint from *For Monsters Only* #5)
Page 44 – The Fiends and the Females (reprint from *For Monsters Only* #8)
Page 46 – Monster Madness! (reprint from *For Monsters Only* #8)
Page 47 – Rosemary's Baby Devlin – Lugoze (reprint from #76)
Page 50 – Cracked Space Shut-Ups! (most beautiful girl) – Bill McCartney (Bill Ward) (reprint from #8)
Page 51 – (Nonchalant) *King Kong* photo (reprint from *For Monsters Only* #2)
Back Cover – Oh, No…Do We Have to Start All Over Again? – Charles Rodrigues (reprint from #110)

***Cracked Collectors' Edition* #18 (*Those Great Old Movies*), 1977 (52 pages) (50c)**

Cover and Back Cover – Photos of Various Movie Stars
Page 2 – The Cracked Bookstore ad – John Severin
Page 3 – Contents
Page 4 – Marx Brothers' Laff-In! (reprint from #73)
Page 7 – 5 Fun Grabbers (reprint from #74)
Page 8 – The Silents Talk Back (reprint from #51)
Page 10 – American Car-Daffy – Sururi Gumen (reprint from #121)
Page 16 – Kings of Comedy (reprint from #57)
Page 18 – The Funnies in the Flicks! (reprint from #72)
Page 21 – Six is the Number (reprint from #40)
Page 22 – The Big Big Guys! (reprint from #102)
Page 24 – The Pirate Treasure Chest (reprint from #64)
Page 26 – Valentino Vibrations (reprint from #94)
Page 28 – Jungle Gems (reprint from #63)
Page 30 – What are the Old TV & Movie Detectives Doing Today? – John Severin (reprint from #121)
Page 35 – Four Fun Flicks! (reprint from #73)
Page 36 – Going Great Guns (reprint from #80)
Page 38 – A Visit with Laurel and Hardy (reprint from #55)

Page 40 – The Pleasure is Ours! (reprint from #70)
Page 41 – The Not So Great Gatsby – Sururi Gumen (reprint from #124)
Page 46 – Cracked Gets Greta Garbo to…Talk at Last! (reprint from #90)
Page 48 – Laurel & Hardy Fun-o-Rama (reprint from #67)
Page 50 – The Marx Brothers Ride Again! (reprint from #75)
Page 51 – (hold your hand) Frankenstein photo (reprint from #38)

***Cracked Collectors' Edition* #19 (*More from the Cracked TV Screen*), 1977 (52 pages) (50c)**
Cover – The Millionaire – John Severin (reprint from #19 and partial reprint from #112, 117, 120, 122, 127, 138, 139, 142)
Page 2 – The Cracked Bookstore ad – John Severin
Page 3 – Contents
Page 4 – The Six Billion Dollar Man – John Severin (reprint from #120)
Page 10 – The Cracked History of Television – Bill Ward (reprint from #124)
Page 14 – If Archie Bunker Took Over the Leads in Other TV Series – John Severin (reprint from #108)
Page 18 – If Real Life Operated Like TV Quiz Shows – Don Orehek (reprint from #125)
Page 23 – Star Tracks – John Severin (reprint from #127)
Page 28 – TV's Defective Detectives – Jack Barrett (reprint from #102)
Page 32 – Cracked Traces a Spinoff – John Severin (reprint from #127)
Page 36 – You Know You are a TV Addict When – Bill Ward (reprint from #127)
Page 38 – The Major Moose Show – John Severin (reprint from #126)
Page 42 – If TV Characters Aged While Their Shows Stayed the Same – Sururi Gumen (reprint from #128)
Page 46 – Beaujack – John Severin / Charles Rodrigues (reprint from #122)
Page 51 – Uncover America (reprint from #84)
Back Cover – Excedruin ad – John Severin (reprint from #86)

***Cracked Collectors' Edition* #20 (*Famous Disaster Movies*), 1977 (52 pages) (50c)**
Cover – Earthshake – John Severin (reprint from #125)
Page 2 – The Cracked Bookstore ad – John Severin
Page 3 – Contents
Page 4 – Earthshake – Ty Dahlwave (John Severin) (reprint from #125)
Page 10 – The Biggies Break it Up! (reprint from *For Monsters Only* #10)
Page 11 – The Man with the Sign – Caracu (reprint from #68)
Page 13 – Cracked Presents Future Insect Monster Movies – Sururi Gumen (reprint from #125)

Page 17 – What Really Happened to General Custer – Larry Barth (reprint from #88)
Page 18 – If California Moved Into the Pacific – LePoer (John Severin) (reprint from #89)
Page 21 – Black Thoughts – Caracu (reprint from #69)
Page 22 – Cracked Interviews the Stunt King – Sururi Gumen (reprint from #128)
Page 27 – Overlooked Disaster Movies – Bill Ward (reprint from #125)
Page 30 – The Towering Infernal – John Severin (reprint from #126)
Page 36 – The Cracked World of Movie Going – Sururi Gumen (reprint from #131)
Page 39 – Ocean ad – John Severin (reprint from #15)
Page 40 – Disaster Movies You May Be Soon Seeing – John Severin (reprint from #128)
Page 43 – Airplot 1975 – Sururi Gumen (reprint from #127)
Page 49 – The Loser – John Severin (reprint from #131)
Page 51 – Cut! Cut! CUT! – John Severin (reprint from #15)
Back Cover – The Stone Age – Oskar Blotta (reprint from #125)

***Cracked Collectors' Edition* #21 (*Cracked's Big Pictures*), 1977 (52 pages) (50c)**

Cover – Thumb Painting – John Severin (reprint from #38)
Page 2 – The Cracked Bookstore ad – John Severin
Page 3 – Contents
Page 4 – A Cracked Look at a Garage Sale – Ron DeLay (John Severin) (reprint from #125)
Page 6 – Cracked Visits a Track Meet – Bill McCartney (Bill Ward) (reprint from #87)
Page 8 – Cracked Looks at a Big City Newspaper Office – Don Orehek (reprint from #104)
Page 10 – A Martian Writes Home from Earth – John Severin (reprint from #40)
Page 12 – Cracked Visits a Prison Yard – Lugoze (reprint from #75)
Page 14 – A Cracked Look at a Department Store – Don Orehek (reprint from #118)
Page 16 – Cracked Takes a Seat at Custer's Last Stand – Bill McCartney (Bill Ward) (reprint from #90)
Page 18 – Cracked Takes a Look at Night Clubs – Bill McCartney (Bill Ward) (reprint from #54)
Page 20 – Cracked Goes to the Hospital – John Severin (reprint from #94)
Page 22 – Cracked Looks at an Air Line Terminal – Don Orehek (reprint from #120)

Page 24 - Cracked Visits a Public Golf Course - Bill McCartney (Bill Ward) (reprint from #88)
Page 26 - "Camp" Comic Heroland - John Severin (reprint from #58)
Page 28 - Cracked Goes to an Encounter Group Therapy Session - Don Orehek (reprint from #123)
Page 30 - Let's Travel Down Under...and Take a Cracked's-Eye View of Australia! - Bill McCartney (Bill Ward) (reprint from #86)
Page 32 - The TV Class Reunion of '85 - Sururi Gumen (reprint from #130)
Page 34 - Cracked Visits Washington, D.C. - John Severin (reprint from #84)
Page 36 - A Cracked Look at a Hamburger Franchise - Bill Ward (reprint from #129)
Page 38 - Cracked Goes to a Weight Watcher's Meeting - Don Orehek (reprint from #121)
Page 40 - Cracked Takes You Back to the Year 1075 BC! - Bill McCartney (Bill Ward) (reprint from #74)
Page 42 - Cracked Looks at New York City - John Severin (reprint from #92)
Page 44 - As Cracked Goes to the Race Track! - Bill McCartney (Bill Ward) (reprint from #93)
Page 46 - The Cracked Bookstore ad - John Severin
Page 47 - Cracked Looks at World War I Sky Fighters - John Severin (reprint from #107)
Page 51 - The Man & the Fly - Oskar Blotta (reprint from #95)
Back Cover - Great Moments in Industry 1889 - Charles Rodrigues (reprint from #126)

***Cracked Collectors' Edition #22* (*Cracked Goes to the Movies*), 1977 (52 pages) (60c)**

Cover - The Godfather Meets Jaws - John Severin (reprint from #131)
Page 2 - The Cracked Bookstore ad - John Severin
Page 3 - Contents
Page 4 - If Hit Movies Were Combined - John Severin (reprint from #131)
Page 10 - All At Sea (reprint from #104)
Page 13 - It's a Weird, Weird, Weird, Weird, Weird World (reprint from #86)
Page 14 - Fun Under the Big Top! (reprint from #81)
Page 16 - The Cracked Camera (reprint from #102)
Page 19 - "The Ex-Con Butler Did it in a Combat Zone!" (reprint from #81)
Page 20 - Around the World in Hats (reprint from #43)
Page 22 - Heavy on the Horror, Please (reprint from #95)
Page 24 - G.I. Laugh-In! (reprint from #75)

Page 26 – Rollicking with Robert Redford (reprint from #92)
Page 28 – Laurel & Hardy Tell it Like it is! (reprint from #88)
Page 30 – Cracked's Guess Who's the Sidekick Contest! (reprint from #90)
Page 32 – Horror Hee-Haw (reprint from *For Monsters Only* #10)
Page 33 – Pix of the Flicks (reprint from #102)
Page 36 – The Quickest Fun in the West (reprint from #77)
Page 39 – Foto Fun! (reprint from #69)
Page 40 – Medicinal Mirth (reprint from #85)
Page 41 – Chip Shots (reprint from #83)
Page 44 – Wild and Wacky Westerns! (reprint from #103)
Page 46 – Mighty Monster Laughs!! (reprint from #45)
Page 48 – Guns and Gags for Hire! (reprint from #62)
Page 50 – By the Numbers (reprint from #50)
Page 51 – (107 days, two seconds, Gravy Train, Smokey) photos (one from *Satan Bug*) (reprint from #65)
Back Cover – Great Moments in Art 1705 – Charles Rodrigues (reprint from #119)

***Cracked Collectors' Edition* #23 (*Cracked Visits Outer Space*), May 1978 (52 pages) (60c)**

Cover – We Look at U.F.O.'s – John Severin
Page 2 and 51 – The American Space Base on Mars – John Severin (reprint from #32)
Page 3 – Contents
Page 4 – Space: 1998 – Sururi Gumen (reprint from #133)
Page 10 – Planets of the Creatures - John Severin (reprint from #72)
Page 16 – Astrological Horoscopes – John Severin (reprint from #83)
Page 20 – The TV Space Trend – Lugoze (reprint from #66)
Page 24 – Annie Get Your Spacesuit – Lugoze (reprint from #67)
Page 32 – Cracked Space Shut-Ups! (most beautiful girl) – Bill McCartney (Bill Ward) (reprint from #8)
Page 33 – The Martian Report on Earth – Bill McCartney (Bill Ward) (reprint from #51)
Page 37 – Escape from the Boredom of the Apes – John Severin (reprint from #97)
Page 42 – If Other Civil Servants Tried to Hustle on the Side Like the Astronauts – Dick Wright (reprint from #110)
Page 46 – Cracked Examines All the Possibilities of Flying Saucers – Bill McCartney (Bill Ward) (reprint from #68)
Page 50 – Hudd & Dini (rocket) – Vic Martin (reprint from #87)
Back Cover – Space Visitors Welcome Here (new)

***Cracked Collectors' Edition* #24 (*Cracked Looks at Celebrities*), July 1978 (52 pages) (60c)**

Cover – Cracked Pot – John Severin (new)
Page 2 and 51 – Hey-y-y (Fonze poster) – Cracked Poster #134 – John Severin (reprint from #134)
Page 3 – Contents
Page 4 – The Academy Awards Show – John Severin (reprint from #134)
Page 9 – Famous Stars in Ads We'd Like to See (reprint from #95)
Page 12 – I Don't Care Who You Are – John Severin (reprint from #96)
Page 14 – Celebrity Childhoods – William Hoest (reprint from #57)
Page 18 – Three Terrific Teams (reprint from #103)
Page 21 – Celebrities and Their Screen Idols – John Severin (reprint from #107)
Page 24 – How Famous People Got Their Nicknames – LePoer (John Severin) (reprint from #92)
Page 26 – Famous Person's School Excuses (reprint from #108)
Page 28 – Hi! I'm Johnny Cashew! – John Severin (reprint from #93)
Page 33 – Celebrity Garbage – John Severin (reprint from #131)
Page 36 – Cracked Interviews the Stars (new)
Page 41 – Celebrities' Home Movies – John Severin (reprint from #136)
Page 44 – If Famous People Had Listened to Their Mothers – John Severin (reprint from #94)
Page 47 – Family Albums of Celebrities – John Severin (reprint from #14)
Page 50 – The Lone Ranger (reprint from #38)
Back Cover – Don Rickles Insult photo (reprint from #77)

***Cracked Collectors' Edition* #25 (*Those Cracked Monsters*), September 1978 (52 pages) (60c)**

Cover – Monsters in Haunted House – John Severin (reprint from *For Monsters Only* #3)
Page 2 – The Cracked Bookstore ad – John Severin
Page 3 – Contents
Page 4 – The Men Behind Kong – Bill Ward (new)
Page 7 – Make Mine Well Done! – John Langton (reprint from #62)
Page 8 – The Wacky Weirdos (reprint from *For Monsters Only* #6)
Page 10 – Transylvanian TV – Bill McCartney (Bill Ward) (reprint from #36)
Page 14 – Mayhem Mirth (reprint from *For Monsters Only* #5)
Page 15 – More Monster Mirth (reprint from *For Monsters Only* #2)
Page 16 – Ugghh!!-Break - Bob Zahn (reprint from *For Monsters Only* #3)
Page 17 – Transylvanian Tee Heeeeeees (reprint from *For Monsters Only* #1)

Page 18 – School For Monsters – Nireves (John Severin) (reprint from #26)
Page 22 – Quick Quiz (watered the front lawn) (reprint from *For Monsters Only* #3)
Page 24 – Ghoul Days! (reprint from *For Monsters Only* #4)
Page 25 – The Painter's Fantasy – Oskar Blotta (reprint from #85)
Page 26 – Mad Mirth Makers! (reprint from *For Monsters Only* #10)
Page 28 – Fetch! – John Severin (reprint from *For Monsters Only* #1)
Page 29 – More Fiendish Delights (reprint from *For Monsters Only* #9)
Page 30 – Frankenstein Conquers The World! (reprint from *For Monsters Only* #4)
Page 32 – What Goes on in a Monster's Mind – Don Orehek (reprint from #138)
Page 35 – Four Screaming Out Loud! (reprint from *For Monsters Only* #4)
Page 36 – A Transylvanian Family Album (reprint from *For Monsters Only* #1)
Page 39 – Transylvania's Montgomery & Morgue – John Severin (reprint from *For Monsters Only* #2)
Page 42 – Mightiest Mad Monsters Strike Again! (reprint from *For Monsters Only* #3)
Page 47 – The Fright-Makers (reprint from *For Monsters Only* #7)
Page 49 – The Condemned Man – John Severin (reprint from #64)
Page 50 – Horror Hee-Haws (reprint from *For Monsters Only* #3)
Page 51 – The One That Got Away! (reprint from *For Monsters Only* #5)
Back Cover – Shut-Ups (I'll find you) – John Severin (reprint from #13)

***Cracked Collectors' Edition* #26 (*Sharks!*), November 1978 (52 pages) (60c) (Another issue with predominantly new material.)**

Cover – Earthshake – John Severin (partial reprint of #125)
Page 2 – The Cracked Bookstore ad – John Severin
Page 3 – Contents
Page 4 – Lettuce to Sharks
Page 6 – Everything You Should Know About Sharks (Before It's Too Late)
Page 9 – How a Shark Attacks
Page 11 – The History of Sharks – Bill Ward
Page 16 – The World's Best Shark Jokes
Page 22 – One Day On the Atlantic Ocean – Howard Nostrand
Page 23 – The Great White's Boyhood – John Severin
Page 26 – Cracked's Shark Identification Chart – Bill Ward

Page 28 – Everything You Should Know About Sharks-Part II
Page 33 – How to Ward Off Sharks – John Severin
Page 36 – A Cracked Look at Sharks – Don Orehek
Page 40 – Sharks....Another View
Page 46 – A Visit to the Beach – LePoer (John Severin) (reprint from #38)
Page 48 – What to do in Case of Shark Attack – Warren Sattler
Page 50 – Shark Shut-Ups (shark disguise) – Don Orehek
Page 51 – Avoid Shark Attacks (reprint from #129)
Back Cover – Great Moments in History 1,000,342 B.C. – Howard Nostrand (reprint from #142)

***Cracked Collectors' Edition* #27 (*Shut-Ups*), December 1978 (52 pages) (60c)**

Cover – Mountain Climbing – John Severin (reprint from #64)
Page 2 – The Cracked Bookstore ad – John Severin
Page 3 – Contents
Page 4 – Shut-Ups (It's a mirage) – Charles Rodrigues (reprint from #131)
Page 5 – Shut-Ups (Have a good time!) – Mike Ricigliano (reprint from #138)
Page 6 – Shut-Ups (big crowd) – Philip Garbage (Charles Rodrigues) (reprint from #67)
Page 7 – Shut-Ups (AAEE-HOOEO!) – Nan Reik (Charles Rodrigues) (reprint from #58)
Page 8 – Shut-Ups (stopping the fight) – Charles Rodrigues (reprint from #132)
Page 9 – Shut-Ups! (erector set) – Arthur Knockwurst (Charles Rodrigues) (reprint from #59)
Page 10 – Shut-Ups (nice monkey) – Vic Martin (reprint from #54) and various reprints by Charles Rodrigues
Page 11 – Shut-Ups (first men on moon) – Charles Rodrigues (reprint from #79)
Page 12 – Shut-Ups (five pounds of tea) – Charles Rodrigues (reprint from #66)
Page 13 – Shut-Ups (spilled the beans) – Vito Modigliani (Charles Rodrigues) (reprint from #97)
Page 14 – Shut-Ups (fear of dark rooms) – Charles Rodrigues (reprint from #72)
Page 15 – Shut-Ups (flight show movies) – Charles Rodrigues (reprint from #133)
Page 16 – Shut-Ups (deathly sick) – Charles Rodrigues (reprint from #83)
Page 17 – Shut-Ups (C-A-T) – Charles Rodrigues (reprint from #57)

Page 18 – Shut-Ups! (tie clasps) – Rodrigliani (Charles Rodrigues) (reprint from #56)
Page 19 – Shut-Ups (bad luck to see bride) – Sam Gross Jr. (Charles Rodrigues) (reprint from #110)
Page 20 – Shut-Ups (don't want to run) – John Severin (reprint from #42)
Page 21 – Shut-Ups (uncomfortable) – Charles Rodrigues (reprint from #130)
Page 22 – Shut-Ups (No cavities) – Sam Gross Jr. (Charles Rodrigues) (reprint from #99)
Page 23 – Shut-Ups (astronaut) – Charles Rodrigues (reprint from #80)
Page 24 – Shut-Ups (hospital gowns) – Don Orehek (new)
Page 25 – Shut-Ups! (can't hold ladder) – Golden (reprint from #63)
Page 26 – Shut-Ups (good clean fight) – Mike Ricigliano (reprint from #134)
Page 27 – Shut-Ups (plastic surgery) – Charles Rodrigues (reprint from #109)
Page 28 – Ye Hang Ups #4 (nice easy job) – Nireves (John Severin) (reprint from #117) / Ye Hang Ups #26 (bong) – Nireves (John Severin) (reprint from #118)
Page 29 – Hurry-Ups (house on fire) – John Severin (reprint from #32)
Page 30 – Shut-Ups! (stick-in-the-mud) – Vito Montigliani (Charles Rodrigues) (reprint from #73)
Page 31 – Cracked Shut-Ups (driving in the country) – Bill McCartney (Bill Ward) (reprint from #9)
Page 32 – Shut-Ups! (Running Deer) – Charles Rodrigues (reprint from #62)
Page 33 – Fine Art Shut-Ups (lopsided hat) – John Severin (reprint from #19)
Page 34 – Shut-Ups (jump) – Rodrigliani (Charles Rodrigues) (reprint from #55)
Page 35 – Shut-Ups (home cooked meal) – Don Orehek (new)
Page 36 – Ye Hang Ups #30 (Houdini) – John Severin (reprint from #121) / Ye Hang Ups #28 (want to play a game?) – John Severin (reprint from #122)
Page 37 – Hurry-Ups (Sarge is pinned) – Bill McCartney (Bill Ward) (reprint from #36)
Page 38 – Hurry-Ups (ship is sinking) – Bill McCartney (Bill Ward) (reprint from #37)
Page 39 – Shut-Ups (Here's his picture) – Charles Rodrigues (reprint from #118)
Page 40 – Shut-Ups! (can't stay up here) – Ellis Dee (Charles Rodrigues) (reprint from #64)

Page 41 – Shut-Ups (the score's tied) – Mike Ricigliano (reprint from #135)
Page 42 – Ye Hang Ups #33 (Slam) – Nireves (John Severin) (reprint from #125) / Ye Hang Ups #35 (four arms) – Nireves (John Severin) (reprint from #126)
Page 43 – Popular Songs Shut-Ups (smile umbrella) – Bill McCartney (Bill Ward) (reprint from #22)
Page 44 – Shut-Ups (ain't got no horses) – Charles Rodrigues (reprint from #121)
Page 45 – Hudd & Dini (octopus) – Vic Martin (reprint from #103)
Page 46 – Hudd & Dini (mousetrap) – Vic Martin (reprint from #83)
Page 47 – Shut-Ups (let's go out dancing) – Mike Ricigliano (reprint from #136)
Page 48 – Shut-Ups (Looks like a Picasso) – Don Orehek (new)
Page 49 – Shut-Ups (Main Street) – Bill Ward (new)
Page 50 – Shut-Ups (innocent) – S. Gross (Charles Rodrigues) (reprint from #104)
Page 51 – Shut-Ups (hit a tree) – S. Gross Jr. (Charles Rodrigues) (reprint from #102)
Back Cover – Shut-Ups (black belt) – Charles Rodrigues (reprint from #129)

***Cracked Collectors' Edition* #28 (*Cracked Goes to the Movies*), February 1979 (52 pages) (60c)**

Cover – We "Monkey" with King Kung – John Severin (reprint from #140)
Page 2 – The Cracked Bookstore ad – John Severin
Page 3 – Contents
Page 4 – King Kung – John Severin (reprint from #140)
Page 10 – Another Combined Movie "Godzilla" vs. "The Towering Inferno" – Sururi Gumen (reprint from #137)
Page 12 – A Cracked History of the Movies – Vic Martin (reprint from #109)
Page 16 – Right from the Horse's Mouth (reprint from #46)
Page 18 – Boys and Girls Together (reprint from #44)
Page 20 – The Big Budget Epic vs. The Low Budget Quickie – John Severin (reprint from #135)
Page 24 – The Moon Ate a Big Pink Kumquat (reprint from #87)
Page 26 – The Good Guys (reprint from #97)
Page 28 – Kansas City Bummer – Dick Wright (reprint from #108)
Page 32 – "Friends, Romans, Countrymen, Lend Me Your Laughs!" (reprint from #80)
Page 34 – Airpot – John Severin (reprint from #91)
Page 39 – Ship Shape (reprint from #82)
Page 40 – Five Times Laughs (reprint from #64)

Page 42 – Keystone Komedy Kapers (reprint from #96)
Page 44 – Four Goodness Sakes (reprint from #45)
Page 45 – The French Commotion – John Severin (reprint from #102)
Page 50 – More Combined Movies "My Fair Lady" & "King Kong" – John Severin (reprint from #133)
Page 51 – Wonderful World of Wacky Laughs! (reprint from #58)
Back Cover – Great Moments in Cosmetics 1,000,000 B.C. – Mike Ricigliano (reprint from #129)

***Cracked Collectors' Edition* #29 (*Mork from Ork*), May 1979 (52 pages) (60c) (Another issue with predominantly new material.)**
Cover – Mork from Ork – John Severin
Page 2 and 51 – Nah-No! Nah-No! – Cracked Poster – John Severin
Page 3 – Contents
Page 4 – Lettuce to Mork / Subscription ad
Page 6 – All Seriousness Aside…A Look at Robin Williams
Page 8 – A Cracked Dictionary of Orkan Terms – John Severin
Page 9 – Mork's Reports to Orson on What He's Found Our About Earth
Page 17 – Mork's Boyhood – Howard Nostrand
Page 20 – If Other Actors Played Mork
Page 26 – A Cracked Look at the Planet Ork – Bill Ward
Page 28 – A Cracked Peak at Mork's Diary – John Severin
Page 38 – How to Spot an Orkan – Warren Sattler
Page 40 – Famous Orkan Jokes
Page 47 – The Cracked Bookstore ad – John Severin
Page 48 – Other Specialized Handshakes from the Planet Ork
Page 50 – Shut-Ups (Easter eggs) – Don Orehek
Back Cover – Virginia Slums ad (reprint from #96)

***Cracked Collectors' Edition* #30 (*Cracked TV Screen*), July 1979 (52 pages) (60c)**
Cover – Laverne & Shirley – John Severin (reprint from #136)
Page 2 – The Cracked Bookstore ad – John Severin
Page 3 – Contents
Page 4 – Leverne & Shirley (Thank you, whistle) – Sigbjorn (John Severin) (reprint from #136)
Page 10 – If TV Commercials Lasted 61 Seconds – Bill Ward (reprint from #131)
Page 13 – How TV Shows Could be Killed Without Cancelling Them – John Severin (reprint from #138)
Page 17 – M*U*S*H (millions of clocks) – John Severin (reprint from #142)

Page 23 – Why is it on T.V. You Never See – Bill Ward (reprint from #133)
Page 28 – Come and Get Me, Copper! (reprint from #64)
Page 29 – One Date at a Time – John Severin (reprint from #142)
Page 35 – What Today's Programs Would Look Like if They Appeared in 2001 A.D. – John Severin (reprint from #132)
Page 38 – What Really Happens During the Filming of Television Commercials! – Arnoldo Franchioni (reprint from #69)
Page 42 – What to Do Until the TV Repairman Arrives – Don Orehek (reprint from #97)
Page 44 – Happy Daze – John Severin (reprint from #144)
Page 50 – Cool-Its (take me out) – Mike Ricigliano (reprint from *Cracked Collectors' Edition* #16)
Page 51 – The Magic Lamp – Don Orehek (reprint from #138)
Back Cover – Great Moments in Inventions 1801 – Charles Rodrigues (reprint from #135)

***Cracked Collectors' Edition* #31 (*Monster House Gallery*), September 1979 (52 pages) (60c)**

Cover – Monster Picnic – O.O. Severin (John Severin) (reprint from #54)
Page 2 – The Cracked Bookstore ad – John Severin
Page 3 – Contents
Page 4 – Howl Makers (reprint from *For Monsters Only* #10)
Page 6 – King Kong's Boyhood – Bill Ward (reprint from #141)
Page 10 – Monsterous Merriment (reprint from #98)
Page 12 – Vampires of the World – Bernard Baily (reprint from #108)
Page 16 – The Search for Bigfoot – John Severin (reprint from #141)
Page 17 – The Talking Blob – John Severin / Joe Catalano (reprint from #149)
Page 23 – Big Things are Happening! (reprint from *For Monsters Only* #7)
Page 24 – Merry Old England Life ad (reprint from #47)
Page 25 – If Frankenstein's Monster Did Guest Appearances on T.V. – Howard Nostrand (reprint from #151)
Page 31 – Great Scenes from Great Horror Movies – John Severin (reprint from #42)
Page 33 – The Monster – Sururi Gumen (reprint from #130)
Page 34 – Hiss the Villains (reprint from #94)
Page 38 – The Big Big Guys! (reprint from #102)
Page 40 – Monster Phrases – Vic Martin (reprint from *For Monsters Only* #5)
Page 42 – A MonStar is Reborn – John Severin / George Gladir (reprint from *For Monsters Only* #1)

Page 48 – The Fiends and the Females (reprint from *For Monsters Only* #8)
Page 50 – Orders – John Severin (reprint from #38)
Page 51 – A Little Off the Top! – BOJ (reprint from #53)
Back Cover – Hudd & Dini (skeleton) – Vic Martin (reprint from #95)

***Cracked Collectors' Edition* #32 (*Summer Fun!*), November 1979 (52 pages) (75c)**

Cover – Celebrities as Little Kids Picnic – John Severin
Page 2 – The Cracked Bookstore ad – John Severin
Page 3 – Contents
Page 4 – How the Kotter Gang Spent Their Summer Vacation – John Severin (reprint from #137)
Page 10 – A Cracked Look at the Beach – Don Orehek (reprint from #97)
Page 13 – The Cracked Guide to Canoeing – Warren Sattler (reprint from #146)
Page 17 – Super Skateboard Stunts – Howard Nostrand (reprint from #144)
Page 21 – Go Fly a Kite – John Severin (reprint from #74)
Page 22 – Prof. Whiffle-Bird Discovers a New Species – Tony Tallarico (reprint from #64)
Page 24 – Exciting Games for Daredevils – Zackary Taylor (Bob Taylor) (reprint from #94)
Page 26 – Boating – Don Orehek (reprint from #112)
Page 28 – Cracked Looks at Hunting and Fishing – LePoer (John Severin) (reprint from #86)
Page 30 – A Cracked Look at Little League Managers – Bill Ward (reprint from #119)
Page 33 – Snide Guide to Camping – John Severin (reprint from #61)
Page 36 – Cracked's Guide to Bicycling – Bob Taylor (reprint from #105)
Page 40 – Cracked's Guide to Backpacking – John Severin (reprint from #108)
Page 45 – Cracked Interviews the Camp King – John Langton (reprint from #111)
Page 50 – The Man & the Fly – Oskar Blotta (reprint from #95)
Page 51 – At An Afternoon Business Luncheon – Howard Nostrand (reprint from #144)
Back Cover – Gorkel House – Tony Tallarico (reprint from #64)

***Cracked Collectors' Edition* #33 (*Shut-Ups*), December 1979 (52 pages) (75c)**

Cover - Bandaged Mouth - John Severin, Charles Rodrigues
Page 2 - The Cracked Bookstore ad - John Severin
Page 3 - Contents
Page 4 - Shut-Ups (I think I can K.O.) - Don Orehek (reprint from #145)
Page 5 - Shut-Ups (set up camp) - Mike Ricigliano (reprint from #139)
Page 6 - Shut-Ups (deadbeats) - Charles Rodrigues (reprint from #119)
Page 7 - Shut-Ups (Who goes there?) - Don Orehek (reprint from #152)
Page 8 - Shut-Ups (baseball) - Bill McCartney (Bill Ward) (reprint from #43)
Page 9 - Shut-Ups (fire escape) - Charles Rodrigues (reprint from #112)
Page 10 - Shut-Ups (outlawing handguns) - Mike Ricigliano (reprint from #140)
Page 11 - Shut-Ups (good likeness) - Sigmund Froyd (Charles Rodrigues) (reprint from #90)
Page 12 - Shut-Ups (take it from the top) - Don Orehek (reprint from #149)
Page 13 - Shut-Ups (Abra-kadabra) - Mike Ricigliano (reprint from #141)
Page 14 - Shut-Ups (credit card) - Lefty Wright (Charles Rodrigues) (reprint from #92)
Page 15 - Shut-Ups (send me in) - Bill McCartney (Bill Ward) (reprint from #3)
Page 16 - Shut-Ups (prison reforms) - Noah Sark (Charles Rodrigues) (reprint from #106)
Page 17 - Shut-Ups (put his footprints) - Mike Ricigliano (reprint from #142)
Page 18 and 22 - Shut-Ups (shoplifting) - Charles Rodrigues (reprint from #114)
Page 19 - Shut-Ups (correct time) - Nelson Varicose (Charles Rodrigues) (reprint from #60)
Page 20 - Shut-Ups (Hollywood contract) - Don Orehek (reprint from #150)
Page 21 - Shut-Ups (true or false) - Sue Sioux (Charles Rodrigues) (reprint from #91)
Page 23 - Shut-Ups (lookout man) - Charles Rodrigues (reprint from #51)
Page 24 - Shut-Ups (I like my new job) - Don Orehek (reprint from #151)
Page 25 - Cracked Shut-Ups (diamond ring) - Bill McCartney (Bill Ward) (reprint from #5)

Page 26 – Cracked Shut-Ups (Europe) – Bill McCartney (Bill Ward) (reprint from #2)
Page 27 – Cracked Shut-Ups (beastly hot) – Bill McCartney (Bill Ward) (reprint from #7)
Page 28 – Shut-Ups (Folkswagon Bunny) – Don Orehek (reprint from #146)
Page 29 – Shut-Ups (what he sees in her) – Norman Rockwell (Charles Rodrigues) (reprint from #107)
Page 30 – Hurry-Ups (fly in soup) – Bill McCartney (Bill Ward) (reprint from #41)
Page 31 – Proverb Shut-Ups (small packages) – John Severin (partial reprint from #15)
Page 32 – Shut-Ups (new highway) – Charles Rodrigues (reprint from #122)
Page 33 – Shut-Ups (manage our budget) – Charles Rodrigues (reprint from #127)
Page 34 – Cracked Shut-Ups (daddy run) – Al Jaffee (reprint from #5)
Page 35 – Shut-Ups (don't need haircut) – Vic Martin (reprint from #49)
Page 36 – Shut-Ups (My debts) – Mike Ricigliano (reprint from #143)
Page 37 – Shut-Ups (winning tickets) – S. Gross Jr. (Charles Rodrigues) (reprint from #103)
Page 38 – Shut-Ups (66…45…38) – Mike Ricigliano (reprint from #144)
Page 39 – Shut-Ups (Helen doesn't mean anything) – Charles Rodrigues (reprint from #124)
Page 40 – Shut-Ups! (40) – Duke Mantee (Charles Rodrigues) (reprint from #61)
Page 41 – Shut-Ups (20 cents) – Rodrigliani (Charles Rodrigues) (reprint from #46)
Page 42 – Shut-Ups (martini) – Cosi Van Tutti (Charles Rodrigues) (reprint from #76)
Page 43 – Television Shut-Ups (cashier's check) – John Severin (reprint from #21)
Page 44 – Shut-Ups (king's dinner) – Julius Siezure (Charles Rodrigues) (reprint from #96)
Page 45 – Shut-Ups (endless snow) – Sam Gross (Charles Rodrigues) (reprint from #95)
Page 46 – Shut-Ups (best nap) – Don Orehek (reprint from #148)
Page 47 – Shut-Ups (hang around) – Charles Rodrigues (reprint from #71)
Page 48 – Shut-Ups (Can I Stop?) – Vic Martin (reprint from #44)
Page 49 – Shut-Ups (make up my mind) – Don Orehek (reprint from #147)
Page 50 – Shut-Ups (SHA-LLALA-KOO) – Charles Rodrigues (reprint from #111)

Page 51 - Shut-Ups (winning tickets) - S. Gross Jr. (Charles Rodrigues) (reprint from #103)
Back Cover - Shut-Ups (sports car) - Charles Rodrigues (reprint from #87)

***Cracked Collectors' Edition* #34 (*Those Cracked Monsters*), February 1980 (52 pages) (75c)**
Cover - Monster House - John Severin (reprint from #43)
Page 2 - The Cracked Bookstore ad - John Severin
Page 3 - Contents
Page 4 - Fiendish Florist Telephone Delivery ad - John Severin (reprint from #43)
Page 5 - Star People Weekly and Creatures and Things Magazine - John Severin (reprint from #148)
Page 10 - The Monsters Laugh it Up! (reprint from #56)
Page 12 - The Nightmares of Monsters - Bill McCartney (Bill Ward) (reprint from *For Monsters Only* #5)
Page 14 - Horrible Humor (reprint from #97)
Page 17 - Bill Ward's Chiller Dillers - Bill Ward (reprint from *For Monsters Only* #3)
Page 18 - The Howls Are Here! (reprint from *For Monsters Only* #9)
Page 19 - Cracked Presents Future Insect Monster Movies - Sururi Gumen (reprint from #125)
Page 23 - Monster Laughs!!! (reprint from *For Monsters Only* #9)
Page 24 - Quick Quiz (Harry Hairy) (reprint from *For Monsters Only* #6)
Page 26 - Monster Party - John Severin (reprint from #43)
Page 28 - Chilling Chuckles (reprint from *For Monsters Only* #10)
Page 30 - The Evil Experiment! - John Langton (reprint from #75)
Page 31 - Killer-Dillers! (reprint from *For Monsters Only* #9)
Page 32 - The Greatest Monster Battle of all Time! - John Severin (reprint from *For Monsters Only* #2)
Page 34 - Fiendish for Fun! (reprint from *For Monsters Only* #10)
Page 36 - The Big Things Do Their Thing! (reprint from *For Monsters Only* #9)
Page 38 - The Big Ones Scream Again! (reprint from *For Monsters Only* #6)
Page 41 - Great Scenes from Great Horror Movies - John Severin (reprint from #42)
Page 43 - Cracked Interviews the Monster King - Bill Ward (reprint from #143)

Page 48 – Monster Greeting Cards – Don Orehek (reprint from #95)
Page 51 – Official Cracked Reporter T-Shirt ad
Back Cover – The Stone Age – Oskar Blotta (reprint from #125)

***Cracked Collectors' Edition* #35 (*Mork*), May 1980 (52 pages) (75c) (Another issue with predominantly new material.)**

Cover – Mork Puzzle – John Severin (swipe from #12)
Page 2 – Official Cracked Reporter T-Shirt ad
Page 3 – Contents
Page 4 – Lettuce to Mork / Subscription ad
Page 6 – Mork and Mindy – John Severin (reprint from #158)
Page 12 – Mork's Guide to the Universe
Page 19 – Mork from Ork Name Game – John Severin
Page 35 – My Life with Mork
Page 42 – The Official Are You an Orkan Quiz
Page 50 – Space Shut-Ups! (most beautiful girl) – Bill McCartney (Bill Ward) (reprint from #8)
Page 51 – The Cracked Bookstore ad – John Severin
Back Cover – Landing On Mars – Howard Nostrand / Murad Gumen (reprint from #156)

***Cracked Collectors' Edition* #36 (*Those Cracked Monsters*), July 1980 (52 pages) (75c)**

Cover – Ghoul, Vampire and Alien – John Severin (reprint from *For Monsters Only* #5)
Page 2 – Official Cracked Reporter T-Shirt ad
Page 3 – Contents
Page 4 – Monster Mirth Rides Again (reprint from *For Monsters Only* #4)
Page 6 – Gunspook – Don Orehek (reprint from *Zany* #2)
Page 9 – The Monster's Advertising Agency – John Severin (reprint from #33)
Page 14 – The Wild Weirdos' Scream-In! (reprint from *For Monsters Only* #7)
Page 16 – The Eerie World of Don Orehek - Don Orehek (reprint from *Monster Howls* #1)
Page 18 – Modern Day Monsters – Joe Maneely (reprint from #5)
Page 20 – Chiller Dillers – John Severin, Joe Kiernan, Benson, Pete Wyma, Art Pottier, Lennie Herman, Norm Sutt, Bob (reprint from *For Monsters Only* #1)
Page 22 – Monster Sandwich-Board Men – John Severin (reprint from #34)
Page 24 – Monster Mirth! (reprint from *For Monsters Only* #6)

Page 26 – Monster Party! – John Severin (reprint from #31)
Page 27 – Ghouls and Giggles (reprint from *For Monsters Only* #7)
Page 28 – Something to Scream at! (reprint from *For Monsters Only* #7)
Page 30 – You'll Die Laughing! (reprint from *For Monsters Only* #7)
Page 31 – Frankenstein and Rock 'n Roll! – Joe Maneely (reprint from #2)
Page 34 – Martin's Screams – Vic Martin (reprint from *For Monsters Only* #2)
Page 35 – A Howling Good Time! (reprint from *For Monsters Only* #6)
Page 36 – Monster Mother Goose – Bill McCartney (Bill Ward) (reprint from *For Monsters Only* #1)
Page 38 – The Monster Howls' Baseball Team – John Severin (reprint from #37)
Page 43 – The Wacky Weirdos Howl Again! (reprint from *For Monsters Only* #5)
Page 45 – Cracked Puts the Bite on Dracula – Howard Nostrand (reprint from #155)
Page 49 – The Screamers (reprint from *For Monsters Only* #5)
Page 50 – Fangmann's ad – John Severin (reprint from #36)
Page 51 – The Cracked Bookstore ad – John Severin
Back Cover – The Angry Elephant and Tarzan's Son – Oskar Blotta (reprint from #147)

***Cracked Collectors' Edition* #37 (*Shut-Ups Plus Hudd & Dini! Plus Hang-Ups!*), September 1980 (52 pages) (75c)**
Cover – Four-Eyed Sylvester – John Severin, Charles Rodrigues, Vic Martin (reprint from #24)
Page 2 – Shut-Ups (losing your hair) – Don Orehek (reprint from #153)
Page 3 – Contents
Page 4 – Shut-Ups (spilled the beans) – Vito Modigliani (Charles Rodrigues) (reprint from #97)
Page 5 – Shut-Ups (the water's fine) – Vincent Van Stop (Charles Rodrigues) (reprint from #82)
Page 6 – Shut-Ups (long hair) – Modest Mussorgsky (Charles Rodrigues) (reprint from #85)
Page 7 – Sagebrush #32 (Yahoo!) – John Severin / Ye Hang Ups #32 (no tipping) – Nireves (John Severin) (reprint from #124)
Page 8 – Shut-Ups (not going to forgive) – Don Orehek (reprint from #154)
Page 9 – Shut-Ups (uncomfortable) – Charles Rodrigues (reprint from #130)
Page 10 – Shut-Ups (Can I sit) – Glenn Mukheryee (Charles Rodrigues) (reprint from #94)

Page 11 – Shut-Ups (only girl) – Carlos Gerdel (Charles Rodrigues) (reprint from #86)
Page 12 – Shut-Ups (drive-in movie) – Charles Rodrigues, Vic Martin (reprint from #93)
Page 13 – Sagebrush #31 (this is war) – John Severin / Ye Hang Ups #31 (Pierre) – Nireves (John Severin) (reprint from #123)
Page 14 – Shut-Ups (driving lesson) – Charles Rodrigues (reprint from #78)
Page 15 – Shut-Ups! (windshield wipers) – Rodrigliani (Charles Rodrigues) (reprint from #84)
Page 16 – Shut-Ups (snowing) – Charles Rodrigues (reprint from #65)
Page 17 – Shut-Ups (practice your violin) – Charles Rodrigues (reprint from #113)
Page 18 – Shut-Ups (I object) – Don Orehek (reprint from #155)
Page 19 – Sagebrush #28 (reptiles were here) – John Severin / Ye Hang Ups #29 (toothache) – Nireves (John Severin) (reprint from #120)
Page 20 – Shut-Ups (duck call) – Vic Martin (reprint from #52)
Page 21 – Shut-Ups (hospital gowns) – Don Orehek (reprint from *Cracked Collectors' Edition* #27)
Page 22 – Shut-Ups! (stick-in-the-mud) – Vito Montigliani (Charles Rodrigues) (reprint from #73)
Page 23 – Hudd & Dini (cannon) – Vic Martin (reprint from #93)
Page 24 – Sagebrush #27 (reptiles are better) – John Severin (reprint from #119) / Ye Hang Ups #27 (fishing) – Nireves (John Severin) (reprint from #119)
Page 25 – Hudd & Dini (lifeguards) – Vic Martin (reprint from #100)
Page 26 – Shut-Ups (five pounds of tea) – Charles Rodrigues (reprint from #66)
Page 27 – Shut-Ups (Squeaky's breaking out) – Don Orehek (reprint from #156)
Page 28 – Shut-Ups (Peanuts) – Ellsworth A. Sap (Charles Rodrigues) (reprint from #69)
Page 29 – Sagebrush (thinnin' hair) – John Severin (reprint from #115) / Ye Hang Ups #3 (He hates to drink alone) – John Severin (reprint from #115)
Page 30 – Shut-Ups (walking on air) – Vito Modigliani (Charles Rodrigues) (reprint from #75)
Page 31 – Shut-Ups (Ladies first) – Rodrigliani (Charles Rodrigues) (reprint from #77)
Page 32 – Shut-Ups (provide a blindfold) – Charles Rodrigues (reprint from #128)

Page 33 – Shut-Ups (start off this auction) – Don Orehek (reprint from #158)
Page 34 – Shut-Ups (KUH-RRRAK!) – Charles Rodrigues (reprint from #125)
Page 35 – Hudd & Dini (painted wall) – Vic Martin (reprint from #76)
Page 37 – Sagebrush #33 (traps all set for Winter) – John Severin / Ye Hang Ups #33 (Slam) – Nireves (John Severin) (reprint from #125)
Page 38 – Hurry-Ups (daddy fell out) – Don Orehek (reprint from #34)
Page 39 – Shut-Ups (snooping around) – Sam Gross Jr. (Charles Rodrigues) (reprint from #100)
Page 40 – Shut-Ups (grown man playing with a doll) – Charles Rodrigues (reprint from #120)
Page 41 – Shut-Ups (electronic calculator) – Charles Rodrigues (reprint from #117)
Page 42 – Shut-Ups (big game) – Don Orehek (reprint from #157)
Page 43 – Sagebrush #38 (rattler's territory) – John Severin / Ye Hang Ups #38 (ah-choo) – Nireves (John Severin) (reprint from #129)
Page 44 – Shut-Ups (cat dragged in) – Rodrigliani (Charles Rodrigues) (reprint from #81)
Page 45 – Hudd & Dini (prison bars) – Vic Martin (reprint from #81)
Page 47 – Shut-Ups (rocks) – Vic Martin (reprint from #50)
Page 48 – Shut-Ups (difficult time) – Charles Rodrigues (reprint from #115)
Page 49 – Shut-Ups (haven't smoked) – Busby Berkley (Charles Rodrigues) (reprint from #70)
Page 50 – Shut-Ups (good year) – Charles Rodrigues (reprint from #126)
Page 51 – Official Cracked Reporter T-Shirt ad
Back Cover – Shut-Ups (unlimited talent) – Sam Gross Jr. (Charles Rodrigues) (reprint from #98)

***Cracked Collectors' Edition* #38 (*Summer Fun!*), November 1980 (52 pages) (75c)**

Cover – Celebrities at the Beach – John Severin (new)
Page 2 – The Cracked Bookstore ad – John Severin
Page 3 – Contents
Page 4 – The Greatest Sequel Ever Made – John Severin / Joe Catalano (reprint from #155)
Page 11 – The Cracked Guide to Tennis – Nat Ball (John Severin) (reprint from #120)
Page 16 – The Cracked World of Summer – Don Orehek (reprint from #155)

Page 20 – Cracked Guide to Baseball – Bill Ward (reprint from #129)
Page 25 – Subscription ad – Warren Sattler
Page 26 – Cracked Looks at Camping – Don Orehek (reprint from #119)
Page 28 – How the Airlines Can Save Money! – John Severin (reprint from #97)
Page 22 – One Day On the Atlantic Ocean – Howard Nostrand (reprint from *Cracked Collectors' Edition* #26)
Page 32 – Nostalgic Amusement Parks – Bill Ward (reprint from #122)
Page 36 – A Visit to the Beach – LePoer (John Severin) (reprint from #38)
Page 38 – Cracked Frisbee Rating System – Bob Taylor (reprint from #133)
Page 41 – The Cracked Guide to Boating – Sailor Sam (John Severin) (reprint from #129)
Page 45 – Cracked Interviews the Resort King – Bill Ward (reprint from #127)
Page 50 – Shark Shut-Ups (shark disguise) – Don Orehek (reprint from *Cracked Collectors' Edition* #26)
Page 51 – Official Cracked Reporter T-Shirt ad
Back Cover – Uncover America (reprint from #84)

***Cracked Collectors' Edition* #39 (*Cracked Goes to the Movies*), December 1980 (52 pages) (75c)**

Cover – Western Gunfight – John Severin (reprint from #39)
Page 2 – The Cracked Bookstore ad – John Severin
Page 3 – Contents
Page 4 – Three Terrific Teams (reprint from #103)
Page 7 – All At Sea (reprint from #104)
Page 9 – Chip Shots (reprint from #83)
Page 12 – Valentino Vibrations (reprint from #94)
Page 14 – 12 O'Clock High Jinks (reprint from #65)
Page 16 – Getting There is Almost All the Fun! (reprint from #92)
Page 19 – Fhive for the Fhun it! (reprint from #95)
Page 20 – A Kook Look at Sports (reprint from #76)
Page 22 – Kings of Comedy (reprint from #57)
Page 24 – Watermelon Jokes to End Them All! (reprint from #97)
Page 26 – Heavy on the Horror, Please (reprint from #95)
Page 28 – Marx Brothers' Laff-In! (reprint from #73)
Page 31 – The Quick Quippers! (reprint from #69)
Page 32 – How the West was Lost (reprint from #39)
Page 34 – When the West Was Fun! (reprint from #53)

Page 36 – Laurel & Hardy Tell it Like it is! (reprint from #88)
Page 38 – The Big Guns! (reprint from #70)
Page 40 – Wild Wheels (reprint from #104)
Page 42 – Around the World in Hats (reprint from #43)
Page 44 – The Screamers (reprint from *For Monsters Only* #5)
Page 47 – Mugging Minors (reprint from #98)
Page 48 – Rollicking with Robert Redford (reprint from #92)
Page 50 – Lights Camera Action! – John Severin (reprint from #60)
Page 51 – Official Cracked Reporter T-Shirt ad
Back Cover – Optimists Anonymous (Pat Paulsen photo) (reprint from #74)

***Cracked Collectors' Edition* #40 (*Cracked TV Screen*), February 1981 (52 pages) (75c)**

Cover – TV Orchestra – John Severin (reprint from #75)
Page 2 – The Cracked Bookstore ad – John Severin
Page 3 – Contents
Page 4 – The Greatest TV Show Ever Made – John Severin (reprint from #161)
Page 11 – If All Violence Were Eliminated from TV – Howard Nostrand (reprint from #149)
Page 14 – One Afternoon at a Colorado Ski Competition – Sururi Gumen (reprint from #149)
Page 15 – If Gary Coleman Played Other Parts – R. McGeddon (John Severin) (reprint from #161)
Page 19 – Cracked's Favorite TV Scenes from Last Season (reprint from #137)
Page 22 – If the Carter Family Became TV Regulars – John Severin (reprint from #150)
Page 26 – The TV Class Reunion of 1985 – Sururi Gumen (reprint from #130)
Page 28 – The Further Adventures of Mork and Mindy – John Severin (reprint from #161)
Page 34 – TV Contraptions We'll Soon Be Seeing – Val Mayerik (reprint from #157)
Page 37 – Nic Disposable ad (reprint from #158)
Page 38 – If King Kong Made Guest Appearances on TV – Howard Nostrand (reprint from #140)
Page 42 – The Cracked Handbook of Acting – Warren Sattler (reprint from #159)
Page 46 – Cracked Interviews the Saturday Morning Cartoon King – Bill Ward (reprint from #159)

Page 51 – Official Cracked Reporter T-Shirt ad
Back Cover – Happy-Daze Shut-Ups (I have a date) – Powers (John Severin) (reprint from #157)

**_Cracked Collectors' Edition_ #41 (_Shut-Ups Plus Hang-Ups! Hudd & Dini!_), May 1981 (52 pages) (75c)**

Cover – Sylvester Plugs His Ears – John Severin, Charles Rodrigues
Page 2 – The Cracked Bookstore ad – John Severin
Page 3 – Contents
Page 4 – Shut-Ups (best tattoo jobs) – Don Orehek (reprint from #159)
Page 5 – Shut-Ups (I LOVE a parade) – Don Orehek (reprint from #163)
Page 6 – Shut-Ups (innocent) – S. Gross (Charles Rodrigues) (reprint from #104)
Page 7 – Shut-Ups (C-A-T) – Charles Rodrigues (reprint from #57)
Page 8 – Shut-Ups (any other questions) – Don Orehek (reprint from #160)
Page 9 – Shut-Ups (married 25 years) – Don Orehek (reprint from #167)
Page 10 – Cracked Shut-Ups (driving in the country) – Bill McCartney (Bill Ward) (reprint from #9)
Page 11 – Hurry-Ups (Sarge is pinned) – Bill McCartney (Bill Ward) (reprint from #36)
Page 12 – Shut-Ups (play like you never played) – Don Orehek (reprint from #166)
Page 13 – Shut-Ups (Looks like a Picasso) – Don Orehek (reprint from *Cracked Collectors' Edition* #27)
Page 14 – Hudd & Dini (octopus) – Vic Martin (reprint from #103)
Page 15 – Hudd & Dini (mousetrap) – Vic Martin (reprint from #83)
Page 16 – Shut-Ups (let's go out dancing) – Mike Ricigliano (reprint from #136)
Page 17 – Shut-Ups (good clean fight) – Mike Ricigliano (reprint from #134)
Page 18 – Shut-Ups! (can't stay up here) – Ellis Dee (Charles Rodrigues) (reprint from #64)
Page 19 – Shut-Ups! (Running Deer) – Charles Rodrigues (reprint from #62)
Page 20 – Ye Hang Ups #30 (Houdini) – John Severin (reprint from #121) / Ye Hang Ups #28 (want to play a game?) – John Severin (reprint from #122)
Page 21 – Ye Hang Ups #4 (nice easy job) – Nireves (John Severin) (reprint from #117) / Ye Hang Ups #26 (bong) – Nireves (John Severin) (reprint from #118)

Page 22 – Shut-Ups (It's a mirage) – Charles Rodrigues (reprint from #131)
Page 23 – Shut-Ups (stopping the fight) – Charles Rodrigues (reprint from #132)
Page 24 – Shut-Ups (don't want to run) – John Severin (reprint from #42)
Page 25 – Fine Art Shut-Ups (lopsided hat) – John Severin (reprint from #19)
Page 26 – Hudd & Dini (sleeping Mexican) – Vic Martin (reprint from #101)
Page 27 – Hudd & Dini (witches) – Vic Martin (reprint from #102)
Page 28 – Shut-Ups! (can't hold ladder) – Golden (reprint from #63)
Page 29 – Shut-Ups (nice monkey) – Vic Martin (reprint from #54) and various reprints by Charles Rodrigues
Page 30 – Shut-Ups (first men on moon) – Charles Rodrigues (reprint from #79)
Page 31 – Shut-Ups! (erector set) – Arthur Knockwurst (Charles Rodrigues) (reprint from #59)
Page 32 – Shut-Ups (drive away your customers) – Don Orehek (reprint from #162)
Page 33 – Shut-Ups (your eyes) – Don Orehek (reprint from #165)
Page 34 – Hurry-Ups (ship is sinking) – Bill McCartney (Bill Ward) (reprint from #37)
Page 35 – Shut-Ups (Main Street) – Bill Ward (reprint from *Cracked Collectors' Edition* #27)
Page 36 – Shut-Ups (Have a good time!) – Mike Ricigliano (reprint from #138)
Page 37 – Shut-Ups (the score's tied) – Mike Ricigliano (reprint from #135)
Page 38 – Shut-Ups (deathly sick) – Charles Rodrigues (reprint from #83)
Page 39 – Shut-Ups (fear of dark rooms) – Charles Rodrigues (reprint from #72)
Page 40 – Hudd & Dini (garbage cans) – Vic Martin (reprint from #82)
Page 41 – Hudd & Dini (boy scouts) – Vic Martin (reprint from #85)
Page 42 – Shut-Ups (bad luck to see bride) – Sam Gross Jr. (Charles Rodrigues) (reprint from #110)
Page 43 – Shut-Ups (AAEE-HOOEO!) – Nan Reik (Charles Rodrigues) (reprint from #58)
Page 44 – Shut-Ups (astronaut) – Charles Rodrigues (reprint from #80)
Page 45 – Shut-Ups! (tie clasps) – Rodrigliani (Charles Rodrigues) (reprint from #56)
Page 46 – Shut-Ups (pastrami on rye) – Don Orehek (reprint from #164)
Page 47 – Shut-Ups (home cooked meal) – Don Orehek (reprint from *Cracked Collectors' Edition* #27)

Page 48 – Shut-Ups (No cavities) – Sam Gross Jr. (Charles Rodrigues) (reprint from #99)
Page 49 – Shut-Ups (jump) – Rodrigliani (Charles Rodrigues) (reprint from #55)
Page 50 – Shut-Ups (our little diet) – Don Orehek (reprint from #161)
Page 51 – Official Cracked Reporter T-Shirt ad
Back Cover – Shut-Ups (Here's his picture) – Charles Rodrigues (reprint from #118)

***Cracked Collectors' Edition* #42 (*The Cracked Lens*), July 1981 (52 pages) (75c)**
Cover – Posting a Caption for Chaplin – John Severin
Page 2 – The Cracked Bookstore ad – John Severin
Page 3 – Contents
Page 4 – More of The Cracked Lens (reprint from #156)
Page 6 – And Yet Still More from The Cracked Lens (reprint from #159)
Page 10 – And Yet Again Still More from The Cracked Lens (reprint from #160)
Page 12 – And Yet Once Again Still More from The Cracked Lens (reprint from #161)
Page 16 – And Yet Once Again Still Some More from The Cracked Lens (reprint from #162)
Page 21 – And Yet Once Again Still Even Some More from The Cracked Lens (reprint from #163)
Page 25 – The Last of The Cracked Lens (reprint from #164)
Page 31 – The Very Last of The Cracked Lens (reprint from #165)
Page 36 – Positively the Very Last of The Cracked Lens (reprint from #166)
Page 41 – Absolutely, Positively, the Very Last of The Cracked Lens (reprint from #167)
Page 45 – Absolutely, Positively the Very Last of Those Cracked Monsters (reprint from #168)
Page 48 – Absolutely, Positively, Unquestionably, the Very Last of The Cracked Lens (reprint from #169)
Page 51 – 5 Fun Grabbers (reprint from #74)
Back Cover – Reel Gone Goodies (reprint from #75)

***Cracked Collectors' Edition* #43 (*Those Cracked Monsters*), September 1981 (52 pages) (75c)**
Cover – Godzilla and Pow-Man – John Severin (reprint from *Pow!* #2 with Sylvester's head pasted over.)
Page 2 and 51 – King Kong – Cracked Poster #140 – John Severin (reprint from #140)
Page 3 – Contents

Page 4 – Cracked Takes a Look at the Transylvanian Teen Scene – John Severin (reprint from #40)
Page 9 – Frankenstein the Untold Story (new)
Page 17 – The Condemned Man – John Severin (reprint from #64)
Page 18 – King Kong's Boyhood – Bill Ward (reprint from #141)
Page 22 – Look Before You Scream (new)
Page 24 – Hairy Scarey Fun (new)
Page 26 – Bill Ward's Chiller Dillers – Bill Ward (reprint from *For Monsters Only* #3)
Page 27 – The Fright-Makers (reprint from *For Monsters Only* #7)
Page 29 – School For Monsters – Nireves (John Severin) (reprint from #26)
Page 33 – A Fiend for Life (new)
Page 36 – Will-Odd – John Severin (reprint from #99)
Page 41 – Monster Puzzle Section
Page 50 – Shut-Ups (put his footprints) – Mike Ricigliano (reprint from #142)
Back Cover – Transylvanian Tee Heeeeeees (reprint from *For Monsters Only* #1)

***Cracked Collectors' Edition* #44 (*Summer Fun!*), November 1981 (52 pages) (75c)**

Cover – Carnival – John Severin
Page 2 – The Cracked Bookstore ad – John Severin
Page 3 – Contents
Page 4 – Jawz – John Severin (reprint from #129)
Page 10 – You Know It's Really Summer When – Don Orehek (new)
Page 13 – The Scuba Diver – Howard Nostrand (reprint from #159)
Page 14 – Literal Interpretations of Baseball Expressions – LePoer (John Severin) (reprint from #164)
Page 16 – Lyin Beat Magazine (reprint from #160)
Page 22 – The Cracked Guide to Horseback Riding – Nireves (John Severin) (reprint from #158)
Page 26 – A Cracked Look at a Backyard Barbecue – Don Orehek (reprint from #155)
Page 28 – Cracked Guide to Roller Skating – Bill Ward (reprint from #160)
Page 26 – Cracked Takes a Look at the Big Cats of the Big Top – Warren Sattler (reprint from #158)
Page 34 – The Adventures of the Masked Bandito – John Severin (reprint from #157)
Page 40 – The Cracked Guide to Skateboarding – Don Orehek (reprint from #134)
Page 44 – Find the "Sylvester Twins" Contest – Don Orehek

Page 45 – The Cracked Book of Summer Games and Puzzles That Anyone Can Do – Warren Sattler (new)
Page 51 – Official Cracked Reporter T-Shirt ad
Back Cover – Great Moments in Travel 1915 – Howard Nostrand (reprint from #161)

***Cracked Collectors' Edition* #45 (*Shut-Ups Plus Hang-Ups! Hudd & Dini!*), December 1981 (52 pages) (75c)**

Cover – Two-Faced Sylvester – John Severin, Charles Rodrigues (reprint from #69)
Page 2 – The Cracked Bookstore ad – John Severin
Page 3 – Contents
Page 4 – Shut-Ups (money and credit cards) – Don Orehek (reprint from #170)
Page 5 – Shut-Ups (best nap) – Don Orehek (reprint from #148)
Page 6 – Shut-Ups (Abra-kadabra) – Mike Ricigliano (reprint from #141)
Page 7 – Sagebrush #50 (There's gold here) – John Severin (reprint from #159)
Page 8 – Shut-Ups (bottle of soda) – Vic Martin (reprint from #48)
Page 9 – Shut-Ups (drive so fast) – Vic Martin (reprint from #47)
Page 10 – Shut-Ups (correct time) – Nelson Varicose (Charles Rodrigues) (reprint from #60)
Page 11 – Hudd & Dini (Vacancy) – Vic Martin (reprint from #79)
Page 12 – Shut-Ups (Folkswagon Bunny) – Don Orehek (reprint from #146)
Page 13 – Shut-Ups (make up my mind) – Don Orehek (reprint from #147)
Page 14 – Ye Hang Ups (mind closing the door) – C.E. Severin (Catherine Severin) (reprint from #170)
Page 15 – Shut-Ups (lookout man) – Charles Rodrigues (reprint from #51)
Page 16 – Hudd & Dini (inflatable man) – Vic Martin (reprint from #97)
Page 17 – Shut-Ups (big crowd) – Philip Garbage (Charles Rodrigues) (reprint from #67)
Page 18 – Shut-Ups (outlawing handguns) – Mike Ricigliano (reprint from #140)
Page 19 – Shut-Ups (set up camp) – Mike Ricigliano (reprint from #139)
Page 20 – Hudd & Dini (books) – Vic Martin (reprint from #105)
Page 21 – Shut-Ups (Hollywood contract) – Don Orehek (reprint from #150)
Page 22 – Shut-Ups (new highway) – Charles Rodrigues (reprint from #122)

Page 23 - Shut-Ups (Helen doesn't mean anything) - Charles Rodrigues (reprint from #124)
Page 24 - Hudd & Dini (foot race) - Vic Martin (reprint from #104)
Page 25 - Shut-Ups (don't need haircut) - Vic Martin (reprint from #49)
Page 26 - Sagebrush (Ah-Choo!) - John Severin (reprint from #85)
Page 28 - Shut-Ups (take it from the top) - Don Orehek (reprint from #149)
Page 29 - Shut-Ups (Who goes there?) - Don Orehek (reprint from #152)
Page 30 - Hudd & Dini (missing key) - Vic Martin (reprint from #77)
Page 31 - Hudd & Dini (kite) - Vic Martin (reprint from #86)
Page 32 - Shut-Ups (shoplifting) - Charles Rodrigues (reprint from #114)
Page 34 - Sagebrush (RAP) - John Severin (reprint from *Cracked Collectors' Edition* #9)
Page 36 - Shut-Ups (put out the dog) - Don Orehek (reprint from #169)
Page 37 - Shut-Ups (big struggle) - Don Orehek (reprint from #168)
Page 38 - Hudd & Dini (skeleton) - Vic Martin (reprint from #95)
Page 39 - Shut-Ups! (40) - Duke Mantee (Charles Rodrigues) (reprint from #61)
Page 40 - Shut-Ups (good likeness) - Sigmund Froyd (Charles Rodrigues) (reprint from #90)
Page 41 - Shut-Ups (endless snow) - Sam Gross (Charles Rodrigues) (reprint from #95)
Page 42 - Sagebrush (Gulp!) - John Severin (reprint from #99)
Page 43 - Shut-Ups (plastic surgery) - Charles Rodrigues (reprint from #109)
Page 44 - Hudd & Dini (garbage cans) - Vic Martin (reprint from #82)
Page 45 - Shut-Ups (king's dinner) - Julius Siezure (Charles Rodrigues) (reprint from #96)
Page 46 - Sagebrush (Mother Nature's secret) - John Severin (reprint from #105)
Page 47 - Hudd & Dini (Indu Magic) - Vic Martin (reprint from #89)
Page 48 - Ye Hang Ups #3 (screams) - C.E. Severin (Catherine Severin) (reprint from #172)
Page 49 - Shut-Ups (SHA-LLALA-KOO) - Charles Rodrigues (reprint from #111)
Page 50 - Shut-Ups (fire escape) - Charles Rodrigues (reprint from #112)
Page 51 - Hudd & Dini (saint Bernard) - Vic Martin (reprint from #108)
Back Cover - Shut-Ups (I think I can K.O.) - Don Orehek (reprint from #145)

***Cracked Collectors' Edition* #46 (*Monsters*), February 1982 (52 pages) (75c)**

Cover – Gravedigger and Ghouls – John Severin (reprint from *For Monsters Only* #8)
Page 2 – The Cracked Bookstore ad – John Severin
Page 3 – Contents
Page 4 – Drecula – John Severin (reprint from #165)
Page 11 – Transylvanian Trouncers (new)
Page 16 – Cartoon Screams – Don Orehek (reprint from *For Monsters Only* #4)
Page 17 – Transylvania's Montgomery & Morgue – John Severin (reprint from *For Monsters Only* #2)
Page 22 – Quick Quiz (Peter Lawford) (reprint from *For Monsters Only* #1)
Page 24 – TV Horror Listings (reprint from *Zany* #1)
Page 26 – Dungeon Dan-Dan-Dandies! – John Severin (reprint from *For Monsters Only* #3)
Page 28 – The Very First of The Cracked Monsters Lens (Have I got heartburn)(new)
Page 32 – A Little Off the Top! – BOJ (reprint from #53)
Page 33 – If Frankenstein's Monster Did Guest Appearances on T.V. – Howard Nostrand (reprint from #151)
Page 39 – A Visit to Transylvania – Bill McCartney (Bill Ward) (reprint from #55)
Page 42 – A MonStar is Reborn – John Severin / George Gladir (reprint from *For Monsters Only* #1)
Page 42 – The Effects of Horror Movies! (reprint from *Zany* #1)
Page 50 – To the Top – Pete Wyma (reprint from *Monster Howls* #1)
Page 51 – Gigantic Monster Mobile Bonus! – Vic Martin (reprint from *For Monsters Only* #6)

***Cracked Collectors' Edition* #47 (*Shut-Ups*), May 1982 (52 pages) (75c)**

Cover – Sylvesters Puts on Poiyoit Pants – John Severin (new with partial reprint from #15) (Rip-off of the cover of *Mad* #93.)
Page 2 – Winners of the "Sylvester Twins" Contest – Don Orehek
Page 3 – Contents
Page 4 – Shut-Ups (Easter eggs) – Don Orehek (reprint from *Cracked Collectors' Edition* #29)
Page 5 – Shut-Ups (sports car) – Charles Rodrigues (reprint from #87)
Page 6 – Popular Songs Shut-Ups (smile umbrella) – Bill McCartney (Bill Ward) (reprint from #22)
Page 8 – Sagebrush #53 (avalanche) – John Severin (reprint from #162)
Page 9 – Hurry-Ups (house on fire) – John Severin (reprint from #32)

Page 10 – Shut-Ups (true or false) – Sue Sioux (Charles Rodrigues) (reprint from #91)
Page 11 – Sagebrush #38 (rattler's territory) – John Severin (reprint from #129) / Sagebrush #32 (Yahoo!) – John Severin (reprint from #124)
Page 12 – Shut-Ups (baseball) – Bill McCartney (Bill Ward) (reprint from #43)
Page 13 – Shut-Ups (20 cents) – Rodrigliani (Charles Rodrigues) (reprint from #46)
Page 14 – Sagebrush #28 (reptiles were here) – John Severin (reprint from #120) / Sagebrush #30 (look up in the sky) – C.E. Severin (Catherine Severin) / John Severin (reprint from #121)
Page 15 – Shut-Ups (I like my new job) – Don Orehek (reprint from #151)
Page 16 – Sagebrush (buffalo stampede) – John Severin (reprint from #91)
Page 18 – Shut-Ups (credit card) – Lefty Wright (Charles Rodrigues) (reprint from #92)
Page 19 – Shut-Ups (what he sees in her) – Norman Rockwell (Charles Rodrigues) (reprint from #107)
Page 20 – Sagebrush (what heat) – John Severin (reprint from #89)
Page 22 – Sagebrush (Howdy Shage) – John Severin (reprint from #113) / Sagebrush (thinnin' hair) – John Severin (reprint from #115)
Page 23 – Hurry-Ups (last cigarette) – Bill McCartney (Bill Ward) (reprint from #38)
Page 24 – Shut-Ups (My debts) – Mike Ricigliano (reprint from #143)
Page 25 – Sagebrush (stomping) – John Severin (reprint from #88)
Page 26 – Sagebrush (Z) – John Severin (reprint from #81)
Page 28 – Hurry-Ups (fly in soup) – Bill McCartney (Bill Ward) (reprint from #41)
Page 29 – Sagebrush (Hi! Hey!) – John Severin (reprint from #108) / Sagebrush (here come food) – John Severin (reprint from #110)
Page 30 – Sagebrush (nobody loves me) – John Severin (reprint from #116) / Sagebrush #34 (Uh! Oh!) – John Severin (reprint from #126)
Page 31 – Shut-Ups (deadbeats) – Charles Rodrigues (reprint from #119)
Page 32 – Shut-Ups (hang around) – Charles Rodrigues (reprint from #71)
Page 33 – Shut-Ups (martini) – Cosi Van Tutti (Charles Rodrigues) (reprint from #76)
Page 34 – Sagebrush (crossing the desert) – John Severin (reprint from #86)

Page 36 – Shut-Ups (prison reforms) – Noah Sark (Charles Rodrigues) (reprint from #106)
Page 37 – Shut-Ups (Can I Stop?) – Vic Martin (reprint from #44)
Page 38 – Sagebrush (water) – John Severin (reprint from #82)
Page 39 – Sagebrush #27 (reptiles are better) – John Severin (reprint from #119) / Sagebrush #29 (beware!) – C.E. Severin (Catherine Severin) / John Severin (reprint from #122)
Page 40 – Shut-Ups! (exercise) – Pick and Pat (Charles Rodrigues) (reprint from #88)
Page 41 – Sagebrush (hey rock) – John Severin (reprint from #112) / Sagebrush #31 (this is war) – John Severin (reprint from #123)
Page 42 – Sagebrush (fancy shooting) – John Severin (reprint from #83)
Page 44 – Hurry-Ups (five dollar raise) – Don Orehek (reprint from #35)
Page 45 – Sagebrush #33 (traps all set for Winter) – John Severin (reprint from #125) / Sagebrush #26 (invited a friend to lunch) – John Severin (reprint from #118)
Page 46 – Sagebrush (filters) – John Severin (reprint from #90)
Page 48 – Hurry-Ups (papa, papa) – John Severin (reprint from #33)
Page 50 – Shut Up and Get it Over With! – Jared Lee (reprint from #101)
Page 51 – The Cracked Bookstore ad – John Severin
Back Cover – Shut-Ups (manage our budget) – Charles Rodrigues (reprint from #127)

***Cracked Collectors' Edition* #48 (*Great Moments 'n Shut-Ups*), July 1982 (52 pages) (90c) (All of the Shut-Ups are new in this edition.)**
Cover – Various Great Moments and Shut-Ups – Mike Ricigliano, Howard Nostrand, Warren Sattler (partially new with reprints from #138, 142, 155, 166)
Page 2 – The Cracked Bookstore ad – John Severin
Page 3 – Contents
Page 4 – Great Moments in Medicine 1882 – Charles Rodrigues (reprint from #122)
Page 5 – Shut-Ups (where's my reward) – Mike Ricigliano / Randy Epley
Page 6 – Shut-Ups (chocolate bars) – Mike Ricigliano / Brent Mitchell, Lisa Grant
Page 7 – Great Moments in Sports 1837 – Howard Nostrand (reprint from #155)
Page 8 – Great Moments in Science 1699 – Mike Ricigliano (reprint from #138)
Page 9 – Shut-Ups (Breaker 19) – Mike Ricigliano / Todd Stevens, Scott Hollander

Page 10 - Shut-Ups (ice cream cone) - Mike Ricigliano / Brian Adair, Tibby Lee
Page 11 - Great Moments in Hunting 999,999 B.C. - Howard Nostrand (reprint from #166)
Page 12 - Great Moments in Technology 186 B.C. - Howard Nostrand (reprint from #172)
Page 13 - Shut-Ups (I hear bells) - Mike Ricigliano / Ken Cote, Randy Epley
Page 14 - Shut-Ups (Did you miss me) - Mike Ricigliano / Randy Epley
Page 15 - Great Moments in Sports 1,217,003 B.C. - Conky Nostrand (Howard Nostrand) (reprint from #171)
Page 16 - Great Moments in History Ice Age - Mike Ricigliano (reprint from #137)
Page 17 - Shut-Ups (station wagon) - Mike Ricigliano / Randy Epley
Page 18 - Shut-Ups (another game of chess) - Mike Ricigliano / Ronda Wages, Mike King
Page 19 - Great Moments in Art 1705 - Charles Rodrigues (reprint from #119)
Page 20 - Great Moments in Sports 1967 - Warren Sattler (reprint from #175)
Page 21 - Shut-Ups (Polly wants a cracker) - Mike Ricigliano / Danny Ford
Page 22 - Shut-Ups (all my years of chemistry) - Mike Ricigliano / Kim LaVinn
Page 23 - Great Moments in Psychiatry 1227 - Howard Nostrand (reprint from #152)
Page 24 - Great Moments in Aviation 1924 - rottenrigues (Charles Rodrigues) (reprint from #130)
Page 25 - Shut-Ups (I'm just wild about Harry) - Mike Ricigliano / Eric Pfeffinger, Tracy White
Page 26 - Great Moments in History 1976 - Mike Ricigliano (reprint from #133)
Page 27 - Great Moments in History 1883 - Charles Rodrigues (reprint from #131)
Page 28 - Shut-Ups (What's the answer) - Mike Ricigliano / Thomas Stavinotta
Page 29 - Great Moments in Games 1,057,649 B.C. - Howard Nostrand (reprint from #148)
Page 30 - Great Moments in Aviation 1947 - Samuel B. Whitehead (reprint from #173)
Page 31 - Shut-Ups (people look like ants) - Mike Ricigliano / Jason Farmer, Eden Dommell

Page 32 – Shut-Ups (I am so cool) – Mike Ricigliano / Anderson
Page 33 – Great Moments in Technology 1029 – Howard Nostrand (reprint from #170)
Page 34 – Great Moments in History 1,000,342 B.C. – Howard Nostrand (reprint from #142)
Page 35 – Shut-Ups (I am a good swimmer) – Mike Ricigliano / Anderson
Page 36 – Shut-Ups (I bowled a strike) – Mike Ricigliano / Timmy Rogan, Erik Schilling
Page 37 – Great Moments in Journalism 1935 – Charles Rodrigues (reprint from #128)
Page 38 – Great Moments in Hospitality 472 A.D. – Howard Nostrand (reprint from #158)
Page 39 – Shut-Ups (Abraham Lincoln) – Mike Ricigliano / Fred Sanders
Page 40 – Shut-Ups (Can't you write faster) – Mike Ricigliano / Fred Sanders
Page 41 – Great Moments in Cosmetics 1,000,000 B.C. – Mike Ricigliano (reprint from #129)
Page 42 – Great Moments in Music 1,057,648 B.C. – Howard Nostrand (reprint from #144)
Page 43 – Shut-Ups (I want to tell you a secret) – Mike Ricigliano / Sinclair and Xavier Szebrat, Tracy Kent
Page 44 – Shut-Ups (Can't you write faster) – Mike Ricigliano / Luke Green
Page 45 – Great Moments in Inventions 1801 – Charles Rodrigues (reprint from #135)
Page 46 – Great Moments in Sports 1947 – Howard Nostrand (reprint from #160)
Page 47 – Shut-Ups (Jimmy Carter) – Mike Ricigliano / Randy Epley, Greg Grabianski
Page 48 – Great Moments in Dentistry 1755 – Howard Nostrand (reprint from #143)
Page 49 – Great Moments in Industry 1889 – Charles Rodrigues (reprint from #126)
Page 50 – Shut-Ups (nobody seems to listen) – Mike Ricigliano / Aaron Quanbeck
Page 51 – Marvin Manley Bodywrecking Club ad (reprint from #162)
Back Cover – Great Moments in History 974 A.D. – Howard Nostrand (reprint from #145)

**To be continued in Part II**

# INDEX

# ABOUT THE AUTHOR

Here's what working on a *Cracked* book for over a year does to you. Before…

**MARK ARNOLD** (born December 15, 1966 in San Jose, California) is an American writer who grew up in Saratoga, California. He has contributed to several publications in the United States, including *The Comics Journal*, *Hogan's Alley*, *Back Issue* and *Comic Buyer's Guide*. Arnold also worked with Jerry Beck and Leslie Cabarga on their *Harvey Comics Classics* series for Dark Horse Comics.

Arnold has written two books about comic books and animation. The first, *The Best of The Harveyville Fun Times!*, focused on the comic book publisher Harvey Comics. The second was *Created and Produced by Total TeleVision productions: The Story of Underdog, Tennessee Tuxedo and the Rest.*

… and after!

Arnold also compiled the traveling original art show entitled *From Richie Rich to Wendy the Witch: The Art of Harvey Comics* which debuted in June 2008 at San Francisco's Cartoon Art Museum, moving to New York City's Museum of Comic and Cartoon Art in December 2008 and traveling again to Pittsburgh, Pennsylvania, in May 2009. The show ended in Pittsburgh in July 2009.

The Saratoga History Museum honored Arnold by including him in a display of famous Saratogans, which ran from November 2009 through January 2010.

Arnold has a BA degree in Broadcast Communication Arts from San Francisco State University, and has studied art through Art Instruction Schools. He currently resides in Saratoga, California, and is working on a book about The Beatles.

If you didn't like this book, you surely won't enjoy:

*The Best of the Harveyville Fun Times!*

*Created and Produced by Total TeleVision productions:*
*The Story of Underdog, Tennessee Tuxedo and the Rest*

CPSIA information can be obtained at www.ICGtesting.com
Printed in the USA
BVOW02201614091 1

270949BV00010B/4/P